FROM RONALD REAGAN TO RODNEY KING

MEDIA AND
PUBLIC AFFAIRS

John Maxwell Hamilton,
SERIES EDITOR

LOU CANNON

FROM RONALD REAGAN TO RODNEY KING

CHRONICLING AMERICA IN THE "AGE OF OPTIMISM"

LOUISIANA STATE UNIVERSITY PRESS
BATON ROUGE

Published with the assistance of the V. Ray Cardozier Fund

Published by Louisiana State University Press
lsupress.org

Manufactured in the United States of America
First printing

Designer: Kaelin Chappell Broaddus
Typefaces: Miller Text, text; Desire Pro, Area Extended, display
Printer and binder: Sheridan Books, Inc.

The manufacturer's authorized representative in the EU for product safety is Mare Nostrum Group B.V., Doelen 72, 4831 GR Breda, The Netherlands. Email: gpsr@mare-nostrum.co.uk.

Jacket photograph courtesy Ronald Reagan Presidential Library.
All interior photos are from the private collection of Lou Cannon.

Cataloging-in-Publication Data are available from the Library of Congress.

ISBN 978-0-8071-8712-8 (cloth: alk. paper) —
ISBN 978-0-8071-8782-1 (pdf) — ISBN 978-0-8071-8781-4 (epub)

CONTENTS

Photographs follow page 238.

PREFACE

As I put the finishing touches on this memoir, Los Angeles County is afire, with blazes ranging from the San Gabriel Mountains to Malibu. At least two dozen people have perished and thousands of homes and other buildings burned to the ground, a reminder of the fragile ecology of the West, where I have lived most of my life. It also brings to my mind a long-ago fire in August 1977 when I was Los Angeles bureau chief for *The Washington Post.*

I hired a freelance photographer and drove three hundred miles north to see a wildland fire that had been burning for a week. Known as the Marble Cone Fire, the wind-fanned blaze was gobbling up trees and other vegetation in the mountains east of Big Sur as it would do for another two weeks. I'd never seen a forest fire in action and wanted to get as close as possible.

The next day the photographer came too close. We were on a fire road with the captain of a fire-suppression unit who was explaining to a small group of reporters how aerial drops and backfires were being used to divert Marble Cone from homes in Carmel Valley. The photographer abruptly broke away from the group and scrambled down a gully for a better view of the flames on a nearby ridge. In an instant the wind changed, and the fire came after the photographer. I yelled at him to come back; the fire captain charged down the gully and pulled him up to the road. After we had retreated to a safer location, the fire captain told us to treat fires with respect.

"Fires have a mind of their own," he said.

The past also has a mind of its own. I began my memoir with a reference to the Marble Cone fire because it was my first story of consequence after I went from covering politics for *The Post* to being the paper's western correspondent. Four and a half decades later, I remember little about the wildfire except its name and had to look up factual details of where it burned and how long it took to contain. All my memory did on its own was to summon the recollection of my photographer's independence and the response to it.

After the measured rebuke by the fire captain, my editor delivered a more pointed judgment when I told him what had happened. "You have to fill out a lot of forms if you lose a photographer," the editor said, which was his way of suggesting that I hire photographers with less courage and more common sense.

Such incidents, routine in a reporter's life, should give a journalist pause if deciding to write about one's own life. The journalist's memory is apt to arrange matters for its own convenience, making the memoirist the hero of the story and burying anything it would prefer to forget. At ninety-one years of age, I sometimes find clarity in events of a half century earlier that they lacked at the time. Is that because we know more as we age? Or because we are filling in the blank spots with our imagination? It's helpful to check the record (if one exists) of events mentioned in the memoir. But dangers can also lurk in records that have been altered to cover up the truth. It's a constant tussle for the memoirist who must decide whether the official version or one's recollection or some blend of the two is the closest approximation to the truth.

I did not keep a diary except for brief periods when I was tracking developments for one of my books. I wish I had. The lack of a day-to-day record imposes an extra burden on the memoirist whose duty is to remember what it was like at the beginning. Historical accounts of everything from battles to baseball games are often written omnisciently, as if outcomes were foreordained. In writing these memoirs, I have tried to heed the warning of the British historian C. V. Wedgwood. "History is written backward but lived forward," she wrote. "Those who know the end of the story can never know what it was like at the time."

I wrote this memoir for multiple reasons. First, I want to leave a record for my three children, seven grandchildren, seven great-grandchildren, and any other future offspring. These numbers do not include my son, David, who died in his prime, or my grandson Nathan, who died young. This book is dedicated to their memory.

Second, I suspect that historians may show interest in my personal observations of Ronald Reagan, whom I covered for most of his political career as a reporter for the *San Jose Mercury-News* and *The Washington Post*. I wrote six books about Reagan's life and legacy.

After the Reagan presidency, I was assigned for a second time by *The Washington Post* to Los Angeles, where in the early morning hours of March 3, 1991, Rodney King was pursued at high speeds on freeways and a city street before being forced to stop by the California Highway Patrol. Los Angeles police officers tried to take King into custody.

King, intoxicated and strong, threw LAPD officers who were trying to handcuff him off his back. He was then hit with a charge from a Taser gun fired by an LAPD sergeant. King shook off this 50,000-volt charge, rose to his feet, and charged in the direction of one of the officers. The officers beat him into submission with their batons. Four officers were charged with illegal use of force and other crimes. When they were acquitted fourteen months later, a terrible riot erupted in South Central Los Angeles. I wrote about these events for *The Post* and in a long book, *Official Negligence: How Rodney King and the Riots Changed Los Angeles and the LAPD*. In this memoir I share my recollections of King, the officers, and their attorneys.

I had not intended to write an autobiography. After the University of California at Santa Barbara purchased my Reagan papers, I was supposed to be the subject of an oral history that would accompany the papers and be available for researchers. The oral historian began the project but did not complete it. I then took up the task of trying to finish it and ultimately decided it was best to start from scratch and do as complete a memoir of my life as possible. I'm grateful to the university, where my papers are housed in the Special Collections of a vast modern library, and appreciative of those who made this possible, especially David Tambo, Sara Miller McCune, and Patricia Van Every. I have donated my extensive Rodney King archive to the university so all my papers would be in one place. I am equally grateful to the Louisiana State University Press for publishing these memoirs.

So here is the story of my life, personal and professional. I have taken my cue from the scholar William Zinsser, who wrote: "The crucial transaction in memoir and personal history is the transaction between you and your remembered experiences and emotions."

Shakespeare was on a similar track when he had Polonius say that, if one is true to himself, he cannot be false to anyone. Although I have attempted to be modest, perhaps (paraphrasing Winston Churchill) because I have much to be modest about, this memoir is also animated by a writer's conceit. The nature of that conceit is expressed on a brass plate on the wall of the room in which I write: *Litera, scripta, manet.* The written word endures.

Or so this writer hopes.

FROM RONALD REAGAN TO RODNEY KING

1

DISCOVERING REAGAN

These memoirs are a journey in discovery—about myself, my family, and those I observed up close as journalist and biographer. They contain observations about Anthony Beilenson, Ben Bradlee, David Broder, Pat Brown and his son Jerry, Phil and Sala Burton, George H. W. Bush, Jimmy Carter, Cesar Chavez, Dick Cheney, Gerald Ford, Katharine Graham, Al Haig, Hubert Humphrey, Paul and Robert Laxalt, Pete McCloskey, Richard Nixon, Nancy Reagan, George Shultz, Stuart Spencer, Caspar Weinberger, and Pete Wilson, among others. These memoirs also include my reflections on the trials of the Los Angeles police officers accused of beating Rodney King and the deadly riots that ensued after the officers were acquitted. But since I'm best known for my five books about Ronald Reagan, the movie actor who became governor of California and fortieth president of the United States, I'll begin by explaining how I came to be his biographer.

My first book about Reagan—the dual biography *Ronnie and Jesse: A Political Odyssey*—was written in 1968 during the second year of Reagan's governorship. I was then state capitol reporter for the *San Jose Mercury-News*. Although my editors expressed satisfaction with my coverage, I realized that my knowledge of Reagan was superficial. I also wanted to know more about Reagan's Democratic rival, the brilliant and moody Assembly speaker, Jesse Unruh, and thought that writing a dual biography of Reagan and Unruh would help me learn more about both men. Curiosity is a useful motive for a writer. Years later, progressive social historian Carey McWilliams told me that every book he'd written—

and he'd done perceptive books on farm labor and anti-Semitism, among other subjects—had been undertaken because he wanted to know more about something.

Ronnie and Jesse received favorable reviews and an especially complimentary one from John Leonard in the *New York Times,* which was gratifying and confidence-building for a first-time author. But I considered the book a one-off because both of my subjects seemed near their political apogee.

Unruh wanted to be governor, but he had so many enemies I doubted he could pull it off. Reagan had potential as a presidential candidate but lacked an obvious path to the White House. He had sought the Republican presidential nomination in 1968 after being persuaded that Richard Nixon was such damaged goods that New York governor Nelson Rockefeller might wind up with the GOP nomination. Reagan appealed to rank-and-file Republicans, but his political team was no match for Nixon's experienced operation. Rockefeller was a chimera, always waiting in the wings. Nixon won the nomination and the presidency. If he served two terms, Reagan would be old news when Nixon stepped down. Such was the conventional wisdom in 1969 when *Ronnie and Jesse* was published. Later that year, I put Reagan in the rear-view mirror and joined the Washington bureau of Ridder Publications.

So much for conventional wisdom. Reagan proved to be a long-distance runner. In 1970, he ran for reelection against Unruh—a matchup forecast in my book—and bureau chief Walter Ridder sent me back to California to cover the campaign. Unruh made a contest of it, but Reagan won again. In 1972, five weeks before the Watergate break-in that would eventually force Nixon to resign and put Gerald Ford in the White House, I joined the national staff of *The Washington Post* and wound up covering the Ford presidency. In 1975, an editor asked me what Reagan would do in 1976. I told the editor that Reagan would run for president, even if it meant challenging a sitting president of his own party.

I'm not sure the editor believed me, but when Reagan announced in November 1975, I was assigned by *The Post* to cover him. His campaign began poorly, and he lost the early New Hampshire and Florida primaries to President Ford. This prompted much of the media, which in 1962 had prematurely written Nixon's political obituary, to conclude that Reagan was finished. But Reagan soldiered on, upsetting Ford in the

North Carolina primary and battling him all the way to the Republican convention in Kansas City, where he would have won if the convention had nominated by secret ballot, as Ford's managers privately acknowledged. As it was, Reagan lost narrowly. Hoping to unify the party after he was nominated, Ford beckoned Reagan to the convention podium. Instead of making the concessionary speech of a defeated candidate or asking for party unity, Reagan gave an evocative warning about the danger of nuclear weapons. That performance demonstrated to me, and to the delegates in Kemper Arena, that Reagan still had the presidency in his sights.

In November, after receiving minimal help from Reagan, Ford lost to Jimmy Carter. Reagan returned home to Southern California, where he kept himself in the public eye with newspaper columns and radio broadcasts.

I also returned to California. A few months into the Carter administration, I was assigned to *The Post*'s Los Angeles bureau, where I wrote about immigration, water policy, forest fires, and other Western issues. But when Reagan announced his presidential candidacy late in 1979, I was asked to cover him again. The managing editor of *The Washington Post* considered this as a short-term assignment. He said I could continue to live in Los Angeles and go back to covering the West after the campaign. The editor was quite certain Reagan would never win the White House. He assured me that Reagan probably couldn't win the nomination, much less defeat a sitting president.

After Reagan routed the Republican field and won an electoral landslide against President Carter, the managing editor changed his mind. He asked me to sell or rent my home in Los Angeles and move back to Washington to cover the White House. My wife and I preferred living in California, and I had job offers that would have kept me there, but the prospect of a ringside seat at the Reagan presidency was tantalizing. Also, my agent told me that publishers were interested in another Reagan book.

I was fortunate to work at *The Washington Post*, a place where people took an interest in me beyond what I produced for the paper. Editors at many news organizations looked upon book writing as a diversion from the reporter's day job. The *Post* editors, many with books to their own credit, understood that book writing was a normal aspiration for a journalist. The editors who guided me were Ben Bradlee, our executive editor of Watergate fame, and Richard Harwood, editor of the national staff, who had hired me.

Harwood survived under fire in the South Pacific as a U.S. Marine Corps officer during World War II. I greatly admired him. Harwood reminded me that one reason he'd hired me was that he had been impressed by *Ronnie and Jesse*. He and Bradlee proposed that I cover the White House and sign a book contract if one was offered. Leave the delivery date as vague as possible, they said, and we'd figure out when I had time to write it. I took their advice. Soon, I was *The Post*'s senior White House correspondent, gathering string for a second Reagan book.

My eldest son, Carl Cannon, once said I hadn't chosen Reagan as much as the subject had chosen me. There's considerable truth to that. Long before he ran for president, I realized that Reagan's ideas and ambitions were not limited by the horizons of California. Now, he was promising to take America in a new direction as president. I was intrigued and hoped to write a sequel to *Ronnie and Jesse*. Reagan would be accessible, I suspected. While president-elect, Reagan confided to an aide that he was pleased that some of the reporters who had covered him in Sacramento, such as George Skelton of the *Los Angeles Times*, would be in the White House press corps. He didn't expect special treatment from them—nor did he get it—but he liked having California artifacts around. During this transition period, Reagan told me he'd heard I was going to write another book.

"Yes," I said. "I'm going to keep writing about you until I get it right."

"Good line," Reagan responded.

He never said anything else about the book to me, saving his criticisms for his diaries. That second book, called *Reagan* without a subtitle, was published in 1982. After Reagan left the White House, I wrote *President Reagan: The Role of a Lifetime* and three other books about him.

I met Reagan in Sacramento in 1965 when he was fifty-five and I was thirty-two. In those days, the San Jose newspapers consisted of the morning *Mercury* and the afternoon *News* with a joint *Mercury-News* Sunday edition. Reagan was conducting an exploratory candidacy for governor, speaking to service clubs and improvised forums throughout California.

With more than a year to go before the 1966 election and name recognition of 90 percent, he had the luxury of moving slowly and making what he called "out-of-town tryouts" in appearances that attracted little press coverage. Reagan skipped the major cities of Los Angeles, San Diego, and San Francisco. Sacramento, the largest city on the tour, was included only because it was the state capital. As his quip about "tryouts" suggests, Reagan thought of himself as an actor and sprinkled his speeches with anecdotes from his Hollywood days. Most Californians thought of him as an actor, too, and Reagan did not discourage this perception. Asked what kind of a governor he would be, Reagan replied, "I don't know. I never played a governor."

The luncheon where I met Reagan was sponsored by the Sacramento Press Club, and the audience consisted of reporters, lobbyists, and legislative aides. I wasn't assigned to write about the event; an editor at the *San Jose News* had noticed Reagan would be in Sacramento and suggested I get an impression of him. Reagan had made his national political debut in 1964 with a stirring televised speech on behalf of Republican presidential candidate Barry Goldwater.

It was the only bright spot for Goldwater in a campaign in which he ran uphill against President Lyndon Johnson, who while secretly planning to send a half-million troops to Vietnam, tarred the Arizona senator as an "extremist" who might plunge the United States into war. A week after Reagan's speech, Goldwater lost in a landslide and his negative coattails carried other Republicans to defeat.

Unlike many Republicans, Reagan never distanced himself from Goldwater during or after the 1964 election. Instead, he berated the moderates in his party who had deserted the Arizona senator. Reagan's loyalty was as much personal as ideological. Except for Goldwater's personal intercession, the celebrated Reagan speech that David Broder called "the most successful political debut since Williams Jennings Bryan electrified the 1896 Democratic convention with his 'Cross of Gold' speech" would not have been delivered. Goldwater's aides somehow believed that Reagan was more controversial than Goldwater and didn't want him to speak. Reagan phoned Goldwater, who put the speech on the schedule. Appreciative that Goldwater overruled his advisors, Reagan stayed loyal to him even though he had no illusions about the quality of Goldwater's disastrous campaign. When I interviewed Reagan in 1968 for *Ronnie and Jesse,* he off-handedly observed that Goldwater had shown that Republicans couldn't run against Social Security, no matter what doubts they harbored about its merits.

At the time of the 1965 Sacramento luncheon, I didn't know the backstory about the speech that launched his political career. I'd watched The Speech, as it became known, and thought Reagan managed to deliver dire, even wild, warnings with a sensible, pleasant demeanor that belied his message. It was hard to determine from a single speech whether Reagan would be an effective political candidate. What I did know was that Governor Pat Brown was rooting for Reagan to become the Republican gubernatorial nominee. An aide in the governor's office had told me that Brown, a Democrat seeking a third term, realized he had accumulated political baggage during two terms in offices and believed Reagan was the only Republican he could beat.

Brown tended to overvalue politicians who hailed from his hometown of San Francisco, which by then was no longer the bellwether in state politics it had once been. He worried that the Republicans would nominate George Christopher, a moderate former San Francisco mayor. This was a misplaced concern. Christopher was a parochial politician who, like Brown himself, was uncomfortable on television. But both Brown and Christopher thought Reagan was cut from the Goldwater cloth and could be portrayed as an extremist in a replay of the 1964 campaign.

I'd seen a few of Reagan's movies but had never seen him in person before the luncheon. I was immediately struck by his cheerfulness, suggestive of the "slightly unnatural sunniness" literary critic Edmund Wilson had discerned in Franklin D. Roosevelt. Reagan animatedly shook hands with everyone at the head table, behaving as if the kind of talk he'd given hundreds of times was a novel experience. Seated at a table near the dais, I watched him converse amiably throughout the lunch, smiling often and eating little. Then he gave an innocuous but well-received speech about what he would do as governor, which didn't sound like all that much. Reagan made it seem as if "waste, fraud and abuse," a favorite target, was a line item in the state budget.

After his brief speech, Reagan took questions. As his campaign manager Bill Roberts later explained, this was really the point of the event. Democrats were asserting that Reagan was "just" an actor who mouthed lines written for him by others. Roberts and his partner Stuart K. Spencer wanted to show that Reagan spoke extemporaneously and could think on his feet. Despite not knowing much about state government, Reagan handled himself well. His self-confidence was leavened with humility, a rare commodity in politics, and although he was scant on details before a knowledgeable audience, Reagan avoided any gaffes. In response to some questions, he said unapologetically that he didn't know the answers but would find out. When a reporter asked Reagan how he could presume to launch his political career by becoming governor of the nation's most populous state, Reagan replied that it would be desirable to have someone who was inexperienced take a fresh look at government.

More than anything Reagan said, it was what happened after the speech that provided a glimpse of the appeal he would have as a candidate. Nearly everyone in the room came forward to meet him, some posing for a picture and one bringing a movie poster, which he asked Reagan to autograph. Reagan always obliged such requests. During the gubernatorial campaign, a wire-service reporter brought him a studio photo from the 1951 movie comedy *Bedtime for Bonzo,* showing Reagan with the chimpanzee who upstaged the human actors in that film. Reagan signed it, "I'm the one with the watch."

As reporters clustered around Reagan, I realized he was still a movie star. Reporters of Reagan's generation had seen his films; those of my generation also remembered him as host of *General Electric Theater,* on which he came across as authoritative and reasonable.

While Reagan chatted, I became aware that he was watching me watch him. I know this sounds odd, but Reagan often sensed when someone was evaluating him. Readers of *President Reagan: The Role of a Lifetime* will recall that my insights into Reagan's capabilities drew on the theory of multiple intelligences propounded by Harvard psychologist Howard Gardner. Reagan understood body language and had a high degree of what Gardner calls "inter-personal intelligence." Once when he was president, Reagan met with a large group in the Oval Office. After the meeting Reagan asked his aide Mike Deaver what a man who'd stood on the fringes of the group had against him. Deaver responded that the man hadn't said a word. But when Deaver checked out his background at Reagan's insistence, he learned that the man in question opposed the administration on the issue being discussed.

At that first encounter with Reagan in Sacramento, I knew nothing about his modes of behavior. I was standing back from the others to avoid giving the impression of being part of a fan club. But when I realized Reagan was watching me, I stepped forward and introduced myself.

"Ronald Reagan," he said in reply.

He had a crisp handshake and looked me in the eye. I went back to my office in the state capitol and later talked on the phone with the editor who had suggested I attend the luncheon. He asked my impression of Reagan. "I don't know why anyone would want to run against someone who everybody knows and everybody seems to like," I said.

After Reagan was in the White House, the editor enhanced our conversation and told people I had predicted he'd become president. His recollection was flattering, but untrue. I had no idea if Ronald Reagan would become the Republican nominee, let alone governor of California, and certainly had no inkling I'd be writing about him for the rest of our lives. But I did realize that Reagan had star power.

I was intrigued and wanted to see what would become of him.

2

THE FIREPLACE AND THE FIRE

Although I was born (on June 3, 1933) in New York City, most of my childhood was spent in Reno, Nevada, which billed itself on a downtown arch spanning its main street as "The Biggest Little City in the World."

I am the elder son of Jack and Irene Cannon, who in the 1940s owned a nondescript store in Reno called Cannon's Thrift Shop. It began as a pawnshop, a business that thrives in gambling towns. But my parents became uncomfortable with taking personal possessions on loan for a pittance, knowing they would rarely be redeemed. So they began buying clothes people had outgrown or guns they no longer needed. Most homes in Reno had guns in those days; my father had a rifle at home and carried a pistol for protection at the store, a block away from Skid Row.

My father was a farm boy turned salesman. He would open a real estate brokerage later in life, but his most cherished memory in business was selling Chryslers at a New York dealership. Chryslers were a high-class automobile before the Great Depression, and my father preferred them to any other car. After the Reno store began making money, he traded in his old Buick for a late-model Chrysler.

Cars of any kind were a big deal in Nevada, where distances are vast and gasoline was cheap. Owning a car was a rite of passage for teenagers, especially boys, and close to a necessity in a state where public transportation was almost nonexistent. Most of my friends had cars by the time they were sixteen; I was the butt of jokes because I didn't drive until almost seventeen. Our cars had all been made before 1942, when Detroit converted to wartime production.

The first and best car I ever owned was a murky black 1936 Chrysler Airflow that my father found on the back of a Reno car lot in 1950. It had low mileage as many cars did then because of the gas rationing during the war. We bought it for $295, the equivalent of about $3,860 in 2025 dollars, with my father doing the bargaining. The money was mine. I had worked summers and weekends since I was eleven. There was nothing unusual about that, either. Boys in Nevada were expected to work when not in school. After I bought the Chrysler Airflow, I became the envy of friends who had teased me about not driving earlier. It was a splendid car with an eight-cylinder engine that delivered 105 horsepower. It had running boards, two glove compartments, and a Borg-Warner overdrive that made a satisfying whir when engaged by a lever next to the steering wheel. My father was pleased I was driving a Chrysler, as if it somehow validated a happy time in his life.

My father was a classic case of the trope about getting the boy off the farm but not the farm out of the boy. Two stories set in southern Oregon tell much of the story of his life. After my parents sold Cannon's Thrifty Shop in the early 1950s, they bought a ranch of several hundred acres near Hugo, a wide spot on the road a few miles north of Grants Pass. The ranch had a one-bedroom farmhouse to which my father added a bedroom and updated the kitchen. The only heat in the house came from an old fireplace, insufficient for the dank Oregon winters. My father replaced the smallish fireplace with a massive one that heated the entire house through vents to the bedrooms. The new fireplace, faced with rough stones and striking tiles, could have been the work of a master architect. It was entirely the design of my father, who had no training in architecture or carpentry and had dropped out of school in the eighth grade. I was in college when my father built it. When I complimented him about it during a visit, he shrugged. He could display vanity about his sales prowess but took anything he built for granted. Years later I saw *Death of a Salesman* and was reminded of my dad in the scene where Biff Loman reminisces about how his father had enjoyed building a bathroom, and a new garage and a porch. "You know, Charley," says Biff, "there's more of him in that front porch than in all the sales he ever made."

The other story is darker. The farmhouse burned to the ground the night of February 2, 1953, my wedding night in San Francisco. My mother had come to the wedding while my father stayed home to tend the livestock. He was in the farmhouse, drinking with his brother

Mike. I still don't know how the fire started, but the ammunition in the house went off. My father said he was lucky to get out alive. "Lucky" was also the name of his dog, an Australian blue shepherd, which my father grabbed and took with him from the burning house. He didn't save much else. Later my dad poked through the rubble and found the remnants of a speaking or debate trophy I had won in high school. He gave it to my mother, who cleaned it up and put it into a frame next to my picture. Alcohol was my father's nemesis, but he seemed to have licked his problem with the bottle by the time he reached Oregon—except when his brother visited. My mother, who liked nearly everyone, couldn't stand Mike and said the words "Uncle Mike" as if they were one, almost in a hiss. Mike's hands were twisted from arthritis, a disease that would cripple my mother and was prevalent on both sides of the family. I got along fine with Mike but realized my mother was right in saying he was a terrible influence on my dad.

Rural Oregon, to which my city-bred mother had made a reluctant adjustment, was never the same for her after the fire. My father rebuilt the house, but he was having trouble getting around the ranch, already showing signs of the emphysema that would kill him at age sixty. My father was a chain-smoker. My mother smoked, too. They both quit after the diagnosis, but it was too late for my dad.

Like many children of alcoholics, I lived in two worlds. I never thought of my father as being especially kind, as my mother was, but he was approachable and steady when sober. When he was drinking, he could be irrational and violent. He'd beat me and my brother for no reason, although I never saw him lift a hand to my mother. I learned to recognize the signs and hide when my father was drinking. My brother Bob, eighteen months younger and my only sibling, was less adept at avoiding Dad when he was drunk. I think Bob was damaged as an adult by what he witnessed as a boy and by what happened to him. I thought, then and now, that I should have protected him better than I did.

It was the drinking that caused me to leave our house in Reno when I was sixteen and stay with friends. It turned out to be the right move, for as soon as I left my father began taking pride in my scholastic accomplishments, as my mother had always done. My mother thought my leaving prompted my father to find help for his drinking. I think he would have done so anyway, as he had sought help before. Dad just hadn't found a way that worked. One thing he tried was called "aversion therapy." He told me he was given his favorite bourbon with drugs that made him vomit. It worked for a while, at least when Uncle Mike wasn't around.

Many years later I read Ronald Reagan's searing story in his early autobiography *Where's the Rest of Me?* about how his drunken father had passed out in the snow. Reagan, slight of build, had dragged his bulky father into the house. This story resonated with me, as did Reagan's entire account of his father's alcoholism even though he sugarcoated it a bit, as children of alcoholics, including me, often do. Reagan's father was also named Jack and also of Irish extraction. I once heard Reagan, when he was governor of California, refer to alcoholism as "the Irish disease." When Reagan was president, chatting with me after I'd interviewed him, he suggested that one reason for my interest in him might be that we both had alcoholic fathers. It was unusual for Reagan to be introspective, let alone comment on the family life of an interlocutor. Reagan wasn't much of a chatterer. He would give you your allotted time or slightly more, try out a one-liner or two, and be gone. Of course, he was president and busy but there was more to it than that. Reagan, although invariably good-natured and usually kind, was also guarded. He had learned this protective mode of behavior as the child of an alcoholic, and it served him well.

Jack Reagan and Jack Cannon were tolerant men who lived in prejudiced worlds. When I was growing up, in the 1930s and 1940s, most people casually used the widely despised derogatory term for Black people. Not in our house, however, nor in the Reagan household a generation earlier. My parents told us that the word was disrespectful, a severe condemnation in a society in which respect mattered. I once got into a fight because I called out a boy who used the N-word. Although I don't recall for certain, it's likely I lost the fight. I was thin and scrawny and unathletic, but my father had taught us to fight back. In my experience bullies usually avoid kids who are willing to fight. Still, I fought often enough. In one of those fights, I swung wildly at a boy who had been tormenting me, my fist catching him square in the nose. His nose bled, and he ran away. When I told my father what had happened, he merely said it was an effective place to hit people.

Reagan describes in his autobiography how Jack Reagan refused to stay in a hotel after the hotel clerk boasted that it wouldn't take Jews. In his son's telling, Jack, who was Catholic, became enraged at the clerk's anti-Semitism and spent the night in his car instead. This story always struck me as contrived, but undoubtedly a version of an account Jack Reagan told his two boys. Jack Cannon would tell stories, too. His mother had died from complications in childbirth, and he had been raised on a farm by his sisters and took off on his own when a teenager. He was nomadic, as was Jack Reagan, until late in life. But Jack Reagan was always a salesman; my father could sell but had also worked in mills and on farms and as a jitney driver. Once, he was driving through Arkansas by himself and gave a ride to a hitchhiker who was Black. My father told him to get in the back of the car. Going through a town, police pulled him over and said he shouldn't be chauffeuring a Black man. My father gave the cops some lip, and they tossed him jail for the night. I loved this story and would beg my father to repeat it. It never occurred to me as a boy to ask an obvious question: What happened to the hitchhiker? I'm not sure my father knew but I wish I had asked.

My mother was diminutive and gentle and hardworking. She claimed to be four-foot, eleven-inches, although she was two or three inches shorter than that. She didn't drive when we were kids, but she learned after my father passed away. My father had acquired a used Mercedes, and my brother and I found some planking and put it in the driver's side of the car so my mother could reach the pedals. Even with the planking, she could barely see over the steering wheel. More than once when my mother was driving, I saw cars swerve when they spied what appeared to be a driverless Mercedes.

My mother had secrets, two of which I will mention. One of them her parents had kept from her as a little girl. The secret was that she was not born in Philadelphia, as she supposed, but on a family visit back to Budapest. My mother's maiden name was Kohn, and she was one of many children in a large Jewish family that had immigrated to the United States from Hungary late in the nineteenth century. I was named after her father, Louis, who in pictures is a distinguished-looking man with a handlebar mustache. I never met him or any other grandparent. My parents left for Nevada when I was about four years old, and my mother's parents died before we went back to New York City for a visit when I was eight. My father's father was long dead—I never learned from what—and my father of course had never known his mother. We traced Tiffin Cannon's ancestry to Donegal. My father must have known more than he told me, for he helped me once on a school assignment about the Great

Potato Famine in Ireland, and he knew more about the famine than my teacher did. I wasn't curious as a child about my parents' ancestry, but it bothered me that I had no living grandparents like other kids. I vaguely remember pretending my grandparents were alive and making up stories about them.

My mother's biggest secret, which she did not reveal during her lifetime and which my father never knew, is that she was older than he was. They had first met when my father was driving a jitney, a small bus owned by a gypsy cab company, up and down the East Coast, one of his many jobs during the early years of the Great Depression. According to the account of Mom's sister Carrie, which I heard when I was eleven, my mother had exhausted herself working at the family store in Philadelphia, and the family agreed she should be allowed a vacation. They scraped together enough money to send my mother to Florida for a week.

During the trip, one of the male passengers made a pass at my mother. He was insistent and it became clear to the driver, Jack Cannon, that Irene Kohn didn't welcome the man's attentions. At a stop along the way, Jack told him pointedly to stay away from her. My mother developed an immediate crush on Jack, who she realized had put his job at risk on her behalf. They exchanged addresses. I don't know if it was then or later that my mother lied about her age to him. It wasn't a small lie; she chopped six years off her age, which was either twenty-nine or thirty at the time. Growing up, we were told that my father was born in 1903, which was true, and that my mother had been born in 1906. My brother, Joel Robert Cannon, whom we called Bob, discovered after her death that she had been born in 1900 in Budapest, not in 1906 in Philadelphia, as we had always been told.

Both of my parents had the pioneering spirit. Irene Cannon was the only one of her large family who left the East. My father was a wanderer and had been all over the country after leaving the farm and the care of his sisters at sixteen. He once told me he'd been in forty of the (then) forty-eight states. So it was in character for my father to pull up stakes and head for Nevada with his wife and two toddlers. My mother's written history of the family's journeys was consumed in the Oregon fire, so I am reconstructing this as best I can, using landmark dates in a few places and otherwise leaning on my unreliable memory. I was born on June 3, 1933, at Lennox Hill Hospital in the Bronx. Bob was born on

January 16, 1935. I think it was 1938 when the Cannons left New York for Reno, although it could have been 1937.

The move to Reno was momentous for my mother. Long-distance calls were expensive and we had little money, so my mother wrote letters every day to her sisters. She learned of the death of one of them while taking me to nursery school. Mom was walking and reading and then crying and she walked me back home instead of taking me to school. I believe there were four girls and two boys in the Kohn family. The youngest boy was troubled; he was referred to in hushed tones by his siblings, but when I was an adult my mother confided to me that he had killed himself. The older boy, Eugene, to whom my mother was close, was brilliant, funny, and reasonably successful. Only one of the Kohn children was able to go to college: It should have been my mother, her sisters said, but his parents sent Gene because he was a man. By the time my mother sent me back alone on the train from Reno to New York for an extended visit in 1944 at a time when I was having trouble with my father, the surviving siblings were Gene and two sisters, Carrie and Bella. Carrie and her husband, Bill Halberstadt, lived on Long Island. Gene and his wife, Frieda, lived in Forest Hills. Bella, my favorite aunt, lived alone in Brighton Beach. I was passed from one to the other. All were responsible but indifferent except for Bella, who was childless and affectionate. One of Carrie's sons, Lou Halberstadt, also reached out to me. He was fourteen or so but saw that I was lost and took care of me. Among other things, he took me trick-or-treating on Halloween after explaining what it was, as I had never heard of it.

The Cannons had visited New York City once before as a family, driving across the country in 1941. I have a lifelong inner ear problem and would get car sick, so the trip was agony for me. But New York City was wonderful. We saw all the sights—I liked the Statue of Liberty best—and my mother told us about Ellis Island, where her family had entered after a voyage that began in Budapest. One Sunday we went to the Bronx Zoo. It was my first visit to a zoo, and I was awed by the elephants and the lions, which my brother said wanted to eat us. Afterward, we went to a Chinese restaurant, also a first-time experience. Before we ordered, a Chinese waiter came to our table and whispered in my father's ear. My father told the waiter to repeat what he had said out loud so my brother and I could hear it.

"The Japanese bombed Pearl Harbor," the waiter said unsmilingly. My father told me later that the waiter thought he should not make that announcement to children. The waiter may have been right. My brother, a month shy of seven, wanted to know who the Japanese were. I was a good geography student and knew where Japan and Hawaii were but didn't know why the Japanese were bombing anyone. We'd heard Hitler's rantings on the radio—my mother was fluent in German—and I'd heard my parents say we would one day be at war with Nazi Germany, but what did that have to do with Japan? After we had ordered, my father patiently explained that Germany and Japan were on the same side. He told us that our country was at war and that the war would be long.

3

JESSE AND PAT

As it turned out, I didn't see much of Ronald Reagan after that Sacramento luncheon where I first met him until he became governor. During the 1966 campaign I was a backup for Harry Farrell, the well-regarded *Mercury-News* political writer. Since I was based in Sacramento, this often meant covering Governor Pat Brown, whom I'd known since the 1950s. Despite my interest in Reagan, I relished the chance to cover what became Pat Brown's swan song.

Brown was an old-fashioned glad-handing politician with an impressive résumé marred by a reputation for indecisiveness. He had an affable manner, a round face accentuated by rounder glasses that gave him an owlish appearance, and a proclivity for scrambled syntax. Viewing the Eel River flood in 1964, Brown said, "This is the greatest disaster since I was elected."

There were many similar Brownisms. But Brown could also clasp a constituent's hand, look into his eyes, and make him feel as if he was the most important person on the planet. He would then promptly forget the person's name, as he also forgot the names of longtime aides and financial contributors. Guests at fundraisers were given oversized name tags so Brown could spot them from a distance. On one occasion a wealthy donor who was angry at Brown over a highway matter covered up his nametag at a fundraiser. Brown could not recall his name.

Nevertheless, the corridors of California politics were littered with adversaries who had underestimated Pat Brown. His genial exterior concealed a steely persistence that had empowered him to bounce back from political defeat and a patience that had enabled him to bide his time until conditions were ripe for him to run for governor. As a five-to-one underdog, Brown was elected district attorney of San Francisco in 1943, defeating an incumbent who had beaten him four years earlier. Brown ran for state attorney general in 1946 and lost, then ran again and won in 1950 and 1954. In 1958, he ran for governor and defeated anti-union newspaper publisher William Knowland, who caused a schism in his party by forcing a more moderate Republican incumbent out of the race. Brown was reelected in 1962 against Richard Nixon, who ran a listless campaign. On the whole, Brown was an excellent governor. He was a builder—of freeways and dams and universities—and believed in the "Great Society" brand of liberalism President Johnson was practicing in Washington.

California epitomized the American dream that William Faulkner called "sanctuary on earth for individual man," The Golden State seemed a promised land of limitless possibilities to servicemen who disembarked from there during World War II. Many of them returned with their families, as did defense workers who had flocked there during the war. From 1945 to 1965, California attracted more than a thousand new residents a day, doubled in population to eighteen million, and surpassed New York as the nation's most populous state. The pace of growth was intoxicating; the only constant, wrote Carey McWilliams, was "rapid, revolutionary change."

To accommodate newcomers and enrich themselves, developers uprooted vast fruit orchards and replaced them with subdivisions and shopping centers. State government helped finance thousands of new schools, a community college system that made higher education widely accessible, and a university system that educated the scientists and engineers who manned the aerospace barricades during the Cold War. During the eight years of Pat Brown's governorship, California completed a vast network of freeways and constructed a gigantic aqueduct that an enthusiastic cabinet secretary called "the eighth wonder of the world" to move water from the wetter northern part of the state to dry and populous Southern California. By the mid-1960s, California had become a font of technological and cultural innovation so diverse and global in outlook that it became fashionable to call it a "nation-state."

California's economic output was exceeded by only five nations, and its per capita income was higher than all the countries in the world.

I was a Californian during most of this period of untrammeled growth. My wife was a San Francisco native, and our four children were born in different places in California. We moved as my jobs dictated: San Francisco, Newark (on the south end of San Francisco Bay), Merced, Pleasant Hill in Contra Costa County, San Jose, and finally Sacramento. Initially, we took growth for granted, as young people do. But our outlook changed. When we moved to Pleasant Hill in 1961, buying a small house, we were surrounded on three sides by orchards. Within a year the orchards had been replaced by tract homes.

Ours was a typical experience in California. A few miles north of our San Jose home, developers were filling in San Francisco Bay. Property taxes soared as local governments struggled to meet demands for schools and services. As cities sprawled far beyond their original boundaries, agricultural land was assessed at "highest and best use," forcing farmers to sell orchards and vineyards that became subdivisions.

This disorienting loss of open space spurred environmental blowback that in most places was no match for developers and the local governments—and the local newspapers that supported them. No one outdid Joe Ridder, the publisher of the *San Jose Mercury-News,* in his breathtaking enthusiasm for a housing boom that wiped out the orchards of Santa Clara County, once known as "the Valley of Heart's Delight." His circulation manager succinctly explained Ridder's reasoning. "Trees don't read newspapers," he said.

Pat Brown, however, did read the papers, and he realized without knowing quite what to do about it that Californians had become agitated about unremitting growth and the taxes needed to pay for it. He briefly considered retirement but wanted another term to put him in the pantheon with Earl Warren, California's only three-term governor (although, later, Pat Brown's son Jerry would serve four non-contiguous, terms), and a man Brown revered even though Warren was a Republican. Brown was pessimistic about his chances until Ronald Reagan came along.

"How could an actor possibly beat me?" Brown asked his longtime friend and advisor Fred Dutton.

By the time I started covering Brown late in 1965, he was spending more time battling Assembly speaker Jesse Unruh, a fellow Democrat, than in preparing to run for reelection in 1966. Unruh was ready to run, and he believed Brown had reneged on a promise not to seek a third term.

Unruh regarded Brown as a ditherer. This opinion had taken public root in 1960 because of Brown's wavering in the case of Caryl Chessman, a notorious Los Angeles rapist. Rape itself was not a capital crime in California, but Chessman had moved some of his victims before raping them, prompting prosecutors to charge him with kidnapping under the state's "Little Lindbergh Law" and making him eligible for the death penalty. Chessman languished for twelve years on Death Row at San Quentin Prison, becoming a writer and inspiring a campaign to grant him clemency because he had not killed anyone. The night before Chessman's scheduled execution in the gas chamber, Brown went home alone after agreeing with his clemency secretary that he would not stop the execution. His twenty-one-year-old son, Jerry, who had recently left a Jesuit seminary, called his father and asked him to spare Chessman's life. Moved by his son's plea, Brown told him he would give Chessman a reprieve while the legislature considered whether the death penalty should be abolished.

Unruh was furious. Brown was not on the ballot in 1960, but all eighty Assembly members were, and Unruh feared that the issue would hurt Democrats in close races. Looking back years later, Unruh told me he hadn't wanted these Democrats—"my Democrats," he called them—hung out to dry for a bill that had no chance. In deference to Unruh, Brown saw to it that the new bill to abolish the death penalty was introduced not in the Assembly but in the more conservative State Senate. There, after an emotional debate, it was rejected in committee by a single vote. Brown refused to grant another reprieve to Chessman, who was executed on May 2, 1960.

Brown truly *was* a ditherer—Unruh had called him a "tower of Jell-O" during the maneuverings over Chessman—but he was also a principled opponent of the death penalty. He'd opposed capital punishment as San Francisco district attorney, one of the few California prosecutors to do so. He continued to oppose it as attorney general and as a candidate for governor. Brown spared more condemned men than any governor of California in history until Gavin Newsom came along.

Brown wanted to spare Chessman, too, but took seriously his oath to uphold state laws, even the death penalty.

Unruh was a phenomenal politician. A Texas sharecropper's son whose family was so poor he lacked shoes as a child, Unruh was nicknamed "Big Daddy" because of a supposed resemblance to the domineering father in the Tennessee Williams play *Cat on a Hot Tin Roof*. Unruh had enormous appetites for power, food, booze, and sex—especially power—but was a pragmatic and usually progressive politician who introduced and shepherded to victory legislation prohibiting racial discrimination by businesses long before this was done nationally. He also authored legislation to protect people who bought household products on installment contracts, as Unruh and his wife, Virginia, had done.

Jesse (pronounced "Jess") Unruh defied typecasting. He was principled and devious, sophisticated and crude, thoughtful and impulsive, visionary and myopic. He could be petty: He once refused to replace the broken typewriter of a secretary of a legislator who had voted against him on a minor bill. But Unruh was also farsighted, leading a national movement to improve the seedy image and second-class status of state legislators. The key to accomplishing this, he believed, was to free lawmakers from dependence on lobbyists for information by providing them with capable professional staff.

Unruh had escaped rural poverty during the Depression by doing well enough in high school to earn a scholarship to Wayland Baptist College in Plainview, Texas. When Pearl Harbor was attacked, Unruh enlisted in the U.S. Navy. Helped by the GI Bill of Rights, a democratizing measure that enabled some two million Americans to obtain a college degree, he completed his education at the University of Southern California after the war. Unruh studied political science and had a brief flirtation with the Communist Party, which in the immediate postwar years was active on the USC campus. Unruh broke with the Communists in part over Harry Truman, whom the Communists detested and Unruh admired.

Plunging into Democratic politics, Unruh ran for the State Assembly in 1948 when he was only twenty-six years old. It took him three tries, but Unruh was elected to the Assembly in 1954. Once in office, Unruh rapidly climbed the slippery pole of legislative leadership, transforming candidate financing in the process. On his thirty-ninth birthday, in 1961, Unruh became Speaker of the Assembly, which he ruled—with iron hand or velvet glove, depending upon the need—until 1963, when he overreached by locking up Republican legislators in the Assembly chambers because they had refused to vote for a budget bill.

The "Lockup," as it became known, backfired. Republicans refused to capitulate and won the media propaganda battle by depicting Unruh as a dictator. Unruh had been drinking when he ordered the Lockup. In its sober aftermath, he acknowledged his poor judgment and launched a personal makeover. Trying to change the physical image of "Big Daddy," Unruh gave up drinking and cigars and went on a four-month diet in which he ate one meal every other day and lost eighty pounds. But although his discipline was impressive and his figure trim for the first time in his life, Unruh remained personally insecure. When I interviewed him the first time for *Ronnie and Jesse,* he insisted on holding the microphone of my tape recorder so he could switch it off if he wanted to say something he didn't want recorded. He never exercised this option but told me later that holding the microphone gave him a feeling of control. This was a huge need for Unruh. He told a friend he sometimes dreamed he was still a penniless boy back on the farm in Texas.

I was fascinated by Unruh. He excelled in the politics of maneuver, understood the motivations of legislators, and possessed broad insights into the changes occurring in California. Unruh had a better understanding than Governor Brown of the strains caused by unending growth. Residents and commuters in the Los Angeles basin and the state's other urban centers wanted relief from smog and traffic congestion. Farmers wanted water, and environmentalists sought protection for endangered landscapes and wild rivers. Homeowners throughout the state protested soaring property taxes, which paid for the hundreds of new schools and roads and shopping malls being built every month in California. Unruh knew these problems defied easy solution, but he believed the legislature should address them.

Despite my respect for Unruh's political skills, I initially disliked him. His aides were arrogant, ignoring phone calls and hinting I'd be frozen out of information from the Speaker's office if my coverage wasn't favorable. Worse, Unruh tried to bully me. Reporters at the time had assigned seats on the Assembly floor. When I wrote a story Unruh didn't like, he waved me down one day after the Assembly session and said he wanted to talk. The talk consisted mostly of Unruh bragging about how he'd blocked part of a series written by Harry Farrell in the *San Jose Mercury* that revealed how the speaker raised money from lobbyists and dispensed it to fellow Democratic legislators. Unruh said he had an "in" with my publisher.

Harry was a splendid reporter, on a first-name basis with every politician in California, and an even better human being. Tall, angular, and ruddy in appearance, he had spent his entire newspaper career at the *Mercury,* where he was a copyboy in the early 1940s before going off to war. When we first met, in the early 1960s, he had twenty years of service at the paper with nearly another twenty ahead of him. He would have long since been poached by one of the big battalions in the news business, but Harry's wife was confined to their home by agoraphobia and other maladies, anchoring him to San Jose.

Harry's series "Money, Power, Politics" appeared in May 1963 when Unruh was at the height of his powers and two months before the disastrous Lockup that caused him literally to look in the mirror and launch his fearsome makeover. The post-Lockup Unruh might have shrugged off the series, but in May the speaker was still so full of himself that he took umbrage at even mild press criticism. The series, accurate and carefully written, focused on Unruh's fundraising methods and reliance on Howard Ahmanson, savings-and-loan association tycoon. When Harry identified the legislators Unruh had funded in return for their loyalty, the speaker panicked and phoned Hank Ridder, the publisher of the *Long Beach Press-Telegram,* who was close to Ahmanson. Hank Ridder in turn called his cousin Joe Ridder, who agreed to suppress the last story in the series. The *Mercury* ran a half-assed article recapitulating what had already been printed so it wouldn't appear that the series had been truncated.

I'd been on the wire desk, dealing with national news, when the series ran and didn't know what had happened to the final installment. After I became Sacramento correspondent, Harry told me the behind-the-scenes story and warned me to beware of Unruh. When Unruh leaned on me by reminding me about the fate of Harry's series, I told him heatedly where he could go with his threats. Unruh seemed amused by my defiance but dropped the subject. From then on, he became more responsive to my questions and more revealing about himself. This culminated in the candid interviews he gave me for *Ronnie and Jesse.* Unruh was a reader, and it mattered to him that someone would write a book about him. He didn't care that it was also a book about Reagan. Unlike Pat Brown, Unruh took Reagan seriously and realized he could become governor. Like the reporters who attended the luncheon where I met Reagan, Unruh had seen Reagan's movies. Although he did not approve of Reagan's politics, he recognized his star power.

A word here about Hank and Joe Ridder. Neither was a journalistic profile in courage—the only Ridder I knew meriting this description was Walter Ridder, who headed the Washington bureau—but there were differences between them. Hank was pragmatic. Although a Republican, he endorsed Democrats when it served his interests. Joe was a fervent conservative Republican. In 1968, he messaged me through an editor that he wanted to see me. I dutifully drove the 120 miles from Sacramento to San Jose. Joe, who had a drinking problem, was downing vodka from a water glass late in the morning. He told me that friends had claimed that Governor Reagan was betraying the conservative cause.

"Is Reagan becoming a liberal?" Joe wanted to know.

"No worry about that, Mr. Ridder," I said.

"Thank you," Joe said with a relieved look on his face. "I knew you'd know."

This exchange makes Joe Ridder sound like a simpleton, which he wasn't. He actually realized something about Reagan that many in the national media didn't grasp until years later—and some never did. What Joe understood was that with Reagan ideology took a back seat to accomplishment. Joe would have preferred it to be otherwise. His number-one complaint was the tax bill Governor Reagan had agreed to in 1967 after protracted negotiations with Unruh. It was, as Joe said, a budget that could have been proposed by a liberal Democrat. Not only did the bill trigger the largest tax increase ever approved by any state—about $1 billion, more than $9 billion in 2024 dollars—but it was a progressive measure that raised income-tax rates on the wealthy and on banks, corporations, and insurance companies while providing property-tax relief to senior and low-income Californians. I defended Reagan's actions to Joe Ridder. Because of an unfinanced accounting changeover proposed by his finance director to avoid a tax increase on his watch, Pat Brown had left Reagan with about two-thirds of the revenue needed to balance the state budget. Reagan had been smart to get the taxes he needed in one fell swoop so he wouldn't have to do it when he ran for reelection. Joe agreed it was smart, but he didn't like it.

After we finished with Reagan, Joe asked me what I thought of Unruh. I replied guardedly, thinking about the fate of Harry's series. The series may have been on Joe's mind, too, because he abruptly said he shouldn't have done what he did to Harry. Joe told me he didn't care for "that Big Daddy guy" but had owed a favor to Hank. Since the series was ancient history, I realized that suppressing the last article must have weighed on Joe. But I wasn't sure that he was as concerned about Harry's feelings as he was about having helped a prominent Democrat. The meeting ended pleasantly, with Joe asking me to stay for dinner. I knew from experience how quickly the mood of a heavy drinker can change, so I pleaded family obligations and drove back to Sacramento. Joe never mentioned Harry's series to me again.

Jesse and I had buried the hatchet on the series, but we had one more brush over its residue at the end of the 1966 legislative session. Unruh's priority that year was Proposition 1-A on the November ballot, which was based on the recommendations of a bipartisan constitutional revision commission with ties to Unruh. It trimmed the state's wordy constitution, made the legislature full-time, and raised lawmakers' salaries. The legislature was already a de facto full-time body, working in special session most of the year.

Unruh could charm as well as bully. He persuaded the state's major newspaper publishers to support the measure, mollifying their concerns by capping the pay increase at 5 percent and including a code of ethics, which in practice proved toothless. Unruh financed the campaign for Prop 1-A by hitting up lobbyists and corporations, then clinched the deal by getting both Ronald Reagan and Pat Brown to back it. Overall, the conception, promotion, and passage of Prop. 1-A was a masterful Unruh accomplishment.

On the last day of the 1967 legislative session, Jesse invited me to have a drink with him at the Senator Hotel, a favorite lobbyist watering hole across from the capitol. We were joined by a Senate aide and his date for the evening. Unruh was in an expansive mood. After the first drink he started bragging about how he had bamboozled newspaper publishers by promoting Prop 1-A as a good government measure. He mentioned that Joe Ridder was aboard and implied that Harry and I were aboard as well.

Annoyed by Unruh's assumption that reporters were stooges for their publishers, I quoted Unruh the lead of my next day's story in the

San Jose Mercury, which said the legislature had celebrated the end of its longest season in history by voting itself a pay raise. Jesse uttered a profanity. But the Senate aide's date laughed at Unruh's discomfort and he relented, saying Prop. 1-A would win voter approval no matter what anyone wrote. We had another drink and let it go.

By this time, after nearly a year in Sacramento, I was adjusting to the capitol beat. I'd been helped by Jim McCauley, who covered the capitol for the *Long Beach Independent Press-Telegram*, the paper owned by Hank Ridder. A few days after I arrived in Sacramento, McCauley made me aware of a late-breaking story of interest in San Jose. I thanked McCauley, who quipped we'd be fired for fraternizing. We became friends and helped one another regularly. We did our own reporting and never read each other's copy even though we shared an office, but we exchanged tips and gossip, often over lunch at Frank Fat's, a Chinese restaurant that is still my favorite place to eat in Sacramento.

Even with McCauley's assistance, covering the legislature was a struggle. I had good sources in Governor Brown's office but had never before covered a legislature and hadn't realized that most of the officials formed a close-knit club to which some lobbyists were admitted but few reporters. Most of the 120 legislators were wary of newcomers in the press corps. The reporters, like the legislators, ranged widely in quality. Some just skimmed the surface of their beats, while others were diligent and dedicated. George Skelton, then of UPI, and Bill Boyarsky, then of AP, were outstanding reporters who would have long and productive careers mostly at the *Los Angeles Times*. Riverside Press Enterprise correspondent Martin Salditch and television newsman Warren Olney were other excellent journalists in Sacramento who became personal friends.

For my part, I was determined to know as many legislators as possible and to write contextually about them. I didn't mind not being a member of the club, for I've never been a joiner. I started by making a list of legislators I knew. It consisted of three Democrats. Gordon Winton was in his first year in the Assembly in 1957 when I worked for the *Merced Sun-Star*. He was ethical, friendly, and popular with Japanese American farmers in Merced County who'd had their land confiscated in World War II. Winton had represented them pro bono in claims against the government after the war.

Assemblyman Jerome Waldie, another on my list, remembered me. In the mid-1950s I'd worked for a chain of weeklies in Contra Costa

County, a suburban county east of Oakland. Waldie remembered me phoning him and asking if he was running for a vacant Assembly seat.

"I don't know and if I did I wouldn't tell you," he replied. I quoted him verbatim in my story. Seeing his response in print, Waldie said, had taught him "not to be smart ass with reporters who were just doing their job."

Waldie, close to Unruh, understood the dynamics of the Assembly and helped me understand them too.

The third legislator on my list was State Senator George Miller Jr., whom I'd known when I was editor of the *Contra Costa Times* in 1959 and 1960. He's now remembered mostly as the father of George Miller III, an iconoclastic, left-of-center Democrat who served forty years in Congress. That's a pity, for few people did as much to resurrect the Democratic Party in California as George Miller Jr. He helped found the California Democratic Council, a volunteer group that supplied the foot soldiers for the party's comeback. Then he became state party chairman and later won election five times to his Senate seat from Contra Costa County. Combative and quotable, he was a favorite of reporters, and usually a happy warrior. But he wasn't happy about Unruh, whom Miller considered a devious bully.

During the 1967 wrangling over the progressive tax bill agreed to by Reagan and Unruh—the bill that prompted Joe Ridder and other conservatives to wonder if Reagan was wandering to the left—Miller believed Unruh broke his commitment to negotiate first with the Senate. Brooding about that slight and about losing a school reform bill that Unruh had killed in a Senate-Assembly conference committee, Miller became enraged when the speaker swaggered over to the Senate to watch proceedings wrap up on the last day of the 1967 session. He rose to his feet and delivered a vitriolic attack.

"I'm sick and nauseated by the presence of Little Nero on our floor," Miller said. "Let him foul his own den."

It was a good show, if overdone. Miller prided himself on keeping his word and detested those who didn't. He was the best raconteur in the legislature and a master of off-color anecdotes, but he was also a caring person who responded when a colleague or aide or even a reporter had a personal problem. One day a young UPI reporter came into the Senate with a distraught look on her face. Her parents were visiting Sacramento, and her father had been denied admission to the Senate because he wasn't wearing a tie. Miller asked the reporter to take him to her parents, who were waiting outside the Senate's heavy doors. Miller took off his tie and gave it to the reporter's father.

"They have to let me in," Miller told them. "I'm a senator."

He was a good one, too. More than anyone, Miller held the Senate together when its composition changed forever in 1967.

What changed the California Senate and the upper houses of most state legislatures in the United States were two U.S. Supreme Court decisions, *Baker v. Carr* in 1962 and *Griswold v. Sims* in 1963, that required them to be apportioned on the basis of population, usually shorthanded as "one man, one vote." Until then, California and many other states had a lower house based on population and an upper chamber that contained more cows than people. Legislative redistricting is normally done in the second year of a decade, based on the decennial census, but the two court decisions forced a redistricting in 1965 that played out in the 1966 elections. Los Angeles County, with about one-third of the state's population, had a single senator before the redistricting. Afterward it had fourteen senators in the forty-member Senate. California's fifty northernmost counties went from having thirty-one senators to eighteen.

As a Sacramento correspondent from late 1965 until late 1969, I witnessed the difficult transition in the Senate, which for a time retained its club-like, rural character even with the addition of so many urban Southern Californians. This was because the Senate was dependent on the Third House, as lobbyists are known in Sacramento. At a time when liberalizing California's restrictive abortion law seemed a far-fetched idea, a prominent lobbyist helped persuade Hugh Burns, the conservative leader of the Senate, to allow Senator Anthony Beilenson of Beverly Hills to proceed with a permissive abortion rights bill. Beilenson was one of the Unruh Democrats in the Assembly elected to the Senate after the "one-man, one-vote" redistricting. He skillfully cleared legislative hurdles and guided his bill to the desk of Governor Reagan, who reluctantly signed it in April 1967.

The abortion legislation exemplified the willingness of the California legislature to tackle controversial issues, including help for the mentally ill and the developmentally disabled. In subsequent decades, the legislature would be diminished by term limits, corruption, and excessive partisanship, but in those days legislators on both sides of the aisle assumed that bipartisanship was a requisite of good government. In the late 1960s the California legislature was on balance effective and progressive, laying down many national markers. The measure with the most far-reaching impact created the California Air Resources Board, which years before the Environmental Protection Agency existed obtained a federal waiver to set strict emissions standards and reduce smog in the Los Angeles basin. The board's standards were copied by other states and the EPA.

While covering the legislature, I made enduring friendships. Judson Clark and William Hauck were legislative aides and graduates of San Jose State College (later university), which in California government played the role of the solid corporal belt in the British Army, providing a reliable flow of mid-level aides and experts for governors and legislators. Bill Hauck became a top aide to two Democratic Assembly speakers and a Republican governor, founded the California Business Roundtable, and served for a quarter century on the California University governing board. He was a problem-solver and recurrent voice of reason in Sacramento. Jud Clark (with Hauck and others) founded State Net, an innovative public information company that published *California Journal*, a magazine of state government and politics with which I had an association throughout its thirty-five-year existence.

I knew every legislator by name and face, not a daunting accomplishment in a state with so few of them. They included George Deukmejian and Pete Wilson, two future Republican governors. One of my favorites was George Moscone, a laid-back Democratic state senator who would be narrowly elected mayor of San Francisco in 1975. We kept in touch. I last saw Moscone on November 23, 1978, at the funeral of Representative Leo Ryan, who had been assassinated in Guyana by members of the Jim Jones cult. Moscone and I chatted after the funeral, and he said he was determined to do something about gun violence. Five days later, Moscone and gay-rights activist Harvey Milk were shot to death by a former San Francisco supervisor who nourished grievances against liberals and gays.

Witnessing Pat Brown in the eighth and final year of his governorship was an instructive and sad experience. Although he'd shown savvy in winning four statewide political campaigns, two for attorney general and two for governor, in 1966 with Reagan looming in the wings, Brown blundered.

He did more than concur with clueless political advisors who told him Reagan would be easier to beat in November. Brown also intentionally nudged Republican primary voters toward Reagan by undermining his competition. In 1940, George Christopher had been a young dairyman trying to get ahead. He cut milk prices, hoping this would attract new customers, and challenged California's anticompetitive price-fixing laws. But the laws were upheld; Christopher was convicted of a misdemeanor and fined. The story was well reported by San Francisco newspapers, one of which lauded Christopher for challenging the price-fixing scheme, but by 1966 this story had been forgotten. Democratic operative Dick Kline proposed revisiting Christopher's conviction and using it as a basis for a hit piece. Don Bradley, Brown's campaign manager, had no reservations about attacking Christopher, but he alone among Brown's advisors realized that Reagan would be the Republican nominee no matter what the Brown camp did. Accordingly, Bradley told Brown it was a waste of time and resources to go after Christopher.

But Brown also sought the counsel of Hale Champion, the state finance director. Champion had been a San Francisco newspaperman and like his boss attached undue political importance to the City by the Bay. He, too, thought Christopher would be more formidable than Reagan.

Hale and his family lived two blocks away from my family in Sacramento, and my eldest son and his son were friends. Hale was a bright and pleasant man who would go on to have an impressive career in Boston, but he could be over-clever. In 1965, in an effort to balance the state budget without a tax increase, Hale urged Brown to change California's accounting system to an accrual method that counted future receipts when they became due rather than when they were collected. Brown embraced the idea. Both men knew that an unfunded changeover in accounting methods would force the next governor to raise taxes because much of the state's revenues would already have been spent. Hale told Brown the changeover was too complicated to become a political issue. Reagan succeeded in making it an issue precisely because it *was* complicated. He didn't try to explain the accounting changeover, but he described it to voters, accurately, as a gimmick to postpone an inevitable tax increase.

Champion supported the smear of Christopher, and Brown agreed. The governor's operatives leaked the story to nationally syndicated columnist Drew Pearson, a favorite Democratic Party hatchet man. Pearson wrote a preposterous column recycling the milk-pricing conviction and describing Christopher as a persistent criminal and a draft dodger during World War II. Most California newspapers declined to run the column, but a newspaper in Vallejo did, and Pearson followed up by coming to California, where he held a press conference and expanded on his charges.

The sordid episode had no discernible impact on the outcome of the Republican primary, which Reagan won handily. But it unified California Republicans, who had not recovered from a bitter 1964 presidential primary in which Barry Goldwater had narrowly defeated Nelson Rockefeller. After winning the nomination and then losing decisively to President Lyndon Johnson, Goldwater wanted to drive GOP moderates out of the party. Reagan had supported this effort, but when he ran for governor he realized the need for a unified party. Immediately after winning the primary, Reagan called Christopher and asked for his support. Smarting from what Brown had done to him, Christopher told Reagan he'd be happy to endorse him. Other moderates followed suit. Years later, over a drink at the North Beach Restaurant in San Francisco, Christopher told me he would have balked at supporting Reagan except for the "Pat Brown–Drew Pearson smear." Instead, Christopher did everything he could to help Reagan defeat Brown.

In the general election campaign, Brown and his advisors disagreed among themselves on the approach they should take toward Reagan, who had never spent a day in public office. Reagan called himself a "citizen-politician," a claim ridiculed by Brown, who asked if people who were ill needed citizen-doctors. He also compared Reagan to a "citizen-pilot" who told passengers it was his first flight "but don't worry—I've always had an active interest in aviation."

These parodies worried Reagan campaign manager Bill Roberts, who knew that voters were concerned with Reagan's inexperience. But Brown couldn't stick to his script and ad-libbed that he was solving California's problems while Reagan was being upstaged by a chimpanzee in the film *Bedtime for Bonzo*. He repeatedly used the word "actor" as a synonym for "know-nothing." This belittling of Reagan's profession impressed neither actors nor voters. Jack Palance walked out of a Democratic telethon in disgust, saying, "Attack him [Reagan] if you wish for lack of experience, but don't go after him just because he is an actor."

The governor and his strategists ignored this warning. Brown rarely gave a speech without a sneering reference to a Reagan movie. His campaign commissioned an oddball half-hour "documentary," *Man vs. Actor,* of which they were inordinately, if mysteriously, proud. At the film's climax, Brown tells an integrated class of young schoolchildren, "I'm running against an actor, and you know who shot Lincoln, don'tcha?"

Brown and his team liked this distasteful line so much they made it into a one-minute spot that was shown several times during the last week of the campaign. It is surely one of the most counterproductive commercials in American political history.

In tandem with this anti-actor message, Brown's strategists sought to demonize Reagan as a right-wing extremist, a page from the playbook used against Goldwater in 1964. Hale Champion thought it would be effective because Reagan had been such a visible Goldwater supporter and had the unwanted backing of Robert Welch, the crackpot founder of the far-right John Birch Society, who had called President Eisenhower "a dedicated, conscious agent of the Communist conspiracy." But Reagan defused the Bircher issue with a statement which said: "Any member of the society who supports me will be buying my philosophy. I won't be buying theirs."

Democrats did not give up trying to wrap the Welch endorsement around Reagan. They figured they had little choice, as the anti-actor strategy was not working. Brown sunk steadily in the polls during the spring and early summer of 1966. In August the state Democratic chairman, Robert Coate, issued a twenty-nine-page document, "Ronald Reagan, Extremist Collaborator—An Exposé." Then came a "white paper" issued by state controller Alan Cranston, who believed his own reelection was assured. Cranston added an undocumented claim that the Birch Society was riddled with anti-Semitism. This angered Reagan, who had quit a Los Angeles country club because it did not admit Jews. A few Democratic politicians were also outraged. George Miller Jr., who had salvaged a number of Brown's programs in the California Senate, bluntly urged the governor to "run on your record and forget this Birch thing."

Guided by Roberts and his partner Stuart K. Spencer, Reagan ran a smart campaign. From midsummer of 1966 to Election Day, the Spencer-Roberts firm knew from polling that Reagan was well ahead and kept the candidate on a light schedule, hoping to avoid mistakes, as they mostly did. Reagan's most significant contribution to the campaign beyond his optimistic presence was to elevate student disturbances at the University of California to a major campaign issue he called "the mess at Berkeley." This hadn't shown as a major issue in the early Spencer-Roberts polling, but Reagan was often asked about the Berkeley situation when he was doing his out-of-town tryout speeches in 1965. Typically, he paid attention to his audiences and added the "mess at Berkeley" to his time-for-a-change litany.

Polling showed that five other statewide Republican candidates were trailing their Democratic opponents. So Reagan brought the other candidates under his wing, campaigning with them and telling audiences "not to send me to Sacramento alone." The Reagan rallies had a Mexican flair, complete with mariachi bands. He finished each speech with the words "*Ya basta!*" the Spanish equivalent of "Had enough?"

Voters answered the question in the affirmative. Reagan received nearly a million more votes than Brown, carrying Democratic working-class precincts in which Brown had swamped Knowland and Nixon. Reagan also did well in suburban and rural areas and received 40 percent of the vote in Mexican American neighborhoods, despite Brown's claim that Reagan was an enemy of Mexican Americans. Reagan carried four of the five other statewide Republican candidates to victory. The Democratic losers included Alan Cranston.

The magnitude of Reagan's victory surprised Brown, but the results did not. Dutton told me that on election night he seemed almost relieved. Brown confirmed as much when I interviewed him a year and half later for *Ronnie and Jesse.*

"I think I was tired of the job," Brown told me. "I think that manifested itself. Being governor eight years, you lose a little of the zip. You've appointed your friends judges, the people you've grown up with. You've appointed other people to higher office, you've put over a great water plan and a master plan for higher education, and you're building three universities. You're seeking out something to do—what do you do now? Now we get down to the tough parts of politics, like a revenue program, and here's where I ran into the stone wall of Jesse Unruh in the Assembly. That's where Ronald Reagan came along."

4

HOME MEANS NEVADA

After the visit to my mother's relatives in New York City, my father drove the four of us back to Nevada in early 1942. We soon moved to Fallon, in farming country sixty-three miles east of Reno. I wasn't happy about it, for I didn't know anyone in Fallon. But I was hardly alone. The war uprooted many Americans, and some of the other children had fathers who were pilots or maintenance workers at what is now the Naval Air Station Fallon. It was built in 1942 for defense against an anticipated Japanese invasion, although I doubt the Japanese would have wasted time in Fallon. The schools there were a mix: farm kids and city kids and kids whose fathers were based at the air station. There were also Native Americans, more than I had ever seen in Reno. "Indians" is what we called them, and that is what they called themselves.

Much later, as an adult in Washington, DC, I became a fan of the Washington Redskins and knew the franchise's owner, Jack Kent Cooke. Many times, I joined in singing "Hail to the Redskins" at old RFK Stadium without giving thought to how that nickname must sound to Native Americans. The controversy over the nickname did not arise in any serious way in Cooke's day, but he was so public-relations conscious that he might have been open to changing the name.

Daniel Snyder, who acquired the team after Cooke's death, enjoyed exhibiting stubbornness for its own sake. He got away with it for years. The *Washington Post,* among the institutions in the capital that decided the name should be changed, commissioned a national poll in

2016, which revealed that nine out of ten Native Americans were *not* offended by the name. To its credit, *The Post* dutifully reported this finding, which only emboldened the cocky and arrogant Snyder. Eventually, other problems caught up with him, including sexual harassment claims and allegations of financial mismanagement. His unpopularity, coupled with a national reckoning on race in 2020, altered the equation. The name was changed first to the Washington Football Team and then to the Washington Commanders.

In the end, the whole drama doesn't seem complicated. No one in Fallon called Indians "Native Americans," a term not yet in vogue, but no one called them "redskins" either. A child could figure out that the word was insulting.

Fallon was not free of racial prejudice. One of the defining incidents of my early boyhood occurred when a teacher, a woman as most teachers were in wartime, said to an Indian child who was slouching at his desk, "Why don't you sit up straight, like a white man?"

A boy who was a friend of the Indian child stood up and walked out of class. Several others, including me, walked out with him. It was spontaneous. We weren't politically conscious—how could you be in fourth grade?—but we knew it was terrible way for a teacher to talk to a kid. We were sent home and someone in authority, maybe the principal, said our parents would be notified. I told my father straightaway. He was angry—but at the school and the teacher, not me. He said we'd done right to walk out.

We lived in Fallon from 1942 until 1945, most of the years the United States was in World War II, and my parents operated a motel called the Cannon Court, which had a replica of a Civil War–era cannon outside. There was gas rationing then and Fallon was a small town, but the motel was usually full because of a local naval air station. Fallon would never have been my choice of a place to live, but I made a good friend there. His name was Lincoln Pierce. His Anglo-sounding name aside, Lincoln in appearance was as Mexican as Emiliano Zapata. His mother was a Mexican woman who had married an Anglo railroad worker who had abandoned them when Lincoln was small. After school we would go to Lincoln's tiny home near the railroad tracks, where his mother made the first tortillas I'd ever eaten. We ate them warm, sometimes with butter and sometimes plain.

It was because of Lincoln that I saw my first dead man. The man had been walking on the railroad tracks when a train had decapitated him. The authorities came and shooed us away from the tracks, but I had seen the man's body and his severed head. Lincoln and I never talked about what we had seen, but I had occasional bad dreams about it.

Besides Lincoln and his mom, the other good thing that happened to my brother and me in Fallon was Gunter Gigas. He was in his twenties or early thirties and was commissioned by my mother to teach the two of us to play the violin. Bob quit after a few weeks, but I stayed with the violin as long as we were in Fallon and for a year or two in Reno. The violin was frustrating to me, but instructing me must have been even more frustrating for Gunter. I love music, and Gunter was at first excited to have me as a pupil. He said I had perfect pitch. Maybe so, but I also have stubby fingers and practiced to no avail. I knew how the violin was supposed to sound, and it never sounded right when I played. Gunter played beautifully.

Fallon was home to the Lahontan Reservoir on the Carson River, which had been providing irrigation for farmers since early in the century. The area later would become chemically polluted, but in those days the streams and tributaries of the river ran clear and were full of catfish and perch and carp. Gunter took us fishing a few times, a poor man's fishing done with worms we dug ourselves. I was better at fishing than playing the violin and consequently less frustrated when engaged in that ancient pursuit. Gunter showed me how to avoid the sharp horn of the catfish when cleaning the fish. "Clean what you catch, and eat what you clean," is what we learned. I don't recall who first said that to me, but I accepted that mantra and passed it on to my children.

Catfish are not everyone's taste, but I liked them. I remember once coming into the kitchen for breakfast and seeing catfish swimming around in a big metal washing tub. I have no idea where they came from. My father was taking them out of the tub and killing and cleaning them, then cooking them in a cast-iron frying pan. He gave me extra, probably because I thought it was neat to have breakfast that way, and the catfish tasted wonderful.

I was grateful to Gunter for teaching me the basics of fishing because my father never once took me fishing. It never occurred to me that my father didn't know how to fish. I assumed, as boys do, that their fathers know everything. I'd daydream about my father taking me fishing, especially after we moved back to Reno, where fathers regularly took their sons (in those days not so much their daughters) to the Truckee River to fish for trout. I knew nothing about casting, and trout are harder to catch than catfish, but I taught myself as best I could. One of the benefits of growing up in Nevada was that the first day of trout-fishing season, even in high school, was an excused absence. I never missed the first day of trout season even though there were times I didn't catch fish.

We moved back to Reno when I was twelve, and my parents opened Cannon's Thrift Shop. Here, the narrative of my memory is blurred. At some point my brother and I lived on my uncle's farm, on Salmon Falls on the American River in the rolling foothills above Sacramento. Folsom and Auburn were the nearest towns. The reason I'm hazy about it is that we also spent several summers on the farm, and those days have merged in memory with the one time I was there in the fall and went to what I believe was the seventh grade in a one-room schoolhouse. Our parents were away in Mexico in what was probably my father's only trip outside the United States. If my brother were alive, he would know the year.

The farm had been my grandfather Tiffin Cannon's place at one point, but in my childhood was owned and operated by my father's oldest brother-in-law, Will Miller, and his wife, Clara, who with the help of her sister Florence raised my dad. I remember asking my father why it wasn't owned by a Cannon. He said it was a long story, which he never told me. Tiffin had farmed in the Sacramento area, where it often flooded, and moved to Salmon Falls seeking higher ground. The farm is now mostly underwater, in the Folsom Reservoir, built in 1956 to protect Sacramento from flooding. During the droughts of the 1970s and the 1990s and again in the longer drought of 2012–17, parts of the farm peeked out of the water, reminding me of the scene in *The Flying Dutchman* when the Norwegian sailors see ghost sailors from the phantom ship. But while the Norwegians were terrified, I was delighted to see part of the farm once again.

Here are a couple of sentences from a story I wrote that ran in the Outlook section of *The Washington Post* on December 23, 1990: "I recognized the rounded outline of Goat Hill, where the goats ran wild and where we gathered mushrooms after the winter rains. Not far away, the old stone bridge at Salmon Falls now spans dry land. The sight of the bridge and the hill stirred happy memories, even though I know these apparitions are ominously dry auguries for California, a nation-state now home to 30 million people where the population is increasing by almost 65,000 each month." I ended the story with a prediction that the "ghost farm would soon be high and dry." It didn't quite make it that year, but the farm emerged almost completely from the water in a more recent drought. On Saturday, November 14, 2015, the reservoir fell to its lowest level in its six-decade history: 14 percent capacity.

I liked everything about the farm. Uncle Will taught me how to milk a cow. Aunt Clara taught me how to find eggs in the chicken coop and showed me how to wring a chicken's neck. I was a squeamish city kid, but Aunt Clara was so matter of fact about life and death that I soon got over my qualms about how chickens flopped around the yard before they died. It was dinner, after all, and there wasn't a grocery store within twenty miles.

I didn't know it, but the Miller farm was an anachronism even then. Will and Clara had 250 acres or so and grew corn and melons and vegetables at a time when huge farms were being carved out of the California desert—"factories in the field," Carey McWilliams famously called them—with migrant labor to feed America.

The Millers were largely self-sufficient. They went to Folsom every few months and bought flour and sugar in bulk, which they stored in bins on a closed-in porch. They also bought kerosene, which provided all the light on the farm. Since they lacked electricity, they had no refrigeration and stored potatoes and apples in cold cellars. They butchered a hog every year and cured bacon and salt pork. But chicken was the staple at a table that featured bacon for breakfast and biscuits and white gravy made by Aunt Clara at every meal.

We were never hungry. In summer there was fresh corn, and Bob and I once got stomach aches eating the kernels raw as we harvested them. They had cherry trees, too. We picked blackberries in summer and harvested mushrooms after winter rains. Aunt Clara showed us the differences between edible mushrooms and toadstools or fly mushrooms, but Bob and I were enthusiastic in our mushroom gathering, and it's a small miracle we didn't poison the family. More likely, Clara picked through our mushrooms before boiling them or sautéing them in bacon fat.

I have other jumbled memories from the farm. Once or twice we played football with boys from other farms on the hilly ground outside the farmhouse. I'd go inside afterward and scribble an account of the game in my awkward longhand, presaging an early career as a sportswriter. The autumn we were left at the farm, Bob and I attended a one-room schoolhouse run by a kind and observant teacher named Nan Kelly. I was the only one in my grade, and Nan Kelly encouraged my interest in history and geography. She also painstakingly taught me how to write an "s" in the correct way. I had done it backwards since learning to write. I could see it was backwards but couldn't do it correctly. It was either poor hand-eye coordination or a glimpse of the dyslexic malfunction that would afflict my youngest son.

When my parents came to take us home from the farm, I was happy to see them, but nourished a fantasy that they would stay and we would all live on the farm. I didn't want to go back to Reno. My brother, on the other hand, was eager to live in a city again. Of course, we went back. I was enrolled by mistake in Northside Junior High School in the eighth grade. Nan Kelly had said I was in the seventh grade in the one-room schoolhouse. I could easily do eighth-grade work but was small for my age. Based on my age and physique, I should have been in seventh grade. The bullies at Northside were larger, stronger, and more numerous than the ones I had faced in Fallon or earlier in Reno elementary school, and they didn't run away when you hit them in the nose. They were organized into a gang with arcane rules that required me to fight a different bully every day. I lost almost every fight in the eighth grade and wasn't doing better in the ninth until an Indian boy named Floyd Sampson befriended me for reasons I either don't remember or never knew. Floyd never picked a fight, but he had a powerful punch. After he befriended me, no one bothered me again.

My brother took a different, more effective approach. Bob was not a fighter, but he was a sweet person who believed in the goodness of others. He would approach a stranger, tell him his name and start relating a story that usually began in the middle, as was his habit. Bob assumed he would be liked or at least accepted and usually he was. He took the same approach with dogs. I was afraid of dogs after being bitten as a young child. Bob was bitten more than I was, even by my father's dog, but it never deterred him. He would go up to any dog and expect him to be a friend. I don't think the dogs knew what to make of him anymore than the bullies did.

After Northside, I attended Reno High School, then the only one in the city. Reno was small with a population of only 34,000 in 1950, the year I graduated. But it didn't feel like a small town. The population of the state was only 160,000, and Reno was Nevada's most populous city and the cultural center of western Nevada. Traveling orchestras and performers often stopped in Reno, which also boasted a flourishing community theater. The casinos were confined to a half-dozen square blocks downtown, and people could live out their lives in Reno without ever visiting them. But they were worth visiting, even for non-gamblers. The most prominent casinos, Harold's Club and Harrah's, billed well-known entertainers at shows that were usually free to the public. I once spent an hour at a casino bar, sipping a coke and listening to legendary 1940s-era bandleader Harry James play trumpet. I found it disrespectful that some customers in the bar and gamblers just outside of it never even looked in James's direction.

For reasons I've never fully understood, I blossomed in high school. I had classes that challenged me, and I also made male friends—and had girlfriends. Although the youngest boy in the school and still scrawny, I was more competitive physically than in junior high because I'd taken a boxing class at the YMCA. Golden Gloves was big in those days and my instructor had won his weight class the year before.

Suddenly, I no longer had to fend off bullies or look to others for protection. I had only two fistfights in high school, holding my own in one and winning the other, a new experience for me. It also helped that I went out for the football team in my sophomore year when I weighed only 102 pounds. Although I didn't make the varsity, I stuck it out for two years on the junior varsity, which at times was split into six-man teams to scrimmage with small schools in Nevada that didn't have enough players for eleven-man football. The other boys at Reno High respected football players, even undersized ones. Although I was an unskilled player, our coach, Bud Beasley, taught us how to tackle, the one aspect of the game in which I did fairly well. Coach Beasley told us that when we thought we were close enough to tackle a runner, take another step and then tackle. Mostly, it worked.

The experience of having small and unathletic players on his team must have been trying for Beasley, who had been a three-sport star in his own playing days. Years later he told me that as he watched me struggle on the field he would mentally compose the letter he would write my parents if I was killed or seriously injured explaining why he had allowed me to play. I gave up football in my senior year and became a sportswriter for the high school newspaper and then the local paper, the *Nevada State Journal,* for which I wrote a column and covered high school games. Writing about football—or any sport—is much easier than playing it. The paper didn't pay me a salary but was generous on mileage, starting at five cents a mile and raising the stipend—for the 1949 state-championship football game won by Reno High School in Las Vegas—to seven cents a mile. Gas was twenty-six cents a gallon. The roundtrip from Reno to Vegas was nine hundred miles, resulting in a stupendous paycheck of $630, by far the most money I'd ever earned. The sports editor at the *Journal* told me he was reprimanded by the newspaper's business auditor for paying that much to a high school student.

The other good thing that happened to me in high school was that I overcame my perpetual shyness and occasional stammer. I was inspired by a charismatic speech teacher named Roger Joseph, a graduate of the celebrated Pasadena Playhouse. Just as Coach Beasley had his little trick about tackling, Mr. Joseph had canny advice for students who struggled to speak clearly. He taught me to memorize the first paragraph or first few sentences of a speech. He said I'd then be able to give the rest of the speech naturally without worrying about my notes. It proved to be transformative advice. I won several local speaking contests and participated on the debate team with my close friend Clinton Wooster, who was droll and well-organized, anticipating his career as a lawyer. Both Clint and I tried out for the senior play and were given good roles. I thanked Mr. Joseph for instilling confidence in me, but he minimized his own contribution.

"Ability is inside you," he said. "It just has to come out."

Years later, Ronald Reagan, who was on the verge of being fired as a radio announcer because he didn't know how to read commercials, told me he'd saved his job by memorizing the first line of a commercial. He'd then read the rest of the commercial, which sounded natural and persuasive. I didn't tell him that this was the same trick taught me by Mr. Joseph.

Friendship is important in high school, and I had good friends. In addition to Clint, my closest friend was a tall, handsome kid named Bruce Lake whose interests, he said, were "girls and cars," in no particular order. They were the right interests for Bruce, who could fix any car and was adored by the girls. Another friend was Roy Johnson, who had come to Reno from somewhere in the East and was interested in diplomacy.

They all had decent careers and married well. Beverly Wooster, Inge Lake, and Lena Johnson all became lifelong friends. Clint went to law school, became the city attorney, was successful in private practice, and ran for the Nevada Supreme Court, an elective office. Bruce became an Air Force pilot; he met Inge while based in what was then West Germany. Inge came to New Jersey with Bruce and founded a successful school. Roy became a Foreign Service officer who served in several war-torn countries. While single, he adopted an orphan boy in Vietnam.

What my friends didn't know—and what I didn't tell them—was that in my senior year I was not living at home. I never discussed my father's drinking or other family problems with anyone. I had spending money and a roof over my head because of my mileage recompense from the local newspaper. I worked the summer after I graduated and the entire time I was attending college, but in my senior year in high school didn't work except for what I did for the paper, which required no heavy lifting. I was one of four valedictorians at graduation; my parents came to hear me speak and said they were proud.

But my folks, especially my father, weren't doing well. My father's closest friend was a police detective named Roy Geach; he and his wife would come to our house and play canasta with my parents. Roy Geach was friendly and informal for a policeman, even saying I could address him by his first name as my parents did. (Of course, I didn't. Boys in those days addressed adults as "sir" or by their titles, and he was "Detective Geach" to me.) But he was easy to talk with. My parents admonished me not to pester him about police work, but once when the Geaches and my parents were playing cards I saw the police revolver holstered in his belt and asked him if he ever shot anyone. Without directly answering my question, he told me that most officers go through their careers without ever drawing their guns in anger.

Detective Captain Geach and a sergeant detective named Allen Glass were shot to death on November 8, 1947. Their killer was a teenager named David Blackwell, the son of a minister. Blackwell, who had a long juvenile record, was a trusty in a reformatory in Washington State when he escaped. Along with two older men, he participated in a crime spree across the Northwest. They committed a string of robberies and shot and wounded a resistant grocer before they arrived in Reno, where they stole $3,500 from a store. Reno police picked up the trail of the three suspects, which led them to a seedy hotel where the robbers had holed up. Geach had a reputation of being a careful officer, but what happened next was anything but careful. The officers barged into a hotel room. Cowan and another officer pinned one man behind the door, forcing him to drop his gun. What follows is from the *Reno Evening Gazette:*

> Capt. Geach and Sgt. Glass proceeded to where Blackwell was lying in bed in an adjoining room. As Capt. Geach threw the bed clothing back from Blackwell he was met with numerous blasts from the robbery suspect's .38 caliber super special automatic. He fell to the floor mortally wounded, and Sgt. Glass, standing behind him was also hit several times and was killed outright.
>
> Capt. Geach succumbed in an ambulance while enroute to a hospital a short time later. Sgt. Cowan opened fire as Blackwell shot and as one bullet struck the youth he dropped his gun and surrendered.

The story goes on to say that neither Geach nor Glass had their weapons drawn. This was improper police procedure, other officers told my dad, but this detail was omitted from subsequent stories, probably in deference to the slain policemen's families. Someone—it may have been Cowan himself—told my father that Cowan then emptied his revolver at close range but missed Blackwell with all but the one shot that slightly wounded him. Cowan's hand had been shaking, unsurprising in the circumstances. The Reno officers arrested the third subject in another hotel room and beat up Blackwell at the station, also unsurprising. There was no mention of the beating in the news stories, but a picture in the paper showed two officers holding up a battered Blackwell, who looked as if he couldn't stand on his own.

Blackwell was executed in the gas chamber in Carson City on April 22, 1949. He had become religious on Death Row—the pastor who counseled him and attended his execution said, "This boy has certainly found Christ."

Robert Laxalt, the distinguished Nevada writer (and later friend) witnessed the execution for United Press. He observed that Blackwell seemed unafraid and walked unaided to the gas chamber. The Associated Press story describing the execution called Blackwell "a handsome, dark-haired youth" with a thin smile. He winked at Cowan as he entered the gas chamber. Blackwell took a deep breath as the fatal cyanide pellets were dropped and "was apparently unconscious within three seconds and certainly unconscious within five seconds," according to the official report of the prison physician.

My father and his friends in the Reno Police Department had cheered the death sentence for Blackwell but found little solace in his execution. This may have been because of the bravery Blackwell displayed in the face of death. It didn't make any of them opponents of the death penalty, as far as I know, but the execution didn't comfort them either. My father started drinking heavily again shortly after Roy Geach's death. During the time I lived at home before moving out in my senior year, my parents never had anyone over to the house to play cards or for any other reason. It was a hard time for both of them. I once overheard my father saying to my mother that he'd tired of the store and wanted to farm. I doubt that my mother, a city person, was keen to leave her friends in Reno for an isolated farm, but she worried about my father's health and his drinking and went along. It took a while, but they eventually sold the Cannon Thrift Shop and moved to Oregon.

5

WILD ABOUT HARRY AND JACKIE AND JOE

Harry Truman's presidential campaign briefly restored my father's spirits. My parents' store was across from the Reno train station, where President Truman stopped on September 22, 1948, as part of his whistle-stop campaign across the West. I was fifteen and closely following the election. It was widely assumed that the Republican nominee, Thomas Dewey, would defeat Truman.

Loosely speaking, my parents were New Deal Democrats, but my father cared more about the New Deal than the Democrats. I cared about Franklin D. Roosevelt, who took the presidential oath of office when I was less than three months old. He was the only president I had ever known. I was in class at Northside Junior High School when the teacher received a note and announced that "our President" had died. She was near tears, and so was I. Many in my class wept openly. We were sent home from school, and I went to my parents' store and asked my father: "Who could be president?" It wasn't a civics question. At twelve, I knew the vice president became president, but I couldn't see how anyone other than FDR could lead our country.

My father assured me that Truman would do okay, but like many other Americans, he was soon disappointed. It wasn't anything Truman did or didn't do; he just wasn't FDR. Early in 1948 a hanger-on at the store began beating the drums for Henry Wallace, the nominee of the left-wing Independent Progressive Party. My mother disliked the man and disliked him even more after he began promoting Wallace. More than my dad, my mother voted the Democratic Party line. She didn't need to be convinced to support Harry Truman.

Dad did, and I went with him to hear Truman speak. The president's whistle-stop was a big deal in Reno. FDR had passed through in the midterm election of 1938 in his failed attempt to purge Democratic senators who were not supporting the New Deal, but most people in Reno had never seen a president, particularly not one fighting for his political survival. Speaking in his flat, midwestern twang, Truman stirred the midday crowd. He denounced the "do-nothing" Eightieth Congress, the first in many years controlled by the Republicans, as "a "bunch of old mossbacks" who "want to turn the clock back."

Read today, as one can do on the Truman Library website, Truman's words seem remarkably detailed for a stump speech, and requiring more knowledge about government than most voters now possess. Truman was running on his own in 1948, or thought he was, and never once mentioned the sainted FDR. He didn't mention Dewey either. What I remember most is that Truman roused his audience, provoking scattered shouts of, "Give 'em hell, Harry!"

Truman responded with a famous line, "They say I give them hell, but I just tell the truth and the Republicans think it's hell." My father and I applauded like crazy. I never heard my dad mention Henry Wallace again.

On November 2, 1948, my father and I stayed up after my mother and brother had gone to bed and listened to the election returns. It was the best time I ever had with my father. He left school after the eighth grade and could be intellectually intimidated by well-educated people, but he had an ear for pretentiousness. H. V. Kaltenborn was an influential and self-important radio commentator of the time with precise diction that my father thought was affected. Kaltenborn, with Bob Trout, anchored what would now be called the NBC News election desk. As the returns trickled in, Kaltenborn became convinced that Dewey would be declared the winner when the "farm vote" came in.

Doing a passable imitation of Kaltenborn, a side of my father I had never seen, my dad said dryly, "When the farm vote comes in, Truman will still be president."

And so he was. By the morning—we were on Pacific Time in Reno—Kaltenborn had retracted his prediction and was congratulating Truman. My father and I were thrilled that Truman was the winner and also that he had carried Nevada. We felt that by staying up all night and listening we had helped pull the president through.

My mother arose early, as was her habit, and saw us sitting together. "What is Louis doing up?" she asked.

My father explained that we'd been up all night listening to the election results. To my mother's surprise, he was protective of me, even saying I could stay home from school that day. But I went to school because I wanted to tell my classmates about it. That afternoon I fell asleep in class and was gently awakened by a teacher who said she understood why I was tired. I wondered if she, too, had been up all night, listening on the radio to the improbable victory of Harry Truman. Soon afterward I dreamed of meeting President Truman, an event so unlikely for a fifteen-year-old Reno boy that I didn't mention the dream to anyone.

One year later I attended Boys State, a mock government sponsored by the American Legion, and was one of two Nevadans chosen to attend Boys Nation in Washington, DC. Traveling across the country by train in late July 1949, I wondered if my dream about meeting President Truman would come true.

It did. All ninety-six boys in Boys Nation were taken by bus to the White House. Truman was seated at his desk in the Oval Office, mechanically shaking hands as we filed past alphabetically. Bill Capitan, a boy from Michigan with a wrestler's build, was behind me. He'd confided to me beforehand that he intended to say something to the president. I didn't believe him. Boys spoke when spoken to in those days. I would no more have initiated a conversation with a president than done a shout-out to the pope. But when it was Bill's turn to shake hands he said, "Hello, Mr. President, I'm from Owosso, Michigan, Tom Dewey's hometown."

Truman looked up, flashed a full-faced smile and gave Bill an enthusiastic handshake. "You've got a good start, boy," he said.

We also met Nevada's two U.S. senators, both on *Time* magazine's list of the nation's ten "most expendable" senators. Our group included Carlos Herrera, the other Nevada boy at Boys Nation. He was a year older and towers over me in a faded newspaper picture of the two of us with Senator Patrick McCarran, the state's senior senator and the most powerful politician in Nevada.[1] Although McCarran, a Democrat, had

1. I was identified in our hometown paper as "Louis S. Cannon." In a sign of the times, Carlos Herrera's first name was rendered as "Carl."

introduced Truman, a former Senate colleague, on his 1948 campaign stops in Nevada, including the one my father and I attended, he detested FDR and the New Deal. McCarran, whose parents were from Ireland, had played an outsize role in limiting immigration from Asia, southern Europe, and other places whose residents were of darker hues. Six decades later, one of McCarran's successors, Senate majority leader Harry Reid, would say that the Las Vegas airport named for McCarran should be renamed because "McCarran was one of the most antisemitic . . . one of the most anti-black, one of the most prejudiced people who has ever served in the Senate."

This was over the top, par for Harry. Although prejudiced, McCarran hardly held a candle to Theodore Bilbo of Mississippi and several other racist senators at the time. McCarran's true passion was stopping communism. His name would be on the internal security bill that passed Congress in 1950 and later would be mostly invalidated by the courts.

After posing for the picture with Herrera and me in his office, McCarran quickly excused himself. It was obvious he had little interest in a couple of teenagers who were in Washington to learn about government. The same could not be said for the other Nevada senator, George Malone, a Republican whose office, *Time* said, was a "rat's nest of mining statistics." I don't know the truth of that description because Senator Malone met us not in his office but at the entrance of the Senate dining room, where he graciously took us to lunch, inquired about our families, and introduced us to other senators, notably Robert Taft, who was also polite and gracious. Senator Taft rose to shake our hands. Standing behind him was a hulking figure, whom Taft introduced as Joseph McCarthy.

McCarthy was not yet notorious. The following February, he would give a speech in Wheeling, West Virginia, to a Republican women's club in which he said: "I have here in my hand a list of 205 [State Department employees] that were known to the secretary of state as being members of the Communist Party and who nevertheless are still working and shaping the policy of the State Department." It was the first of many such speeches.

Most of the political figures I met in Washington that week seemed larger than life, but McCarthy was unimpressive. Even McCarran looked like a senator (or as I imagined a senator looked) and carried himself well. McCarthy had a hangdog appearance and at midday a five o'clock shadow that would later become a feature of the caricature of him by the famous *Washington Post* cartoonist Herblock. McCarthy also had a limp handshake and did not look one directly in the eyes, as my father had taught me men were supposed to do when shaking hands. I was astonished when he became the center of public attention a few months later.

The most impressive politician to the Boys Nation group was Hubert H. Humphrey of Minnesota, a year into his first term in the Senate. Civil rights was the closest I came to having a cause as a teenager, and Humphrey was a hero to me for his performance at the 1948 Democratic Convention in Philadelphia, where he said: "The time is now arrived in America for the Democratic Party to get out of the shadow of states' rights and walk forthrightly into the bright sunshine of human rights."

This stirring appeal for inclusion of a civil rights plank in the Democratic platform triggered a southern walkout and the presidential candidacy of "Dixiecrat" Strom Thurmond, which at the time was seen as another nail in the political coffin of President Truman.

Humphrey talked faster than anyone I'd ever heard, so fast that the boys taking notes couldn't keep up with him. He was enthusiastic about America and what he saw as the coming triumph of liberalism and possessed a spark that dazzled even the boys from Republican families. I had no inkling that in 1972 I'd be covering a less ebullient Humphrey for *The Washington Post* as he made his final try for the presidency. The spark was deeply buried by then but still there.

At Boys Nation we were housed in dormitories at American University vacant for the summer break. Public buildings in Washington, DC, then suffering through a historic heat wave, were air-conditioned, but the dormitories weren't, and I was unprepared for the relentless heat and humidity. Reno, at elevation of forty-five hundred feet, is pretty dry and cools down at night on even the hottest days. When I was a little kid, I once heard my dad say to my mom, "One thing, 'Rene, you always need a blanket here at night." I puzzled about that. We naturally needed blankets at night, so why was my father saying that? I finally understood at American University, where I sweated all night, took a shower in the morning, and dreaded coming back to the dorm.

Boys Nation was not in step with segregated Washington. We were told to take the first seat available on the chartered bus that took us around the district and beyond. Although we were hardly a rainbow coalition, our group included a sprinkling of Blacks and Asians and they didn't sit at the back of the bus. A woman stared at us disapprovingly as we disembarked at Monticello, the Thomas Jefferson home, as a Black boy who had been in the front row got off the bus.

As much as I enjoyed Boys Nation, I was happy to leave Washington and take the train to New York City. Ostensibly, my reason for going to New York was to visit my mother's dwindling group of relatives, none of whom I'd seen since 1945. The relatives were nice people, particularly my Aunt Bella, but that wasn't my motivation for this side trip. My real purpose—and I had saved money from many odd jobs to make it happen—was to see the two best baseball players in the world. Politics was interesting but didn't hold a candle to baseball, the only sport my father would walk across the street to see.

Baseball then was the national game even in the West, where there were no major league teams. Despite having played countless pickup games, I wasn't much of a player. Slow and small, I also suffered from severe astigmatism, undiagnosed until my freshman year in college. At Reno High School tryouts I had one shining moment, hitting a curve ball a long way by following Coach Beasley's mantra of waiting on the ball. The other wannabe ballplayers cheered when I hit that curve, but I made an error on an easy groundball when we took the field, which doomed whatever slight chance I had of making the team. Unlike in football, there was no baseball junior varsity.

My interest in baseball was undimmed by lack of skill. After World War II, minor league baseball teams proliferated in sports-crazed America, and Reno had a Class C team—the Silver Sox—that played in the Sunset League, again mostly California teams. It was a low-level farm club of the New York Giants. My father had been a Giants fan when he lived in New York. He told me he'd seen the great Carl Hubbell pitch. He also told me there was a contest to become a Silver Sox batboy: Just write one hundred words or so saying why they wanted this job. I came in second. My mother told me that the parents of the boy who came in first were friends of the owner, but I didn't care. As runner-up, I became batboy for the visiting teams, which was more fun. The summer of 1947, I would walk the two miles from our home to a seedy hotel where the ballplayers stayed and accompany them on a bus to the ballpark. Afterward, I'd ride back on the bus and sometimes eat with the players and walk home after midnight.

The Sunset League was full of has-beens and never-would-bes, including a slew of players who'd been in the high minors during the war, when many major league players were in service. Few Sunset Leaguers ever made it to the majors. One who did was a Silver Sox pitcher, Al Corwin, who won twenty-six games for Reno as a twenty-year-old ace, more than he would ever win again. Three years later, Corwin made it to the Giants and won five games in that miraculous 1951 season climaxed by the Bobby Thompson homerun known as the "Shot Heard 'Round the World."

My favorite person among the visiting teams was the Anaheim manager, Jack Rothrock, who had been the right fielder on the St. Louis Cardinal team known as the "Gashouse Gang," which won the 1934 World Series. Rothrock took a shine to me because I knew the history of that team. On one of Anaheim's trips to Reno, he took me to dinner after the game and told stories about Dizzy Dean and Pepper Martin and other members of the Gashouse Gang.

The two players that drew me to New York in 1949 were the most celebrated in baseball. One was Joe DiMaggio, then in the twilight of his brilliant career. The other was Jackie Robinson, who had broken baseball's color line two years earlier. I had pictures of them, torn out of a sports magazine, on the wall of my basement bedroom. Like most Giants fans, my father didn't care for the Yankees but made an exception for DiMaggio, the ultimate Yankee, who my dad said was the best ballplayer in the world. My father's favoritism for DiMaggio went down well in our predominantly Italian neighborhood, in which DiMaggio was a demigod.

Living in a time and place where there was much overt racial prejudice, my brother and I were fortunate that our parents were not bigots. When Robinson broke in for the Brooklyn Dodgers in 1947, I was surprised to hear one of the athletes at Reno High whom I had previously admired say that Black people "should stay with their own." (He didn't use the word "Blacks.") I told my father about this, who said it wasn't the boy's fault: He had "backward" parents. "They should have let colored people play in the majors long ago," my father said.

So although I had differences with my father and was dismayed by his drinking, I had his blessing on this New York side trip. Both he and my mother pointed out, however, that long-distance telephone calls were expensive and said I should write down what I saw and tell them when I came back. That is what I did. My notes from this trip are long lost, but they are embedded in memory.

I saw DiMaggio play on August 6, 1949, in a game between the Yankees and the St. Louis Browns, a franchise that five years later would become the Baltimore Orioles. I'd bought a ticket in the center field bleachers for fifty cents, asking to be as close as possible to DiMaggio. I was three rows back. My dad had warned me that I'd be lucky to see DiMaggio play. The Yankee Clipper, as the newspapers called him, had been out of the lineup from the beginning of the season until late in June because of a heel injury, and sportswriters were saying it might be his last year. But there he was, with No. 5 on his back, shagging flies as he warmed up for the game.

Soon after the game started, a Browns player hit a tremendous fly ball into right center. DiMaggio was off at the crack of the bat. We had been told that he made everything look so easy. Well, maybe that's the way it looked from the grandstand, but from the center field bleachers you could see that he was running as hard as possible, gobbling up ground with his elongated stride. He made the play, of course. He was Joe DiMaggio. But I realized that, while he may have made everything look easy, it wasn't really easy for him.

On that day, Yankees starting pitcher Allie Reynolds didn't have his good stuff, and the Browns teed off on him as if it were batting practice. Reynolds was gone by the third inning, with the Browns leading six-to-three. At the end of four innings, the score was eight-to-three. A few fans left, but what did they know? I had faith in DiMaggio, who rewarded me by hitting a line-drive home run in the fifth inning. Other Yankees came through. The Browns couldn't get Tommy Henrich out. A normal right fielder playing first base that day, Henrich went four for five. More amazingly, Yankees shortstop Phil Rizzuto, not usually a long-ball threat, hit two home runs for the only time in his career. The second of them, in the sixth inning, cut the Browns lead to eight-to-seven. No one was leaving the park now.

By then, I was certain the Yankees would pull it out. In the bottom of the ninth with one out, Henrich hit a home run to tie the game. This brought up DiMaggio, who homered to give the Yanks the game, nine-to-eight. I took the subway back to the YMCA hostel at which I was staying with a friend from Boys Nation. He asked me how it had gone. "The way it was supposed to," I said.

Two days later, I went to Ebbets Field to see the Dodgers play the Giants. By now I was staying with my Aunt Bella in Brighton Beach, and she had arranged for a ticket to be picked up at the will-call window. The clerk in the will-call was tucked deep inside a narrow alcove. After I gave him my name, he instructed me to shove a dollar into the alcove. As I did, two arms, one white and one black, hit my arm. They were the guys behind me in the will-call line, trying to take advantage of a scrawny kid from out of town. As I extricated the ticket, they continued to pound my right arm, leaving a heavy bruise that did not heal for several days. But I held firmly onto the ticket.

Nothing in my experience had prepared me for a Dodgers-Giants game in Ebbets Field. People were shouting words I didn't understand, including racial epithets. The grandstand, where I was seated between third base and home plate, smelled of beer and body odor, and there was a persistent noise level, a kind of loud buzz, which continued throughout the game. A wizened, nondescript man was in the seat next to mine, and he saw I was alone. "Where you from, kid?" he asked. From the look on his face when I said, "Reno, Nevada," I don't think he'd heard of the place. He then gave me a rundown on the Dodger players, which included the information that Robinson was Black.

"I know," I said. "I'm here to see him play."

The wizened man gave me a bemused look and told me the Dodgers had "another Negro" who was also pretty good.

The other African American player on the Dodgers' roster was hard-throwing pitcher Don Newcombe, then in his rookie season. He came into the game with a ten-to-three record and began mowing down the Giants hitters, getting ahead with fast balls and following up with curves. The box score says Newcome struck out only five hitters that night, but it seemed like more to me.

Robinson, meanwhile, was magnificent. This would be his MVP season, when he led the league in batting with a .342 average and in stolen bases with thirty-seven. He was a coiled spring on the field, exploding when he fielded the ball at second, from which he started two double plays. In the second inning, Giants pitcher Dave Koslo brushed Robinson back with a pitch and then made the mistake of getting the next pitch over the plate. Robinson hit it out of the park. He had a tight smile as he circled the bases. The Dodgers added another run in the eighth and went into the ninth inning with a two-to-nothing lead. Then Whitey Lockman, the Giants' left fielder, led off the ninth with a home run. I thought the Dodger manager might pull Newcombe at that point, and I guess Newcombe did, too, for he looked at the bullpen and then into the dugout, as if someone was coming out for him. No one did, and Newcombe retired the next three Giants in order, giving the Dodgers a two-to-one victory and winning his eleventh game of the season.

I had resolved before the game to cheer for Robinson when he came up and quietly root for the Giants, my father's favorite team, to win the game. That resolve vanished with Newcombe's first pitch. How could one not be for the Dodgers in Ebbets Field? Many years later when I lived in San Jose, I would root for the San Francisco Giants and Willie Mays, but that night I was possessed by the Dodgers and convinced that in Jackie Robinson I had seen the greatest player in the world. After the game, the Dodgers fans stood up and roared, in no hurry to leave the park. I was transfixed. The wizened man next to me had left me alone during the game but now turned and said: "Bet you never saw anything like this in Reno, kid."

He sure had that right.

6

THE RISE OF RONALD REAGAN

Fast forward to 1967. Remember Ronald Reagan's quip that he didn't know how well he'd do as governor because he'd never played a governor in a movie? In real life he found the role demanding. That came as no surprise to his political team, Bill Roberts and Stuart Spencer, who'd never fully bought Reagan's campaign assertions that having a state helmsman devoid of government experience would afford a fresh look at California's problems.

"Oh, what will that poor soul do if he's ever elected governor?" Roberts said to campaign press secretary Lyn Nofziger.

In fact, Reagan had much that he wanted to do, but Roberts and Spencer were not in Sacramento to help him. They had returned to their political consulting business in Southern California, leaving the new governor with a young staff that for the most part was as inexperienced in government as Reagan.

"We were not only amateurs, we were novice amateurs," Nofziger said later. Reagan had some advantages, however. He was a resonant speaker with broad public support, and his years as president of the Screen Actors Guild, an intensely political union, had made him conversant with many issues and taught him the value of compromise. But the topics Reagan knew about were national issues, and his focus had been on the federal government. He had thought little about state issues and ran for governor because that was the path open to high office.

In the early days of his governorship, Reagan was at once brilliant and adrift. The brilliance was his realization that the unfunded accounting changeover inherited from Pat Brown that left California with an immense budget shortfall presented a political opportunity. While other Republicans were bemoaning that Brown had left them in a pickle, Reagan recognized otherwise in his first week in office. In his inaugural message, Reagan denounced the changeover as "a gimmick that solved nothing but only proposed the day of reckoning" and promised to "squeeze and cut and trim until we reduce the cost of government." Behind the scenes, he was telling aides that economies were insufficient to balance the budget and that a tax increase was needed. Reagan realized voters have short memories. An early tax increase could successfully be blamed on Pat Brown; if he waited, the reason for its necessity might be forgotten. Reagan campaigned ideologically and governed practically, which turned out to be a preview of his presidency.

Unruh was pleased that Reagan had opted for a tax increase. The speaker favored it on its merits and also believed it would come back to haunt Reagan when he ran for reelection. With that in mind, I tried to get Reagan to discuss the political calculus of his decision to raise taxes when I interviewed him for *Ronnie and Jesse* in the summer of 1968. Reagan wouldn't bite but came close. I told him Unruh believed the tax increase would hurt him when he ran for reelection. First, Reagan told me he had not decided if he would run again. Then, he asked me when the tax bill had been passed. "1967," I said.

Reagan then asked me when the election was. "1970," I said.

"You see," Reagan said. He left me to fill in the blank that the tax increase would be old news when the election rolled around.

Reagan was so good at politics that he denied he was a politician, knowing the label was unpopular. When I wrote that Reagan was an effective politician, he told me he wasn't a politician at all in the normal sense of the word. Instead, Reagan claimed to be a "citizen politician" like the fabled Cincinnatus who had left his plow to rescue Rome in crisis and returned to the fields once he had accomplished his mission. This was a fantasy. Reagan had no intention of returning to Hollywood. Once he entered politics, he stayed until he reached its pinnacle.

For all his political savvy, Reagan's first months as governor were difficult. He knew a tax increase was necessary, but he didn't know how a budget was constructed or how bills were passed. He showed terrible judgment on a critical appointment. He focused largely on what interested him, not bothering to get up to speed on much he needed to know.

Readers interested in the ups and downs of Reagan's first year in office can find my accounts in *Ronnie and Jesse* or *Governor Reagan: His Rise to Power*. I'll limit myself here to a pair of Reagan mistakes that foreshadowed similar problems in his presidency. The first and most serious of these was his disastrous choice of a state finance director, California's most important appointive post. The second was a lack of focus as his administration grappled with the sensitive issue of the state's mental hospitals.

Overall, Reagan's early appointments as governor were reasonably good. Some were outstanding. That's because most of them originated with Thomas Reed, a brainy physicist who had become wealthy in land development. This unusual résumé for a political aide insufficiently describes Reed, a free spirit who called himself a conservative but was libertarian in his social views and moderate on environmental issues. Opposed to U.S. involvement in Vietnam and believing that President Johnson had hoodwinked the American people about the need for U.S. troops, Reed had become involved in Barry Goldwater's 1964 campaign. Long before Goldwater lost in a landslide, Reed realized that Goldwater wasn't an acceptable candidate to most voters. But Reed was inspired by Reagan's speech for Goldwater a week before Election Day.

After Goldwater lost, Reed envisioned a Republican comeback in 1968 with Reagan as the party's standard bearer. For Reagan to have a realistic chance of becoming the presidential nominee, Reed believed he needed to show as governor that he could attract and hire good people to work for him. Reed accordingly volunteered to serve as appointments secretary for the first hundred days of Reagan's governorship. He saw his job as fending off party officials and Reagan admirers who thought a job in the administration should be a reward for supporting Reagan during the campaign. Reed wanted Republicans for these jobs, if possible, but only those of demonstrated ability. With the assistance of Paul Haerle, a like-minded San Francisco lawyer, Reed made some inspired choices, the best of them a visionary secretary of resources director named Norman (Ike) Livermore. Largely because of Livermore, Governor Reagan's administration in California had an exceptional environmental record that contrasts with the record in Washington when President Reagan appointed the antediluvian James Watt as secretary of the interior.

State finance director is the most critical appointment for a California governor, and Reagan's first choice would have been perfect. He wanted to appoint A. Alan Post, the legislative analyst, widely respected for impartiality and an encyclopedic knowledge of state budget practices. Post had criticized Brown's unfunded accounting changeover and taken a dim view of various Unruh proposals. But he was resolutely nonpartisan, and it made Post uncomfortable when Reagan said during the campaign that he wanted to appoint him finance director. Post told me he didn't want to be part of anyone's campaign. When Reagan won and offered him the job, Post politely turned him down.

Rancher William P. Clark, who would have an important role in the Reagan presidential administration, then suggested Caspar Weinberger, a San Francisco attorney with an accomplished résumé who was well informed on state financial issues. Reed, Nofziger, and chief of staff Phil Battaglia agreed. As a state legislator in the 1950s, working with information supplied in part by Alan Post, Weinberger had investigated corrupt liquor lobbyist Artie Samish and helped reform the state beverage-control system. But Weinberger was persona non grata with Reagan's wealthy backers, known as the Kitchen Cabinet, because he had supported Nelson Rockefeller against Goldwater in the 1964 primary.

In the face of this opposition, Reagan offered the finance post to the Ohio state finance director. He turned down the job. Choice number three was a Lockheed executive who also had no interest. Reagan was disappointed. He had predicted during the campaign that chief executive officers and other high-ranking businessmen would step forward to serve his administration. Few did.

Desperate to fill the position, Reagan hired a diminutive, eager-to-please consultant named Gordon Paul Smith, who wasn't anyone's first choice save his own. Smith knew little about the state budget and even less about the legal authority of his new job. He shunned outgoing finance director Hale Champion, who tried to cooperate with the new administration, and he was unaware of the California constitutional provision that the Department of Finance is under the purview of the governor-elect. Smith had no allies on the Reagan staff. The professional civil servants in the Finance Department tried to help him but soon decided that he was in over his head.

Smith also gave himself too little time to prepare a 1,005-page, $4.6 billion budget that stunned Sacramento. It called for 10 percent across-the-board reductions, penalizing departments that had operated frugally and rewarding those with padded payrolls. Smith was ridiculed by both parties in the legislature, but the idea for the across-the-board cut was Reagan's. He had propounded it at a meeting during the early days of his exploratory candidacy, using a favorite riff that he repeated in his inaugural message: "There are simple answers, just not easy ones." Reagan's first state budget provided no answers at all.

Many of Reagan's efforts to squeeze, cut, and trim state spending were similarly illusory. Some, such as a freeze on state hiring, were temporary. Others, such as selling the state airplane, were symbolic. A particularly pointless gesture was a Battaglia brainstorm calling for state employees to work voluntarily on Lincoln's and Washington's birthdays. Less than 2 per cent of the state workforce showed up on either holiday.

The legislature refused to consider the budget, and to Smith's dismay, Reagan acknowledged in an early March speech that 10 percent across-the-board cuts were impractical. On March 27, Smith submitted a new budget, but by then the legislature had lost confidence in the embattled finance director. Unruh was incensed by Smith's insistence that the budget could not be balanced unless $160 million was cut from Medi-Cal, California's version of Medicaid, providing health care for the poor and disabled. Reagan approved the reductions, which were blocked by the courts and became unnecessary once the tax increase was approved. Smith continued to advocate for them. Reagan at first backed his finance director, but after conceding that the Medi-Cal cuts were unnecessary, Smith was allowed to resign in early 1968 for "personal reasons" after thirteen months on the job. Weinberger replaced him.

Smith's second budget had eased the job anxieties for most of the state's 169,000 employees but caused consternation at the Department of Mental Hygiene, which ran California's ten hospitals for the mentally ill. The budget proposed to reduce the department by 3,700 employees, most of them hospital staff. This was of interest to my editors because there was a mental hospital in the *Mercury* circulation area.

The Department of Mental Hygiene was a tempting target for budget-cutters since the population of the mental hospitals was declining because of tranquilizing drugs and new medical procedures. The number of patients fell from 33,000 in 1963–64 to 20,000 in 1967–68. But the patients who had left the hospitals were those who responded best to drug treatment, while the patients who remained were more apt to need intensive care. California's mental hospitals were already understaffed; in 1967 they had yet to meet staffing standards that had been recommended in 1952. The proposed budget cuts would have reduced the staff by about 9 percent and left the hospitals 16 percent below the 1952 standards.

Democrats, supported by the union that represented the hospital workers, denounced the cuts. Even Republican-leaning newspapers such as the *Mercury* who otherwise supported Reagan economies were skeptical. I thought at the time that reducing mental hospitals' staff was one of those rare occasions when Reagan's political instincts deserted him. The truth, as I learned in researching *Ronnie and Jesse,* was more complicated—but also more disturbing. Fanned by Nofziger's concerns, Reagan had expressed qualms that the mental hospital staff might be stretched too thin by the cuts, but he never followed up on this perception. Reagan, who was oddly disengaged, had done little more than skim the surface of the budget proposal made in his name. The minutes of the key meeting in which the hospital budget cuts were ratified suggest that Reagan barely participated in the decision-making process.

During a discussion about the hospitals' medical staffing needs, Reagan asked, "Do you know how hard it is to mispronounce "psychiatric" once you know how to pronounce it right? I had to do it in *Kings Row* and at first I couldn't do it. It is like deliberately singing a flat note." It was Reagan's only recorded contribution to the discussion.

The battle between the Reagan administration and a skeptical legislature over the mental health budget dragged out inconclusively through Reagan's first gubernatorial term as patient loads continued to fall. Large-scale patient releases and later court rulings forbidding involuntary commitment left many of the mentally ill to fend for themselves on California's streets, a problem that has reached crisis proportions in the twenty-first century in all the state's major cities—and, because California sets bad trends as well as good ones—across the nation. It might have been otherwise.

Alan Post, testifying at a legislative hearing, proposed closing two of California's ten mental hospitals and using the savings to create community clinics for the mentally ill. Assemblyman Frank Lanterman, a conservative Republican, latched onto this idea in Reagan's second term as governor and authored a measure (the Lanterman Act) that Reagan signed into law in 1971. It resulted in the closing of several state hospitals, but neither Reagan nor his successor, Jerry Brown, ever requested the legislature to adequately fund community treatment centers. Nor for the most part did the governors who came after them. Only five state mental hospitals remain in California today (although the state's population has doubled), while community treatment remains starved for funding.

Reagan's proposal to reduce the mental hospital staff prompted critical stories in many newspapers about conditions at these institutions where thousands of people were warehoused. I wanted to see for myself, but the Department of Mental Hygiene turned down my request to visit Agnews, a state mental hospital near San Jose with a notorious past. Originally known as the Agnews Hospital for the Chronic Insane, its main building was a multistory unreinforced masonry structure that crumbled in the 1906 earthquake, killing more than a hundred patients. The hospital was rebuilt, but the standards for admission were excessively vague; it was often said that Agnews was a dumping ground not only for the mentally ill but for vagrants and drug users arrested by local police.

I told state senator Alfred Alquist of San Jose, a friendly Democratic legislator, that my request to tour Agnews had been denied. A few days later, Alquist asked me to accompany him on an unannounced drop-in at Agnews. We went on a Saturday and were told the hospital was closed to outsiders. Then someone informed the young doctor in charge that Alquist was on the committee that oversaw funding for the Department of Mental Hygiene, and the doctor agreed to show us around. Early in the tour, we heard loud pounding from behind a door. The doctor said it was nothing, but Alquist insisted the door be opened. We found a boy in his teens dressed in shorts and sitting on the floor. The only furniture in the room was a plastic bucket.

That wasn't all. Mental hospitals by their nature can be awful, and it was obvious even to someone (me) who had never previously visited one that Agnews was seriously short-handed. A forty-person ward on which some patients were calling for help and others yelling incoherently was watched by a single attendant. This was in the daytime, and the doctor said in response to a question from Alquist that the hospital was even more thinly staffed at night. By the time we had finished the tour, the doctor, a Brit, no longer felt threatened by our presence. He seemed impressed by Alquist, who asked hard questions without being combative. Perhaps the doctor realized that it might be useful to have a story in the local paper calling attention to the hospital's staffing shortcomings, which were about to become worse under the Reagan budget. Whatever the doctor thought, Alquist and I were shaken by what we'd seen. Alquist, a union man, had been skeptical of the proposed cuts in hospital staffing before touring the hospital; he told me afterward that the cuts were ill-advised and morally wrong.

"All the governor has to do is make a personal visit to one of these places and he will see we need more staffing—not less," Alquist said.

The mental hospital fiasco encouraged me to think more seriously about writing a book about Reagan. The supposed savings from the cuts in the Department of Mental Hygiene didn't amount to much in terms of overall state spending. How could someone who was so politically savvy about the need for taxes bungle what should have been a much easier issue? Some conservatives were already pounding the drums for a Reagan presidential candidacy. Giving short shrift to the mentally ill and the people who took care of them obviously didn't advance these prospects. I didn't know at the time that Reagan was disconnected from his own budget proposal—as well as somewhat disconnected from the presidential boomlet—but wanted to learn more about him.

I'd written magazine articles but didn't know how to write a book and even less about how to get one published. My only experience in writing something at book length was an attempt ten years earlier at a novel, which I sent to a publisher who didn't bother to send me a rejection letter. A second publisher, however, sent me an encouraging rejection letter, if that's not a contradiction in terms, which said if I did thus and so with the manuscript I would have a chance of getting the novel published. I never followed up, having realized from rereading my manuscript that writing fiction was not my métier.

In 1967, I was happy and living well in Sacramento. Reagan and the legislature were interesting, and my bosses were pleased with my work. Home life was good. On summer days when I could get away early, I'd be at Donner Lake in the High Sierra within the hour, trout fishing with my boys. We also found a lake in the foothills where we could go bass fishing. In a small pond near bass lake, I taught my young daughter to fish for bluegill. The children were doing well in school. My wife had friends in our neighborhood and liked living in Sacramento. She encouraged me to write a book on Reagan and Unruh and helped me carve out an office we'd been using for storage.

As first conceived, the book was to be jointly written with a friend who knew Unruh well. But he was slow off the mark. In an effort to jump-start him, I suggested we tape-record a conversation in which we discussed the themes of the book and divided responsibility for the reporting. My friend then confessed that he felt too close to Unruh to do the book with me. I felt an immediate sense of relief, which I took as a sign that I really wanted to write it on my own.

So I wrote a proposal for a book on Reagan and Unruh and sent it to Luther Nichols, the Doubleday editor in San Francisco. I chose Doubleday because they published so many political books. What I didn't know then—there was so much I didn't know—was that most of these book proposals came through agents or were written by previously published authors. If I'd realized the odds, I probably wouldn't have sent the manuscript to Luther, who later told me that it was the only time he ever offered a contract to an unpublished author on the basis of a proposal that came over the transom. The contract was for $5,000—around $48,000 in 2025 dollars and generous for an unpublished writer. More than the money, the contract meant that the book would be published.

I knew I could write the book. My only concerns were about how much access I would have to Reagan and Unruh and whether I'd be able to do the book without taking a leave of absence, as there were now four children at home and even with my advance we needed the money from my newspaper salary.

Bill Boyarsky, then with the Associated Press, who had written the first book on Reagan as governor, assured me that access wouldn't be a problem. Talking to me one day in the Capitol rotunda, Boyarsky said, "They'll tell you things for your book they won't tell you for your stories." It was typical Boyarsky: succinct and prescient.

And though I hadn't thought about it when I submitted my proposal, a dual biography made access easier. I foresaw, accurately, that Reagan and Unruh would be opponents in the 1970 governor's race. This gave the rival camps an incentive to talk. Unruh said right away he'd give me the access I needed.

Reagan also granted access but wanted me to interview him when he was flying around the country campaigning for Republican candidates in the fall of 1968. Journalists had followed Reagan in droves leading up to the GOP convention but lost interest after Richard Nixon had been nominated. Reagan nonetheless was in demand as a campaign speaker, particularly in the South and West, and his people told me he would have more time for extended interviews while flying to campaign stops than at the governor's office in Sacramento. The real reason for the airborne interviews, I later learned, was that Reagan was still afraid of flying. His aides thought I might be a useful distraction.

My editors at the *Mercury* and publisher Joe Ridder supported my book project, a welcome surprise. The editors didn't mind using wire services on most stories as long as the *Mercury* had first word on local appointments, especially judicial appointments. It was customary in the press office in those days, under both Pat Brown and Reagan, to give newspapers with Sacramento bureaus advance warning on such appointments, so it required little effort on my part. Harry Farrell backstopped me on any big developments. Because of this support, I wrote *Ronnie and Jesse* without losing any paychecks, something that would never happen again in my life.

I was all set to fly off with Reagan when the Sacramento press corps learned of the arrangement. The old guard didn't like that I'd have hours of exclusive time with the governor on an airplane. The oldest of them was Earl (Squire) Behrens of the *San Francisco Chronicle,* who dropped into my office to convey the message. He was eighty years old in 1968 and would live to be ninety-three. He walked with a limp and seemed incredibly old to me. But the limp was not a consequence of age. Squire had been severely injured when a mine exploded under his motorcycle sidecar while fighting in 1919 with the Allied expeditionary force against the Bolsheviks in Siberia. He would have "spells," as he called them, now and again. I saw him fall asleep during a legislative hearing one day, gently woke him, and asked if I could help. Squire had shown disdain for me, as he did for many young reporters, until that day. But he appreciated my concern, confided the story of his injury, and treated me with respect from then on. I asked him how I could assuage the concern of the press corps.

"Be a pool reporter for everyone if anything happens to Reagan while you're traveling with him," Squire replied. I assured him I'd do just that. With Squire vouching for me, I heard no more objections from any other reporter.

In preparation for the trip, I bought a primitive tape recorder. I'd never used one before and, like most reporters in those days, relied on my handwritten notes. But my penmanship has always been poor, perhaps as a result of being converted from my left hand to my right as a child. I compensated in two ways. On deadline, as I was when filing a story for the *San Jose News*, an afternoon paper, I composed the story quickly in my mind and dictated to the rewrite desk. If I did an extended interview for a later story or magazine article, I would type out my notes at the end of the day. I was a fast typist (and remained so until my stroke in December 2022 at eighty-nine). This was the result of having learned touch-typing in high school in an otherwise all-girl class at a time when many reporters did hunt-and-peck typing. I took a portable typewriter with me on the plane to transcribe interviews at night in my hotel room.

A word about that airplane. Campaign finance laws were virtually nonexistent in 1968. Wealthy supporters freely loaned planes and cars and even yachts to politicians without having to report these contributions. My notes on the type of plane Reagan used are long gone, but it was a comfortable and commodious aircraft, at least for me. Reagan, however, was not comfortable in the air. He had been afraid to fly since being tossed around in a small plane in 1937 while en route to Catalina for Chicago Cubs spring training.

Reagan never flew again until he entered politics nearly three decades later. His contract with General Electric stipulated travel by train as he toured GE plants around the country, and as late as the 1966 campaign for governor he traveled by car or bus wherever he could. Stu Spencer said the fact that Reagan flew at all testified to his political ambition. Interviewing Reagan in 1968, on a flight from Boston to Jacksonville, I made the mistake of asking him if he was still afraid to fly. Reagan said he did what the demands of office required and then looked out the window and added, "But's it's still an awful long way down."

He seemed to have unnerved himself, for I got little from him in the way of usable answers for the rest of that flight. Later in the trip, when the plane was delayed for a minor repair in New Orleans, Reagan anxiously paced the tarmac until aides persuaded him to go back inside the plane while the repair was being made and submit to more of my interviews. I doubt that it was relaxing for him, but it was preferable to flying.

I started my interviews with questions about his family and boyhood and proceeded chronologically. My thought was that Reagan would become used to me and perhaps more responsive when I turned to controversial issues of his governorship. It didn't quite work out that way.

Reagan was pleasant and easy to interview, but I had an uneasy feeling that I knew beforehand what he was going to say. On the second night out, I thumbed through a copy of Reagan's 1965 memoir, *Where's the Rest of Me?* and found that he was repeating verbatim the accounts of his life he had dictated to his ghostwriter for that book.

This trip on which I had such exceptional access suddenly seemed a waste of time. I had visions of returning to Sacramento and telling my editor at Doubleday that I hadn't learned anything I didn't already know. So the next day I spoke up before the interview began, telling Reagan that everything he had told me was already in his own book and that I was hoping for a more original take. Reagan cocked his head, as he often did when told something he hadn't expected to hear. It was a mannerism that gave him an extra couple of seconds to respond. Most politicians have some placeholder them allows them additional nanoseconds to figure out what they want to say. On the stump, Reagan would say, "Well," pause, and proceed with his answer. John F. Kennedy, whom I'd met on a California train swing in 1960, would repeat part of the question and say, "Let me say this about that," a habit he carried into his presidency.

On this occasion after cocking his head, Reagan nodded agreeably, and said, "So you want something new, Lou?"

He gave me the impression I should have said so before beginning the interviews. But he took my point. Ever afterward—from this interview in 1968 through the last one I did with him in 1989 after his presidency—Reagan provided nuggets of new information. Admittedly, I didn't always know when Reagan was telling me something important. In one of our talks on the plane, he made an off-hand comment that he was an avid science-fiction reader who worried that the world might be destroyed in a nuclear war, a recurrent theme of the genre. This had no relevance to governing California, but it was useful information fifteen years later when President Reagan proposed the Strategic Defense Initiative. Reagan's nuggets of information were sprinkled amidst masses of rote responses, familiar anecdotes, and reams of data. He loved data, and I would later write of Reagan, "He never met a statistic that he didn't like."

Sometimes the most interesting thing Reagan had to say was an aside. For instance, after a somewhat tedious rundown on the limited returns on Social Security investment, Reagan said, "Now you can't run against Social Security. Barry (Goldwater) proved that."

The practical and ideological coexisted contentedly in Reagan's mind with equal opportunity to come to the forefront. Stu Spencer once told me that Reagan made a courtesy call during the 1980 presidential campaign to influential televangelist Jerry Falwell, who launched into a diatribe about the immorality of abortion, with Reagan nodding in agreement. Alone afterward with Reagan in the car, Spencer asked him if he was seriously considering proposing the overturn of *Roe v. Wade* as Falwell wanted him to do.

"Do you think I'm crazy?" Reagan replied.

Abortion was an issue that dogged Reagan throughout his political career. He told me in another 1968 airplane interview that he had never thought much about the subject until it was thrust upon him early in his governorship. The key feature of Tony Beilenson's permissive abortion rights bill allowed an abortion if a doctor certified it was necessary to preserve the physical or mental health of the mother. This was six years before the U.S. Supreme Court discovered in *Roe* a constitutional right to privacy. The conventional wisdom in the 1960s was that the issue would be decided in the states. Indeed, Justice Ruth Bader Ginsburg suggested in 2016 that the nation might now be more accepting of abortion rights if this course had been followed.

In 1967, when Senator Beilenson introduced the Therapeutic Abortion Act, abortion was illegal in most states. In California, it was allowed only to save the life of the mother. Abortion was largely a taboo subject in legislative chambers and the press; the *Los Angeles Times* would not use the word, referring to abortion only as an "illegal medical procedure." But there was growing pressure for change. In San Francisco, nine physicians had been criminally charged with performing abortions on women with German measles, which can cause deformity in a child. Four women, two of them Catholic, collected thousands of signatures on a petition asking that the physicians not be punished and urging a change in the law.

As it does to this day, the Roman Catholic Church led the opposition to changing the law, but the partisan battle lines were different then. This was an era when conservatives believed that government, as was often said, had no business in "the board room or the bedroom." A majority of Republicans who were not Catholic favored liberalized abortion. Liberal Democrats who were Catholic overwhelmingly opposed abortion. With support from non-Catholic Republicans, Beilenson's bill passed the Senate. A GOP legislator who'd been a prosecutor then guided the bill through the Assembly and insisted Reagan sign it.

Reagan didn't know what to do, and neither his staff nor—unusually—his wife were helpful to him. When Reagan asked his wife what he should do, she suggested he talk to her father, which he did. Dr. Loyal Davis, who had adopted Nancy Reagan as a teenager, believed abortion should be legal. Spencer-Roberts, the firm that had managed Reagan's election campaign, was hired by the Catholic Church to lobby against the Beilenson bill and arranged a weekend meeting between Reagan and Cardinal Francis McIntyre, who predictably opposed any change in the law.

Reagan's staff divided entirely on religious lines with the Catholics—Phil Battaglia, the chief of staff, and Bill Clark, the cabinet secretary—urging a veto. The Protestants—Lyn Nofziger, the communications director, and Ed Meese, the legal affairs secretary—wanted Reagan to sign it. Reagan was left to make the decision on his own. In contrast to his behavior on the proposed budget cuts in the mental hospitals Reagan immersed himself in the arguments over the Beilenson bill.

"I have never done more study on any one thing than on the abortion bill," Reagan told me in the 1968 interview. This study didn't help him much at the time. At a May 9, 1967, news conference after the bill had passed the Senate and was awaiting Assembly approval, Reagan claimed to have discovered "loopholes" in the bill. Beilenson said bluntly that these loopholes were actually the purpose of the legislation. Reagan also suggested that California could allow Colorado, which had already liberalized its abortion law, to serve as a "laboratory" on the issue. This angered Republican senators who had made themselves political targets by voting for the bill and didn't want the abortion issue to come up in subsequent sessions of the legislature. Reagan seemed confused at the news conference. He felt so pressured that he uncharacteristically lied to reporters about having met with Cardinal McIntyre.

Nevertheless, at the urging of Republican legislators, Reagan signed the Beilenson bill on June 14, 1967. By the time I interviewed him aloft in 1968, he had either forgotten that he lied about meeting the cardinal or realized that the meeting had become so widely known that there was no point in denying it. I didn't press him on the falsehood. My interest was in the process of how he had arrived at his decision to sign the bill after absorbing so many of the arguments against it. One reason, Reagan said, was that he hadn't expected it to lead to widespread abortions. He had been told, I suspect by Dr. Davis but certainly by Republican legislators who had voted for the bill, that doctors would be careful in certifying women as eligible for abortion.

Reagan would often have visual images in his head when he made controversial decisions. I suspect that on the Beilenson bill he had conflicting images. On the one hand, there were images of women dying from illegal "backyard" abortions. On the other were images of babies killed in their womb because their mothers did not want to bring them to term. Reagan had trouble reconciling the two. Some of the statements he made just before signing the bill sounded more appropriate for a veto message.

By the time I interviewed Reagan in 1968, it was apparent that doctors were approving most requests from women for abortion and that the Beilenson bill had, without intending to, virtually authorized abortion on demand. I say "without intending to" because Beilenson himself told me he was surprised by the huge surge in California abortions. He was a lawyer, not a doctor, and he had expected the medical profession to interpret narrowly the provision allowing abortions to preserve the mental health of the mother.

In 1967, the year the Therapeutic Abortion Act became law, there were 518 legal abortions performed in California. The number jumped tenfold to 5,000 by 1968 and to 15,000 in 1969. During Reagan's second term as governor, beginning in 1971, abortions in the state averaged more than 100,000 a year. Abortions became so common under the Beilenson legislation that abortions at first increased only slightly after the *Roe*. Eventually, however, abortions surged again as women realized they no longer had to go through a charade of claiming anticipated mental illness in order to halt an unwanted pregnancy. In 1980, the year Reagan was elected president, 199,080 abortions were performed in California. The total number of abortions performed in the state from 1968 to 1980 was 1,444,778.

Reagan pointed out to me in 1968 that he was relatively new to office when he signed the Beilenson bill and said he would have vetoed the measure if he had realized what it would do. But this outcome was accurately forecast by the Catholic Church and other opponents of the legislation, and Reagan had confessed at his May 9, 1967, news conference that he was troubled by this possibility. By the time I interviewed him in 1968, he seemed to have forgotten what he said at the news conference. Instead, Reagan emphasized that he had since studied the issue and concluded that abortion was equivalent to murder.

Reagan held that view for the rest of his political career, but there was always an ambivalence about the way he expressed himself in the public arena. When he ran for president in 1976, Reagan attempted to atone for his signature on the Beilenson bill and win the support of pro-life activists by advocating a constitutional amendment that would prohibit abortion except to preserve the life of the mother. This was California law when Reagan became governor. But Reagan rarely mentioned abortion in campaign speeches in 1976 and not at all in 1980.

As president, Reagan never sought enactment of such an amendment. Perhaps the most telling expression of Reagan's practicality on the issue was that as president he addressed the annual pro-life rally in Washington every year by telephone rather than in person so he was never seen with leaders of the movement on the evening news. For their part, most leaders of the pro-life movement were content to have a president who said he was on their side.

When Reagan nominated Sandra Day O'Conner as his first appointment to the Supreme Court, some pro-lifers expressed concern about what her rulings might be on abortion. Aware of this, Reagan asked O'Connor's view on abortion when he interviewed her for the high court post. O'Connor said that abortion was abhorrent to her personally but that she would not let personal opinions influence her judicial decisions. Reagan let it go at that. He was principled, to be sure, but from beginning to end, he was also a practical politician.

7

TURNING POINTS

A few weeks after Boys Nation, I was invited by a Reno service club to relate my experiences in Washington. I was brief. The main speaker at the luncheon was a lawyer, recently returned from the South, who gave a bleak report on U.S. race relations. The lawyer, who was white, pointed out that Black people were disenfranchised in the South by various methods. He observed that racial discrimination was also legal in Nevada. Black people could vote in Nevada—there were so few they were not viewed as a political threat—but they weren't welcome in restaurants or stores, many of which posted the ubiquitous sign: "We reserve the right to refuse service to anyone." Some signs were more bluntly racist, including one that said "No Indians or Negroes allowed."

This lawyer was no militant. One of his arguments was that denying to African Americans the services and opportunities available to whites fed Soviet propaganda about racial discrimination in the United States. Two years later, a Black radical gave me a better reason: He told me that if someone was standing on his toes, he wanted him to get off not because someone was watching but because it hurt.

In 1950, my senior year at Reno High School, Nevada's population was 160,000, including 4,300 Black residents and about 5,000 American Indians. I'd had Indian friends going back to the third grade in Fallon but didn't know any African Americans until I met Eliza Moss, whom I believe was the only Black student in our senior class of 220 or so at Reno High School. She was smart and pretty and I liked her, but I was shy around girls. Years later at a reunion, she told me that she liked me in high school because I'd been friendly to her. It would have been hard not to be friendly toward Eliza. If I'd known that she thought well of me at the time, I would have asked her out.

Apart from Eliza, the only Black person I knew as a boy in Reno was an athlete from the University of Nevada whom I met in my parents' store. He said he was a friend of my dad. Marion Motley, a fullback from Canton, Ohio, had broken the color line at UNR, then the only university in Nevada, before becoming one of the greatest professional football players of all time with the Cleveland Browns. After Motley, UNR brought in several Black football players, one of them the athlete who knew my dad. People cheered them on Saturdays, but the athletes couldn't eat in the restaurants downtown nor could Black entertainers stay at the clubs where they performed. Langston Hughes, in a 1956 memoir, noted Black people who wanted to eat in Reno were limited to a couple of cheap Chinese restaurants. This was in the 1930s, when our family moved to Nevada. By the late 1940s, Blacks in Reno also had access to a restaurant in the Greyhound Bus Station and a rundown gambling casino in Skid Row. This casino, which also catered to Asians, was within walking distance of my parents' store, and I once went over to check it out. I was stopped at the door because I was underage.

In the summer of 1950, I met Alice Lucretia Smith, who with her husband, Alfred, had five years earlier founded the Reno-Sparks chapter of the NAACP. Alfred had died in 1946. Mrs. Smith, a granddaughter of slaves from Mississippi, had a sunny disposition and confidently predicted that Reno would be fully integrated one day. But African Americans were being served at many restaurants in the South before they were in Reno, which some civil rights leaders dubbed "the Mississippi of the West." Even unfavorable publicity for the city from a famous 1961 sit-in at the café of the Overland Hotel where the owners locked in Blacks who had come to eat did not shake the entrenched culture of discrimination. After this embarrassing incident, influential Reno business leaders said they would accept a law outlawing discrimination in public accommodations, but the Nevada legislature didn't get around to approving such a measure until 1965, a year after Congress passed the Civil Rights Act. One reason for Nevada's glacial approach may have been that, unlike in the South, where everyone knew they lived in a Jim Crow society, many white Nevadans never faced up to the backwardness of our state on race relations. We inhabited a bubble, imagining that we lived in a place of opportunity for all.

The 1950 Reno High School yearbook beside me as I write this passage shows a sea of white faces, except for Eliza and two Asian boys. One of them was Buddy Fujii, among the most popular kids in the class. There is a conspicuous absence of Indians, who were more numerous in Nevada than Blacks or Asians but not in high schools except for the Indian reservation near Carson City. The Paiute classmates I'd known in junior high didn't go on to high school.

My interest in civil rights began early. I'd read about the South and particularly remember a story in an old *Reader's Digest* someone had left in my parents' store. It was written by a man who had been hitchhiking, in Mississippi. Two men stopped and said they'd be happy to take him wherever he was going but had to make a detour first. The detour was to the lynching of a Black man accused of having sexual relations with an elderly white woman. The account was horrifying, all the more so because the participants in the lynching were ordinary people who said jovial goodbyes to one another after this awful murder as if they'd been attending a Sunday social.

My parents believed that Black people—indeed, all people of color—tended to be treated unfairly by whites. They taught my brother and me to treat people equally: to shake hands and call adults of any race "Mr. and "Mrs." This doesn't sound like much, but it displayed more commitment to equality than was common in Nevada at the time. Our parents also set a positive example by defying the Nevada norm in refusing to post one of those right-to-refuse-service signs in their store. Also, I'd never forgotten that my father had approved of my classroom walkout in Fallon.

My absorption with civil rights issues contributed to a turning point in my life. My father's drinking weighed on me, and I had quietly resolved by my senior year to move out of the family home. This wasn't a quixotic decision. I'd thought hard about it and saved my mileage payments from the local paper and tips from busing at an upscale restaurant as well as earning money from odd jobs, including tutoring a boy who struggled with reading and math. His schoolwork improved, and his parents recompensed me generously. As a result of this varied work, I had saved several hundred dollars at a time when one could buy a gallon of gas for less than thirty cents and a loaf of bread for half that much.

Finding a place to stay was more of an issue than the rent. I needed a place willing to accept a sixteen-year-old boy without asking questions, located near my high school. The only boarding houses I knew about were noisy and rundown. So I sought out an older friend, a student at the university who shared my interest in classical music—he introduced me to Gustav Mahler, among other composers—and had also improved my chess game. My friend was vaguely radical (or so it seemed to me) and made the case to me in 1948 for Henry Wallace. I told him that if I were old enough to vote I'd cast my ballot for Truman. Except for this disagreement, we ostensibly thought alike about politics, especially civil rights.

My older friend did not pry, which I appreciated. When I told him my plan, he said he'd look around and soon came up with the name of a couple who rented rooms. I will call them Richard and Nadine, not their real names. They were in their early sixties and lived in a ranch-style house on the north edge of town with a small white cottage in the back that was rented to a married couple. The main house had a kitchen, study, and master bedroom as well as three rooms they rented out. By chance, Nadine said, a room was available. It was a small tidy room that seemed ideal.

Nadine and I chatted, and our talk turned to politics. She told me she participated in informational picketing of one of the casinos in 1948, calling upon the owners to admit Black people. My mother had told me of the picketing, which was of brief duration and brought no change in casino policy. I was nonetheless impressed that Nadine had promoted civil rights in Reno. We quickly settled on a nominal rent. Nadine's rules were few. I made my bed, as I'd done at home, had instant coffee and juice in Nadine's kitchen for breakfast, and took lunch at school. In the evening Nadine cooked a modest meal, often a stew or casserole, for the boarders. She asked that we call her by midday if we were not going to be there for dinner.

Before leaving home, I told my mother and my brother about my intentions. My mother was supportive. My brother wanted to come with me. I told him that wasn't possible but would make it a point to see him every day at school. He was a junior, a year behind me. The seniors and juniors didn't hang out together, but I knew all his classes, and I kept my promise to see him daily at school. I also told my father what I was doing. He accepted my decision and said he'd also left home at sixteen. It wasn't quite the same thing because my father's mother had died giving birth to him, and he was raised by his sisters. But I didn't say that: It comforted my father to think I was following in his footsteps—and it comforted me as well.

So I packed my stuff, put some of it in the basement, and with a suitcase full of clothes moved into the room set aside for me by Richard and Nadine. It was an easy adjustment. Richard and Nadine drank little and usually wine, if anything. They never raised their voices. These were new and pleasant experiences for me. Even better, they didn't smoke. I'd struggled with respiratory ailments since early childhood, and my parents were chain-smokers. Not until I entered a nonsmoking environment did I realize how much cigarette smoke bothered me.

But while happy with the move and pleased that Richard and Nadine treated me as an adult, I sensed there was something mysterious about them. I never found out exactly what they did—or had done—for a living. Nadine was the child of missionaries and had lived in China. I never learned anything about Richard's background. Both said they were educators, without providing details. Richard was also a competent mechanic but with a bad back that kept him from getting under cars except in emergencies. As it turned out, they were mysterious because they were members of the Communist Party, as were most of the other boarders and the couple occupying the cottage. I knew little about the Soviet Union and what I did know wasn't particularly useful. I'd read *Ten Days That Shook the World*, John Reed's romanticized account of the Russian Revolution. I'd also followed the military events of World War II, when the United States and the Soviets were allies. Like many other Americans, my parents had no illusions about the Soviets but welcomed the alliance because of their distaste for the Nazis. My father, who had a sense of history, said Hitler had made the same mistake as Napoleon in invading Russia.

The wartime U.S.-Soviet alliance was a fading memory by the time I moved into Richard and Nadine's house. With the Cold War flourishing, many Americans had become fearful of Communist subversion. But Nevada, a frontier state with a live-and-let-live attitude, had a better record on civil liberties than on civil rights. With the possible exception of Senator McCarran, no one in Nevada was looking for Reds under the bed. The University of Nevada escaped the ordeal of the University of California, which in 1948 was preoccupied by a campaign to root out radical professors via an anti–Communist Party loyalty oath.

Given what I thought was my tolerant outlook, I wasn't alarmed when Richard and Nadine began leaving me articles and books with a radical slant. At first the books and stories emphasized civil rights, as they knew its importance to me. I've forgotten most of the articles but remember one that credited Lester Rodney, a sportswriter for the *Daily Worker,* for his early advocacy of eliminating the color line in major league baseball. This resonated with a boy who'd seen Jackie Robinson play. They also had a recording of Paul Robeson, the great bass-baritone (and Communist), singing radical songs. The lyrics didn't faze me—I'd listen to Robeson singing "Mary Had a Little Lamb"—but soon Richard and Nadine were leaving articles that extolled Soviet communism. I wasn't much interested in the articles but liked some of the novels Nadine lent me, especially *And Quiet Flows the Don,* an epic tale for which Russian writer Mikhail Sholokhov would win the Nobel Prize for literature.

On Sundays, Richard and Nadine led the boarders, including the couple from the back cottage, in discussions about current events. The participants, who included a few people from outside the home, didn't call themselves Communists but talked in Marxist jargon. One of the participants was the friend who found me the room. He had obviously known Richard and Nadine a long time, and it suddenly dawned on me that the whole business of me being there was a setup. I didn't say anything to the older friend but didn't trust him after that. The discussion participants called themselves "progressives," as liberals do today, but held actual liberals in contempt. A recurrent refrain was that liberals pretended to be progressive but outdid conservatives in their Red-baiting. Richard and Nadine went relatively easy on Harry Truman, knowing I admired him, but it was clear they didn't hold him in high regard. Small wonder. Truman resisted Soviet expansion. On June 26, a few weeks after I graduated from high school, Truman sent U.S. troops to defend South Korea against an invasion from Communist North Korea.

In retrospect I wish I'd been skeptical about the propaganda being poured into me. My friends thought me serious, but the truth was I would rather gamble—it was possible to get into certain casinos if you "looked older"—than explore political philosophy. Later, I would read Arthur Koestler and Robert Conquest and become aware of the murderous calamities Stalin had inflicted on the Soviet people, but at the time I accepted at face value too much of the propaganda that Richard and Nadine were peddling. Partly, this was because they were skillful in influencing others. Realizing I didn't give a fig for Marxist theory, they stressed their commitment to social justice, which was genuine up to a point. Still, I found even an adulterated dose of ideology a stumbling block. Richard's explanations of "scientific socialism" seemed mumbo-jumbo to me, and I found the books he recommended unreadable. But I enjoyed the company of most of Richard and Nadine's group, all the more so because my closest friends were no longer in Reno: Clint Wooster was at Stanford and Bruce Lake had joined the Air Force. I also identified with the group's local political activism. Richard and Nadine reached out to people who didn't know how to navigate the system or lacked the clout to do it. For example, they tried to help some Indians who lived south of Reno in a primitive housing tract obtain municipal sewage service.

Richard and Nadine and their acolytes wouldn't have lasted long in Stalin's Russia. They were reformers in the political context of Nevada but wore blinkers when it came to the nature of Soviet totalitarianism. I didn't think of that at the time. What I thought was that Richard and Nadine were kind and approachable, as were all the boarders save the husband of the couple in the back. Cottage Man, as I called him privately, was grumpy and didactic. He spouted Marxist guff at the drop of a sock: dialectical materialism, the "correlation of forces" and workers this and workers that. We disliked each other instantly.

The boarder I liked best was a factory worker who moved to San Francisco about the same time I did. Years later, he told me that Nadine and Richard had tried to recruit him into the Communist Party. He turned them down. One of the reasons, he said, was that he knew I had already rejected a similar recruiting attempt. Another was that Communists were atheists, and he believed in God. The factory worker was right about me. I had turned down what seemed to me a half-hearted attempt by Nadine to join the Communist Party, telling her I just wanted to work for good causes without joining anything. She didn't argue. We never once discussed the existence of a supreme being, which was just as well. Although I wasn't religious at that time, I had an odd belief that God had plans for me.

But in my refusal to become a Communist, I was no profile of courage. When Nadine asked me to join the party, I said I'd think about it. She could read me and knew I meant "no." Then, out of the blue, the number-two editor at the local paper approached me and said the FBI had told him that I was living in a "hotbed" of communism. He passed on what he said was a message from the FBI, asking me to spy on the conversations in Richard and Nadine's house.

I think he used the word "report" rather than "spy," but the meaning was clear. The editor said the FBI would pay my rent and give me some extra money for doing this. I was offended by what seemed to me a bribe and asked the editor what would happen if I refused. He said the newspaper would stop giving me freelance assignments and that I would be making trouble for myself down the road if I didn't tell authorities everything I knew about these Communists.

I asked for a few days to think about the offer. After I'd considered it, I told the editor I respected the FBI but did not want to spy on people who'd been kind to me. This decision would have serious consequences for me, but I don't see what else I could have done. Despite their naivete about the Soviet Union, Richard and Nadine never talked about overthrowing our government. As far as I knew, their political energies had been mostly expended on civil rights. Beyond that, I thought the FBI should have come to me directly and not tried to bribe me for spying on my friends. I didn't want the money. If the FBI had appealed to my patriotism, the choice would have been difficult, for I have always been loyal to our country.

In retrospect, the editor's message rattled me. I'd left home to escape a stressful situation but now faced the unhappy choice of joining a cause I doubted or spying on people who had treated me well. I sometimes sought solace in fiction, and John Steinbeck was a favorite author. I'd read *The Grapes of Wrath* and decided to read his anti-Communist novel, *In Dubious Battle.* It was an eye-opener that led me to Arthur Koestler and other anti-Communist writers. Then, while I was pondering my next course of action, events intervened.

That summer I worked as a busboy at a small, upscale restaurant called the Townhouse. The owner treated the staff well, feeding us steaks before our shifts. After I'd been there a month, the owner told me he appreciated my hard work and would help me become a waiter if I stayed at the restaurant. Instead, I developed a severe strep throat and a bronchial infection and couldn't work at all. Meanwhile, my mother told me that she and my father had sold the store and were going to Oregon to look for a ranch to buy.

They hadn't yet sold the Reno house and wanted to know if I would keep an eye on it. I moved out of Richard and Nadine's house so as not to infect anyone. That's when I realized that Nadine cared about me. She would leave containers of' chicken soup on the curb outside my parents' house. In the meantime, I'd been accepted by the University of Nevada, which was midway between the family house and Richard and Nadine's. In-state students could wait until just before classes started to decide whether they would attend. The day my doctor said I was no longer contagious, I enrolled for the fall semester and soon afterward moved on campus to a dormitory known as Lincoln Hall.

It was a good decision, the first I'd made in a long time. The person designated as my roommate decided at the last moment not to attend school, and I unexpectedly had a room to myself. Room and board were slightly more expensive than at Richard and Nadine's, but I needed to work anyway and I liked being free from the propaganda. I stayed in touch with Richard and Nadine after I moved out but stopped going to the Sunday discussion groups. I found a job cleaning a mill in the evening. It covered my expenses but made for a long day.

In *The Message in the Bottle,* novelist Walker Percy asks why we're so often disappointed on big occasions we've long anticipated yet unaccountably happy in small uncharted moments. That was me in Lincoln Hall, blissful and unconcerned with the future. The only cloud was a paucity of dates, but my schedule left little time for girls. Spare time was pick-up basketball with friends in the university gym or chess, which abruptly became an encompassing passion in Lincoln Hall. We played matches in the dormitory all day and into the night, taking turns monitoring classes for one another. Then the passion subsided like a summer storm, and we became normal students again.

There was, however, an exciting residue of this chess-playing. Casino owner Bill Harrah allowed an upstairs room of Harrah's Club to be used by the Reno Chess Club for its meetings. I would typically arrive from the mill, shaking off the dust from my jeans to the amusement of the better-dressed club regulars. Even at my present age, I still do math in my head; at the time I could do equations and because of my math skills was a competent player at the club level. One night the chess club had as its guest the Belgian grandmaster George Koltanowski. I'd followed his career and read his daily chess column in the *San Francisco Chronicle,* which he wrote for fifty-two successive years before his death at ninety-six in 2000. Koltanowski had escaped the Holocaust, which claimed several family members, because he was on a chess tour in Central America when the Nazis overran Belgium. In Cuba, a chess-playing U.S. consul impressed by Koltanowski's skills granted him a visa to the United States.

Koltanowski was famed for his "blindfold" skills in which he played several opponents at once without looking at the board. He holds the record for having defeated thirty-four players in this manner. That night in Reno he faced some two dozen local chess players. After we'd played for a while, he offered me and three other players a draw. We took the offer, considering it an honor. Koltanowski won all the other games. In appearance he was a slight, unprepossessing man with a droll manner. He said to call him "Kolty," but none of us did, despite Reno's informal ways. To us, fortunate recipients of draws with the master, he was Mr. Koltanowski, which is the way I think of him today.

The other influence on my life that summer was a linguistics class taught by Dr. Charlton Laird, an exciting lexicographer and novelist best known for a book called *The Miracle of Language* and the 1971 edition of *Webster's Thesaurus,* which remains in use to this day. To his students, Dr. Laird was a mesmerizing teacher who could talk nonstop about the roots of the English language. He plunged me into a lifelong love affair with the written word.

As a young man in Iowa, Dr. Laird had suffered a terrible car accident that damaged his vocal cords. He had to relearn how to speak and in the process developed a unique accent that made him sound as if he were a posh Brit who had been brought up in the Midwest. He also had a pronounced stammer. Two of my classmates got in a spirited argument, one saying that Dr. Laird's stammer disappeared during his dynamic lectures and the other asserting that the class became was so absorbed in what he was saying that we didn't notice it. I was designated to settle the argument by focusing on Dr. Laird's stammer during a class while others took notes on the contents of the lecture. I concluded that both my classmates were right: Laird stammered less when he got going, and the class stopped noticing entirely.

Dr. Laird inspired me to read *Beowulf* in Anglo-Saxon. He also encouraged me to become a journalist, as he had once been in Iowa, saying it would serve me in good stead no matter what else I did in life. He also had a droll sense of humor. When I asked him what the final examination would "resemble," he replied, "Mr. Cannon, the final examination will resemble nothing so much as a rotary snowplow bearing straight down upon you."

Apart from Dr. Laird's class, I preferred to hang out at the local newspaper, the *Nevada State Journal*, than at the university. The newsroom wasn't quite *The Front Page*, but it had its moments. There was a managing editor with elongated arms and a short fuse who jumped up and down on his desk yelling at reporters who had screwed up. There was a husband-and-wife team, he an editor and she a reporter. Once when he corrected something in her story, she said, "Yes, dear." She had coined a phrase describing Reno as the "tough little town on the Truckee," which was not bad except that she used it in almost every story.

There was another reporter, a former U.S. Marine, who had a bottle of whisky in his right top desk drawer next to a revolver. He'd write a sentence or two, take a slug of the whiskey, and then put the bottle back in his desk and repeat the process. Everyone drank. There was a bar across the street called the 116 Club, which was the street number. The front door of the bar was said to be so perfectly aligned with the front door of the newspaper so that if you were sober you could walk straight from the paper into the bar without scraping anything. To determine if this were true, I walked across the street blindfolded with a friend alongside so I wouldn't be hit by a car. I walked straight into the bar.

Some first-rate journalists worked at one time or another for the *Journal* and its companion paper, the *Reno Evening Gazette*. The most influential was Frank McCulloch, of whom the Center for Investigative Journalism said in 2004: "With his ahead-of-the-curve reporting from Vietnam for *Time* magazine and influential management stints at the *Los Angeles Times, Sacramento Bee,* and *San Francisco Examiner,* Frank McCulloch was one of the great journalists of the past fifty years. Unfortunately, far too few people know that."

I didn't know Frank well at the time—we became friends years later—but admired him greatly. As I told the *American Journalism Review* in 2006, all young journalists in Nevada in those days aspired to be Frank. He had the journalistic virtues: He was skeptical. He was fair. He was kind to those less fortunate. He met the Finley Peter Dunne test of "comforting the afflicted and afflicting the comfortable." He wasn't ideological at all. If he took sides, it was on behalf of the less fortunate.

Two other less-famous journalists grounded me in the basics of reporting. Ty Cobb, the *Journal* sports editor named after the famous baseball player, taught me to go beyond the box score. "Talk to people," he said. "Talk to people and don't just talk: listen to them."

John Burns, the city editor in Reno and later my city editor at the *Merced Sun-Star,* taught me to avoid "fancy writing." I think it was John who first cited H. L. Mencken's advice to me: Finish your story, sit back, and think of a terrific ending. Then turn the story in before you write it because the story is already done.

Bill Friel, the *Gazette* sports editor, hired me one summer as Sunday sports editor, an elegant title considering I was all by myself on Sundays, when the paper didn't publish. It was fun and a useful experience, as I usually wrote several stories in two or three hours. I wrote about boat races at Lake Tahoe, a big deal in those days, and stock car races. There was a women's stock car race called the Powder Puff Derby at which one of my duties was to kiss the winner.

As I learned too late to thank him, Bill put his job on the line by standing up to the editor who had said I couldn't work at the paper unless I informed on the local Communists. Bill told the editor that I would outgrow my leftist leanings and deserved a chance as a reporter. He had been in the Navy during the war and was an effective storyteller and actor. Reno had an excellent little theater, which staged *Detective Story,* a Sidney Kingsley play that had been a Broadway hit with Ralph Bellamy in the lead role. I don't see how Bellamy could have been any better than Bill as the boozy, tough-guy detective Jim McLeod. The final moments of the play are melodramatic and sentimental, too much so for modern audiences. I thought the ending was perfect. Many years later, my mother said she and my father had been invited to the play but hadn't gone because they didn't want to be reminded of Roy Geach.

In thinking about the journalists who tolerated and encouraged me, I've tried to find a defining moment in which I turned away from political causes to become a writer who spurns ideology and sees his role as bearing witness. I don't remember any epiphany. Rather, through a gradual process, my heroes became people with a sense of history who saw deeply and made a virtue of getting the facts right. Most of these people were journalists or started out that way. Among the best of them—certainly the one who traveled the greatest distance in his writing—was Robert Laxalt, a member of the famous Nevada family whose eldest brother, Paul, would become governor of Nevada and a U.S. senator.

Bob Laxalt worked for UPI in the state capitol of Carson City and came often to Reno. It's a comment on the prevailing standards of accuracy at the time that his nickname at the Reno papers was "Frenchy." Bob was Basque. He was sweet and funny and tough: He'd boxed in Golden Gloves matches and been in the war. Bob was ten years older than me and related to me like the older brother I didn't have. When we met in 1949, he was a proficient reporter who was beginning to chafe at the limitations of wire-service journalism. We all knew he was destined for something, but I doubt any of us at the Reno papers realized what a terrific writer he would become. *Sweet Promised Land,* his book about his father Dominque and the Basques in Nevada, was published in 1957.

"My father was a sheepherder, and his home was the hills," it begins. In this lovely book, as Raymond Chandler said about *The Postman Always Rings Twice,* there is no wasted sentence nor unnecessary word.

The title of *Sweet Promised Land* is taken from a resonant ballad in Walter Van Tilburg Clark's semi-autobiographical Reno book, *The City of Trembling Leaves.* Clark, who wrote *The Ox-Bow Incident* and *Track of the Cat,* strongly influenced Laxalt. The ballad, which I and my schoolmates knew by heart, asserts that God made Nevada but left it unfinished, hence "sweet promised." This is the refrain:

> Oh, this is the land that old Moses shall see,
> Oh, this is the land of the vine and the tree,
> Oh, this is the land for My children and Me,
> The sweet promised land of Nevada.

Bob and I bonded and stayed in touch after I left Nevada. I was working for a California newspaper when *Sweet Promised Land* was published and read it in a single sitting late one night. I wrote him a letter, saying the book had touched me. Bob said I should come back to Nevada, which wasn't possible with my growing family and late-starting career. When my first book, *Ronnie and Jesse: A Political Odyssey,* was published, Bob wrote me a complimentary letter and noted that we were about the same age when our first books came out. Keep writing, he said. With Bob, writing and almost everything else in life was all about the verities. Honesty. Accuracy. Simplicity. Rewrite and cut and rewrite more, he would say. Write the story the way you'd tell it. Never give up on yourself or allow yourself to become discouraged by rejections.

Over the years, Bob Laxalt wrote seventeen books, four of which were nominated for Pulitzer Prizes, and brilliant stories on forgotten people for *National Geographic. Sweet Promised Land* and its sequels led to the founding of a Center for Basque Studies at the University of Nevada. His achievements were recorded in an excellent biography, *Robert Laxalt: The Story of a Storyteller,* by Warren Lerude, who knew him well.

Bob kept urging me to return to Nevada. When the dean's job at the university's journalism school opened, Bob nominated me. It was flattering, but I was writing and reporting and wasn't interested; the university hired someone far more qualified for running a journalism school than I ever would have been. Bob and I stayed connected. In 1983, the university honored us as "Distinguished Nevadans." The real honor, I told him, was to be on the stage with him. I shared these views with an audience in Reno on November 6, 2006, as a speaker at the Robert Laxalt Distinguished Writer's Program. Bob and his wife, Joyce, were there. I read this passage from *Sweet Promised Land:* "The air was sweet with the smell of new-mown hay and the call of night birds came softly to our ears. The workingmen trudged like shades in single file through the darkness, their wooden shoes clacking hollow on the cobblestones, and the song they sang was the low, mournful song of the close of day."

After several moments of silence, Bob's father speaks: "How well I remember the sound of the shows and the shadow of the scythe against the night. When I was a little boy I would run out into the dark and meet my father in the road and say, 'Good evening, my father,' and he would take my hand in his, with fingers so hard and bent, and we would walk together into the house."

I could tell you some more Laxalt stories and try to write a bang-up ending to this chapter, but I won't. Turn in your story, advised Mencken and John Burns. You're done. So is this chapter.

8

PATHS NOT TAKEN

My introduction to Shakespeare was in a high school class in which we read and acted *Julius Caesar*. I played Brutus, a traitor who is one of Caesar's murderers and is later described in the play, not quite believably, as the noblest Roman of them all. To be a plausible Brutus, I convinced myself he was not actually a traitor because he'd joined the assassination plot to restore the republic. Brutus himself indulged this self-deception; my acceptance of his rationalization did not survive the class. What did survive was an appreciation of Shakespeare. I am still stirred on rereading the passage in which Brutus urges coconspirator Cassius to attack the massing forces of Mark Antony and Octavian before they become stronger.

"There is a tide in the affairs of men, which taken at the flood, leads on to fortune," Brutus declares. "Omitted, all the voyage of their life is bound in shallows and in miseries. . . . And we must take the current when it serves, or lose our ventures." Brutus lost the battle and committed suicide, but he was right in what he said about taking the current.

In the summer of 1951, the nomadic tide of life took me to San Francisco. During the next four years, I went to college, married, became a father, was drafted into and discharged from the Army, and discovered my life's work.

San Francisco State University today is a sprawling campus with thirty thousand students in the southwestern corner of the city. When I enrolled in the fall of 1951, it was downtown, at Buchanan and Waller Streets, and part of the California state college system that in 1972 was renamed a university system. In a semiofficial history, SF State was described as a "noisy happy firetrap" of a campus. The student body of forty-three hundred was largely working-class, and many were veterans attending under the G.I. Bill of Rights, the great leveler of the postwar years.

Most students in my classes worked at least part-time and were attentive to their studies. When you work for an education, you tend to value it. I found a job in a warehouse that paid my bills. With millions of other young men, I'd registered for the draft when I turned eighteen. That was in Reno. The Korean War was raging, but my draft status wasn't on my mind when I transferred to SF State. Because of the draft policy during the Korean War, college students were exempt from induction as long they were enrolled in fifteen and a half units a semester. The course of study could have been basket weaving as long as the number of units reached the requisite total. Mine didn't, as I learned after my fall class schedule was set. SF State didn't give full credit for a course I'd taken at the University of Nevada, and my work schedule made it difficult to add an extra class. I thought of calling my draft board to ask if I could be allowed to make up the credit in my junior year but figured this might call attention to my unit shortfall, which I hoped would go undetected. So I did nothing and put the draft out of my mind.

Remember Richard and Nadine, the Marxists who provided me with a place to stay when I left home? Richard and I had run across each other in the spring of 1951 on the University of Nevada campus in what had seemed a chance encounter, although in retrospect I'm not certain it was. When I told Richard I was moving to San Francisco, he said he knew a friend there who rented rooms to students and would give me her phone number, which he did. That summer I piled my meager belongings into the 1936 Chrysler and set out for San Francisco. Before leaving, I called Richard's contact, a middle-aged Russian woman who indeed had a room. Better yet, she had a garage for my car and was on a trolley line that stopped at the San Francisco State campus.

The Russian woman called herself a "progressive." Copies of the *People's World,* the West Coast newspaper of the Communist Party, were scattered about her coffee table. I found a notice in one of the papers about an upcoming musical event and reception that the Russian lady said would be attended by young people. I didn't know anyone my age in San Francisco and went to the event, which I think involved folk music.

Truthfully, I don't remember the music because my eyes were taken with a pretty girl with luminous eyes and olive skin who sat in the row in front of me. I was too shy to introduce myself, but on the way out picked up a flyer for an upcoming envelope-stuffing for some long-forgotten cause. It was sponsored by "Youth for Peace and Freedom," abbreviated to YPR. I wanted to meet the girl and went to the envelope-stuffing. The dozen people who were there went around the room introducing themselves. She said her name was Virginia Oprian and smiled at me. Emboldened, I asked if she'd accompany me to an upcoming concert. She said yes. It was the beginning of a succession of small dates, several of them a walk or cable car ride to Chinatown, where lunch cost a couple of dollars.

Virginia, known as Ginny, lived in the Twin Peaks area of San Francisco but had grown up in North Beach, a touristy part of the city with a permanent population that included many Italian Americans. Because of Ginny's complexion, I assumed she was of Italian descent like so many girls I'd known in Reno. In fact, she was Romanian on both sides of her family. Her parents were divorced, and her father, Nick, of whom she spoke fondly but rarely saw, was an autoworker, remarried and living in suburban Detroit. Ginny lived with her mother, Helen, whose maiden name was Lotrean, and her stepfather, Paul Cline. Virginia was an only child, and Helen was devoted to her.

My involvement with Ginny plunged me into a world I'd meant to leave behind for good. Paul Cline had been executive secretary of the Communist Party in Los Angeles, including Hollywood, beginning in the late 1930s. When the United States and the Soviet Union were allied during World War II, Communists were directed to cooperate with liberals and other "anti-fascist elements." Paul did so enthusiastically; his background in the labor movement had persuaded him that unity among progressives was vital. Far from the battlefields of Europe and the South Pacific, domestic Communists became starry-eyed patriots in pursuit of that unity. During the heady period of the U.S.-Soviet alliance, Earl Browder, the U.S. leader of the Communist Party, even proclaimed that "Communism was 20th century Americanism."

Did he really believe such nonsense? I have no idea, but the united front with liberals did not withstand the brutal Soviet takeover of Poland and other Eastern European countries after World War II. As the Cold War intensified, Moscow ordered the replacement of Browder with

Eugene Dennis, a hard-edged Stalinist. In 1946, Browder and his followers, including Paul, were expelled from the party. Paul was distressed but remained loyal to what he saw as communism's larger goals. Instead of faulting Stalin, he accepted a preposterous fiction common among Browderites that it was "the men around Stalin" who were responsible for what had happened. We now know that most of these men feared that their entire families might be murdered or sent to the gulag on Stalin's whim.

Although the blinkers would fall from Paul's eyes after Nikita Khrushchev disclosed Stalin's vast crimes in his "secret speech" in February 1956, they were firmly in place when Paul and I met in 1952. After agreeing not to discuss Marxism or the Soviet Union, we got along famously. Paul had read widely and been active in union struggles for higher wages and better working conditions, and his knowledge of the American labor movement was immense. He also liked baseball. I never saw a copy of the *People's World* in Paul and Helen's home. He preferred the *Christian Science Monitor,* then an excellent newspaper. If Paul were alive today, he'd probably subscribe to *The Economist* or the national edition of the *New York Times.*

Helen also considered herself a Communist while acknowledging she didn't know much about Marxism. I doubt she was a party member. No intellectual, Helen reflexively supported left-wing causes, but didn't limit herself to issues that made Communist hearts go pit-a-pat. She had a keen interest in mental health and later founded one of the first community treatment centers for mental illness in California. She and Paul met at a social event, according to Ginny, and fell so hard for each other that friends teased them. "Here come the dear darlings," they would say as Paul and Helen arrived.

My resolution to never again become mixed up with Communists went out the window once I began dating Ginny. But I was warier than I had been in Reno and relieved to find that Ginny had no interest whatsoever in the party even though she had absorbed Paul and Helen's romantic view of the Soviet Union. Her friends were mostly "red-diaper babies," children of Communists who had grown up in the war years when being pro-Soviet was not a handicap. But in the climate of the Cold War, such opinions could be hazardous for those who held them. San Francisco was supposedly progressive, but real and alleged Communists had it harder there than their counterparts in Reno. The father of one of Ginny's best friends had lost his job as a teacher because he refused to sign a loyalty oath. The father of another friend was a former German Communist who had survived a concentration camp. He owned two oversized German shepherds that never bothered Ginny but scared the hell out of me. One of them once pinned me against a wall when Ginny and I visited her friend while the father was running an errand. The father came home and took control of the dogs. I gave Ginny's friend and her father a wide berth after that, making excuses when Ginny wanted to visit their house. I was ashamed of my cowardice, but deathly afraid of those damned dogs.

Ginny and I were busy—she worked as a bookkeeper at a garment center and was taking night classes at the University of California—and we at first saw each other mostly after the weekly meetings of YPR. They were run by a community organizer in his thirties who I'll call Jeff. He was married and generous and had an eye—too much of an eye, some thought—for the pretty teenage girls in YPR. As he later acknowledged, Jeff was also a Communist who had set up YPR at the party's direction. It's hard to know why. Unlike the discussion group led by Richard and Nadine, the YPR meetings had no particular political slant. For the most part, we engaged in gauzy discussions about world peace that avoided serious talk about the Korean War or the larger Cold War.

On Election Day in 1952, YPR members distributed leaflets in downtown San Francisco urging people to vote for the presidential candidate they believed most likely to bring peace to the world. I don't know who the leaflet writers had in mind; Jeff said he thought that voters using this yardstick would pick Dwight Eisenhower, who defeated Adlai Stevenson in a landslide. I'd have voted for Ike had I been able to do so, but I was nineteen and the voting age was then twenty-one. The YPR meetings served mainly as a social outlet for children of Communists and their allies, which for all I know may have been its real purpose. Ginny and I couldn't wait for the meetings to end so we could be with each other.

At this far remove it's hard to pinpoint the moment when the two of us realized we were in love. As the reader will know if he or she has been in love, it's a delightful and somewhat mysterious sensation. My heart leaped when Ginny entered the room, which sounds corny as I write these words more than six decades later. But it was true.

We didn't sleep together. Both of us believed that intimacy with someone you might marry came after the vows. Women of this generation were more inclined to caution since the pill that could prevent pregnancy had not yet been approved for contraceptive use. (That happened in 1960.) Ginny, only seventeen, thanked me for not pressuring her. Paul and Helen were relieved when Ginny told them that I was behaving like a gentleman—Helen's word, which was also my mother's highest word of praise—and even more pleased that our schedules didn't allow us much time together.

I'd moved from the Russian woman's house to a boarding house for male San Francisco State students on Potrero Hill, known as the Rock because its facade mimicked the exterior of Alcatraz prison. Many of the students were music majors and some were members of the excellent SF State orchestra. I attended several orchestra rehearsals, sometimes with Ginny. She liked music and had ushered at the San Francisco Opera House to see the performances.

Our happy little world was interrupted by reality when the Reno draft board took away my student deferment and reclassified me 1-A. Since the northern Nevada pool of potential draftees was small, I realized this was a prelude to a draft notice.

I might have appealed, contending I'd lost a unit on a technicality in transferring colleges, but that seemed a bureaucratic way to delay the inevitable. At the time of the Korean War, most young men anticipated serving in the military. We weren't far removed from the national conscription of World War II, when deferments for nonmedical reasons were rare. Several friends in Reno joined reserve units and were sent to Korea. Others from my high school class went to work instead of going to college and were drafted.

The Korean War was a working-class war because of the draft policy of deferring full-time college students. Except for those who wanted to serve, this policy spared children of the elite from military service. Draft evasion was rare. Not until the Vietnam War did draft avoidance become prevalent. Conflating their own comfort with (in many cases) genuine opposition to the war, these scions of the well-off wrote articles and books to explain their actions. One of the best explanations is by Tim O'Brien, who in his memorable novel, *The Things They Carried,* relates how he contemplated fleeing to Canada before deciding to accept military service. O'Brien is too hard on himself in my opinion. He describes doing his duty as an act of moral cowardice. But he went to war and was wounded and survived to write about it.

My draft notice during the Korean War did not provoke similar self-examination. I reacted as a gambler does when he loses a dubious bet. With the draft looming, Ginny and I decided to marry. Ginny was only seventeen, so she needed parental consent. Paul liked me but believed his stepdaughter was too young for marriage. Helen felt the same way and also wasn't sure I was the right husband for Ginny. Nonetheless, I proposed in December 1952. She accepted and said she would talk to Paul and Helen. Since I knew how they felt about it, I was reconciled to waiting until Ginny turned eighteen on March 13, 1953. Ginny, who rarely let go of something once her mind was made up, didn't want to wait. She told her mother that unless she gave her consent we'd go away and get married when she turned eighteen and not invite her to the wedding. Ginny never said a word to me about this threat; Helen told me this story years later. Helen said she'd changed her mind because she wanted to give consent while she still could.

We were married on February 2, 1953, at San Francisco City Hall by a Municipal Court judge with Ginny's mother and a friend of mine as witnesses. The city's characteristic foggy weather inspired the judge, who assured us that a bright sun lurked behind the fog and would shine on us forever. The fog became thicker after the ceremony. It was so dense that night that some invited guests never made it to the reception Jeff and his wife held for us at their home on Potrero Hill. My best man inched his way up the hill, narrowly missing a stopped car. "All I could think about was that goddam judge," he said.

My draft notice came soon afterward. Inducted in San Francisco, I was sent to Fort Ord for basic training. Today much of this once-sprawling base is the Fort Ord National Monument with the rest occupied by the California State University at Monterey Bay, the Fort Ord Dunes State Park, two subdivisions, and a strip mall. When I was there, Fort Ord was one of the U.S. Army's two major basic training centers in the West, churning out soldiers for the Korean War, which was winding down, as it had for two world wars. Motorists driving to Monterey or Carmel on the nearby freeway could often hear shooting from the coastal firing range, which is now part of the national monument.

I missed Ginny terribly in the early weeks of basic training but didn't mind the Army. This was a surprise to me since there was hardly anything in my background to suggest I'd be a suitable soldier. As a Boy Scout, I'd hated camping, and Army bivouacs were worse. I was smaller, less muscular, and slower than most of my fellow recruits, many of them farm boys. The interminable marching didn't bother me—I was a cross-county runner and a two-miler in high school in Nevada—but I was in a weapons platoon in an infantry company, which meant sometimes carrying a mortar part in addition to my nine-and-half-pound M-1 rifle. We were taught to take apart and reassemble that rifle blindfolded.

Most of us were nineteen or twenty years old and highly competitive, as young men tend to be. I probably rated in the lower fourth of our group in physical skills but had an advantage on the firing range. As a boy I envied other boys whose fathers took them fishing, not realizing that my father probably didn't know how to fish. But he had taught me how to shoot, a skill I didn't know I needed before being drafted. Dad was a crack shot with a rifle and a good one with the .38-caliber revolver he carried to the store in Reno at a time when robberies were frequent. He taught me how to hold the rifle and keep my arms and body still and how to breathe. He told me to aim slightly low because novice shooters usually miss high. We'd practice until we ran out of ammunition. "You done okay," he would say if I'd shot well, high praise from him.

By the time I was drafted, I'd almost forgotten about the shooting lessons, which came back in a flash at the Fort Ord rifle range. "Take a deep breath, then exhale," my father had said. "Keep your arms still. Squeeze the trigger, never jerk it. Aim slightly low."

My rifle-shooting score was second-best in the platoon, and I was rated a "sharpshooter," the highest designation. Afterward I overheard a popular soldier in the platoon—he was the one with the slightly better shooting score—tell another recruit, "That scrawny kid can really shoot." That marked my moment of acceptance in the platoon.

Away from the firing range, basic training was boring. But after the first month, weekend passes were doled out to recruits who could pass a rigorous inspection of their uniform, bed, and footlocker. Inspectors would sometimes throw a quarter on the bed; if properly made, the coin would bounce. The inspectors would take off a point (called gigs) for each shortcoming; three gigs and you didn't get a pass. I was determined to get every pass possible since Ginny was pregnant and San Francisco only 112 miles away.

An Army enlistee who wanted to be a career soldier took me under his wing. He also had a pregnant wife—unfortunately for him, she was far away in the East—and sympathized with my desire to obtain every possible pass. He'd learned a lot about the Army in the short time he'd been a soldier, and he urged me to blend into the pack. The noncoms who inspected us gigged laggard soldiers whose shoes were badly shined or beds improperly made, but they also had an eye for show-offs who polished their brass and shoes a bit too much. One enlistee stood out. His brass always glimmered, and he stepped forward whenever volunteers were sought. The rest of us never volunteered. The enlistee who was helping me detested Eager Beaver. "He wants to make general in a week," was one of the more printable things he said about him. The inspectors laid in wait for this show-off, gigging him for microscopic failings. It wasn't fair really, but many in the platoon ragged Eager Beaver when he didn't get a pass. I never missed a pass. I'd learned to get ahead in the U.S. Army by blending into the ranks.

Nevertheless, I was one of sixteen soldiers commended for "outstanding performance" in basic training. There were four platoons in Company C of the Sixty-Third Infantry Regiment, and the brass picked two soldiers from each platoon. My commendation may have been influenced by an incident in the last week of basic training, when we were trucked from Fort Ord to Camp Roberts, eighty-six miles southeast. The coastal marine layer often kept us cool at Ord. Not so at inland Camp Roberts, where summer temperatures often reached the high 90s. We practiced maneuvers at Camp Roberts the last week of basic, culminating in an all-night twenty-six-mile march over a mountain to Highway 1 on the Pacific coast.

Highway 101, north of Paso Robles, skirts the southeastern edge of Camp Roberts. From a driver's perspective, the land looks fairly flat, but further west, where we trained in the summer of 1953, Camp Roberts becomes a series of undulating hills and gullies with streams and an occasional canyon.

We started at twilight, elated to leave Camp Roberts. The elation dimmed as we trudged uphill in the growing dark on a narrow trail carved through the brush and scrub oak. The coastal range that we traversed is steeply banked. Pine Ridge, just south of where we marched, rises to 3,586 feet, low by the standards of the Sierra Nevada but formidable when climbed from sea level. We marched single file, not talking. Then, in a rush, it happened. The soldier in front of the soldier in front of me tumbled off the trail in the dark and landed on a ledge perhaps ten feet below. He was lucky; beneath this wide ledge was another narrower ledge that trailed off into a gorge. The soldier behind the solider who had fallen kept going. I must have scrambled down the ledge to attend to the fallen marcher. I say "must have" because all I remember is being there with the fallen man, helping him to sit up. Someone put flashlights on us. The executive officer was there. It seemed he was always there when we needed him.

The exec officer, a lieutenant, was an African American. We looked up to him, even the farm boys from the South who had never expected to be commanded by a Black man. The exec had won over the southern draftees on a day one of them skipped sick call to march with his buddies. After a few miles he was drooping. The exec officer wordlessly took the southerner's rifle and carried it at port arms the rest of the march. He was a hero to all the draftees after that, all the more so because the captain who was our commanding officer, a white southerner, was a bombastic fool who once kept us standing at attention under a hot sun while he prattled on about our duties. He didn't stop until two of the soldiers in the ranks keeled over.

On the night I was helping the soldier who had stumbled during the march to the coast, the exec officer joined us, put his arm around the man, and asked if he was hurt. He shook his head. Then the exec turned to me. "You okay?" he asked. "Yes, sir," I said. "You did good, soldier," the exec said. Then he was gone.

Other men scrambled down the ledge, helped the fallen soldier to his feet, and recovered his rifle. I rejoined the march, which had halted because of the incident. We marched all night to the coast highway and boarded trucks that took us back to Ord. I was later told that the soldier I helped rescue had fallen asleep on the march.

9

THE LIGHT OF THE WORLD

"Babies arrive on their own schedule," said my wife, expressing newfound wisdom from her hospital bed after our first-born, Carl Michael Cannon, made a dramatic entrance into the world in San Francisco on October 24, 1953. We had not been expecting him that Saturday. Neither of us had anticipated anything more exciting than an Italian dinner in North Beach.

We'd started the day at our rented house in Seaside, near Fort Ord. The move to Seaside had been prompted by my wild drives back and forth to San Francisco on weekend passes during basic training. I'd received a speeding ticket while dashing back to make an 11 p.m. bed check one Sunday, and another soldier we knew was injured in a car accident the same day. That was enough for Ginny.

Most rentals near Fort Ord were expensive, but she resourcefully found a tiny house that was so poorly built you could see the sky through the pine roof. We liked being together, but Ginny was eight and a half months pregnant and her support system other than me was in San Francisco. She missed her mother. So we drove to San Francisco to visit Ginny's mom and grandparents, who owned a modest hotel on Kearney Street in the financial district. We planned to have dinner with her family, overnight at the hotel, and attend the 49ers game Sunday, then leave from Kezar Stadium for a leisurely drive back to Seaside. With basic training behind me, I no longer had to worry about Sunday bed check but needed to be at Fort Ord for Monday morning reveille.

We were unpacking in the hotel room when Ginny felt the first labor pains. At first she wasn't sure what they were. I was twenty years old and my wife eighteen, and we were as clueless as clams. We didn't know, for instance, that nine months of a woman's gestation was an average, not an absolute. Nor did it occur to us that a 115-mile drive in an old car with worn shock absorbers was not the smartest idea for a woman deep into her pregnancy. The baby was due November 7, engraved on our minds' calendar as a precise date like Thanksgiving or Christmas. Never for a moment did we think that the baby might arrive earlier (or later). We were so ignorant I'm amazed we knew enough to time the labor pains. They were coming at six-minute intervals when I desperately reached the Army hospital at the Presidio, where an operator transferred me to a doctor with the rank of major. Our conversation went like this:

MAJOR: Do you have a car, soldier?

ME: Yes, sir.

MAJOR: Do you know what I'd do, soldier?

ME: No, sir.

MAJOR: I would put my wife in the back seat of the car and drive immediately to the Army hospital at the Presidio. Do you know where the Presidio is?

ME: Yes, sir.

Still in uniform, required off base in those days, and with Ginny in the back seat of my 1936 Chrysler, I sped along Van Ness Avenue until a motorcycle policeman pulled me over and asked why the hurry. I pointed to my wife in the back seat and said I was trying to reach the Presidio hospital.

"Follow me," he said. With siren blaring, the motorcycle cop led me down Van Ness to Bay Street, where we turned toward the Presidio. As cars in front of us swerved and pulled over to the side, I felt exhilarated and imagined the siren was announcing the birth of our baby.

When we reached the hospital, Ginny was taken away on a gurney. A nurse told me later that I had tried to accompany the gurney and was stopped because Army rules prohibited fathers in the delivery room. The nurse also said that I'd reached the hospital in the nick of time and was now the father of a healthy baby boy.

The sergeant in the headquarters company to which I was assigned had told me I could take a week's leave when the baby arrived. But when I called to ask about it, he put me on hold, came back to the phone and told me I needed to return for Monday reveille. Then he hung up. The sergeant, a decorated Korean War soldier, was a stand-up guy whom I knew wouldn't have hung up without a reason.

He had checked with the duty officer about my leave, which he assumed to be routine. But the duty officer abruptly remembered he had been denied leave when his wife had their baby. Recalling this indignity, the duty officer said he wanted me back immediately, never mind Monday reveille, but the sergeant told him I'd hung up. This was long before cell phones, and the sergeant told the duty officer he had no idea how to reach me.

So I was at Ord for Monday reveille. Afterwards the sergeant told me he'd arranged a week's leave so I could return to San Francisco. It was good I did so. Carl had been an easy birth, Ginny said, but she nonetheless had a rough first week as he cried repeatedly at night. By the third or fourth night she was frazzled and asked me to get up with him when he needed to be held or changed. Being a father was exciting, and I was happy to do it. This tiny bit of help was all it took, for Ginny was composed and competent after that. We enjoyed being parents, but I was awed at the responsibility of fatherhood and apprehensive about how I would provide for mother and child. By the end of my week's leave, Carl had mostly stopped crying at night and become a model baby. He was happy and so were we. Ginny is gone now and Carl is a father (and a grandfather) of his own, but my feelings about him haven't changed much. I'm pleased he became a reporter and writer who in some ways surpassed me, but it's who he is, not what he's done, that matters.

Carl was the first of four. Although she usually wasn't superstitious, Ginny told me soon after we were married that a fortune teller had predicted she would have four children. Our second child, David, was born in 1956. Soon after his first birthday, he was stricken with a mysterious disease the doctors could not explain beyond telling us that the white blood cells in his body were devouring the red ones. Our doctor put him in the University of California hospital in San Francisco and pumped him full of antibiotics. His condition worsened. The doctor wore a mask of optimism around Ginny, but she realized that the prognosis was dire.

Then one day David's red cell count surged. Within a week he had nearly recovered. Ginny was all smiles when the doctors told us this at the hospital. At home, she broke down. She had prayed with me for David's recovery and believed our prayers had been answered. When she stopped crying, she smiled at me and said: "Our baby's saved." The doctors didn't know why David had become sick nor did they know why he'd turned the corner so suddenly. I was curious about what had happened, but all Ginny cared about was that he had survived.

As David grew to manhood, he became an accomplished long-distance runner. At the beginning we ran together, but I realized when he was a high school freshman that I was holding him back and let him run alone. Dave won numerous trophies in high school, competed as a Division 1 runner in college, and ran well into middle age. His best distance was two miles, but he worked to improve his speed and in his mid-fifties became one of the top milers in the country in his age group. He seemed a picture of health at sixty when he was diagnosed with pancreatic cancer. Two months later, on Carl's sixty-third birthday, he was gone. I said at David's memorial service that he was taken from us too soon at sixty, but that we had fifty-nine extra years of his joyous presence. I keep reminding myself to look at it that way.

Judith Cannon, our daughter, was born in Merced, California, where I was a reporter on the local newspaper. When Ginny learned she was pregnant, she suggested, only half-jokingly, that we rent a house across the street from the hospital so she could go immediately to the delivery room when the time came. As it happened, we were about three miles away, and I put Ginny in the car at the first labor pains. The baby arrived soon after she entered the hospital.

Ginny was delighted to have a daughter, and through trial and error with the boys we'd become experienced parents. We were unprepared, however, for the problem caused by a wet 1957–58 winter and a leaking septic tank at the back of our rented home. Much of the Merced soil was what locals called "hard pan," reddish brown clay impervious to gardening tools. Water ponds on hard pan, and the puddles remained months after the winter rainy season, providing ideal breeding grounds for mosquitoes. My beat at the *Merced Sun-Star* included the county-wide mosquito abatement district, and I'd learned that mosquitos were potent carriers of malaria and other diseases. Soon after we brought Judy home from the hospital, I killed a large *anopheles* mosquito near her crib. Blood spurted onto the wall.

"That shows it's a female," I said.

Ginny was horrified, both at the blood on the wall and my ill-timed display of entomological knowledge. She stood guard over the crib and sent me out to find mosquito netting. We put it over the crib and made sure the boys were covered with insect repellant when they went to bed, but Ginny and I soon decided that we needed to get far away from the leaking septic tank.

So we purchased our first home, something we'd avoided doing because we didn't have much money and didn't know how long we'd be in Merced. The down payment was $2,000, twice our savings, so I borrowed $1,000 from my parents, the only time in my life I accepted money from them. The house cost $12,500, the equivalent of $137,000 in 2025 dollars, which wouldn't buy a starter house anywhere in California today. To us it was a ton of money that wiped out our savings, but we were happy with a modest home that had the great virtue of being connected to the city sewer system. There were no more problems with mosquitoes.

We enjoyed having a girl in the house. Judy didn't cry much, and we learned when she was still in elementary school that she had a lovely singing voice. She was in the glee club at school and the choir at church. When it was time for her to go to college, we sent her to her school of choice, the Boston Conservatory of Music.

Jack Nicholas Cannon, named after our fathers, was our fourth and final child, born in 1965. He wasn't planned, and I doubt that Ginny particularly wanted to be pregnant. But when she found out that she was, I reminded her of the fortune teller's prediction and she was fatalistically happy during her pregnancy after that.

"We're supposed to have this baby," she said, and I did not disagree.

The baby was due on November 1, although we both realized he could arrive early. I had gone to Sacramento for the *San Jose Mercury,* dividing my time between learning the beat and finding us a place to live. I found a house on a cul-de-sac in the William Land Park area and brought Ginny to Sacramento to get her stamp of approval. Then I took her back to San Jose and returned to Sacramento to attend to some details on the house. I should have driven back to San Jose on Sunday, October 31, but was tired and at Ginny's suggestion stayed the night, which proved a mistake. Jack was born the following day while I was on my way to San Jose.

Jack grew to be six feet, two inches, taller than his brothers. I adored him. He had more health issues than all his siblings combined, including a persistent bad back and a shaky digestive system. He also had another problem we were slow to recognize. Jack was dyslexic and struggled to read. His excellent memory and clever response to visual clues enabled him to conceal his dyslexia in the early grades, but because he couldn't see words properly, he couldn't sound them out, and he fell behind in the fourth and fifth grades. No one diagnosed his condition, and Jack didn't tell anyone. His teachers thought he wasn't applying himself and to our discredit we suspected the same. Saying "try harder" to a dyslexic is a waste of time—and cruel. Jack was doubtless trying harder in school than his siblings had ever done, but he lacked the building blocks with which they were equipped. So he battled with dyslexia pretty much on his own. Talking to his frustrated mother after a poor report card, Jack blurted out his feelings.

"My dad and Carl are writers, and I can't even read." It was an epiphany for Ginny. We put him in a special school, where he improved.

Jack compensated for his reading difficulties with musical gifts. He could play any stringed instrument and became an accomplished bass guitar player in a rock band. We sent him to Berklee College of Music in Boston, which uniquely prepares students for music careers by teaching them contemporary music. Jack was a brilliant bass player but didn't read music and so became a street musician. It was a hard life, but Jack recast himself as "Jackson" and augmented his meager income with bartending. As Jackson Cannon, he became a nationally known mixologist. He was the bar manager for a beloved Boston restaurant and held a stake in a high-class bar when the COVID-19 pandemic struck, taking the bar and restaurant. But he rebuilt his bar and his career. He also reads.

David had no children. Carl has three. When the pandemic hit, Carl had three granddaughters, two from his older daughter, Kelly, and one from his son, Nick. Both Kelly and Nick welcomed pandemic-era boys into their families, giving Carl and his wife, Sharon, two grandsons—a full house. Judy lost a son but has two daughters. Her eldest, Tiffany, has two children (and two stepchildren). Kelly and Tiffany's children made me a great-grandfather at a young age. Jack, marrying late, has two children younger than Tiffany's older child. All told, I have seven living grandchildren and seven great-grandchildren who are, for me, the light of the world.

Readers other than family members can be excused for wondering if I would ever stop going on about my offspring and return to the narrative. When we left it, I was a soldier in 1953, basking in Carl's birth. The euphoria was short-lived.

To explain what happened, we need to return to the day of my Army induction, when I filled out a flurry of forms and declined to sign a document affirming under penalty of perjury that I was not a member of the Communist Party or any of a long list of groups designated by the attorney general as "Communist fronts." I scanned the list for Youth for Peace and Freedom and didn't find it, but there were so many groups on the list I couldn't be certain I didn't belong to one of them.

I take a dim view of loyalty oaths, although I would cheerfully pledge to defend and uphold the Constitution of the United States against all enemies, foreign and domestic. Such pledges were sufficient for Americans until loyalty oaths acquired a cachet during the early stages of the Cold War, when they were used to purge many people who were not Communists from government. Mostly, the oaths stemmed from a 1947 executive order signed by my hero Harry Truman who was trying to fend off Republican accusations that he was "soft on communism" in preparation for his 1948 campaign. Presidential biographer David McCullough said Truman signed the order with "misgivings." McCullough quotes Truman advisor Clark Clifford as saying that its purposes were entirely political, since Truman did not believe communism posed a serious domestic threat.

I didn't know all this background when I was asked to sign the loyalty oath at induction. But as I looked at that piece of paper, I thought of the father of a friend of Ginny's who was no more a Communist than Truman. He'd been a professor at the University of California–Berkeley when, to the consternation of civil libertarians, the university in 1948 required all faculty members to take an oath similar to the one I was asked to sign. The professor refused and lost his tenured position. He was teaching at an obscure college when we met.

"I'm not a Communist, but I don't want to sign this," I told the sergeant who had handed the document to me. The sergeant seemed bored.

"You don't have to," he said, and I didn't.

My refusal to sign the oath did not arise as a problem during basic training, when we were told we'd probably be sent to Korea. But the Korean War was winding down—an armistice was signed in July—and some of us were given other orders. The platoon leader who had bested me on the rifle range, for instance, was sent to Germany. My orders consigned me to an advanced leadership course in another part of Fort Ord, where I received acceptable marks. The ostensible purpose of the course was to train cadres to take recruits through basic training. I didn't relish going through basic again in any capacity, but this was the U.S. Army, so I did what I was told. I was made an acting corporal, which meant the rank without the pay, and helped shepherd a group of recruits through basic. Then I was assigned to a headquarters company, good duty with Ginny and our baby close by in Seaside.

One night I had a dream in which an officer confronted me and said I was being undesirably discharged from the Army because I'd been a member of the Labor Youth League. I protested to no avail. The officer demanded my base ID, and MPs drove me to the front gate and dropped me off outside. I awoke in a sweat and told Ginny what I had dreamed.

She tried to calm me. "It's only a dream," she said.

But it wasn't. Three days later my dream unfolded in precise detail in real life. I have no explanation for the prescience of this vision. I didn't know that draftees who had declined to sign the loyalty oath were being undesirably discharged. To the contrary, I believed I was in good standing with the Army after receiving a commendation in basic training and graduating from leadership school. I didn't want to leave the Army and was angry that my loyalty to our country was being questioned. It was a sudden turnaround. Two weeks earlier, the officer who handed me my discharge papers had called me a promising soldier and suggested I might want to enlist—"re-up" it was called—after my draft service and pursue an Army career. The officer was a captain who certainly wouldn't have urged me to stay in the Army if he had known I faced an undesirable discharge. I wanted to say this but couldn't get the words out. The dream about this event had seemed real; the real events had a nightmarish quality. I felt that I was outside my body, watching events unfold. I couldn't speak.

What happened? I managed to get my discharge upgraded to "honorable," but wondered for years why the Army acted as it did. In retrospect it doesn't seem much of a mystery. Joseph McCarthy, the hulking senator with the hangdog look Senator Robert Taft introduced me to at Boys Nation, had risen to prominence with sensational charges that hundreds of Communists had infiltrated American public institutions. His platform was the Senate Permanent Subcommittee on Investigations, which under McCarthy's chairmanship shifted its focus from investigating fraud and waste in the executive branch to hunting for Communists. As McCarthy held hearings around the country and grilled hundreds of witnesses, the Democrats on the subcommittee resigned in protest, allowing McCarthy a free hand. Riding high early in 1954, McCarthy accused the Army of lax security processes, depicting the routine promotion of a New York dentist from captain to major as part of a wider Communist plot. The Army countered that the counsel of McCarthy's Senate subcommittee had pressured the Army for preferential treatment for a recently drafted former McCarthy aide. McCarthy temporarily turned over the chairmanship of his subcommittee to another Republican senator, and the subcommittee held televised hearings on the competing charges.

In these salad days of network television, the hearings attracted a large viewing audience. That was bad for McCarthy, who performed better on the stump than on TV. Representing the U.S. Army, Boston attorney Joseph Welch repeatedly exposed the Wisconsin senator as a crude bully who made flimsy charges he could not back up. The denouement came on June 9, 1954, when McCarthy claimed that a young attorney with Welch's firm was a member of a pro-Communist group. Welch's response echoes in history.

"Until this moment, senator, I think I never really gauged your cruelty or your recklessness," he said. When McCarthy tried to continue, Welch angrily interrupted, "Let us not assassinate this lad further, senator. You have done enough. Have you no sense of decency?"

It was the beginning of the end for McCarthy, whose national popularity quickly evaporated. Censured by Senate colleagues, ostracized by his party, and held in contempt by President Eisenhower, a broken McCarthy died three years later at the age of forty-eight. This history is familiar. Less familiar is the impact of the hearings on the hundreds of draftees who had declined to sign the loyalty oath they were presented with at induction. The hearings were held from April through June. While Welch was exposing the emptiness of McCarthy's allegations, the Army was quietly ridding itself of draftees who might be deemed subversive.

The charge that I was a member of the Labor Youth League, an arm of the Communist Party, was bogus. Nevertheless, I realized that someone making a cursory investigation might have reached this conclusion since I knew and liked the group's national chairman, Bill Lowe. We'd met at a civil rights event in San Francisco months before I was drafted. No doubt he was a Communist or he wouldn't have headed the LYL, but

Bill never gave me a Marxist pitch or discussed foreign policy with me, perhaps because he was aware of my aversion to the Soviet Union.

Although he was from the East Bay, not the Deep South, Bill was African American, so civil rights were personal for him. At a forum, someone argued that the United States should treat minorities better because ill treatment of Black people was being exploited for propaganda purposes by the Soviets. Bill believed, as I did, that all Americans should be treated with dignity, period. We never saw each other after I was drafted, but I've always thought well of him.

After my discharge, I was in a fog that grew thicker by the day. I had hoped to complete my college degree, but that seemed unrealistic with a wife and child to support. Ginny was working at a drugstore, but we had little money between us, and I knew it wouldn't be easy to find work without an honorable discharge. I felt embarrassed at having been kicked out of the Army and outside of immediate family didn't tell anyone what had happened. Ginny and Carl rescued me from the fog. Instead of feeling sorry for myself, Ginny said, I should fight back and appeal my discharge. As for Carl, he was such a happy little boy that it was impossible to be depressed in his company.

We returned to our home turf. I sold my beloved 1936 Chrysler and bought an old Chevy that soon broke down. But it served its purpose of getting us back to San Francisco, where we stayed with friends for a couple of weeks until Ginny found an apartment on Dolores Street in the heart of the Mission District. I took any and all jobs, working part-time in a cannery and then at a tire shop from which I was fired because I wasn't fast enough. Twice at what would have been better jobs, I was asked to show my discharge papers. I said I didn't have them with me and would bring them back but never returned. Then, a friend asked me if I could drive a big truck. Yes, I lied, rationalizing that learning how to drive a Jeep in the Army was experience enough. I managed to drive a semitrailer from the East Bay down to Imperial County and kept it on the road. It was a long drive in those days before the interstate highway system. The truck was loaded with plumbing parts, I was told, although I never inspected the load. To make this drive, which paid better than cannery work, I had to join the Teamsters Union, which turned out to be a fortunate break.

By the winter of 1954–55 I'd earned enough money to realize my family wasn't going to be on welfare. Ginny was helping at Carl's nursery school. She later acquired a certification to teach at nursery schools, work she liked and at which she was proficient. Politically, she'd turned away from left-wing groups such as YPR and joined the Federated Young Democrats of San Francisco, many of whose members had worked for Adlai Stevenson in the 1952 presidential campaign. Several Young Democrats became our social friends. One was Phillip Burton, an ambitious young lawyer who was determined to win political office in a state then safely Republican. His first try came in 1954 when Burton was twenty-eight years old. Trying to drum up support for his brother, a teacher named Bob Burton rang our doorbell one day and was greeted by Ginny, who looked even younger than her nineteen years.

"Are your parents home?" he asked.

"No, but my husband is," she said with a smile. "Do you want to meet him?"

Bob told us that Phil was running for a seat in the lower house of the California legislature, against an elderly incumbent Democrat who'd held the seat for many years without—according to Bob—accomplishing much. Phil and his wife, Sala, lived a block away, so we walked over with Bob to meet him. Phil was a brainy lawyer and fast talker and he dazzled Ginny, who wasn't easily impressed. I could hardly get a word in but looked at Burton's campaign bio and approved of his positions on civil rights and civil liberties. He invited us on the spot to join his campaign. I held back, thinking he wouldn't have asked if he'd known about my discharge. But Ginny accepted and was soon making and distributing yard signs and talking up Phil to everyone she met.

Burton would go on to a storied career in the state legislature and the U.S. House of Representatives, but he had little going for him in 1954 except a determined cadre of relatives—and Ginny. Phil knew his chances of winning were remote, but his prospects improved when the incumbent died suddenly. This turn of fate should have made Burton a winner in the primary against two minor candidates. The hitch was that the incumbent died too late to have his name removed from the ballot. Sala Burton realized at once that many voters didn't know the identity of their assemblyman and therefore wouldn't know that the incumbent, William Berry, had died unless someone told them. The newspapers were opposed to Burton; some of them never even mentioned that Berry had passed away. Sala said the campaign should take all its limited funds and do a mailer to every Democrat in the district. The mailer would express deep sorrow at Berry's passing and say that Phil Burton was now the "endorsed Democrat" for the office. For some reason, Phil asked me, whom he barely knew, what I thought of the idea. I said it was tasteless. So did the other men advising Phil, including Bob Burton. The only person who supported Sala was Ginny. But men rarely listened to women in those days, and Sala's proposal for a mailer was rejected. So Phil Burton began his illustrious career by losing to a dead man.

Our rooting interest in basketball fared better. A friend at the city's oldest institution of higher learning—the Jesuit-founded University of San Francisco—secured us passes to USF Dons basketball games, and we were able to watch the marvelous team led by Bill Russell that won sixty consecutive games and two NCAA basketball championships. Bay Area basketball fans were slow to recognize they had a great and largely homegrown team on their doorstep, and Ginny and I rattled around in the spacious Cow Palace, where the early games were played to sparse crowds.

In addition to Russell, USF had two superb guards, K. C. Jones and Hal Perry. Russell and Jones are remembered by fans for long, title-winning Hall of Fame careers with the Boston Celtics, but the USF winning streak began when Perry became a starter. He never played pro ball but did a stint with the Harlem Globetrotters before the owner of the team reportedly told Perry it was a waste of his considerable intellect to play on a barnstorming team and put him through law school.

Ginny, normally uninterested in sports, was fascinated by Russell, who made soaring rebounds, awesome blocks, and reverse dunks. He would make his mark in the NBA as a defensive genius, but at USF he averaged twenty points a game and twenty rebounds during the winning streak. We also rooted for USF because of the school's consistent stands for racial equity. In 1951, the USF football team had skipped the Orange Bowl because its two star Black players were not welcome in Miami. The 1954 basketball team was also not welcome in any Oklahoma hotel at a Christmas week tournament, so the team stayed at a college dormitory, which Perry later said bonded the players. USF had one white star, Jerry Mullen, an all-American forward (who also went on to play professionally) who was both an excellent rebounder and a scorer.

I liked Russell because he was cool and outthought opponents as well as outplaying them. In the first playoff game that year at the Cow Palace, a bulky white center on a Texas team tried to intimidate Russell by shoving him and extending his elbows on rebounds. Then on one missed shot, Russell grabbed the back of the shorts of the Texas center as he went air-bound. The center missed the rebound, landed awkwardly, and glowered at Russell, who looked back at him innocently. The Texas center was a mess after that, missing rebounds and an easy shot. His coach soon took him out of the game, which USF won handily.

USF basketball was a pleasant diversion, but I needed a steady job. The Teamsters acquaintance who'd given me the gig driving a big truck to Imperial County called to tell me of a job driving a laundry truck in San Mateo. The drivers had Teamsters coverage, so the pay and benefits were adequate. He called me, I later learned, because of a rumor that the laundry company would try to go nonunion when the contract expired. The Teamsters wanted drivers who would vote to keep the union if it came to a test. I got the job. We'd moved to a less expensive but more spacious apartment on Potrero Hill in San Francisco, and I took an early morning bus to San Mateo, where I drove a laundry route that went from working-class San Carlos to upscale Hillsborough. It was a way station, but it paid our bills.

Meanwhile, I appealed my discharge to an Army review board. A supportive civil liberties attorney agreed to represent me pro bono. He wanted me to find others who had similarly been discharged in the hope of establishing a pattern to such cases. Today it would be relatively easy to locate such people through social media, but at that time there was no easy way for a private citizen of limited means to find someone who didn't want to be found. I thought of seeking advice from the head of Youth for Peace and Freedom, but it seemed odd to ask someone I believed to be a Communist to find people falsely accused of pro-Communist association. Ginny had no such qualms. She went to him and received sound advice: Set up a committee and advertise it in left-wing and liberal circles. He volunteered to do it; Ginny politely declined and said we wanted to do it ourselves.

We called the group we formed the Veterans Civil Liberties Committee and said we stood for "honorable discharge for honorable service." The phrase had a nice ring but didn't get us very far. The plight of draftees who had for one reason or another been branded subversive and booted out of the military to appease McCarthyism was not a high-priority item for civil libertarians. More surprising, the issue was also not a priority for many of those who'd suffered the indignity of an undesirable discharge. After a year of trying, we'd found a half-dozen people who were discharged under circumstances similar to mine. Four had refused to sign the loyalty oath; the other two had signed it but had family members with left-wing sympathies, or so they said. Only one of the six had appealed his discharge; another said he was "thinking about it." Most of them had found jobs and hoped their discharges would never become public. No one wanted his name used for any purpose. Because of their failure to come forward, I despaired of getting anywhere with a public case.

Meanwhile, my lawyer had appealed my discharge to an Army review board. He had a conflict with the hearing date and asked if I knew another attorney who might be willing to present my appeal. I suggested Phil Burton, a shot in the dark because I'd not discussed my situation with him, but Phil agreed to represent me. We paid his travel expenses to Washington, DC, but he declined payment for his legal services. Ginny, who knew Phil better than I did, was excited he'd agreed to handle the case and was optimistic about the appeal.

I didn't know what to expect. I'd written to the executive officer who'd praised me on the march to sea but had not heard back. Additionally, I was anxious about my testimony to the board. I anticipated being asked if I were a member of the Communist Party. I'd said I wasn't when refusing to sign the loyalty oath at my induction and was happy to say it again. But I wasn't about to apologize for my refusal to sign the loyalty oath or repudiate my friendship with Bill Lowe. Nor was I willing to name the names of other undesirably discharged veterans who had come to my attention through the Veterans Civil Liberties Committee. When I raised these concerns to Burton, he said I was getting ahead of myself. This was a review board, not an investigating committee. Just be respectful, tell the board why you deserve an honorable discharge and keep your answers short, Burton said, and you'll be fine.

At the hearing in Washington, Burton gave a brief but pointed presentation that made no mention of my refusal to sign the loyalty oath. He said I'd been serving in the Army ably and without incident when I was abruptly discharged because of an anonymous accusation that I was a member of the Labor Youth League. There was "not a shred of evidence" for this charge, Burton said, and I'd been given no chance to rebut it. In a thinly veiled reference to Senator McCarthy's actions, Burton said too many lives had been ruined by anonymous accusations and that the Army itself had also suffered from them. Surely, the board did not want to endorse such scurrilous behavior by refusing me an honorable discharge.

It was an effective and passionate speech to which my summary here many decades later does not do justice. The board members appeared spellbound by Burton's narrative, and one of them nodded in apparent agreement when he made the point about the Army being harmed by anonymous charges. I was transfixed as well. I had never stepped back and fully put together what had happened, and to hear the story from another person made me realize the unfairness of what had been done to me. Burton had obtained his law degree to go into politics and had never tried a case before a jury. He would have been quite good at it.

There was no way I could match Burton's performance, and I did not try. When Franklin Roosevelt was asked by one of his sons how to deliver a speech, he reportedly replied: "Be brief, be sincere, be seated." So when the white-haired colonel who chaired the board asked if I had anything to add to what my attorney had said, I said only that I had served honorably and deserved an honorable discharge. Then I sat back with some apprehension to await the board's questions.

I need not have worried. Unbeknownst to Burton or me, the board had in its possession two letters commending me, one from the executive officer and one from the sergeant who had secured my leave when Carl was born. The board was not bound by twenty-first-century rules of evidence that would have required it to inform us about the letters. I never saw either letter, but the board chairman said they painted a positive picture of me as a soldier.

"You're not a Communist, are you, Mr. Cannon?" the chairman asked in a tone that said he knew this was a ridiculous question.

"No, sir," I said.

The only other question was a softball from another board member who wanted to know if I would be willing to complete my Army service.

"Yes, sir," I said with unfeigned enthusiasm. In truth, I missed the Army. Ginny didn't like this response, but Burton assured her that the board had no authority to restore me to duty even if it wanted to do so.

The chairman announced we would be informed of the board's decision by mail, and Burton and I left the hearing room. Because my mouth had become dry during the hearing, I drank a long gulp of water after it was over. As Burton and I were leaving the building, I suddenly had an urgent need to urinate. While Burton waited, I returned to a men's room near the hearing room. As I was washing my hands, I noticed the board chairman at the next sink. He nodded to me, then said he had a question for me.

"What do you plan to do with the rest of your life, Mr. Cannon?" he asked.

I had many times gone over in my mind the responses to the questions I had expected at the hearing and were never asked. This was not a question I had anticipated, and I said the first thing that came into my head.

"Become a newspaper reporter, sir."

Expressionless, the colonel took in my answer, then shook my hand and said: "Be a good one."

10

SAN FRANCISCO PRECINCT CAPTAIN

My Army discharge was soon upgraded to honorable, but my goal of becoming a reporter remained elusive. I was still driving a laundry truck and applying for fill-in jobs at obscure newspapers when Phillip Burton and his wife, Sala, moved out of the Twenty-Third Assembly District where he'd lost in the 1954 primary to William Berry, the Democratic incumbent who died a month before the election. The Burtons' new home was in the Twentieth Assembly District in eastern San Francisco. The district included Potrero Hill, North Beach, Chinatown, and Bernal Heights. Although Democrats outnumbered Republicans nearly three-to-one, it had long been represented by popular liberal Republican Thomas Maloney, an incumbent with a daunting nickname: "the unbeatable Tommy Maloney."

In 1956, two years after his embarrassing defeat, Burton told me he was thinking about running against Maloney. I encouraged him. "You were beaten by a dead man," I told Burton. "Use it. . . . Tommy Maloney won't take you seriously."[1]

Burton told me later that my encouragement played a role in his de-

1. John Jacobs quotes these words in his seminal book, *A Rage for Justice: The Passion and Politics of Phillip Burton*, 1995. Jacobs interviewed me for this book, but took this passage, abridged here, from an interview of me by Gene Marine, a freelance journalist, for an article, "How the Unbeatable Was Beaten," in the February 1957 issue of *Frontier* magazine. Marine interviewed me at my home on Carolina Street, where he also examined my copious charts, which I no longer have, on the Potrero Hill precincts.

cision, but I'm pretty sure he'd already decided to run. The only person who might have dissuaded him was Sala. Knowing this, I asked Burton what Sala thought about him running against Maloney. She was all for it, Burton said. That meant he was running.

Burton then asked me to join the campaign. I was flattered but hesitated, believing that becoming involved in partisan politics conflicted with my goal of becoming a newspaper reporter. Burton persisted. After what he'd done for me, it was hard to say no, and Ginny made it harder. She said I owed Burton for representing me so ably before the Army review board. Without meaning to be unkind, she also observed I was not yet a working journalist. I called Burton and told him I was aboard.

Looking back, I realize that more was involved than Ginny's urging or my sense of indebtedness to the lawyer whose speech to the Army Review Board had given me a new start in life. I believed in Phil Burton, shared his politics, was impressed by his boldness in challenging Maloney—and wanted to be involved in his campaign.

Burton was a young man in a hurry. He was twenty-nine when he decided to run against Maloney, turning thirty on June 1, 1956, four days before the primary. (I would turn twenty-three two days later.) He had a following among the Young Democrats of San Francisco and the California Democratic Council, a liberal group that grew out of the volunteer clubs that supported Democratic presidential candidate Adlai Stevenson in 1952. Women found Burton attractive. He was tall and striking with wavy black hair. Ginny thought he was sexy and liked that Burton did not treat women as inferiors or try and take advantage of them. Phil had dated many women, but when Ginny and I met him he had eyes only for Sala, whose Jewish parents had made it out of Poland just ahead of the Nazis. Sala was ten years older than her husband.

Men also liked Burton. I think they identified with his competitive spirit even though he had little use for sports except basketball. Burton's game was politics, and he excelled at it. Politics in Burton's broad definition included every social or economic issue under the sun. Most decisions are political, he said.

Burton's father was a physician. He wanted his eldest son to follow in his footsteps and was disappointed when he became an attorney and additionally disappointed when he entered politics instead of practicing law. On the plane coming back from Washington after the Army Review

Board hearing, I asked him why he had not become a doctor. "I can't stand the sight of blood," he said.

Phil also didn't like talking about his father, a reluctance which I understood, as I was then unwilling to discuss my father's alcoholism. Although Phil's childhood was different from mine, it was no happier. His father, Tom, at age thirty-six, virtually abandoned his family to attend medical school. The Burtons lived in Milwaukee. The school was in Chicago, where Tom lived and ate in a cheap hotel, supporting himself by selling medical texts and occasionally coming home on weekends. Phil's mother, Mildred, supported the family by working at the Roman Catholic diocese where she attended daily Mass. Phil, then ten, was supposed to be "the man of the house" in a family that included two younger brothers.

After Tom completed medical school, he uprooted the family to San Francisco, where he interned in a hospital and afterward ran a clinic. John Jacobs, Burton's biographer, depicts Tom Burton as a liberal idealist who treated patients who could not afford payment for free, belonged to the American Civil Liberties Union, and opposed the forced relocation of Japanese Americans after Pearl Harbor. Tom Burton passed on his progressive politics to his sons, if not his profession.

Phil and his brothers grew up believing, as Ronald Reagan and my parents did, that FDR was the nation's savior. Although Bob Burton was an altar boy as a child, neither he nor his brothers were religious as adults. All three boys embraced the secular faith of their father in activist government. Bob, who had knocked on our door in 1954 to recruit Ginny and me for Phil's first campaign, became a teacher at San Quentin Prison. John followed Phil into the legislature and Congress and after conquering drug demons became an effective Assembly speaker who spoke up for the least-affluent Californians. "He never forgot where he came from," said George Steffes, Governor Reagan's legislative liaison.

I liked being around Phil. He was hyperactive and talked compulsively—and loudly—but was the unusual chatterbox who was also a good listener. He knew the ethnic composition and voting habits of every neighborhood in San Francisco. His ability to do the complicated calculus of political redistricting in his head would make him the foremost expert on this subject in the state. But what drew me most to Burton was his commitment to racial equality. Before most of the white world had heard of Martin Luther King, before the freedom rides, before California had laws against discrimination, Phil Burton was a persistent advocate for racial justice.

The 1956 campaign gave him an opportunity to practice what he preached. On February 29, 1956, a headline-seeking U.S. attorney in San Francisco subpoenaed the records of Chinatown's twenty-six family associations. These records would have revealed that many of Chinatown's workers were undocumented immigrants subject to deportation. Chinatown was distraught. When Ginny and I went for dinner soon afterward at a favorite Chinatown restaurant, we found it closed. The owner told me his employees were in hiding, along with most other workers in Chinatown. Burton denounced the subpoenas as an anti-Chinese intrusion into the affairs of the family associations and called for them to be quashed. A federal judge did just that on March 20, ordering the records to be returned unopened to the associations. Burton was applauded in Chinatown for speaking out when other politicians, Maloney included, were silent.

Soon after telling Burton I'd join his campaign, I received a call from Rudy Nothenberg, a friend in the Young Democrats, who said Phil wanted him to be his campaign manager. That was a plus. Rudy was a brilliant organizer. He and his parents had been interned in Shanghai during World War II by the Japanese along with sixteen thousand other stateless German Jews.

Burton's opportunity for victory was made possible by a crucial change in the unique system of cross-filing that had long enabled Republicans to dominate California politics. Cross-filing allowed candidates to file for both the Republican and Democratic nominations. Since candidates were not identified by party on the ballot, voters often didn't know if they were voting for a Republican or a Democrat.

Cross-filing originated with Hiram Johnson and his Progressives, who tried to reform California politics through what they called "direct democracy." Johnson was elected governor in 1910. Progressives believed that powerful monopolies such as the Southern Pacific Railroad had corrupted the state's politics with lavish donations to the major parties, which sponsored legislative candidates who protected these monopolies. They were right but, with parties out of the picture, the special interests financed candidates in other ways—sometimes directly. Lobbyist-supported incumbents carved out cozy districts for themselves, won the nominations of both parties, and were elected repeatedly without serious opposition.

As Democratic Party registration increased, cross-filing enabled the minority Republicans to keep legislative control. In 1952, a group of liberal Democrats qualified a ballot initiative to repeal cross-filing. Republican leaders outsmarted themselves by sponsoring a rival ballot measure that preserved cross-filing but allowed party identification. As it happened, the initiative to abolish cross-filing lost, while the initiative providing for partisan identification won. It proved a game changer. Party identification transformed California from a Republican citadel to one of the nation's safest Democratic states. By 1958, Democrats had won control of the legislature, which except for four years they have held to this day. In 1959, they abolished cross-filing. But in 1956, it was far from certain that Burton could deny Tommy Maloney from winning the Democratic nomination through cross-filing.

The eldest of eighteen children, Maloney had worked at his father's saloon while still a boy. Later he was a lumberman and then a stevedore, heading San Francisco's Longshoremen's Union local in 1919. He had the backing of more than a hundred labor unions, many businesses, the Roman Catholic Church, and was an icon of the Irish American community. In 1924, Maloney was elected to the California Senate, where he cosponsored workmen's compensation and unemployment legislation. When a 1932 reapportionment designed to curb San Francisco's power in the legislature reduced the number of senators from the city from seven to one, Maloney ran for the Assembly and won. He won a dozen more times as an assemblyman, usually obtaining both the Republican and Democratic nominations.

One reason Burton wanted me in the campaign is that Ginny and I lived on Potrero Hill, a few blocks from Maloney's home. We'd met Maloney and knew he was esteemed by his working-class neighbors. Democrats had a significant edge in voting registration on Potrero Hill, which Maloney had always carried by wide margins. Indeed, many Hill residents believed Maloney was a Democrat. Burton said that, if we could cut Maloney's margin on the Hill to 55–45 percent, he could win the nomination. That seemed too cautious to me. When Ginny and I met with Burton at our rented flat on Carolina Street, I predicted we'd beat Maloney in Potrero Hill.

After Burton left, I confessed to Ginny that I didn't feel very confident about my forecast. Never mind, she said. Phil, whom she always called by his first name, had wanted to hear me say we could win Potrero Hill. Ginny also advised me not to presume on my friendship with Phil but to take any problems that arose to Nothenberg. That's what I did. Rudy and I talked almost daily. Our precinct operation was the heart of the Burton campaign. We had more than a hundred Young Democrats to choose from, most of them energetic women and men in their twenties. Burton had put Potrero Hill entirely in my hands after agreeing with me that we should avoid provoking Maloney. So I set about finding precinct workers who felt comfortable with a low-key approach. We didn't want Maloney to know he faced serious opposition, so we didn't work his home precinct or the neighboring one. Our campaign literature didn't mention Maloney. The precinct workers were instructed to emphasize that Burton was a Democrat and say nothing about Maloney. If his name came up, the precinct worker was to say that Maloney was a nice man for a Republican and that Burton was a promising Democrat who was running to gain experience. This tactic usually worked but not always. One man became enraged when a precinct worker told him Maloney was a Republican, calling him a liar and threatening to beat him up.

Maloney, who hadn't had a serious challenger in twenty years, didn't bother with precinct work. Ginny, our best precinct worker, was pregnant with David and particularly effective with young mothers. For two precincts with large Russian populations, I found a Russian speaker. For precincts loaded with dockworkers, we found a couple of dockworkers. I worked three precincts in which many voters were Irish American. They were working-class people who didn't mind that I drove a laundry truck for a living.

Maloney's campaign was mostly pro forma. He sent out a single mailer, which emphasized his endorsements. It wasn't enough. Burton won the Democratic primary with 8,371 votes to 6,292 votes for Maloney while a third Democrat siphoned off 3,358 votes. All three candidates cross-filed. Maloney received 5,450 votes on the Republican line compared to only 542 votes for Burton. We were pleased, but Maloney had outpolled us on primary day, meaning there was work to do in the general election.

I'd used two weeks of vacation and my weekends to organize Potrero Hill in the primary. Burton wanted me to take off the last two weeks of September and all of October and see that I was paid the equivalent of my truck-driving wage from Democratic Party funds. Thanks to the Teamsters, I managed to get the time off. (The Teamsters local was pro-Maloney but liked having a friend in the Burton campaign.) Ginny and I disagreed about taking income from a political party, which I thought undermined my efforts to become a reporter. I wanted to donate my time. Ginny observed this wasn't realistic, especially with another mouth to feed, David having been born in July. I gave in but vowed to myself that I'd never again accept another nickel from a political party. I never have.

Maloney and his campaign team had not expected Burton to win the Democratic nomination. Belatedly aroused, they went into attack mode, alleging in fliers that Burton was soft on communism and supportive of Red China. Other fliers implied that Burton was a capitalist tool. A complex oil initiative was on the California ballot in 1956. A Maloney flier framed Burton's position on the measure this way: "Standard Oil Wants You to Vote for Burton."

We didn't know what to do about these accusations. Sala Burton felt strongly that we needed to respond, while Rudy Nothenberg argued that answering the smears would bring the charges to the attention of additional voters.

Meanwhile, the fliers kept coming, becoming more strident as the campaign progressed. The weird Standard Oil charge didn't bother me, but some of our precinct workers on Potrero Hill were being asked if Burton was a Communist. Late in the campaign, we received a tip that on the Sunday before the election a new flier accusing Burton of being pro-Communist would be passed out on the steps of the Catholic church on Potrero Hill before the family Mass. I felt a need to do something, although I wasn't sure what. I called Burton to tell him about the tip. Maloney must be desperate, Burton said. He sounded calm, but I could tell from his tone of voice that he was worried.

What did I think should be done? Burton asked. Leave it to me, I said. On Sunday without telling anyone except Ginny, I went to the church forty-five minutes before Mass and saw a chubby teenager with a thick batch of fliers in his hands.

"What's this about?" I asked him.

"It's about this Communist named Burton," he said. The boy didn't sound all that interested, and he also didn't seem particularly athletic. Impulsively I snatched the entire batch of fliers from his hands and ran as fast as I could. Out of breath after a couple of blocks, I looked back and realized that no one was pursuing me. I stopped and skimmed the flier which in big red type proclaimed: "Don't send a Communist to Sacramento."

That was enough for me. I stopped reading, started walking, and dumped the fliers in a trash can. When Burton asked me that night how the fliers had been received, I told them they hadn't been distributed and left it at that.

There was much more to the Burton campaign than Potrero Hill. John Jacobs gives an extended account in *A Rage for Justice*. Writing three decades later, he based much of what he wrote on interviews with campaign participants, including me. Three things stand in my mind about that campaign. The first is that Burton was an outstanding candidate whose work habits and tireless energy set a high standard for the rest of us. Second, with the exception of one of the city's four newspapers, Burton's campaign was barely covered—the papers didn't take us seriously—but if they had, Maloney might have roused from his complacency sooner. Burton also had perfect pitch when it came to the city's ethnic enclaves, especially Chinatown.

The city had a ban on firecrackers but had long made an exception in Chinatown, where the New Year festivities were a tourist draw. For reasons now forgotten, in 1956 the city decided to enforce the firecracker ban. This happened shortly before the U.S. attorney's issuance of the mass subpoenas aimed at rooting out undocumented immigrants. Chinese leaders, mindful of past racism, saw a plot. Without buying into any conspiracy theories, Burton said the Chinese were right to complain. He promised that if he were elected he'd introduce a bill permitting firecrackers for two weeks during the Chinese New Year. The combination of opposing the subpoenas and supporting firecrackers made Burton a political star in normally Republican Chinatown.

Burton also made inroads with a small but growing African American community at a time Blacks did not routinely vote Democratic. Burton was a member of the NAACP, and his law partner was Joseph Williams, a Black friend from Golden Gate Law School. Anticipating battles that continue to this day, Burton had made a vivid impression in the predominantly Black neighborhood of Hunter's Point on Election Day 1952. After being told that the only polling place in Hunter's Point would close at 8 p.m. with voters still in line, Burton rushed to the polling place and loudly demanded that booths be kept open until everyone in line had voted. Intimidated by Burton's manner and threats of legal action, the poll workers complied. This action won favorable notice from Dr. Carlton Goodlett, a Black physician and publisher of the weekly *Sun-Reporter*. The newspaper enthusiastically covered Burton and endorsed him.

Our underfunded campaign also struggled to gain the backing of organized labor, which had long worked closely with Maloney's union support. Bucking the consensus, the militant International Longshoremen's and Warehouse Union endorsed Burton. We received help from George Hardy, a respected labor leader who headed the local Building Trades union. Hardy had no use for Republicans, even liberal ones, and backed Burton.

So the campaign plowed along, a bit short on money but rich in human resources. We beat the unbeatable Tommy Maloney, narrowly but decisively. The results were Burton 17,807, Maloney 17,148, a margin of 659 votes, or slightly less than 2 percent. In a close election, everything matters, and my bailiwick of Potrero Hill mattered a great deal. We won the Hill by 164 votes, with 2,229 for Burton and 2,065 for Maloney. I had delivered, albeit belatedly, on my promise to Phil of beating Maloney in his own backyard.

Chinatown mattered, too, as did Hunter's Point—Burton carried 80 percent of the vote in both neighborhoods—and was the only Democrat in California to defeat a Republican incumbent legislator in 1956, when President Dwight Eisenhower won reelection and carried California a second time. Burton gave credit where credit was due. Asked why he won, he mentioned four names: Hardy, Lee, Nothenberg, and me. It was the right list, but the self-effacing and systemic Nothenberg was indispensable. Rudy, who always had people in reserve, sent me Alan Cranston, the future U.S senator. Cranston was a fitness addict and in good shape. I asked him to work the hilliest part of the vacated precinct. Sala Burton and Ginny Cannon also played vital roles. When I was one precinct worker short, Ginny, although busy with a toddler and a new baby (and a precinct captain in another neighborhood) volunteered to pick some of the slack. Sala's advice was sound—and this time was usually heeded.

Burton's election gave me a rare feeling of accomplishment. My debt had been repaid—many times over, Burton said—and for the first time in my adult life I'd shown leadership and organizational ability. I'd had a political education in the process. Ginny had been a big part of the effort, and we'd become closer while sharing childcare and precinct work. She said she was proud of me, but neither of us had illusions about the future. The letdown came the Monday after the election, when I went back to driving a laundry truck.

A few days after the election, a wealthy Democrat who'd paid attention to what I'd done for Burton offered to set me up in business with the proviso that I'd be available for party work in future campaigns. I said I'd talk it over with Ginny. We liked the man who was making the offer, and the money was tempting, but I wanted to quit politics while ahead as both of us knew I wasn't cut out to be a businessman.

"Too bad he doesn't own a newspaper," Ginny said.

I turned down the offer and set out to become a journalist.

11

THE MINOR LEAGUES AND BEYOND

I am a lifelong baseball fan. Perhaps because I spent so many years in the lower rungs of journalism, I appreciate ballplayers who had long apprenticeships in the minors before reaching the big leagues. My favorite was shortstop Maury Wills, who spent nine years in the minors before the Los Angeles Dodgers promoted him to the majors. Wills restored the art of base stealing to major league baseball and helped the Dodgers win three World Series. I also liked Paul Lo Duca, a less-famous Dodger who labored in the minors a dozen years before becoming a catcher and an outfielder in the majors.

Although they earned their way with talent and hustle, Wills and Lo Duca were also lucky. The overwhelming majority of minor leaguers never make it to "the show." They endure endless bus travel, crummy motels, and awful food for little more than minimum wage. Outside the towns where they play, baseball fans know of these minor leaguers, if they know of them at all, through the iconic film *Bull Durham* or the aptly titled John Feinstein book, *Where Nobody Knows Your Name.*

Reporting isn't as hard as playing baseball, but when done right isn't easy either. Reporting demands accuracy—under deadline pressure. It rewards diligence, which often means making the extra phone call or knocking on the extra door. It requires careful listening and considerable research. Reporters need to be skeptical but also possess a sense of fair play. These qualities mattered as much at the tiny newspapers where my career began in California as at *The Washington Post.* Arguably, they may matter even more at the small papers where there are fewer editors to catch mistakes.

My fifteen years in the minor leagues began at the *Lafayette Sun* and its sister weeklies in 1957 and moved on to the unrelated *Newark Sun,* the *Merced Sun-Star,* the *Contra Costa Times,* the *San Jose Mercury-News,* and the Washington bureau of Ridder Publications. The first two papers were weeklies, the Merced and San Jose papers dailies. The *Contra Costa Times* was in transition, publishing three or four days a week on its way to becoming a daily.

I was editor at the *Contra Costa Times* and a bit of everything at the long-defunct *Newark Sun,* owned by two printers who were brothers. In San Jose, after beginning on the wire desk, I became the state capitol correspondent in Sacramento. In 1972 I was hired by *The Washington Post,* where for the next twenty-nine years—the last two in freelance status—I covered politics and the presidency, interrupted by two stints as the newspaper's chief correspondent in Los Angeles where I ranged widely throughout the West, covering politics, the environment, immigration, along with forest fires and other breaking news.

During most of these forty-three years, I considered myself a general assignment reporter, rewarding and fascinating work, to be sure. But I wanted more. When I became excessively interested in the people I was covering—Ronald Reagan, of course, but also Pete McCloskey and Rodney King—I expanded my knowledge by writing books. I wrote nine books in all, five of them about Reagan. I also wrote a social history of the 1992 Los Angeles riots that were triggered by the acquittal of the white LAPD officers who had beaten and arrested King.

I have never ceased being a reporter. After becoming a freelancer in 2000, I still wrote occasionally for *The Post,* including the obituary of Ronald Reagan. I did a few magazine pieces and op-eds for the *New York Times* (including Nancy Reagan's obituary) and have written for *Time* and *National Review* and *Smithsonian* magazine and online outlets, including *RealClearPolitics.* I briefly headed *California Journal,* a monthly publication that failed to survive the social media age. I wrote a monthly column for *State Net Capitol Journal,* which covers state politics and government. For many years I wrote a column that was nationally syndicated by *The Washington Post.* My best columns are heavily reported. I'm a forgettable pundit but a good reporter.

In 1957, my work at the Reno papers while in high school was several years in the past and did not impress editors at the various newspapers where I applied for a job. My job search was mostly done on weekends since after the Burton campaign I'd gone back to making a living as a laundry-truck driver. One day while eating a brown-bag lunch in the truck, I spotted a help-wanted ad for a reporter in a San Francisco newspaper. It led to an evening interview with Herman Silverman in his home in the suburban foothills of Lafayette, east of Oakland.

Silverman, the publisher of the *Lafayette Sun* and related newspapers, was dapper and fast-talking. My old sports clips from the Reno papers and a few pieces I'd written for minor magazines were of no interest to him. What he wanted to know was whether I understood the basic elements of reporting and could write grammatically. To ascertain this, Silverman gave me a "story test," then a widely used method of determining an applicant's competence.

Silverman related a series of facts in random order. Some were important, others trivial. Some didn't belong in the story at all. I had not anticipated such a test but was ready for it. I started by having him spell the names of the people and communities in the account he was relating. The story's "lede," which is how old-timers render the opening of a story, was obvious, and I quickly wrote it on Silverman's typewriter. He was impressed and said that, if I was willing to accept the salary of a beginning reporter, the job was mine. I told him I had to check with my wife. Fine, he said. Call me back within twenty-four hours and give me your decision.

Ginny had supported my newspaper-job search but was not thrilled by Silverman's offer. My salary would be $55 a week, less than half my $120 weekly wage as a truck driver, which was occasionally enhanced by tips. The wage difference was attributable to the fact that many truck drivers were unionized.

My desire to become a reporter at the expense of our standard of living provoked the first crisis of our marriage. Ginny was born in San Francisco and liked living there. She enjoyed being a mother and had supportive friends. She was also working as a part-time nursery teacher, a job at which she excelled. I was proposing to uproot the family for a job that barely supported us. But the uprooting bothered Ginny more than the pay cut. She didn't want to leave San Francisco, and it was hard to blame her for that.

We came up with an imperfect compromise. Ginny wouldn't move.

I would get a room near the paper and come home on weekends. Since I didn't like being away from the kids during the week, it was an unappealing plan, but neither of us could think of a better one. I called Silverman and said I'd take the job after giving notice to my employer. So I drove a laundry truck for two more weeks and then went to work at the *Lafayette Sun*.

It wasn't long before I missed the laundry route. Silverman, who professed an urbane liberalism, was a tabloid journalist at heart. Soon after I joined the *Sun*, a photographer told me his favorite Silverman story. A helicopter had crashed in a field, decapitating the pilot. The photographer had taken a picture at a respectful distance. Herman inspected the photo and quickly decided that the remains of the pilot weren't sufficiently visible. He took a magic marker and circled the body and then circled the head, a short distance away.

"That's the way to do it," he told the photographer. The picture ran on the front page, with Silverman's markings. Above the photo, below the newspaper's banner, a headline in large type proclaimed, "Merry Christmas."

I detested the *Sun* but was fascinated with the proficiency of Herman and Dick Osborne, his chief editor, in maneuvering stories so that the various *Suns*—in Orinda, Walnut Creek, Pleasant Hill, and Concord—would all prominently feature a local angle.

What I disliked about the paper—hated, really—was that it was fake in a way that went beyond the rantings of Donald Trump about "fake news." Most articles in the *Suns* were rewrites of stories in the *Oakland Tribune,* then dominant in the area, or other local dailies. Worse, they were rewrites that didn't credit their source. On my first experience of such a rewrite, I asked my editor what we would do if the story we were rewriting contained a serious error. That's not our problem, I was told—and most of the time it wasn't. When the relative of a suicide victim complained that an essential fact in our story was wrong, I bucked it to Herman, who said with a straight face that the error wasn't the *Sun*'s fault because the story had been rewritten from a daily newspaper. I don't know whether I was more astounded by the explanation or by the grieving relative's acceptance of it.

Nonetheless, the rewrites drove me crazy. When I was made the main reporter for the Pleasant Hill and later the Concord versions of the *Sun* I tried to cover as many stories as possible to avoid rewrites. But we ran so many stories that I made only a small dent. Give it up, another reporter advised. Accept the *Sun* for what it is.

In addition to the rewritten stories, the *Suns* featured community columns written by women about neighborhood events too trivial to qualify as news. The requirements for becoming a columnist were undemanding and did not include writing skill or a command of grammar. If you lived in the community, could meet a weekly deadline, and didn't mind working for free, you could write a column for any of the *Suns*. One columnist wrote frequently about planned vacations until the Walnut Creek police chief complained to Herman that burglars were avid readers because it informed them when houses would be vacant.

Nonetheless, the *Suns* were a useful learning experience. I learned how to read police blotters and zoning maps and much about the workings of planning commissions and school boards. In Concord, where I was tipped that the police were going to raid the town's most prominent bookmaker and our photographer was absent, I learned on the fly how to use a Speed-Graphic camera. Most important, I learned how to develop sources, some of whom would be helpful a few years later when I became editor of the *Contra Costa Times*. Eric Sevareid once wrote that in his early days on television he practiced on his viewers. I certainly practiced on readers of the *Sun*. Once, in writing about a complex Walnut Creek zoning dispute, I managed to get almost everything wrong. My editors didn't say anything—if they even noticed—but a savvy city planner took me aside and went through the story with me, pointing out what I had messed up or missed. I thanked him profusely. In those days, I needed all the help I could get.

I didn't stay long at the *Sun*. It was six months, I think, but I'm not entirely sure as I have no written record of anything I did there. At the time it seemed much longer. I missed the kids terribly during the week. Ginny found me useless on the weekends, when I played with the children and did almost nothing else around the house. During the week I'd work twelve hours a day or more at the paper, usually eating dinner alone at an Italian restaurant that featured spaghetti with a salad and bread for $1.19. Once a week I ate there with the editor, Dick Osborne, who contributed an extra dollar so we could have wine with the meal. This restaurant saved me, for I turned over my meager paychecks to Ginny, who made sure I had enough for rent and a little pocket money. Like most American families, we didn't have credit cards then.

Silverman was cheap. I found out my first week at the *Sun* that other reporters were getting a car allowance. Barging into Herman's office, I said I was using my car on the job and wanted a car allowance, too. He calmly agreed. My next check contained the allowance—an extra dollar a week.

After two or three months, I began looking around for other newspaper employment. Silverman had a trick I'd been warned about by one of his ad salesmen. If you missed a day for illness or any other reason, he kept track of it in a little brown ledger book. When someone quit to go elsewhere Silverman would take out the book and tell the departing employee that he owed him for the number of days marked in his ledger. If you couldn't or wouldn't work these days, Herman would dock your last paycheck.

When I found another job through a friend of a friend, I went to Herman's office to give notice. After wishing me well, he took out his ledger and said I owed him seven days. This was out of line. I'd missed two days for the flu and one other on a flimsy excuse that was really a job search. Except for these three days, I'd worked for one or another of the *Sun*s every weekday from morning to night. But I didn't argue with Herman's accounting. Because of the forewarning by the ad salesman, I'd made it a point to give notice the day after I was paid. Instead of holding onto the check for Ginny, I'd promptly cashed it. Having this money in my wallet enabled me to tell Herman where he could put his seven days. As I left his office I was cheered by the staff, even the printers. I didn't know why. A reporter later told me that Silverman had left his office intercom on while I was in his office.

My next stop on my journalism odyssey was Newark, a tiny city at the south end of San Francisco Bay. The Mitchell brothers, both printers, had purchased a small printing press with the purpose of putting out a local weekly. I'd driven to Newark on the day I'd called in sick and met with them. They were from the Deep South and naive about California but friendly and well-meaning. They showed me a trial version of the newspaper, which was short on advertising and weak on content. I said I could fill the paper with news but wasn't sure I could do anything about the advertising. The Mitchells assured me that the owner of a department store in the town's largest shopping center was ready to advertise in a big way once he saw there was real news in the *Newark Sun*.

We had a skeletal staff. A high school senior who reminded me of myself in my Reno days did local sports. He was paid a pittance. We paid a local photographer ten dollars for pictures we used, fifteen if the photo was on page one. Whenever possible, I took photos to save us the expense. Lucille Mitchell, wife of one of the brothers, was "society editor," which meant she wrote soft news—PTA events, a community concert, a business dinner by the Chamber of Commerce—mostly from mailed press announcements or phone calls. The *Newark Sun* occupied two cramped offices at the back of the ground floor in the Mitchell home. I took the smallest office, telling Lucille I would be out news-gathering most of the day. The Mitchells paid me a hundred dollars a week, still less than what I'd made as a truck driver but nearly twice my salary at the *Lafayette Sun*.

Our news content was the warp and woof of a small California city that was overshadowed by Fremont, which surrounds Newark. Burglaries and beauty contests. Tree plantings, automobile accidents, ribbon cuttings, and road widenings. Development of a Master Plan. City Council and planning commission meetings.

As anywhere, some news was grim. A baby who had been released from one hospital fell ill a few hours later and died in an ambulance on the way to another hospital. My story pointed out that the first hospital had come under fire previously for similar incidents. An unidentified man was found dead in a field, allegedly gored by a bull. I read the police report and interviewed the man who had found him. The death seemed suspicious to me, but in these pre-DNA days it was hard to identify someone who didn't have a police record.

I also wrote editorials, one of which opposed a proposal by the Pacific Gas and Electric Company to exempt transmission lines, public utility poles, and underground facilities from the city's use-permit process. PG&E sought such exemptions throughout its service area, and many small cities rolled over and acceded to any requests from this powerful utility. Newark did not. It was a working-class, heavily Democratic community with an independent streak. It rejected the PG&E proposal.

It was fun while it lasted, which wasn't long. There simply weren't enough people or enough of a commercial base in Newark to support even a weekly newspaper. The 1960 census two years later put Newark's population at 9,884. The town was so small that Ginny and I hadn't been able to find a rental there; instead we'd rented a tract home in Fremont. On March 13, 1958, I wrote a farewell column in the *Newark Sun,* thanking a score of people by name and all our readers. I regretted leaving Newark. The experience had been invaluable, and the Mitchells had even taught me the rudiments of typesetting. But the job never had a sense of permanence.

After the Newark experiment ended, I was hired as a general assignment reporter at the *Merced Sun-Star,* an established daily in California's bountiful Central Valley. The city editor there was John Burns, who'd been a senior reporter and fill-in editor at the *Nevada State Journal* when I was a teenage sportswriter. Burns was principled, intelligent, hardworking, and thorough. His journalistic hero was *New York Times* feature writer Meyer Berger, who'd won a Pulitzer Prize in 1950 for his account of the murder of thirteen people by a deranged veteran. Burns wasn't quite in Berger's league (few were), but he was an excellent writer who appreciated the value of details. He was also a faithful Catholic who in Reno had gently challenged my youthful radicalism, urged me to discard ideology of any kind, and recognized my possibilities as a reporter. I knew his editing would improve my writing and I wanted to work for him.

Ginny liked John Burns on sight. Somewhat to my surprise, she also liked Merced. This was my first newspaper job with regular hours. Ginny hadn't gone with me to Lafayette, and in Newark I'd been pretty much a one-man band. The *Sun-Star* was an afternoon paper published six days a week. This required getting to work early but also meant I was usually home for dinner with the kids. Ginny, who was now pregnant with our third child, made friends with the spouses of other reporters, one of whom was also pregnant.

Most of my Merced files—unlike those for Newark—are long gone, and I don't know the exact date I started at the *Sun-Star.* I think it was early April 1958 as I recall many fields in the Central Valley were still underwater from the El Nino rains of the 1957–58 winter.

The publisher of the *Sun-Star* was a combative little Rotarian named Dean Lesher whose persistent boosterism was leavened by a constructive civic-mindedness. Lesher had graduated cum laude from the University of Maryland, earned a law degree at Harvard, and developed a legal practice in Kansas City, Missouri, before becoming bored with representing clients and corporations. He was fascinated by newspapers, which he believed could shape and improve a community. Lesher bought a small paper in Nebraska that failed before he succumbed to the lure of California and brought his family west. In 1941, when he was thirty-nine, he'd bought the *Sun-Star* for a pittance.

Although the war years were boom times in California, the Merced newspaper suffered from lack of advertising. Wartime rationing had given department stores little to sell; hence they had no need to advertise. It was even worse for car dealers, a traditional source of newspaper ad revenue. With auto factories converted to production of tanks, dealers had no new cars to sell, and gas rationing limited used-car sales.

Lesher invited Merced's successful merchants and other prominent figures to a meeting where he gave a visionary promotional lecture on the coming postwar boom. Merced would benefit more from this improving economy, he said, if it had a newspaper that looked after the city's interests. But Lesher said he couldn't wait until the end of war. He bluntly told the assemblage that he would give up on the *Sun-Star* and leave Merced unless the merchants started advertising immediately. They did.

Merced and the *Sun-Star* thrived after the war, and Lesher repaid the supportive merchants with generous coverage of their promotions and an absence of negative news. This was par for the course at the time. "Nothing ever happens in department stores," Carey McWilliams had noted in a local lecture that was not covered by the *Sun-Star*. This was before I arrived in Merced, but I listened to a recording of the event in which McWilliams had decried newspaper favoritism to its big advertisers. By saying that nothing happened in department stores, McWilliams meant that local papers didn't report the horrific incidents which sometimes occurred there. He then proceeded to recount some of these incidents in gruesome detail, including one where a woman shopper had been mangled by an escalator. Many years later, I had the good fortune to become friends with McWilliams, whose admirable books have mostly stood the test of time.

As for Lesher, boosterism aside, he turned out to be an able publisher who rarely interfered with the newsroom. When a well-known and litigious attorney, one of the wealthiest men in California's Central Valley, tried to squelch stories about his intoxicated driving escapades, Lesher backed the newsroom. On another occasion I was in a corridor near Lesher's office when he physically ejected from his office a larger man with whom he'd been arguing. A secretary told me the man had threatened to withdraw his advertising if Lesher didn't change the newspaper's coverage on some issue.

Lesher was a member of the Merced City Planning Commission and dealt with this potential conflict of interest in an interesting way. He instructed the city editor that Planning Commission meetings were to be covered but that reporters should avoid favoritism. Specifically, he ordered that, if anyone criticized Lesher, the story should include the criticism.

Nonetheless, Planning Commission meetings were an ordeal for reporters, knowing the publisher would read every word they wrote. Technically, these meetings were part of the city beat, but John Burns rotated the coverage so that no reporter would be stuck with the meetings too often. I recall drawing the short straw of covering the commission only once. Afterward Lesher told someone that my story was more interesting than the meeting. If so, it cleared a very low bar.

The managing editor of the *Sun-Star* was a folksy South Dakotan named Cliff Schlegel, a fount of oddball stories. For example, he told us about an FBI agent in the South Dakota city where Schlegel worked before coming to Merced. When the FBI had a press release, the agent would stand under the street clock in front of the paper, synchronize his watch with the clock and march into the newsroom at the precise time the document was marked for release. Editors explained that the information had to be delivered beforehand to be printed at the time it was supposed to be released. The agent didn't budge. "Mr. Hoover said this was for Tuesday noon release, and that's the time it is now," he told the editors.

Schlegel's stories and country-lawyer appearance masked solid journalistic instincts. He understood, as Dick Harwood would tell me years later at *The Washington Post*, that the acid test of an editor's competence is the performance of his hires. Schlegel had found a gold mine in the level-headed John Burns, whom he valued and consulted on hiring decisions.

As an editor, Burns would have succeeded at any newspaper. He caught grammatical errors and improved our writing. He also found holes in stories, even when the reporters attempted to conceal them by writing around a missing fact or failing to explain the context of what they were writing about. Burns would approach our desks with a puzzled look on his face, point to the offending paragraph, and ask softly, "Is there something more to this the reader should know?"

The other star at the paper, although he didn't think of himself this way, was a brave photographer named Clayton Peterson. He was always close to the action at a fire or other catastrophe, sometimes too close, and it showed in his photos. In these pre–interstate highway days, Highway 99 running through Merced was a major thoroughfare between Northern and Southern California and the scene of numerous devastating accidents. Clay was at most of them. He also took lovely pictures of children, animals, and trees.

A gifted photographer, he became tongue-tied in job interviews. When I was at the *San Jose Mercury* a few years later, the photo editor was trying to fill a vacancy and asked me if I knew any good photographers. I mentioned Clay. The photo editor interviewed him and liked his work but didn't hire him because Peterson was inarticulate in response to basic biographical questions. "He just sat there," the photo editor said. I told him he should have put a camera in Clay's hands when he interviewed him. Clay always knew what to do when he had a camera.

I was a poor substitute for Clay when I filled in for him. Anxious to impress, I had claimed rudimentary photographic experience in my *Sun-Star* job interview. My punishment for that slight exaggeration was to be designated as backup for nighttime calls when Clay was off or taking photos elsewhere. Fortunately for me, Clay was rarely off. But I responded to enough ghastly car accidents to change my driving habits. When I went to Merced, I was an excessively fast driver. When we left, I was driving so slowly Ginny had to remind me to keep up with the traffic on the highway.

After a few weeks as a general assignment reporter, I was moved to the police beat. That was fine with me as I'd grown up around cops. The police chief, seeing this, took me into his confidence. But there was no major crime in Merced in 1958 and the beat produced few stories. Then in June that year the sports editor had a row with the managing editor and walked out. John Burns remembered I had covered sports in Reno and passed this on to Schlegel, who asked me if I'd like to be sports editor. I was reluctant, fearful I'd be typecast as a sportswriter. Schlegel then asked what beat I'd like most. The county beat, I replied, which at the *Sun-Star* included politics. Schlegel said he'd start looking for another sports editor but asked if I'd do the job until they found one. He promised me the county beat when it next came open. So for the next few months I was sports editor, even taking over the departed editor's column.

The *Sun-Star* sports page in summer, often two pages, was a mix of local sports and major league baseball. The Giants had moved west that year to San Francisco, and baseball fans in Merced couldn't get enough of them. Boxing was also a big deal in those days. On June 30 there was a celebrated bout in the San Francisco Cow Palace between Joey Giambra and Joey Giardello, two of the world's top middleweights. The departed sports editor had received press accreditation for the fight, and Schlegel urged me to cover it, even calling the Cow Palace to substitute my name.

I've long since been turned off by boxing, but I was a fan in the 1950s without qualms about the brutal nature of the sport. I'd grown up listening to fights on the radio with my father, and the boxing instruction I'd received as a boy had been of practical value in helping me deal with bullies. The instructor took me once to Golden Gloves boxing matches in Reno, and I'd gone several times afterward on my own. Although I'd never seen a professional prizefight except on newsreels and television, I knew about Giambra, a brilliant boxer with movie-star good looks who'd reputedly been denied a shot at the middleweight title because he refused to replace longtime manager Mike Scanlon with someone designated by the Mafia.

Giambra's deft left jab and fancy footwork enabled him to leave the ring some five years later with two distinctions: He was never knocked out and he was one of the few professional fighters, then or now, to leave the ring with his face virtually unmarked. Although it was rarely his first recourse, Giambra had a hard right punch to go with the jab and knocked out thirty-one of his sixty-five opponents.

Giardello, who is familiar to modern fans mostly because of a movie about his controversial fight with Hurricane Carter, was a roughneck who had served a prison term for assaulting a gas station attendant. He considered Giambra a wimp. The two had fought back-to-back fights six years earlier, splitting unanimous decisions. Giardello was favored to win the rubber match at the Cow Palace.

Most fight crowds prefer punching to boxing artistry. My dad was a fan of Jack Dempsey, one of the greatest punchers of them all, and it was an article of faith in our house that Dempsey had been robbed of the heavyweight title by the referee in his rematch with Gene Tunney in

1927. Dempsey floored Tunney in the seventh round but stood over his fallen foe for five seconds before going to a neutral corner. Following a rule that was new at the time, the referee then began the count. Tunney arose at the count of nine and went on to win the fight by unanimous decision.

No doubt my dad would have rooted for Giardello if he'd been at that 1958 fight. The crowd certainly did. Every time Giardello landed a punch the crowd would roar. He had Giambra backpedaling during the early rounds and delivered a series of nice combinations when Giardello caught him once near the ropes. But Giambra clinched and danced out of trouble, and Giardello never had him against the ropes again. The frustration showed on Giardello's face. If only he could catch this pretty boy, he'd end the fight with a knockout. But he never did.

Awaiting the decision, the crowd cheered Giardello, who gave the victory sign and jumped up and down as he returned to his corner. Wait! Wait! said Giambra's manager Scanlon, waving his hands in an attempt to shush the crowd. In the press section the prevailing view was that Giardello had won. I thought Giambra might be the winner, but since I'd never before covered a fight kept my opinion to myself. Then the decisions came. One judge scored it for Giambra by two points. The other judge, who must have watched a different fight, scored it for Giardello by an improbable five points. That left the decision to the referee, Jack Downey, who scored the fight 96–94 for Giambra. When Downey raised Giambra's arm in victory, Giardello unleashed a string of expletives and glared at the referee. Giambra smiled thinly but was strangely subdued for someone who'd just won a hard bout against a formidable foe.

Afterward, the reporters went to the dressing rooms. Giambra was nowhere to be found. Meanwhile, Giardello, interviewed as he showered with two bodyguards standing fully clothed on each side of him, was cursing the ref.

"Do you think you won the fight, Mr. Giardello?" a young reporter asked.

"What the fuck do you think" responded Giardello, who came out of the shower and lunged dripping wet at the reporter. The bodyguards grabbed him by the arms, pulling him back as water cascaded over them. The rest of us backed away and left. Driving back to Merced, I wondered what had happened to Giambra.

Months later, Giambra offered an explanation for his disappearance.

He said he'd been asked to take a dive but had refused and left the Cow Palace immediately afterward in fear for his life. Later he wrote a self-published book in which he described himself, with some accuracy, as the "uncrowned champion" because he'd defeated many fighters who became champions of their division. One of them was Giardello, who in 1963 defeated Dick Tiger to become the middleweight champion of the world.

I served as sports editor of the *Sun-Star* until the replacement arrived, then returned to general assignment with a pang of regret. I could have gone to as many Giants games as I wanted. The local sports scene was interesting. But I had a feeling I'd lose interest in sports if I had to write about it for my livelihood. That may not make sense, since I've covered politics for decades without losing interest. But it's the way I felt and still do.

The county beat, which soon came open, was varied and busy. I made daily checks of legal filings, the sheriff's office, the district attorney, and the county administrative offices. I wrote political stories, covered the meeting of the Board of Supervisors, and attended several criminal and civil trials. I was also the local stringer for United Press International, recommended to the wire service by Schlegel. UPI was especially keen on stories about climbers in Yosemite but also welcomed articles about eccentrics, such as a fiery-tempered Superior Court judge who'd been reprimanded for threatening attorneys.

One morning I was in this judge's court when a sheriff's deputy arrived with shackled prisoners from the county jail who were there to be arraigned. As the judge began speaking, the deputy inadvertently interrupted by rattling the shackles of the prisoners. The judge exploded, yelling at the deputy: "If you do that again, I'll put you in those chains."

I liked the rhythms of daily journalism, where each morning brought new surprises within the context of an unchanging routine. Our deadline was noon, but we could go to 1:00 p.m. for big or breaking page-one stories. There was no rewrite desk at the *Sun-Star* so I'd have to hoof it back to the newsroom by 11:00 and write in a hurry. Writing on deadline always gave me a rush. John Burns knew I could deliver and never hurried me. Sometimes, when the story was done, he'd smile and say, "You made it."

My beat also included the countywide Merced Mosquito Abatement District, then the largest such entity in the state. Disease-carrying mosquitoes were a serious problem in Merced, which lies in the lee of California. Rivers to the north flow into the San Francisco Bay or its tributaries; streams south of Merced run southward and eventually empty into the Pacific Ocean. Much of the soil in Merced is the impenetrable reddish clay known as hard pan. Water puddles on the surface, providing ideal breeding grounds for mosquitoes.

I became fascinated with the substantial efforts being made to reduce the mosquito threat without subjecting people to dangers from toxic pesticides. Four years before publication of *Silent Spring*, the Rachel Carson bombshell that made the nation aware of the danger, the enlightened staff and board of this obscure district were struggling to warn the public of the destructive impact of chemicals routinely used by the farmers of the Central Valley.

I don't remember the names of these good people. I do remember an oversize bulletin board on which staff tacked examples of what could happen when someone became overexposed to pesticides. The starkest example involved a crop-dusting pilot who had crashed his low-flying biplane into a drainage ditch, rupturing an insecticide tank. The pilot survived the crash but was bathed with toxic parathion. He scrambled out of the ditch to a nearby country road and walked a half mile toward the nearest farmhouse when he collapsed and later died.

What was known in the twentieth century as "crop-dusting" has since evolved into "aerial application," a sophisticated method of crop-spraying. In the 1950s, crop-dusting was mostly conducted by farmers or pickup pilots who had learned to fly Piper Cubs during World War II. Surplus planes were sold at bargain prices to civilians after the war, and some became crop-dusters. Mishaps were frequent. Soon after coming to Merced, I'd witnessed a crop-dusting demonstration and marveled at the pilot's skill. What I didn't know then was that the pilot and the rest of us were flying blind on the dangers of insecticides.

I saved two batches of clips from my *Sun-Star* days, including a six-part series called "They Guard Your Health," which examined how hospitals, physicians, nurses, and other professionals provided health services in Merced. The county, one of five in California with a combined county hospital and health department, was fortunate to have an enlightened medical director, Dr. A. Frank Brewer, an apostle of preventive medicine. The Merced County Hospital conduced regular clinics on general medicine, dentistry, pediatrics, gynecology, and eye examinations as well as twenty-six clinics a month on diabetes, cerebral palsy, rheumatic fever, tuberculosis, venereal diseases, and other common and deadly ailments. Other clinics were held in four towns scattered around the county. People without health insurance were deemed "county patients," meaning that the clinics were free. This was a boon in an agricultural county where many lacked medical insurance. Long before Medicare, Medicaid, and the Affordable Care Act, what Brewer called "extra health services" provided medical care for nearly everyone in Merced County. Brewer had sold conservatives on the clinics by arguing they would keep people out of the hospital and save the county money, as they did.

Although I was proud of the work at the time, reading it later I can't help but notice that the series is devoid of skepticism. Except for a passing reference to long lines in emergency rooms, there is not a whiff of criticism of the medical services provided in Merced County. To some degree this shortcoming reflects the boosterism of the *Sun-Star*, which was so proud of Merced's hospitals and Brewer's progressivism that it was not interested in finding defects. But I reported and wrote the series and at a minimum should have tested the claims of the local medical establishment by finding someone unhappy with the medical service he or she had experienced. That I did not do so may have reflected my own satisfaction with doctors and hospitals. I was twenty-five years old and grateful to the physicians in San Francisco who had saved our son David from the unknown illness that almost took his life. Our daughter Judy, five months old at the time, had been born in Mercy Hospital, Merced's Catholic medical facility. Ginny said it was an easy delivery and praised the kind treatment she had received at Mercy. We are all products of our experiences, but I would come to demand more of myself as a reporter.

My other batch of *Sun-Star* clips, an investigative series involving the Merced County Board of Supervisors, provides a cautionary lesson for memoirists tempted to rely too heavily on their recollections. What I remembered was that a supervisor wanted to help a relative who owned an electrical company. He and his allies on the five-man board approved several contracts to remodel the old county hospital into a building intended for other usages. By law, they should have put the remodeling contracts out to bid for any spending exceeding $4,000. Instead, the supervisors split the contract into segments and awarded them on a cost-plus basis to firms of their choice, which subcontracted the electrical work to a company owned by the supervisor's sister. In the triumphalist narrative of memory, I exposed the supervisors in a series of hard-hitting bylined articles that eventually forced them to cancel the cost-plus contracts and put the hospital remodeling out to bid. If I hadn't kept the clippings, that's what I'd be writing in this memoir.

But I *did* keep the clips, which tell a somewhat different tale. For starters, not one of the fourteen stories I wrote about the board's bidding practices over a nine-month period is bylined. Jogged by rereading the stories, I remembered that, when I told the managing editor, Cliff Schlegel, about what the board was doing, he told me to pursue the story but warned that my articles wouldn't carry a byline. The *Sun-Star* had a small staff and no investigative reporter, typical in those long-before-Watergate days. As Cliff saw it, I needed to maintain good working relations with the supervisors since I covered all their activities, and hence my articles about bidding irregularities would have no bylines.

With one key exception, there was nothing particularly "hard-hitting" about most of the stories. I also misremembered a central fact: While the supervisors did approve some small contracts on a cost-plus basis, they also approved the main contract for remodeling the hospital on a cost-plus contract of more than $57,000, on its face a violation of the law. I am summarizing the story here—and rounding the numbers—for I find the articles in retrospect somewhat tedious and devoid of analysis. For one thing, the supervisor's sister is not mentioned in any of the stories.

However, my memory *is* accurate, as the clips confirm, on the story that made the difference. Cliff and John Burns were frustrated that the supervisors had ignored our coverage and continued to award contracts on a cost-plus basis. (One of these, for a Juvenile Hall remodeling, was $23,000.) So John suggested the paper run a story that might encourage readers to take the supervisors to court. Cliff knew the former county counsel, who anonymously described to us how one could file a taxpayer's lawsuit against the board. I put all the lawyer's points in accessible prose to produce the most readable and productive article of the series.

At their next meeting, the supervisors gave up. On the advice of counsel, they rescinded the cost-plus contract for remodeling the hospital and promised that all such contracts would be sent to bid in the future. Four companies subsequently bid on the remodeling with the winner the company the board had chosen previously, albeit at a slightly lower bid.

The supervisors were angry at the *Sun-Star* but wanted to stay on good terms with me. Inadvertently, I contributed to their self-deception. At the meeting where the board rescinded the cost-plus contract, the supervisor whose sister owned the company that did the electrical work denounced the paper, Cliff, and the publisher, Dean Lesher. Another supervisor who was my best source on the board said he knew I had nothing to do with the stories. He looked to me for comment, and I said: "I'd have to say that the entire series was my idea."

Why I chose that locution I do not know, but my best source on the board pounced on it. "Aha, you'd *have* to say it," he said. Then he praised me for my all-around coverage. Other supervisors chimed in; even the supervisor with the favored sister who detested me lauded my reporting.

I realized instantly that I should not have responded at all. The lesson I learned that day would come in handy years later in Sacramento when a legislator who disliked a story I'd written asked me a pointed question during an Assembly hearing. "I have nothing to say," I said. Reporters are almost always better off when they let their stories do the talking.

The most engaging person on the county beat was Steven P. Galvin Jr., the district attorney of Merced County. His father, Steven Sr., had been district attorney in the early 1930s. Galvin Jr. had an acquired horror of vigilantism. While he was attending Santa Clara University, students he knew had joined a mob of thousands that battered down a jail in nearby San Jose and lynched two men accused of kidnapping and murdering department-store heir Brooke Hart. As the two men were hanged in St. James Park, the mob taunted them with cries of Hart's name.

"They didn't know Hart," Galvin recalled sixteen years after this sordid event. "They were just a mob."

Galvin believed the governor ("Sunny Jim" Rolph), who had refused to mobilize the National Guard to prevent the lynching and promised to pardon anyone involved in it, should have been prosecuted. Earl Warren, then a district attorney in Alameda County, called for an investigation. Nothing came of it. Rolph died of a heart attack a few months later.

My friendship with Galvin dated from a story I wrote for the *Sun-Star* about a string of trial losses by the district attorney's office. The story irritated Galvin's deputies, but he reacted philosophically, as he often did to criticism. After the story ran, Galvin explained to me how easy it is for a prosecutor to post an impressive conviction record. He said all a prosecutor had to do was pile on the charges against a defendant, then offer to take a plea on a lesser offense. The defendant's attorney, often an overworked public defender, would usually advise his client to take the plea instead of risking a long sentence if he were found guilty on all the charges. Galvin didn't work that way; he charged defendants with whatever crime he thought they had committed—no more, no less.

Because of a liberal and activist state Supreme Court, California gave many protections to criminal defendants, such as informing them of their rights when they were arrested, that the U.S. Supreme Court under Earl Warren would later enshrine in the national consciousness. At a time the California Supreme Court was being denounced by police officials and prosecutors, Galvin refrained from criticizing the court. Indeed, he went further. If evidence turned up that might help a defendant, Galvin shared it with the defendant's lawyer. Justice meant more to him than his conviction rate.[1]

Not that Galvin was sanguine about losing, particularly if the crime involved homicide or rape. One of the office's losses, tried by his able deputy Ben Curry, particularly stuck in Galvin's craw. It bothers me, too, after all these years.

A U.S. airman, a ground mechanic, stationed at Castle Air Force Base, north of Merced, was accused of raping a woman at knifepoint while her baby slept in a nearby crib. He allegedly had threatened to harm the baby if she didn't submit. The airman's defense would not be allowed today in California courts; his lawyer portrayed the woman as promiscuous and introduced prior acts that would now be inadmissible. Nonetheless, I thought that on balance she was a good witness. The lawyer's badgering confused her at times, but she did not deviate from her story that her assailant had threatened to harm her baby if she did not submit.

The defense must also have thought the victim was an effective wit-

1. This principle of requiring prosecutors to disclose exculpatory information to the defense would also be enshrined in federal law by a U.S. Supreme Court decision called *Brady v. Maryland.* But *Brady* wasn't decided until 1963. Steve Galvin was doing this in the 1950s of his own volition.

ness because at the last moment the defendant decided to testify. Curry dismantled him on the stand. The defendant said the woman had submitted willingly but couldn't explain why he needed a knife if she had consented to have sex. I wrote a story for the *Sun-Star* after the case had been submitted to the jury. John Burns edited the story and asked me what I thought the verdict would be.

"Open and shut," I said. "The guy's guilty."

This trial taught me a lesson that would be useful more than three decades later in the trial of the LAPD officers accused of beating Rodney King: Don't assume what a jury will decide. After a day's deliberation, the jury found the defendant not guilty. He looked surprised. Curry was furious. He had flown B-17s and B-25s in combat during World War II and took as a personal affront that an airman, even a member of the ground crew, would commit such a crime.

I was disgusted for another reason. I was acquainted with the jury foreman, a loudmouth local businessman who often sounded off about how liberal judges and juries were soft on crime. A few days later I ran into him and told him that the one time in his life he had a chance to combat crime, he'd let a rapist go free. He was defensive, acknowledging that the defendant had probably committed rape but insisting there was reasonable doubt because the woman hadn't done enough to resist him.

"You can't thread a moving needle," he said.

I am not making this up. This blather was worse than sexist, but I reminded myself that there were women on that jury. What did they think? The foreman said the women had been unsympathetic to the victim because she was promiscuous.

Soon after the trial, the acquitted defendant went to the district attorney's office and asked for the return of his knife. Curry refused to give it to him. "I had no legal grounds," he said, "but I told him if he was going to rape someone else, he'd need to get a new knife."

I advanced my understanding of the criminal code by taking a university-accredited night-school class on criminal law taught by Galvin, who was a good teacher. He knew that local police officers would sign up for the class and hoped they'd acquire a better understanding of why the California courts were complicating their lives with progressive civil liberties rulings. Sure enough, at the very first class a ranking officer asked Galvin what prevented him from conducting random searches of homes that he suspected harbored criminals. "The Constitution,"

Galvin replied. He went on to give a cogent explanation of the Fourth Amendment.

I don't know whether Galvin's class changed police behavior in Merced, but it certainly made me a better trial reporter. That class would pay unforeseen dividends decades later when I covered the trial of the LAPD officers in the Rodney King case for *The Washington Post.* But I didn't have an immediate opportunity to demonstrate my newly acquired knowledge of the criminal code, for Dean Lesher soon came to me with a surprising offer.

Summoning me to his office, Dean asked if I would like to become editor of the *Contra Costa Times,* a newspaper Lesher owned in Walnut Creek, California, near where I'd worked for the *Sun* weekly papers.

"What happened to John?" I asked. John was John Plumb, the editor of the *Times.* I'd met him when working for the *Sun* papers and considered him a top-flight editor.

"He's burned out and taking a public relations job," Lesher said. I told Lesher I'd never been an editor except for my short stint in Newark. Lesher reminded me that I'd done well when I stepped in as the *Sun-Star* sports editor. He said I had the ability to do the job and that the *Contra Costa Times* editorship was mine if I wanted it.

I wasn't sure I did. Ginny and I were comfortable in Merced. She'd made friends and was teaching part-time at a nursery school, a job she enjoyed. Professionally, I was still learning as a reporter and having John Burns as city editor was a boon to my continuing development. Personally, I was as happy as I'd ever been in my life. I enjoyed our children and liked my newspaper colleagues. Every second or third Friday, the newsroom staff played poker, with each of us taking turns being the host. Despite growing up in Nevada, I had rarely played poker before going to Merced. Some of the Merced players were experienced, and I lost money at first—not much, for the stakes weren't high—but gradually found my way. After a few months, Burns told me that my poker-playing skills had improved as much as my reporting.

For all that, the Contra Costa job offer was enticing. It meant a raise, so I'd finally be making as much as I had as a laundry-truck driver. From Ginny's point of view, it put us closer to her beloved San Francisco and to her mother, who had moved to Berkeley. My parents would be about the same distance away as they were in Merced. I liked the idea of going back to the county where I'd been a greenhorn as a reporter and showing what I could do with a rising newspaper. It would be a challenge, which I realized. I might not have such a chance again—or so I thought. So after using most of the week Dean had given me to make up my mind, I thanked him for offering me the job and said I'd take it.

By any definition I was still a long way from the big leagues of journalism, but I was at least moving up in the minors.

12

BEST NEWSPAPER IN WALNUT CREEK

Failure is supposedly a better teacher than success. If so, I earned a doctorate in journalism in a year and a half as managing editor at the *Contra Costa Times,* where I made mistakes of judgment that reflected my youth and inexperience.

I suspected from the beginning that I might be in over my head. After taking the job, I sought the counsel of a friend, Ed Bradley, the editor of the *Antioch Ledger* in eastern Contra Costa County. "There are two types of newspaper editors," Bradley told me. "One type worries if the newspaper is going to come out tomorrow. The other knows it's going to come out because it has for the last century and focuses on how to make tomorrow's edition better than today's. You be the second kind of editor."

That was good advice from a smart journalist, but I wasn't sure of its relevance. The *Contra Costa Times* published several times a week but not daily, with confusing deadlines. It was a throwaway newspaper known as the "Green Sheet" and was delivered to most households in central Contra Costa County, focusing on the bustling suburban community of Walnut Creek. At the beginning of 1960 when I arrived, the *Times* was published three times a week; it had advanced to four times a week by the time I left in the late spring of 1961.

The editor I replaced was John Plumb, a World War II combat veteran who'd fought in the Battle of the Bulge in the 101st Airborne Division. The publisher was Stan Lesher, whose main battles were with his father, Dean Lesher, who owned the paper. As managing editor, I directed a small staff, did a substantial amount of reporting and editing, and wrote editorials. I was also the face of the newspaper at service-club meetings. This chore was time-consuming, and I farmed out as much of it as I could to Stan, who chaffed at his father's frequent interference in decision-making, but paid attention to the bottom line. He was tightly wound but a decent guy. Realizing that Dean was the ultimate decider, previous editors had largely ignored Stan. I made it a point to consult with Stan and keep him informed of what was happening in the newsroom. He appreciated this, and we became allies.

The editorial staff under my predecessor consisted of two full-time reporters, two part-timers who wrote sports and church news, respectively, and a freelance photographer. Before I set foot in the office, I'd convinced Dean to let me hire another full-time reporter, so I could do more of the "big picture," as Dean put it. At twenty-six years of age, I wasn't quite sure what the big picture meant but knew we needed an extra reporter. The better of the two reporters who worked for my predecessor was gone by the time I got there after being hired by one of the San Francisco papers.

The remaining reporter at the *Contra Costa Times* when I arrived was an alcoholic thirty years my senior. Stan and Dean told me they'd unsuccessfully urged Plumb to fire him. But he was the only reporter I had, and I told him he was starting with a clean slate. He was on his best behavior the first week. In the second week he missed a meeting he should have covered. I took him aside and told him I'd never fired anyone but couldn't tolerate missed meetings or drinking on the job. He promised to shape up and did for a few weeks. But one day he showed up intoxicated on an assignment, and I had no choice but to let him go. The paper had no set severance policy, but I persuaded Stan to give him a month's salary if he promised to enter a rehabilitation program. He said he'd join Alcoholics Anonymous. I never heard from him again.

The next two months were frenzied. I reported and edited during the day, read application letters at night, and squeezed in hasty job interviews whenever I could spare a few minutes. That is not a good way to hire reporters. We'd placed a help-wanted ad in *Editor & Publisher*, the industry magazine, and I pored through a mostly unimpressive batch of applicant letters Plumb had left me.

My main reliance during these first weeks was a woman named Ruth who did the church news part-time and helped on proofreading. She was in her fifties and had no journalistic background but was bright and witty and could write. I offered her a full-time job as a reporter. Ruth said she was flattered but had a family and wanted to work only part-time. The other part-timer was my sports editor, a willing high school senior. Unfortunately, he was a terrible speller and there was no electronic spell-check in those days. I told him to use the dictionary.

"How do you look a word up if you don't know how to spell it?" he asked.

"Do your best," I said.

His best wasn't terrific but was better than my own hires. The first was in his mid-thirties with a middling résumé. I will call him Joe, not his real name. The second reporter I hired came from one of Plumb's leftover letters. I will call her Brenda, also not her real name. She worked at an Ohio paper and had adequate clips. There weren't many women in journalism in those days. The newsroom in Merced was all-male, and I had resolved to hire a female reporter in Walnut Creek. Brenda was mostly a feature writer, doing what were then called "human interest" stories. She assured me she could also do hard news. Having two reporters allowed me to take more time hiring a third. I interviewed perhaps half a dozen applicants. The one who impressed me most (I will call him Tom) was about my age. He had a disheveled appearance, but his clips, from a small newspaper in the Central Valley, showed command of complex issues, including farm labor and immigration. He'd come to the Bay Area to get married—he was the father of a toddler—and acknowledged he'd applied for several reporting jobs without success. I told him I'd check his references and get back to him.

After he left, I called his main reference, his editor on the paper where he'd worked. The editor said nice things about Tom's reporting ability but seemed tentative. I asked him if he would hire Tom again, and the editor said he wouldn't. I pressed him for specifics, but all he would say was that Tom was "odd." I was baffled. Tom obviously didn't know that his former editor was bad-mouthing him. But with a reference like this, he was never going to find a newspaper job unless I hired him, which I did after telling him that he should drop his former editor from his reference list. Tom was by far the best hire I made at the *Contra Costa Times*. He was hardworking, reliable, and wrote well. At times he'd put a (liberal) opinion in a straight news story, but it was easy to remove since his stories contained plenty of facts. I liked that he was passionate about his work.

My other two hires had problems, which soon became mine. Joe was nervous on deadline, and I'd sometimes have to take over and finish his stories. I could have lived with that, but a bigger problem soon presented itself.

One Sunday morning I was awakened at home by Stan Lesher, who was shouting into the phone "Pisso, Pisso."

"What are you talking about?" I asked.

"His name is Bisso and we called him Pisso on the front page," Stan said.

He was referring to a story by Joe, who had rendered the name of Mr. Bisso, a reputable local businessman, as "Pisso" throughout his story. I don't recall the subject of the story. What I remember is that Mr. Bisso was understandably infuriated. He had called Stan at home and asked why we were ridiculing him. When Stan tried to calm him by suggesting it was a typographical error, Mr. Bisso hit the roof.

"The same typo six times in one story?" he yelled at Stan. "That makes no sense."

And of course, it didn't. When Mr. Bisso threatened to sue, Stan assured him that he would see to it that the offending reporter was fired. That was what Stan wanted me to do. I said we needed to find out what had happened before firing anybody.

It turned out that Joe was hard of hearing and had heard the "B" as a "P." I'm more sympathetic to Joe's problem now that I've experienced age-related hearing loss myself, but even then I was more puzzled than angry. I asked Joe why he hadn't told me of his problem, and he replied that I wouldn't have hired him if I had known of his disability, which was probably true. Then I asked why he didn't compensate by having people he was interviewing write their names. He usually did that, Joe said, but he'd been sure in this case that the man's name was "Pisso."

I didn't fire Joe. I told Stan I would go hat in hand to Mr. Bisso and offer to write a prominent correction that didn't repeat the offending error. Bisso turned out to be a decent guy. When I explained the reason for the error, he became sympathetic to Joe and said he wouldn't sue.

"Please don't fire him," Bisso added, making my life easier. I had Joe call Bisso and apologize and instructed him to keep a low profile, out of sight of Stan. I also told Joe to make doubly sure of the spelling of any name he used in a story. Joe was grateful he still had a job but became even more nervous on deadline. I spent too much of my limited time finishing his stories and checking every name.

Brenda was even worse. There had been a bad typographical error in a feature story she'd written, in which "widows" appeared as "windows," and she blamed me for not catching it. She also thought I should have fired Joe, even though she'd made errors of her own in news stories. She was capable enough but careless in checking facts except for feature stories, in which she took exceptional pride. I told Brenda she needed to improve her work and let me deal with Joe. Instead, she found Dean Lesher's home phone number and started calling him with her complaints about the other reporters and me. It was like having a spy in the newsroom.

I took what solace I could in my own reporting, which focused on the growing pains of Walnut Creek. A city planning aide who'd taken me aside three years earlier and pointed out my mistakes in a story for the *Sun* papers approached me as I was leaving a city council meeting and told me that my reporting had improved. I was grateful for the faint praise.

"It had nowhere to go but up," I told him.

In addition to reporting and writing a healthy share of stories for each edition, I also wrote editorials. That didn't come as easily to me as reporting, in part because I tend to tell all sides of a story, which is not necessarily the function of an editorial. There's an apocryphal story that President Truman once asked for the advice of a one-armed economist because so many had the habit of saying "on the one hand and on the other." That was the problem with my early editorials, which I think Stan and Dean liked because I wasn't picking fights. That changed as I mastered the form.

I recently reread the editorials. To my surprise, many of them read better than my contemporaneous news stories, perhaps because I set aside a couple of hours (usually alone late at night) to craft them. The news stories were written amidst the hurly-burly of our newsroom, where I was simultaneously editing, fact-checking, laying out the paper, and dealing with the photo lab. Although I'd wanted to be Ed Bradley's "second kind of editor" who worried only about the quality of his newspaper, I was increasingly a harried editor who worried if the paper would come out at all.

Many of my first editorials were of the "goo-goo" or good-government type common to Lesher papers. Some local newspapers were promoters of untrammeled suburban growth, which meant more department stores and car dealers and hence more newspaper ad revenue. But not all. Dean Lesher was pro-growth, but his years on the Merced Planning Commission had taught him that growth required management and planning. He wanted communities in his circulation area to have good schools, subdivisions with parks or open spaces, and shopping malls that did not assault the senses. Perhaps because I believed similarly, I never consulted Dean or Stan on editorials, supporting school bond issues in Walnut Creek and Concord, rapid transit, water conservation, master planning, pay raises for local officials, and restoration of library services that had been foolishly reduced by penny-pinching county supervisors. Stan wrote me a pithy note about the latter editorial, saying that maybe the supervisors felt they had a better chance of being reelected if voters were illiterate. Otherwise, I never heard from either Lesher about my editorials.

But it wasn't long until I expanded into the realm of criminal justice, about which I had strong opinions made stronger by the tutelage of Merced district attorney Steve Galvin. John Nejedly, the district attorney in Contra Costa, also respected civil liberties. An ex-convict named Frank Salas with a record of burglary, robbery, and narcotic violations was wanted by various law enforcement agencies in Contra Costa County for a string of robberies. Cornered in a Benicia farmhouse, he surrendered after police fired shotgun blasts through the windows. Salas was then held incommunicado for four days before he was arraigned.

Nejedly was furious when he learned Salas had not been promptly apprehended. Furthermore, he believed the arresting officers had failed to procure evidence that would stand up in court. The district attorney dismissed all charges against Salas in the interests of justice and for lack of evidence. Law enforcement agencies in Contra Costa County were appalled, and the county grand jury called Nejedly to testify about his actions. I wrote an editorial supporting Nejedly, which included this paragraph:

"The public official's son accused of running a stop sign will never lack for adequate defense counsel. The Frank Salases will in too many cases fail to have their rights protected unless the district attorney acts to protect them."

This appeared in the October 2, 1960, *Contra Costa Times*. Soon afterward I wrote an editorial headed "Restore Voting Rights" about the travails of a leading citizen in a small California town who'd been involved in a recall campaign of a local official. During the campaign, it was revealed that the leading citizen had been convicted of a felony twenty years earlier. To his great embarrassment, he was barred from voting. California law at the time allowed ex-felons to vote only if they were granted a "certificate of rehabilitation." Applications for these certificates were public knowledge, and few ex-felons applied. I argued for a measure on that year's state ballot that would automatically have restored voting rights to a felon upon completion of the sentence. Voters rejected the measure, Proposition 8, at the behest of California law enforcement agencies, but it has since become state law.

I took this stand on my own. When Dean Lesher offered me the job of editor, he had observed that 1960 was a presidential election year. He said he'd reserve the right to make the presidential endorsement, but I could decide state and local endorsements, including ballot propositions. He was as good as his word. Lesher had a reputation of being pushy with editors and insistent on getting his way, but he was considerate in all my dealings with him.

In the summer of 1960, there was an outburst of organized anti-Catholic sentiment in Contra Costa County. It was the usual drivel. Pamphlets were mailed to voters and letters sent to newspapers alleging that Democratic presidential nominee John F. Kennedy's first loyalty was to the Roman Catholic Church, not to the United States of America. These claims reinforced a boyhood belief, imbued in me by parents and teachers, that Al Smith had failed to win the presidency in 1928 because he was a Catholic. I wrote an editorial that contained the following passage: "One no longer has to read about the 1928 election campaign to discover the curious and staggering anti-Catholicism that comes so swiftly to the fore in this phase of our politics."

I was not then a Catholic, as I have been for the last several decades of my life, but the editorial reflected my naive surprise that people I thought urbane and tolerant harbored anti-Catholic stereotypes. Ginny and I went to a dinner where the hostess made a crude anti-Catholic remark during a discussion about the upcoming election. I didn't know what to say, but Ginny rebuked the hostess for questioning Kennedy's patriotism. We left soon after and were not invited back.

Dean Lesher telephoned me from Merced after reading the editorial for the first time in the paper. This was unusual; he usually saved any comments for his monthly visits to Walnut Creek. Dean said he agreed entirely with what I had written. But Dean also surmised that I was pro-Kennedy and said he wanted me to know that the Lesher papers would be endorsing Richard Nixon, a Californian, for president.

This was no surprise. Although his papers occasionally endorsed Democrats, Dean was a Republican and along with most Americans he admired President Dwight Eisenhower. I didn't know what he thought about Nixon, who Eisenhower had elevated to the vice presidency, but I'd heard Dean say that Senator Kennedy, although a good man, lacked the experience to be president. I had reservations of my own about JFK's experience and particularly doubted the accuracy of his exaggerated assertion that a "missile gap" favored the Soviet Union over the United States. I'd assigned myself to a portion of JFK's "whistle-stop" train tour in California and was impressed by Kennedy's upbeat speeches and easy manner with reporters. I distrusted Nixon and wanted to put to rest the notion that a Catholic couldn't be elected president. As Dean surmised, I voted for Kennedy.

Dean offered to write the editorial endorsing Nixon. I took him up on the offer but thought better of it when a half-hearted draft of an endorsement editorial landed on my desk. It was a weak editorial written by a strong man, suggesting among other things that Nixon was not the equal of Eisenhower. Who was? Although I didn't like Nixon, I thought that if we were endorsing him we should do better. I called Dean and suggested he omit the Eisenhower-Nixon comparison and make some other changes that would deliver a more ringing endorsement. Dean thanked me for saying this and asked me to make any edits I thought desirable, which I did.

In 1960 at my discretion the *Contra Costa Times* also endorsed incumbent Representative John Baldwin, a moderate Republican running against a left-of-center Democrat in the local congressional race; and for the state Assembly endorsed the liberal Democrat Jerome Waldie, just completing his first term in the legislature. Six years later, when Baldwin died in office, Waldie would win his seat in the House of Representatives. Waldie was a valuable legislator in Sacramento and Washington and an early critic of the Vietnam War. After the 1960 election, Dean sent me a complimentary note about the choices of Baldwin and

Waldie, both of whom won, and also thanked me for my help on the Nixon editorial.

The one serious difference Dean Lesher and I had on editorial policy occurred months before the election, triggered by the case of serial rapist Caryl Chessman. Pat Brown had delayed Chessman's execution so that the legislature might consider banning capital punishment. At the time I entered the editorial fray on March 13, 1960, an abolishment bill had recently been rejected in a state senate committee, making Chessman's execution virtually inevitable.

The most evocative testimony before the Senate committee in favor of abolishing the death penalty came from Clinton Duffy, a respected former warden of San Quentin Prison, where California conducted executions. I knew of Duffy from an admirer, San Quentin chaplain Byron Eshelman, an acquaintance at church camp. Moved by Duffy's testimony, I wrote an editorial headed "The Death Penalty." Here is what it said:

> Few could match dignity or eloquence of Clinton Duffy, former warden at San Quentin, as he told California state senators that the death penalty is no deterrent to crime.
>
> The child of a San Quentin guard, Warden Duffy was once known as the man who "cleaned up San Quentin." When he left the warden's post after 12 years of service under one Democratic and two Republican governors, Duffy had seen nothing in his many last watches on death row to make him change his mind about capital punishment.
>
> In effect, Duffy said that sentence to death was virtually a matter of chance with the weak and the poor often that supreme penalty's only victims. Duffy spoke from his long experience as an official at executions, when he stated that the death penalty, whatever else it might be, is inequitably enforced and always has been. . . .
>
> California's legislators may have eased their own election fears by the quick committee killing of the anti-death bill. But the day when the state must face the issue squarely has only been postponed.
>
> Civilized society that believes in equality under the law must one day discard the death penalty.

When I sat down to write this editorial, I had intended to question the effectiveness of the death penalty, not call for its abolishment. That's what the editorial did, minus the last sentence. But when I reached that point, something was missing. It seemed almost cowardly to abhor the death penalty as much as I did and end the editorial with some pabulum about how the state would have to face up to the issue at some distant remove after killing Chessman. So I added the last sentence.

I hadn't always been that unequivocal in my feelings about capital punishment. When teenaged David Blackwell shot to death my father's friend and another Reno police officer, our family and Roy's fellow officers and many friends outside the Reno Police Department had wanted revenge. We were jubilant when Blackwell, only eighteen, was sentenced to die. But Blackwell's execution did not provide Roy Geach's widow or my father or the officer who had apprehended him with any satisfaction. We had not foreseen that Blackwell would accept responsibility for his crimes, undergo a religious conversion, and walk bravely into the gas chamber unaided, winking at the police officer who had arrested him. His behavior robbed us of vengeance. My father became depressed and drank heavily, Roy's widow became a recluse, and the arresting officer soon retired. He said he'd lost interest in being a cop.

I agree with Warden Duffy that the death penalty is no deterrent. I appreciate the arguments of those who oppose it because it discriminates against minorities and anyone too poor to afford good counsel. As a Catholic, I applaud Pope Francis for saying there are no exceptions to the Church's opposition to capital punishment. But the main reason I'm against the death penalty is because of what it does to those who survive the execution. It never satisfied any of us who loved Roy Geach.

On Dean's next trip to Walnut Creek, he dropped by to discuss the progress of the paper. As he was leaving, he said, "By the way, I believe the death penalty is necessary."

I mumbled something about how he had said I could determine editorial policy on state and local issues.

"I did and I do," Dean replied. "I just wanted you to know my position."

Dean was being generous. My editorial was technically within the authority he had granted, but I'm sure Dean had expected me to take a stand on such matters as the massive state water bond on the ballot that year rather than cosmic issues of life and death. I should have told him beforehand that the paper was opposing the death penalty. Part of the problem was that there was not much time to tell anybody anything. I felt increasingly that my job was an assembly line of reporting, writing, editing, and assigning with little time for reflection—or my family.

Soon after Chessman's execution, Dean brought up the subject of the death penalty on another of his visits to Walnut Creek. Dean said that he wanted me to know that his support of the death penalty was not unconditional and that there had been a strong case for sparing Chessman because he had not killed anyone. I might have mentioned that in the editorial, I said. No, Dean responded, you wrote what you thought was right.

As this conversation suggests, I had no problem working for Lesher despite his reputation for contentiousness. We tend to judge people on the way they've treated us, and Dean and Stan treated me well. But for the first time in my adult life, I had serious health issues clearly related to my job. It started with insomnia and stomach aches. I was getting home too late to play with the children, having a couple of drinks and wolfing down my dinner before bed. Ginny suggested skipping the drinks and having bland dinners, which we did to no effect. I was self-medicating with antacids, which also didn't help. Call a doctor, Ginny said. Even now, past ninety, I'm never keen on seeing a doctor. When I was young, I avoided them entirely even though the job provided health insurance. But the stomach aches caused such distress I took Ginny's advice.

A day before my doctor's appointment, another blow fell. Tom, our best reporter, came to me and said he was separating from his wife and needed time off to find a place to stay and arrange his affairs. I was baffled. Tom and his wife had a two-year-old boy. Ginny had briefly provided day care for the toddler until Tom's working wife could find more permanent arrangements. Ginny liked the boy and his mother and told me the family was close. But I didn't pry into Tom's personal life. Take the time you need, I told him, but please come back as soon as you can.

Years later, I learned Tom was gay. This may have been what the editor Tom had naively used as a job reference meant by saying Tom was "odd." Tom and I trusted each other professionally, but there was no way he would have confided his sexual orientation to me at that time. In 1961, consenting sex between men was a crime in California and homosexuality was labeled a mental disorder by the American Psychiatric Association. Unless they were independently wealthy or worked in a tolerant oasis such as the entertainment industry, gays did not have the option of coming out.

With Tom gone, the stress of putting out the *Contra Costa Times* increased. I was sleeping less and becoming more exhausted by the day. The young doctor who saw me was interested in my plight. He told me I had a "pre-ulcerous" condition, prescribed some medicine, and questioned me about my work situation. I told him the truth.

"Do you know what's going to happen if you die?" he said. "The paper will find another editor."

These words were a punch in the gut. At twenty-seven, I had given no thought to dying. When I told Ginny about the doctor's words, she said, "You need to find another job." It was an epiphany. The combination of the doctor's observation and Ginny's advice made me resolve to leave the *Contra Costa Times*.

The medicine helped my stomach, and my decision to leave helped even more. I slept better, and getting out the paper became easier. Since I didn't yet have another job, I wasn't ready to give notice and couldn't mention my decision in the newsroom because Brenda would have called Dean behind my back. But I shared my decision with Stan, hoping he'd keep it confidential. Stan, who had medical issues of his own, was sympathetic. He asked if a significant raise would make a difference; I told him my problem was stress, not salary. Stan put me in for a raise anyway and thanked me for raising the profile of the paper. He may have thought I'd change my mind once I tested other opportunities.

When I eventually left, Stan told me that I'd much improved the paper, "making it the best paper in Walnut Creek." I told him that wasn't saying much since the only competition in that category was the *Sun* papers, which both of us detested.

"How about the best newspaper in central Contra Costa County?" I suggested.

"I like the ring of best newspaper in Walnut Creek," Stan said with a smile.

For the next six weeks I did comparison shopping. There were numerous jobs available—a far cry from the situation now—but some of them seemed as stressful as the one I had. The best of these jobs was a deputy managing editor position at a thriving daily; the executive editor who interviewed me hinted the managing editor was likely to retire in a year or two. What the executive editor dangled as an alluring prospect had the opposite effect; it made me realize that I really didn't want to be a managing editor.

The most tempting offer came from the *Pine Bluff Commercial* in Arkansas, which was looking for an editorial writer who would challenge the state's segregationist governor, Orval Faubus. The publisher read several of my editorials and said he'd particularly liked what I'd written about the death penalty. He flew me to Pine Bluff, where after an interview and dinner with his family, he offered me the job of editorial page editor. I was impressed by the publisher, the paper, and the reporters I met. If I'd been on my own, I would have taken the job on the spot, but I had three children of whom the oldest was seven. Ginny didn't want to bring them up in Arkansas. So I turned down the job. The publisher hired Paul Greenberg, a better choice than me, and his editorials subsequently won a Pulitzer Prize.

I settled for a less interesting—and much less stressful—job in California. Because of an impending retirement, the *San Jose Mercury* was seeking an assistant wire editor. The job required editing wire copy and laying out the late street edition twice a week. Shifts began at 3 p.m. or 4 p.m. and ended at midnight or 1 a.m. We had several editions, but the editors lavished their attention on the home edition, which closed at 10:30 p.m. on most days and earlier on Wednesday and Thursday when the paper was packed with big display ads from the grocery and department stores. The job required speedy editing because the *Mercury* was overwhelmed with wire copy. In addition to the usual Associated Press and United Press International wires, we had a wire provided by the *New York Times* and another syndicate. Starting in 1962, we received the new joint wire service offered by *The Washington Post* and the *Los Angeles Times*. It was more than we needed, but it blocked suburban competitors who otherwise would have purchased these services.

The *Mercury* had a terrific wire editor named Dale Cockerill, who was terse and professional with the three or four of us—sometimes only two—on the wire desk. My other colleagues during my four years on the wire desk included an old guy who refused to tell his age but vaguely recalled working with Ernest Hemingway on the *Kansas City Star*. He didn't think Hemingway was any great shakes as a reporter but remembered he was "a brave fella" who was always jumping on ambulances and fire trucks. The old guy was a good editor but slow.

Dale treated him with respect and gave him a lighter load of work than the rest of us. The all-male cast of editors also included a Brit who'd been a "vacky"—one of the children evacuated from London during the Blitz to safer towns in the West of England. He loved the word "amazing," his invariable response to anything out of the ordinary. Another editor was a quiet recovering alcoholic who had supposedly been a good reporter. He told me once at lunch that there were fewer temptations on the desk.

The quiet alcoholic left the paper and was replaced by a loud drinker who was a graduate of the tabloid press and a provocative headline writer. When President Lyndon Johnson gave a Georgetown speech offering an olive branch to North Vietnam and threatening to bomb the Communists back into the Stone Age if it wasn't accepted, his headline proclaimed: "LBJ GOES BOTH WAYS."

Loud Drinker usually skipped dinner with the rest of us at 10:45 p.m. after we had closed the city edition. He'd say he'd already eaten and make a quick visit to a nearby bar where most of us stopped after the shift. The rest of us were brown baggers who ate in the library, which was otherwise empty except when the librarian worked late or a reporter was checking the files.

The librarian, white-haired and with supersized owlish eyeglasses, had a creative filing system. One night while we were having lunch in the library, he discarded into a wastebasket the file of Pierre Mendes France, the former French prime minister who had begun his nation's disengagement from Algeria.

"We won't be needing this anymore," he said. I asked why. The librarian, addressing me as if I were a young child who couldn't possibly understand such things, said Mendes France was long out of office. There would be no file of him in the *Mercury* library when he was elected to the French Parliament five years later.

My favorite anecdote about that benighted library involved a horrible icepick murder in which the killer, as the newspaper story put it, rendered his victim a "human pincushion." The killer was convicted and sent to prison. Some years later he was involved in a prison incident that sent a reporter in these long-before-Google days scurrying to the library to find the stories of his crime. He came up empty. In desperation he asked the librarian, who told the reporter to look under "H" where the stories were found in a folder labeled "Human Pincushion."

Most of the four years I spent on the wire desk were uneventful except for the nights Dale was off and I laid out the street edition. Those nights brought me into frequent conflict with the city editor, who pushed me to put secondary local stories on page one. I pushed back but came to dread those confrontations and the derogatory remarks the city editor would make to others about my news judgment.

I was in Dale's spot one night in February 1962 when the story broke of the spy swap at a German bridge of the American pilot Francis Gary Powers for Soviet colonel Rudolph Abel. Powers had piloted a U.S. U-2 spy plane shot down over the Soviet Union in 1960. He'd parachuted to safety and was taken prisoner by the Soviets, who'd tried him and sentenced him to prison. Abel was a senior KGB spy who'd been caught and convicted in the United States five years earlier. Their story was told in the popular 2015 movie *Bridge of Spies.*

With the deadline fast approaching, I remade the front page, wrote a headline on the spy swap, and told the city editor I needed to move one of his stories off page one. He was unusually polite and agreeable. The next day a local reporter told me the city editor had been impressed with my speed and decisiveness and was singing my praises. We had no further conflicts. I later learned that the city editor was coping with personal issues that would have immobilized me.

I was a Protestant in those days, and we worshipped at a Congregationalist church. Our minister was a cheerful sort who gave circuitous sermons that left me struggling to understand their meaning. One Sunday his sermon topic was "The Street Where You Live." The sermon was about someone who had been profoundly influenced by the name of his home street. The minister asked us to think about the meanings of our street names. I am not making this up.

Yet, this silly sermon prompted Ginny and me to reflect on our lives in San Jose. The street where we lived was aptly named "Pasatiempo Drive," and in career terms I'd certainly been passing time. Ginny said she was passing time as well. She was a part-time nursery schoolteacher who wouldn't take a full-time job because she wanted to focus on being a good mom. Both of us enjoyed our young children. We were far from perfect parents, but we realized that time spent with our children was precious and unrecoverable.

The more I thought of it, the more I was grateful for my job on the *Mercury*'s wire desk, where I had no managerial responsibility and no work to take home. It may have been the most enjoyable time in my life. But it was also a peaceful interlude that couldn't last.

13

DEFINING MOMENTS

Harry Farrell did double duty for twenty years as the ubiquitous political correspondent of the *San Jose Mercury-News,* writing about the political scene from San Jose, then decamping to Sacramento for the legislative session. He knew every governor, legislator, and lobbyist in the state and was considered one of California's best political writers. But ever-longer legislative sessions and his wife's deepening agoraphobia combined to make travel problematic. In 1965 Harry told the executive editor he could no longer go to Sacramento for extended periods. The editor valued Harry and accepted his solution of hiring a full-time state capitol correspondent.

On the wire desk, my long-standing interest in politics deepened in 1964 as Barry Goldwater attempted to remake the Republican Party in his conservative image. Dale Cockerill, our laconic wire editor, appreciated my knowledge of politics, gave me political stories to edit, and sometimes called me the political editor even though it wasn't a formal title. Dale was devoted to "fair and balanced" reporting long before Fox News gave those words a partisan taint. He thought much of the political coverage was hostile to Goldwater and asked me to sift out one-sided stories. Balanced coverage couldn't rescue Goldwater, whose worrisome wisecracks reinforced the stereotype of the Arizona senator as a dangerous gunslinger. In May, Goldwater said, "I don't want to hit the moon. I want to lob one (presumably a missile) into the men's room of the Kremlin and make sure I hit it."

That was a glib quip not intended to be taken seriously, but Goldwater also mused aloud on ABC's *Issues and Answers* program about the possibility of using tactical nuclear weapons on Chinese supply lines in North Vietnam. Such comments encouraged conjecture (stoked by his opponents) that a President Goldwater might lead the nation into nuclear war. Few people bothered to explore what Lyndon Johnson might do if elected president in his own right. We didn't learn until later that he was planning to send half a million U.S. soldiers to Vietnam.

I was fascinated by Goldwater and also by Nelson Rockefeller's belated attempt to stop him in the California Republican primary. Rockefeller's campaign in California was managed by the ascendant young team of Bill Roberts and Stuart Spencer, who packaged Goldwater's scary statements into TV and radio commercials that made "extremism" the central issue of the campaign. Beginning as a distant underdog, Rockefeller surged under Spencer-Roberts guidance and held a double-digit polling lead the week before the June 2 primary. Then on Friday before the primary, ignoring Spencer's plea to stay in California, Rockefeller flew back to New York for the birth of his first child with Margaretta (Happy) Rockefeller. Nelson Junior arrived the next day. Eighteen years younger than Nelson and mother of four, Happy had worked on Rockefeller's staff; both had divorced longtime spouses to marry each other. This was old news, but Goldwater's managers unleashed a barrage of radio and television ads bluntly reminding voters of the presumed infidelity of Nelson and his second wife. Goldwater narrowly won a primary he'd seemed certain to lose and clinched the presidential nomination.

I decided to take a vacation during the Republican National Convention in San Francisco and cover it for a paper that wasn't sending its own correspondent. I called the editors of the *Pine Bluff Commercial* in Arkansas, who years earlier had tried to hire me as editorial page editor, not knowing if they would remember me. They did—and embraced the idea of having their own reporter at the convention.

The Arkansas delegation was headed by Governor Winthrop Rockefeller, assuring his brother Nelson a rare friendly reception in the South even though the delegation held divided loyalties on the nomination. The governor graciously introduced me to the Arkansas delegates, who then treated me as if I were a local, answering my questions and even inviting me to social events.

I don't remember the stories I wrote for the *Pine Bluff Commercial.* What has remained in my memory bank is Nelson Rockefeller's defiant speech on the second night of the convention in the cavernous Cow Palace. Goldwater's managers, in charge of the proceedings, had given Rockefeller five minutes at 9 p.m., midnight in the East. It was near 10 when he actually spoke, and his speech ran longer than the allotted time because Rockefeller was repeatedly drowned out by boos and cries of "We Want Barry!"

Rockefeller was undeterred—and unsparing. Without mentioning Goldwater by name, he denounced the "extremist threat" to the Republican Party and called out "anonymous middle-of-the-night telephone calls, unsigned threatening letters, smear and hate literature, strongarm and goon tactics, bomb threats and bombing, infiltration and take-over of established political organizations by Communist and Nazi methods."

At these words, the booing increased. But some delegates loved it. I noticed an athletic-looking Black man on the edge of the Arkansas delegation, leaping up and down on the balls of his feet and yelling, "You tell 'em, Rocky!" It was my baseball idol Jackie Robinson. The people near him weren't booing, and I sidled over to get as close as possible to Robinson. As I did, Rockefeller continued to lecture the angry delegates, saying "Some of you don't like to hear it, ladies and gentlemen, but it's the truth."

"That's right, that's right!" Robinson shouted over the booing. When Rockefeller finished, I approached Robinson, one of the few African Americans at the convention, and asked his opinion of the speech. It was an unnecessary question, considering what I had just witnessed, but Robinson didn't mind.

"Wasn't he wonderful?" he said before being swallowed up by protective security guards.

I was thrilled by Rockefeller's performance and my brief encounter with Jackie Robinson. As I made my way off the crowded floor, a message flashed on a billboard in my mind, telling me that my life's work was writing about politics. It was an eerie experience, as though I was seeing an actual flashing billboard. The billboard in my head popped up again two nights later as Goldwater declared to roars of approval in his acceptance speech, "Extremism in the defense of liberty is no vice. And let me remind you also, that moderation in the pursuit of justice is no virtue."

So, I said yes when Harry sounded me out soon after the convention about becoming the new Sacramento correspondent for the *Mercury-News*. In addition to wanting to be a reporter again, I had a personal reason for moving to Sacramento. My father had died two years earlier and my mother, increasingly crippled by arthritis, was alone. Their home was in Citrus Heights, fifteen miles northeast of Sacramento, and I had driven up on weekends as often as possible. Now I would be able to see her regularly.

Ginny favored the move. We sold the house with moderate difficulty and because Ginny was pregnant with Jack, I was charged with finding a home in Sacramento. I found a shaded house on a cul-de-sac that backed up to a school and was an easy drive to work.

My office was downtown in the capitol itself. In those days reporters had seats on the Assembly floor and access to the coffee lounge used by legislators. We sat near the state senators in their chamber and could flag down most senators when necessary. Jesse Unruh had succeeded in his mission of providing Assembly committees with a well-informed staff. Reporters also had access to most of these aides, plus the watchdog legislative analyst's office, the governor's cabinet, and key players in the civil service. Overall, California state government was remarkably accessible to journalists.

I took advantage of that openness during the next four years, beginning in the fall of 1965. While my primary job was to cover local legislators and matters pertaining to the *Mercury*'s circulation area, I interpreted my mandate broadly and wrote about the issues that were redefining California. These included multiple efforts to save California from itself as development and population growth menaced the redwoods, the wild rivers of the state's north coast, and even San Francisco Bay. I also wrote stories about abortion, farm labor, fluoridation, higher education tuition, mental health, smog control, and taxes, issues that preoccupied the legislature in that tumultuous decade of the 1960s.

Whenever possible, I tried to have a vantage point beyond the capitol. In March 1966, for instance, Cesar Chavez launched a 340-mile march from the tiny San Joaquin Valley town of Delano to Sacramento, seeking to dramatize the plight of farmworkers, most of them Filipino and Mexican American, who had struck nonunion grape orchards to protest low pay and abysmal working conditions. Chavez, leader of the United Farm Workers, urged American consumers to boycott grapes in the grocery store that hadn't been picked by union labor.

Chavez hoped to arrive in Sacramento on Easter Sunday and make the case for the grape boycott directly to Pat Brown. Two grape growers capitulated along the march, but Brown decided to appease the larger number of growers who held out against the union. Instead of meeting Chavez, the governor spent the day at Frank Sinatra's home in Palm Springs. Ronald Reagan, running against Brown, did no better. To the disgust of campaign consultant Stu Spencer, who respected Chavez, Reagan sarcastically dismissed the march an "Easter Egg roll."

Joining the march in its late stages, I was struck by the quiet charisma of Chavez, who projected an aura of leadership. When I interviewed him, he observed that San Jose was his "home barrio" and added that the *Mercury* was pro-grower. I told him I was just covering the march, although Chavez may have guessed my sympathies because I brought Carl, then twelve, along with me. In any event. Chavez said I was welcome. I asked him if he thought the boycott would succeed. "In time," Chavez said, nodding softly. He was right on both counts. The boycott prevailed but not until 1970.

At the suggestion of my friend Jud Clark, who worked for an Assembly committee, I started covering the Little Hoover Commission, a watchdog body that provided a trove of stories. Out of that coverage came the most significant stories of my Sacramento tenure. The California Highway Patrol purchased patrol cars annually through a bidding process mysteriously won every year by the same Sacramento Dodge dealer. A source suggested I read the bid specifications. They were complex, involving many changes to provide for CHP hardware and armament, and worded in a way that gave a bonus to the local car dealer who always won the bid. The state was paying thousands of dollars more for these special cars than if it had been buying them at retail price off a car lot and refitting them. I interviewed Dodge dealers in other California cities who had once competed for the CHP contract. They had given up, convinced the bids were rigged. The winning bidder had rewarded government officials with cars equipped with features unavailable to the public such as alarms and searchlights. I tracked down a former member of Brown's cabinet who acknowledged owning such a car. He told me he'd received a good deal from the Sacramento Dodge dealer.

I wrote several stories about the favoritism shown this dealer, and other papers began picking them up. Most papers attributed the stories to the *San Jose Mercury* and sometimes credited me. (The *Los Angeles*

Times, the last paper to pick up the story, attributed nothing, saying that "the Times had learned" what was happening.) The stories had an impact. No one went to jail, but the CHP specifications were revised, and new bids were taken. The Sacramento Dodge dealer won again, but he had lowered the price of the cars by about $2,000 a vehicle. The *Mercury* ran an editorial in praise of my stories, which it noted had saved taxpayers a lot of money. I won my first award, from the American Political Science Association.

This led to another defining moment. Each year, the American Political Science Association doled out awards to promising reporters in various state capitals and invited them to expenses-paid conferences with interesting speakers. The 1968 conference for reporters west of the Mississippi River was in Sun Valley, Idaho, and the speakers included David Broder, Douglass Cater, and Carey McWilliams. All three became lifelong friends. The only one I'd met before Sun Valley was Broder of *The Washington Post*, who'd dropped into my Sacramento office during one of his California trips. He was the only big-shot eastern reporter who regularly sought the perspective of correspondents from small papers with state capital bureaus. Broder would not like me calling him a big shot; he was extraordinarily modest for a man widely considered the nation's best political reporter. Broder had brought his wife, Anne, and their four boys. She was an outspoken enthusiast for Senator Eugene McCarthy and his daring effort to win the 1968 presidential nomination. During a hike at Sun Valley, Anne planted a McCarthy banner on a mountainside.

McWilliams is an iconic figure. I had read every one of his books and have many times reread *California: The Great Exception* and my favorite, *Southern California: An Island on the Land*. McWilliams was as modest as Dave Broder. Cater was not, but he had much to be immodest about. He was a journalist and scholar who'd held an important education post in President Lyndon Johnson's administration. I'd read Cater in the *Reporter* magazine and also *The Fourth Branch of Government*, his trailblazing book about political coverage in Washington. Cater took an avuncular interest in me and suggested I should become a Washington correspondent.

At the time, my ambition was more limited. I liked covering California issues and working for the *San Jose Mercury-News* in Sacramento, where I enjoyed considerable freedom. That changed for the worse in

1969 when Harry Farrell and I spent weeks, often working late hours, investigating Richard J. Dolwig, an influential and corrupt Republican state senator. While chairing a committee that considered changes in state condemnation laws, Dolwig had been an undisclosed attorney for clients who would have benefited from the changes. He had authored legislation to enable a development firm to fill San Francisco Bay with 28 million cubic yards of sand while "reclaiming" an island for a subdivision development. Harry and I had obtained copies of checks and a telegram showing that Dolwig was paid $25,000 for introducing the bill and was seeking at least $10,000 more for its advancement. Dolwig had also conspired with a notorious gambler who had been convicted of racketeering. The gambler was willing to pay Dolwig to obtain a reduced sentence for an associate convicted of telephone tampering. Dolwig testified under oath that he did not remember the name of the judge whom he'd asked to lighten the sentence, but contradicted this claim in a statement to an FBI agent.

Our editors agreed we had the goods on Dolwig, and we sought a response from him while preparing a draft series called "The Secret Life of Richard Dolwig." But Dolwig wouldn't meet with us. Instead, he called our publisher, Joseph B. Ridder, who killed the series without so much as a telephone call to Harry or me. An editor informed Harry, who called me in Sacramento. I was livid and didn't trust myself to call Ridder. Harry took it upon himself to confront Ridder in his San Jose office. He got nowhere. Ridder didn't dispute our findings but told Harry he didn't want to expose a prominent Republican senator. Strangely, or so I thought at the time, when Harry told Ridder that I wanted to take the series to another publication, Ridder said he had no problem with that.

When I first wrote about the suppression of the Dolwig series in my book, *Reporting: An inside View*, published in 1977, I attributed Ridder's action to partisanship. Seen from this distance, I'm less certain about his motive. It's striking that Joe didn't care if the damning findings about Dolwig were published as long as it wasn't in the *Mercury-News*. It's conceivable that killing the series was a quid pro quo; Dolwig sometimes did favors for publishers, and Ridder may have owed him something. It's also possible that in return for not publishing the series Ridder extracted a promise from Dolwig not to run again. Dolwig had served in the legislature as assemblyman and then senator since 1948. He did not seek reelection in 1970, and his Senate seat was won by a Democrat.

His post-legislative career did not go well for Dolwig, who moved to Hawaii and became involved in a dubious real estate deal with no Joe Ridder to help him off the hook. Five years after our series was suppressed, Dolwig was convicted of conspiracy, racketeering, and mail fraud and sentenced to prison. Harry sent me the banner headline on the story in the *Mercury-News* about Dolwig's conviction and wrote on it: "Poor Dick. If our story had run, he'd be out by now!"

Loyal to the *Mercury* despite Ridder's action, Harry and I never followed through on our threat to get the Dolwig series published elsewhere. Before deciding on my next course of action, I received a call from Walter T. Ridder in the Ridder national bureau asking me if I'd "like to trade the heat of Washington for the heat of Sacramento." Walter had a reputation for honesty and, although I barely knew him, I blurted out the story of the Dolwig series and how his cousin Joe had suppressed it.

"That was wrong," Walter said. "Joe should have known better than that."

Walter then assured me that, if I came up with a similar investigative story in Washington, he'd proudly send it to all the Ridder papers and stand behind it. I thanked him and said I'd discuss the Washington job with my wife.

This conversation with Walter took place in the early summer of 1969. Ginny and I were in our mid-thirties. She had never been to Washington and was enticed by the thought of living there. I needed to leave the *Mercury* to keep my self-respect but had no ready alternative in Sacramento. Going to the Washington bureau would keep me seamlessly employed, no small consideration with three children to support. Ginny and I agreed, however, that we should stay in Sacramento until my dual biography of Governor Ronald Reagan and Assembly Speaker Jesse Unruh came out that fall. When I called Walter back, he also agreed I should remain in Sacramento for the launch of the book.

I'd written *Ronnie and Jesse* in five months, pouring into it my accumulated historical knowledge about California politics and government. When someone asked Ginny how I could do such a comprehensive 90,000-word book in such a short time, she said that I'd been writing it in my head for years. Both Ginny and Jud Clark read the entire manuscript, caught errors, and suggested useful changes. It was good they did so because the editors at Doubleday changed virtually nothing in a manuscript that at a minimum needed tightening. Despite its wordiness, I was pleased with *Ronnie and Jesse,* realizing that both of my subjects were works in progress. In particular, much was yet to be accomplished by the enigma known as Ronald Reagan.

The publication of *Ronnie and Jesse* changed my life. All at once I was considered an expert on California politics, especially Reagan, and much in demand on television. I tried to wear my supposed expertise lightly but was gratified, perhaps overly, by a batch of head-turning reviews. These are excerpts from three of more than fifty favorable reviews:

"This is a deep and penetrating work on California politics, which demonstrates the quality of background and talent used by a political journalist in the reporting of public affairs," wrote *Los Angeles Times* book critic Robert Kirsch. After citing the Machiavelli dictum quoted at the beginning of my book—"Everyone sees what you appear to be, few know what you are; and those few dare not oppose the opinion of the many"—Kirsch said of me: "He does dare." Writing in *National Review,* Jeffrey Hart called *Ronnie and Jesse* "the first detailed and responsible study of Ronald Reagan's career to appear in print." Best of all, I thought, was the review by John Leonard, then the dean of book critics, in the *New York Times* on November 11, 1969. Leonard praised me for "sticking to the facts" instead of psychologizing Reagan or Unruh. Elsewhere in the review, he called *Ronnie and Jesse* "the best book on state government I have seen."

Ginny and I had little time to celebrate. Walter Ridder was pressing me to come to Washington, and I did so in November, little more than a month after the publication of *Ronnie and Jesse.* Ginny stayed behind with the kids and the house, which we put up for sale. While she looked forward to the move, it was a blow to our eldest son, Carl, sixteen, who'd been doing well academically and socially at McClatchy High School in Sacramento. It's hard to move when you're in high school.

As for me, I was happy to escape the corrupting influence of Joe Ridder journalism. The suppression of the Dolwig series had left a sour taste, but in thinking about it I realized that Harry and I (and perhaps our editors) had been naive in assuming that the series would make its way on journalistic merit. We'd forgotten—or at least I had—that Harry had years earlier suffered the embarrassment of having the last article pulled on his useful exposé of Unruh's fundraising methods. Joe was a friendly guy with a hail-fellow-well-met facade despite being hobbled by alcoholism, but he was also a prototype counting-house publisher who valued profits over journalistic ethics.

The Swift meatpacking company had learned this lesson a couple of years earlier. When Swift tried to locate a packing house in an industrially zoned area of San Jose near the fountain-adorned *San Jose Mercury-News* headquarters, Joe swung into action. Perceiving the smells and sounds of this facility as a threat to the value of his property, Joe launched the "Great Slaughterhouse Scare." Reporters were dispatched to the Midwest to inspect other Swift plants and grind out horror stories about their supposed effects on local communities. A moribund homeowners association was ginned up to launch a "popular protest" against the Swift plant. Even environmentalists, whom Joe normally had no time for, were solicited in the crusade.

Joe Ridder won the one-sided fight. I was happy with the result, if not the means used to attain it, as the paper took a new interest and gave better play to the stories I was writing from Sacramento about pending legislation to give local communities more control over shoreline development.

The *Mercury-News* supported this legislation editorially, which the paper would not have done without the slaughterhouse scare, and it was signed into law by Governor Reagan. The *Mercury-News* also backed a bill by Don Edwards, a liberal San Jose Democratic congressman who rarely received support from the paper, to establish a wildlife refuge at the south end of the bay. This, too, passed after various delays.

On the plane to Washington, DC, to join the Ridder bureau, I read *Murder in the Cathedral,* T. S. Eliot's verse drama of the murder of Thomas Becket, Archbishop of Canterbury, at the order of a king he refuses to obey. Eliot is a bit elevated for me, but I'd been interested in Becket, a martyr to his conscience, since seeing the film of the same name four years earlier. Many who are unfamiliar with the play or the movie know its most memorable line: *The last temptation is the greatest treason: to do the right deed for the wrong reason.*

It occurred to me that doing right for the wrong reason perfectly described Joe Ridder's newfound enthusiasm for environmental protection of San Francisco Bay. Years later I returned to this notion in *Reporting: An Inside View.* "One wonders," I wrote, "what the Santa Clara Valley would be like today if the *Mercury-News* had shown some of this same environmental consciousness during the years when the orchards were being torn down to make way for the crazy-quilt development and the urban sprawl."

Recalling the orchards that surrounded our tract home on three sides and were cut down within a year, Ginny said that Joe never would have had any interest in preserving even a single tree. More trees meant fewer houses, she observed, and smaller circulation.

Walter Ridder, God bless him, was even more caustic at lunch the day after my arrival in Washington. He said Joe had not been considered a bright light by the Ridder family, which gave him an obscure newspaper in San Jose that no other Ridder wanted. But the runt of the litter became the top dog. As San Jose and Santa Clara County grew, the *Mercury-News* became the most profitable property of the Ridder group. Joe never tired of reminding other family members of how much money the *Mercury-News* was making.

"Joe measures everything by money," Walter said.

14

THE RICHES OF THE INDIES

"He that would bring home the wealth of the Indies must carry the wealth of the Indies with him." These words of Samuel Johnson, engraved on the south face of Union Station in Washington, DC, were pointed out to me by Walter Ridder, who said this insight guided his hiring practices. I said I had no idea what that meant. Walter explained that he brought reporters into the Ridder Washington bureau who'd proven themselves covering local and state government and politics. With this background, Walter said, they would do just fine in Washington.

Walter was bred for journalism. He was the grandson of Herman Ridder, a German immigrant who in 1875 had started a German-language Catholic newspaper in New York to serve like-minded expatriates. He later bought the *New Yorker Staats-Zeitung*, the nation's most influential German-language newspaper. Active in politics, Herman opposed the efforts of Theodore Roosevelt, when he was police commissioner of New York, to close saloons on Sunday. Germans, he said, needed their "Sunday beer." Although Herman died insolvent, his heirs continued his work, launching what became the Ridder newspaper and broadcasting empire.

Over the years, the Ridders produced enough offspring to enable family members to operate most of the nineteen newspapers and broadcasting outlets owned by Ridder Publications. Unlike many newspaper families, the Ridders disdained the "newspaper chain" label and decentralized their properties and their politics. The Minnesota papers in St. Paul and Duluth were pragmatic, alternatively supporting mainstream Democrats and Republicans. Joe Ridder in San Jose was staunchly conservative. Walter was the family liberal, backing George McGovern against Richard Nixon in 1972. Unlike Joe, however, Walter never allowed politics or business dealings to interfere with journalism. Near the end of Walter's career, an editor at the St. Paul newspaper invited him to write his own epitaph.

"His heart was in the newsroom, not the counting house," Walter wrote. When he died, in 1990, the line made it into his obituary.

After graduating from Harvard in 1939 with a bachelor's degree in history and literature, Walter worked at a succession of small newspapers and in 1941 became Washington correspondent for the *St. Paul Pioneer Press-Dispatch*. In 1942, he enlisted in the Army but was soon discharged because he was terribly hard of hearing. Even in 1969, when I first knew him, Walter wore an old-fashioned hearing aid with an earpiece connected by wire to an amplifier-receiver and battery pack on his clothing. He had perfected the art of pretending to listen and would turn off his hearing aid in conversations with a bore, participating by nodding or shaking his head at appropriate moments. When I asked him what a particularly mind-numbing dinner companion had imparted, Walter tapped his hearing aid and said: "I haven't the slightest idea, my boy. That fellow was an early turn-off."

Despite his poor hearing, Walter became a war correspondent and was present at the U.S. liberation of Dachau in 1945. After the war, he returned to Washington, then went back to Europe in 1948 as head of the information department of the European Recovery Plan, better known as the Marshall Plan. The experience made Walter an avowed internationalist who believed the Marshall Plan had saved Western Europe from starvation and quite possibly Soviet domination.

When I came to Washington in the winter of 1969, Walter was nominal head of the Washington bureau but also publisher of the *Gary Post-Tribune*. It was an impossible juggle, and Walter would eventually bring in William Broom, a capable journalist, as bureau chief. For much of 1970, however, our tiny bureau of three operated on its own. We had weekly lunches with Walter, often at the Occidental Restaurant, where the walls were bedecked with pictures of politicians. These were pleasant meals with useful discussions, but Walter gave few assignments. Since we were in Washington more than he was, Walter assumed we'd know what to do.

Our bureau was in the National Theatre building, sharing space and benefiting from the clerical services and alert receptionist of the Washington bureau of a Ridder financial newspaper. We filed our stories by Western Union. I was responsible for the three Ridder papers in California. Albert Eisele, the bureau's senior correspondent, handled the two Minnesota papers. Ernie Hernandez, a Filipino American whose father had been an officer in the Philippine Army and survived the Bataan death march, was responsible for the Gary paper and a newspaper in Boulder, Colorado, that the Ridders had recently acquired. But the way we worked eluded neat boundaries. If one of us had our teeth in an ongoing story, he stayed with it even when it was on someone else's turf. Because of this practice I spent time with Senator Hubert H. Humphrey of Minnesota, which proved useful when I was assigned to cover him in 1972 after joining *The Washington Post.*

Our informal style of operating was made possible by the odd ways the Ridder papers made use of the Washington bureau, and the unselfish collegiality of Eisele, who was just as pleased when Ernie or I came up with a good story as with one of his own. Al gave me tips about the preferences of various editors, the idiosyncrasies of particular members of Congress, or the best places to take a source to lunch. He was always willing to make a phone call if I needed help at deadline, a practice Ernie and I tried to emulate. In our little bureau, we took care of one another.

Although Al did not pick fights, he never hesitated to write about the real or perceived shortcomings of the politicians he covered. When Senator Walter Mondale had an operation, Al wrote that other Democratic politicians in Minnesota were hoping the doctors would sew some guts in him while he was on the operating table. After he became vice president in 1977, Mondale referenced this story when asked why he'd hired Eisele as his press secretary.

"I had to do something to get him out of journalism," Mondale quipped.

I knew Ernie from the chaotic 1968 Democratic National Convention in Chicago, where I was responsible for the daily file to Ridder afternoon papers. It would have been a thankless task of rewrite except for Ernie, who roamed the streets of Chicago as thousands of unarmed antiwar demonstrators clashed with club-wielding policemen. It helped that he was fast on his feet. Out of breath and with his shirt ripped, Ernie returned to our bureau in the Chicago Hilton in the wee hours after the first day of the convention with a wild story of his adventures on the streets, which climaxed when he leapt over the hood of a car to evade two pursuing cops. I told him to sit down and write the story just the way he was telling it to me. Ernie wrote a terrific story that was used by all our afternoon papers.

The next night, Ernie went out with the cops. Unlike the demonstrators, they were armed, but their situation was nonetheless stressful. The police had been out of control the first night and, with Democratic delegates denouncing their conduct, they were under orders to exercise restraint. That wasn't easy because agitators were hurling projectiles at the police from the back ranks of the demonstrators, angering the cops, who took it out on the youthful innocents shouting slogans in the front ranks. Ernie's souvenir of the evening was a potato embedded with a razor blade. Again, he wrote a superb story, this time from the perception of the embattled ranks of law enforcement.

These two stories were worthy of a Pulitzer, but I don't know if anyone bothered to enter them for any prize. The afternoon Ridder papers rarely bothered with awards; they were resigned to playing second fiddle to their morning counterparts, which generally had larger circulations and bigger staffs. Beyond that, the Washington bureau was usually out of sight and mind to Ridder papers, no matter what time of day they published. The Ridder insistence on not being a newspaper chain was so drummed into the heads of local editors that most of them didn't inform readers of the existence of the Washington bureau, instead describing us as members of their staffs. After I moved to Southern California in 1977, people I knew in Pasadena asked me where I had lived in their city. I have never lived in Pasadena. The locals assumed I had because the *Pasadena Star-News* used many of my stories from the bureau, always identifying me as the paper's Washington correspondent.

The exception that acknowledged the existence of the Washington bureau was the *St. Paul Pioneer-Press*, the best of the Ridder papers. Bill Sumner, the paper's editorial page editor, had worked in the Washington bureau and was its consistent booster. But even the *Pioneer-Press* made skimpy use of stories not filed by Eisele. After I went to *The Washington Post*, Sumner told Al that my stories were getting better play in the *Pioneer-Press* than when I worked for the bureau.

Nonetheless, the bureau had its moments. Al's understanding of Hubert Humphrey and his Democratic rival, Eugene McCarthy, enabled him to break several stories involving one or the other senator. He eventually wrote *Almost to the Presidency*, an insightful book about both of them. Ernie had an eye for scandal and racial conflict. When I made the rounds of the Ridder papers, Ernie took me to a couple of rough bars in Gary. One had only white customers who didn't bother to conceal their hostility toward Blacks. At the other bar everyone was a person of color. Ernie was welcome in both bars. I wouldn't have gone to either of them alone.

My coverage for the Ridders focused initially on Congress, taking advantage of my Sacramento experience because several of the 38 Californians in the House had served as state legislators. For the best and brightest of them, the House with its 435 members and seniority rules was a comedown. The California legislature has 80 Assembly members and 40 state senators. Members such as Thomas Rees of Los Angeles, who'd been a positive force in both houses in Sacramento, struggled to be noticed in Washington. Rees and I enjoyed each other's company and had regular lunches where he often waxed nostalgically about his legislative days. At a time when the whereabouts of Howard Hughes was a mystery, Rees quipped that Hughes had been hiding out for years as a Los Angeles congressman.

I naturally paid particular attention to those California House members who represented cities where the Ridders had newspapers. Most were Republicans, despite Democrats being a majority in the House and in the California delegation. Although this would soon change, the only Democrat from a major circulation area of a Ridder paper was Don Edwards of San Jose. He'd been in the House since 1963 and would remain there until 1995. Edwards was a fierce civil libertarian and opposed every U.S. military involvement that occurred during his three-plus decades in the House: the Vietnam War, the intervention by President George H. W. Bush to overthrow a dictator in Panama, and the first Gulf War. Edwards had done his homework on me. In our first conversation, he complimented me for helping Phil Burton win a state legislative seat and also referenced the series on the corrupt state senator Richard Dolwig that *San Jose Mercury* publisher Joe Ridder had suppressed. I steered the conversation in a different direction, asking Edwards how he'd managed with his liberal record to stay on good terms with conservatives in his district.

"Constituent service," he replied. "I represent everyone in my district, not just the people who agree with me." Edwards was never seriously threatened in any election. He was married three times and lived to be a hundred years old.

No one except Edwards mentioned my involvement in Burton's 1956 campaign before I was a journalist, which was fine with me. I saw Phil socially from time to time but stayed away from covering him, concerned that whatever I wrote might be perceived as a conflict of interest. Walter Ridder gently advised me not to worry about it and rattled off a list of people who had worked for a politician before or after going into journalism. "Treat Burton as you would any other congressman," Walter said, adding that if I avoided him I wasn't doing that.

Another Democrat I'd known for a long time was Senator Alan Cranston, who'd once worked precincts for Burton out of our home in San Francisco and was a key figure in the rise of his party in the 1950s. Passed over in 1958 as the party's candidate for U.S. Senate, the office he wanted, Cranston became state controller, a position with a significant amount of patronage that he wielded to his advantage. But there were two Alan Cranstons. One focused on world peace—he'd been a United World Federalist before becoming a partisan politician—who was perceptive about the dangers of nuclear proliferation. The other enjoyed raising money more than any other politician I have ever known. In the late 1980s, Cranston raised $1 million from Charles H. Keating Jr., at the same time he was intervening with federal regulators to save Keating's savings-and-loan association from collapse. In 1991, the Senate Ethics Committee would rebuke Cranston's behavior as "improper and repugnant."

Elected in 1968, Cranston had been a senator for only a few months when I came to the Ridder bureau. He was my first call, in part because Walter had told me that one of the California papers wanted a profile of him and in part because Cranston had long been a source of useful information. He didn't like my account in *Ronnie and Jesse* of his attempted smear of Ronald Reagan in the 1966 gubernatorial campaign, but he was too professional to let that get in the way of a relationship with a reporter for three California newspapers. Still in the glow of being a new senator, Cranston invited me to lunch in the Senate dining room. He knew he was lucky to be there. In 1968, right-wing firebrand Max Rafferty had challenged Senator Thomas Kuchel, a moderate fixture in the Senate, in the Republican primary. Few gave Rafferty a chance, but he narrowly bested Kuchel, who had never before been challenged in his party and did not take Rafferty seriously until it was too late.

"What would have happened if Kuchel had won the primary?" I asked.

"You'd be having lunch with Senator Kuchel," Cranston replied.

The other California senator at the time was Republican George Murphy, a onetime song-and-dance man and Hollywood pal of Reagan, who was challenged in the 1970 election by a promising young Democratic House member, John Tunney, son of the former heavyweight boxing champion.

I spent more time with House members than with the two senators. The Ridder paper in Long Beach devoted considerable ink to its local House member, Craig Hosmer, a moderately conservative Republican with an acerbic wit. Hosmer was a member of Richard Nixon's congressional class, first elected in 1946. During the eight years Nixon was vice president, the House members of that class took turns hosting an annual dinner in his honor. When it was Hosmer's turn, he called Nixon's secretary, Rosemary Woods, to ask for a funny story about Nixon.

"There are no funny stories about the vice president," Woods told him.

Hosmer was a reliable Republican vote but made it clear to me three years before Watergate that he had no illusions about Nixon.

A House Republican who held even less regard for Nixon was arch-conservative John Rousselot, a straight shooter despite being a spokesman for the John Birch Society, and so hardline he said the U.S. should break off diplomatic relations with the Soviets, withdraw from the U.N., and use tanks to knock down the Berlin Wall. Running for governor of California against Pat Brown in 1960, Nixon repudiated the JBS and refused to endorse Rousselot and Ed Hiestand, the two California House members who were Birchers. Both were defeated for reelection although their loss was more the result of a Democratic-controlled gerrymandering than anything Nixon said.

Rousselot returned to the House in 1971 in a redrawn and heavily Republican district in the circulation area of the *Pasadena Star-News* after edging out Patrick Hillings, a Nixon buddy, in the GOP primary. Rousselot had become public affairs director of the Birch Society and shifted its focus away from Communist conspiracies to local issues such as "support your local police," a slogan Rousselot is credited with originating. Rousselot acknowledged that Welch was "a little bit crazy" but told me that most rank-and-file Birchers were hardworking, middle-class patriots. He believed Nixon was a craven opportunist. In 1972, Rousselot welcomed Pete McCloskey's quixotic challenge to Nixon for the Republican presidential nomination. Rousselot and the liberal McCloskey, who represented a suburban San Francisco district in the House, had been high school friends in Pasadena.

Nixon claimed to be a party man, but his relationship with the GOP was more a marriage of convenience than a love affair. Republicans respected Nixon's political skills and grit in resurrecting himself after defeats in 1960 and 1962 but believed he consistently put his interests ahead of his party's. Nixon ratified this perception in 1972 when his reelection committee hoarded money he didn't need at the expense of fund-starved congressional candidates even though he was miles ahead of his Democratic opponent, George McGovern. Democrats were in disarray that year, giving Republicans a rare chance to win the House, which Democrats had held for all but two years since World War II. But they gained only a dozen seats and fell short while Nixon won by a landslide. When the Watergate scandal blew up in Nixon's face in 1974, congressional Republicans refused to go to the mat for a president whose only concern was himself. Facing impeachment and lacking sufficient Republican support, Nixon had no choice except to resign.

Watergate was still in the future when I covered Congress for the Ridder papers, but the Vietnam War cast a somber shadow over Washington, which also had been shaken by four days of rioting in April 1968 after the assassination of Martin Luther King.

"If I had a dollar for every denunciation I've heard on the (House) floor of the Vietnam War, I could retire a very rich man," a veteran congressional reporter told me soon after I started covering the Hill. His point was that Congress would mostly talk while the president—any president—could plunge our country into war. In early April, U.S. troops began pursuing the Viet Cong from Vietnam into Cambodia. Later that month, Nixon ordered a full-scale invasion of Cambodia, triggering a civil war in which the Khmer Rouge would kill two million people.

On May 4, 1970, National Guard troops called out to quell a demonstration at Kent State University in Ohio, fired into a crowd of protestors, killing four students and wounding ten others, one of whom was crippled for life. Walter Ridder and I were having lunch at the Carlton Hotel when we heard the news. He spotted Richard Harwood, the national editor of *The Washington Post,* eating alone at another table and we went over to him. Walter introduced me, and he and Harwood talked about Kent State.

"It's started," Harwood said. "We're killing our own."

I liked Harwood immediately. He had a ramrod Marine posture and a firm handshake, and he looked directly at you as he spoke in a voice that was at once soft and resonant.

"Maybe you'll want to hire him some day," Walter said to Harwood about me.

"Maybe," Harwood replied.

"He wrote a good book about Ronald Reagan," Walter said.

"I'll read it," Harwood said.

I was embarrassed by this attention and told Walter after we left that I was happy at the Ridder bureau. "You never know what's going to happen, my boy," he replied.

A few days later, I was sounded out by another *Post* editor and a month after that by an editor for the *New York Times.* I told them both that I was satisfied with the job I had.

Kent State changed the political mood of the country. Thomas Reed, advising Governor Ronald Reagan in his 1970 reelection campaign, observed that the student protestors Reagan had previously demonized became our children who were being shot on a college campus. Thanks to Reed and Stuart Spencer, Reagan mostly stopped talking about the "mess at Berkeley" he claimed to have corrected.

The Ridder papers were interested in Reagan, and Walter sent me to California to cover the 1970 campaign between Reagan and Jesse Unruh. Unruh had less money than Reagan, and almost no one gave him a chance to win. Consequently, Reagan waged an uninspired campaign in a good Democratic year. When I saw Reagan, he virtually ignored the Unruh challenge and talked vaguely about reforming welfare in his second term. I came away believing that Reagan was taking too much for granted.

Unruh meanwhile was plugging along in an effort to portray Reagan as the tool of the ultra-wealthy. Jess was too realistic to predict victory but told me he was making progress after his slow start, which was true. Even as the nominee for governor, Unruh kept track of his beloved

Assembly, which was then narrowly controlled by the Republicans. He said the Democrats stood a good chance of regaining control, as they did. In his own race, Unruh won back many of the working-class Democrats who had deserted Pat Brown four years earlier, but it wasn't nearly enough. Reagan won by half a million votes, slightly more than half his margin over Brown—and a narrower win than in either of Reagan's two successful presidential campaigns.

The Ridder papers in California also wanted stories about the Senate race between Murphy and Tunney. At the time California voters were often ticket splitters, not the lockstep Democrats they are today. Ticket splitting had enabled Murphy to win his Senate seat in 1964 against the nonchalant Pierre Salinger while Lyndon Johnson was carrying California easily. Salinger, who had served as John F. Kennedy's White House press secretary, had been appointed by Pat Brown the day after he moved to California. Ineligible to vote in the election in which his name was on the ballot, he was widely viewed as a carpetbagger.

But ticket splitting hurt Murphy in 1970. Tunney was a vigorous thirty-six, while health issues made Murphy, who'd had throat cancer in 1966, appear older than his sixty-eight years. The contrast in health and age between the two candidates might in itself have been sufficient for Tunney to win. Then the *Los Angeles Times* discovered that Murphy, once a vice president of Technicolor, had received an annual $20,000 consultant's fee (more than $162,000 in 2025 dollars) from the entertainment firm while in the Senate. Technicolor also paid Murphy's air travel and half the rent on his Washington apartment. These disclosures put Murphy on the defensive while Tunney was running a strong campaign. The highlight for me was the joint appearance of Tunney's father, Gene, with the famous fighter Jack Dempsey, whom Tunney had beaten to win the heavyweight boxing championship of the world. My dad, a Dempsey man, would have enjoyed seeing these two old prize fighters together. Tunney won the election handily with a bigger margin over Murphy than Reagan had over Unruh.

After the campaign, I returned to Washington and became caught up in the politics of opposition to the Vietnam War. Pete McCloskey, distrustful of Nixon and appalled by the expansion of the war into Cambodia, had become the Republican man of the moment to critics of the war. Walter Ridder, whose opposition to the war was becoming more vocal, urged me to pay close attention to McCloskey. I did so happily, for he fascinated me. My coverage of McCloskey would open a new chapter in my life that would take me with him to Vietnam and Laos and his subsequent campaign for the presidency.

Walter Ridder looked out for me at every turn. He gave me my head in the bureau and introduced me to the national editor of the newspaper that would become my home for the better part of three decades. By assigning me to McCloskey he both expanded my horizons and brought my work to a wider audience, including the editors of *The Washington Post*. Remembering the quotation on Union Station, I realized that Walter had brought me the wealth of the Indies.

15

THE McCLOSKEY EXPERIENCE

Paul Norton McCloskey Jr. was a Korean War hero, an environmental activist, a courageous contrarian, and ultimately a friend. I accompanied him to Southeast Asia in 1971 as he gathered evidence to make a case against the Vietnam War and the bombing of Laos. Subsequently, McCloskey opposed President Richard Nixon for the 1972 Republican presidential nomination. Although he never had a realistic chance of winning, his campaign gave him a platform from which to expose the systematic bombing of Laotian villages, which the U.S government had denied.

McCloskey burst onto the political scene in 1967 by defeating Shirley Temple Black and nine other candidates in a special congressional election in San Mateo County, south of San Francisco. With wire-clipped hair, a Stanford law school education, and a hero's résumé, McCloskey was handsome and well-spoken. Democrats crossed party lines to vote for him.

Once in Congress, McCloskey ignored the traditions of the House, which operated on the Sam Rayburn principle of "to get along, go along." McCloskey did neither. After North Korea seized the USS *Pueblo* and its eighty-three-member crew on January 24, 1968, McCloskey proposed that Congress should declare war against North Korea if President Johnson thought this would help recover the ship and its crew. The White House ignored him, and McCloskey received a torrent of critical letters from his constituents.

McCloskey was nostalgic about the war in which he had served with distinction. Reminiscing about Korea, McCloskey told me, "We started out with extremely long-range exchanges of fire and a lot of patrolling. This was a great enjoyment to me. I had followed World War I and the Civil War. I'd studied military tactics all my life. "The ultimate was [to be] a platoon leader in Korea."

A measure of that enjoyment remained when McCloskey's platoon engaged the enemy at close quarters. He was wounded twice and talked readily about his combat experiences without making himself the hero of his stories. But his Marine Corps comrades testified to McCloskey's exemplary courage as did the medals—the Navy Cross and the Silver Star—he received. In one battle an artillery round that also injured several other Marines shattered McCloskey's leg and cut a tendon.

"He disregarded the intense pain and loss of blood and continued to treat the casualties," said the Silver Star citation. "When a stretcher party was able to reach the area, he directed the evacuation of casualties and returned to his platoon. Only upon the direct order of his battalion commander and senior medical officer did he allow himself to be evacuated for treatment. Second Lieutenant McCloskey's alert actions and courageous devotion to duty undoubtedly saved the lives of four critically wounded comrades."

McCloskey initially supported U.S. involvement in Vietnam. After an emotional 1965 visit to a fellow Marine whose leg had been amputated in Korea, McCloskey sent a letter to the Corps asking to be recalled to active duty. He was rejected. The brass had no interest in activating a fifty-eight-year-old suburban lawyer who'd been a platoon leader in Korea and was now a lieutenant colonel in the Marine reserves. So McCloskey followed the Vietnam War from a distance, with mounting skepticism about U.S. involvement. As a newly minted member of Congress, he traveled to Vietnam in January 1968, identifying with the Marines he met there and forming a low opinion of the South Vietnamese Army's capabilities.

When Richard Nixon became president in 1969, thirty-one thousand U.S. lives had been lost in Vietnam, and Americans were war-weary. The Nixon administration began peace talks in Paris and in a nationally televised speech on November 3, 1969, Nixon announced he would replace Johnson's "Americanization" of the war with "Vietnamization." The plan called for phased withdrawal of U.S. combat forces and an expanded effort to train and equip South Vietnamese forces to become responsible for their own defense.

McCloskey favored Vietnamization but wanted a faster withdrawal of U.S. troops. "If the South Vietnamese are capable of preserving their independence, this capability will be demonstrated as easily in one year as it will be in three," McCloskey said in one of thirty-three letters he wrote to Nixon. McCloskey had become convinced that the South Vietnam Army was not sufficiently motivated or skilled to resist the Viet Cong—the Communist guerilla forces operating within South Vietnam—let alone the North Vietnamese Army. But McCloskey was not ready to break with Nixon, and the last paragraph of his letter expressed respect for the way he had conducted the first eleven months of his presidency.

McCloskey's view of the president changed dramatically in 1970. In February, McCloskey made a second trip to Vietnam, this one sponsored by peace groups. I interviewed him after his return and found his opposition to the war had hardened. McCloskey had visited the Fifth Regiment of the U.S. Marine Corps—*his* regiment—at a time when Marines were sustaining far fewer casualties than when McCloskey served in Korea. But McCloskey was skeptical of official announcements that highlighted purported enemy casualties. McCloskey said U.S. government figures claimed that Viet Cong and NVA troops were being killed in "situations where no enemy is encountered or any battle fought."

With assistance from officers in the Marine Corps, McCloskey compiled statistics showing that Marines had encountered 1,277 booby traps in 1969 and detonated 604 of them. In these encounters, unannounced by the Pentagon, 99 Marines had died and another 1,135 had been wounded.

Something else happened on this second Vietnam visit that altered McCloskey's perception of the war. He had until then fixated on the plight of the Marines in Vietnam, not on what was happening to Vietnamese civilians. Here is the most significant passage in the hour-long interview I did with McCloskey after he returned:

> I flew over miles and miles of tree lines where hamlets and everything had been destroyed. I have real reservations that this policy is anything but a war crime. If you look back on Nuremberg and our policy in 1946, we insisted that it was a war crime to wantonly destroy villages. The only purpose of destroying these villages was that they gave occasional shelter to the Viet Cong that came into

> them or provided rice to the VC. For the United States to pursue a definite, specific policy of scorching the earth of the civilian population because many of the civilians had relatives fighting in the Viet Cong—well, I'm not sure we can justify this policy over the long pull. To me it's exactly what we executed Germans for doing because they had harbored enemy units that had taken shelter there.

This 1970 trip was one of two tipping points that moved McCloskey from a half-hearted supporter of Vietnamization to full-throated condemnation of Nixon and the war. The other was the May 1970 invasion of Cambodia, which McCloskey believed to be illegal. Long before McCloskey made his third trip to Vietnam, the one in which I accompanied him in April 1971, he had concluded that the war was unjustified.

McCloskey's opposition mirrored public concerns, and most Ridder editors welcomed stories about a military hero who was questioning the Vietnam War. My interview of McCloskey after he returned from his 1970 trip to Vietnam led to an extensive account of his views in Ridder newspapers. Walter Ridder lauded my coverage and wanted more. When McCloskey offered me a spot on the plane for his third trip, the hefty cost that was my pro rata share of the airfare wasn't in the Ridder Publications budget. Walter paid the fare out of his own pocket.

"McCloskey understands war," Walter told me. "Maybe he'll find out something that has eluded others."

During that trip I began to think of writing a book about McCloskey, who was pondering a challenge to Nixon for the GOP presidential nomination. Walter urged me to do the book and generously gave me time for research and writing. That's how I came to write *The McCloskey Challenge,* my second published book.

We took off from Dulles Airport in an unseasonable snowstorm on April 6, 1971. On board in addition to McCloskey and me were Representative Jerome Waldie, an antiwar Democratic from a congressional district east of San Francisco; Paul LaFond, who'd recently retired as a colonel after thirty-nine years in the Marine Corps; Chuck Daly, who'd served with McCloskey as a fellow officer in Korea and remained one of his best friends; Harold Willens, a peace activist from Southern California; and Jerry Cook, a young Fresno businessman. The only media person on board besides me was John Dominis, an accomplished *Life* magazine photographer. McCloskey was in an exultant mood. He was headed back for another look at the war that he had not been allowed to fight and had learned to oppose.

"McCloskey carried with him a long rolled-up map with a marking for every village in the Laotian panhandle," my notes of that night indicate. "He is already in Laos and in Vietnam."

On the plane, McCloskey told war stories, answered mail, and read a revealing report on Laotian refugees from a Senate subcommittee headed by Senator Edward Kennedy. His most graphic story was about a Marine who had lost a testicle in Korean combat, inevitably bringing to mind Jake Barnes, the hero of Ernest Hemingway's *The Sun Also Rises.* After telling this story, McCloskey said with great emotion, "That was a horrible story. I was never worried about getting killed. I prayed to God I wouldn't be wounded."

McCloskey's mission seemingly misfired our first day in Vietnam, with help from his inner circle. McCloskey had frequently compared the U.S. evacuation of refugees from the northern provinces of South Vietnam to the forced relocation by the Nazis of 100,000 civilians from northern Norway in 1944. This had been one of the charges against German General Alfred Jodl, who'd been found guilty of war crimes at Nuremberg and executed. During a Saigon briefing on April 7, 1971, McCloskey argued about the Vietnamese evacuation with George Jacobsen, the staff officer for U.S. pacification efforts in Vietnam. Jacobsen defended the action as a way to protect the refugees from the Viet Cong and received unexpected help from LaFond, who said, "I don't think that's a war crime." Tight-lipped, McCloskey said, "See we're not all doves in this group."

Witnessing this exchange, I mistakenly thought the McCloskey mission had gone off the rails. But the Marine Corps is as gossipy as a boarding school, and LaFond, at once soft-spoken and decisive, was popular with Marines who has served under him in the Third Marine Division in Vietnam. It turned out that every Marine we subsequently met in Vietnam during the McCloskey trip (and many who were not Marines) had heard of the Jacobsen-LaFond exchange. Instead of harming the McCloskey mission, LaFond's independence lent it credibility.

LaFond and I bonded on this trip and stayed in communication afterward. As a second lieutenant on Okinawa during World War II, LaFond had won the Silver Star for taking command of two platoons in addition to his own when their officers were wounded and successfully repelling counterattacks for the next forty hours "in the face of fanatical Japanese resistance." He'd commanded the Third Marine Division in Vietnam in 1968 and 1969. When LaFond retired in 1970, General Charles Krulak, commandant of the Marine Corps, called him "the epitome of a Marine leader, caring, compassionate, yet tough when he needed to be tough." What Krulak didn't say was that LaFond believed the Vietnam War was a mistake.

We tracked down some of the Vietnamese civilians who'd been evacuated, one of whom shed light on what had happened to the hamlet they had been forced to abandon. Evacuees from Xuan Loc hamlet of Ap Thanh village in Thua Thien province had been resettled in a hamlet known as Gia Long B.

McCloskey was interviewing the hamlet's elders, who said their original village had been "burned down by the VC," when the questioning was interrupted by a man who identified himself as Ho Lee and said he was an assistant platoon leader in the Popular Forces, the South Vietnamese militia. Ho Lee said the original hamlet had been burned down not by the Viet Cong but by the U.S. Third Marine Regiment. (This was LaFond's old outfit but before he had taken command.) "If they don't burn the houses, the VC will use them for shelter," Ho Lee explained.

I interviewed our interpreter at Gia Long B. His name was Nguyen Than Nhat, a recently married twenty-one-year-old staff sergeant in the South Vietnamese Army. He described the evacuations as an inevitable part of a war he didn't want and conceded that U.S. and South Vietnamese artillery had killed villagers.

"The VC take refuge in the hamlets," he said in measured English." "If we don't kill the people, we can't kill the VC."

Then Nhat expressed distaste for killing but said the Communists would never allow the war to end until they'd killed all their opponents. His family had been part of an exodus of some 600,000 Roman Catholics who fled the north for South Vietnam after the Geneva Accords of 1954 split the country into two at the Seventeenth Parallel. He was four years old at the time and said he had managed to avoid warfare until being drafted into the South Vietnamese Army. I asked Than Nhat if he had killed any Viet Cong. He said he'd killed two VC a month earlier when they'd attacked a supply station where he was stationed. "I don't want to fight, but I've got to kill the Communists or they will kill me," he said.

The next day we went to Duc Duc near the DMZ, where the Communists had indeed shown a willingness to kill their fellow Vietnamese, including women and children. One week earlier, a mixed force of 1,500 North Vietnamese Army troops and Viet Cong irregulars had struck Duc Duc and its satellite hamlets. Jack Foisie, the respected *Los Angeles Times* correspondent in Vietnam, reported that the lone surviving VC prisoner said the attack was intended "to make a point with the local people that they should have heeded our warning to move away." To make this point, the attackers killed 21 military defenders and 109 civilians, 35 of whom were executed during the nearly twelve hours the attackers occupied the place.

The carnage in Duc Duc, however appalling, paled in comparison to My Lai, a small village in Quang Ngai province and scene of the worst U.S. atrocity of the Vietnam War. The McCloskey party visited My Lai the day after Easter Sunday. Slightly more than three years earlier, on March 16, 1968, U.S. soldiers with Charlie Company of the Eleventh Infantry Brigade under the direction of Lieutenant William Calley had massacred 504 civilians. Among the victims were 182 women—17 of them pregnant—and 173 children, including 56 infants. Not a single shot was fired at the U.S. soldiers.

Army higher-ups covered up what had happened at My Lai for more than a year until Ron Ridenhour, a soldier of the Eleventh Brigade who had not participated in the killings, brought My Lai to public attention. Ridenhour had written President Nixon, the Joint Chiefs of Staff, and several congressmen without getting a response before confiding in journalist Seymour Hersh, who broke the story in November 1969. This led to a special investigation which recommended that twenty-eight officers be court-martialed. The Army charged fourteen of these officers. Calley testified he had followed the orders of his superior officer, Capt. Ernest Medina. Medina and the other accused officers were acquitted. Calley was the only one convicted.

A week before the McCloskey party arrived in Vietnam, Calley was sentenced to life imprisonment. U.S. public opinion favored Calley. George Wallace visited him in the stockade and urged President Nixon to pardon Calley. The White House received thousands of letters in Calley's support. Georgia governor Jimmy Carter proclaimed American

Fighting Man's Day and urged Georgians to drive for a week with their lights on. Three days after the verdict, Nixon reduced Calley's sentence to house arrest pending an appeal.[1]

McCloskey was nonplussed. We'd discussed My Lai on the plane to Vietnam hours after Captain Aubrey M. Daniel III, the lead prosecutor at Calley's trial, criticized Nixon for interference in the military justice system. McCloskey had disparaged Nixon for lesser matters than leniency to Calley, but he did not criticize the president for reducing the sentence to house arrest. McCloskey agreed with the verdict, however, saying it was obvious to any "professional Marine" that Calley was guilty. When I asked McCloskey how he assessed the public outcry against the verdict, he said: "I think it shows that large segments of the American people have become so inured to violence, so accustomed to considering the terrible Communist enemy as a threat that they justify in their own minds the killing of men, women, children, old people as a lesser evil than Communism."

I kept my own counsel but held a different view. I don't believe that everyone who objected to Calley's sentence endorsed mass murder of civilians. Many of those who objected to the verdict or the sentence believed it was unfair to put the entire blame on Calley and let his superiors off the hook. This sentiment was expressed in letters sent to the White House, members of Congress, and the news media.

Quang Ngai province was not secure for Americans at any time during the war. Before the McCloskey party visited My Lai, the South Vietnamese military sent out patrols that prowled the countryside, looking for Viet Cong. This disturbed Waldie, who said he didn't want lives risked for the congressional party. The U.S military advisor in charge assured Waldie that the patrols were "a low-level operation." We encountered no trouble, but there was nonetheless a tension to the My Lai visit we'd not found elsewhere in Vietnam. Late one hot and humid day, we walked in single file after repeated warnings about landmines, looking

1. Calley served three years under house arrest. After lengthy appeals, his conviction was upheld by the appellate courts. But his sentence was reduced by the secretary of the army, and he never served another day in custody. On August 19, 2009, while speaking to the Kiwanis Club of Columbus, Georgia, Calley apologized for his role in the My Lai massacre, saying: "There is not a day that goes by that I do not feel remorse for what happened that day in My Lai. I feel remorse for the Vietnamese who were killed, for their families, for the American soldiers involved and their families. I am very sorry."

through the gloom at shelled ruins of homes. McCloskey unfurled his inevitable map and led us to the fetid ditch where the massacre had begun.

"No big deal," McCloskey said.

"What are you talking about?" I asked.

"That's what Calley said on the witness stand," McCloskey replied. "It was no big deal."

My Lai cast a pall on the trip that never entirely lifted while we were in Vietnam. That was in part because what had happened at My Lai was a much greater war crime than the evacuations McCloskey was investigating and there was nothing any of us could do about any of it. But the My Lai visit had also been necessary. I think it reinforced the feelings of all of us that this awful war needed to end.

McCloskey crowded more experiences into this third journey to Vietnam than most people would have accomplished in twice the time. He had an appetite for work and an intolerance for the cocktail-party, swimming-pool events scheduled for him by his military and civilian hosts. McCloskey canceled them. He roamed all over the five provinces of I Corps, mostly by helicopter, asking questions of Vietnamese and Americans. We traveled to the Ashau Valley, to Hue, to a mountain district with a largely Montagnard population, to refugee reception centers, to resettlement sites, and to the Demilitarized Zone. We also met with some of the forty young combat officers who had written President Nixon a revealing letter while waiting for embarkation to Vietnam. After expressing a commitment to obey their oaths and do their duty, these officers urged total withdrawal from Vietnam "at the earliest possible moment."

McCloskey visited on his own the hospital where the sole North Vietnamese survivor of Duc Duc was held. He was defiant and reminded McCloskey of one of his sons.

This trip was a learning experience for me. I especially valued a day in Saigon where I talked with reporters who'd been covering the war and, with the help of a volunteer translator, interviewed ordinary Vietnamese.

The helicopter rides were harrowing, however. The worst flight was at the DMZ, where the pilot swooped and soared—to the degree a helicopter could do either—among undulating hills, drawing antiaircraft and machine-gun fire from North Vietnamese batteries below. The pilot later pointed to machine-gun bullets in the cowling and told me it was a game pilots played to relieve boredom. Some game. McCloskey, immersed in his maps, didn't notice either the antiaircraft fire or my anxiety. But the observant Paul LaFond saw that something was wrong with me. After a bumpy flight, he put his hand on my shoulder and whispered, "You'll be all right." I thanked him but never again felt comfortable in a helicopter.

The arc of our trip changed in Laos. In Vietnam, the military had been in charge and, despite differences between the brass and McCloskey, he was respected for his war record, as were LaFond and Daly. As a result, McCloskey was allowed to do pretty much whatever he wanted to do in Vietnam. The military was also lax with the rest of us. I attended a briefing on the Phoenix program—the operation for infiltrating Viet Cong infrastructure in the villages and killing VC cadres—from which reporters were supposedly barred. LaFond took me in, saying, "He's with me."

We were allowed no such liberties in Laos, where the Central Intelligence Agency was running the show. The CIA was conducting a not-so-secret "secret war" in Laos and feared, with good reason, that McCloskey might publicize the relentless bombing U.S. planes were doing at CIA behest on the Plain of Jars. So the CIA did what it could to divert McCloskey from his mission, initially separating him from his staff. Only McCloskey and Waldie were transported by military aircraft to Vientiane, where the two congressmen had dinner at the home of U.S. ambassador George McMurtrie Godley. The rest of us followed the next day by commercial airline.[2] Daly took advantage of an unwanted night in Saigon to interview former political prisoners, but McCloskey could have used him or LaFond as backups at the dinner.

That dinner—on April 13, 1971—was contentious. I was able to reconstruct what happened by interviewing McCloskey, Waldie, and a CIA participant. "The Godley dinner was a setup in which Godley was the teacher and all the underlings were instructed to lay it on to Pete," Waldie told me. McCloskey made their task easier for he had unaccount-

2. The U.S. military command had initially tried to prevent Dominis and me from accompanying McCloskey and Waldie to the northern provinces of Vietnam. They gave in when McCloskey and LaFond insisted. The CIA was immune to such pressure. Once we were in Laos, however, the CIA was amenable to flying us anywhere so long as we left Laos. After the mission ended, we were flown on a U.S. government plane from Vientiane to Bangkok.

ably failed to read a summary in his briefing book of a United States Information Service (USIS) report that confirmed much of the evidence he was seeking.

McCloskey wanted to show that U.S. warplanes had regularly bombed Laotian villages at the direction of Godley and his predecessor, William H. Sullivan. The U.S. government had acknowledged some bombing but greatly minimized its extent. Godley and Sullivan explained the influx of refugees from the Plain of Jars by saying the villagers had fled the Pathet Lao, the Laotian Communists, not because they were being bombed by the United States. Sullivan so testified before the Kennedy subcommittee. This was a false dichotomy. Fleeing the aerial bombing and the Pathet Lao were not mutually exclusive motivations. The testimony was also misleading because it suggested that all villagers opposed the Pathet Lao. In fact, some villagers preferred the Communists to the Royal Laotian government. As the USIS survey reported, the Pathet Lao showed villagers who stayed how to construct shelters and find hiding places from the bombs. The senior USIS officer who had compiled the survey had no doubt about the primary cause for the thousands of refugees. He wrote: "The bombing is clearly the most compelling reason."

Godley's contribution to the CIA deception was to distribute to every member of the McCloskey party, myself included, a slick twenty-six-page report that explained the plight of Laos and its refugees without a single reference to the bombing campaign. McCloskey and I thumbed through it in disbelief. Pete and Waldie had already interviewed sixteen refugees in the village of Ban Na Nga on the Vientiane plain. Matt Storin of the *Boston Globe* and I witnessed most of the interviews, including one with a sixty-two-year-old woman named Tian Di, who after first trying to run away allowed herself to be interviewed and bared her breast to show shrapnel wounds. Her husband had been killed in a raid. Another refugee was a ten-year-old boy who showed leg wounds that McCloskey and Daly, who had seen such wounds before, believed were caused by pellets of white phosphorus. A Buddhist monk said his village had been bombed for years and that not a single house remained.

Since no one in the McCloskey party spoke the Lao language, we relied on four interpreters, all of whom I subsequently interviewed. Two of the four promoted the embassy line that the refugees were fleeing the Pathet Lao, not the bombing. One translator, a Catholic priest, went further, saying "thank God for the U.S. bombing" because it had helped deter the Communists. Even so, the priest acknowledged that every one of the refugees cited the U.S. bombing attacks as a reason for leaving the Plain of Jars.

On April 18, the Sunday after we returned from Laos, McCloskey said on the CBS show *Face the Nation:* "There are some 9,400 villages [in Laos], and it looks to me like we have destroyed thousands of them." Waldie and I agreed that McCloskey went beyond any evidence uncovered on our trip. But McCloskey had an intuitive grasp of the bigger picture, and we know now that his assessment was accurate.

Laos is a country the size of California that at the time of the McCloskey visit had a population of three million. From 1964 to 1973, the U.S. dropped more than two million tons of ordnance on Laos during 580,000 bombing missions—equal to a planeload of bombs every eight minutes, twenty-four-hours a day, for nine years and more than the total number of bombs dropped by U.S. planes during World War II. Per capita, Laos was the most heavily bombed country in history. As one Laotian villager recalled, the bombs fell like rain.

Designed to support the Royal Lao Government against the Pathet Lao and to interdict traffic along the Ho Chi Minh Trail, the bombings had at most a minor military purpose and no impact whatsoever on the outcome of the Vietnam War. But they destroyed most villages in ten of Laos' eighteen provinces and created from 700,000 to 1 million refugees. In other words, the bombing displaced from one-fourth to one-third of the entire civilian population of a country with which the United States was not at war, in the process killing scores of thousands of villagers. How is that not a war crime?

The killing continued long after the bombing stopped. As many as a third of the bombs, mostly cluster bombs with multiple "bombies" the size of a tennis ball, did not explode on impact, leaving Laos contaminated with vast quantities of unexploded ordnance that later detonated without warning. Laotian farmers were aware of the danger but needed to feed their families and had no choice except to work the fields. More than twenty thousand people were killed or wounded by unexploded ordnance after the bombing ceased.

The United States withdrew from Vietnam in 1975 after losing a war it had fought for more than a decade. With the Americans also out of Laos, the Pathet Lao made short work of the remnants of the royal government and established a one-party socialist state that remains in power. Two generations later, America is still counting the human costs and debating the legacies of the Vietnam War, but Laos does not loom large in our national consciousness. The secret war there would not be remembered at all in this country except for Barack Obama, who in his second term as president visited Laos. On this trip, in September 2016, Obama did not formally apologize for U.S. actions in Laos, but he vividly acknowledged the results of the bombings.

"Villages and entire valleys were obliterated," Obama said. "Countless civilians were killed. That conflict was another reminder that, whatever the cause, whatever our intentions, war inflicts a wrenching toll, especially on innocent men, women and children."

Obama went on to say that, given its history in Laos, the United States had a "moral obligation to help Laos heal." He pledged $90 million in aid over three years to help Laos detect and dismantle unexploded bombs. This nearly equaled the $100 million the United States had paid for this purpose during the previous twenty years.

I never returned to Laos. Over the years I've continued to track developments there and was pleased when the Pathet Lao government, its professed socialism notwithstanding, decided to allow farmers to profit on what they grow and sell. The population of Laos has more than doubled since the McCloskey trip to a current seven million. Laos remains poor, ranking 116th among 167 countries in 2019 on a global prosperity index.

John Dominis and I broke off from the main group after McCloskey and Waldie had finished interviewing refugees and holed up at a small house on the outskirts of Vientiane with a bottle of Scotch. It was the only time I drank on the trip. Dominis was a star photographer, famous for close-ups of wild animals and an iconic black-and-white photo of African American athletes Tommie Smith and John Carlos raising black-gloved fists in protest at the 1968 Olympics. While we drank, Dominis asked if I would write the text of his photo story in *Life* about McCloskey. He had queried his editors and said *Life* would pay me and probably give me a byline. I told him I needed to ask Walter Ridder, who was paying my expenses. When we reached Thailand, I filed a story and sent a query to Walter, who tersely responded: "Do it." So I did. *Life* paid more than

I expected, but did not give me a byline. I'd imagined as a boy having a bylined story in the only magazine to which my parents subscribed, but kept my disappointment to myself.

Overall, those two-plus weeks in Vietnam and Laos made a formative impression. I'd been skeptical about the merits of the Vietnam War long before this trip and what I'd seen, particularly in Laos, heightened those doubts. Back home, concern over the war seemed to be fading, reflecting Nixon's steady and staged drawdown of U.S. troops. There had been 549,000 such troops in 1969 and would be 69,000 in 1972. But opponents of the war, of whom McCloskey was the most vocal Republican, were determined to bring all Americans home.

McCloskey ran against Nixon for the 1972 Republican presidential nomination. So did Rep. John Ashbrook of Ohio, who believed Nixon had betrayed conservatives. Ashbrook and McCloskey knew each other and were friendly if not close. They also shared a common theme: Nixon could not be trusted. I tracked both candidates for Ridder Publications, with emphasis on McCloskey.

The two congressmen were distant longshots. Nixon's reelection committee was awash in money. Neither congressman was adequately funded; nor had either ever run a national campaign. Ashbrook was dependent on movement conservatives, most of whom held their noses and stuck with Nixon. McCloskey began his campaign as a single-issue peace candidate, denouncing the Vietnam War and its bloody sideshow in Laos. But in June 1971 he allowed reporters to draw him into discussion of other issues. It was a mistake. Garry Wills contended in a *New York Times* column that McCloskey should be a "kamikaze" who should "pick [his] smokestack and head right down it" without concerning himself with other issues.

"Hedging just reduces his credibility," Wills wrote. "Gestures toward a normal candidacy cripple his protest; they look like the promptings of ordinary ambition." Whatever slivers of hope McCloskey or Ashbrook harbored in New Hampshire were extinguished by Nixon's dramatic visit to the People's Republic of China. Nixon visited China from February 21 to February 28, 1972, enabling Americans to see television pictures of China for the first time in more than two decades. Nixon returned to the United States a week before the New Hampshire primary on March 7. During the trip and the weekend afterward, the president was a constant presence on television in New Hampshire, blotting out most TV coverage of the Republican primary. I'd watched the first day of the Nixon trip on television in a New Hampshire café with Ashbrook, who was convinced the timing of the president's visit was no accident. McCloskey's camp held the same view.

"It's over," McCloskey's New Hampshire chairman told me days before the primary. Considering Nixon's enormous advantages, his winning margin was unimpressive. He won easily with 67.6 percent of the vote, which is another way of saying that his two opponents received nearly one-third of the vote from New Hampshire Republicans after a campaign in which they were scarcely visible. McCloskey received just under one-fifth of the vote (19.8 percent) and Ashbrook just under 10 percent.

McCloskey abandoned his presidential campaign the next day, which coincided with the publication date of *The McCloskey Challenge.* He remained on the ballot in a few states, including Massachusetts, where he won 13.5 percent of the vote. After Nixon sewed up the GOP nomination, Pete returned to Congress, where he continued to be an iconoclast on issues ranging from Israel to the environment. In 1982 he ran for the Senate, finishing second to Pete Wilson in a seven-person Republican primary. In 1988 he exposed a fraudulent claim of conservative televangelist Pat Robertson, who was running for president and claimed to be a Marine "combat veteran" of the Korean War. It was Robertson's misfortune that he and McCloskey had been on the same troop ship in the Pacific.

"My single distinct memory,'" McCloskey wrote, "'is of Pat, with a big grin on his face, standing on the dock at Kobe, telling us that his father [Sen. Willis Robertson of Virginia] had gotten him out of combat duty." This revelation wrecked Robertson's presidential campaign in a year when the televangelist was a serious candidate who won four primaries.

After leaving Congress in 1983, Pete settled in California, as I have done. He spoke out often, ran a quixotic (and losing) 2006 congressional campaign in a Republican primary, and afterward changed his party registration and became a Democrat.[3]

I valued McCloskey until he passed away, at age ninety-six, on May 8, 2024. He made his share of mistakes, as we all do, but he spoke truth to power. He was a fearless man, on the battlefield and on the tangled fields of politics.

3. His campaign battle cry was vintage McCloskey: "Congressmen are like diapers," it said. "You need to change them often, and for the same reason."

16

HUBERT HUMPHREY'S LAST HURRAH

Early in 1972, Richard Harwood, assistant managing editor of national affairs at *The Washington Post,* sounded me out again about joining the paper's prestigious national staff. I was interested but indecisive. The first time Harwood approached me, I'd brushed him off by telling him how much I liked my job at Ridder Publications. I was still happy in my work and appreciated Walter Ridder's generous support on the Pete McCloskey project but had become aware of the limitations of being a regional correspondent for a newspaper group with at best a secondary interest in Washington coverage. I was also nearly thirty-nine and believed for some reason that no paper at which I'd want to work would hire me after I turned forty.

But I'd heard stories about *The Post* that gave me pause. Particularly disturbing was a report that Executive Editor Benjamin Bradlee encouraged "creative tension" and would assign different reporters to the same story to see which one did better. I wanted no part of such a demeaning competition. Also, I liked my colleagues in the Ridder bureau and valued our cooperative approach to reporting.

Weighed against this was my admiration for the courage shown by *The Washington Post* in printing the Pentagon Papers and my respect for David Broder, the paper's nonpareil political writer. The thought of working alongside Broder was appealing. I wouldn't learn until years later that Broder had been urging Harwood to hire me.

In February 1972, I went to New Hampshire to report on the presidential primary for Ridder Publications. I spent a day with Senator

Edmund Muskie of Maine, the front-runner for the Democratic presidential nomination. It began at a high school where Muskie lashed out in anger at a polite question asked by a student supporting George McGovern. That night I flew home to Washington on the Muskie plane. Muskie and two aides were playing poker, and press secretary Dick Stewart approached reporters in the back of the plane, seeking a fourth player. When no one volunteered, Stewart turned to me and said, "You play poker, Cannon. Join us."

I prefer playing with friends or fellow reporters rather than with politicians but joined the game. Muskie was having a bad night. After losing several hands, he drew to an inside straight. When he didn't get the needed card, he uttered an oath and threw down his cards with such force they bounced on the cabin floor. I was amazed. The odds of making an inside straight are not great, and we were playing for small stakes. Muskie continued to play but remained in a dour mood for the rest of the flight.

When I told Walter Ridder about my day with Muskie, he suggested I write a column about it. I did, recounting Muskie's conduct at the high school and the poker game and suggesting that his temperament might be too volatile for the presidency. Columns in Ridder newspapers didn't usually attract attention in Washington. I remember hearing from only two people: Broder, who praised me for going beyond the conventional wisdom, and Stewart, who claimed after-the-fact that the poker game had been off-the-record.

Later that month—this was February 1972—Muskie had a famous meltdown at a news conference in front of the *Manchester Union Leader* where he denounced eccentric conservative publisher William Loeb.[1] Press accounts said Muskie had tears in his eyes, although his aides insisted it was melting snow. Whatever the truth, Muskie was politically damaged. Broder showed my column to Harwood with a comment that I had been ahead of the pack.

I didn't know this at the time. Nor did I know that Marie Ridder, Walter's wife and a friend of Harwood since their days covering the fateful presidential campaign of Robert Kennedy, was also boosting me.

1. In his February 26 speech, Muskie called Loeb a liar and denounced him for impugning the character of Muskie's wife, Jane. Newspapers reported that Muskie cried openly, with David Broder writing that Muskie "broke down three times in as many minutes."

(Harwood later told me about the lobbying of Broder and Marie and said it had been unnecessary because he'd been interested in me since reading *Ronnie and Jesse.*) Eventually, Walter Ridder pushed me into making a decision. When I told him about Harwood's overture, Walter seemed surprised I hadn't accepted on the spot. A few days later when I was at the Ridder home, he took me aside.

"Can I talk to you as a friend, my boy?" Walter said.

"Sure, Mr. Ridder," I said. "You're my friend."

"Take the job," Walter said. "They won't come to you a third time."

The next day, I phoned Harwood and said I'd be honored to join the national staff if he still wanted me. He did, but there were hurdles to clear. The first was lunch with Harwood and Ben Bradlee, who asked me about my goals. I said I wanted to do a book on lobbying. Afterward Harwood told me drily that my answer was supposed to be working for *The Washington Post.* But Harwood called later in the day to tell me I'd impressed Ben by answering his question honestly instead of trying to ingratiate myself.

Hurdle No. 2 was finding dates to leave the Ridder bureau and start at *The Post.* I'd hoped to leave at the beginning of April and take a week between jobs. But Al Eisele, the senior correspondent at Ridder, needed extra time to wrap up his dual biography of Hubert Humphrey and Eugene McCarthy,[2] and Walter asked me to stay an extra week. Typically thoughtful, Walter said he'd call Harwood and tell him why I had delayed picking a starting date. They reached an agreement that satisfied them and cost me my week off. I worked my final day for the Ridders on Saturday, April 15, 1972, alone in the bureau, writing a memo for my successor, and I started at *The Washington Post* on Monday, April 17, in the offices at 1150 Fifteenth Street that will be familiar to anyone who saw the movie *All the President's Men.*

The staff had just moved there from offices around the corner that were so traditional they could have served as a set for *The Front Page.* The new offices had open cubicles with the top editors ensconced in separate open offices with a window view. Old-timers grumbled that the new offices were better suited to an insurance company than a newspaper, but I thought this modern newsroom looked grand. A few days earlier, Charles McDowell of the *Richmond Times-Dispatch* had asked

2. *Almost to the Presidency: A Biography of Two American Politicians,* by Albert Eisele, 1972.

me to meet him for coffee. Charlie, one of Washington's best journalists, had heard I was having second thoughts, fearful of being caught up in a rat race of creative tension at *The Post*.

"Don't worry about that," Charlie said. "You just be you and you'll be fine."

Charlie's words comforted me, and he turned out to be right. Assuming a certain level of ability, one's success at any given newspaper depends in part on chemistry and chance. I started work at *The Washington Post* when the paper was booming and adding staff. Two competent reporters were hired on the national staff at roughly the same time I was, and neither made it through the six-month probation period. For me, everything clicked right away and mostly ever after at *The Post*.

I plunged almost immediately into the political campaign. Harwood said that, before he sent me on the road chasing candidates, he wanted me to get the feel of the newsroom on a primary day. So on the night of Tuesday, April 25, with Harwood watching, I assembled a story from the files of reporters who had covered that day's Democratic presidential primaries in Massachusetts and Pennsylvania. Harwood wanted a holding story for the first edition and a write-through for the late city edition, which most subscribers received. But we had enough information for an in-between edition, and I rewrote the first edition lead, telling Harwood I would do another rewrite for the late city. He just nodded, but I could tell he was pleased by my initiative.

My baptism by fire at *The Post* came the following day. Broder, on the road, had been telling the national desk to pay attention to Ted Kennedy, who insisted he was not a candidate for president but was beginning to sound like one. Kennedy had received a standing ovation at the United Auto Workers convention in Atlantic City after denouncing President Nixon for not ending the Vietnam War. UAW president Leonard Woodcock said the union was "ready to enlist in his cause" if Kennedy ran for president.

This next day after perusing a Broder memo, Harwood sent me to Atlantic City. It was early evening. Harwood asked me if I could make the trip. I made a quick call home and said yes. I kept a small overnight bag in the trunk of my car but had no money. This was a day before credit cards were ubiquitous—or even commonplace. No problem, said Harwood. There was a business office on the fifth floor, and Harwood said he had the combination to the safe. When the combination didn't work, Harwood returned to the newsroom and slapped down a twenty-dollar bill on the national desk. Motioning to other editors, Harwood said, "Contribute," and they did.

The national staff intern made a reservation for me on a plane to Atlantic City, flying out of National Airport. It was a small plane, and I had the last seat in the back. Readers will remember my aversion to such planes, dating from a 1960 emergency landing in Reno and reinforced by helicopter flights on the McCloskey trip to Vietnam. It was raining. As the plane skirted thunderstorms and bounced around the night sky, I felt close to losing my dinner, an embarrassment I was spared because there hadn't been time for dinner. I remember thinking I'd made a huge mistake in giving up the comfort of the Ridder bureau for this bumpy flight.

The intern had booked me into a seedy hotel near the Atlantic City boardwalk. I arrived near midnight, slept uneasily, and was awakened early by a tremendous boom. As I tumbled out of bed, my first thought was that the convention center had been bombed. I peered into the hall. There was no one in sight, so I dressed hurriedly, went to the lobby, and confronted a sleepy-eyed hotel clerk, asking him about the explosion.

"They took down the Traymore," he said. "Didn't you know? It was in all the papers and on the radio."

I'd arrived too late to get a newspaper and didn't have a radio. The Traymore, an upscale hotel in art deco style, had been the toast of Atlantic City until it faded as a resort destination in the pre-gambling 1960s. Its takedown, which began that morning of April 27, 1972, put the hotel into the *Guinness Book of Records* for the most explosives used in a controlled demolition. I may have been the only person in Atlantic City who was unaware of its planned destruction.

At least I was up early. After breakfast, I walked down the boardwalk toward the convention center and encountered Paul Schrade, the spade-bearded western regional director of the UAW. He was downcast. I knew Schrade from California, where he'd been wounded the night Robert F. Kennedy was assassinated on June 5, 1968. Long active in labor and liberal causes, Schrade was further radicalized by the killing of Kennedy and became a fierce opponent of the Vietnam War.

"What's the matter, Paul?" I asked.

"They're dumping me," Schrade replied. "After all I've done for the UAW, they're dumping me."

At last, I said to myself. *A story.* I expressed sympathy for Schrade and then interviewed him. He was eager to talk because he felt he was being pushed out of the union leadership for bogus reasons. The rap on Schrade was that he spent too much time on antiwar activities while neglecting union affairs. That may have been true, although Schrade denied it, but the underlying reason he was in hot water was that he'd supported Douglas Fraser, the UAW vice president, against Woodcock for the union presidency in 1970. Fraser's supporters had been gradually purged. Schrade was a favorite with reporters, including me, because he was candid and quotable. Later that day, he was defeated for the regional presidency by Jerry Whipple, president of Los Angeles Local 509 and a Woodcock loyalist. I filed my first story for *The Washington Post.*

It wasn't long before I had my second. When I reached the convention center I inquired about Woodcock's whereabouts. He was in a small office in a back room. I didn't say I wanted to interview him; I told the guard that he wanted to see me. Woodcock spotted me talking to the guard and waved me in. He vaguely remembered me from an interview I'd done while with Ridder Publications and became talkative after I told him I now worked for *The Washington Post.* Woodcock had little to say about Schrade but was distraught that his preferred presidential candidate, Ed Muskie, had imploded in the Pennsylvania and Massachusetts primaries with Humphrey winning the former and McGovern the Bay State. Woodcock said he had telephoned Muskie and advised him to abandon the race. Kennedy, popular with the union's rank and file, was the next option and Woodcock favored him. But realizing that Kennedy was unlikely to run, he praised McGovern's candidacy—giving me my second story of the day, which ran in *The Post* under the headline "Auto Union May Drop Muskie for McGovern."

This story, in turn, gave birth to another. Ohio was the next big state on the Democratic primary calendar, and Cass Stevens, president of the Ohio UAW, was a key member of the Muskie delegate slate. Stevens said he would remain loyal to Muskie but that other union members were on their own. He predicted McGovern would win the Ohio primary, as he subsequently did. I filed a next-day story that ran with the headline "McGovern Picks Up Some UAW chiefs."

When I returned to Washington on Friday, the out-of-town editor, J. D. Alexander, and the political editor, Mary Lou Beatty, were singing my praises. Mary Lou told Broder I'd filed three stories in two days. Broder said it would have been four if the editors had responded more promptly to his memo and sent me to Atlantic City to cover Kennedy. Broder's praise mattered to me, and it mattered even more that Harwood told me I was off to a good start.

The next week, managing editor Howard Simons came by my desk and said, "It seems like you've already been here for a long time." I thanked him and said I hoped I would be. It was good to have his approval. We would never be close, and there was sometimes tension between him and Harwood, but Simons paid more attention to the paper's contents than any other editor and kept mental track of the productivity of reporters. Simons was a key adjutant in the resurgence of *The Washington Post* under the leadership of Katharine Graham and Ben Bradlee, but he often felt that his achievements were underappreciated. Simons, for example, had pried Broder away from the *New York Times*. Later, Simons would believe with some justification that he didn't get sufficient credit for coverage of the Watergate scandal, which he kept going at critical points of the investigation. The Watergate break-in occurred on June 17, two months after I joined the staff of *The Washington Post*.

Putting out a daily newspaper the size of a small book is stressful for the editors and reporters who do it, and in my early months at *The Post* I had yet to discover the fault lines of the newsroom. Nor, for a while, did I know what I was supposed to be doing. Harwood and I had discussed various assignments before I was hired. The environmental beat was vacant, and I was suited for that, but in the process of mentioning this possibility Harwood observed that Bradlee wasn't terribly interested in the environment. It hardly seemed worthwhile to take a beat the top editor disdained. We'd discussed other ideas: Harwood was keen on having me do an overview of the White House, whatever that meant. But our discussions prior to my hiring didn't matter. Once I joined the national staff, I realized Harwood counted on me to find a place for myself. In his hiring practices he resembled a football general manager who drafted players for athletic ability rather than for any specific position. Harwood believed good reporters could cover anything that came their way. So did I.

What came my way in May 1972 was Hubert Horatio Humphrey, the senator from Minnesota, now seeking the presidency. Humphrey had been part of my mental baggage since July 14, 1948, a month after my fifteenth birthday, when his rousing speech at the Democratic National Convention permanently shook up Democratic Party politics. I'd met Humphrey, then a freshman member of the Senate, a year later at Boys Nation and was dazzled by his rapid-fire delivery and command of issues.

The Humphrey who now came into my life as a seasoned political reporter was a battered remnant of this liberal avatar. After fifteen years as a senator from Minnesota, four as Lyndon Johnson's vice president, and a turbulent year in 1968 when he won the Democratic Party's nomination but lost the presidential election to Richard Nixon, Humphrey was a once-flashy fighter who'd taken too many blows. Although he had climbed to his feet in 1970 and again won election to the Senate, Humphrey continued to be disparaged as an apologist for LBJ and especially for the Vietnam War, from which he'd belatedly distanced himself. In 1972, having convinced himself that he'd always questioned the merits of the war, Humphrey was making a final effort to win the presidency.

Biases in the news business abound, but in those days they were more complex than generally realized. The standard conservative complaint of liberal bias in *The Washington Post* news pages was rarely valid when Harwood was overseeing the national report; he made no secret that he wanted to abolish any slant. But there are other kinds of media biases besides ideology or partisanship. One is a preference for the new or novel at the expense of the traditional or timeworn. In 1972, George McGovern was new and George Wallace's appeal to working-class Democrats was newsworthy. Humphrey was old hat. Apart from Broder and his panoramic view of the campaign, no one at *The Post* was taking notice of Humphrey, or so his well-connected advisors complained to Bradlee and publisher Kay Graham. These complaints were passed down to Harwood, who initially discounted them. No one told Harwood which candidates to cover. But he paid attention to facts on the ground and, after Muskie's collapse and Humphrey's victory in the Pennsylvania primary, Harwood decided to put a reporter full-time on the Minnesota senator. He picked me because I knew Humphrey and was available.

It was great fun at first. Humphrey was accessible and quotable, and I was getting stories into the paper and compliments from the editors. On the road, *The Post* provided resources I'd only dreamed about. You could file by Western Union or dictate stories to a rewrite bank. You were backstopped by first-rate copy editors who caught your errors even while irritating you with pedantic questions. *The Post* even had a researcher, the brilliant Joan Shorenstein. She was technically Broder's researcher but checked quotes and dates for me as well. Such help was invaluable in the days before computers when you were alone in the field and dependent on your memory.

Humphrey was competitive in the Midwest. He won the Indiana and Ohio primaries on May 2 and ran close to McGovern in the Nebraska primary a week later. On the same day, May 9, Humphrey had an even more satisfying primary victory in West Virginia, where twelve years earlier he'd lost to John F. Kennedy. That victory in 1960 was decisive for Kennedy; it showed a Catholic could win a heavily Protestant state. In 1972, it was Humphrey's turn to view his victory in West Virginia as an augury of future success. He gave an emotional post-primary speech that included a grace note for the martyred JFK: "West Virginia was a place where I personally suffered a political defeat but the nation gained a great president."

Many reporters used this as the lede. I put it in the third paragraph and led with HHH's telephone call to country singer Jimmy Wofford, who had cried on Humphrey's shoulder the night he lost to JFK. "At last you got hold of the right song," Humphrey told Wofford.

The fun went out of the campaign on May 15 when George Wallace, campaigning in Laurel, Maryland, was shot five times by Arthur Bremer, who described himself in his diary as an "unemployed malcontent who fancies himself a writer." Before Wallace was shot, many of us in the press corps had nourished an illusion that the bad days of 1968, when Martin Luther King and Bobby Kennedy were murdered, were behind us. The Wallace shooting was a grim reminder that would-be assassins are a permanent part of the American political landscape.

The former Alabama governor was the most popular segregationist in the nation. The day after he was shot, he won Democratic primaries in both Maryland and Michigan. Exit polls in Michigan suggested that Wallace's position on issues mattered more to voters than sympathy for him because of the shooting. The former governor of Alabama had campaigned fiercely against the "forced busing" of schoolchildren to achieve racial balance, while excoriating supposed "welfare chiselers." Campaigning in Michigan, Wallace never singled out African Americans, but he didn't have to. My *Post* colleague George Lardner, who understood Wallace's modes of behavior, recalled that in one southern speech, after his standard denunciation of welfare cheats, Wallace paused for the inevitable applause and added: "You know who I mean."

The shooting left Wallace paralyzed from the waist down and effectively ended his campaign. He'd won ten primaries, all in the South except for Michigan, and received nearly as many votes as Humphrey and McGovern. If Wallace had been able to continue campaigning, he might have wound up with the most total votes. Although there was no plausible scenario under which the Democratic Party would have allowed him to become its presidential nominee, Wallace had demonstrated the disenchantment of white working-class Democrats with the party's supposed civil rights consensus.

Politically, McGovern benefited from Wallace's incapacity. The South Dakota senator had a head start over Humphrey and was gradually widening his delegate lead. By mid-May, McGovern and Humphrey had each won three primaries, but McGovern had won caucuses in five states compared to only one for Humphrey. Most states divided delegates proportionally, so McGovern picked up delegates even in states he lost. For example, Humphrey had won Ohio narrowly, gaining seventy-five delegates in the process but, even while losing, McGovern had picked up sixty-five delegates. Since California law then required political parties to use a winner-take-all system, the June 6 primary became all-important. Whoever won California's 271 delegates was virtually certain to be the Democratic nominee.

I spent the last two weeks of May and the first week of June in California mostly with Humphrey but switched off for a couple of days with McGovern. Humphrey had taken up residence in the Beverly Hilton in Beverly Hills, from which he ventured forth daily to campaign by bus or plane. I'd made a strategic reservation on Humphrey's hotel floor and twice buttonholed the Minnesota senator as he stepped off the elevator. Humphrey was even more talkative than usual during a campaign he knew could be his last hurrah. He conducted nightly briefings for reporters in an aide's hotel room with Humphrey sitting on the couch and most of the reporters on the floor. These became vivid seminars in political science as Humphrey looked back at his three decades in politics. The ground rules of these sessions banned recordings or note-taking and showed a vulnerable side of Humphrey, who confided that his campaign was broke. When he wasn't talking to reporters, Humphrey was on the phone with donors who had bankrolled him in the past, pleading for money to run more television commercials. One night he was late briefing us because he'd been talking to a wealthy contributor many of us knew.

"I just hated asking [the contributor] to give again," Humphrey said. "I hate begging for money."

The Humphrey campaign was not equal to these briefings. Although Humphrey held his own in three televised debates with McGovern, most of his public events were haphazard affairs. The nadir was a Humphrey visit to a Lockheed plant where McGovern's vote against a Lockheed loan guarantee was a significant issue, but Humphrey's staff couldn't even tell reporters the purpose of the visit. In contrast, when I switched off Humphrey and traveled with McGovern, reporters were given demographic data and a political sketch of every county they visited.

I compared the two campaigns nine days before the election in what turned out to be a prescient story. "McGovern Camp Capturing California's Political Flavor," said the headline. The superiority of the McGovern campaign and other factors had "combined to create the potential for a decisive [McGovern] victory" in the June 6 California primary, I wrote.

On Election Day, McGovern defeated Humphrey by nearly 5 percent of the vote. Humphrey ran well in Los Angeles County and Orange County, but his relatively narrow margin of victory was more than offset by lopsided McGovern margins in the San Francisco Bay Area. George Wallace, Ed Muskie, and Shirley Chisholm, the first woman in a Democratic primary, received 14 percent of the vote among them even though Wallace and Muskie were no longer in the race.

Politicians often have illusions of indispensability, and Humphrey resisted the verdict of the California electorate. With the Democratic National Convention in Miami Beach approaching in July, Humphrey challenged California's winner-take-all rules and asked the Democratic Credentials Committee to redistribute the state's 271 delegates proportionally. Had this happened, McGovern would have fallen short of the delegate number he needed to be nominated.

It was a cynical gambit. Four years earlier, the assassination of Robert Kennedy had thrown the Democrats into turmoil, and Humphrey became the party's nominee without winning a single primary. Democrats vowed this would not happen again and rewrote their rules so that the candidate who won the most delegates in the primaries would be the nominee. Humphrey had supported this change. He also acknowledged he would have opposed altering the winner-take-all system if he had won the California primary.

Humphrey returned to his home in Lake Waverly, Minnesota, after the California primary. I returned to Washington, where Harwood asked me how Humphrey justified his challenge. He doesn't justify it, I said, he's just doing it.

On June 27, in the run-up to the Miami Beach convention, the party's Credentials Committee met in Washington and, by a six-vote margin, stunned the political world by upholding the Humphrey challenge. The rationale of the committee majority was that Democratic Party rules, drawn by a commission McGovern had headed before he became a candidate, frowned on winner-take-all and that this took precedence over a California law requiring it. Since McGovern had received nearly 44 percent of the primary vote in California, the committee allotted him only 44 percent of the delegates—120 of the state's 271 delegates. The other 151 delegates were awarded to a coalition dominated by Humphrey supporters that also included delegates whose first choice would have been Wallace or Muskie. Reporters dubbed it the "ABC" Coalition—Anybody But McGovern. The Credentials Committee demonstrated the power of organized labor, which was in Humphrey's corner and had quietly packed the committee. It also highlighted the national inexperience of McGovern, who had overlooked the credentials process in favor of the Platform Committee, where his people had carved out left-of-center positions on income redistribution and defense spending.

"It is dirty; it is cold politics," wrote Theodore White; "a handful of people, manipulating a committee of 150 individuals, had denied the validity of the law and voting of California, a state of twenty million people."[3] White called the result the "Humphrey steal," and his outrage was widely shared. Harwood and Meg Greenfield, deputy editorial page editor of *The Post,* suggested I write a column about what had happened. It ran at the top of the op-ed page under the headline, "The Two Faces of Humphrey."

> There are two Hubert Humphreys parading around these days, and one of them is getting in the way of the other. Humphrey No. 1 is the extraordinarily knowledgeable senator whose quarter-century record of achievement in civil rights, arms control and social legislation probably is unmatched on Capitol Hill.
>
> This Humphrey is a resolute internationalist with few illusions

3. *The Making of The President 1972,* by Theodore H. White, 1973, p. 173.

> about the present and potential striking power of the Soviet Union, a Humphrey who believes that the defense budget reductions advocated by Senator George McGovern go too far too fast and rely more than they should on the "glamour" defense of the submarine.
>
> Humphrey No. 1 is sincerely worried that a threatened "elitism" within the Democratic Party portends a political disaster for his Democrats. He believes that he can have a significant impact on his party's platform and his country's future if he stands up for what he believes at the Democratic National Convention.
>
> Humphrey No. 2 also is going to the convention, but with a different goal in mind. This Humphrey, buoyed by a victory in the Credentials Committee, is willing to ignore his own past positions to accomplish his aims and to redistribute the delegates won fairly by McGovern in the California primary on a proportional basis. Humphrey No. 2 now says he was "simply wrong" in declaring before the California vote that he should have challenged the primary at that time or not at all.

The column continued in this vein, describing Humphrey's various rationalizations but also saying he'd made "substantive points" about the defense budget and in pointing out that the poor, the aged, and working youth were underrepresented at the Democratic convention:

This column appeared on July 1, 1972, and angered Humphrey campaign chairman Jack Chestnut. Because Humphrey's victory in the Credentials Committee raised the possibility he could become the Democratic nominee, my editors wanted me to interview the candidate and write a profile of him before the convention began in Miami Beach on July 10. Humphrey had been available for interviews on the campaign trail but was now back in Lake Waverly, and Chestnut wouldn't let me see him.

Referencing my column, Chestnut asked, "Which Humphrey do you want to see?"

"Either of them," I replied.

"Well, they're not available," Chestnut said with a smirk.

Humphrey's campaign staff was an odd mix of the starry-eyed and the sleazy. The staff's lower rungs were crowded with idealists who'd followed him for years, some who had carried the torch as far back as 1960. They were augmented by young volunteers whose chief recommendation was their adoration of Humphrey. There was nothing starry-eyed about Chestnut, a gimlet-eyed Minneapolis lawyer with access to corporate contributors. I think Chestnut used my column as an excuse to shut me out—what he really disliked was that I'd been quietly probing into his dubious fundraising for Humphrey's 1970 Senate campaign. I never found a smoking gun, but the Watergate special prosecutor did. Chestnut would be convicted by a jury for obtaining and disguising an illegal $12,000 campaign contribution ($100,000 today) and sentenced to four months in prison.

But that didn't happen until 1975. In the first week of July 1972, Chestnut blocked me from seeing Humphrey, as I informed my editors. Simons liked my Humphrey coverage but said the paper would have to send another reporter to interview him if he wouldn't see me. Harwood didn't like the idea of a campaign manager choosing the correspondent who would interview his candidate, but time was fleeting and I understood Simons's point. Expressing more confidence than I felt, I told both editors I had contacts in Minnesota who could connect me to Humphrey.

The next day I flew to the Twin Cities and through one of these contacts obtained Humphrey's private unlisted phone number. When I dialed it, the phone was answered by an aide whom I'd known while at Ridder Publications. He said he had a high opinion of me but was under orders to keep me away from Humphrey. I told the aide I wanted to hear this from Humphrey himself and asked that he bring the senator to the phone. If he doesn't want me to see me, I said, I'll accept his decision without argument.

Humphrey came to the phone. "Where have you been, Lou?" he asked heartily.

"I need to interview you for a story," I said.

"Come on out," Humphrey said and put the aide who'd answered the call back on the phone to give me directions to Lake Waverly, an hour's drive away.

Senator Humphrey greeted me at the door and led me into his comfortably modest home. We talked for two hours. Humphrey was so voluble I was reminded of the time eighteen years earlier when he'd addressed the Young Democrats of San Francisco, quipping that some pastors don't understand the difference between immortality and eternity and talk forever. Humphrey then talked for a solid hour.

In Lake Waverly, Humphrey was relaxed and thoughtful, as he'd been in those late-night sessions with reporters during the California primary. He was generous to McGovern and treated the Credentials Committee's decision to deny the South Dakota senator a majority of the California delegates as a procedural issue of no great importance. Perhaps Humphrey's accumulated political savvy made him realize that the Credentials Committee action was too outlandish to hold.

And hold it did not, thanks to two savvy pols: the charismatic Willie Brown, cochair of the McGovern delegates from California, and the storied Larry O'Brien. The convention chairman, O'Brien was known for his longstanding connections to the Kennedy family and a lifelong devotion to the Democratic Party. On Sunday, July 9, the day before the convention opened, he ruled that the 120 delegates the Credentials Committee had awarded to McGovern could be seated and vote on the California challenge. The 151 delegates the Credentials Committee had awarded to the ABC coalition were not eligible to vote.

O'Brien gave a second—and crucial—gift to McGovern on July 10, the first night of the convention, when he ruled in favor of a motion to unseat the pro-Humphrey coalition and award all the Golden State's delegates to McGovern. Other challenges had been settled before the California vote and it was now after midnight. A roll-call vote supported O'Brien's ruling, launching another fight that challenged the ruling of the chair. McGovern might have lost these votes except for a three-minute speech by Willie Brown that galvanized the convention. Brown had memorized the names of all the Blacks, Hispanics, women, and young people he called "my delegates" and pointed out that they precisely met the quota-like diversity tests demanded by the new Democratic rules. These quotas repelled many convention viewers but were of scriptural importance to a majority of delegates in Miami Beach.

"Give me back my delegation!" Brown thundered at the conclusion of the most memorable speech of the 1972 Democratic convention. The delegates did.[4]

4. The best description of Brown's role at the convention is provided in *Willie Brown: A Biography*, by James Richardson, 1996. White's *The Making of the President 1972* provides a superior account of the political maneuvering that led to rejection of the Humphrey challenge but mostly ignores Brown's contribution to the outcome.

Watching Brown's speech from his hotel suite, Humphrey realized he had lost and moved quickly to endorse McGovern.

"We have fought the good fight," Humphrey said; "we bow out now with a spirit of friendship and understanding, as a good Democrat."

Although I believed Humphrey would have been the stronger candidate against President Nixon, McGovern had earned the nomination. As for Humphrey, my treasured memory of him would always be his declaration at the 1948 Democratic National Convention that Democrats must "get out of the shadow of states' rights and walk forthrightly into the bright sunshine of human rights." This speech provoked a southern walkout but led the Democrats to adopt a civil rights plank for the first time. I was fifteen, and my father and I had listened to Humphrey's speech on the radio. This was the good Humphrey, and it was comforting to have him back.

On July 11, 1972, the day before McGovern was nominated, I covered Humphrey's exit. My story in *The Post* was headlined "HHH Quest Ends":

> Hubert H. Humphrey's long quest for the presidency ended in defeat today with a tear for his staff and a pledge to his country.
>
> With his voice trembling, and his head held high, Humphrey released his delegates and vowed to continue seeking "a nation governed with justice and compassion."
>
> Later, in a candid discussion of his own campaign in his hotel suite, Humphrey said he had learned much he never knew from his third and final attempt to become President.
>
> ". . . There is a change of mood in the country," Humphrey said. "I can't quite identify it but there is a change and I don't think I would be as good a man in public life as I will be had I missed the chance to test that change. I'm a more sensitive person now to what really is going on than I would have been had I just become smugly content with being a United States senator, $42,500 a year for six years. . . . I have been out and I have tasted the fruit of the land."

Humphrey's self-assessment to a small group of reporters, one of them me, came eight hours after a withdrawal statement to an overflow news conference in a room also packed with Humphrey staff members, many of them young volunteers who'd worked without pay. Before the news conference, Humphrey had called his wife, Muriel, in Lake Waverly to tell her he was withdrawing. She'd been expecting it—her main concern, as she'd told her husband two weeks earlier, was not that he would lose but that he would be too critical of McGovern. Humphrey also called financial backers S. Harrison (Sonny) Dogole and Eugene Wyman and met privately with a few advisors, including longtime friend Edgar Berman and deputy campaign manager Lloyd Hand to tell them he would spend the rest of his life working for social justice in America. He repeated that pledge at the withdrawal ceremony, adding "I'm going to be a senator. I'm not going back to the drugstore."

When Humphrey said that it was better to have sought the presidency and lost than not to have run at all, the volunteers began to weep. Berman and other Humphrey old-timers in the room wept with them. Humphrey himself had remained dry-eyed, but the response of the staff overcame him.

"I'd like to ask you if I could wipe away a tear," he said, as his staff rose in a sustained and spontaneous ovation.

I had a few moments with Senator Humphrey the day after this splendid leave-taking. He thanked me for my coverage, saying nothing about my "Two Faces of Humphrey" column. Then he repeated his public pledge to help McGovern. I'm sure he appreciates that, I said.

Neither of us knew then that McGovern's successful effort to overcome Humphrey at the convention had distracted the South Dakota senator from a key decision that would doom his general election campaign against Richard Nixon.

17

THE NON-CAMPAIGN OF RICHARD NIXON

Landslides in presidential elections are not normally subject to second-guessing. No one thinks Alfred Landon could have beaten Franklin Roosevelt in 1936 with a different strategy. Nor would Barry Goldwater have upset Lyndon Johnson in 1964 by tacking to the center after he was nominated, although this might have saved some moderate Republican candidates in that Democratic landslide. Landon won two states, Goldwater six. In 1972, Richard Nixon swamped George McGovern, who carried only Massachusetts. Even so, journalists and historians still speculate about how McGovern might have fared had he chosen someone other than Senator Thomas Eagleton of Missouri as his running mate.

On paper, Eagleton seemed a safe choice. He was a Roman Catholic with a liberal voting record from what was then a swing state and had the backing of organized labor, which was suspicious of McGovern. At forty-two, Eagleton was one of the youngest members of the Senate; he had served in the U.S. Navy, graduated from Harvard Law School, and had never lost an election. But unknown to McGovern, Eagleton suffered from clinical depression in an era when stigma attached to any form of mental illness. Eagleton had checked into a hospital three times between 1960 and 1966 for physical and nervous exhaustion, twice receiving shock therapy. Later, he would be diagnosed as bipolar.

McGovern selected Eagleton because everyone else had turned him down, starting with his first choice of Ted Kennedy, and also because the Humphrey challenge had deprived him of time to do much vetting of a Senate colleague he barely knew. McGovern believed he needed to clinch the nomination before he could credibly proffer the second spot on the ticket. He wasn't assured of victory until the early morning hours of July 11, when the convention rejected the Humphrey credentials challenge and seated McGovern's California delegates. McGovern was nominated on July 12. The next morning, his staff and advisors assembled in a Doral Hotel conference room under the direction of Frank Mankiewicz to review vice presidential possibilities. This was cutting it close: McGovern's choice for vice president would be announced that night.

McGovern's sleep-deprived advisors discussed a range of possibilities before reaching consensus on Boston Mayor Kevin White, whose name was forwarded to McGovern. But the Massachusetts delegation, informed of the recommendation, objected to White because he had originally backed Ed Muskie. Professor John Kenneth Galbraith, leader of the Massachusetts delegates, conveyed this objection to McGovern and made a passionate plea that he choose someone else.

McGovern then offered the number-two spot to several senators, all of whom declined. One of them, Senator Gaylord Nelson of Wisconsin, recommended Eagleton, whose name had been bandied about by McGovern's advisors at the morning meeting before they settled on White. McGovern agreed. He called Eagleton at his crowded suite in a nearby hotel and asked him to be his running mate. Eagleton accepted. Before making it official, however, McGovern put Mankiewicz on the phone to ask the Missouri senator if he there was anything in his background that could embarrass the campaign. Eagleton said there was not.

Although Eagleton had concealed his hospitalizations in his Missouri campaigns, there was a below-the-surface buzz about them in the state's political community that McGovern's advisors probably would have detected if they'd had even a single day to perform their due diligence. Instead, they'd simply taken Eagleton at his word. Within hours of Eagleton's nomination, McGovern aides were hearing about his hospital stays. Knight Newspaper reporters Clark Hoyt and Robert Boyd compiled a two-page dossier on Eagleton's hospitalizations and flew to South Dakota to confront McGovern. This enabled the McGovern campaign to have Eagleton announce the hospitalizations himself, which he did at a press conference on July 25.[1]

1. Boyd said that informing McGovern of Eagleton's hospitalizations was "the fair and decent thing to do." They didn't anticipate McGovern using the information to preempt their story. Many reporters believed McGovern had taken advantage of

Eagleton offered to resign, but McGovern defended him, saying he was "1,000 percent" behind his running mate. During the next two weeks, as pressure mounted on Democrats to dump Eagleton, McGovern climbed further out on a shaky limb, which made him look foolish and weak when he forced Eagleton to quit eighteen days after he had put him on the ticket.

I wasn't involved in this story, having returned to Washington, where the editors informed me that I'd be covering the Nixon campaign in the fall. Although these assignments came in question form ("Will you?" works better than "You will," Simons was fond of saying), reporters were expected to answer in the affirmative. I looked forward to the assignment and valued my editors. Mary Lou Beatty was witty and sharp. Harwood was Harwood, gruff and reliable.

McGovern was scheduled to announce his replacement for Eagleton on August 5, 1972. Harwood called me that morning and said Ben Bradlee had been tipped that Larry O'Brien would be the new running mate. That didn't sound right to me. O'Brien, a savvy Irish American politician, had managed the successful senatorial and presidential campaigns of John F. Kennedy, and didn't view himself as an officeholder. Nor did anyone else. He'd come into the Democratic National Convention in 1972 as party chairman and wanted to continue in that role. (It was O'Brien's office that had been broken into by the Watergate burglars in June.) Instead, McGovern spurned O'Brien for Jean Westwood, an early supporter, and I saw no way he would pick O'Brien for the number-two spot. Harwood agreed with my analysis but said we always checked out Bradlee tips. So that night I went to the eight-story residential annex of the Wardman Hotel where O'Brien lived and waited for him in the lobby.

Three other reporters, two from local radio stations, were also waiting in the lobby. *They must have the same source as Bradlee,* I thought. When O'Brien arrived, he told us he had no idea who was going to replace Eagleton, but was sure it wasn't him. Graciously, he invited us to join him in his residence. O'Brien said the television had gone out earlier in the day (*Why didn't he get it fixed?* I wondered), and he was planning to listen to McGovern on the radio.

Boyd and Hoyt. In 1973 the two reporters shared a Pulitzer Prize for their enterprising journalism.

We took the elevator upstairs to O'Brien's suite, and he tuned to the station that was carrying McGovern's speech. All we heard was static. When did this thing stop working? O'Brien asked no one in particular. No one responded, so O'Brien told an aide to call down for his car and put it in the driveway. We can listen to McGovern on the car radio, O'Brien said. I found this comedy of errors off-putting. Larry O'Brien was a big shot, even though he didn't act like one. But how was it that he didn't have a working television or radio? Still, we had no alternative except to go down to the driveway and surround O'Brien's car while he turned up the radio volume, and McGovern announced his choice of Sargent Shriver. While we were listening, John Daly of *What's My Line* fame and his wife, Virginia Warren, Earl Warren's daughter, who also lived at the Wardman, came down the driveway. They asked O'Brien if everything was all right.

"I saw you all around the car and thought there might have been an accident," Daly said.

"There has been," replied O'Brien.

We all laughed, but the Eagleton accident doomed any hope McGovern had of running a competitive campaign. It was a longshot to begin with, but there were hints before Eagleton that McGovern might make it competitive. Pollster Lou Harris put McGovern within seven points of Nixon in June and within ten points in July. But the bottom dropped out after the Eagleton debacle.

David Broder believed Nixon was always on track to win but that the Eagleton affair cost McGovern a chance to make a respectable showing that would have made him the Democratic frontrunner in 1976. Pat Caddell, McGovern's twenty-two-year-old pollster, claimed McGovern could have won eight or ten states sans the Eagleton affair. I was skeptical, but Broder noted that voter turnout in 1972 was significantly lower than in the three previous presidential elections. Millions of Democrats just didn't vote.

One of McGovern's problems was that Nixon's "Vietnamization" policy had removed the Vietnam War as an urgent issue for American voters. McGovern saw the fallacy of this, for U.S. support forces were still engaged, but he did not do well in communicating this perception to the American people. He never came close to the righteous thunder he had expressed while opposing a war-funding bill in 1970.

"Every senator in this chamber is partly responsible for sending 50,000 young Americans to an early grave," he said then. "This chamber reeks of blood. Every senator here is partly responsible for that human wreckage at Walter Reed and Bethesda Naval and all across our land—young men without legs, or arms, or genitals, or faces or hopes."

The Eagleton affair enabled Nixon to hide in plain sight during the 1972 election campaign, ignoring McGovern and avoiding the press. Reporters assigned to the Nixon campaign found ourselves covering Vice President Spiro Agnew instead of the president. Nixon limited his appearances to set-piece events such as a ticker-tape parade through Atlanta in an open car. His avoidance of all but the friendliest of journalists spared Nixon questions about the Watergate burglary, which *Washington Post* reporters Bob Woodward and Carl Bernstein were pursuing with determination.

Even before the Watergate break-in, I was having trouble penetrating the Nixon presidency. Working for *The Washington Post* opened many doors but closed them at the Nixon White House. I knew Nixon and H. R. Haldeman from California and John Ehrlichman from researching my book about Pete McCloskey. Haldeman and Ehrlichman, both lawyers and Christian Scientists, had been classmates at UCLA. They'd been dubbed the "Berlin Wall" because of their German surnames and their effectiveness in serving as wary gatekeepers for Nixon. While at Ridder Publications, I'd enjoyed reasonably good White House access, particularly to Ehrlichman, a former Seattle land-use attorney with a decent environmental record.[2] He'd been a useful source, but he warned me that this was about to change. At the Sans Souci, then a favorite Washington restaurant for reporters and their sources, Ehrlichman told me that because *The Post* was "hostile" to President Nixon he could no longer be a source of mine. I asked Ehrlichman if I'd ever misquoted him or misused information he had given me. No, said Ehrlichman, *but that wasn't the point.* Ehrlichman seldom returned my calls after that. We never had lunch again.

2. In *The Making of the President 1972*, Theodore White lauded Ehrlichman's good-government impulses. "His shop was one of the few at the White House where ideas were seriously entertained—good ideas, too, on energy, on land-use policy, on urbanization, on preservation of the American environment." But this shop was dissolved after it became involved in the operation of the Plumbers, who burglarized the office of Daniel Ellsberg's psychiatrist.

Thankfully, I wasn't yet the White House correspondent for *The Post.* That challenging beat in the Nixon years was capably occupied by Carroll Kilpatrick, a mannerly southerner known for his professionalism and kindness to newcomers, including me. Carroll was so highly regarded by the White House press corps that even Ronald Ziegler, the smooth-talking White House press secretary, treated him with respect. I had little use for Ziegler, who'd worked in Haldeman's advertising agency and tended to be evasive even when openness would have served him better. Frustrated, I tried to gain perspective on the Nixon presidency by interviewing Republican members of Congress I'd known while working for the Ridders. But they were frustrated, too. House Republicans seeking reelection in 1972 complained they had little communication, let alone assistance, from the Committee for the Re-Election of the President, with its marvelously apt acronym of CREEP.

The Nixon reelection committee was headed by Clark MacGregor, who had replaced disgraced former Attorney General John Mitchell. MacGregor had been a moderate House member from a suburban Minneapolis district and supporter of the civil rights legislation in the 1960s. He'd been closely covered by the Ridders, most recently in an unsuccessful 1970 Senate race he'd lost to Hubert Humphrey. Afterwards, MacGregor joined the Nixon White House as a member of the legislative liaison team. I had called him twice when working for the Ridders; he'd returned the calls promptly and answered my questions. But when I called him as a reporter for *The Post,* it took two days for MacGregor to get back to me and, when he did, he launched into a tirade about the alleged anti-Nixon bias of the paper, particularly savaging Bob Woodward's Watergate stories. This was in late July 1972 when Woodward's and Bernstein's reporting on the Watergate affair was in its infancy. I was astounded. So was David Broder, who had a good relationship with MacGregor. Broder counseled me not to become discouraged.

"It's not you who's different," he said. "It's them."

I was struck by the number of people who blamed the skullduggeries ("dirty tricks") of the administration that were coming to light on Nixon subordinates, most often Haldeman or Ehrlichman. To me, that didn't hold up. In California, Haldeman had been a mainstream Republican who during the 1966 campaign for governor had asked Ronald Reagan to soft-pedal his attacks on UC-Berkeley student activists. As a member of the University of California board of regents, Haldeman worked with liberal Fred Dutton to find a compromise between Reagan and Democratic leader Jesse Unruh on the thorny issue of university tuition. Haldeman and Dutton had briefed reporters on their proposal, which I thought more sensible than the plans offered by Reagan or Unruh. As for Ehrlichman, he and his wife had taken in Pete McCloskey's wife, Cubby, while McCloskey was serving as a U.S. Marine in Korea.

Haldeman and Ehrlichman would serve prison time for covering up the Watergate scandal (and in Ehrlichman's case for approving the break-in of the office of Daniel Ellsberg's psychiatrist). But as Reagan said about both men, "They weren't criminals at heart." It wasn't the men around Nixon who turned his presidency into a lawless conspiracy. It was Nixon, always Nixon, who as Haldeman's diaries later revealed, was in on the Watergate crime and the cover-up from the beginning. His reelection slogan—"Nixon's the One"—was more revealing than intended.

Years later, my belief that the Nixon administration's unrelenting hostility toward the media originated at the very top was verified by the National Archives release of a July 30, 1972, memo from the president to Haldeman. Composed at Camp David, the memo was a three-page rant against the press prompted by a political story I'd written about the Nixon reelection effort published in *The Post* that Sunday morning. My article was a straightforward scene-setter on the state of the Nixon campaign as the general election contest against George McGovern took shape. But Nixon tells his White House chief of staff that my story should be a catalyst for "ironclad rules" when dealing with "media representatives that we know are antagonistic to us."

My story wasn't antagonistic at all. I quoted—by name—Haldeman, Clark MacGregor, and Republican National Committee chairman Robert Dole. The story's tone was neither unfriendly toward Republicans nor pessimistic about the GOP's chances in November. What seems to have galled Nixon was my release of state polling (which the campaign itself had been releasing), a reference to possible Republican vulnerability on the issue of abortion, and a couple of blind quotes from Republicans about how Nixon may have been overconfident in his presidential campaigns of 1960 and 1968. In his own words Nixon comes across as a paranoid, thin-skinned micromanager who is needlessly combative.

The guidelines he was instructing Haldeman to decree included having a member of the White House press office sit in on every interview and, incredibly, having a Nixon campaign aide slyly follow Dole and

MacGregor around town and discreetly tape-record every public remark they made.

Nearly a year after this memo was written, White House lawyer John Dean revealed to a congressional committee investigating Watergate the existence of a White House "enemies list." Included on the original catalog of twenty names were famous actor Paul Newman, Common Cause president Morton Halperin, and two Black congressmen, John Conyers of Michigan and California Democrat Ron Dellums, whom I knew from my days in the Bay Area. Two journalists—CBS correspondent Daniel Schorr and *Washington Star* columnist (and future *Post* colleague of mine) Mary McGrory—were on the initial list. Many more journalists would be on a second list subsequently made public. But his memo about my story reveals that Nixon regarded virtually the entire press corps as his enemy, as its third paragraph reveals:

> First of all, it is vitally important than only the most intelligent and sophisticated person on our campaign staff dare to go in the ring with one of these people. Second, we should not waste time with one of them at the expense of turning down interests with media representatives who are our friends. Third, even when our most intelligent people are meeting with people like Cannon they must constantly keep in mind that they are confronting a political enemy and that everything they say will, therefore, be used against us. I had to emphasize this over and over again because we never seem to get it across to our people no matter how many times they get burned.

In truth, Richard Nixon's own worst enemy was Richard Nixon. The president's centrality in the Watergate scandal wasn't known in the summer of 1972, not even at *The Washington Post,* which led the investigation. Nor was it known to Bob Dole. More than anyone else, Dole rescued me from the sour mood I was in because no one of importance in the Nixon campaign would talk to me. Dole's job required him to defend Nixon, which he did effectively and with a partisan edge. He'd also taken a few shots at my paper. To Dole, this was "just business" in the words of that year's blockbuster movie, *The Godfather.* Off the record (and, later, on the record) Dole expressed misgivings about Nixon and his gatekeepers, while maintaining good relations with reporters, including me. Unlike Ehrlichman or MacGregor, Dole didn't give a fig where I worked. He saw relationships with reporters as personal, based on mutual trust.

I was impressed by Dole's personal story. How could you not be? As a twenty-one-year-old second lieutenant and Tenth U.S. Army Mountain Division platoon leader on an Italian mountainside two months before World War II ended in Europe, Dole had been gravely wounded in the back and right arm by German artillery fire while trying to pull his radioman to safety. This action earned Dole a Bronze Star for valor, but it was perilously close to being a posthumous award. A fellow soldier gave Dole a huge dose of morphine and wrote "M" for "morphine" on his forehead in Dole's blood, so that whoever found him would not give him a second, fatal dose.

Over the next thirty-nine months in a U.S. veterans' hospital, Dole lapsed in and out of consciousness, lost a kidney, lost the use of his right arm and most of the feeling in his left arm. He'd been a lean and muscular three-sport high school athlete—good enough in basketball that legendary University of Kansas coach Phog Allen invited him to try out for KU's team. But when Dole looked in a mirror during his long convalescence, he did not recognize himself. Dole was close to giving up when Hampar Kelikian, a Chicago orthopedist and survivor of the Armenian genocide, inspired him to "focus on what I had left and what I could do with it, rather than complaining what had been lost."

What Dole did with what he had left was pursue a political career that surpassed any heights he would have achieved in sports. He became so expert in concealing his disabilities that even his fellow senators did not realize he had no use of his right hand and that his left was partly numb. Dole wore shoes without laces because he could not tie them. When he ate in public, he favored finger food because he could not cut food with a knife.

Dole had a sense of humor that rivaled Ronald Reagan's although it was not as self-deprecating. He skewered Democrats and Republicans alike with a mordant wit that irritated Nixon and Haldeman. On August 2, 1972, Dole held a news conference to preview the Republican National Convention, which that year was largely a coronation of Nixon.

"It's so exciting that I can hardly wait to get there," Dole deadpanned. He then described floor demonstrations that would be "spontaneous for ten or fifteen minutes."

Was Nixon accessible? "They say the president is hard to see, but that's not true," Dole said. "I called one of those assistant presidents the other day and asked to see him. They said you can see him at 8 p.m. on Channel Four or 9 p.m. on Channel Seven."

The paragraph above was cut from my story on Dole's press conference, but the editors kept my kicker: "Dole made a jesting reference to allegations of GOP involvement in the break-in and alleged bugging of Democratic national headquarters here June 17. When the [Dole] news conference was delayed at the start because of microphone problems, he stepped forward and announced: 'A lot of our sound men are busy.'"[3]

I was told by a Republican source that when Haldeman read this story he denounced Dole as disloyal, a perception ratified when CBS used this line as well. "Nixon and Haldeman believe that *The Washington Post* and CBS are joined in a conspiracy to bring down the president," my source told me.

Dole remained as party chairman through Nixon's reelection. Two months later, Nixon dumped him and brought in George H. W. Bush to head the RNC. Dole saw the hidden hand of Haldeman at work. "While the president was telling me what a great job I did, the other fellows were going out to get the rope," he said.

Dole had never cared for the White House palace guard, but by the time of his firing he'd also lost much respect for Nixon. Without going into details, Dole told me he'd been asked to question McGovern's patriotism and was unwilling to do that.

"You came pretty close," I said skeptically.

"You should have seen what they asked me to do," Dole replied.

When I pressed him for specifics, Dole said "the White House bunch" had wanted him to disparage McGovern's war record. It's little wonder that this disgusted the former infantry officer. Lieutenant George McGovern had flown thirty-five combat missions as a B-24 pilot over German-occupied Europe. Officially called the Liberator, the B-24 was better known by its four-man crews as the "flying coffin." A friend of mine, Bob Martin, was a tail-gunner on B-24 missions out of Italy over German-held Ploiesti oil fields in Romania. He prayed that he might see his twenty-first birthday.

McGovern was two months short of his own twenty-first birthday

3. One of the tasks assigned to the Watergate burglars was to repair a defective microphone that had been placed there on a previous break-in by the same burglars.

on August 1, 1943, when he participated in a massive raid on the Ploiesti fields—one of the costliest operations of the war for the U.S. Army Air Force. The attackers lost fifty-three aircraft and 660 air crewmen without halting production in the oil fields. McGovern's B-24 participated in this raid. His plane, like Martin's, came back intact.

Nixon was not a draft evader, like Bill Clinton and Donald Trump. He was in the naval reserve when Pearl Harbor was attacked and stationed in Iowa when he volunteered for service in the South Pacific. It wasn't Nixon's fault he saw limited action, but it was unsavory that his 1972 campaign wrapped itself in the American flag and equated McGovern's antiwar views with lack of patriotism. Dole sought Senate reelection in 1974 as the Watergate cover-up closed in on Nixon. I was assigned to cover the race in which Dole was the decided underdog. Interviewing Dole in his Senate office, I asked what Nixon could do to help him.

"He can stage a flyover of Kansas," Dole quipped.

I was walking away in the Senate corridor after the interview when Dole burst out of his office and flagged me down. He said he'd reached a truce with the White House and that his flyover wisecrack would undo it. So he asked me not to use the line in my story. Normally, I wouldn't have gone along with a politician withdrawing something he had said on the record, but Dole had been candid with me when no one of stature at the White House would take my calls. I said it was a great line but agreed not to use it.

Back at *The Post* I told the story to Ben Bradlee and another editor. The other editor said I should use the line anyway. Ben reproached him. "No, we won't use it," he said. "Lou told him we wouldn't use it, and we play by the rules."

Ben and I should have listened to the other editor. In those days, newsmagazines released their contents to the wire services Sunday night, hoping *The Post* or the *New York Times* would pick up a story and credit the magazine. Ben called me at home that Sunday and said the line we'd suppressed had been used prominently in that week's issue of *Time*. Bradlee said he didn't blame me; it just ratified his low opinion of Dole.

Hot under the collar, I called Dole the next day and asked why the line I'd agreed to suppress had appeared in *Time*. "You're right to be angry," Dole said. "I should have called you. What happened is that I went to the Senate floor, and a reporter buttonholed me on the way and I thought this line is just too good not to use."

"You're on the record from now on," I told him.[4]

Early in 1974, Dole's chances of reelection seemed remote. His anticipated Democratic opponent was Robert Docking, a capable two-term governor who would have been heavily favored. But rocked by a financial scandal that touched on those close to him, Docking retired.

Enter Representative William Roy, known as "Dr. Bill," a diminutive barrel-chested obstetrician from Topeka and the only member of Congress to hold both medical and legal degrees. Roy was popular and had delivered more than five thousand babies in his district. He'd been a Republican most of his life but switched his registration in 1970 to run as a Democrat on an antiwar platform. He defeated a Republican incumbent and won again in 1972.

Dole entered the race in a despondent mood. He'd been fired from his job as Republican national chairman in January. A few months later, he divorced his wife of twenty-four years. Nixon resigned the presidency on August 9, and President Gerald Ford pardoned him unconditionally on September 8. After the pardon, Dole said he had received "about all the help from President Ford that I can stand." Ahead in the polls, Roy tried repeatedly to link Dole to Watergate, which cast a shadow over the campaign. The headline on my October 8 tory summarized his predicament: "Dole Haunted by Watergate in Kansas Senatorial Campaign."

Also hovering over the election was the issue of abortion. Along with the thousands of babies he delivered, Roy had performed a few legal abortions in 1969 after the Kansas legislature passed a relaxed abortion bill on a bipartisan vote. Soon afterward, Roy ended his medical practice to run for Congress. In 1973 the Supreme Court issued its landmark *Roe v. Wade* decision legalizing abortion. Opponents of *Roe* were not yet the highly organized force they would become in later years, but Roy was the only obstetrician in the nation running for Congress, and groups that would later be called "right to life" took aim. Dole's views on abortion were not fully formed, but he saw an opportunity when he followed Roy on the speaker's stand at the Kansas State Fair in September. The can-

4. My point in relating this long-ago story is not that Dole jobbed me out of a nice quote. It's that our mutually respectful relationship remained intact. After retiring from politics, Dole spent the last years of his life greeting former comrades-in-arms—tour groups of his dwindling band of brothers—and their families at the World War II Memorial in Washington, DC. Dole died on December 5, 2021, at ninety-eight. I consider it a privilege to have covered him.

didates had mostly discussed agricultural issues, but Roy had vaguely supported abortion rights. When it was his turn, Dole said of Roy: "You heard him stand here today and say he's for abortion on demand."

Some postelection pundits would call abortion, which was rarely mentioned by either candidate after that exchange, the decisive issue of the campaign. The evidence for that claim is dubious, since Roy maintained a substantial lead in the polls well after the abortion issue was raised. What I believe was decisive and so reported in *The Post* was a ferocious attempt by Roy—a "smear," Dole said—to pin Watergate on his opponent. The architect of that strategy was Robert Brock, a lawyer who doubled as Roy's campaign manager and Democratic state chairman. Brock also was on Nixon's "enemies list" and he sent a letter to others on the list saying that voting against Dole was "the closest thing to voting against Nixon that any of us will have the opportunity to do."

On September 29, Dole and Roy were interviewed jointly on the CBS program *Face the Nation*. I was a panelist along with Bill Plante of CBS News on a program moderated by longtime host George Herman, who was known for his impartiality. But when Roy said Dole "knew or should have known" about Watergate, it reminded Herman of Senator Joseph McCarthy badgering witnesses by saying they knew or should have known of someone's alleged Communist connections.

"Which is it," Herman asked Roy. "Did Senator Dole know, or should he have known? The question flustered Roy, who gave an incoherent answer. But he continued to use this formulation, which had been devised by Brock, as he campaigned around Kansas.

In those days, print journalists labored in relative anonymity but risked becoming part of the story they were covering by going on television. *Face the Nation* was rebroadcast in prime time on the CBS outlet in Wichita. Because of the pointed questions I'd put to the candidates on that show, I became known to both political camps in Kansas. The next day I was covering Dole at a luncheon speech in Kansas. During the question period an earnest young conservative arose and said he thought the *Face the Nation* panelists had favored Roy.

"Do you think they were fair to you?" he asked Dole.

Dole spotted me in the audience and responded, "Well, we have one of the panelists here, so let's ask him. Do you think you were fair, Mr. Cannon?"

"Very fair," I said.

"There you go," said Dole.

I should have said nothing, especially since I was familiar with Dole's tactic of trying to draw reporters into the story. Two days later I was with Roy at a campaign event when he came up to me and complained that Herman and I had ganged up on him and helped Dole.

"I would not expect that from the *Washington Post,*" he said.

I was disappointed that Roy shared the conservative stereotype of my paper's liberalism but could see he was too upset to discuss the matter. So I told him I was sorry he felt mistreated while making a silent resolution to never again appear on a television program that was interviewing a candidate whose race I was covering.

Dole felt he had come out second best at the state fair debate but believed he had come out on top on *Face the Nation*. Whether true or not, the CBS program buoyed Dole's spirits. "It energized him," said Lieutenant Governor David Owen, who was retiring from politics and had lent Dole his formidable political organization. In Owen's telling, he was rummaging through the desk of his predecessor when he found a *Reader's Digest* article about Dole's war wounds and his long and painful recovery. Owen slapped the headline "Guts" on the article and distributed it in all 105 Kansas counties. It was news to many Kansans because Dole had not talked about his war service in previous campaigns.

Owen also commissioned two television ads portraying Roy as a mudslinger. One showed a billboard of Dole being splattered with mudballs that were equated with Roy's statements about Dole. The mudballs come off, revealing a clean and smiling Dole.[5]

Before these ads, Roy had been on offense. After they ran, Roy was besieged with questions from reporters about whether he had mispresented Dole's record. Polls by two Wichita television stations that had Roy far ahead in September gave Dole a slight lead in October. I wrote about Dole's comeback in a story headlined, "Dole Battles Back from Brink of Political Oblivion" that ran a week before Election Day.

Dole won by a scant 13,532 votes out of 794,434 cast. But in a horrible year for Republicans even a narrow victory was impressive. Dole would

5. Owen said the original wording of the ads called Roy a "liar." Dole would not agree to this, and the word "mudslinger" was substituted. Owen's comments were made at the Dole Institute of Politics on October 9, 2014.

remain a player on the national political scene for two decades, becoming a master legislator who guided Senate passage of major legislative proposals by four presidents. He was also the Republican nominee for vice president in 1976 and president in 1996. None of this would have happened if Dole had lost his Senate reelection bid. And as Dole told me weeks after the 1974 election, "I would never have won had Roy not tried to tie me to Watergate."

Voters often sympathize with senators who have been rejected for national office. Hubert Humphrey and Edmund Muskie were untouchable in their Senate races after their presidential bids had failed. More surprisingly, George McGovern, who lost his home state to Nixon in the 1972 presidential landslide, held on to his South Dakota Senate seat in 1974, upsetting the Republican candidate, Leo K. Thorsness, a former prisoner of war in Vietnam.

The twin victories of McGovern and Dole led to an alliance that produced a major reform and significant expansion of the food stamp program, the school lunch program, and the supplemental nutritional program for Women, Infants, and Children (WIC). McGovern said Dole lined up Republican support for these programs "as effectively as it could be done." The two senators also launched the first U.S. global initiative dedicated to feeding hungry children: the McGovern-Dole International Food for Education and Child Nutrition Program, which enabled humanitarian agencies such as the UN World Food Program to provide school meals overseas, using U.S. crops and assistance from the federal government. The program has served more than forty-five million hungry kids abroad and earned Dole and McGovern the World Food Prize in 2008.

History sometimes turns losers into winners—and vice versa. Barry Goldwater, swamped by Lyndon Johnson in the 1964 election, lived to see some of his supposedly wild-eyed ideas implemented during Reagan's presidency. Historians across the political spectrum now share Pete McCloskey's and George McGovern's critical views of the folly of U.S. participation in the Vietnam War. In 2007, McGovern visited Santa Barbara, and a friend invited my wife and me to have lunch with McGovern at a Montecito country club. He was as relaxed as I'd ever seen him. George W. Bush was president, and we discussed contemporary politics and the chances of a Democrat winning the White House.

When the talk turned to child nutrition and food stamps, McGovern lamented increasing Republican criticism of such programs and said that wouldn't have happened if Dole were still in the Senate. McGovern said he and Dole had accomplished much together but that more needed to be done, in the United States and globally, to see that every child in the world was fed. It was a pleasant and enlightening lunch. Neither of us mentioned Richard Nixon.

18

THE PEOPLE OF *THE POST*

I depart from my more-or-less chronological narrative to write about my colleagues at *The Washington Post,* where I worked twenty-six years plus two more as a freelancer on the national staff. My stories are available in the archives, but my experiences with these exceptional people have until now been stored solely in my memory bank. This chapter is the suggestion of my eldest son Carl, who is editing these memoirs. When my narrative bogged down because I kept interrupting it to write about my colleagues, Carl suggested I devote a separate chapter to the people of *The Post* who meant the most to me.

Let's start with Richard Lee Harwood, who hired and inspired me even after he left the paper in 1988. He still inspires me. He was a U.S. Marine severely wounded at Iwo Jima and a terrific journalist. Soon after I joined *The Post,* I watched Harwood edit a story in which the reporter referred to someone as an ex-Marine. "There are no ex-Marines at this paper," Harwood said, deftly excising the "ex." Harwood would not then discuss Iwo Jima, but he let me know that his wartime experiences had helped shape the way he looked at the world.

Harwood was broad-shouldered and resolute. He was also Hollywood handsome. If you've seen his son John Harwood, who is also a journalist, on television, that's how his father looked in his sixties. Dick Harwood's childhood had been grim. "His one sibling, a sister, died as a teenager; his mother committed suicide, his preacher father took to drink and farmed his son out with relatives in another state." So wrote

Madeleine Blais, who worked for Harwood at the *Trenton Times* and later won a Pulitzer Prize at the *Miami Herald.*

But with an assist from the U.S. Marine Corps, Harwood became an inspirational leader who was idealistic about the purposes of journalism but often viewed the practice of it with a gimlet eye. He was also a good writer who detested clichés and tropes on which reporters so often rely. When a reporter wrote about a "surprising development," Harwood said, "That means that the reporter was surprised." As assistant managing editor (AME) of national news at *The Washington Post,* Harwood was often contrarian and never reluctant to differ with reporters or other editors. He was hard, and *The Post* was soft, said Peter Silberman. He could be especially hard on lazy reporters, but you could always get a straight answer from Harwood.

William Greider, a perceptive reporter and later AME national, had followed Harwood to *The Post* from the *Louisville Times,* where Harwood had covered politics and was known in political circles as "Black Death Harwood," or "Death" for short. *Post* management was wary of Greider and his left-of-center perspective, but Harwood valued Bill—as did I. After a trying day in which Harwood alone stood up for him, Bill told me he understood why Marines had followed him up the dangerous beaches in the South Pacific.

Ben Bradlee lured him to *The Post* in 1966. In his first year at *The Post,* Harwood won the George Polk Award for a story on how the FBI had infiltrated civil rights groups. In 1968 Bradlee assigned Harwood to cover the budding presidential campaign of Robert F. Kennedy. Bradlee believed that reporters who covered RFK too often became his cheerleaders, and he believed Harwood would resist this temptation. Instead, Harwood became so fond of Kennedy that he wrote a letter to Bradlee saying he should be replaced by a more objective reporter. It was written the day before Bobby Kennedy was assassinated.

Assessing Harwood's abilities as a reporter in his memoir, *A Good Life,* Bradlee said he was "primitive in his search for the truth, impossible to deceive, and without peer in his ability to write a declarative sentence." In 1970 Harwood became *The Post*'s first ombudsman and wrote columns about the mishaps of journalism and in-house memos calling out the paper's biases. One of Harwood's columns apologized to Attorney General John Mitchell for a serious error in a story about him.

I was one of Harwood's first hires after he became AME of national news in 1972. It was a promotion for Harwood and a challenge: he'd been critical of the national staff and Bradlee wanted him to improve its performance. I wasn't aware of this backstory, but I looked up to Harwood and wanted to show him that he hadn't made a mistake in hiring me. A month after I joined the staff, Harwood wrote me this note: "I told you to hit the ground running. You've done that and done it well. I feel vindicated and wise and you should feel good. Keep charging." Forty-eight years later I still have that note, tucked it into a small framed picture of Harwood, his wife Bea, and Peter Silberman, then Harwood's loyal deputy.

Pete's title was national editor. Short and dark-haired with glasses that gave him an owlish appearance and with an occasionally lit cigar in his mouth, Pete was a deft editor and the paper's best grammarian. Bradlee made him the arbiter of grammatical disputes, accepting his rulings as conclusive. This was impressive as there was a slew of English language mavens at *The Post,* and Pete's first language was German. He and Harwood complemented one another. Harwood was creative and attuned to the big picture; Silberman was conscientious and thorough, filling in the cracks. Each could do the job without the other, as Harwood showed when Silberman became AME financial and as Pete demonstrated years later when he became AME national. But together they were amazing, the best editorial team for which I ever worked at any newspaper. Pete spent thirty years at *The Post.* He was fair and meticulous with exceptional news judgment and unflappable under deadline pressure. He became a close friend.

Pete had grown up in Japanese-ruled Shanghai, to which his family had escaped from Berlin. Before the Nazi regime became actively genocidal in 1939, Jews were allowed to emigrate if they could find a country that accepted them. Few countries did, but Shanghai, not even a country, was an exception. By the time the Japanese bombed Pearl Harbor in 1941, Shanghai was home to an estimated twenty-three thousand German Jews who lived in a squalid ghetto for stateless people. Shanghai took in more Jewish refugees than Canada, Australia, New Zealand, South Africa, and India combined. Pete avoided talking about the Shanghai years much as Harwood avoided questions about his wartime service. But Pete did tell me learned English, which he spoke with a slight German accent, at a Catholic school in the Jewish ghetto. When my youngest son, Jack, was assigned in high school to interview someone about his World War II experiences, he chose Pete. In that interview, Pete talked eloquently of passing under the Golden Gate Bridge as he arrived in San Francisco after the war. It was his Ellis Island.

Pete and I were racetrack buddies even before I came to *The Post*. As horse-race handicappers, we had skills that complemented one another—he was good with speed figures and I paid attention to trainers—but he managed his money better than I did. On Saturdays when I wasn't working we'd often go to Laurel Park in Maryland. Pete was also a disciplined player in our poker group and a strong finisher in any gambling endeavor. I lost count of how many times Pete salvaged a losing day by hitting a long shot in the last race. He'd often win the last poker hand, as well.

I lived in Northern Virginia, and when I worked late in the wintertime and the Washington bridges over the Potomac were icy, I sometimes stayed the night at Pete's house in Washington. We played chess or went to dinner. As a reaction to his Shanghai diet, Pete avoided fish and rice. Pete was a quiet patriot who was thankful for becoming a U.S. citizen. He'd been drafted into the U.S. Army and gone willingly, serving as a soldier during the Korean War. When I asked him in 1992 if he intended to vote for Bill Clinton, Pete said he never voted for anyone who had evaded the draft.

David S. Broder was an idol of mine before he became a colleague and a friend. I met him in the mid-1960s when I was state capitol correspondent for the *San Jose Mercury News*. The Sacramento press corps looked down on reporters from what we called "the East," believing they came to California with their heads crowded with stereotypes and their stories written in advance. Broder was different. He would regularly drop into our bureaus wanting to know our perspectives. "Eastern" only from a California perspective, Broder was from the American heartland, where he'd once coedited *The Maroon*, the student paper at the University of Chicago.

When I came to Washington for the Ridders in 1969, Broder was the gold standard of political reporters, as he would be for decades. In *The Boys on the Bus*, his bestselling book about the reporters on the 1972 presidential campaign, *Rolling Stone* writer Timothy Crouse described Broder as "the high priest of political journalism, the most powerful and respected man in the trade," adding that his "reputation transcends even the prestige of the *Post*." But what I didn't know until I joined the paper was that David's influence on his colleagues was even greater than his influence on his readers. Broder saw to it that the newest members of the national staff received top assignments, even if he took a back-row seat. At the 1972 Republican convention, Harwood assigned me to write the lead story one day. It was an honor for such a newcomer to the national staff, and I couldn't turn it down. Broder realized I'd been following a House reform story, and he sat in a smoke-filled room for four hours, taking notes for me. By putting himself out for his colleagues, Broder taught us it was the story that mattered, not our egos. He inspired us to work as a team and lifted the confidence and quality of the entire newsroom. Years earlier, Broder had written a piece that began, "Let us be modest, ladies and gentlemen of the press, for we have much to be modest about."

It impressed my son Carl, then at the *Baltimore Sun*. When a young reporter complained to Carl that he'd been treated shoddily by one of the prima donnas in our business, Carl told him to forget it and look instead at the example set by Broder. "When I was a teenager, David Broder never came to our house that he didn't ask me what I was doing or how I felt," Carl told the reporter. "He is the greatest of them all, and he never had a swelled head."

It's worth adding that anyone with a swelled head wouldn't have lasted long around Dave's wife, Ann Broder. She was a savvy and accomplished woman whose kindnesses to me were manifold.[1]

An episode at the 1980 Republican National Convention in Detroit illustrates the way Broder helped his colleagues—and the dependability of Ben Bradlee. Ronald Reagan had clinched the presidential nominee weeks before the convention but hadn't picked a running mate. The electronic media and the *New York Times* were abuzz with the notion that Reagan might put former President Gerald Ford on the ticket, and aides to both men had explored this possibility. I thought it was a goofy

1. Ann took me under her wing at the 1968 National Governors' Conference in Cincinnati, introduced me to such celebrities as Richard Goodwin, and shared my disgust that Lyndon Johnson had shown up inebriated for the event. Years later—on October 5, 1980, to be exact—I was asleep on the Broder living-room couch when Ann awakened me and told me to phone my eldest son, Carl, who informed me that his wife Sharon had given birth to Nicholas Cannon, their first child and my first grandson.

idea. Ford had been president and now he was supposed to be vice president under someone he didn't even like? Two of my well-placed Reagan sources were promoting George H. W. Bush. This made sense. Bush had competed in nearly every primary and had a following among Republicans who thought Reagan too conservative. Putting Bush on the ticket would instantly unite the party and was the kind of practical solution that appealed to Reagan.

Not knowing more than this, I went to Broder and told him I thought Bush would wind up on the ticket. I didn't have hard evidence, but Broder respected my insights about Reagan.

"Pursue it and write it," Broder said, "and leave everything else to me."

So I did more reporting and wrote a widely disbelieved story saying that Bush was likely to be Reagan's choice. Broder had prepped Bradlee, who assured him he would back me if I climbed out on a limb. Bradlee overdid it, as demonstrated by this overheard conversation between Ben and his friend Tom Winship, then editor of the *Boston Globe.*

"Lou knows Reagan, but I think he's going to be wrong about Bush," Winship said.

"Even if he's wrong, he's right." Bradlee said. "I like my reporters to be bold."

When a friend told me of this conversation, I was alarmed. I appreciated Ben's clannish loyalty, but the identity of the running mate wasn't going to be a matter of opinion. If I was wrong, I was wrong. So I waited nearly an hour in a hotel corridor to talk to a valued Reagan source who was promoting Bush. He said Reagan was having second thoughts about Ford and that he would eventually turn to Bush.

"He's almost there," my source said.

This was useful information but well short of confirmation. It was after midnight now, and Broder and my editor Dan Balz were unavailable. To hell with it, I thought, and went with my gut. I scribbled Ben a note on a hotel notepad, offering my resignation if the running mate wasn't Bush. About three in the morning when no one was in our workspace I placed my note in Bradlee's inbox.[2]

When Reagan put Bush on the ticket the following night, I was in the convention hall. Howell Raines and Bill Kovach of the *New York Times* came over in view of their editor, Abe Rosenthal, and shook my hand.

2. Bradlee told me later that he tore up my note. Soon after the convention, he gave me a raise.

That was gutsy because Rosenthal had been debunking my Bush stories. I looked at Abe, but he looked away. Broder, who had been poached from the *Times* by Bradlee, called from our workspace and said Bradlee was so happy he was going to kiss me when I returned there.

"Tell him, I won't come back to the workspace then," I replied.

We celebrated that evening, with Broder as always drinking less than the rest of us.

Every *Post* reporter knew that Bradlee backed his reporters, and I think we took more risks—I certainly did—because of it. Four years earlier, when Reagan and President Ford were locked in a tight battle for the Republican presidential nomination, I learned before the 1976 party convention in Kansas City that Ford had sewn up the nomination. This contradicted what Reagan's campaign manager John Sears was saying and what most newspapers were printing.

Sears was a brilliant and unconventional strategist. He'd persuaded Reagan to pick a running mate before the convention in the person of Pennsylvania Senator Richard Schweiker, a tactic that prompted several Pennsylvania delegates who favored Ford to declare they were undecided. But Ford had the White House at his disposal, and he used it to woo these delegates with private dinners. After they had visited the White House, most of these delegates continued to say publicly they were undecided even though they had pledged privately to Ford. The *Post*'s excellent delegate counter, reporter Steve Isaacs, did not take such statements at face value. He separately interviewed the supposedly undecided delegates and found that when pressed most of them acknowledged they favored Ford. Steve said there were ten votes for Reagan in Pennsylvania and that Ford would get the other 105 delegates. He was precisely right.

Armed with the information from Isaacs, I reinterviewed my Reagan sources. My key interview was with a high-placed advisor who asked me whom he should talk to about getting a job in the Ford campaign.

"You're leaving?" I asked.

"It's over," he said. "Ford has enough delegates to win."

The quote was off the record, but not the information. I wrote a story declaring that Ford had clinched the nomination, and *The Post* ran it under an eight-column banner. The story coincided with Nancy Reagan's birthday, and *The Post* ran a page-one photograph of her blowing out the candles on her birthday cake on the campaign plane. I was in the picture, giving the story added (and unintentional) heft. Sears exploded when he saw the story and didn't talk to me for years. Reagan was angry, too, but restrained. He probably suspected the story was true even though Sears and press aide Lyn Nofziger told him it wasn't. I received a couple of telephoned death threats in which I didn't place much credence although I told Broder about them. When I returned to *The Post*, Bradlee put his arm around my shoulders and walked me through the newsroom, making the unmistakable point that he supported my story. While we were walking, I said softly to Ben that the story was right.

"I know the story was right," Ben said in a low voice intended just for me. "We're not accustomed to bannering stories that are wrong. But you be careful." I didn't know if Broder had told him about the death threats but promised Ben I wouldn't take unnecessary chances.

In a public tribute to David and Ann Broder on their eightieth birthdays, I said Dave was the best political reporter who ever lived but a second-rate reporter compared to the kind of friend he'd been. I could have said something similar about many others at *The Post*, Harwood and Silberman and Bradlee certainly, but also Dan Balz and Don Oberdorfer and Joel Garreau and Haynes Johnson and Jay Mathews and Tom Edsall and, later, Sander Vanocur, who became a television columnist at *The Post* because Bradlee gave him a job after he'd worn out his welcome at the networks.

I don't want to come off as Rebecca of Sunnybrook Farm in my remembrances of the national staff. The *Post* had misfits, like every news organization. We had a reporter who was captive of the agency he covered and by virtue of this missed a big story and was fired. We had an editor who made tracks on every story that crossed his desk, putting them in his own tone-deaf voice. I went to implausible lengths to avoid him editing my copy. We had another editor who took so much pride in being in the know that he mentioned an exclusive I had in the works to a friend who mentioned it to the Associated Press, and I was scooped on my own story. The editor begged me not to tell anyone about what he had done, and I didn't. I gave this editor and every editor I had at *The Post* my professional best. A reporter should do his job even when his editors don't.

No one is immune to stereotypical thinking, but Harwood believed journalists could resist this fault by staying open to information that enlarged their worldview. Donald Oberdorfer was such a journalist, bringing the same verities to diplomatic coverage that David Broder did to political coverage. "Always there, calm, knowledgeable, unbiased, armed with the right questions, knew everybody, clear and fair," in the assessment of Leslie Gelb, who competed against Oberdorfer for the *Times*. "He made neither enemies nor friends of officials."

I'd been at *The Post* many years before getting to know Oberdorfer. He became the paper's correspondent in Tokyo shortly after I joined the national staff. Soon after he returned to Washington, I became western correspondent in Los Angeles. But during the Reagan years we were both in Washington and collaborated on stories, especially during Reagan's meetings with Soviet leader Mikhail Gorbachev. We worked well together; Oberdorfer understood diplomatic and national security issues, and I knew Reagan. At the first Reagan-Gorbachev meeting in Geneva (November 1985) we learned then-startling news that Reagan had proposed to Gorbachev that the United States and the Soviet Union scrap all their nuclear weapons.

Both Don and were fascinated by the transformation of U.S-Soviet relations after four decades of Cold War, which Oberdorfer later examined in a useful book, *The Turn*. Three years after Geneva at the Moscow summit, Reagan strolled the Kremlin grounds and when asked if the Soviet Union was still an "evil empire" said he was "talking about another time, another era." Of all the events I covered at *The Post*—and I wrote more than four thousand stories—this seemed the most surreal. It's regrettable that Vladimir Putin and a succession of U.S. presidents have made hash of the Gorbachev-Reagan transformation. If Oberdorfer were still around, he'd no doubt write another book explaining why this has happened.

The day after the Kremlin stroll, Reagan and Gorbachev held their final closed meeting of the summit. Don and I separately interviewed participants and exchanged memos in London, where the Reagan party spent the night. Neither of us had slept much, and I was coming down with a head cold. Don insisted I go to bed and said he would write the story. With typical generosity, he put my name first in the double byline. The next day as the press bus prepared to depart for Heathrow, Don noticed I wasn't on it. He had the driver hold the bus, went back into the hotel, and found me interviewing someone in the bar, oblivious of the time.

I didn't often miss a press bus in my career, but I was intermittently rescued in large and small ways by Broder, Oberdorfer, and others. This support system helped enormously when my first marriage disintegrated and when my mother died. Newsroom collegiality is an undervalued virtue. "Newsrooms look like such communal places, but they really aren't," Jim Hoge told me when he was editor of the *Chicago Sun-Times*. The underappreciated collegiality of *The Post*'s national staff meant that reporters spent more time reporting and less time worrying about bylines or looking over their shoulders to see who was gaining on them. The teamwork of the national staff produced many shared stories and was a reason *The Post* was so productive in the 1970s and the 1980s, which Broder believed was a golden age of the newspaper.

Journalistic historians who focus on this period rarely mention *The Post*'s political coverage. Instead, they single out two sets of stories, only one of which involved the national staff. That would be the Pentagon Papers, which happened nine months before I joined *The Post*. The other story was the Watergate scandal, featuring Bob Woodward and Carl Bernstein, two metro staff reporters, doing the heavy lifting. They were backed up by Bradlee; Howard Simons, the executive editor; Harry Rosenfeld, the metro AME; and Barry Sussman, the city editor. Harwood wanted the national staff to take over the Watergate investigation, but Bradlee stayed with the reporters who had broken the story.

My personal relationship with Woodward got off on the wrong foot. At a critical juncture of the Watergate story in 1973, White House press secretary Ron Ziegler announced that President Nixon had ordered members of his staff to testify before the grand jury, and I wrote a story about it. In their book *All the President's Men,* Woodward and Bernstein relate how they opposed putting this story in the paper because White House aides had previously appeared before the grand jury. In their view the Ziegler announcement was entirely a public relations effort. What Bob and Carl didn't note was that Bradlee came out of his office into the newsroom and in earshot of anyone who happened to be there asked all three of us to make our case. My argument was simple: It was the first time any administration official had proclaimed such cooperation, which made it a story in my view. Bradlee agreed on the spot and, going further than I would have, directed that the story lead the paper. Woodward and

Bernstein wrote a separate story (a fact also omitted from the book) quoting sources who disagreed with Ziegler. That story also ran on page one.

But Woodward and Bernstein also credited me in their book for writing some of the "finest pieces about the effects of Watergate and the GOP." As I told Bradlee during the newsroom debate, I'd take the word of either of them over Ziegler, a practiced liar. He was nonetheless Nixon's spokesman, and we needed to cover what he said and did. Harwood, who had heard the entire argument without saying a word, took me aside when it was over.

"Thanks for backing me up," I said with a sarcasm I rarely expressed to Harwood.

He laughed and said, "You did fine without me."

Then Dick told me to keep doing what I was doing. When people look back on our news coverage, Harwood said, I want it to be known that the national staff treated the White House fairly—even while Woodward and Bernstein were exposing Nixon.

This episode proved a tiny blip in my relationship with Woodward, the most influential investigative journalist in the English-speaking world and the rare person whose head hasn't been turned by fame. Woodward and Bernstein set in motion the train of events that led to Nixon's resignation, and Woodward could have named his price at the many media outlets that coveted his services. Instead, he remained with *The Washington Post* and wrote many books brimming with inside stories from half a dozen presidencies plus the Supreme Court and the Federal Reserve. The best of them is *Rage,* Woodward's second book about President Donald Trump, which features an admission by Trump that he had early awareness of the potency of COVID-19 and deliberately withheld this information from the American people. Woodward also was influential inside *The Post.* Leading by example, he mentored other investigative reporters and at crucial moments shared information acquired from his legion of sources with colleagues, including me. Bob listens more than he talks, rarely uses the first-person pronoun, and is a beacon of integrity. He is a trusted friend.[3]

3. Woodward's wife, Elsa, also a friend, is a distant cousin of my wife, Mary Shinkwin Cannon.

President Gerald Ford responding to my question among a crush of reporters

Posing with my wife Mary Cannon, President Ford, and his chief of staff, Dick Cheney

My son Carl Cannon (*center*) receiving the Gerald R. Ford Prize for Distinguished Reporting of the Presidency in 2000

With President Ford and fellow journalist David Broder

President Reagan huddling with reporters at the White House

Discussing current affairs with President Reagan aboard Air Force One

Sharing a laugh with President Ronald Reagan
and Chief of Staff James Baker

Meeting President Reagan's good friend and
longtime British prime minister Margaret Thatcher

One of many get-togethers at the Reagans' California ranch

Greeting First Lady Nancy Reagan at the Reagan ranch

Enjoying some down time at the president's ranch

Interviewing Vice President Walter F. Mondale on Air Force One

With former president Reagan at his Century City office

Exchanging a few words with President George H. W. Bush

Interviewing President Bush at the White House.
On the right are David Hoffman and David Broder.

With son Carl and Vice President Dick Cheney
at his office in the White House

Since this chapter spans two marriages and several decades, this is as good a place as any to say the little I intend to say about my marriage of thirty years to one woman and my marriage of nearly four decades to another.

My first wife, Virginia, and I were children of our generation. She was an inveterate reader whose interests ranged from political biographies to detective novels and who worked as a nursery schoolteacher and later a bookkeeper. But family always came first for her. Ginny, as she was known, took for granted that she and the children would move whenever I changed jobs. I consulted with her, of course, and turned down an editorial writer's job in Pine Bluff because she didn't want to raise the children in Arkansas. Otherwise, she'd always been willing to move.

That changed when I became White House correspondent for *The Post* at the onset of the Reagan presidency. Neither of us had anticipated this assignment. We lived in Woodland Hills, California, and I was supposedly the national staff's correspondent in Los Angeles even though I'd spent 1980 covering the presidential campaign. My editors had told me beforehand I would not be covering the White House if Reagan won, but they liked my coverage of the campaign and, after he won, they changed their minds. It was a request, not an order, but I had only a year or two more in Los Angeles before I'd be reassigned to a beat unknown. After covering Reagan for so long. I was curious to see how he'd do as president, and *The Post* was offering me a front-row seat. I was pleased and paid little attention to Virginia's muted response. She'd been happy from 1969 to 1977 when we'd lived in Vienna, Virginia, and I worked for Ridder Publications in Washington. But in 1981, as we drove across the country from California to another home in northern Virginia, Ginny confessed she'd become rooted in Woodland Hills and hadn't wanted to leave.

"Why didn't you tell me?" I asked.

"Because I knew you wanted the job and didn't want to stand in your way," she replied with typical loyalty.

We arrived in Oakton, Virginia, on one of the coldest days in the winter with both of us remembering how pleasant it was in California. Our relationship never recovered.

Mary Shinkwin was working for former Senator John Tunney in Santa Monica when Virginia and I separated. The California delegation in Congress had been part of my beat at Ridder Publications, and

I'd known Mary when she was Tunney's secretary on Capitol Hill. She was shy, smart, pretty, and loyal to Tunney, who was protective of her. Mary and I had stayed occasionally in touch after I went to *The Post*, but I hadn't seen her in years. After Tunney lost his bid for reelection in 1976, he asked Mary to work for him at an investment firm he founded in Los Angeles.

One bright Sunday afternoon in 1982, I was drinking wine at a Santa Barbara hotel with Francis Xavier Clines, a premier *New York Times* correspondent. We were there covering President Reagan, who was on one of his periodic trips to his California ranch. Global events requiring a presidential response sometimes occurred on these trips, but all was quiet this particular day, which Frank and I were enjoying with a good pinot noir.

Each summer the Reagans hosted a barbecue for the White House press corps at a nearby ranch, where they'd descend from the clouds of Rancho del Cielo and spend a couple of hours with reporters and TV producers and their guests. Frank, who knew my personal situation, asked if I was going to bring anyone to the barbecue. I mentioned Mary but doubted she'd be interested.

"Call her," Clines insisted. "Otherwise you'll always wonder what she would have said."

So I called Mary, who thanked me but graciously declined the invitation. I was let down only briefly, for she soon called back and said she'd reconsidered. I'm still grateful to Frank for pushing me to make that call.

Mary told me that she had called back because she thought this might be the only time she'd meet Ronald Reagan. She is a devoted Democrat, but Reagan was a special president. In the security line at the barbecue the Secret Service spotted a vial of pepper spray in Mary's purse and confiscated it. After the Reagans had left, I tried to impress Mary by recovering the pepper spray. The agent in charge knew me and also knew that many California women at the time carried pepper spray for their protection. He returned the vial.

Fast forward to another Sunday in Santa Barbara. It is January 17, 2016, and Mary and I have been married more than thirty years. We were at a small dinner party after a benefit performance of the two-person play *Love Letters*, for Antioch Santa Barbara, of which I was then a trustee. The actors were Carol Burnett and Brian Dennehy. Mary had a crush on Dennehy, the barrel-chested actor who played cops and various tough-guy roles on television and in the movies, as well as a disarmingly benign alien in *Cocoon*. I made sure they were introduced.

Dennehy said to Mary, "I'll betcha don't know anyone who has been married for thirty years—twice."

Pointing to me, Mary said quietly, "Yes, I do. My husband."

We returned to our table. Later, a dinner companion of Dennehy came by and said, "I've never seen Brian speechless before."

In the interval between my divorce and remarriage I was depressed. My mother was on a downward arc at a Bethesda care home where my brother and I had moved her after her caretaker died. Even though I didn't discuss personal matters at work, word somehow got around, and my colleagues reacted with near-familial support. Pete Silberman and Dave Broder were especially kind. Harwood was convinced I needed time off and said he would order me to take it if I didn't do it myself. I reluctantly took a week. When I returned, Harwood said he had more time in mind, but he didn't order me to go away so I stayed.

Another colleague who reached out was Haynes Johnson, a star journalist and the son of a great reporter. While with the *Washington Star*, Haynes had won a Pulitzer Prize for his civil rights coverage, centering on events in Selma, Alabama. He became the first son of a Pulitzer Prize winner to also win the award. His father Malcom of the *New York Sun* had won the Pulitzer in 1929 for writing about underworld control of the New York docks, which became the basis for the Marlon Brando classic *On the Waterfront*. In 1969 Bradlee lured Haynes to *The Post* and gave him free rein to do anything he wanted. This could have disrupted beat coverage, but Haynes avoided trouble by consulting with reporters before he invaded their turf. If the reporters objected to what Haynes wanted to do, he'd do something else.

Haynes was a graceful writer and a gracious man. When I wrote his obituary for *Time* magazine in 2013, I praised his newspaper and television commentary, concluding: "His colleagues appreciated his talents, but we valued him as much for his many kindnesses."

Dan Balz, our political editor in 1980, would eventually have the unenviable task of succeeding David Broder. Dan was also from Illinois and like Broder was self-effacing, hardworking, and fair-minded. Balz and I hit it off during the 1980 campaign when he was the political editor and I was covering Reagan. Some of our editors dismissed Reagan's chances, and this attitude occasionally seeped into our headlines. A headline on a story I wrote from Illinois—"Scope of Reagan Appeal Problematic"—became a running gag between Dan and me. When we talked the day before the election and it was apparent Reagan would win, Dan said we should say that Reagan's victory was problematic.

Bill Greider was AME national during that campaign and the first year of the Reagan presidency. His well-known liberalism made the Grahams uneasy, but Bill wasn't distorted by his politics. He was a hard-charging journalist in the Harwood mode and one of the paper's best writers. During the impeachment hearings of President Nixon, reporters on the national staff took turns analyzing the day's proceedings. It was Bill's turn on the day an official of the Committee to Re-Elect the President confessed to lying about CREEP's role in the 1972 election campaign. "Perjury went down as smoothly as the second martini," Greider wrote.

Bill and I were on our second martini when he took me to dinner during the 1980 campaign and asked me to explore Ronald Reagan's life more deeply. Bill said many readers knew little about Reagan's early days despite his two previous campaigns for the presidency. I had never before been encouraged at *The Post* to write extensively about Reagan. Out of that dinner and those martinis came a series called "A Reagan Almanac" that examined Reagan's life and set the tone for my future coverage of Reagan. Bill was left-of-center, to be sure, but he also was responsible for some of the best writing I did about Ronald Reagan.

If anything, Bill was too enthusiastic about my coverage; he became angry when he learned it hadn't been entered for a Pulitzer and picked an unnecessary battle with Howard Simons, the executive editor. I urged Bill not to make a fuss. I wasn't that into prizes, although while covering Reagan I'd go on to win my share.[4] What I needed more was for Bill to retain allies in management. Even before Reagan took office in January 1981, Greider had begun eight months of conversations with

4. These awards included the White House Correspondents Association's Aldo Beckman Award in 1984 for overall excellence in presidential coverage and the Merriman Smith award for excellence in presidential news coverage—a single story written under deadline pressure—in 1986. I knew and respected Beckman and Smith. I also won the first Gerald R. Ford Prize (1988) for distinguished reporting on the Nixon, Ford, and Reagan presidencies. My son Carl also won both the Ford Prize and the Aldo Beckman award—for his coverage of George W. Bush.

David Stockman, the administration's budget director. Stockman, a former House member from Michigan and conservative wunderkind, was trying to make sense of Reagan's contradictory trifecta of promises from the 1980 campaign. Reagan had promised to cut taxes, boost defense spending, and balance the budget. Stockman's mentor was former Republican Congressman John Anderson, who ran as an independent presidential candidate in 1980. Debating Reagan, Anderson said the only way the budget could be balanced while taxes were being cut and defense spending increased was "with mirrors." But Stockman believed it could be done and temporarily became a convert to the doctrine of supply-side economics. Supply-siders believed that reducing taxes would jump-start the nation's moribund economy and produce more revenue than would be lost by the tax cuts.

As 1981 unfolded, Reagan won legislative victories on his tax and budget bills, while Stockman became increasingly gloomy in his conversations with Greider as he began to realize that supply-side economics couldn't deliver on its promises. Instead of producing a balanced budget, supply-side was causing the federal budget deficit to balloon and would soon become handmaiden to a serious recession. On October 23, 1981, the federal budget deficit reached a symbolic $1 trillion.

On November 6, Reagan threw in the towel on the balanced budget, inaccurately telling reporters, "I've never said anything but that it was a goal." (In May, Reagan had told a Republican publication he expected not only a balanced budget but a small surplus by 1984.)

Greider had briefed me on what Stockman was telling him, information that enriched my stories. But Bill hadn't told me he was writing for the *Atlantic Monthly* instead of *The Washington Post*. When he mentioned this after his conversations with Stockman had ended, I became alarmed and asked Bill if Ben Bradlee knew this. Bill assured me he'd kept Ben in the loop. Ben remembered it differently but told me much later that he hadn't thought a story about Reagan's budget director would have such explosive impact. This suggests Greider had at least talked to Ben beforehand about his plan to take the story to *The Atlantic*—but probably not enough. Great Men do not always pay attention. Sometimes you have to sit them down and explain to them that their world is about to change and not for the better.

On November 10, 1981, Senator Gary Hart of Colorado read an advance copy of Greider's *Atlantic* story into the *Congressional Record*.

"The Education of David Stockman" began with an admission from Stockman that "none of us really understands what's going on with all these numbers" and proceeded to expose supply-side economics as renamed "trickle-down economics" under which the wealthy received huge tax cuts that were supposed to filter down to everyone else. Forty years later, "The Education of David Stockman" stands as a trenchant exposé of supply-side economics.

At the time many Republicans, including Reagan aides Edwin Meese and Michael Deaver, wanted Stockman to be fired. But White House chief of staff James Baker realized that Stockman could do more damage as a disgruntled outsider than as an apologetic budget director and urged Reagan to keep him. The president did so, absolving Stockman and blaming Greider for the embarrassing article. Similar concerns about misplaced loyalty were raised at Greider's workplace, but there was no Jim Baker equivalent inside *The Washington Post* to speak up for Bill, who left the paper quietly and was snapped up by *Rolling Stone.*

Greider went on to write a series of populist books with such titles as *The Betrayal of Democracy* and *The Soul of Capitalism: Opening Paths to a Moral Economy.* Stockman was muzzled for the rest of Reagan's first term while supply-side zealots on Capitol Hill denounced him as a traitor. After Reagan's reelection in 1984, he left the White House and wrote a book repaying Reagan's forgiveness by portraying the president as befuddled and out of touch. Greider had many admirers on the national staff, including me, but Bradlee assuaged our anxiety over his departure by offering the AME national job to Pete Silberman.

My reporting colleague on the White House beat at the beginning of the Reagan presidency was the admirable Lee Lescaze, a man for all seasons. When Bradlee tapped Lescaze to become AME of the Style section, Silberman asked me if there was any reporter who had impressed me with his coverage of the Reagan campaign. I mentioned David Hoffman of Knight-Ridder, who'd done excellent campaign coverage but had not been rewarded by his organization with the White House beat. Hoffman wanted to cover the White House, and *The Post* hired him. He was a serious person, sometimes too serious, but one of the hardest-working reporters I've ever known. He served as my colleague for several years, had an extensive career at *The Post,* and won a Pulitzer Prize for *The Dead Hand,* his book on Soviet nuclear strategy, and another for editorial writing in 2024.

Years later, when Robert Kaiser was AME national, he asked me if there was anyone already covering the White House whom *The Post* should hire. The answer to that easy question was Ann Devroy, a standout reporter for *USA Today* and Gannett News Service who didn't get the attention she deserved because some people in our business looked down on her organization. I knew from experience that you can find good reporters anywhere, and Devroy was a great and competitive reporter and fun to be around. She had a young daughter and had reached an agreement with *USA Today* allowing her to skip most road trips. Kaiser went *USA Today* one better: He asked her to become *The Post*'s political editor. It was an offer Devroy couldn't—and didn't—refuse. She excelled in that job and later distinguished herself on the White House beat during Bill Clinton's presidency. Her story did not have a happy ending. Cancer felled Devroy at the young age of forty-nine. Her friends, of whom I'm one, still miss her.

Then there is Maralee Schwartz, barrier breaker, who in 1979 began as a researcher for *The Post*. Our desks were opposite, and we answered each other's phones and became friends. Maralee was enthusiastic and full of ideas. During the 1980 campaign, with encouragement from Dan Balz, she started a Political Notes column that was copied by the *New York Times*. The *Post* at the time had a rule forbidding researchers from having a byline. Both Balz and I unsuccessfully appealed to managing editor Leonard Downie to make an exception for Maralee. Years later I saw a double-bylined story in the paper with Maralee's name and asked Len what had happened. "Maralee wore me down," he said with a smile. Breaking other barriers, Maralee went on to become congressional editor and political editor.

Researchers were an unimagined luxury in my journalistic career before *The Post*. David Broder, who shared everything, made his researcher Joan Barone available for members of the political team. If I asked Joan to look up something, she often intuited my follow-up question and had the answer. Susan Morrison, a later researcher, would perch over my desk in a space too small for most people, write down questions, and swiftly return with answers. Joan and Susan are gone but remembered. I don't know the whereabouts of James Schwartz, to whom I'm also indebted. He was a researcher at *The Post;* I hired him to keep eighteen hundred files in order when I wrote *President Reagan: The Role of a Lifetime*.

When Harwood returned to *The Post* from the *Trenton Times* in the mid-1970s, he brought with him Joel Garreau as an editor on the national desk. Harwood was prodding me to become the western correspondent and wanted me to think well of Garreau, a free spirit whose duties included editing the out-of-town reports.

"Don't be put off by his beard and his doper pouch," Harwood said. "He's a capitalist."

Garreau raised goats on a small northern Virginia farm from which he commuted to *The Post.* He was an imaginative editor who also wrote interesting books. When I noted that a section of his first book, *The Nine Nations of North America,* was indebted to my reporting, Joel replied disarmingly: "Steal from the best, I always say."

Another marvelous *Post* journalist is Jay Mathews, who both proceeded me and succeeded me at the Los Angeles bureau. Jay is at once erudite—he learned Mandarin when he was assigned to the Beijing bureau—and down-to-earth. His first love is education, and he still writes an education column for *The Post.* In defiance of journalistic norms, Jay often shows his stories to the subjects of his reporting. Once in Los Angeles he allowed the Scientologists to read a critical story he'd written about them. I thought this was inviting trouble, but the Scientologists were unused to considerate treatment from the media and made no objection to the story.

Ruth Marcus was a talented young reporter covering the Supreme Court, with whom I often shared information during the Reagan presidency. She became a *Post* columnist, highly respected especially on Supreme Court issues, and a leader of the paper's editorial board until owner Jeff Bezos blew up the paper's editorial page section as I was finishing this memoir. The late Helen Dewar covered the Virginia legislature with distinction and later the U.S. Senate when I was covering the Reagan White House. We exchanged information, more to my benefit than hers, and occasionally a byline.

I also enjoyed working with the late Spencer Rich, a master digger whose data was better than the government's, and with the classy George Lardner, who won a well-deserved Pulitzer for an agonizing story no father would ever want to write—the murder of his daughter. As I contemplate my time at *The Post,* I realize how much I owed so many of my colleagues and how warmly I remember them. I should also give a shout-out to Stuart Auerbach, John M. Berry, Herb Denton, Karen

DeYoung, Douglas Fever, George Will, Meg Greenfield, Fred Hiatt, Judith Havemann, Jerry Knight, Joanne Omang, Joe Pichirallo, William Prochnau, Donnie Radcliffe, Megan Rosenfeld, Kathy Sawyer, Larry Stern, Juan Williams, and George Wilson.

If the most difficult job for a reporter at *The Post* was succeeding Broder, as Balz has done so capably, the equivalent challenge for an editor was following Ben Bradlee, a unique and charismatic leader who'd led our paper to the journalistic heights. This daunting test fell to Leonard Downie, whose forty-four-year journalism career was spent entirely at *The Post.* When Bradlee stepped down and Downie became executive editor, he made no attempt to emulate Ben but went where Bradlee had not gone and focused on improving local coverage, which Len did so well that *The Post* won a slew of Pulitzer and other prizes.

Downie wasn't born to wealth, and he empathized with reporters who felt underpaid. With the backing of Donald Graham, Downie surveyed comparable salaries at the *New York Times,* with the result that many national staff members received raises. Len was also an early apostle of diversity, hiring and promoting women and minorities. Downie chose Kaiser as his managing editor, saying he wanted someone smarter than himself. They became a good team after an anxious start in which they reacted harshly against a reporter who in a moment of panic copied passages from another paper without attribution in a "Letter from Florida" she'd written for *The Post.* The reporter was suspended while Downie and Kaiser examined her previous stories for evidence of plagiarism, finding none. I knew the reporter and talked to her. She said she'd felt under pressure because the letter was overdue but admitted she had done the wrong thing, adding that she had never done it before and would never do it again.

Nonetheless, her firing seemed likely. Because this was the first offense of a promising and contrite reporter, I thought it warranted a lesser penalty. I talked to Kaiser, who said that several others felt the same and that he and Downie would hear us out. Only three reporters—Dale Russakoff, David Maraniss, and me—showed up for a meeting with Len and Bob, and it soon became clear they were disinclined to give the offending reporter a second chance. Kaiser said neither he nor readers would be able to trust anything she wrote and asked if there were any grounds for *not* firing her.

"The doctrine of redemption," Maraniss replied, making me an instant fan. The reporter was fired anyway. She later caught on with a newspaper in another city and to the best of my knowledge had a productive career.

The editors used this incident as a launching pad to improve the staff's standards of attribution. They were right to do so. When I'd worked for Ridder Publications, I'd often been annoyed that *The Post* or the *Times* would use information from a local story without attribution. But the efforts of Downie and Kaiser to codify our practices were initially heavy-handed. We began attributing facts that were in the public domain and needed no attribution, prompting the head of the copy desk to quip, "Tomorrow is Tuesday, the Associated Press reported." In time this hyper-focus on attribution passed, having left a useful imprint.

Willie Mays once said he would play baseball for nothing if he could afford it. That's the way I feel about journalism, especially my twenty-nine years with *The Washington Post.* We had fun, broke stories, and took chances because we knew we had the backing of our editors. Ben Bradlee and the other editors in turn had consistent support from our amazing publisher, Katharine Graham. Downie had similar backing from Kay's son and successor, Donald Graham. Don was amazing, too. He'd served in the Army in Vietnam and as a patrolman for the Washington, DC, police department before working in every department of the newspaper.

The Grahams respected the news staff and treated us well; I was proud to work for them. During her reign, Kay periodically descended from her office on the seventh floor to distribute comments and compliments on the fifth-floor newsroom. Once, she sought me out after I'd written a scathing story about Reagan.

"Lou," she said, "I don't know why those people at the White House even talk to you, but I'm glad they do."

Those people talked to Mrs. Graham, too. She began having lunch with Nancy Reagan, who quietly took soundings of powerful people much as Kay did. Both were shrewd judges of character, could swear like sailors, and were rarely reluctant to express their opinions. Because of my long relationship with the Reagans, I was sometimes a guest at the Graham home (and at the home of Ben Bradlee and Sally Quinn as well), where I learned by listening. Once in a private conversation, I commended Mrs. Graham for her courage in printing the Watergate stories, and she modestly responded that any newspaper owner would have done the same. I then told her how Joseph Ridder, publisher of the *San Jose Mercury-News,* had suppressed a series I'd cowritten because the crooked state senator we exposed was a Republican.

Mrs. Graham shook her head. "It's a wonder you stayed in journalism," she said.

The sternest test for Kay Graham was neither Watergate nor the Pentagon Papers but the wanton destruction of the printing presses by militant pressmen on October 1, 1975. Informed of this catastrophe, Mrs. Graham drove herself to the paper, where she found the paper's nine massive presses had been vandalized; one had been set on fire, while a union member held a screwdriver to the pressroom foreman's throat.

The pressmen had accomplished something President Nixon was never able to do: shut down *The Washington Post.* Mrs. Graham wrote in *Personal History,* her autobiography, that she was "shocked and saddened" by what she saw. That shock extended to the newsroom. When I arrived for work in the middle of the morning, I tried to see what had happened, but guards kept everyone away from the pressroom. By chance, I encountered Kay on her way out of the pressroom and told her I was sorry about what had happened. She pledged grimly that the paper would soon print again, which it did, missing only one day. Mrs. Graham's team avoided the picket line in front of the paper by using helicopters that landed on the paper's roof and whisked printing plates to satellite presses scattered around the metropolitan area.

During the next four-a-half months there were times when I also longed for helicopter access to *The Post.* I'd been a member of three unions and had never crossed a picket line, which I did for the first time when I came to work that morning. The line was strung out along Fifteenth Street near the main entrance to *The Post.* When I crossed it going home, I was swung at from behind, the blow landing on my shoulder. I turned around and swung back, hitting my assailant in the nose. A melee ensued. After I extricated myself and walked to a nearby Metro station, I discovered my watch was missing. The watch had sentimental value because it had been my father's. Fortunately, a friend on the picket line had witnessed the scuffle. She retrieved the watch and returned it to me the next day.

Newsroom employees at *The Post* belong to the Washington-Baltimore chapter of the American Newspaper Guild. I was a proud member, knowing how much the union had done historically to improve pay and working conditions, but along with others in the newsroom held a low opinion of the militant mediocrity who was executive secretary of our chapter. We had questioned his purpose and tactics in the past and were not surprised he backed the destructive pressmen.[5] But the guild is a democratic union; we ignored the executive secretary's threats to dock our pay and decided by voice vote the day after the presses were wrecked to continue working. Subsequently, this decision was ratified in two recorded votes.

I spoke at one meeting, saying the pressmen, like former President Nixon, should be held accountable to the rule of law. The contract of the pressmen had expired. If they had struck without destroying the presses, the guild would have honored the picket line. Even as it was, guild members might have reconsidered their position had not pressmen or goons in their employ physically attacked guild members and phoned spouses threatening bodily harm to their families. Several guild members were assaulted crossing the picket line, as I had been. Kathy Sawyer was hit on the head with a block of wood; Jules Witcover was beaten up in a garage as he was retrieving his car. Both were top reporters and popular in the newsroom.

Battle lines hardened during the winter as *The Post* continued to publish. Management offered the pressmen a new contract that would have made them among the highest paid pressmen in the nation. After the pressmen's union rejected the offer, *The Post* hired nonunion replacements, some of whom had put out the paper during the strike. Mrs. Graham was accused of union-busting. She countered by citing her prolabor history and blaming the pressmen for using violence to accomplish their goals rather than bargaining in good faith. (Fifteen people eventually were indicted on various charges relating to destruction of the presses.) *The Post* survived as a unionized paper by signing new contracts with the typesetters and other unions, including the guild. The picket lines around *The Post* ended in February 1976, providing immense relief to

5. He had approved a dubious strategy in a 1974 strike in which we "withheld our excellence" from the newspaper. That strike lasted only seventeen days after the membership—over the objections of the executive secretary—voted to accept an offer from management making *Post* reporters the highest paid in the nation. The executive secretary had also tried to get our guild unit to endorse George McGovern for president in 1972. We told him that journalists don't do political endorsements and voted against it.

those of us who had been crossing them. The scars of the conflict would be slow to heal.

Richard Harwood spent his last four years at *The Washington Post* doing a second turn as the paper's ombudsman. Although he was no longer my boss, I valued his insights and slipped into his office whenever possible to get his take on whatever was happening. This was in 1988 when I was covering the White House during the last year of the Reagan presidency.

Harwood had served in the Pacific Theater from 1943 to 1946 with the Fifth Marine Amphibious Corps and saw combat on Saipan, Tinian, Guam, and Iwo Jima, where he'd been wounded and lost a lung. His wartime experiences had long been a taboo subject, but that was beginning to change. One day Harwood showed me a draft of a long article (later a short book) he had been commissioned to write about Tinian, which U.S. Marines had captured from the Japanese in July 1944.[6] *A Close Encounter: The Marine Landing on Tinian* combines military analysis and a plentitude of maps with masterful descriptive writing.

"Tinian was easy on the eyes, but the heat and humidity were brutal, the cane fields were hard going, and it was the season of monsoons." Harwood wrote.

Dick asked my opinion of the Tinian draft, and I said that James Jones, our mutual favorite war writer, would have liked it. We discussed the war, but Harwood still held back on talking about Iwo Jima, and I didn't press him. He seemed to feel that he and the other 26,000 servicemen who'd been wounded on this bloody island, owed the 6,800 Americans who had died there the respect of silence. But there was more to it than that, as I learned later.

I remain abidingly grateful to Dick Harwood for bringing me to *The Washington Post* and to David Broder for mentoring me once I got there. I'm grateful, too, to the men and women cited here and to others I have failed to mention for making our years together at the paper rewarding. We were witnesses who wrote what Philip Graham had called the first rough draft of history. As Mikhail Gorbachev said to Ronald Reagan in Moscow, we also had a good time.

6. A year later, Tinian would be the takeoff point for the U.S. planes that dropped atomic bombs on Hiroshima and Nagasaki.

19

THE RISE AND FALL OF JERRY FORD

In the summer of 1974, *The Washington Post* promoted its help-wanted section with broadcast commercials that had the tag line: "I got my job through the *Washington Post.*" After Gerald Ford succeeded Richard Nixon, someone at the White House created a poster showing a smiling Ford proclaiming that he, too, had obtained his job through *The Post,* a reference to the iconic reporting of Woodward and Bernstein. I spotted the poster while interviewing Ford after he'd become president and mentioned it to Bradlee, who surprised me by saying he wanted it. This was unlike Ben, whose near-spartan office was unadorned with his many honors. When I told Ford, he chuckled and signed it to Ben with an inscription. Bradlee exhibited it in his office for many years.

Ford was a burst of summer sunshine, dispelling the twilight gloom of the Nixon presidency. "My fellow Americans, our long national nightmare is over," he said after taking the presidential oath of office. "Our Constitution works; our great Republic is a government of laws and not of men. Here the people rule."

Ford was the most common American to occupy the Oval Office since Harry Truman. In time he would suffer, as Truman had, from a public perception that he was too ordinary for such high office, but the first weeks of the Ford presidency were alive in symbolic practice of American democracy. Ford made his own breakfast. He was introduced to the strains of the Michigan fight song, rather than "Hail to the Chief." He allowed old friends to call him "Jerry" rather than "Mr. President."

There was a purpose to this symbolism. Ford had never been elected to anything other than his Grand Rapids congressional district, but he realized that his fellow Americans, exhausted by the Watergate scandal and the seemingly endless Vietnam War, longed for normalcy in Washington and a measure of tranquility at home and abroad. Jerry Ford created a natural atmosphere so effortlessly that he received little credit for what might have been his most significant achievement as president.

The short happy life of the Gerald Ford presidency ended on September 8, when he unconditionally pardoned Richard Nixon for any crimes he may have committed. Nixon had been named an unindicted coconspirator by the federal grand jury that investigated the Watergate burglary, and the pardon did not sit well with the jury foreman, who had wanted to indict Nixon, or with Democrats who'd sung Ford's praises during the first month of his unelected presidency. Polls showed the pardon unpopular, and media criticism was harsh. David Broder asked my opinion, and I told him I thought the pardon was a hard pill to swallow but probably helpful to the country. Broder said we were a minority of two at *The Washington Post.*

The understandable suspicion was that Ford had struck a deal with Nixon to pardon him before he resigned. Ford denied this under oath before the House Judiciary Committee in the only sworn congressional testimony ever given by a sitting president. But pardoning Nixon had not been Ford's initial impulse. On August 28, at the first press conference of his presidency, Ford had said it would be "unwise and untimely" to commit to a pardon in advance of legal action against Nixon. When Ford changed his mind, he said he felt that doing so was in the best interests of the country, adding that the Nixon family's situation was "a tragedy in which we all have played a part. It could go on and on and on, or someone must write the end to it. I have concluded that only I can do that, and if I can, I must."

This vague declaration was the tip of an iceberg of concern about Nixon's mental health. Writing in *The Post* two days before the pardon was issued under the headline, "Nixon in Exile: Lonely, Depressed," I quoted an anonymous Nixon friend as saying the former president was "terribly depressed with much to be depressed about."

Two days after the pardon, George Lardner and I reported that former White House counsel J. Fred Buzhardt after visiting the former president in San Clemente told Ford that "Nixon was in a considerable state of anxiety." The story also quoted Senator Robert Griffin of Michigan, the Republican whip, as saying that Ford's concern about Nixon's mental and physical condition was a key factor in the pardon.

When Ford and I later discussed the pardon off-the-record, he mentioned my story about Nixon's depression and said he'd received similar reports. Ford said much the same to Tom DeFrank, the White House correspondent of *Newsweek,* to whom he was close. "I was hearing that he was terribly distraught," Ford told DeFrank. "I don't know whether you could call it irrational (but) he was despondent, had an unhealthy state of mind."[1]

Ford was most concerned, he told me, that drawn-out legal proceedings against Nixon would make it difficult if not impossible for the country to heal. Healing was a touchstone for Ford, who titled his autobiography *A Time to Heal.* Writing about the pardon in this book, Ford said, "I simply was not convinced that the country wanted to see an ex-president behind bars."

He added: "We are not a vengeful people; forgiveness is one of the roots of the American tradition. And Nixon, in my opinion, had already suffered enormously. His resignation was an implicit admission of guilt, and he would have to carry forever the burden of his disgrace. But I wasn't motivated primarily by sympathy for his plight or by concern over the state of his health. It was the state of the country's health at home and around the world that worried me."

History has been kind to Ford on the Nixon pardon. In 2001, the John F. Kennedy Library gave Ford its annual Profile in Courage award. Ted Kennedy, who had opposed the pardon, said he had come to accept it as a decision in the national interest. In a July 2014 panel hosted by *The Post,* Bob Woodward called the pardon "an act of courage."

Such revisionism came far too late for Republicans who faced the voters in November 1974. Democrats netted forty-nine House seats and four Senate seats in these midterm elections, plus the governorships of California, New York, and two other states. Political demographer Michael Barone said that the country after Watergate was "more Democratic than in the presidential landslide years of 1936 or 1964 . . .

1. Email to the author from Tom DeFrank, December 16, 2020.

more Democratic (for the moment) than when it was led by its paladins Franklin Roosevelt and John Kennedy."

The election results weakened Ford, raising doubts among Republicans about his ability to lead them into battle in 1976, creating a promising opportunity for Ronald Reagan.

As Reagan wound up his second term as governor of California in 1974, he was quietly assessing his presidential possibilities. Ford's ascension had disrupted Reagan's unannounced game plan, which assumed Nixon would serve out his second term, leaving the path open for a run in 1976. Instead, Reagan was left with the unpalatable alternatives of challenging Ford for the nomination, which he knew would split the party, or waiting until 1980 when he would be nearly seventy—probably too old by the political standards of the time.

I'd kept in touch with the Reagan camp with calls to loyalists such as Mike Deaver and Lyn Nofziger and interviewed Reagan in Sacramento for an evaluation of his governorship I wrote for *California Journal.* Reagan was noncommittal but avoided praising Ford.

I spent July through September of 1975 on leave from *The Post* at the Aspen Institute. Before I left for Colorado, Ford asked me if I thought Reagan would run in 1976. I answered yes. Ford shook his head in disbelief and said Reagan would not have the support of the Republican Party. I didn't want to argue with a president and said nothing more, but I knew Reagan would not be deterred by lack of institutional support. When I returned to the White House beat early in October, Dick Cheney, who was poised to replace Don Rumsfeld as White House chief of staff, asked me if Reagan would run. I was amazed because Cheney was usually politically attuned. I told him Reagan was already planning his announcement, which took place in New York City on November 25.

Aspen had been a worthwhile interlude. I'd gone there at the invitation of journalist and educator Douglass Cater, a friend and mentor whose trailblazing 1965 book, *The Fourth Branch of Government,* had influenced my thinking about the role of the press. Doug suggested I write a follow-up book. It took longer than I'd estimated to write *Reporting: An Inside View* and longer still to get it published, but it would never have been written without that Aspen experience and Doug's encouragement. Aspen had many other attractions. The great novelist Saul Bellow was in residence and generous with his time. The institute's library was full of books on politics and government. My wife and our two youngest children came for much of the summer. Judy, our teenage daughter, would be a music major in college. She remembers an enchanted evening when she sat next to Aaron Copland at dinner and talked about music. My youngest son, Jack, then ten, hiked with me to the top of Aspen Mountain, where he spotted a golden eagle. It was a magical summer.

Back at the White House, President Ford was floundering. By the time Reagan announced he was running for president, Ford's job approval ratings had slumped back to the low forties, close to what they had been in the post-pardon days.[2]

Ford was nonetheless trying to put his stamp on a foreign policy he'd inherited, complete with Henry Kissinger, from Richard Nixon. Ford had kept Kissinger in the dual posts of secretary of state and national security advisor, but as part of a White House staff shakeup on November 2, he gave the national security portfolio to Brent Scowcroft. Ford told me he felt at ease with Scowcroft, but Ford had promised continuity with Nixon's foreign policy, which meant keeping Kissinger as secretary of state. At the same time, Ford fired his predecessor's secretary of defense, James Schlesinger, and CIA director William E. Colby, replacing them with Rumsfeld and George H. W. Bush, respectively. Colby, always a good soldier, went quietly, but the bristly Schlesinger became a critic of Ford and a darling of conservatives who preferred Reagan.

Ford's foreign policy could be described as Nixon Lite. He wanted to be seen as upholding the Nixon détente with the Soviet Union, which Americans generally favored, and going an extra step toward U.S.-Soviet cooperation, thereby drawing a contrast with Reagan. In August, Ford had signed the Helsinki Accords, which recognized the inviolability of the European borders established at the end of World War II, angering many Poles. As his next move, Ford sought to cement Nixon's China overtures with a seven-day trip in December to China, Indonesia, and the Philippines, culminating with a speech in Honolulu on the thirty-fourth anniversary of the bombing of Pearl Harbor.

I'd been at Aspen during Helsinki and looked forward to Ford's trip, which I prepared for by reading *Flowers on an Iron Tree* by Ross Terrill. As I entered the airport in what was then called Peking, I was met by a bespectacled and bulky man in a padded jacket.

2. I now had a *Post* colleague, the redoubtable Ed Walsh, helping me on the beat. We shared White House coverage for a while, and he eventually succeeded me.

"Hello, Mr. Cannon, I understand you know a lot about the Republicans," he said. Bulky Man asked me if Reagan would replace Ford as the Republican nominee in 1976. I told him that Republican voters would make this decision.

"But what will the party do?" he persisted. I didn't have the slightest idea.

The days in China were heavy on ceremony, propaganda, and too many rounds of the potent Chinese alcoholic drink baijiu. Few Americans had been to China then, and I wanted to escape the official regimen and see Beijing and its environs. We weren't allowed to see much in the city, but on the third day of the trip a Yugoslav diplomat known to *The Post*'s foreign desk arranged for a few reporters to visit a market outside the city. It was modest by American standards, but the Chinese farmers were proud of it, and one of them spoke English. While the farmer was showing off oversize cabbages, I heard a familiar voice behind me. It was John Chancellor of NBC News, who'd risen to TV heights as a news anchor but remained a diligent reporter. We were friends. Jack, as his friends called him, wanted to know the price of everything in the market. But as the conversation continued, Chancellor sensed that the English-speaking farmer wanted to tell us something he didn't want our Chinese escorts to hear. Chancellor took him aside so he could speak to just the two of us. This was near the end of the Cultural Revolution, and we had only the vaguest sense of the horrors and privations it had visited on the Chinese people. The farmer told us that past years had not been kind to the Chinese people. There were times, he said, when the people had only "white tea" to drink. Neither Chancellor nor I knew what he meant.

"You call it water," the farmer said.

The big moment of Ford's visit was a December 2 meeting with Chinese leader Mao Zedong. A since-declassified memo of their conversation shows that Mao, who would die ten months later, was candid about his deteriorating medical condition.

Ford, accompanied by Kissinger and Scowcroft, met Mao for nearly two hours, longer than Mao had spent with Nixon. The declassified memo is shorter and may not include their entire conversation. The memo is notable for Mao's repeated expressions of animus to the Soviet Union, which Ford joined at critical moments. Mao suggests at one point that the United States was more talk than action in dealing with the Soviets, prompting this exchange:

FORD: "We can also use force against a country which causes much trouble."

MAO: "That is not bad. Then we have reached another agreement."

But this was not enough for Mao, who continued to denounce the Soviet Union and talked about driving the Soviets out of its beachheads in Africa. After Nixon's historic visit in 1972, the United States and China had issued the Shanghai Communiqué, pledging to seek "normalization" of relations and calling for more trade and "people-to-people" contacts. The lack of a communiqué after Ford's visit was widely seen as a sign of underachievement, even though the body language between Ford and Mao had been positive, as it was the next day when Ford and Kissinger met with Deng Xiaoping, the pragmatic vice premier who after Mao's death would become the most powerful figure in China.

I suspect that, in view of Mao's bristling attacks on the Soviet Union, Ford did not really desire a communiqué. Reagan had announced his presidential candidacy two weeks earlier, and Ford was positioning himself politically as a peace-seeking president who was being challenged by an opponent with reckless foreign policy views. In this context Ford wouldn't have wanted it known he had told Mao that the United States was willing to use force against the Soviet Union. Mao favored a communiqué that emphasized mutual U.S.-Chinese militancy toward the Soviets—the last thing Ford needed.

Ford's legacy would have been better served had he returned to Washington from Beijing. Instead, he flew to Jakarta, where on December 6 he and Kissinger gave the dictatorial Indonesian ruler Suharto the green light for a bloody invasion of the former Portuguese colony East Timor. The traveling press corps was kept in the dark; we weren't even told that East Timor had been discussed.

Operation Komodo, as the invasion of East Timor was known, occurred the next day, while the Ford party had moved on to the Philippines. It did not succeed as quickly as Kissinger anticipated because lightly armed Timorese fiercely resisted 20,000 Indonesian troops, many of them airborne. But the invaders were brutal, well-armed, and willing to kill civilians. By the time Indonesia annexed East Timor seven months later, estimates of Timorese deaths ranged as high as 100,000. The best that can be said about Ford's conduct in the East Timor affair was that he was incredibly misinformed. No such defense can be made for Kissinger.

The arc of history, however, favored the Timorese. Suharto fell from power in 1998. In 1999 the United Nations conducted a referendum in which 78.5 percent of Timorese voted for independence, triggering violence by pro-Indonesia militias in which thousands of people were murdered and most of the Timor infrastructure destroyed. The United Nations restored order by sending in a largely Australian armed force. So much for those who say the UN never accomplishes anything. East Timor became independent in 2002. On August 30, 2024, the Democratic Republic of Timor-Leste (the Portuguese words for East Timor) celebrated the twenty-fifth anniversary of the referendum that led to its independence. It is a poor but free country and one of the most democratic nations in the region.

Ford was greeted in Manila by President Ferdinand Marcos and a reception of 100,000 Filipinos. Then it was on to Honolulu where Ford spoke at the USS Arizona Memorial on the morning of December 7, 1975, describing his 27,000-mile trip as a step toward construction of "a safer and saner world."

At a second speech that day at the East-West Center, Ford proposed what he called a new Pacific Doctrine, calling for normalization of relations with China, economic cooperation and healing in Vietnam, and affirming that the U.S. relationship with Japan was a "pillar of our strategy." Ford hoped that the phrase "Pacific Doctrine" would define his strategy in the region, which might have happened if Ford had been elected in his own right.

A month before the Asian trip, Ford had damaged his chances of winning in 1976 by dumping Vice President Nelson Rockefeller from the ticket and replacing him with Bob Dole. The future Senate majority leader was a war hero and an accomplished lawmaker on Capitol Hill, but that's not why he was chosen. Ford made the switch in an effort to appease Reagan and seven conservative Republican senators including Barry Goldwater who had opposed Rockefeller's confirmation. On November 2, 1975, Ford phoned Rockefeller and asked him to stand aside in 1976. Rockefeller dutifully sent Ford a resignation letter the next day and throughout the campaign stuck with the cover story that he had decided on his own not to run. Choosing Rockefeller had been Ford's most creative decision as president and dropping him showed weakness. Ford eventually reached the same conclusion although the big unknown is whether Ford could have staved off Reagan for the Republican nomination if he had kept Rockefeller on the ticket.

I knew Dole and came to know Rockefeller and got along with them both. My experience as a reporter with Rocky began on December 19, 1974, the day he became vice president. I was at *The Post* working on an unrelated story when I received a telephone call from a woman named Shirley in the presidential scheduling office. I knew Shirley from the Nixon White House, where she'd been helpful when many of her co-workers weren't speaking to me. She said Rockefeller had chosen me for the vice presidential press pool, which came as a surprise. Press pools represent their colleagues in limited-access venues. The usual White House press pool at the time included representatives of the wire services, newspapers, newsmagazines, television, and radio.

I had never heard of a press pool for the vice president, let alone one he had selected. And why me? I didn't even know Rockefeller, but Shirley said he had specifically asked for me. I never learned why. My editors were unimpressed. They wanted the story I was working on. Fortunately, Connie Chung, a crackerjack reporter and reliable friend, was the TV reporter on the pool. When I told her I had to write a story before joining the pool, Connie said she'd cover for me. As it turned out, she wrote the pool report and signed both our names to it. I joined the pool late in the day at the office of Senator Hugh Scott of Pennsylvania, who was holding a reception for the new vice president. When I arrived, Henry Kissinger was extolling Rockefeller's virtues to a captive audience. Rockefeller seemed strangely subdued. He thanked me for coming, then said under his breath that it had been a long day.

Perhaps Rockefeller had a premonition of how unfulfilling the vice presidency would be for someone who had served fourteen years as governor of New York. It would have been hard for Rockefeller to flourish as vice president under any circumstances, and White House chief of staff Donald Rumsfeld and his staff kept the vice president isolated and mostly away from Ford. Rumsfeld had been a sidekick of Ford in the House, while Ford and Rockefeller barely knew one another. Rockefeller was the bigger man but less adroit than Rumsfeld in the craft of maneuver. As a result, he was largely reduced to being a ceremonial vice president with time on his hands.

The most notable of these ceremonies were funerals. After King

Faisal of Saudi Arabia was assassinated on March 25, 1975, Rockefeller was dispatched to the funeral. Soon after he returned from what he described as a grueling trip, long-time Nationalist Chinese leader Chiang Kai-Shek died on April 5 in Taiwan. Rumsfeld proposed sending secretary of agriculture Earl Butz to Chiang's funeral, and it was announced by the White House. But Madame Chiang Kai-shek and remnants of the once-powerful China lobby complained they needed someone of greater stature and asked for Rockefeller, who was knowledgeable about China. Ford acceded and asked Rockefeller to go to Taiwan.

Two of the three press seats on the Rockefeller plane were quickly gobbled up by the Associated Press and the *Los Angeles Times,* and the Rockefeller staff chose the *New York Times* from a long line of applicants to fill the third seat. But the *Times,* which had spent a small fortune covering Rockefeller over the years, was in cost-cutting mode and turned it down. Shirley called me and offered *The Post* the remaining seat. Soon I was off to Taiwan for the first and only time in my life.

The trip coincided with the contentious last days of the U.S.-backed regime in South Vietnam—the government would collapse on April 30—and the withdrawal of the remaining U.S. troops and embassy personnel stationed in Saigon. Congress had rejected Ford's request for additional aid to South Vietnam, prompting Rockefeller to say at a New Jersey fundraiser that Congress would be blamed if South Vietnam was lost. With Vietnam in mind, our trio of reporters on Air Force Two asked Hugh Morrow, Rockefeller's long-time press secretary, for time with the vice president, who give us an hour. Rockefeller said the U.S. withdrawal from Vietnam "had the makings" of an issue in the 1976 election.

"Let's say 2,000 Americans, or 3,000, half of them are killed, half of them are taken captive," Rockefeller said. "That raises a lot of issues."

The normally poker-faced Morrow winced at Rockefeller's answer, knowing that Ford had declined to speculate about possible casualties during the withdrawal. Part of Rockefeller's problem, we later learned, was that the Dubonnet he was drinking was liberally spiked with vodka. This may have prompted Rockefeller to intemperately share his thoughts about Cyprus where in 1974 a Greek military coup seeking to unite Cyprus with Greece had triggered a Turkish invasion of the island and its division between Turkish Northern Cyprus and the Greek Cypriot Republic of Cyprus. Because U.S. weapons were used in the invasion,

Congress cut off military aid to Turkey, a NATO ally. Ford was dismayed. The United States had important military bases in Turkey, and he worked to restore this aid.

On the plane we asked Rockefeller about Turkey's view. "If I were a Turk," replied Rockefeller ("a stipulation that would bar him from office in the first place and, in the second, is not the viewpoint he is charged with expressing," *Washington Post* editorial editor Meg Greenfield noted drily) "and had built my army totally on American weapons and spare parts and was dependent on them and had paid cash for delivery of weapons and then got cut off when I was trying to defend a minority of mine who had really been having a rough time on an island, I'd have to think twice."

We asked Rockefeller how he would feel if he were a Greek. "If I were a Greek and I believed in democracy," said Rockefeller, "I would be so very happy that my country as a result of the blunders of the military dictatorship in Cyprus that the government was overthrown . . . that I would be down on my knees praying to whoever they pray to." Morrow later told me that even after Rockefeller left office he would regularly receive letters informing him that Greeks prayed to God the Father and his son Jesus Christ.

Rockefeller's ramblings drew critical attention from the White House (Rumsfeld) and the State Department (Kissinger and others). But Ford, who had occasionally consumed an extra drink and expressed himself colorfully, ignored these concerns. Shaky interviews aside, Ford realized that Rockefeller had been the right man to send to Taipei. Although Rockefeller said nothing in public beyond a continued pledge of friendship with Taiwan, he privately assured its leaders that the United States would stand by Taiwan if the island were attacked by mainland China. Rockefeller also made a positive public impression. He was a hit at the National Museum, where the vice president's knowledgeable interest in Chinese jades and bronzes impressed his guides. Rockefeller had been collecting Chinese objects of art since 1930.[3]

An unrelated incident from this trip remains lodged in my memory. On our first morning in Taipei, Morrow and I were in the lobby of the Grand Hotel when Rockefeller came over and said Senator Lloyd

3. I analyzed the highs and lows of Rockefeller's trips in the *Washington Post* on April 20, 1975, in a story headed "Rockefeller's Taiwan Trip Was Reflection of the Man."

Bentsen of Texas had decided to run for president on the basis of my story about the vice president's airplane interview. That made no sense. Bentsen had been a declared candidate for the 1976 Democratic presidential nomination since February. He had raised considerable money, but his candidacy never caught fire. By the time of the Rockefeller trip, Bentsen had scaled back his campaign, basing his slim chances on a deadlocked convention. After Rockefeller left, I asked Morrow why the vice president didn't know that Bentsen was a candidate. "It was probably something he misheard in his briefing," Morrow said.

I didn't know what he was talking about. Morrow then explained to me that Rockefeller struggled to read because of dyslexia and was extensively briefed verbally every day about news events and other matters.[4]

This information had personal resonance. My youngest son, Jack, was having a hard time in school, and his mother and I were at a loss for an explanation. Jack was ten years old and bright but had difficulty reading or doing basic arithmetic. He was working harder in school than his three siblings ever had to work, and neither his parents nor his teachers had insight into his struggle. Eventually, we learned the nature of dyslexia and gave Jack help, but he was on his own during critical years of his boyhood.

Hugh Morrow told me that the press and public knew about Rockefeller's dyslexia. I thought that unlikely and upon my return asked colleagues at *The Washington Post* if they knew about it. None did, which speaks to a deficiency of journalism. We need to tell readers or viewers not only where politicians stand on the issues but how they acquire information.

Ford did not go abroad again as president after returning from his trip to China, Indonesia, and the Philippines. He was preoccupied for the rest of his term, first with Reagan's challenge to his nomination and afterward with his campaign for the presidency versus Jimmy Carter. I covered these campaigns for *The Post,* wrote about them in three books, and will limit myself here to a few personal observations. For starters, Ford was

4. In 1975, Rockefeller delivered a speech on the PBS special *The Puzzle Children* where he recounted his struggles with dyslexia and offered inspiration and advice to other dyslexic "puzzle children."

an easy politician to cover. He was good-natured and kind to people, including his staff, and was undistorted by his office or the extensive demands of long campaigns. Ford's simplicity and openness concealed an underrated intelligence and an exceptional command of the federal budget, on which I twice saw him give mistake-free briefings without notes.

Ford paid attention to his presidential duties without being consumed by work. He had learned early in life to compartmentalize and easily distinguished work from play. Ford was passionate about skiing, at which he displayed a child's wonder and an athlete's grace. When a reporter asked Ford what would happen if a global crisis erupted when he was on the slopes, he pointed to the Secret Service agents who accompanied him when he skied and said they'd find him. This was mostly true, although Ford delighted in racing away from his ski escorts much as Ronald Reagan would enjoy cantering away from agents who escorted him on horseback.

In December 1975, I was among a small number of White House reporters who accompanied Ford on a holiday trip to his favorite ski haven in Vail, Colorado. Such trips were usually light duty, and I brought my son Jack. One evening the reporters on the trip hosted a dinner for Ford, and I was delegated to meet the president outside the dining hall. Jack spotted Ford first and said, "Hello, Mr. President, I learned to ski today." Ford was charmed. He spent several minutes talking to Jack about the joys of skiing before a reporter came out of the dining hall, gave me a look, and led the president inside.

Ford's Achilles' heel was a stubborn streak, which made it hard for him to cut his losses. On October 6, 1976, in his first debate with Jimmy Carter, Ford declared: "There is no Soviet domination of Eastern Europe and there never will be under a Ford administration."

The Kremlin then had three military divisions in Poland and treated the governments from the Baltics to Romania as Soviet satellites. Ford meant to say the spirit of the people of Eastern Europeans had not been crushed by Soviet occupation. Moderator Max Frankel asked a follow-up question that provided an escape hatch, but Ford didn't take it.

"No Soviet domination of Eastern Europe" became the news of a debate in which otherwise Ford had done well. Worse, Ford stuck with his misstatement for two days despite the unanimous opinions of his advisors that he needed to issue a correction. Finally, Brent Scowcroft, Stu Spencer, and Dick Cheney convinced Ford to back down.

Jerry Rafshoon, Carter's media guru, would call Ford's blunder decisive, but polling evidence of this is lacking. The polls show Ford holding his own in this debate and gaining in two more debates with Carter. Covering the campaign, I was struck by Ford's unblinking optimism. Since Ford had been a winner all his life, said his pollster Robert Teeter, he could not believe he might lose. But lose he did. My story on the election outcome ran November 4, 1976, in *The Washington Post* under the headline "A Political Comeback That Just Missed."

> Close counts only in horseshoes and hand grenades. Winning isn't everything. It's the only thing. By all these familiar bromides, what happened yesterday is that Gerald Rudolph Ford lost an election he was expected to lose. By any other standard, what happened yesterday was a disappointing ending to what surely ranks as the most remarkable comeback in the history of American presidential politics.
>
> Ford trailed Jimmy Carter by 33 points in the Gallup Poll last July. He was 39 points behind in the August Harris Survey. Margins less wide than those signaled that it was all over for Barry Goldwater in 1964, all over for George McGovern in 1972.
>
> But it was not all over for Ford. Despite the combined handicaps of a staggering Democratic registration advantage, the burden of a long association with Washington in an anti-Washington year and the suspicions of millions of Americans that he lacked the capacity to be president, Ford made a race of it.

The electoral vote was the closest since 1916. Carter carried twenty-three states with 297 electoral votes, while Ford won twenty-seven states with 240 electoral votes. In an election in which nearly 80 million people voted, the change of 5,600 votes in Ohio and 3,700 votes in Hawaii would have made Ford the winner. But the man who claimed to have received the job because of *The Washington Post* never seemed like a loser to me.

20

SEMINOLE INTERLUDE

At the beginning of the 1976 campaign when *The Washington Post* faced a challenge to its normal practice of covering every presidential candidate, there were simply too many candidates. In addition to the Republican face-off between Ford and Reagan, seventeen Democrats sought their party's presidential nomination, then the largest field in history. Lacking resources to cover every candidate, the editors accepted David Broder's suggestion to use zone coverage in New Hampshire and Florida. A reporter in each of these early primary states became point person for covering candidates in both parties. I was assigned Florida. Until then, I had covered Reagan, but went to Florida without complaint. Zone coverage gave me a chance to see the Democratic field, including former peanut farmer Jimmy Carter.

Early in 1974, Broder had invited Carter and Dale Bumpers to lunch in Kay Graham's upstairs dining room. Carter was finishing his first and only term as governor of Georgia. Bumpers was doing the same as governor of Arkansas. The well-spoken Bumpers impressed most of the attendees as presidential material. Carter did not. I was in the luncheon minority who found Carter interesting. As it turned out, Bumpers decided to run for the Senate, leaving the path to the presidency open for a fellow moderate southerner.[1]

Carter assembled a political team from his gubernatorial staff plus the inimitable Jerry Rafshoon, a creative ad man, and Tim Kraft, a top-

1. In 1974, in an election I covered for *The Post,* Bumpers defeated Senator William Fulbright to win the Democratic nomination and then easily won the general election. He served in the Senate for twenty-four years.

notch organizer. Competing in the Iowa caucuses, which other Democratic candidates had passed up, Carter came off as folksy and relaxed, a pleasant contrast to more pompous politicians. He received only 27 percent of the vote in Iowa—"uncommitted" with 37 percent was first—but Carter led all actual candidates, and Rafshoon ran with the results. He plastered New Hampshire with billboards declaring Carter the winner in Iowa. The billboards boosted the name recognition of the little-known Georgian, enabling Carter to win the primary with 28.4 percent of the vote.

By the time I covered Carter, Florida had become critical to his candidacy. The Democratic field was still crowded, but only four candidates had traction. One of the four, the personable liberal Arizona congressman Mo Udall, had finished second in New Hampshire and was popular with reporters but lacked the resources to compete effectively in Florida. That left Carter, George Wallace, and Senator Henry "Scoop" Jackson, a neoliberal stalwart trying to fill a void left by the absence of Hubert Humphrey. He was like Hubert in other ways, too. I flew on the Jackson plane to Florida and watched a reporter trying to get the attention of the senator, who was in the front row. A Secret Service agent stopped the reporter from entering what would have been the first-class cabin. The reporter yelled "Senator!" and Jackson heard him. He got out of his seat and walked back to the reporter after gently informing the agent that reporters were free to approach him at any time.

The once-fearsome Wallace, now campaigning from a wheelchair, was not yet the repentant sinner who would renounce his past racism. But he was also not the firebrand he'd been before being shot in 1972. Wallace still denounced "those pointy-heads in Washington who think they know better than the people," but he was rarely specific and avoided racist remarks. I reported that Wallace was trying to take the high road and avoid criticizing his opponents. His genteel tactics reflected Wallace's diminished political status. Franklin D. Roosevelt had never been photographed in his wheelchair, but the modern media did not observe such polite taboos. When a confidant pointed out later to Wallace that FDR had been elected despite his disability, Wallace responded, "Yeah, they elected Roosevelt, but they didn't watch him on television every night getting hauled on a plane like he was half-dead."[2]

2. That anecdote was revealed by Howell Raines of the *New York Times* in his September 1998 obituary of Wallace.

Carter's goal in Florida was to defeat Wallace and force him out of the race. But Wallace still had a following, Carter reminded me in an interview as he drove from the Jacksonville airport to a meeting with Jewish supporters. It was the first time I'd seen Carter face-to-face since the Graham luncheon, and he looked lean and determined. He described the primary as a "showdown" and said he needed to beat Wallace in Florida to maintain the momentum of Iowa and New Hampshire. The drive took twelve minutes, and just before we'd reached our destination Carter asked if we could talk off the record. I agreed, prompting the following exchange:

CARTER: "Why does David Broder have it in for me?

ME: "I don't think that's true, governor. Broder is fair to everyone."

CARTER: "Not to me. He never writes anything good about me."

I was shaken. Broder was a friend, as well as my idol and mentor, and I'd never heard any other politician complain he was unfair—nor would I in during my twenty-six years at *The Washington Post.*

When I told David what Carter had said, he counseled me not to fret. "There are always candidates who expect us to be cheerleaders and are bothered when we're not," he said.

I never found out the basis of Carter's complaint about Broder, but I had my suspicions. Political reporters sometimes develop crushes on candidates, and Carter became the flavor of the month for the national press after his victories in Iowa and New Hampshire. To his journalistic boosters, Carter seemed refreshingly authentic. But Broder did not go gaga over Carter; one of his many strengths as a journalist was that he made independent assessments and was never in a rush to praise or condemn. "Let's see how it plays out," he often said.

There's a certifiable weirdness about politics in Florida, which exists to this day. In 1976, it surfaced at the meeting where Carter spoke to his Jewish supporters. When I tried to enter the hall, I was told the speech wasn't open to the press. By luck, I spotted a Democrat I knew and asked him why the meeting was closed. He explained that those attending didn't want to be identified because Jews in Florida were supposed to be supporting Jackson, a strong supporter of Israel. I ignored the implication that Jewish voters were expected to vote on this issue alone—or march in lockstep.

"What if I promise not to identify them?" I asked, even though the attendees wore nametags. "Then you can come in," the man said, and I did.

Carter began his speech by saying that he admired Jews, whom he called "the people of the Book." I thought this a bit much, but the audience seemed to like it. Then Carter talked about honesty in government before getting to the nub of his speech. "I would like to see a condition in Florida and the nation where you'd never see George Wallace's name in a headline again," he said. Carter knew his audience. I talked to several people after the speech who said they admired Jackson but were leaning to Carter because he could beat Wallace.

Although Carter advisor Patrick Caddell's own polls showed Jackson running a close third, Carter's strategy was to portray Jackson as a desperate minor candidate whose only function in the race was to split the anti-Wallace vote. Arriving in Florida, Carter said Jackson had "failed to get a single vote in New Hampshire." That was because Jackson hadn't been on the ballot. Carter accurately anticipated that some radio stations would carry his statement without noting that Jackson had skipped the New Hampshire primary.[3]

Carter frustrated Jackson. Campaigning in Massachusetts, Carter proposed putting a federal solar energy research center in the Bay State. In Florida he said the center should be located in the Sunshine State. Jackson said the location should be decided on its merits.

"I'm not going to tell voters one thing in Massachusetts and another in Florida," Jackson said. But in these pre-internet days, Carter got away with it. Later in the campaign, Carter's position on abortion varied as he moved from state to state. A reporter on the Carter plane asked Rafshoon for an explanation. "Well, ladies and gentlemen," Rafshoon quipped, "The way I see it, Governor Carter has the issue of abortion surrounded."

Florida proved pivotal in the Democratic primaries. Carter won with 34 percent of the vote to 30 percent for Wallace and 24 percent for Jackson. Wallace dropped out a week later after losing Illinois, where he had barely campaigned. Jackson won an unusual primary in New York State in which participants voted for delegates rather than candidates. It had little impact on the race, and Jackson dropped out after Carter beat him in the Pennsylvania primary on April 27. Both Wallace and Jackson subsequently endorsed Carter.

3. Carter's cheap shot wasn't even technically true. Although Scoop Jackson wasn't on the ballot, he received 1,857 write-in votes in the 1976 New Hampshire primary.

I saw little of Carter after Florida. With the field of Democratic contenders whittled down to Carter and a handful of pursuers, *The Post* abandoned zone coverage, and I returned to the Republican contest between Reagan and Ford. But not entirely. As Carter emerged as the likely Democratic nominee, *The Post* decided it needed round-the-clock coverage of him in Plains, Georgia, where Carter and his wife, Rosalyn, were born and lived most of their lives. With the nearest major airport in Atlanta more than 130 miles away, this was not a coverage of convenience. Since no reporter wanted to be buried in Plains on body-watch coverage, Broder proposed that all *Post* reporters who were covering the campaign spend a week there. He volunteered for the first week in Plains, and the rest of us, following his example, rushed to sign up. There was no lodging in Plains, so reporters stayed in nearby Americus, which boasted two motels ("the Best Western and the worst western," as Jules Witcover put it) and most news organizations rented rooms in the former. *The Post* kept the same room throughout the campaign. When I arrived, newspapers with previous stories had been neatly piled up in a corner by Helen Dewar, the reporter I replaced.

Plains, a town of six hundred people in southwest Georgia, had been a peanut-farming hub for most of its existence. But Carter's candidacy had transformed this rural backwater into a frenzied tourist mecca in which enterprising locals hawked memorabilia and campaign buttons and took visitors on unnecessary tours of a small, circular-shaped town they could easily have walked on their own. The most popular campaign button sported a hideous yellow illustration of a big-toothed grinning peanut with white lettering on a green background. The message on the button said: "The Grin Will Win Jimmy Carter for President in '76."

Beneath the commercial exterior of the new Plains, one quickly encountered the Old South. As governor, Carter had rebuffed white supremacists and left the all-white Plains Baptist Church to help start an integrated congregation, but vestiges of racism remained. Bruce Drake, a fine political reporter with the *New York Daily News,* was asked one day at our motel whether he was "the Jew boy from New York" who was covering Carter. Bruce allowed that he was. Except for those with southern roots, reporters in Plains were strangers in a strange land.

During my week in Plains I saw the candidate twice, once at the Carter family home. He and Rosalyn were gracious and Carter came over to me and commented favorably about my coverage in Florida. I thanked him, of course, but wondered if he was trying to mollify me to make up for his earlier criticism of Broder. When Carter asked me how I liked Plains, I disingenuously replied that it was lovely. Later that year when I was covering Ford, I saw Carter at the debates and a final time during a week in which *Post* reporters switched candidates to see the campaign from the other side.

The next time I saw Jimmy Carter he was president of the United States.

21

THE REAL REAGAN

PART I

Ronald Reagan was on the ropes when I resumed coverage of his presidential campaign in North Carolina in March 1976. After losing the Iowa caucuses to President Ford, he had suffered the narrowest of defeats in the first-in-the-nation New Hampshire primary, which Reagan had expected to win. Ford then won five consecutive primaries, and a rumor started that Reagan would soon drop out. This squared with the fiscal realities of the Reagan campaign, which was broke.

As the March 23 North Carolina primary loomed, reporters crowded around Reagan at airport press availabilities and repeatedly asked him when he was going to quit the race. Reagan became more aggravated with each repetition of this question, which he answered every time by saying he was staying in. When a television reporter loudly ignored Reagan's reply and asked again when he was going to quit, Reagan became red in the face.

"I'm *not* going to drop out!" he said.

He added that he wouldn't say it again but would answer questions on any other subject. Reagan later claimed this was part of his strategy, but it didn't sound like strategy to me. It sounded like an infuriated candidate who refused to be pushed into quitting.

I interviewed Reagan on the next short flight to another airport in North Carolina. My editors shared the conventional view that Reagan would soon be out of the race and suggested that it might be time to write Reagan's political obituary. With this in mind I asked Reagan the question he'd just said he wouldn't answer.

"When are you going to withdraw?" I asked.

"You too, Lou?" Reagan said, almost sadly.

I was embarrassed. I told Reagan that I'd needed to ask the question because my editors wanted his personal response in my story. Reagan said he understood but his tone of voice made it sound to me as if he didn't. I'd been covering him since he ran for governor of California, and Reagan expected me to know when he was serious.

No matter what Reagan said, I didn't see how he could continue. His campaign was deeply in debt, and some of his supporters had given up. But Reagan ignored the debts and the discord. He telephoned a once-key donor from California who no longer contributed and asked him to give again. He campaigned relentlessly. Two days before the primary, Reagan departed from form and predicted he would win North Carolina. Reagan rarely forecast an election outcome because, as he once told me, he did not want to be seen as either defeatist or overconfident. Later in the campaign if polls showed him leading in a state, Reagan would sometimes say, "President Dewey told me not to be overconfident." After an aide told Reagan that few people remembered Thomas Dewey, who was upset by President Harry Truman in 1948 despite being heavily favored, Reagan started saying he was "cautiously optimistic," a formulation he stuck with the rest of his career.

Reagan won the North Carolina primary convincingly, turning what had seemed Ford's surefire nomination into an open battle. Reagan and Ford would split the next twenty-two primaries, carrying their fight for the nomination to the Republican convention in Kansas City. Although Ford narrowly prevailed among the delegates, Reagan won the hearts of the Republican rank and file, giving him a leg up for the nomination four years later. I will not reprise the plowed ground of Reagan's near-miss for the nomination in 1976 or his successful campaigns for the presidency in 1980 and 1984, which I have written about in several books.[1] Instead, I will recount my interactions with Reagan and attempt to assess him personally, drawing on previous writings when necessary.

1. I wrote about Reagan's campaigns and his presidency in *President Reagan: The Role of a Lifetime,* published in 1991 and updated in 2000. *Reagan,* published in 1982, covers the second term of Reagan's governorship and the beginning of his presidency. I wrote about the Reagan governorship in *Governor Reagan: His Rise to Power,* published in 2003, and in my first book, *Ronnie and Jesse: A Political Odyssey,* 1969.

Ronald Reagan was destiny's child. Exalted by his mother, Reagan believed from an early age that he was fated to do great things. Much that happened in his life reinforced this feeling. Lacking any radio experience except imitative renditions of President Franklin Roosevelt's fireside chats, Reagan provided an imaginary account of a football game on a broomstick microphone to land a broadcasting job during the Great Depression. He became a well-known sportscaster in Iowa but dreamed of being a movie actor. In 1937 he went to Hollywood and auditioned at Warner Bros., where a promising young actor whom Reagan resembled had recently died in an automobile crash. Jack Warner noticed the resemblance and hired Reagan, who became a movie star and president of the Screen Actors Guild. When his film career faded, Reagan found a new one as spokesman for General Electric, which gave him a national platform every Sunday night introducing the popular *GE Theater* on television. Reagan's contract required him to speak at GE plants throughout the country. He wrote his own speeches and mingled with company workers, traveling a unique path that became a springboard into politics.

Reagan grew up a Democrat, and he was grateful to FDR for appointing his father, Jack, and his brother Neil to positions overseeing federal programs that distributed relief to jobless families in Lee County, Illinois, where the Reagans lived. After Reagan became a movie star, some Democrats in Hollywood wanted to run him for Congress but decided he was too liberal to win. They may have been right, but Reagan wasn't liberal for long. His politics changed with the tax burdens of prosperity and from knowing businessmen who chafed under government regulations they blamed on the New Deal. Reagan gave voice to their complaints but walled off a section of his heart for FDR, whom he never stopped admiring.

By 1964, Reagan was conservative enough to deliver his nationally televised speech for Barry Goldwater, and two years later ran for governor of California as a Republican. After winning the primary, Reagan defeated the incumbent by a million votes, climbing the first rung of a ladder that led to the White House. Reagan displayed little outward ambition even as he became a political star. His mother, Nelle, who had imbued her younger son with Christian teachings and interested him in theatrics, also taught him humility. Reagan rarely boasted, but occasionally his inner ambition would peek out from wherever it was hiding and allow a glimpse of the real Reagan, who told me that in college a fortune teller had predicted he'd be president. Reagan said he attached no special meaning to her forecast. If this were so, I wondered, why did he remember it? I did not dispute him. During more than thirty years of covering Reagan, I mostly asked questions and saved any comments for my writing.

In my first interview with Governor Reagan, I asked about his family, and he talked for twenty minutes about his mother. When I asked about his father later in the interview, I drew a rote response that sounded as if Reagan were reading from a fact sheet. He was actually accessing one of many stored cassettes in his memory bank. In discussing his father, Jack Reagan—a nomadic shoe salesman and alcoholic—Reagan repeated the relevant passages from his autobiography, *Where's the Rest of Me?* The title was the line Reagan uttered in the film *Kings Row* when he awakens to find his legs have been amputated by a deranged doctor who disapproved of Reagan's character, Drake McHugh, because he had slept with his daughter.

I first became aware of Reagan's mental cassettes while traveling the country with him in 1968, doing interviews for my first book as Reagan campaigned for Republican candidates. All of us store narrative identities of our lives as we remember them, but Reagan's narratives were especially numerous and dramatically detailed. He had a powerful memory. Senator Paul Laxalt of Nevada, Reagan's closest ally in Congress, described Reagan's mind as "frighteningly retentive." Reagan's brother Neil believed that Dutch, as Ronald was known in boyhood, had a photographic memory. Because of his exceptional ability to memorize, Ronald Reagan quickly learned his lines as a film actor in the B division of Warner Bros., where, he said, the studio didn't want films good, they wanted them Thursday.

The information in Reagan's mental cassettes was both an asset and a liability. On the plus side, they provided Reagan with a fund of dramatic and entertaining stories to share with varied audiences. They also gave him a store of one-liners, to which he constantly added, and occasional Socratic questions for his entourage. My favorite in the latter category occurred at Yosemite National Park, where Governor Reagan came out of a meeting with aides, looked up at a magnificent mountain, and told his aides he saw a face on the mountainside. Most of them agreed and started describing features of this imagined face, but one confessed he just couldn't see a face on the mountainside.

"Neither can I," Reagan said. "I just wanted to see who the yes men were."

The downside was that Reagan sometimes accessed the wrong tape when tired or inattentive or at worst couldn't access them at all. At the Washington summit meeting in December 1987, Reagan startled Soviet leader Mikhail Gorbachev by reprising old anti-Soviet jokes both of them knew by heart. Secretary of State George Shultz and National Security Advisor Colin Powell were appalled, fearing that Reagan was undermining the constructive relationship he had established with the Russian leader at earlier summits.

I'd had a preview six years earlier of how a tired Reagan could misfire. The occasion was an interview after the Economic Summit (G-7) in Canada on July 20–21, 1981, Reagan's first group meeting with leaders of the world's industrial democracies. Using separate channels, *New York Times* reporter Hedrick Smith and I had wangled interviews with Reagan on Air Force One on his return flight to Washington. When Smith and I boarded the plane, we were told by Reagan aide Mike Deaver that we could do the interview together or not at all. Fine, we said, we'll do it together. But Reagan wasn't fine. He was exhausted to the point where he could barely talk, and when he did, he related an old anecdote I'd heard dozens of times about an optimistic boy who's playing cheerfully in a pile of horse manure because he knows there's a pony in there someplace. Reagan told this story as if it were new. When we asked Reagan what he had learned at the G-7, he said he'd been pleasantly surprised to find that French leader Francois Mitterrand was staunchly anti-Soviet. This was hardly a news flash, but it was almost the only coherent statement Reagan made during the flight.

Such performances, usually out of public sight, reinforced a stereotype of Reagan that one prominent Democrat coded as "amiable dunce." But Reagan could also think on his feet and participate in an intricate dialogue as he did at the October 1986 summit meeting with Gorbachev in Reykjavík, Iceland, where both leaders hoped to abolish or severely shrink the nuclear arsenals of their countries. The forty-eight-page transcript of the Reagan-Gorbachev negotiations at Reykjavík shows that Reagan was neither a dunce—nor always amiable.

The silliest thing said about Reagan, and it was said often, is that "what you see is what you get." Actually, the real Reagan guarded what he allowed on the surface so outsiders wouldn't see too much. This real

Reagan could be focused or distracted. When focused, he was a strategic thinker with longstanding goals in domestic and foreign policy who was particularly impressive when his competitive instincts were aroused. He demonstrated his competitiveness dramatically in a 1980 debate with George H. W. Bush during the New Hampshire primary campaign. After a pro-Bush moderator threatened to turn off Reagan's microphone, Reagan indignantly borrowed a line from an old Spencer Tracy film, declaring, "I paid for this microphone, and it's mine."

There were other times when it seemed as if Reagan's brain was on vacation. At an August 1984 photo op at Rancho del Cielo, the Reagan spread northwest of Santa Barbara, Reagan was asked by a reporter about progress on U.S.-Soviet nuclear arms talks, and Reagan faltered—nothing coming to mind. As he hesitates, Nancy whispers: "Tell them we are doing everything we can." He dutifully repeats the words, not the first time nor the last that Nancy Reagan bails out her husband.

I spent a big chunk of my working life trying to understand Reagan's modes of behavior. Soon after his first meeting with Gorbachev in Geneva, I did a book interview with Reagan and asked him which part of his résumé he thought was most neglected. "The Screen Actors Guild," Reagan said reflexively before describing a successful negotiation with movie moguls when he was SAG president.

"What did you learn from these negotiations?" I asked.

"That the purpose of a negotiation is to get an agreement," he replied.

Reagan must have made a similar point when he briefed columnists about Geneva in the White House theater because an irate Pat Buchanan complained afterward, "The president called them movie producers. He called the Communists movie producers." I witnessed this rant and told Buchanan that Reagan did not mistake Gorbachev for a reincarnated Jack Warner—he was talking about the negotiating process.

Reagan loved to negotiate. In 1971 during his second term as governor, Reagan bargained with Democratic Assembly speaker Bob Moretti on a welfare-reform bill that dealt harshly with fraud but also increased the grants to the poorest recipients. As president a decade later, with Democrats controlling the House as they did throughout his presidency, Reagan negotiated with moderate Democrats known as Boll Weevils (later called "Blue Dogs") to obtain support for his tax-reduction and budget bills. They came from states, principally Texas, that Reagan had carried in 1980. Reagan promised them he would not campaign against them in the 1982 midterms if they voted for both of his bills, as most of them subsequently did. Republican Party officials in Texas were furious when they learned of this promise, but Reagan kept it.

Reagan didn't sit down with Gorbachev until five years into his presidency, but he was eager from the outset to meet with any Soviet leader willing to negotiate. On April 14, 1991, fifteen days after being seriously wounded in an assassination attempt, Reagan lifted the grain embargo President Jimmy Carter had imposed on the Soviet Union for the invasion of Afghanistan and sent a handwritten letter to Soviet leader Leonid Brezhnev saying he hoped that ending the embargo would lead to a "meaningful and constructive dialogue which will assist us in fulfilling our joint obligation to find lasting peace."

Brezhnev, in declining health, did not take up the offer. Neither did subsequent Soviet leaders. Yuri Andropov might have done so but was afflicted during his brief time at the Soviet helm with kidney disease. His successor, Konstantin Chernenko, was also ill when he took over the Soviet reigns. "They kept dying on me," Reagan said, as if Soviet leaders passed away to spite him. But though the locution was odd, Reagan's point was accurate. It contradicts a familiar fable which holds that Reagan changed course toward the Soviet Union in his second term, opting for a more conciliatory approach. The truth is that Reagan reached out to the Soviets from the beginning but made no progress until Gorbachev came along.

The common thread of Reagan's dealings with movie moguls, Democrats in the California legislature and the U.S. House of Representatives, and Mikhail Gorbachev was his insistence on a constructive outcome. Reagan was willing to walk away from an adversary who he thought demanded too much, as he did at Reykjavík, but he always returned to the bargaining table. Those who succeeded in negotiating with him—notably Moretti and Gorbachev—recognized Reagan's desire for a productive result. Reagan's first secretary of state, Al Haig, did not. Haig told me he'd opposed lifting the grain embargo as well as Reagan's letter to Brezhnev, going so far as to have the State Department send a separate letter to the Soviet leader that did not mention a possible meeting between the leaders of the United States and the Soviet Union. Reagan complained in his diary that Haig acted as if he were president. A few months later, Reagan replaced him with George Shultz.

Reagan's epiphany on the need for a constructive relationship with the Soviet Union occurred long before his presidency. As an idealistic young actor in Hollywood, he joined the United World Federalists, a utopian peace group. Reagan was also an avid science fiction fan and, in 1951, when he was dating Nancy Davis, he saw the movie *The Day the Earth Stood Still.* He was so taken by its peace message that he accurately recounted the plot of the film to me in detail more than thirty years later. The movie's alien hero, portrayed by Michael Rennie, is an envoy from an advanced civilization that has tamed its violent tendencies by turning peacekeeping over to an interplanetary force of robots who are programmed to destroy nations that resort to war. This civilization has been monitoring scientific developments on Earth with alarm and worries that, having unlocked the secrets of the atom, humans will acquire space travel and carry our warring tendencies into the galaxy. The alien has come to put Earth's nations on notice: Work together in peace or be destroyed by the robotic police force.

"We shall be awaiting your decision," the alien declares before flying away in his saucer. "The decision rests with you."

Reagan took this fantasy seriously. Colin Powell repeatedly deleted references to what Powell called "little green men" from Reagan's memos or speeches. This didn't stop Reagan from telling Gorbachev in Geneva that the United States and the Soviet Union would cooperate if threatened by an invasion from outer space. The usually voluble Gorbachev was at a loss on how to respond. Reagan told me this in satisfaction, believing he had scored a point with Gorbachev. Perhaps he had. Powell ultimately came to the view that the outer space references were meaningful to Reagan and did not try to remove them from a resonant speech the president gave to the United Nations on September 21, 1987. F. Scott Fitzgerald wrote that "the test of a first-rate intelligence is the ability to hold two opposed ideas in the mind at the same time, and still retain the ability to function." By this standard, Reagan was a genius. He clung to the notion of an enforced world peace throughout his life while denouncing the Soviet Union as the "focus of evil in the modern world." In his 1964 speech for Goldwater, Reagan accused "our well-meaning liberal friends" of pursuing a policy of "appeasement [that] gives no choice between peace and war, only between fight or surrender." But Reagan as much as his "liberal friends" also equated thermonuclear war with the obliteration of civilization, which eventually led him to the realization that the policy of mutual assured destruction (MAD) on which peace between the United States and the Soviet Union depended was immoral—and unsustainable.

"It's a truly mad policy," Reagan told me after the 1980 Republican platform repudiated MAD, which it called the "Hobson's choice between mass mutual suicide and surrender."

When Reagan became president, most analysts regardless of ideology considered the Soviet Union a permanent feature of the global landscape. Reagan didn't. He had read about economic shortcomings in Russia and concluded that the Soviets couldn't keep pace with the United States in a sustained arms competition. Reagan spelled this out publicly for the first time at *The Washington Post* on June 18, 1980. He had not yet been formally nominated but had wrapped up the Republican nomination. My publisher, Katharine Graham, asked me to invite Reagan to lunch so we could question him about what he hoped to accomplish if he became president. Lyn Nofziger thought *The Post* would try to trap Reagan and opposed the visit. But the invitation pleased Reagan. I asked him what I should tell Mrs. Graham.

"Tell her I'm coming," Reagan replied, "and would like to bring Lyn along."

So Reagan, with Nofziger in tow, came to lunch and a free-for-all discussion in Mrs. Graham's dining room that she and several editors and reporters attended. The luncheon conversation soon turned to Reagan's call for increased spending on defense. When an editor suggested this would intensify the arms race, Reagan agreed. Nofziger was sitting next to me, and I could feel his body tense when Reagan said, "It would be of great benefit to the United States if we started a buildup."

Reagan then spelled out his view that the Soviet economy was under so much stress that Russian leaders wouldn't be able to match a U.S. arms buildup. "I think there's every indication and every reason to believe that the Soviet Union cannot increase its production of arms," Reagan said. "Right now, we're hearing of strikes and labor disputes because people aren't getting enough to eat. They've diverted so much to military [spending] that they can't provide for consumer needs."

Reagan's response was the clearest statement until then about why he believed an arms race would serve U.S. interests. And there was more. Reagan said a U.S. buildup would prompt the Soviets to "*come to the bargaining table*" (my emphasis) and seek negotiations to reduce nuclear weapons. The United States, he said, would be bargaining from a position of strength. This was Reagan the Negotiator talking, and I abruptly realized that Reagan envisioned a negotiated end to a Cold War that others in both parties believed was perpetual.

After Reagan left, I met with the editors in charge of putting out the next day's paper, most of whom did not realize the import of Reagan's comment about bringing the Soviets to the bargaining table. Fortunately, Harwood was there. When another editor suggested a shopworn topic as a lede, Harwood bluntly told him I knew more about Reagan than he did and said I should write the story as I saw it. I did. Under the headline "Arms Boost Seen as Strain on Soviets," my story began: "Ronald Reagan said yesterday that a rapid U.S. arms buildup would be good for the United States because it would strain the defense-burdened Soviet economy and force the Soviets to the bargaining table."

The story had been budgeted for page one, but the editor who had been chastised by Harwood put it on page three instead. I didn't care, remembering that radical journalist I. F. Stone had said you never knew where you'd find a page-one story in *The Washington Post.* In the meantime, thanks to Harwood, I'd been installed as *The Post*'s resident expert in Reagan Land.

It wasn't much of a stretch.

I'd periodically interviewed Reagan during his eight years as governor of California, his six years out of office, and his eight years as president of the United States. Reagan tended to be more helpful, like many another politician, when I turned off the tape recorder. He had an editor in his brain who cautioned him from saying too much to reporters, even those he trusted. This mental editor relaxed when the tape recorder was off, especially if I changed the subject to a topic unrelated to the purpose of the interview. When he was unguarded, Reagan could be uncompromisingly candid—even caustic.

After an interview on state issues for *California Journal,* for instance, I asked Governor Reagan about Vice President Spiro Agnew, who was struggling but had not yet been exposed as a crook. Reagan had defended Agnew but realized it was time for the vice president to go. "An actor has to know when to leave the stage," Reagan said.

While Jimmy Carter was president, NBC's Andrea Mitchell and I interviewed Reagan on background and asked him about the prospective political candidacy of Ted Kennedy. The sole surviving Kennedy brother's national ambitions had been derailed on Martha's Vineyard when he drove a car off a bridge and into the water on the tiny island of Chappaquiddick. Kennedy escaped, but a twenty-eight-year-old woman with him in the car drowned. Without mentioning any of this, Reagan simply said he didn't think Kennedy would run.

Mitchell persisted: "But what if he does run?"

"Then I guess I'll just have to remind people that I was a lifeguard," Reagan quipped.

I felt comfortable in Reagan's presence, even when asking an adversarial question, but he always maintained an inner distance. He was easy to interview because he was happy and rarely hostile, but finding new ground was a challenge. When I was White House correspondent for *The Washington Post,* I filed almost daily, and it was not unusual for his surrogates to take issue with my stories. Reagan rarely complained, even when he thought I was off base. For some reason he seemed to care more about how I felt about him than what I wrote. Reagan's diaries contain many criticisms of my stories (and my book *Reagan*). His diary entry for November 14, 1982, said he'd read *Reagan* and found "a pot full of inaccuracies. All in all though his editorializing was friendly."

Our personal discussions often involved our mothers. When my mother died, Reagan phoned me at home from the White House to express condolences. She'd been ill, and I thought I'd been prepared for her passing. Reagan comforted me by saying, "You are never prepared for the death of your mother."

Reagan had previously told me he had been shaken when his mother died even though she had suffered for years from dementia. On rare occasions our conversations wandered into trivial matters such as the virtues of the Water Pik, a teeth cleaner that he'd received as a present. "You'd be amazed at what comes out," Reagan said. Reagan said his father loved gadgets, and he did, too. We didn't talk often about Jack Reagan, whom Reagan said suffered from "the Irish disease" of alcoholism, telling me this as if we had never discussed the subject before. He then asked about my father for the first time. I told him my father, also named Jack and of Irish descent, was an alcoholic. "Maybe that's why you're interested in me," Reagan said.

There were many reasons I was interested in Reagan beyond the obvious one that I was assigned to cover him, but the main reason was that I wanted to understand how his mind worked. I was not alone. The nature of Reagan's intelligence perplexed his inner circle and others who saw him at close quarters.

"People say he is a simpleton, which isn't right, and when they realize he isn't, they're apt to go to the other end of the spectrum and compare him to Socrates, which doesn't work either," William F. Buckley told me.

Buckley's magazine *National Review* valued Reagan but didn't crack the code. Neither did newspaper reporters. Governor Reagan held frequent press conferences when I was state capital correspondent for the *San Jose Mercury-News.* Although he mostly held his own with the contentious Sacramento press corps, Reagan suffered lapses that left reporters scratching their heads. Once, for instance, he was extolling the merit of his legislative program when a reporter asked him what was in it. Reagan turned without apparent embarrassment to aides on the side of the room and asked if any of them knew the contents of his legislative program.

I did extensive research for *Ronnie and Jesse* without solving the mystery of Reagan's thought processes. No biographer ever completely knows the innermost thoughts and feelings of his subject, but I came closer to figuring out what made Jess Unruh tick than I did in solving the Reagan enigma.

My eureka moment occurred while researching *President Reagan: The Role of a Lifetime.* I'd heard about a Harvard psychologist named Howard Gardner who had challenged the conventional belief that "intelligence" is a general capacity possessed by everyone in greater or lesser degree and measurable by tests. Gardner believes people are intelligent in different ways. I read his brilliant book, *Frames of Mind: The Theory of Multiple Intelligences,* and interviewed him. Gardner identified seven specific intelligences (later raised to eight) with distinctive characteristics. Gardner ranked Reagan high in a form of intelligence he called "interpersonal," high in "bodily kinesthetic intelligence," high in an aspect of "language intelligence" and low in the "logical-mathematical intelligence" at which lawyers and scientists usually excel.

"Reagan's good with language, but not logically," Gardner told me.

"He makes sense of the world narratively. Scientists can be deductive and understand logic but often can't tell stories. Stories are not necessarily logical."

Gardner believes that the combination of intelligences exhibited by Reagan are unusual for a president but not necessarily for an actor. "Actors find it easier to mimic than to understand," Gardner said, "They are kids who often have difficulty with the usual school stuff, but they can parrot things back and get reinforcement from others. Many people in acting are not happy with who they are. What sets Reagan apart is that he is extraordinarily happy with himself—and with the role of Reagan."

Gardner may underrate the happiness of actors, but he had Reagan right. I felt a sense of discovery a scientist must feel when a gigantic mystery abruptly becomes comprehensible. I had spent a quarter century tracking Reagan and was said to know him well. What I knew was that he understood all manner of things that suggested powers of analysis without possessing any visible analytical ability. The mistake I made was trying to fit Reagan into a preconception of how an "intelligent politician" behaves. But Reagan was unlike other politicians. He was intelligent on his own terms. I shared these insights with Stu Spencer, Reagan's savvy political advisor, who understood Reagan.

"That's exactly right," Spencer said. "Exactly. I'm always asked to explain him, and I talk about him as intelligent but not in the way politicians are intelligent." Spencer and others experienced in briefing Reagan provided him with a narrative whenever possible.[2]

"When I briefed Reagan, I wanted him to remember the substance," said Ed Meese, who briefed him regularly in the governor's office in Sacramento and periodically at the White House. "There were really two modes with him," Meese said. "When he had a script, he felt compelled to use it, probably because of his acting background. When he grasped a subject, he was able to deal with it on his own. But when he was briefed technically, he often felt compelled to repeat what he had been told."

Technical issues—and more—often exceeded the capacity of a mental card file that was constructed when Reagan was giving speeches across the country for General Electric and using local newspapers and *Reader's Digest* for research. Although this source material had expanded over the years, Reagan entered the White House with an in-

2. Stu Spencer died on January 12, 2025, as I was putting the finishing touches on this memoir. He was important to Reagan and to me.

sufficient grasp of public policy and, worse, no idea about how much he didn't know.

Early in 1983, Brent Scowcroft was amazed to learn that Reagan did not realize that the principal Soviet threat to the United States was posed by land-based intercontinental ballistic missiles. When *Time* magazine asked Reagan why such basic information had eluded him, he replied: "I never heard one of our negotiators or any of our military people or anyone else bring up that particular point." Any briefer would have assumed Reagan understood this "particular point" since he'd often cited data about Soviet missile production to bolster his contention that America was losing the nuclear arms race.

Some insiders accounted for the gaps in Reagan's knowledge by deciding that he was intellectually lazy. "He was a highly intelligent man, who when confronted with big workloads and easy workloads, would always pick the easy workloads," said Richard Allen, Reagan's first national security advisor.

But Gardner found more confusion than laziness. People who lack Reagan's exceptional memorization ability "recode" the information they receive into their own language in order to remember it, Gardner told me. Over time, Reagan's memory advantage yielded to the disadvantage of his deficient analytic skills. He turned seventy soon after becoming president, probably too late to acquire such skills even if he had perceived the necessity of doing so.

Reagan's memory lapses were not uniform. All of us have episodes in life we would prefer to forget, and Reagan's mind tended to erase unpleasant memories. In 1962, Reagan testified the day before his fifty-fifth birthday to a grand jury investigating his old employee Music Corporation of America (MCA) for alleged conflicts of interest in simultaneously representing clients, studios, and networks. Reagan had signed a secret memo in 1952 allowing MCA to produce an unlimited number of television shows. He remembered almost nothing about it or a follow-up memo he signed in 1954. The two points of which he was certain—that other agencies had received similar waivers and that no financial consideration was given MCA—were wrong. In subsequent testimony, Reagan became steadily more forgetful. One of his explanations for not remembering these events was that he was "in Glacier National Park making a cowboy picture for RKO." The movie, *Cattle Queen of Montana*, was made two years later.

When Reagan became governor of California, his aides soon learned that he did not always remember what he had done—or said. The most striking example was a comment Reagan made on April 7, 1970. Speaking without notes to an agricultural group about on-going turmoil on university campuses, Reagan declared that "if it takes a bloodbath" to end campus uprisings, "let's get it over with." When an aide told Reagan afterward that the word "bloodbath" could be politically damaging in an election year, Reagan denied having used the word. Reagan's press secretary had to play him a recording of the speech to convince him that he had indeed said "bloodbath." Reagan then dismissed what he had said as "a figure of speech."

This incident foreshadowed a damaging lapse twenty years later when President Reagan could not remember key elements of a secret arms sale to Iran he'd approved in an attempt to facilitate the release of Americans held hostage in Lebanon.

But Reagan was much more than the sum of his lapses. He mastered the art of governing California in his second term, working with the Democrats in the legislature to enact constructive legislation on welfare issues, tax reform, and the environment.

As president, his resolute optimism helped to restore the faith of the American people in themselves and their government, an ironic accomplishment for someone who declared in his inaugural address that "government is not the solution to our problem; government is the problem." President Reagan also broke the back of inflation, albeit more with traditional means such as interest-rate increases imposed by Federal Reserve chairman Paul Volcker rather than through the wizardry of supply-side economics. The Reagan recovery that began in 1982 after a short recession lasted ninety-two months to July 1990 when George H. W. Bush was president. In his dealings with the Soviet Union—with Gorbachev, especially—Reagan was a transformational president. The two leaders massively reduced the nuclear arsenals of their countries, twenty-fold in the case of the Soviet Union, and left the world safer than they found it.

As a reporter, I covered the Reagan presidency from beginning to end for *The Washington Post* and wrote a column syndicated by *The Post* called "Reagan and Company." Even now, after writing several books about Reagan, I marvel at the enormous contradictions of the man and his presidency. At his best he was a visionary leader who ignored stereotypes and accomplished much that seemed impossible when he took office. At his worst he pursued a laudable goal—freeing Americans held captive under appalling conditions—with such recklessness and lack of common sense that he endangered an otherwise successful presidency.

22

THE REAL REAGAN

PART II

The seminal crisis of Reagan's presidency was the secret sale of antitank and antiaircraft weapons to Iran, the central element of what became known as the "Iran-Contra scandal." Two horrific bombings in Lebanon set the stage. The first, on April 18, 1983, shattered the U.S. embassy in Beirut, killing 63 people, including 17 Americans. Then on October 23, a truck armed with two thousand pounds of explosives ripped through the gate of a four-story barracks near the Beirut airport housing Marines who were the backbone of a U.S. peacekeeping force in Lebanon. Plowing into the lobby, the truck exploded with such force it lifted the building from its foundation. The blast killed 241 U.S. service members, 220 of them Marines, and wounded more than 100 others. It was the deadliest attack on U.S. Marines since Iwo Jima. Reagan called the bombing "the saddest day of my presidency, the saddest day of my life."

With defense secretary Caspar Weinberger taking the lead, the surviving Marines were "redeployed," as Reagan put it, in February 1984 to ships offshore. The withdrawal from Lebanon removed the only barrier to Reagan's reelection. With the nation prosperous and at peace, he won a second term in 1984, evoking the mantra of "Morning Again in America." But there was no such dawn in Lebanon, where radical elements of the Iran-backed Shia group Hezbollah began kidnapping Americans to use as hostages. The hostage-taking escalated on June 14, 1985, when two grenade-wielding Shiites hijacked TWA Flight 847 with 153 passengers and crew aboard, including 135 Americans, after it took off for Athens bound for Rome.

One passenger, U.S. Navy diver Robert Dean Stethem, was brutally beaten and then shot to death, his body dumped on the tarmac in Beirut. The hijackers released a majority of the passengers but kept 39 Americans as hostages, putting all but 7 of them under control of Amal Shiite leader Nabih Berri. After seventeen days of what Reagan called "intense" diplomacy, the TWA hostages were freed.

Reagan had promised never to negotiate with terrorists. The deal that freed the TWA hostages exposed the hollowness of that pledge and contained within it the seed of Reagan's approval of secret arms sales to Iran. The hijackers of TWA 847 were murderers, but not mindless terrorists. They captured American hostages to pressure Israel to release 700 Shiites taken captive for "security offenses" during the Israeli invasion of Lebanon and held in a Haifa prison. This put Reagan on the spot, especially after 32 of the hostages sent him an emotional letter urging him to avoid military action and ask Israel to release the Shiites. Reagan telephoned Syrian President Hafez Assad, who shared credit with Berri when the hostages were released on June 30.

While the TWA passengers were in captivity, Reagan tried to maintain a normal schedule and was thrust by White House chief of staff Donald Regan into the center of an emotional firestorm. Regan, treasury secretary in Reagan's first term, had been allowed by the president to swap jobs with White House chief of staff James Baker. On January 8, 1985, the Reverend Martin Jenco, head of Catholic Charities in Lebanon, was kidnapped in Beirut. Jenco's close-knit Catholic family in Illinois sought a meeting with Reagan. They were turned down initially but, on June 28 when Reagan flew to Chicago for two speeches, Reagan amended the schedule to allow family members of the TWA hostages and Jenco's family to meet with Reagan in a high school library adjacent to one of the speaking sites. At the meeting, two of Jenco's brothers asked Reagan why he was willing to make a deal to release the TWA hostages but not a similar deal to free their brother. Reagan replied that he was doing everything he could to free the priest.

After a half hour of such questioning, the son of one of the TWA hostages said to Reagan, "Mr. President, I don't know how you can stand your job." Reagan was so shaken that Regan asked him if he needed time to compose himself before his speech. The president shook his head and wobbled through a speech about tax reform to which he added a promise that "terrorists and those who support them must and will be held to account."

Later, I talked to Mike Deaver, who had left the White House in May. He said that he and Baker would never have set up such a meeting because Reagan was vulnerable to "sob stories." Iran and Iraq were then engaged in a bloody war. Although the United States was ostensibly neutral, the administration launched Operation Staunch, which urged other nations to cease transferring arms to Iran and called for a negotiated end to the war. A month later, Shultz designated Iran a sponsor of international terrorism, and the United States imposed export controls on Iran.

As this was happening, Robert "Bud" McFarlane, Reagan's national security advisor, pursued an initiative to supply presumed moderates within the Iranian government with antiaircraft and antitank weapons in return for Iranian pressure on Hezbollah to release seven Americans held hostage in Lebanon. One of these hostages was William Francis Buckley, the CIA station chief in Lebanon, who had been kidnapped on March 16, 1984, as he was leaving for work. William J. Casey, Reagan's chief of central intelligence, had been told that Buckley was being tortured by his Hezbollah captors to reveal the identities of CIA agents.[1] Provided with this information and given his personal feelings about the hostages, Reagan was unsurprisingly receptive to McFarlane's initiative. On January 17, 1986, Reagan confided to his diary that he had given "the go-ahead for selling TOW anti-tank missiles to Iran." When he thought about the American hostages in Lebanon, he saw in his mind's eye the awful conditions of their captivity, which made him susceptible to any scheme to free them.

McFarlane was one of the first Marine officers in Vietnam and did a second tour. Between tours he received a master's degree in international relations and was assigned as Henry Kissinger's military aide during the Nixon presidency. He stayed on as an assistant to Brent Scowcroft when Ford became president and in the Reagan years served as deputy national security advisor under Bill Clark. When Clark became secretary of the interior, Reagan replaced him with McFarlane. It was the first time McFarlane had held a number-one post, and he found it difficult. McFarlane told me over a drink that Reagan had forgotten

1. Buckley was severely tortured for more than a year before dying sometime in June 1985 of untreated pneumonia. His desecrated remains were returned to the United States on December 28, 1991. He was buried in Arlington National Cemetery with full military honors.

his name during a national security discussion and complained that the president depended only on wealthy, self-made men such as Shultz, Weinberger, and Regan. I pointed out that Meese and Deaver, of humble origins and not wealthy, had become influential in staff roles.

The soft-spoken McFarlane's interactions with Reagan were complicated by the president's declining hearing, which first became evident in the 1980 campaign when Reagan misheard questions from reporters. Troubled by the potential this posed for political calamity, Deaver conferred with Nancy Reagan, who saw to it that her husband was equipped with hearing aids. Reagan told me the hearing aids helped in normal conversation but not when there was ambient noise. At a Christmas party for the White House press corps, Reagan motioned me to come halfway up the stairs as he was leaving. Whispering to me about the evening, he said: "I couldn't hear a thing."

Most of those who dealt regularly with Reagan compensated for his hearing issues by speaking loudly and distinctly. Reagan helped himself by becoming reasonably adept at lip-reading, but understanding Casey was a recurrent problem. Following Clark's example, Reagan called the CIA director "Mumbles." Reagan also had trouble, even one-on-one, understanding McFarlane, who gave long-winded briefings in a low monotone. Although Reagan liked McFarlane, he didn't enjoy his briefings or always understand what he'd been told.

Hearing issues aside, Reagan saw himself as a big-picture president who left most details to subordinates. But even by big-picture standards, he was distressingly uninformed about the early debate within his administration over selling weapons to Iran. It began on June 17, 1985, when McFarlane drafted a directive that would have reversed U.S. policy by encouraging other nations to supply arms to Iran. McFarlane wanted more than an arms-for-hostages swap. He envisioned a radical change in U.S. policy toward Iran. McFarlane had been told, wrongly as it turned out, that anti-American cleric Ayatollah Ruhollah Khomeini was at death's door and that moderates would come to the fore once he died. McFarlane said these moderates would appreciate U.S. arms aid to Iran in its struggle with Iraq. Bill Casey approved of McFarlane's directive, but Shultz and Weinberger denounced it. Weinberger wrote that sales of U.S. arms to Iran "would be seen as inexplicably inconsistent by those nations whom we have urged to refrain from such sales."

Absorbed in the TWA Flight 847 crisis, Reagan knew nothing of the critical reception McFarlane's proposal had received from his secretaries of state and defense. Nor did he know that U.S. intelligence questioned whether any moderates in Iran were still alive.

Israel intervened during the summer of 1985. On July 3, David Kimche, deputy director of the Israeli foreign ministry, visited Washington and told McFarlane that Iranian officials wanted a dialogue with the United States, which he said would lead to hostage releases in Lebanon. McFarlane briefed the president on this conversation before Reagan entered Bethesda Naval Hospital for cancer surgery. During the surgery, Reagan transferred presidential powers to Vice President Bush. The hostages were so much on Reagan's mind that soon after reclaiming presidential powers on July 13 he asked Don Regan if there was any news about them.

There is no evidence Reagan gave a fig for the strategic initiative to Iran envisioned by McFarlane and Casey. What mattered to Reagan were the hostages. On July 17, Reagan wrote in his diary an entry he would later say marked "the beginning of what became known as the Iran-Contra affair." "Some strange soundings are coming from some Iranians," Reagan wrote. "Bud M, will be here tomorrow to talk about it. It could be a breakthrough on getting our seven kidnap victims back. Evidently the Iranian economy is disintegrating fast under the strain of war."

With Reagan's blessing, Israel on August 20 sent 96 American-made TOW (tube-launched, optically tracked, wire-guided) missiles to Iran through an unsavory arms dealer named Manucher Ghorbanifar. They were the first installment of a deluge of missiles to Iran sent first by Israel and then by the United States—a distinction without a difference since the United States replenished Israeli weapons stocks. Combined, Israel and the United States sent 2,004 TOWs to Iran plus 18 HAWK antiaircraft missiles and 200 HAWK spare parts.

These weapons wouldn't have been sent had Reagan heeded Shultz and Weinberger. But they did not get Reagan's full attention until a December 7, 1985, meeting in the White House family quarters chaired by McFarlane. At this meeting, CIA deputy director John McMahon told Reagan that Iranian moderates had already been slaughtered by Khomeini and advised against the arms sales despite his boss Casey favoring them. Even Don Regan, who had supported the initiative, used

Wall Street parlance to advise against it. "Cut your losses, Mr. President," Regan said.

Reagan ignored them all, displaying a stubbornness that made mincemeat of the stereotype that he was a laid-back president who saved himself for public performances. There were, in fact, two sides to Reagan's temperament. One was a passive disengagement from many of the issues before him. The other was a passionate commitment to causes he visualized in personal terms, such as American hostages. At the December 7 meeting, Weinberger made every argument he could think of, including the lawyerly assertion that "there are legal problems here, Mr. President, in addition to all the policy problems."

Reagan bluntly replied that he didn't "feel we can leave any stone unturned in trying to get the hostages back. The American people will never forgive me if I fail to get these hostages out over this legal question."

He added a typical Reagan quip that, if laws were broken and people went to jail, "visiting hours were Thursday." During a six-week period beginning on January 6, 1986, Reagan signed three findings approving the U.S. sale of missiles to Iran. More than three years later, Reagan told me he had discounted the warnings of Shultz and Weinberger that the initiative would harm his presidency.

"I will tell you that both Cap and George Shultz thought of that and thought that if it ever became [public], it would look like we were trading arms for hostages," Reagan told me in a February 10, 1989, interview after he left office. "Well, they turned out to be right. I didn't see at the time how it possibly could, when we were dealing with some people who had to literally hide from their own government to save their lives. . . . I said to both those fellows [Shultz and Weinberger] when we were talking, 'Look, if I've got a child kidnapped for ransom, I don't believe in paying ransom. But if I suddenly discover there's somebody who might be able to get that child back from the kidnapper and knows a way to get it back, yes, I'd reward that individual.' But I never convinced them. And now, as I say, they turned out to be right."

Not for the first time, Reagan was resistant to inconvenient facts. The essential fact, as we now know, was that the kidnappers weren't hiding from anyone because the entire initiative was the brainchild of the Iranian regime.

McFarlane, also resistant to this reality, learned he had been misled during a dangerous mission to Iran that a congressional committee described as "extraordinarily heroic and very foolish," because he had no guarantee of safe conduct from Iran. McFarlane, Lieutenant Colonel Ollie North, George Cave of the CIA, and three others flew to Tehran from Tel Aviv on May 25, 1986, in an unmarked Israeli 707 that contained one of a dozen pallets of HAWK spare parts the Americans had agreed to provide in exchange for the hostages. McFarlane expected to meet the three highest-ranking Iranian officials below Khomeini. Instead, the Americans were taken to the former Tehran Hilton, where they spent four nights and met minor officials. After two nights of wrangling, McFarlane napped as North agreed with the Iranian officials to accept release of two hostages in return for delivery of the remaining pallets of HAWK spare parts. The plane was in the air from Israel when McFarlane awoke, rejected the deal, and had the parts-bearing plane turned around in midair. The failed mission, Reagan wrote in his diary, "was a heartbreaking disappointment for all of us."

The secret arms sales were disclosed by a Lebanese magazine on November 3, 1986, the day after American hostage David Jacobsen was released by his Shia captors. The other American beneficiaries of the arms sales, Father Jenco and Presbyterian minister Benjamin Weir, had been released in July and September, respectively. Shia militants soon captured three hostages to replace them. Thanks to the U.S. arms sales, American hostages had become valuable currency.

During the next three months, Reagan struggled to save his presidency. He had lost his most priceless resource—public credibility—and with it the confidence that had carried him through other crises of his life. Relying on false information provided by Admiral John Poindexter, McFarlane's successor as national security advisor, Reagan gave a disastrous televised speech on November 13 in which he understated the number of missiles supplied to Iran and denied the central truth of the arms sales. "We did not—repeat did not—trade weapons or anything else for hostages, nor will we." Reagan said.

Watching this speech, I was struck by the validity of Reagan's view that television is a revealing medium. Instead of the self-assured Great Communicator, Reagan came across as a carping and defensive president who blamed the media for his troubles much like any other cornered politician. The speech didn't fool the American people. A *Los Angeles Times* poll found that only 14 percent of viewers accepted Reagan's version of events. At a press conference six days later, Reagan had recovered his composure but not his command of the facts. Asked by CNN correspondent Charles Bierbauer if the United States had been involved with Israel in supplying weapons to Iran. Reagan lied that he had "nothing to do with other countries or their shipments of arms."

Reagan's problems were compounded later that month when Assistant Attorney General William Bradford Reynolds, searching documents in North's office in the Old Executive Office Building, came across a detailed memo from North to Poindexter revealing that $12 million of the proceeds from the arms sales "will be used to purchase critically needed supplies for the Nicaraguan Democratic Resistance Forces."

There was a surreal quality to the subsequent inquiry by Attorney General Ed Meese, who leisurely investigated the Contra connection while North shredded thousands of documents and Poindexter erased hundreds of emails. Even so, Meese found revealing information. Taken together, North and Poindexter made the Gang That Couldn't Shoot Straight look like expert marksmen. North had left documents all over the place, and Poindexter wasn't aware that the emails he thought he had destroyed were preserved in the mainframe of the National Security Council's computer.

Reagan reacted to news of the diversion by denying prior knowledge of its existence and firing North and Poindexter. Reagan never changed his story on the diversion, relating it to me again in the February 10, 1989, interview. Special Prosecutor Lawrence Walsh did not issue his final report until 1993, during President Bill Clinton's first term, but he concluded "that there was no credible evidence that the president authorized or was aware of the diversion of the profits from the Iran arms sales to assist the contras." That's where the matter stands historically.

Reagan was a strong supporter of the Nicaraguan counterrevolutionaries (hence "contras"), whom he had compared to the U.S. founders. Reagan had sought $14 million in aid for the contras from Congress in 1986—I wrote several stories about this—but was rebuffed. He told his national security advisors to keep the contras together "body and soul." Walsh observed, however, that Reagan also told his advisors to stay within the law.

The contras angle worked to Reagan's advantage for it shifted media attention to the part of the scandal where there was no evidence of Reagan's involvement and away from the arms sales for which he bore responsibility. Those sales probably violated the Arms Export Control Act, as Weinberger and later Shultz had warned, but there was no congressional appetite for impeachment on this issue. Reagan's pollster Dick Wirthlin welcomed the shift of attention to the contras because his surveys showed the public more concerned about the arms sales than the diversion. Reagan's credibility was especially tested in two days of testimony to a Special Review Board chaired by Senator John Tower. On January 16, 1987, Reagan told the board he'd approved the first TOW shipments sometime in August 1985 and had agreed to replenish Israeli weapons from U.S. stocks. McFarlane had given a similar account to the Senate Foreign Relations Committee, while Don Regan had a contrary recollection. He told the Tower board and White House counsel Peter Wallison that Reagan had not given prior approval to the Israelis.

Wallison did his best to find the truth. Aided by Regan and David Abshire, a well-regarded former ambassador to NATO, Wallison combed through the president's calendar with Reagan, hoping to refresh his recollection. Wallison asked Reagan if he had been surprised when he learned that the Israelis had sent TOWs to Iran.

"Yes, I guess I was surprised," Reagan said.

"That's what I remember," chimed in Regan. "I remember you being angry and saying something like, 'Well, what's done is done.'"

"You know, I think he's right," Reagan said to Wallison.

But Wallison realized that Reagan's recollection was shaky. On February 10, the day before the president testified a second time before the Tower board, Wallison drew up what Abshire called an "aide-memoire" to help Reagan remember what he had told them. At the top, Wallison wrote, "On the issue of the TOW shipment in August, in discussing the matter with me and David Abshire, you said you were surprised to learn that the Israelis had shipped the arms. If that is your recollection, and if the question comes up at the Tower Board meeting, you might want to say you were surprised."

When Reagan testified before the board on February 11, Tower asked the president why there was a discrepancy between his statement and Regan's on whether he had given prior approval to the Israeli shipment. Reagan rose from his chair, walked around his desk and said to Wallison, "Peter, where is the piece of paper you had that you gave me this morning?"

Then Reagan picked up the paper and began to read from it verbatim, ending, "If the question comes up at the Tower Board meeting, you might want to say you were surprised."

Tower's jaw went slack. He suspected that Reagan was being manipulated by counsel and had the board's chief of staff ask for a "copy of the script." Wallison could not believe what Reagan had done.

"I was horrified, just horrified," he said later.

He had prepared the paper so Reagan could refresh his recollection before the meeting and had no idea he would read it to the board. But Wallison now realized that Reagan's recall was worthless.

"My conclusion is that he was influenced by the last person he talked to," Wallison told me. "He had no recollection of his own."

The Tower board had been exposed to the real Reagan, as he was seen every day by the handful of aides who had access to him. Tower and Senator Edmund Muskie, the review board's vice chairman, were appalled. Muskie observed that the Israelis had sent special emissaries to the White House to ask if they could help in getting the hostages released.

"This comes to a president who is agonizing over this thing every day, and yet he can't remember anything about it," Muskie said. "My God."

Reagan was a man of strong convictions but fragile command of the facts. After this testimony, some of his aides wondered if he was "losing it," as one of them put it. I've often been asked similar questions, usually in the context of speculation about whether Reagan had Alzheimer's when he was president.[2] Although I'm not qualified to make a medical diagnosis, I don't think Reagan suffered from any form of dementia while in office. He gave several strong public performances during the last two years of his presidency, including a memorable speech at the Berlin Wall on June 12, 1987. He had vigorously walked along the wall that morning with reporters, including me, and viewed the poignant inscriptions that paid tribute to those who had died while trying to cross. He delivered the speech powerfully and showed no hesitancy when East German loudspeakers on the other side of the Brandenburg Gate tried to drown him out.

Reagan slowed in the last months of his presidency—I say this with

2. I'm reprising these events as Joe Biden's presidency comes to a wobbly conclusion amid concerns about his acuity—at a time when America has just elected a seventy-eight-year-old replacement. This is more than a historical episode. It's a public policy matter of continuing relevance.

a nonagenarian's empathy—but he was lucid in my post-presidential interview. Reagan's meltdown before the Tower board was of a piece with his forgetful performance in 1962 before a grand jury investigating the Music Corporation of America. Almost everything Reagan told that grand jury was wrong. When factual knowledge collided with his mental narrative, Reagan could not keep the facts straight at any age.

Why was this so? While I never put this question to Howard Gardner, I suspect the answer has something to do with the nonlinear nature of Reagan's intelligence. Reagan made sense of life through stories, not factual analysis. He composed powerful narratives in his mind and showed a salesman's gift for sharing them with audiences. If reality disrupted his narrative, he clung to his basic story as long as he could and became confused when he couldn't.

The person who knew Ronald Reagan best realized that his stories didn't always parse. Watching him flounder in the November press conference, Nancy Reagan decided that her husband needed to make amends to the American people. She campaigned to this end for the next three months, bringing Stu Spencer and Mike Deaver and Democratic power broker Robert Strauss, among others, to the White House to talk sense to the president.[3] Reagan resisted but eventually gave in, perhaps as much to make domestic peace as for any other reason.

Mrs. Reagan then enlisted Landon Parvin, her favorite White House speechwriter, to compose an apology. Deft and sensitive, Parvin had written many of the self-deprecating quip lines Reagan loved. ("I know hard work never killed anyone, but I thought why take a chance.")

Parvin came up with the ideal formulation: "A few months ago I told the American people that I did not trade arms for hostages," Reagan said in a thirteen-minute speech from the Oval Office on March 4, 1987. "My heart and my best intentions still tell me that is true, but the facts and evidence tell me it is not."

It was a roundabout apology, but these words perfectly expressed Reagan's feelings about what he'd done.

3. Strauss told me that he had always regretted not leveling with President Johnson about the intensity of domestic opposition to the Vietnam War. He saw his meeting with President Reagan as a chance to redeem himself and was blunt with Reagan about the need to apologize. Nancy Reagan called him after the meeting and thanked him.

23

THE BIG THAW

Focusing too much on the Iran arms sales provides a one-sided picture of Reagan's foreign policy, which overall was realistic and achieved notable successes in reducing and equalizing U.S. and Soviet nuclear arsenals. Reagan promised before he became president to increase military spending in order to negotiate from a position of strength and bring the Soviets to the bargaining table. He kept his promise, but the military buildup for which Reagan is credited (or blamed) began when Jimmy Carter was in the White House. Nuclear physicist Harold Brown, Carter's defense secretary, realized the Soviets were outpacing the United States in missile acquisition and deployment. As Brown memorably explained to a congressional committee: "When we build, they build. When we stop, they build."

Although Carter increased defense spending, the Soviets achieved parity in nuclear warheads in 1978 and were well ahead when Reagan took office. The Soviets had added about 2,000 warheads a year under four different leaders, including Gorbachev, when he and Reagan first met in Geneva. Then at its peak, the Soviet nuclear arsenal contained 38,582 warheads; the United States had 23,368 nuclear warheads.

Reagan and Gorbachev did the heavy lifting on the first START (Strategic Arms Reduction Treaty), which was not completed while Reagan was in the White House. Gorbachev and President George H. W. Bush signed it in 1991. Warhead numbers have declined under every subsequent U.S. president and every Russian leader, as Reagan and Gorbachev envisioned. The New START Treaty extended by President Biden and Russian leader Vladimir Putin in 2022 continues this legacy. It restricts the United States and Russia to 1,550 deployed strategic warheads each—far too many for those of us who want a world without nuclear weapons (as Reagan and Gorbachev did), but a pittance compared to the height of the Cold War.

Reducing warheads reduces the risk of accidental conflagration, a recurring nightmare of the nuclear age. Without providing specifics, Reagan told me he'd been briefed about Stanislav Petrov, a Soviet lieutenant colonel who may have prevented World War III. Petrov monitored satellite surveillance computers that warned of pending missile attacks. On September 26, 1983, the computers told him that five missiles were about to strike the Soviet Union. But Petrov distrusted the quality of Soviet equipment and doubted the U.S. would limit an attack to five missiles. So instead of telling his superiors about the incoming attack, as he was supposed to do, Petrov aborted a Soviet response. The satellite had mistaken sunlight reflecting off the top of clouds for a missile launch. This scary incident occurred during a period of extreme tension in U.S.-Soviet relations.

On September 1, 1983, Korean Air Lines Flight 007, a passenger jet with 269 persons aboard, including 63 Americans, strayed off course and was shot down by a Soviet fighter plane near Sakhalin Island. A war scare developed in Europe, where French president Francois Mitterrand compared the situation to the Cuban missile crisis of 1962.

Reagan behaved coolly throughout these dangerous days. Returning to Washington from his California ranch when KAL 007 was shot down, Reagan met with his advisors, some of whom were in a white heat over what they considered Soviet barbarism. Casey, Clark, and Weinberger urged Reagan to cut off scheduled meetings and other dealings with the Soviets. Shultz counseled against overreaction, and Reagan agreed.

"The world will react to this," he said. "It's important that we not do anything that jeopardizes the long-term relationship with the Soviet Union."

On September 5, Reagan gave a nationally televised speech that he told his diary took much rewriting. He called the downing of KAL 007, which the Soviets falsely claimed was a spy plane, "a crime against humanity" and urged Congress to condemn it. But Reagan also said, "We cannot, we must not give up our effort to reduce the arsenals of destructive [nuclear] weapons threatening the world."

To this end, he announced he was sending Ambassador Paul Nitze back to Geneva to resume negotiations with the Soviets on reduction of intermediate-range nuclear weapons in Europe and would continue to seek arms reductions when START talks resumed in October. Nothing could keep Reagan from trying to negotiate.

Reagan's pragmatic focus on nuclear arms was a salient feature of his presidency. He'd been studying the Soviet Union since he was an actor in Hollywood, and his readings and briefings after he became president reinforced his belief that its economy was faltering. He made periodic proposals during his first two years in office, including a November 18, 1981, speech to the National Press Club unveiling what became known as his zero-zero plan for intermediate nuclear weapons in Europe. Reagan said the United States was prepared to cancel its deployment of Pershing II and ground-launched cruise missiles if the Soviets dismantled the SS-20 and other intermediate-range missiles. Nothing came of this offer nor of subsequent Reagan proposals. This was primarily the fault of Soviet leaders before Gorbachev, but Reagan's messages were frequently blunted by hawks within his administration who distrusted the Soviets too much to negotiate with them.

History's lessons are apparent only in the rearview mirror. In the winter of 1983–84 when the nuclear freeze movement was at zenith, prospects for any new U.S.-Soviet arms agreement seemed remote. Even Reagan, the perennial optimist, became distressed at the harsh Soviet perceptions of his presidency, which were shared by growing numbers of critics—mostly leftist—in the United States and Europe. Early in 1984, Reagan received a CIA report on Soviet attitudes which repeated the fantasy that the United States was planning a nuclear first strike on the Soviet Union.

"Do you suppose they really believe that?" Reagan asked McFarlane.

The national security advisor was skeptical of the report, but the Soviet press was comparing Reagan to Hitler, and Reagan felt a need to lower the temperature. In separate year-end interviews with *Time* and *Newsweek,* he said he would no longer use the phrase "focus of evil" to describe the Soviet Union. The phrase originated in a March 8, 1983, speech to an evangelical group in Florida that was written by Anthony

Dolan, the most conservative of the house speechwriters in the Reagan White House. This is the same speech in which Reagan described the Soviet Union as an "evil empire."[1]

I wrote more than two hundred stories for *The Washington Post* in 1983 but will cite only two of them, one of which had significant bearing on Reagan's nuclear strategy going forward and the other about a key appointment who would help Reagan in his dealings with the Soviets.

On March 23, Reagan gave a nationally televised speech proposing a futuristic nuclear defensive system he called the Strategic Defense Initiative (SDI). Reagan said it would "give us a means of rendering . . . nuclear weapons impotent and obsolete."

And on June 5, acting on a tip, I wrote that Jack F. Matlock Jr., U.S. ambassador to Czechoslovakia, would become the administration's director of Soviet and East bloc affairs. He was the choice of Bill Clark, who, as I wrote, considered Matlock the "finest Sovietologist in the State Department." Matlock, a fluent Russian speaker and subsequent U.S. ambassador to Moscow, would help Reagan navigate the tricky shoals of Soviet foreign policy and chronicle the results in a definitive book, *Reagan and Gorbachev: How the Cold War Ended.* Matlock was neither hawk nor dove but a professional foreign service officer guided by history and the facts on the ground. He smoothed the rough edges of a sometimes disorderly NSC staff and put it on the same page as Reagan and Shultz in dealing with the Soviet Union.

Yuri Andropov died on February 9, 1984. He was succeeded by Konstantin Chernenko, who would remain alive for little more than a year. Chernenko died on March 10, 1985, and was replaced immediately by Mikhail Gorbachev. Reagan was excited by the ascension of Gorbachev. He'd received a favorable report on the new Soviet leader from British prime minister Margaret Thatcher, who'd had an extensive conversation with Gorbachev three months earlier in London. Brushing aside Shultz's suggestion that he attend Chernenko's funeral—Reagan hated funerals—Reagan instead sent Shultz and Vice President George H. W. Bush, along with a letter inviting Gorbachev to a summit meeting in Washington. The atmospherics of U.S.-Soviet relations quickly improved, and Reagan and Gorbachev would meet face-to-face eight months later in Geneva.

1. Reagan told me near the end of his presidency that he'd used the phrase "evil empire" only in this one speech. I replied that he'd only had to use it once because those of us in the media had continually repeated it.

Reagan prepared with exceptional effort for this meeting, impressing Shultz and even McFarlane, who was often discouraged by Reagan's relaxed work habits. Reagan typically buckled down for big performances. With Reagan in mind, an actor once told me that the rhythm of an actor's life often required intense work for a few weeks or months followed by extensive down time. Matlock oversaw Reagan's preparation. He wrote twenty-five papers doled out weekly in the six months before Geneva that explained Soviet objectives, strategy, and negotiating tactics as well as Russian culture and history. Reagan dutifully read almost all his briefing papers, but the only ones he ever described to me as interesting were what he called Matlock's "stories."

Gorbachev also prepared for the summit. While on balance more analytical than Reagan, he did not fully trust his briefers except for his handpicked foreign minister, Eduard Shevardnadze. As a result, Gorbachev did not know as much about Reagan as Reagan knew about him. But Gorbachev did realize that Reagan had a source of authority to which no Soviet leader could pretend. Pavel Palazchenko, Gorbachev's interpreter and personal aide, recalled being with Gorbachev and a group of Soviet officials when one of them started to denigrate Reagan. Gorbachev impatiently interrupted, saying, "You are talking about the president of the United States, elected by the American people."

My introduction to Gorbachev came that same day at a photo session that opened the November 19, 1985, Geneva summit. I was impressed. Gorbachev displayed a personal magnetism almost equivalent to Reagan's as well as a sense of humor rare among Soviet officials.

Reagan and Gorbachev plunged enthusiastically into the work of the summit. They met for eight hours on November 19 and 20, half of the time alone and half of the time with interpreters present and bodyguards just out of earshot. Reagan wanted to discuss the causes of U.S.-Soviet distrust. He observed that the two countries had been allies during World War II but that Gorbachev's immediate predecessors had shown no desire to cooperate. He maintained that the United States was seeking equity, not military superiority. In addition to their advantage in nuclear warheads, the Soviets had 5.4 million men under arms compared to 2.4 million for the United States.

Gorbachev said that, instead of discussing causes of mistrust, the two leaders should focus on proposals to end the arms race. His main concern was SDI, against which he made repeated and somewhat contradictory arguments. On the one hand, said Gorbachev, SDI would lead to production of "space weapons" for offensive use. Yet, Gorbachev also argued that the only reason a country would develop a defensive system was so that it could launch a first nuclear strike while protecting its population. In response, Reagan said the United States and the Soviet Union should share the fruits of any U.S. research on SDI and reduce their offensive arsenals as defenses were developed.

SDI illustrated both the intuitive political brilliance of Ronald Reagan and the limitations of his scientific knowledge. He was horrified by nuclear weapons and had idealistic views about abolishing them. Reagan believed "a nuclear war can never be won and must never be fought." These words, first used in a 1982 radio speech, popped up in the joint declaration of Reagan and Gorbachev at Geneva but were most resonant when Reagan spoke to the Japanese Diet on November 11, 1983, in the country that had known the horrors of Hiroshima and Nagasaki.

"I believe there can be only one policy for preserving our precious civilization in this modern age: a nuclear war can never be won and must never be fought," he said. "The only value in possessing nuclear weapons is to make sure they can't be used—ever. I know I speak for people everywhere when I say our dream is to see the day when nuclear weapons will be banished from the face of the earth."

Listening to this speech, I found this passage enormously moving, as did its Japanese listeners, some of whom had tears in their eyes. It expressed the animating impulse behind SDI as Reagan envisioned it and received thunderous applause in the Diet. But SDI's critics in the United States didn't take Reagan's proposal seriously. Scientists said a nuclear defensive system would be overwhelmed by a proliferation of missiles mixed with dummy drones. Soon after Reagan proposed SDI, a Democratic senator dubbed the idea "Star Wars," and Star Wars it obligingly became in the media. A few conservatives tried to make the best of this dubious moniker. The third film in the *Star War* series was released in May 1983 two months after Reagan proposed SDI, and neoconservative Richard Perle observed that "the good guys won." But Reagan detested the "Star Wars" labeling and never used it.

The idea of a system defending the country from a nuclear attack was popular, as Reagan knew it would be. But though SDI polled well in the United States, a closer look at those surveys revealed that many Americans who supported it had little idea how it might work.

The government spent $30 billion on SDI research without coming up with a specific plan before the program was killed by President Clinton in 1993. For all its costs and unreality, SDI was arguably a good investment. For starters, it drove Gorbachev wild. Military spending consumed about one-sixth of the Soviet budget. Gorbachev wanted to reduce military outlays and spend more on the domestic economy. Matching SDI would have made that goal impossible. So the very idea of SDI made it a bargaining chip in U.S.-Soviet negotiations. Reagan, however, believed in antimissile defense as its own end. I tried in conversations with him with the tape recorder off to get him to acknowledge that SDI was mostly a bargaining chip whether he thought of it that way or not. Reagan wouldn't accept this formulation. He believed American know-how could accomplish anything. Once Reagan described the goal of SDI, it was in his mind as good as built. Gorbachev and Reagan argued about SDI on both days of the Geneva summit with the Soviet leader becoming heated in his opposition.

"It's not convincing," Gorbachev said after Reagan promised to share SDI technology with the Soviets. "It's emotional. It's a dream. Who can control it? Who can monitor it? It opens up an arms race in space."

"As I said to you, I have a right to think you want to use our missiles against us," Reagan replied. "With mere words, we cannot abolish the threat."

Both Reagan and Gorbachev sought to portray the summit as a success. U.S. and Soviet negotiators had agreed to reestablish educational, scientific, cultural, and athletic links discarded by Carter after the invasion of Afghanistan and on a statement on air safety designed to prevent a repetition of the KAL 007 disaster, but they disagreed on the contents of a joint statement the two leaders wanted to make at the conclusion of the summit.

At dinner that night, hosted by the Reagans, Reagan regaled Gorbachev with Hollywood stories. They were interrupted by Shultz and the Soviet negotiating team, who arrived to tell the leaders they were at loggerheads over the language of a joint statement. Shultz pointedly blamed Soviet official Georgi Korniyenko, saying he was not following Gorbachev's instructions. Gorbachev turned to Korniyenko and said, "Do it the way we discussed."

This impressed Reagan as evidence that Gorbachev was "a man who was sure of himself and his power." The weary negotiators worked through the night before coming up with an agreement at 4:45 a.m. on Thursday, November 21. The statement pledged the United States and the Soviet Union to seek a 50 percent reduction in nuclear arms, "appropriately applied." No one knew for sure what this meant since the two sides counted nuclear arsenals differently, but it was enough for the two leaders to pronounce the summit a qualified success. In preparing the statement as well as speeches Reagan would give at a NATO meeting in Brussels on the way home and to a joint session of Congress upon his return, Matlock battled with White House speechwriters, who kept injecting anti-Soviet jibes. Three passages offended Matlock, but he agreed to leave them in the speeches without marking them and see how Reagan reacted.

Reagan showed up for a breakfast meeting with the negotiators and the speechwriters with the passages marked out. Turning to Buchanan, Reagan said: "Pat, this has been a good meeting. I think I can work with this guy. I can't just keep poking him in the eye."

On Wednesday, November 20, the two leaders began a second day of summitry, this time at the Soviet mission in Geneva. Shultz was struck by Gorbachev's low-key, emotionless defense of Soviet actions in Afghanistan, which contrasted with his passionate statements about other Soviet policies and his denunciation of SDI. Gorbachev said he'd learned of the Soviet invasion of Afghanistan in a radio broadcast, which Reagan interpreted as a sign that he was saying he had no responsibility for the war. In tonal contrast to Gorbachev, Reagan became emotional as he denounced Soviet conduct in Afghanistan.

From this distance, even after a U.S. intervention in Afghanistan that lasted twenty years and a second Taliban conquest of that beleaguered nation, Soviet conduct in Afghanistan seems unnecessarily cruel. Reagan had seen pictures of Afghan children disfigured by Soviet bombs that had been disguised as toys. As always, he reacted more to human suffering than to policy abstractions.

Nonetheless, Reagan and Gorbachev left Geneva hoping to meet again in Washington the following year. But unrelated developments delayed their reunion. The seminal event occurred April 26, 1986, when an explosion destroyed Reactor No. 4 at the Chernobyl nuclear power station in Ukraine. It became the worst disaster in the history of nuclear power, killing at least 50 people and exposing 100,000 others to varying degrees of radiation.

Resorting to the familiar Soviet practice of covering up unpleasant events, the Kremlin waited two days to issue a statement. When Gorbachev addressed the crisis, he offered neither regrets nor an apology. But he did use language Reagan found moving, saying the disaster "showed again what an abyss will open if nuclear war befalls mankind."

Chernobyl had a profound effect on Gorbachev. From then on, disasters, whether natural or human-made calamities, were reported promptly in the Soviet media. Chernobyl had an impact on Reagan, too. The catastrophe reminded Reagan of Armageddon, specifically of a passage in the Book of Revelation that told of how "a great star fell from heaven, blazing like a torch, and it fell on a third of the rivers and on the fountains of water. The name of the star is Wormwood. A third of the waters became wormwood, and many men died of the water, because it was made bitter."

When Reagan learned that "Chernobyl" meant "wormwood" in Ukrainian, he was certain the disaster at Reactor No. 4 was a portent. In time, Reagan would have a more secular realization: He became convinced that Chernobyl helped make Gorbachev receptive to U.S. proposals for nuclear arms reduction.

At the time, the Reagan administration was too hobbled by internal conflicts regarding SALT II to test this receptiveness. Reagan was caught between rival camps of advisors. Some wanted to keep SALT II intact while negotiating limits with Gorbachev whereas hard-liners urged him to scrap it on the grounds the Soviets had been cheating all along. His heart was with the conservatives, but his head was telling him not to antagonize the Soviets while he was seeking another summit with Gorbachev. Bob Kaiser and several other *Post* colleagues well versed in arms control regularly asked me where Reagan stood on one or another proposal. Often, I didn't know. Mimicking Reagan's approach to the world, I had a big-picture view of Reagan that didn't always include the details. But what I knew was important.

I knew Reagan had a romantic attachment to SDI unlikely to be shaken by any argument—including assertions that it violated the existing ABM Treaty. He wanted to be told how to construct a missile-defense system, not what he could accomplish by trading it away. I knew he was bored by the arcana of arms control but was determined to reduce both Soviet and U.S. nuclear arsenals. I knew he detested communism but trusted Gorbachev. However, Reagan didn't consider trust sufficient for an arms-reduction agreement. Matlock had taught Reagan a Russian phrase, *doveryay, no proveryay,* that he used repeatedly. It meant, "trust but verify."

Progress moved glacially during the spring and summer of 1986. Gorbachev was still affected by Chernobyl, and the Reagan administration by internal conflicts. Every proposal to the Soviets, every Reagan letter to Gorbachev, every speech on U.S.-Soviet relations became a tortuous exercise in reconciling conflicting State Department and Pentagon drafts. This task fell mostly to Colonel Robert Linhard, the capable arms-control specialist on the NSC staff who came to realize that the persistent clashes between State and Defense departments reflected a conflict in Reagan's own thinking. The president was committed both to missile reductions and to SDI, and he refused to regard these goals as incompatible. Reagan wanted the Soviets to make a 50 percent reduction in offensive nuclear capability while accepting U.S. deployment of a defensive system that would make their nation more vulnerable to a surprise attack. This approach found public voice on June 19, 1986, when Reagan addressed a high school class in Glassboro, New Jersey, where President Lyndon Johnson and Soviet leader Alexei Kosygin had begun the SALT process in 1967. Reagan urged Gorbachev to join him in taking "action in the name of peace" to reduce nuclear arsenals. But Reagan also said that SDI "might one day enable us to put in space a shield that missiles could not penetrate, a shield that could protect us from nuclear missiles just as a roof protects a family from rain."

Reagan then sent Gorbachev a July 25 letter drafted by Linhard on what became known as the "zero ballistic missile" plan. It proposed that the United States and Soviet Union abide by the ABM Treaty for five years, followed by a two-year period during which each side would inform the other about its proposals to eliminate ballistic missiles, deploy a missile defense system, and share the fruits of its antimissile research. Either side could then withdraw from the ABM Treaty on six months' notice.

Gorbachev responded to Reagan's proposal in a three-page letter delivered by Shevardnadze on September 19. Its last paragraph contained this surprising proposal:

> The thought came to me to propose to you, Mr. President, that as soon as possible, putting off all other matters, we meet one on one

> close by—for example, in Iceland, or in London—maybe for just a day, for a completely confidential, closed, frank conversation (possibly only in the presence of our ministers of foreign affairs). The result of that conversation—we wouldn't get into details, its rationale and meaning would be a demonstration of political will—would be instructions to our appropriate departments for draft agreements on two or three questions that you and I could sign during my visit to the United States.

Opting for Iceland, Reagan welcomed the offer of another meeting with Gorbachev. Matlock told Reagan that Gorbachev wouldn't have sought the meeting unless he had something new to propose, and Reagan had faith in his ability to negotiate with his counterpart. In contrast to the tutorials in which he had immersed himself before Geneva, Reagan made no special preparations for Reykjavík. Matlock thought Reagan had a "clear idea" of what he wanted to accomplish, which was eliminating all intermediate-range missiles in Europe in an agreement that could be signed at a full-fledged summit in Washington. But Arms Control and Disarmament Agency director Kenneth Adelman found the president unable to follow a summary of the U.S. and Soviet positions presented by Poindexter. These perceptions are not mutually exclusive. Specifics sometimes eluded Reagan, and Poindexter could be hard to follow. In any case, no one on the Reagan team—not Shultz nor Matlock nor Adelman nor Poindexter nor Don Regan—raised any caution flags. The mood in the White House was so cocky that there was no backup plan in case the meeting in Reykjavík went awry.

In advance of Reykjavík, scheduled for the weekend of October 11–12, Reagan came under fire from conservatives who wanted Reagan to press Gorbachev on human rights and Afghanistan. Reagan got the message. On October 7, my story in *The Post* was headlined "Reagan Vows to Pursue Human Rights, Regional Issues with Gorbachev."

Chatting with reporters before visiting Iceland in 1973, President Nixon had called his destination a "God-forsaken place." In reality, Iceland has beguiling natural beauty and distinctive inhabitants. I saw little of the countryside but shared a quick ride with another reporter to Hallgrímskirkja Church, which has a panoramic view of Reykjavík, a striking city. We had time for this diversion because the press corps had flown with Reagan on Thursday, October 9, so the president would be rested for his meeting with Gorbachev, who did not arrive until Friday evening. Unusually, Reagan came without his wife. Matlock had advised Reagan to leave Nancy at home so as to avoid temptation for social or ceremonial events. He assumed Gorbachev would follow suit.

But when the Soviet foreign ministry sent Gorbachev a schedule, he rejected it with the comment, "You have reserved no time for me to consult my wife." Time was found, and Raisa Gorbachev accompanied her husband to Reykjavík.

The Reykjavík Summit was held in Hofdi House, a onetime ambassadorial residence overlooking the sea that was the official guesthouse of the Iceland government. Reagan and Gorbachev began two days of intensive discussions there on Saturday morning, October 11. As Reagan arrived for the first meeting, CBS correspondent Bill Plante shouted at him from among a group of reporters, "Are you going to give away the store?"

"Don't own the store," Reagan replied.

I was standing next to Plante and took note of Reagan's realistic answer and upbeat mood. Before even sitting down with Gorbachev, Reagan seemed to be sending a signal of success to come.

Diplomatic accounts of summits typically must be read with caution. Most often, they rely on recollections of participants or surrogates with a vested interest in the outcome, leaving reporters dependent on what they have been told by those inside the meeting room. Even historians trying to fill in the gaps years later must choose from competing filtered versions of events. The Reykjavík Summit is the sole exception among the twenty-six meetings that nine U.S. presidents had with six Soviet leaders over forty-eight years.

A State Department transcript of the Reykjavík meetings between Reagan and Gorbachev and their foreign ministers once classified as "Secret" has been reclassified "Sensitive" and is available online. Also available is *The Last Superpower Summits,* prepared by the National Security Archive, which purports to include "virtually every word that Reagan, Gorbachev and [George H. W.] Bush said to each other from 1985 through 1991."

Because of the plentitude of material, any well-informed reader can judge the merits of the proposals made at Reykjavík without the mediation of observers such as myself, who wrote about the meeting in *President Reagan: The Role of a Lifetime.* The participants in the

Reykjavík Summit also have plenty to say and have written interesting accounts themselves. Despite this abundance of information, I'm going to revisit the Reykjavík Summit, which I covered for *The Washington Post*. It offers more insight into the real Reagan—and for that matter, the real Gorbachev—than any other meeting of the Reagan presidency.

On October 11, 1986, the first day of the Reykjavík Summit, Reagan began by listing issues he said were "left open" from Geneva, including the ABM Treaty, nuclear testing, and strategic weapons. He said, "both the U.S. and the USSR would like to see a world without nuclear missiles." Gorbachev agreed this was the "main issue" and suggested that Shultz and Shevardnadze join them, and he would outline his proposals. He added that "regional issues, humanitarian issues and bilateral relations" could be discussed in the afternoon. Gorbachev in effect accepted the U.S. agenda, differing only in nomenclature. (What the Soviet leader called "humanitarian issues," the American president called "human rights.")

Given this unexpected opportunity, Reagan talked, perhaps too much, about human rights, saying that many Americans came from other countries and were concerned about what happened in their native lands. After Shultz and Shevardnadze joined them, Gorbachev read his proposals aloud from a paper outlining the "principles" to be followed at a Washington summit.

Gorbachev proposed a 50 percent cut in strategic nuclear forces and reiterated the idea of eliminating U.S. and Soviet intermediate-range missiles from Europe while allowing British and French missiles to remain. Gorbachev proposed abiding by the ABM Treaty for ten years, during which SDI research would be confined to the laboratory. This was a concession; the Soviets had previously insisted on fifteen years of compliance with the treaty.

Reagan responded by saying he favored eliminating *all* strategic nuclear weapons. He proposed replacing the ABM Treaty with an agreement that would allow both countries to continue research and testing within certain limits. If it turned out that strategic defenses were feasible, the country that developed the technology would be obligated to share it with the other country and eliminate all offensive weapons in two or three years. Reagan added that he and Gorbachev "would not be here forever."

"We'll consider your reaction preliminary," a disappointed Gorbachev replied, saying he had made new proposals while Reagan repeated old ones. When they broke for lunch, neither leader was happy.

"He's brought a whole lot of proposals," Reagan told Shultz, "but I'm afraid he's going after SDI." Reagan and the U.S. team then retired to the "bubble"—a tiny room of transparent plastic made secure from electronic eavesdropping—to devise their strategy.

That afternoon, Reagan and Gorbachev tried again, this time with Shultz and Shevardnadze present from the beginning. Reagan reiterated his view that SDI did not have offensive capabilities. He compared SDI to gas masks used to protect soldiers in World War I. But when Reagan talked once more about sharing the technology of SDI research, he provoked a memorable explosion from Gorbachev.

"Excuse me, Mr. President," Gorbachev said, his voice rising, "but I cannot take your idea of sharing SDI seriously. You are not willing to share with us oil well equipment, digitally guided machine tools or even milking machines. Sharing SDI would provoke a second American revolution! Let's be realistic and pragmatic."

This ended the substantive discussion of the day, but both leaders agreed to have two working groups convene in an effort to reach agreements that could be signed Sunday morning. The talks lasted from 8 p.m. until dawn and included several Soviet concessions, bringing the group close to consensus on offensive weapons—but not on antimissile defense.

On Sunday morning, October 12, Reagan and Gorbachev held what had been scheduled as their final meeting at Reykjavík. They were supposed to finish by 12:30 p.m., have lunch, and fly home. The two leaders accepted the steep cuts in offensive weapons the working group had agreed to, but missile defense remained a stumbling block. Believing an agreement might be in reach. Reagan and Gorbachev postponed their flights, instructed their foreign ministers to seek a compromise, and agreed to meet again that afternoon.

Shultz summoned the working group and Poindexter. "We're at a very serious impasse on SDI," Shultz said.

Shevardnadze arrived after lunch and demanded to know if Reagan would accept the ten-year period of strict compliance with the ABM Treaty on which the working group had agreed. After some discussion, Perle and Linhard drafted a counterproposal, which they gave to Shultz, who after reading it aloud said that when he gave it to Reagan "the sound you hear may be the president banging my head against the wall."

The new proposal broke into two parts the ten-year period ABM compliance Gorbachev had proposed. During the first five years, strategic nuclear arsenals would be reduced by 50 percent, as the working group had agreed. Both sides would abide by the treaty for another five years if all ballistic missiles were eliminated during that time. After ten years, each side would be free to deploy a strategic defense. Instead of banging Shultz's head against the wall, Reagan found the plan "imaginative" and wanted to present it to Gorbachev.

"He gets his precious ABM treaty, and we get all his ballistic missiles," Reagan said. "And after that we deploy SDI in space. Then it's a whole new ball game."

Reagan and Gorbachev met at 3:20 p.m. after Shultz and Shevardnadze had talked separately for an hour. Gorbachev offered a counterproposal to do away with all nuclear-armed weapons in two stages. This would include bombers and cruise missiles, in which the United States had an advantage, as well as ballistic missiles, in which the Soviets were well ahead.

Reagan said he thought the two sides were close to agreement. He romanticized about meeting Gorbachev again in ten years and being so old that Gorbachev would not recognize him. The two of them would together "destroy the last missiles." Gorbachev said that Reagan, then seventy-six, had passed the "danger period" in his life and would live to be a hundred.

As they bantered, Shultz returned and said there was a conflict in the translation of the texts. The two leaders recessed while the translation issue was addressed. During the recess, someone suggested that, since the leaders were tired, it might be desirable to prolong the meeting for another day. Reagan's face fell, and he uttered a four-letter word. Matlock ruefully remembered his advice to leave Nancy Reagan in Washington.

"If she had been in Reykjavík, he probably would have been content to continue the meeting another day," Matlock later wrote. "Gorbachev was not the only leader who seemed lost without his wife."

But neither Matlock nor anyone else in the room had the heart to pressure Reagan to stay. Years later, I asked Shultz if another day would have changed the outcome. "I don't think so," he said. In the end, Reykjavík came down to a single word, "laboratory," to which Gorbachev wanted to confine SDI. The counterproposal he had read Reagan earlier in the afternoon contained this sentence: "The testing in space of all space components of anti-ballistic missile defense is prohibited, except research and testing conducted in laboratories." When the meeting resumed at 5:30 p.m., Reagan proposed instead that during the ten years in question each could continue "research, development and testing which is permitted by the ABM Treaty."

Gorbachev asked if the word "laboratory" had been deliberately omitted. Reagan replied affirmatively. This was the make-or break issue in a nutshell, but the leaders put it aside for a few minutes to discuss other differences. Gorbachev called the U.S. proposal imprecise, referring to "strategic offensive weapons" in one section and to "ballistic missiles" in another, but thought this could be sorted out. Reagan agreed.

"It would be fine with me if we eliminated all nuclear weapons," Reagan said.

"We can do that," Gorbachev said. "We can eliminate them."

"Let's do it," Shultz said.

A few minutes later, Reagan said that if the two leaders agreed to eliminate all nuclear weapons "they could turn it over to their Geneva people with that understanding, for them to draft up that agreement, and Gorbachev could come to the U.S. and sign it."

Reagan and Gorbachev had reached an amazing juncture few would have thought possible. Never before had an American president and a Soviet leader agreed to rid the world of nuclear weapons or come even remotely close to such an understanding. Nonetheless, Gorbachev and Reagan were now on a downhill slope and descending fast. Gorbachev said he could not take the word "laboratory" out of the agreement and Reagan said he would not "destroy the possibility of proceeding with SDI" by confining research to the laboratory. Gorbachev asked if that was the last word. Reagan said it was and added that he had a problem of public criticism in his country that Gorbachev did not face.

"The most outspoken critics of the Soviet Union over the years, the so-called right wing, and esteemed journalists [are] kicking my brains out," Reagan said.

Gorbachev then accused Reagan of not making "a single, substantial major step" in his direction. Everyone in the room abruptly realized they were about to lose the agreement they had been celebrating a few minutes earlier. It was more than Shevardnadze could bear. He made a sweeping, emotional appeal, directed as much to Gorbachev as Reagan.

"The two sides are so close to accomplishing an historic task, to decisions of such historic significance," he said, "that if future generations read the minutes of these meetings and saw how close we have come, but how we did not use these opportunities, they will never forgive us."

"This should not be turned down over a word," Reagan replied. "Anyone reading that would believe that the U.S. was committed to the ABM treaty."

Gorbachev said that it was "not just a question of a word but a question of principle." If he agreed to SDI research outside the laboratory, he "would be called a dummy and not a leader." He was not against SDI, he said, but the research had to be in laboratories.

Reagan said he'd asked Gorbachev for a favor of changing a word and that Gorbachev had refused. The favor was too much, said Gorbachev, who repeated his claim that the United States wanted to develop a "space-based ABM system which would permit U.S. to destroy the Soviet Union's offensive nuclear potential."

Under their agreement, Reagan responded, there would be no offensive weapons left to destroy, "and space defenses could not be deployed for ten years or so." It was not the word itself, it was the implication. Gorbachev was asking him to give up the one thing he had promised not to give up. Reagan asked Gorbachev to come up with an alternate word for laboratory. He said again he was asking Gorbachev to change his mind as a personal favor "so that hopefully they could go and bring peace to the world."

Gorbachev would not grant the favor. The State Department transcript has him saying that, if they could agree to ban research in space, he would sign it "in two minutes." He repeated that "the point was not of words but one of principle" He had a clear conscience about what he had done. Responding to Gorbachev's last refusal, Reagan stood and shoved his papers into a manila folder. Gorbachev stuffed his into his briefcase. As they stood together, Gorbachev asked Reagan to give his regards to Nancy Reagan. On the steps outside, the two leaders tautly shook hands. The Reykjavík Summit was over.

Television cameras were trained on the entrance to Hofdi House, and we could see the handshake in the press room. The body language of the two men told us the meeting had ended badly. From my experience with Reagan, I knew his tight jaw line expressed anger. His personal assistant, James Kuhn, later described Reagan as "very taken aback, upset, borderline distraught."

These impressions of a failed summit were reinforced by Shultz, who arrived at the press center at 7:20 p.m. for a half-hour briefing that was mournful and riveting. Shultz would write in his memoirs that it was his dejected appearance rather than what he said that led reporters to conclude the summit had failed, but his words conveyed the same message as his face. As the second paragraph of my story put it under a Reykjavík, Iceland, September 12, 1986, dateline: "Secretary of State George P. Shultz, reporting in a strained voice on a meeting that began with bright promise and ended gloomily after more than seven hours of negotiation today, said he was 'deeply disappointed' and no longer saw 'any prospect' for a summit meeting in Washington for the two leaders in the coming months."

The story ran under a two-line banner headline that read "Reagan-Gorbachev Summit Talks Collapse as Deadline on SDI Wipes Out Other Gains." Other media coverage of the summit's outcome was as negative as mine. Shultz set the tone for television viewers, as his gloomy evaluation was carried live on CNN, NBC, and CBS. The only note of optimism was sounded by national security advisor John Poindexter, who told reporters on Air Force One returning from Reykjavík that there had been a "breakthrough" in limiting intermediate-range nuclear missiles in Europe. A month later, Poindexter would cover up the U.S. arms sales to Iran and wind up in the dock, but he was more on target that Sunday than Shultz, White House chief of staff Don Regan, or the press corps put together. The news desk inserted Poindexter's comments as the tenth paragraph of my story.

Sunday's failure was Monday's success. The day dawned bright and sunny in Washington. As temperatures rose from the high forties to the mid-sixties during the day, the mood lightened at the White House and the State Department. My next-day story was headlined "Reagan to Seek a Silver Lining." Shultz's gloomy performance in the immediate aftermath of the summit had temporarily disqualified him from the role of cheerleader, but Poindexter proved a capable substitute.

Reagan capped the effort to put a happy face on Reykjavík with a well-delivered nationally televised speech. "I told him [Gorbachev] I had pledged to the American people that I would not trade away SDI—there was no way I could tell our people their government would not protect them against nuclear destruction," Reagan said. "I went to Reykjavík determined that everything was negotiable except two things: our freedom and our future."

This was vintage Reagan, snatching victory from defeat with oratory that put the American people at the center of the story. A *New York Times–CBS News* Poll that week found that 44 percent of respondents blamed Gorbachev for the failure of Reykjavík to produce an arms-control agreement, while only 17 percent blamed Reagan. (Eleven percent blamed both and 4 percent neither.)

Reagan and Gorbachev would struggle to find a mutually acceptable formula for nuclear arms reduction. The road ahead would be uneven as U.S. and Soviet foreign ministers and arms-control experts tried to disentangle the gains of Reykjavík from the disagreement over missile defense. That they were able to do so speaks less to the cleverness of the experts than to the idealism of Reagan and Gorbachev, who were committed to massively reducing the nuclear arsenals on both sides.

"The experts didn't believe, but the leaders did," said Alexander Bessmertnykh, the deputy Soviet foreign minister.

Idealistic as they were, Reagan and Gorbachev were also politicians who knew the limits of their running room. Reagan could have agreed to confine SDI to the laboratory for ten years, since it was unlikely any defense system would have been ready to test by then, but he was alert to hazards on his right, and realized that conservatives at home had embraced SDI and expected him to stand up for it. Their worry was that Reagan was so eager to cut a deal with Gorbachev that he would "give away the store," as Bill Plante had phrased it that first morning in Reykjavík.

For his part, Gorbachev could have found a substitute word for laboratory if he'd wanted to do so—as Sergey Akhromeyev, the voice of the Soviet military, conceded. Matlock wrote that, as U.S. and Soviet delegations filed out of Hofdi House after the summit collapse, Akhromeyev looked at U.S. arms-control expert Paul Nitze and said, "It's not my fault." Subsequent events would show that Gorbachev had potent adversaries in Moscow. He needed to show he had blocked a U.S. attempt to put weapons in space.

The challenge for Reagan and Gorbachev was to find a way back to the bargaining table. This would take time and patience on the part of both men. Reykjavík was neither the beginning nor the end of the Reagan-Gorbachev negotiations, but in the famous phrase that Winston Churchill used to describe the second battle of El Alamein, the end of the beginning. There would be summits to come and an important agreement to be forged.

24

MOMENTS OF HOPE

One summer day in 1982, a Russian who said his name was Andrei called and invited me to lunch. He said he wanted to discuss my columns and stories. I consulted with Ben Bradlee, who advised me to have lunch with Andrei, pick up the check, and not tell him anything that hadn't already been in the paper.

Andrei was a well-informed Russian with (he said) legal resident status in the United States. In the Cold War climate of the time, I assumed Andrei worked for Soviet intelligence. He seemed especially familiar with my stories about Bill Clark, then President Reagan's national security advisor.

Over the next year and a half, Andrei and I had irregular lunches in which we exchanged minimal bits of information. Just when I had given up on Andrei telling me something I didn't know, he opened up a bit. Yuri Andropov was terminally ill, according to a news report the Soviets denied, and I asked Andrei who would be the next Soviet leader. Andrei didn't deny the report about Andropov, which was newsworthy in itself, and he put forward Mikhail Gorbachev as a possible successor. Konstantin Chernenko replaced Andropov when he died on February 9, 1984; Gorbachev's turn didn't come until Chernenko died fifteen months later. But Andrei had revealed himself as a Gorbachev booster. After Chernenko was named, Andrei accurately predicted that Gorbachev would one day lead the Soviet Union.

I didn't see much of Andrei in 1984, when I was away from Washington covering Reagan's reelection campaign, and he entirely dropped off my radar screen in 1985, only to resurface after Reykjavík late in 1986. Andrei was intrigued by my stories about how Reagan hoped to capitalize on the gains of Reykjavík. He said Gorbachev felt the same way and wondered aloud if Reagan would be diverted by the ongoing Iran-Contra investigations.

After keeping a low profile in the months after Reykjavík, Gorbachev must have decided that Reagan would survive. On February 28, 1987, he unlinked the INF Treaty from other agreements, thereby pushing SDI to the side. A report from the Soviet press agency TASS, issued in Gorbachev's name, said, "The Soviet Union suggests that the problem of medium-range missiles in Europe be singled out from the package, and that a separate agreement on it be concluded without delay." Reagan accepted the offer three days later, setting in motion negotiations that would culminate with the signing of the INF Treaty by Reagan and Gorbachev in the East Room of the White House on December 8, 1987.

Why did the Soviets decide that intermediate nuclear weapons could be decided separately? I asked George Shultz later, and he answered that it was their fear of the Pershings. Seventy-two aging Pershing 1-A missiles, armed with nuclear warheads and based in West Germany, could have quickly reached the Soviet heartland. Gorbachev wanted them gone. West Germany, however, wanted to retain these missiles as an offset against shorter-range nuclear missiles (SS-12s and SS-23s) the Soviets had in East Germany and Czechoslovakia. Diplomacy by Shultz, meeting for three days in Moscow with Gorbachev and Soviet Foreign Minister Eduard Shevardnadze, resolved the issue. On April 15, Gorbachev announced that Soviet missiles in East Germany and Czechoslovakia would be destroyed.

There was an ironic twist to these negotiations. It was an article of faith among American conservatives that the Soviets cheated on agreements, as in fact they often did. This was why Reagan insisted on "trust but verify." But when the crunch came on INF verification, the CIA and the National Security Agency, not the KGB, blinked. This was Gorbachev's doing. He agreed to an "intensive verification" plan proposed by Shultz that would have placed U.S. and Soviet inspectors at each other's factories to count missiles as they left production lines. U.S. intelligence agencies complained to the White House that the Soviets might glean valuable information from this plan. Once more, Gorbachev saved the day. On June 12, appropriately in Reykjavík, NATO foreign ministers called for "global and effectively verifiable" elimination of all intermediate-range and shorter-range missiles. On July 23, Gorbachev accepted this concept, known as "double global zero." This did away with the need for factory inspection because there would be no new missiles to inspect. A month later, West German chancellor Helmut Kohl announced that Germany would dismantle its Pershing 1-A missiles.

Reagan's respect for Gorbachev had not made him blasé about the Soviet Union. In June, Reagan made a ten-day trip to Europe that included participation in the economic (G-7) summit in Venice. The trip was capped with a visit to West Berlin where, on June 12, 1987, Reagan gave one of the most notable speeches of his presidency.

On the morning of the speech, I was one of a small group of reporters who accompanied Reagan on an inspection of the Berlin Wall, the most tangible symbol of the Cold War. I'd seen pictures of this forbidding structure, but it was uglier up close. It was poignant, too, with tributes scrawled on the western side of the wall to brave and desperate German civilians who had been shot and killed while trying to cross. Reagan was also seeing the wall for the first time. His demeanor was downcast. At one point he looked at the top of the fifteen-foot-high wall, ringed with barbed wire, and shook his head. Most of Reagan's presidential speeches were delivered from the White House or at inside forums. Because of his tour of the wall, the tone of Reagan's speech that day was different from any other speech of his presidency.

The *Post*'s bureau chief in Berlin was the multilingual William Drozdiak, a tall and burly former basketball player for the University of Oregon and the European professional league. To insure me a good view of the speech site in front of the Brandenburg Gate, Bill plowed gently through the crowd of Berliners and U.S.-based embassy personnel like a well-mannered blocking back, clearing me a path. We wound up at a mound of earth just below Reagan, who challenged Gorbachev to create a new era of freedom in Europe. Reagan asked whether stirrings of reform and openness begun by Gorbachev signaled "profound changes" in Soviet policy or were "token gestures." Then, in a soaring voice, he said: "There is one sign the Soviets can make that would be unmistakable, that would advance dramatically the cause of freedom and peace. General Secretary Gorbachev, if you seek peace, if you seek prosperity for the Soviet Union and Eastern Europe, if you seek liberalization: Come here to this gate! Mr. Gorbachev, open this gate! Mr. Gorbachev, tear down this wall!"

Later, Reagan told me that he could hear the anger in his voice as he was speaking these lines. The object of his anger, Reagan said, was not Gorbachev but the East German police who had herded people away from loudspeakers that the West German authorities had placed on the western side of the wall so East Germans could hear the speech. The East German police then turned on their own loudspeakers to drown out Reagan. They did not succeed. In what may have been the most effective performance of his presidency, Reagan's words were heard throughout Europe and all the way to Moscow. Gorbachev did not comment, but TASS labeled the Reagan speech "provocative."

Howard Baker, who had replaced Don Regan as White House chief of staff, had used the same word when he saw the draft written by conservative speechwriter Peter Robinson. State Department aides had sought to delete the direct appeal to Gorbachev to tear down the Wall. Reagan told me later he'd thought about removing these passages but decided to keep them. I suspect his thinking was more theatrical than ideological. Reagan knew a good speech when he saw it, and he appreciated the dramatic setting provided by the historic Brandenburg Gate. Reagan liked the message of his Berlin speech so much he reprised it in a speech televised to Europe on November 4 after Gorbachev had agreed to a Washington summit.

"Wouldn't it be a wonderful sight for the world to see, if someday General Secretary Gorbachev and I could meet in Berlin and together take down the first bricks of that wall, and could continue taking down walls until the distrust between our peoples and scars of the past are forgotten?" Reagan said. This never happened, but two years later Berliners pulled down the hated wall themselves.[1]

But U.S.-Soviet relations were improving, and the accommodating mode on the U.S. side was enhanced in November by significant changes on Reagan's team. Defense secretary Caspar Weinberger resigned, citing

1. By then most Russians were reconciled to the notion that member nations of the Warsaw Pact—the Eastern European nations behind the Iron Curtain—wanted independence. However, one mid-level KGB official stationed in East Germany considered the collapse of the Soviet bloc a tragedy. His name was Vladimir Putin.

his wife's ill health, and was replaced by Frank Carlucci. Colin Powell, who had been Carlucci's deputy, became national security advisor.

Powell was Reagan's sixth and last national security advisor, and he meshed better with the president and Shultz than any of his predecessors. With reporters he respected, Powell was candid and on the record. He didn't know me except by reputation, but in my first interview with Powell when he was Carlucci's deputy he told me that the Nicaraguan contras whom Reagan admired were a "highland fighting force" with no ability to take Managua. Shultz told me that Powell got away with such candor because he always told the truth and had no agenda of his own.

The Washington summit meeting between Reagan and Gorbachev was designed as a victory lap for the signing on December 8, 1987, of a document called the "Treaty Between the United States of America and the Union of Soviet Socialist Republics on the Elimination of Their Intermediate-Range and Shorter-Range Missiles." This would lead directly to the destruction of 859 U.S. nuclear missiles and 1,836 Soviet nuclear missiles. But the treaty's importance transcended numbers, as Reagan noted in a White House signing ceremony. While only 4 percent of the U.S. and Soviet missile arsenals were eliminated by the INF Treaty, it was the first U.S.-Soviet treaty of any kind to provide for destruction of nuclear weapons. It was also the first treaty to provide for verification; the two nations would monitor destruction of the missiles, setting an important precedent for the START Treaty signed by Gorbachev and President Georg Bush two years later.

Responding to Reagan lyrically, Gorbachev said, "We can be proud of planting this sapling which may one day grow into a mighty tree of peace. May December 8, 1987, become a date that will be inscribed in the history books—a date that will mark the watershed separating the era of mounting risk of nuclear war from the era of a demilitarization of human life."

Reagan and Gorbachev displayed a comfortable familiarity with each other that was a byproduct of their meetings in Geneva and Reykjavík.

"We have listened to the phrase of an old Russian proverb," Reagan said, once again. The maxim is *doverey no provery*—trust but verify."

"You repeat that at every meeting," Gorbachev said good-humoredly.

"I like it," Reagan said, as officials from both countries laughed and applauded.

The private part of the victory lap went less smoothly. Reagan and

Gorbachev walked together to the State Dining Room, where they delivered separate television statements to worldwide audiences. Next on the agenda was a plenary session where the two leaders were joined by senior advisors for what was supposed to be a discussion of arms issues. But after starring in his big scene of the treaty-signing ritual, Reagan behaved as if he'd been taken to the wrong set and asked to perform without a script. Gorbachev began with a report on his efforts to reform the Soviet system. Reagan, who often faded in mid-afternoon, appeared disoriented and didn't know what to say. Shultz and Powell recognized the signs.

"Since he didn't know what he should talk about, Reagan told stories," Powell told me later.

Gorbachev was used to Reagan's anti-Soviet anecdotes. The Soviet leader usually laughed politely at them and occasionally contributed his own joke about the backwardness of the Soviet bureaucracy. But Gorbachev took pride in *perestroika* (restructuring) and he found nothing funny when Reagan responded to his progress report by telling an anecdote about a Russian-speaking American scholar who had taken a taxi to the airport for a flight to the Soviet Union. The cab driver was a young man who had not completed college, and the scholar asked him what he intended to do after he completed his education.

"I haven't decided yet," the driver told him. When the scholar arrived in Moscow, his cab driver was also a young man who hadn't completed his education. When the scholar asked him what he would do when it was done, the driver replied, "They haven't told me yet."

Gorbachev was offended that his glowing description of change in the Soviet Union had been answered by this shopworn anecdote. Powell agreed. "It *was* offensive," he said. "The meeting was a disaster."

As soon as it was over, Shultz, Powell and Howard Baker took Reagan aside and expressed their concern. "I guess I shouldn't have told that joke," Reagan said.

But it was not the joke alone that distressed Shultz, who called the entire meeting "a bad show." Reagan had been inattentive and unable to converse with Gorbachev. It was an embarrassing performance, which Reagan agreed should not be repeated. That night Powell wrote talking points for Reagan and took them to Shultz, who edited them. Baker and Powell gave them to Reagan the next morning, urging him to stick to the script and tell no jokes. The president did as instructed. Meeting with Gorbachev in the Oval Office on December 9, Reagan was alert and businesslike.

Writing the lead story of the treaty-signing with Don Oberdorfer, I knew nothing of Reagan's lame performance with Gorbachev behind closed doors. The participants in that meeting were tight-lipped even with reporters they trusted. They didn't lie, but they declined to discuss the conversations. Shultz and Powell told me what happened later, when I was writing *President Reagan: The Role of a Lifetime.* That is one of the reasons reporters write books.

But if our news story missed Reagan's lapse, it captured the impact of Gorbachev on normally blasé Washington. The capital city was gripped by what *Washington Post* columnist Tom Shales called "Gorby fever." Wherever Gorbachev went, crowds lined the streets to applaud. On busy Connecticut Avenue, with Secret Service and KGB agents holding their breath, Gorbachev directed his limousine driver to stop and went out in the street like an American politician to shake hands. When the Gorbachevs arrived late at the White House for a spectacular state dinner, Reagan wisecracked to the Soviet leader, "I thought you'd gone home."[2]

In his White House remarks and at the Soviet embassy, Gorbachev made the case for *perestroika.* "Something very serious is afoot, something very profound," he said, "an awareness that we cannot go on as we are, that we cannot leave our relations the way they are."

Americans who were tuned to these events also received a positive impression of Reagan, who appeared to have recovered the confidence that had deserted him during a year marked by congressional and criminal investigations into the Iran-Contra affair, the collapse of the stock market, and Nancy Reagan's cancer surgery.

Away from the public eye, Reagan and Gorbachev discussed human rights and Nicaragua without rancor but also with no breakthroughs. Progress towards a strategic arms treaty stalled for the same reason as at Reykjavík. Reagan remained wedded to an antimissile system. Gorbachev remained determined to confine SDI to basic research, although

2. Guests included Joe DiMaggio, Billy Graham, Jimmy Stewart, and Mstislav Rostropovich. Gorbachev reciprocated the next evening at the Soviet embassy, where he was applauded by celebrities including Gore Vidal, James Baldwin, John Denver, Robert DeNiro, Arthur Miller, Paul Newman, Yoko Ono, Gregory Peck, and Meryl Streep. Gorbachev was impressed with the turnout, listing all these names and more in his memoirs.

he no longer used the word "laboratory," the loaded term that sunk the Reykjavík Summit.

"We are going forward with the research and development necessary to see if this is a workable concept, and if it is, we are going to deploy it," Reagan told him.

"Mr. President, you do what you have to do," replied Gorbachev. "And if in the end you think you have a system, you want to deploy, go ahead and deploy it. Who am I to tell you what to do? I think you're wasting money."

As this exchange suggests, Reagan and Gorbachev had achieved a comfort level unique among U.S. and Soviet leaders. Each knew the other's positions by heart. Reagan had been impressed with Gorbachev's willingness to sign a treaty requiring the Soviets to destroy many more missiles than the United States. According to Jack Matlock, "Gorbachev came to understand that the goals Reagan had set forth fitted Soviet needs." This was especially true of Afghanistan, which the Soviets needed to quit not because Reagan wanted them out but because the war was draining Russian resources and morale. Gorbachev had described Afghanistan as a "bleeding wound." (As Americans themselves would learn in the twenty-first century, this was an apt description). In April 1988, Gorbachev signed a treaty between Afghanistan and Pakistan ending the Soviet military presence in Afghanistan.

The Washington summit was hard on the homeless. Acting at the behest of the federal government, the D.C. metropolitan police rousted them out of the downtown area, including near *The Post* building on Fifteenth Street. The streets were quiet when Don Oberdorfer and I walked across the street to the Madison Hotel bar for a drink—bourbon for Atlanta-born Oberdorfer, scotch for me—before the late-city edition. Don had spotted a clunky editing change in our story, managing to get it fixed before reached the majority of *Post* subscribers. Don was more meticulous than I was, and right about nearly everything.

Reagan was versed in the lore of treaties, viewed from a conservative perspective. In his final year as governor of California, Reagan read *The Treaty Trap* by historian Laurence Beilenson, whose aim was to show that authoritarian nations rarely live up to political treaties.

Armed with this analysis and his historic suspicion of the Soviet Union, Reagan opposed both the SALT I Treaty signed by Richard Nixon and Soviet leader Leonid Brezhnev in 1972 and the SALT II agreement signed by Jimmy Carter and Brezhnev in 1979. After the signing of the INF Treaty, the shoe was on the other foot. Reagan assumed that right-wing activists would try to block ratification, using his past statements against him. He was right.

Borrowing the techniques liberals had used to mobilize public opinion against Reagan's Supreme Court nominee Robert Bork,[3] conservatives sent 300,000 letters and 5,000 cassette recordings of an attack on the treaty by General Bernard Rogers, the former supreme commander of NATO. Newspaper advertisements compared Reagan to Neville Chamberlain, the gullible British prime minister who had signed an accord with Hitler to bring "peace in our time." In the Senate, conservatives led by Jesse Helms of North Carolina and Steven Symms of Idaho introduced amendments designed to kill the agreement Reagan had forged with Gorbachev.

It's as easy as breathing to oppose adversaries but hard to stand up to one's friends. Reagan did not falter in the face of intense conservative opposition to the INF Treaty. George Will was the favorite columnist of Ronald and Nancy Reagan, so they shrugged off Will's written comment that Reagan was engaged in "moral disarmament." More distressing to Reagan was the campaign against the treaty in *National Review* by William F. Buckley. Reagan invited Buckley to the White House but couldn't change his mind.

Ultimately, the treaty prevailed because the American people never took seriously the notion that Ronald Reagan had gone soft on Communism. A voter survey conducted during the second week of January 1988 found that 79 percent of Americans supported the treaty with only 17 percent opposed. Such lopsided findings emboldened Senate leaders to reject the killer amendments, none of which garnered more than fifteen votes. They then choked off a Helms-led filibuster, enabling the Senate to ratify the treaty by a ninety-three–to–five vote. The vote occurred on May 27, two days before Reagan and Gorbachev began their fourth summit in Moscow.

Long before their final summit, Reagan and Gorbachev realized that

3. On October 23, 1987, the Senate rejected Robert Bork's nomination to the Supreme Court by a vote of fifty-eight to forty-two.

a strategic arms control treaty would have to await the next president. The barrier was still SDI, but in a February 25 interview with me for *The Washington Post,* Reagan chose to present the problem of a strategic arms treaty as a matter of timing. He told me that the "time was too limited" for U.S. and Soviet negotiators to complete their work before the Moscow meetings. Curiously, both leaders seemed content with the impasse. Those of us who knew Reagan—even Shultz, who praised Reagan's "strategic vision"—had to do some fancy tea-leaf reading to figure out what was on the mind of the Great Communicator. What we divined was that Reagan hoped to make a splash in Moscow by changing the subject from arms control to human rights and other issues.

Gorbachev may also have needed a breathing spell. Oberdorfer had learned from his diplomatic sources that he was feeling pressure from the Soviet equivalent of the military-industrial complex over the INF Treaty, in which they gave up many more warheads than the United States. That trend would continue when Gorbachev and President Bush signed the START Treaty on July 19, 1991, five months before the Soviet Union ceased to exist.

The subtitle of my book *President Reagan* is *The Role of a Lifetime,* which I chose during the run-up to the Moscow summit. It was meant to convey that Reagan's experience as an actor often defined the way he saw the world as president. Reagan never objected to the subtitle. He had quipped that he didn't see how anyone could do the job of president without having been an actor, an inside joke he would make public in the final weeks of his presidency. Gorbachev, a consummate performer who was attracted to the dramatic arts as a younger man, understood this dimension of Reagan.

"We are both actors," Gorbachev had said at Geneva. "He is a good one."

After Moscow, Oberdorfer and I examined the summit from a theatrical perspective. While we were doing this, Reagan compared the summit to an epic film produced by Cecil B. DeMille. For Reagan, his Moscow performance truly *was* the role of a lifetime, and he played it to the hilt.

Our story ran on June 9, 1988, under the headline "The Scripting of the Moscow Summit." We said the Reagan show was produced by Thomas Griscom, the White House communications director, and Powell, who headed a summit planning group. Their aim, we wrote, was a production that Moscow and the world would find "coherent and convincing." The script was crafted by Tony Dolan, whose claim to fame was originating the phrase "evil empire" to describe the Soviet Union. Reagan had tried out the script before a Philadelphia focus group assembled by pollster Richard Wirthlin. Both the pollster and Reagan called the focus group "an out-of-town tryout." Reagan was an active participant in the production. He raised questions about the script, rehearsed with enthusiasm, and in a speech to cultural and artistic leaders in Moscow reflected on the lessons of Hollywood.

"In the movie business, actors often get what we call typecast," Reagan said. "The studios come to think of you as playing certain kinds of roles . . . and no matter how hard you try, you can't get them to think of you in any other way. Well, politics is a little like that, too. So I've had a lot of time and reason to think about my role."

Reagan saw himself as a global apostle of freedom, voicing the aspirations of Russians and others yearning to be free. He saw a summit on Soviet soil as a unique opportunity to make the case for freedom and democracy, which required more than the quiet diplomacy he had previously practiced on human rights. At Reykjavík, he'd brought Gorbachev a list of twelve hundred Soviet Jews, known as "refuseniks," who'd been denied permission to emigrate. In Washington he'd given Gorbachev other lists of Soviet dissidents and members of separated families who wanted to rejoin relatives in the United States. In Moscow he presented Gorbachev with a list of fourteen human rights cases on which the United States sought action. Gorbachev became testy. When an American reporter asked him if he would act on the U.S. requests, Gorbachev replied, "There are too many lists."

Reagan was not discouraged by such put-downs. Despite the verbal potshots he and Gorbachev exchanged, they had reached a level of trust unusual for any two leaders, let alone the leaders of the world's most powerful Communist country and its most powerful democracy. Appealing to the abundant better angels of Gorbachev's nature, Reagan believed his counterpart would be receptive to his pleas to allow refuseniks and dissidents to leave. Under the banner of *glasnost,* Gorbachev had already freed a number of dissidents, including Nobel laureate Andrei Sakharov, who with his wife, Elena Bonner, had been released from internal exile. Reagan believed Gorbachev would do much more, as he eventually did.[4]

In his human rights campaign, Reagan had discovered the utility of the Helsinki Final Act he had criticized when had it was signed by President Ford in 1975. Thirty-five nations, including the United States and the Soviet Union, had signed that accord. In a presummit stopover in Helsinki on May 27, 1988, Reagan said it established "new standards of conduct" on human rights. He gave a balanced speech in Finlandia Hall, praising Gorbachev for extending human rights in the Soviet Union while also saying that more needed to be done.

But Reagan's first act in Moscow contained a defect in the script that nearly wrecked the entire performance. At Nancy Reagan's suggestion, both Reagans planned to dramatize the plight of Soviet Jews by visiting a well-known refusenik family, Yuri and Tatyana Ziman. Mrs. Reagan believed a visit to the Zimans would "spice up" the summit, but Gorbachev became furious when he saw the schedule, saying it was insulting for the Reagans to visit a refusenik's family before calling on the Gorbachevs. Deputy foreign minister Alexander Bessmertnykh told Colin Powell that, if the Reagans went through with this, the Zimans would never be allowed to emigrate. Reagan quickly backed down, telling his aides that the entire idea had been his wife's.

Instead the Reagans opted for a stroll on the Arbat, a popular pedestrian mall lined with boutiques and cafes, where the president was even more of a draw than Gorbachev had been in Washington. But Muscovites did not enjoy the liberty of their American counterparts who had been allowed to approach Gorbachev's limousine. The Arbat was packed with Sunday strollers. When word passed that the Reagans were in their midst, they surged forward to meet them. The KGB responded by forming a flying wedge and charging the crowd, hurling people aside and pounding them with their fists.

4. Within months of the Moscow summit, Gorbachev allowed thousands of the refuseniks to immigrate to Israel. Nearly everyone on the lists Reagan had given Gorbachev was freed. Rabbi Arthur Schneier, president of the ecumenical Appeal of Conscience Foundation, said Gorbachev "will go down in history as the man who let my people go."

American reporters, me included, were astounded by this rough treatment of a friendly crowd. So was Reagan, who wrote in his diary that night about the "warm, friendly people [on the Arbat] who couldn't have been more affectionate . . . I've never seen such brutal manhandling as they did on their own people who were in no way getting out of hand."

Reagan stuck to his script for the rest of the trip, which included a memorable speech to ninety-six dissidents from all corners of the Soviet empire. He delivered it at Spaso House, where the Reagans stayed in Moscow. It is the U.S. ambassador's residence and therefore sovereign U.S. territory. Soviet officials allowed the Zimans to attend. The audience also included Abe Stolar, whom I met. Stolar, who was born in Chicago, had been taken to Moscow by his Marxist parents as a child in the 1930s. He had fought in the ranks of the Red Army during World War II and was seriously wounded. But now he desperately wanted to come home and had become a celebrity among Americans pleading the dissidents' cause.

Reagan spotted Stolar, stuck out his hand, and said: "I've just spoken to Mikhail Gorbachev about you. I told him we came from the same state and were born at the same time."

In his speech to the dissidents, as he had in Helsinki, Reagan credited Gorbachev for advancements on human rights while prodding him to do more. Reagan described his human rights agenda as freedom of religion, freedom of speech, and freedom of travel for the Soviet people. "The new Soviet leaders appear to grasp the connection between certain freedoms and economic growth," Reagan said. "We hope that one freedom will lead to another; that the Soviet government will understand that it is the individual who is always the source of economic creativity."

"Moment of hope" became the animating impulse of the summit. Reagan mentioned it at every speech he gave in Moscow, and Gorbachev made it the centerpiece of his remarks at a dinner for the Reagans and in a quick march around Red Square with Reagan and U.S. and Soviet officials in tow. Gorbachev stopped at one point to say that the American people and the people of the Soviet Union must be friends, to which Reagan gave a full-throated endorsement.

But while the leaders agreed on the benefits of friendship between their countries, Reagan's celebration of individual freedom challenged the very premises of Marxism-Leninism. This was evident in a thoughtful—and at times provocative—speech Reagan gave at Moscow State

University soon after speaking to the dissidents. Reagan spoke beneath an enormous marble bust of Lenin, who I imagined looked disapprovingly at this American interloper who was preaching the benefits of free-market capitalism. As the students listened raptly, Reagan shared with them an idealized version of U.S. history, explaining that "Americans seek always to make friends with old enemies," as they had done with the British after the Revolutionary War, with each other after the Civil War, and with the Germans and Japanese after World War II. Now, said Reagan, it was time for Americans and Soviet citizens to become friends:

> Your generation is living in one of the most exciting, hopeful times in Soviet history. It is a time when the first breath of freedom stirs the air and the heart beats to the accelerated rhythm of hope, when the accumulated spiritual energies of a long silence yearn to break free. . . .
>
> We do not know what the conclusion will be of this journey, but we're hopeful that the promise of reform will be fulfilled. In this Moscow spring, this May 1988, we may be allowed that hope; that freedom, like the fresh green sapling planted over Tolstoy's grave, will blossom forth at last in the rich fertile soil of your people and culture. We may be allowed to hope that the marvelous sound of a new openness will keep rising, ringing through, leading to a new world of reconciliation, friendship and peace.

Ever since Reagan began public speaking in the 1930s when he was a sports broadcaster in Iowa, he had valued youthful audiences, and he was energized, he told me later, by the students at Moscow State University. After a masterful speech, Reagan responded to questions, treating students to stream-of-consciousness replies of the sort that had often confounded American interviewers. Reagan reminisced that when he was governor of California he could "start a riot" just by going to a college campus, adding a self-deprecating quip about his own academic diligence as a young man. In response to other questions, Reagan speculated that the U.S. government had done "American Indians" no favor by putting them on reservations, told them he opposed the constitutional amendment limiting U.S. presidents to two terms, and repeated his old riff about how anyone can come from anywhere and become an American.

When he was finished, the students rose and gave Reagan a standing ovation. As I left the auditorium in the company of Gary Lee, the Russian-speaking Moscow correspondent for *The Washington Post,* he overheard two women students enthusing about Reagan. "You can see why he's called the Great Communicator," one said.

The public statements made by Reagan and Gorbachev at the Moscow summit mattered more in terms of the Cold War than anything the leaders did in their four private and largely ceremonial meetings. Reagan told no more anti-Soviet jokes, and Gorbachev was more relaxed and patient than at previous summits. He treated Reagan as a respected and nearly retired elder statesman, even intervening to end a photo opportunity where a tired Reagan seemed bewildered by reporters' questions.

Even a last-minute gambit by Gorbachev to disrupt the Reagan script by inserting a seemingly innocuous, but highly problematic, phrase into the agreement didn't dampen the mood. After being rebuffed, the Soviet leader fell silent for a moment, then brightened and put his arm around Reagan.

"Mr. President, we had a great time," he said, and the two men walked without rancor to the treaty ceremony, the final business of the Moscow summit.

The Washington Post account of this exchange was published on June 3, 1988, my fifty-fifth birthday. This is the story that Oberdorfer and I reported together, which he mostly wrote in London after I went to bed with a bad cold. Don had talked to Shultz and Carlucci, and I interviewed Powell and Baker. All parties agreed that Reagan would have accepted Gorbachev's change in the wording except for the objections of his staff. Baker, the master of Senate maneuver, saw nothing wrong with that. Staff were supposed to point out pitfalls to the decision-makers, Baker told me.

The Moscow summit was the last great performance of the Reagan presidency. On his way home, Reagan added a grace note in a speech at London's Guildhall, where he celebrated the summit as a turning point in East-West relations and declared that a "worldwide movement toward democracy" was ushering in "the hope of a new era in human history, and, hopefully, an era of peace and freedom for all."

That's a lot of hope to pack into a single sentence, but such was the optimism of the time. Reagan's friend Margaret Thatcher responded admiringly, saying that the Moscow summit would "encourage the course of history for years to come." She credited Reagan for leading the Western alliance and for his confident attempt "to enlarge freedom the world over."

Blessed by a symbiotic relationship in which each had need of the other, Reagan and Gorbachev led their countries out of the darkness of the Cold War into the light of the first constructive relationship between the United States and the Soviet Union since their wartime alliance against Nazi Germany. Although both nations still possessed terrifying nuclear power, the two leaders had set back the doomsday clock. Although Gorbachev would go on to sign the START Treaty with President Bush, his domestic reforms—*glasnost* and *perestroika*—had set in motion forces he could not control.

When Gorbachev asked Soviet-controlled nations in Eastern Europe to emulate his reforms, they countered by seeking the withdrawal of Soviet armies garrisoned in East Germany, Poland, Hungary, and Czechoslovakia. As these troops withdrew, the seven Warsaw Pact nations freed themselves from the Soviet yoke. After the Berlin Wall fell on November 6, 1989, it became clear that the Soviet Union was living on borrowed time. Gorbachev survived a clumsy coup attempt on August 18, 1990, but Lithuania declared its independence in November and other Soviet republics followed suit. Eleven of these republics formed a federation led by Russia and headed by Gorbachev's rival Boris Yeltsin. By the time Gorbachev resigned on Christmas Day 1991, the Soviet Union had passed into history.

Reagan and Gorbachev stayed in touch through the Soviet twilight and beyond. On September 20, 1988, Gorbachev expressed his feelings in a long letter to Reagan, saying, "Our relationship is a dynamic stream and you and I are working together to widen it." They would exchange many more letters—some eighty over a nine-year period that had begun in 1985—and have a fifth meeting when Reagan was still president on Governors Island in New York on December 7, 1988. George H. W. Bush, the president-elect, accompanied them and asked Gorbachev if *glasnost* and *perestroika* would succeed.

"Jesus Christ himself could not tell you that," Gorbachev replied.

Bonded by their legacies, Reagan and Gorbachev met again in San Francisco, where the United Nations was born, on June 4, 1990, when Gorbachev was an embattled Soviet leader and Reagan an ex-president.

The next day, Gorbachev called on George Shultz at Stanford. Shultz said he'd heard that Gorbachev's meetings with President Bush had gone well.

"Yes," Gorbachev replied, "but Reagan was there when times were really tough."

The Reagans visited Moscow a second time, in September 1990, at the invitation of the Gorbachevs, staying again at Spaso House. Jack Matlock, who had advised Reagan before his previous meetings with Gorbachev, was now the U.S. ambassador and "privileged," he wrote, to attend their meetings. Reagan and Gorbachev behaved like old friends, "now very much on the same wavelength," Matlock said. Gorbachev talked at length of his efforts to reform the Soviet political system "and complained of the difficulties he faced in changing people's habits."[5]

Gorbachev and his wife, Raisa, traveled to America for thirteen days in 1992, visiting eight cities, meeting with President Bush and former President Jimmy Carter, and speaking at Fulton, Missouri, where Winston Churchill had famously warned that an Iron Curtain was descending over Eastern Europe. That trip began with a sentimental journey to Rancho del Cielo, the Reagan ranch northwest of Santa Barbara. By then I was again the western correspondent for *The Washington Post* with a home in Summerland, some thirty miles from Rancho del Cielo. It would be the last time the Reagans and the Gorbachevs were together, and Nancy Reagan told me all of them enjoyed it.

On Sunday, May 3, Reagan took Gorbachev for a spin around the 688-acre ranch in a Jeep with the license plate GIPPER. The Reagans gave the Gorbachevs two white cowboy hats. Raisa donned hers correctly, but her husband put his hat on backwards. Reagan was too polite to correct Gorbachev in the presence of photographers, but a photo taken by Santa Barbara photographer Steve Malone shows him staring at Gorbachev's hat with an amused expression.

The Reagans and Gorbachevs took a walk, and Reagan told a well-worn story about chopping 137 telephone poles to build the fence around the ranch house. Afterward, Gorbachev slapped a fence post and motioned to the photographers to take another picture of the four of them.

5. Gorbachev's main attempt to change habits was his anti-alcohol campaign of 1985–87 that raised prices on vodka and imposed restrictions on the amounts that could be sold and hours of sale. The campaign reduced criminality and nudged life expectancy upward, but was resented by working-class Russians.

"This picture will be even more famous than the picture of us next to the fireplace in Geneva," he said. The next day, at the Ronald Reagan Presidential Library in Simi Valley, Gorbachev gave a speech warning of the perils of "nationalist extremism" and received the first Ronald Reagan Freedom Award.

"We were able to make a difference," he said to Reagan in accepting it. It was the eighth and final time the two old warriors were together.

A plaque on President Reagan's desk in the Oval Office proclaimed: "There is no limit to what a man can do or where he can go if he does not mind who gets the credit."

It was an apt sentiment; in seventy years of journalism, I rarely met a politician as magnanimous as Reagan. He had long believed that his policies would prompt change in the Soviet Union, but when changes came, Reagan knew who was most responsible for them. When a reporter asked Reagan at the Moscow summit who deserved credit for the changes in the Soviet Union, he replied: "Mr. Gorbachev deserves most of the credit, as the leader of this country."

This answer delighted Gorbachev, who quoted it in his memoirs. Some commentators said Reagan was merely being gracious while on Gorbachev's turf, but he used similar formulations after returning home. In his farewell speech as president from the Oval Office on January 11, 1989, Reagan celebrated a "satisfying new closeness with the Soviet Union" and praised Gorbachev for instituting "internal democratic reforms" and beginning withdrawal from Afghanistan.

"My view is that President Gorbachev is different from previous Soviet leaders," Reagan said. "I think he knows some of the things wrong with his society and is trying to fix them. We wish him well." Reagan's ingrained modesty was also evident in his evaluation of domestic affairs. In the farewell speech, he downplayed his reputation as the Great Communicator and said it was the content of his speeches that mattered.

"I wasn't a great communicator, but I communicated great things, and they didn't spring full bloom from my brow, they came from the heart of a great nation—from our experience, our wisdom, and our belief in the principles that have guided us for two centuries," Reagan said. "They called it the 'Reagan Revolution.' Well, I'll accept that, but for me it always seemed more like the great rediscovery, a rediscovery of our values and our common sense."

Reagan departed the presidency in a flurry of sentiment and varied appraisals of his achievements and shortcomings. My assessment was a page-one story headlined "Reagan Leaving Legacy of Surprises" in *The Post* on January 5, 1989, five days before George H. W. Bush became the nation's forty-first president.

> Ronald Wilson Reagan, a popular president who spoke to the future of America with a compelling vision of the past, returns to California this week, leaving behind a legacy of surprises. Reagan departs on a crest of public approval, with even critics saying that he restored confidence in the presidency. His geniality, optimism and self-deprecating humor commended him to Americans who did not necessarily share his political opinions or his policy prescriptions. As a master communicator with a background in radio, films and television, he proclaimed old values and new policies in carefully scripted Oval Office television speeches consciously modeled on the radio "fireside chats" of his first political role model, President Franklin D. Roosevelt.
>
> But as Reagan prepares to leave Washington as the first president since Dwight D. Eisenhower to complete two terms, commentators and historians are finding him hard to pigeonhole.
>
> While Reagan championed conservative values, he barely tinkered with the edifice of social welfare programs launched during the New Deal and widely supported by Americans. While he promised to eliminate the Cabinet departments of education and energy, he instead enlarged the Cabinet by creating a Department of Veterans Affairs. While he conducted the largest peacetime buildup in history, he was for the most part reluctant to use military force except when the odds, as in the 1983 invasion of Grenada and the 1986 bombing of Libya, were overwhelmingly in the United States' favor. Even on environmental and regulatory issues, where Reagan's preference for market solutions was clear, his record defies easy ideological classification.
>
> "It's such an interesting mixture of brilliance and inadequacy," said Princeton University historian Fred Greenstein, who described Reagan as displaying unsurpassed skills in his public presidency but showing a staggering lack of curiosity and inattention to White House management."

The central irony of Reagan's presidency, I wrote, was its impact on attitudes toward government. Reagan's bedrock belief was that government had become so large and intrusive it was "reversing the order of things" and no longer derived its consent from the governed. "This belief has been the underlying basis for everything I've tried to do these last eight years," Reagan said in his farewell address.

But Reagan's success in restoring confidence in the presidency had renewed faith in government institutions, according to various polls. This trust in government that in my boyhood was personified by FDR and later by Eisenhower and John F. Kennedy and that Reagan rekindled did not survive. The Pew Research Center found in 2021 that only about one-quarter of Americans say they trust the government in Washington to do what is right "just about always" (2 percent) or "most of the time" (22 percent). When Reagan left office, a CBS Poll found that 68 percent of Americans approved what he had done; only 26 percent disapproved.

Thanks to contemporaneous accounts and the assistance of Ken Duberstein, Marlin Fitzwater, James Kuhn, Landon Parvin, and Colin Powell, I was able to describe the last day of Reagan's presidency with substantial detail in the opening chapter of *President Reagan: The Role of a Lifetime*. The bare-bones version is that Reagan, actor that he was, paid close attention to the final act of his presidency and how it might be viewed by the public and future historians. Reagan was seventeen days shy of his seventy-eighth birthday, but he was always looking ahead.

Reagan had a departure script prepared by Kuhn and Duberstein, with editing by the Reagans. The outgoing president left two reassuring notes to his successor and a last letter to Margaret Thatcher, thanking her for her support. The Reagans bade warm farewells to the White House staff. Then it was on to the inaugural, where George Bush was sworn in as the forty-first U.S. president in a ceremony on the west front of the Capitol. Afterward, the Reagans and Bushes returned to the White House for an emotional leave-taking. Bush fought tears as he said goodbye to the man who had put him on his ticket and given him the opportunity to become president.

James Baker, usually restrained, wept openly as Reagan climbed into the Marine helicopter that would bear him and his wife to Andrews Air Force Base. When the helicopter banked over the White House, Reagan turned to Nancy and said tenderly, "There's our little bungalow down there." She smiled back with tears running down her cheeks.

The logistics of reaching Andrews and clearing security did not permit the small contingent of reporters traveling with Reagan to California to attend Bush's inaugural. As one of those reporters, I watched it on television at Andrews, where a crowd of fifteen hundred drawn from the surrounding military community saw Reagan off. One sign in the crowd read "Air Force One Flies Once More for the Gipper," but the Boeing 707 that bore the Reagans and their entourage to California was no longer Air Force One, a designation reserved for the plane carrying the president. It was the same plane Reagan had flown throughout his presidency, stripped of its top-secret communications gear and without military aides aboard. In addition to the Reagans, the passengers included a cadre of aides, guests, journalists, and Nancy Reagan's hairdresser.

During his presidency, Reagan rarely talked to reporters in the air, but on this day he made his way back to us in the cramped rear compartment of the plane and conducted an impromptu news conference. Nancy soon joined him. Reagan was asked about his accomplishments as president and gave a long answer centering on his economic policies.

When the same question was put to Nancy, she murmured, "a peaceful world."

Reporters were transcribing these answers from our tape recorders when the Reagans called us to the center of the plane to celebrate the day with bottles of champagne and a yellow cake inscribed "The Reagan Years 1981–89." Hampered by a bandage on his left hand from minor finger surgery, Reagan cut the first piece and had trouble balancing the cake and champagne. He put the champagne down, as he always did if the choice was between an alcoholic beverage and a dessert. Then he told stories of the presidency and Hollywood and war movies. This prompted me to ask him if he regretted not seeing combat in World War II. He replied without embarrassment that he had not thought about it. His eyesight was so bad, Reagan added, that he would not have been called up at all if he had not been in the reserves.

Secret Service agents took no chances on this day. They'd almost lost Reagan outside the Washington Hilton less than ten weeks into his presidency. This was remembered in the ranks, and the agents were determined to escort the Reagans safely to their new home in Bel Air.

Accordingly, the presidential plane landed on a runway designated "remote terminal ramp" at the southwest corner of the sprawling LAX terminal. The landing site was so far from the main terminal, and the published information about Reagan's arrival so deliberately scant, that it's a wonder seven hundred people found their way to a welcoming rally organized by the Reagan advance staff. It might otherwise have attracted thousands.

I wrote my story about Reagan's first trip as a former president on the plane and filed it at a convenient phone bank after we landed. Assured that the welcoming ceremony would be brief and inconsequential, I was surprised when I returned from the phone to find a jubilant Reagan rambling away to an adoring crowd. "He's thrown away the [cue] cards," Stu Spencer said.

Reagan was invigorated by the sunny weather he preferred to the chill of Washington and pleased with the warm greetings he received from Los Angeles Mayor Tom Bradley, comedian Rich Little, actor Robert Stack, and William French Smith, his first attorney general.

"When you have to stay eight years away from California, you live in a perpetual state of homelessness," Reagan said.

Stack, an old friend, told Reagan he had changed the course of history. Little told Reagan he would have to find work, and Reagan responded he'd been asked to do a remake of *Bedtime for Bonzo,* this time cast as the chimpanzee. He said he would continue to campaign for his beliefs, including repeal of the Twenty-Second Amendment. The crowd chanted, "Four more years."

Then, with such fantasies discarded, it was time to go. A motorcade insignificant by presidential standards bore the Reagans to their Bel Air home. I hitched a ride to the Century Plaza with Spencer, whose driver had commandeered a white Cadillac for the occasion. At the hotel, I called the newsroom and updated my story with Reagan's remarks at the welcoming ceremony. The next day I flew home to Northern Virginia and began work on *President Reagan: The Role of a Lifetime.*

25

THE REST OF THE STORY

Fortune had smiled on Ronald Reagan throughout his adult life. He'd landed a job as a radio broadcaster at the height of the Great Depression when a more qualified applicant didn't show. He'd received a coveted Hollywood film contract after one reading. After a divorce, he met and married Nancy Reagan, who cared for him and made him her cause. When his movie roles dried up, he turned to television and stayed in the public eye as host of a popular TV program. He turned to politics at a time the Republican Party was desperate for new faces, and the Democrats he opposed for governor and then for president were burdened by the accumulated grievances of incumbency. Reagan benefited as a candidate by having the services of Spencer-Roberts and fortunate as a president to have the guidance of James Baker and George Shultz.

At first, Reagan's luck held in the post-presidency. He settled into an easy Southern California lifestyle with a government-provided Century City office on the thirty-fourth floor of a building on Avenue of the Stars that satisfied both security needs and what Nancy Reagan told me was her husband's preference for heights. On smogless days, Reagan could go to the window and glimpse the Pacific Ocean in the distance. Reagan completed his memoirs in this office, where I met Mother Teresa at the elevators as she was leaving and I was arriving for a book interview.

The office was a five-minute drive to a comfortable three-bedroom ranch house on a wooded acre in Bel Air that Nancy Reagan had found for them while her husband was president. Twenty wealthy investors, some of whom had helped the Reagans since he was governor, purchased the house. The Reagans paid the money back. They had plenty of money, especially after an October trip to Tokyo and Osaka, where Reagan received $2 million for a couple of twenty-minute speeches and a few ceremonial appearances. Reagan was publicly criticized for taking so much money from a foreign source, and Nancy saw to it that this was not repeated. Less attention was paid to the twenty-nine speeches or videotaping that Reagan did for Republican candidates free of charge. Whenever possible, Reagan slipped off to his mountaintop ranch northwest of Santa Barbara where he rode, cleared brush, and did other manual labor. In June 1989, to Nancy's delight, the Reagans traveled to London, where he received an honorary knighthood from Queen Elizabeth II.

Luck deserted Reagan soon after this trip when he was bucked off a horse on July 5, 1989, while he and Nancy were visiting William Wilson's ranch in Sonora, Mexico, near the Arizona border. Wilson, one of the few Roman Catholics in the Reagan inner circle, had served during the Reagan presidency as U.S. ambassador to the Vatican. Reagan was flown by military helicopter to a hospital at Fort Huachuca, an Army base near Tucson, where he was treated and released after a five-hour stay. A Secret Service spokesman minimized the extent of Reagan's injuries, but in Los Angeles, Reagan spokesman Mark Weinberg vividly described the incident.

"The horse Reagan was riding bucked wildly several times on a rocky downhill slope and eventually stumbled, throwing him," Weinberg said. Two months later Reagan went to the Mayo Clinic in Rochester, Minnesota, for a routine physical. Doctors found and removed fluid on his brain, which they attributed to the horse-riding incident.

When I interviewed Nancy Reagan years later, she insisted that the horse-riding accident was the source of his subsequent Alzheimer's disease. She may have been onto something. A University of Pennsylvania study published in the March 2021 issue of *Alzheimer's & Dementia* found that head injuries, even mild ones, are associated with a long-term increase in risk of dementia. The study was based on a twenty-five-year tracking of fourteen thousand Americans in four U.S. states. The study noted that genetics also play a role. Reagan's mother, Nelle, had dementia, probably Alzheimer's, the most common type of dementia among seniors.

Dementia resulting from head injuries does not always manifest itself immediately, and such was the case with Reagan. He had no medical issues in 1990 except for a discovery in May of scar tissue from his 1985 cancer surgery. On this trip Reagan toured the torn-down Brandenburg Gate that he had urged Gorbachev to open three years earlier. He addressed the Polish parliament in Warsaw and shipyard workers at Gdansk who'd played a historic role in ending Soviet domination of Poland. Reagan then went to Moscow to see Gorbachev and meet with Boris Yeltsin. In December, Reagan went abroad again, this time to Britain, where he addressed the Cambridge Union Society. He was functional throughout the trip.

In February 1991, I interviewed Reagan for a story that ran in the Style section of *The Washington Post* on February 7, a day after his eightieth birthday. In the interview Reagan expressed a sense of wonder about his life, saying "Most of my dreams came true."

Reagan's birthday was celebrated at the Beverly Hills Hilton at what I wrote was "a lavish flag-waving affair suffused in the glow of past glories and mists of present patriotism." The flag waving was mostly over the Persian Gulf War then being waged by U.S. forces against the Saddam Hussein regime in Iraq. Reagan praised President Bush and Colin Powell, who then headed the Joint Chiefs of Staff, and in response to a question said Powell had the qualities to be president. Margaret Thatcher, who had resigned as prime minister the previous November, was the featured speaker. Turning to Reagan, she said, "Your abiding contribution . . . was to enlarge freedom the world over, and you succeeded—with perhaps a little help from friends."

Reagan spoke effusively about Thatcher and Nancy Reagan. Of his wife he said, "My life really began when I met her and has been rich and full ever since."

This black-tie birthday party turned out to be the last big posh event of the Reagan era. It was attended by Hollywood and political celebrities, including California Governor Pete Wilson, Vice President Dan Quayle, former Senators Howard Baker and Paul Laxalt, and cabinet members from the Reagan and Bush administrations, including George Shultz and Cap Weinberger. The Hollywood contingent included Eva Gabor, Charlton Heston, Liza Minnelli, Tom Selleck, and Elizabeth Taylor. The event raised $2 million for the Ronald Reagan Presidential Library then under construction in Simi Valley.

I saw little of Reagan for several months after this party but kept in touch through Nancy Reagan, with whom I'd developed a friendly relationship. I next caught up with him on May 7, 1991, designated "Ronald Reagan Day" at the state capitol in Sacramento, to which the former president had been invited by the Democratic-controlled legislature. George Skelton of the *Los Angeles Times* ably captured the impression made by Reagan: "He's eighty now, the hearing is shot and the voice isn't as crisp," George wrote. "But the stride, the smile, the timing and aura are still vintage Ronald Reagan."

I wrote about the event in a "Letter from California," which an editor had suggested would allow me latitude to discuss Reagan's political odyssey. So I recalled that Reagan on being elected was asked whether he would be successful as governor had responded that he didn't know because he'd never played a governor. After two terms as governor and two terms as president, I wrote, Reagan was "a smash hit in the role of elder statesman."

He spoke to the assembled legislators after being warmly introduced by Assembly Speaker Willie Brown Jr. as "citizen-governor Ronald W. Reagan." Brown, a liberal Democrat and California's first Black speaker, had been an assemblyman since 1964, two years before Reagan became governor. He was a flamboyant and savvy politician who had been helpful when I was Sacramento correspondent for the *San Jose Mercury*. He took me aside and explained the political significance of Ronald Reagan Day. Brown said the central purpose was to assist Pete Wilson, who was struggling to obtain legislative passage of a state budget at a time of recession-diminished revenues. Wilson inherited a budget deficit in Sacramento, as Reagan had in 1967. Since Reagan had solved his budget predicament with a massive tax increase, Brown thought the conservatives might listen to him.

After lunch with Wilson, Reagan gave a clever speech studded with nostalgic references to former foes from his days in California politics, along with and a nod to "my friend Mikhail Gorbachev." Reagan never uttered the despised word "taxes," but he praised Wilson's budget "leadership," the code word in Sacramento for the tax increase. Read as Donald Trump serves in his second stint in the White House, Reagan's speech is a reminder of how far Republicans have retreated from sensible pragmatism in the ensuing decades. Reagan urged the legislators to lobby members of Congress on behalf of the "Brady bill," which provided a seven-day waiting for handguns. As governor, Reagan had signed a bill providing a fifteen-day waiting period for such purchases. It was "time for the rest of the country to catch up with California," he said.

Reagan's next performance came on the stage of the Ronald Reagan Presidential Library, built from $57 million in donations on a picturesque mountain in Simi Valley overlooking rugged hills on which many Hollywood westerns had been filmed. The library opening on November 4, 1991, featured a gathering of five U.S. presidents—Bush, Reagan, Gerald Ford, Richard Nixon, and Jimmy Carter—for the first time in history.

"Under President Ronald Reagan the nation stayed strong and resolute and made possible the beginning of the end of the Cold War," Carter said, setting the tone for a presidential celebration in which the participants took turns praising themselves and each other. Arnold Schwarzenegger, a future governor of California, had been added to the list of Hollywood celebrities, which was otherwise a similar lineup to the guests at Reagan's eightieth birthday party. Bob Hope received a standing ovation as he walked through the crowd, which included thirty-five hundred invited guests and six hundred members of the media.

For Reagan, "who resolutely believes in happy endings," I wrote, "the ceremony marked the climax of a long effort to build a library after opposition from liberal faculty members forced the library foundation to abandon its original site at Stanford University. Simi Valley, 40 miles west of Los Angeles, is more appropriately Reagan country than Stanford."[1]

Time was running out on Reagan, as it does for everyone, but he did not surrender easily. His public schedule was reduced in 1992, and Nancy kept him away from reporters. Aided by riding and physical labor at Rancho del Cielo, he remained in excellent physical shape and looked younger than his age. While he had slowed mentally, Reagan could still rise to the occasion as a speaker, as he demonstrated in July

1. The editors allotted considerable space for this story, and I inspected the exhibits before the presidents arrived. The Prosperity Gallery celebrated the "American Miracle: Economic Recovery in the Reagan Years," but as I noted did not mention the "runaway deficit and mounting national debt that were also part of Reagan's economic legacy." Overall, I wrote: "The exhibits in the Reagan library, like those of other presidential libraries, make little pretense of objectivity. The years of the Reagan presidency are presented as the best years of our lives."

with an upbeat speech to the Republican National Convention in Houston that contrasted with the exclusionary rhetoric of other speakers and reminded me of his glory days as the Great Communicator. Taking issue with the frequent claim that the nation was in decline, Reagan quoted Emerson in describing America as the "country of tomorrow." But his speech was not shown in prime time, and to Reagan's disappointment he was used sparingly by President Bush's team in the campaign. With an assist from Ross Perot, Bill Clinton carried California, which Reagan had won ten times in primaries and general elections for governor and president.

Alzheimer's disease does not always strike suddenly, like Athena bursting from the brow of Zeus. Instead it comes, as it did for Reagan, like a thief in the night, stealthily robbing its victims of their memories before slowly killing them. Friends and family of Ronald Reagan, most of all Nancy, noticed in late 1992 and early 1993 that he was becoming increasingly forgetful and repeating himself.

The first public inkling came on February 6, 1993, during a celebration of Reagan's eighty-second birthday. Margaret Thatcher was once again the featured speaker, and Reagan made a toast to her and then, a few minutes later, repeated it verbatim. Guests pretended not to notice. I had been invited to the birthday celebration but was unable to attend because of a scheduling conflict. The next day, however, several people present called me and wanted to know, as one of them put it indelicately, if Reagan had "lost his marbles."

I told my editors what had happened and asked if I should write a story about it. They said no; one of them observed that various former public officials in Washington suffered from Alzheimer's and said we hadn't written about them. Reagan's lapse had occurred at a public event, which made it different, but I didn't argue with my editors. I knew little about Alzheimer's at the time, and Reagan hadn't been diagnosed with anything as far as I knew. Reagan's press secretary was no help. So we passed up a chance to raise a question about an awful disease that afflicts millions of Americans, including readers of *The Washington Post.*

It took a year and a half, but Ronald Reagan seized that teachable moment himself on November 5, 1994, in a poignant letter to "my fellow Americans" explaining his condition. The letter came as no surprise to those who had glimpsed Reagan on television at Richard Nixon's funeral on April 27, 1994, where he displayed the blank look common to Alzheimer's victims.

In August, doctors made it official. Reagan received a diagnosis at his annual check-up at the Mayo Clinic that he was "entering the early stages of Alzheimer's." Reagan's daughter Maureen, who had been shocked when she visited her father, thought he was beyond the "entering" stage but did not quarrel with the Mayo Clinic. Ronald Reagan resolved any doubts with his forthright letter, which Nancy accurately described to me as a "typical Ronnie letter." Her husband had a knack for incorporating his experiences into a universal message and explaining large matters in simple ways. Reagan said in his letter that he was writing it to "promote greater awareness" of Alzheimer's. Then with a last tip of the hat to Nancy and the American people, he concluded:

> Unfortunately, as Alzheimer's Disease progresses, the family often bears a heavy burden. I only wish there was some way I could spare Nancy from this painful experience. When the time comes I am confident that with your help she will face it with faith and courage.
>
> In closing let me thank you, the American people for giving me the great honor of allowing me to serve as your President. When the Lord calls me home, whenever that may be, I will leave with the greatest love for this country of ours and eternal optimism for its future.
>
> I now begin the journey that will lead me into the sunset of my life. I know that for America there will always be a bright dawn ahead.
>
> Thank you, my friends. May God always bless you.
>
> Sincerely, Ronald Reagan

I never saw Reagan once he disappeared from public view behind the veil of Alzheimer's. I discussed seeing him with Nancy, who said she wanted me, as a biographer of Reagan who had covered him since "the early days," to remember him as he was. But she softened this edict by saying I could appeal.

"Who could I possibly appeal to?" I asked.

"Me," she said, and we both laughed.

I have vivid memories of Reagan that surely would have survived seeing him when he was ill. But I never questioned Nancy's decision or asked to see Reagan again. I'm not sure why. As journalist and biographer, I should have wanted to see him, but I felt a curious reticence about infringing on the privacy of a man about whom I'd written so much.

Although I didn't see Reagan, I was unable to avoid him. During the difficult decade when Nancy and her handpicked caregivers watched over her husband, rumors frequently circulated that he had died. Every few weeks, news organizations throughout the world would hear such gossip, and a *Post* editor would call me to ask if it was true. This continued when I was on leave to write my book about the Rodney King case and the Los Angeles riots, and even after I left the paper in 2000.

I always checked these reports with Joanne Drake, the smart and durable chief of staff for Nancy Reagan. At first I felt embarrassed. Joanne had a young family and didn't need calls from a reporter in the middle of the night. But Joanne gave me her home phone number and told me to call her anytime I heard a rumor of Reagan's death. I was Joanne's canary in the cold mine, for she said I was usually the first call, which gave her a chance to check on Reagan's condition before she received other inquiries. Joanne called me on June 5, 2004, reaching my wife, Mary, to say that Ronald Reagan had died and that she would soon be issuing a statement on behalf of Nancy Reagan.

"My family and I would like the world to know that President Ronald Reagan has passed away," the statement said. "We appreciate everyone's prayers." Death was attributed to pneumonia with complications caused by Alzheimer's disease. The next day *The Washington Post* ran an obituary I had written a decade earlier after Ronald Reagan was engulfed by the unforgiving fog of Alzheimer's.[2]

2. I had enormous help from the editors in updating this obituary, probably the longest newspaper article I ever wrote about Reagan. Leonard Downie, the executive editor, rewarded me by putting "Washington Post Staff Writer" under my byline although I'd not been a staff writer for four years. It meant a lot to me then and still does.

26

EARTHQUAKES AND FIRES

The White House beat is a central assignment at *The Washington Post*, but the western bureau in Los Angeles existed on the newspaper's domestic periphery during my two assignments there. As a White House correspondent, I was in the paper nearly every day. In the western bureau, I often had to find stories that would appeal to faraway editors with differing tastes and limited space.

One benefit of the three-hour time difference was that Mary and I could have dinner together without interruption by an editor. The drawback was that it often required me to guess the value of a story before reporting it to get it listed on the day's news budget. Bill Elsen, the easygoing and meticulous out-of-town editor during much of my second western tour, understood this problem and helped as best he could.

On balance, I like working in bureaus, as I'd done in Sacramento for the *San Jose Mercury-News* and in Washington, DC, for Ridder Publications. Reporters have more freedom in bureaus than in the home office. Some things had changed for the better since my first western tour. The assignment desk in Washington had taken over management of the stringer network, which freed me from a time-consuming chore. Also, the territory had shrunk. The *Post* now had a correspondent in Denver, so I didn't have to worry about stories in the Mountain West. I covered the West Coast and Hawaii, placing most emphasis on California, and wandered occasionally into Arizona, Nevada, or Utah.

Jay Mathews was my colleague when I returned to the western bureau. I had succeeded him in 1977, when he went to China, and he succeeded me during the 1980 presidential campaign. The western bureau was at its best in 1991 with two of us, and our reporting preferences complimented one another. For instance, Jay was interested in Alaska, while I preferred Hawaii, where I had friends and sources. Jay, who at this writing is still an education columnist for *The Post,* was fascinated by education and would write nine books on the subject, five of them about high schools. Long before global warming became a national fixation, I'd developed an interest in weather and climate. I'd hiked the desert around Reno as a boy and taken a multilayered climatology course at the University of Nevada. I enjoyed environmental stories.

The bureau lost Jay in 1992. His wife, Linda Mathews, was a respected editor at the *Los Angeles Times* when Peter Jennings hired her as his producer on ABC's *World News Tonight.* She moved to New York, and Jay followed later, working for *Newsweek* until he became *The Post*'s Wall Street correspondent. I soldiered on with a succession of resourceful news aides.

Ever since Watergate, *The Washington Post* has been a magnet for complaints of alleged corruption in local communities. The news aides fielded many such calls and tried to filter out the oddballs and conspiracy theorists. In my first tour in the bureau in the late 1970s, news aide Katharine MacDonald devised what we called the "Watergate test" to distinguish genuine tips from fanciful ones. If the caller claimed he had a story that would put Watergate in the shade, we could safely ignore it.

After a reporting internship at *The Post,* MacDonald became a solid reporter at the *San Francisco Examiner* under the tutelage of Frank McCulloch, a journalistic legend. The news aides in my second incarnation in the bureau—Jill Walker, Leef Smith, and Jessica Crosby—were savvy and talented. In 1991 Walker (now Jill Robinson) in my absence wrote the first six stories on the Rodney King beating. Smith (now Leef Barnes) could do anything and was particularly helpful during the 1992 Los Angeles riots. Crosby (now Jessica Young) did invaluable reporting on the Northridge earthquake of 1994.

I am afraid of large spiders and flying in small planes but fearless during earthquakes. These quakes are numerous in California because much of the state sits atop the San Andreas Fault or one of many subsidiary faults. In my high school days I slept through a magnitude 6.0 earthquake in Reno that made a huge crack in our living room wall. I later experienced a slew of moderate earthquakes in California and absorbed misplaced conventional wisdom about what to do if you're inside a building when one strikes.

I was talking to Bill Elsen at 7:43 a.m. on June 28, 1991, when our apartment in Santa Monica began to shake. (My wife was home in Summerland eighty-five miles away.) I told Elsen we were having an earthquake.

"I'll call you back," Elsen said.

"No, stay on the line," I said as I crouched under the archway of our front door. "We could lose our power."

We did in fact lose power because of the Sierra Madre earthquake. Jay Mathews, who lived in Pasadena, was nearer the quake and reported it with customary aplomb in a story that also had my name on it. The Sierra Madre temblor had a magnitude of 5.6 on the familiar Richter Scale with an intensity of VII (very strong) on the lesser-invoked Mercalli Scale measuring surface intensity. Two people died and a hundred were injured. Jay described one of the deaths in the second paragraph of our story: "Julie Nickoley, a stablehand at Santa Anita racetrack, nine miles from the epicenter, died after a piece of structural steel struck her in the head as she was watching morning workouts from the grandstand."

The story ended with an anecdote about Lucy Jones, a lively seismologist spokesperson with the U.S. Geological Survey at Caltech. She and her husband, also a scientist at Caltech, were getting ready for work when the quake struck. She was dressing their four-year-old son, Sven, while their nine-month-old baby, Niels, was by himself in a room with sliding glass doors.

"I spent the quake yelling, 'Where's Niels? Where's Niels?' Jones said."

"The baby, born to seismology, had crawled to safety," our story noted.

Fast forward to 4:31 a.m. on January 17, 1994. I'm on book leave and in bed in our Summerland home, which is built on pillars extending deep into the earth. Summerland is near Santa Barbara, where an earthquake in 1925 flattened homes and killed thirteen people. Our home shook and rattled, with movement continuing for several seconds that seemed longer. I wondered if this was the Big One, when I saw my wife standing in our bedroom doorway.

"What are you doing?" I asked.

"It's an earthquake," Mary said. She was doing what I had done when the Sierra Madre quake struck. We'd been taught to stand in doorways, advice based on a single stark picture of an adobe doorway standing in a collapsed house. It is bad advice, experts say now.

We had been awakened by the Northridge earthquake, which measured 6.7 on the Richter scale and had a Mercalli intensity of IX, the second highest number on this scale used to describe a "violent" earthquake. Our electricity went out, but we had a battery-powered radio and soon learned that a powerful earthquake had struck the San Fernando Valley, centered in Northridge. We wondered if our apartment in Santa Monica had been damaged.

Soon I received a phone call from Karen DeYoung, who headed the national staff. Bill Hamilton, the versatile journalist who had succeeded me, was in Seattle. Because telephone service was down in Los Angeles, Karen couldn't reach Jessica Crosby, the news aide I'd hired and Hamilton had kept. I told Karen that Crosby would know what to do. Karen asked if I could help out. Of course, I said. Karen said a television report had shown that the Santa Monica Freeway had collapsed and asked if I could reach the epicenter of the earthquake from the west on Highway 101.

"I'll try," I said. Then, to Mary's surprise, I went back to bed and slept soundly for fifty minutes. I knew it would be a long day.

Highway 101 extends fifteen hundred miles from Los Angeles to the Canadian border. It bisects the San Fernando Valley, reaching the Pacific coast at Ventura. Highway signs are marked south and north, but the true direction of Highway 101 as it runs by Summerland is west and east. So I drove east through the San Fernando Valley to reach the earthquake epicenter. It was familiar territory, as I'd lived in the valley during my first assignment to the bureau. Exiting at Balboa Boulevard, where a shattered water main had sent a torrent of water down the street, I saw a drowned dog floating in the rapids. Flames peeked through soaked debris above a ruptured gas main. Balboa wasn't drivable, so I took another street to Reseda Boulevard, where the three-story Northridge Meadows Apartments had collapsed on itself like a sunken multilayered pancake, crushing inhabitants on the first floor. The scene was chaotic. Bodies were being removed, and survivors and onlookers were milling about. I looked for Jessica but couldn't find her. Instead, I found a couple who had been sleeping on the third floor of the apartment building when the earthquake struck.

"It kind of felt like a bomb went off," said Susan Pearson. "It tossed me up in the air, and when I came down, it tossed me up again."

"We were airborne, thrown from our bed," said her husband, Erik Pearson. "It was one big explosive jolt that slammed up and down and then pitched the whole building diagonally about twelve feet."

Erik was an emergency medical technician who had teamed up with five others to rescue panicked survivors from the second and third floors. "We formed a human chain, stretching fire hoses between balconies and using a ladder to reach people," Erik Pearson said. "People were screaming. They were crawling all over each other. People came down in front of you and between your legs."

I interviewed other survivors of the apartment collapse, including a woman who said she would move back to her hometown of Boston. Then I returned to my car, which was equipped with a bulky cell phone, the only mobile device then available. There was no service. With deadlines approaching, I remembered I'd previously had good reception when I lived in Woodland Hills. I drove there, parked in a shopping center, and dialed the national desk. This time I got through. Near the end of my dictation, the phone crashed. I drove home to Summerland.

Power had been restored at home, and I called the desk on our landline. An editor told me my story was on page one, sharing a byline with Jessica Crosby, who had submitted a substantial file. Crosby had also reported from Northridge Meadows Apartments. Either we'd been there at different times or missed each other in the chaos. Crosby had also filed two additional stories.

The Northridge earthquake killed 57 people, including 16 at the Northridge Meadows Apartments, and injured more than 9,000, about 1,500 of them seriously. For days afterward, thousands of homes and businesses lacked electricity, and some lacked gas. Fifty thousand people had little or no water. Destruction or severe damage of 82,000 residential and commercial units and 5,400 mobile homes left 125,000 people temporarily homeless.

In terms of casualties, it was the deadliest in Southern California since the Long Beach earthquake of 1933, which killed 115 people. In disruption to the region, the Northridge earthquake, which occurred on a previously unknown blind thrust fault, was the most severe natural calamity in the history of Southern California. Elevated portions of the Santa Monica Freeway (Interstate 10), the world's busiest freeway, collapsed, as did major portions of Interstate 5, the region's main link to Central California. Bridges on four other freeways also collapsed.

Despite all this, Southern California was relatively fortunate. Although some commercial buildings collapsed, loss of life was minimized because the quake struck in the early morning hours of Martin Luther King Jr. Day, a federal holiday. Capitalizing on their good fortune, state and local authorities hired C. C. Myers, a firm known for its quick work, to rebuild the Santa Monica Freeway, the most vital highway link in the region. The freeway was reconstructed in sixty-six days, about half the allotted time.

Karen DeYoung called the day after the earthquake, thanking me for the story and saying I was right about Jessica Crosby, whom she called a "real reporter." That was high praise from Karen, known for her brave coverage of the Nicaragua civil war, among other stories. Hamilton was back in Los Angeles dealing with the complex aftermath of the earthquake, and Karen said I could return to my book.

But Mary and I needed first to check earthquake damage at our Santa Monica apartment. She had rented it when she came to California in 1977 and lived in it alone until I came into the picture in 1984. We had kept it throughout the second term of the Reagan presidency and in 1990 when I was writing *President Reagan: The Role of a Lifetime.* For me the apartment was a beachhead in the Los Angeles area where I could stay during the week while working in the bureau. It meant much more than that to Mary. So it was wrenching to see the apartment after the earthquake. All our kitchen cabinets had opened and emptied, smashing glasses and plates. The only surviving item was a single wine glass from a set Mary's parents had given us for our wedding. We swept up the broken glass and dishware and spent the night with friends.

I had begun work on my next book, *Official Negligence,* and had a scheduled interview the next day with Tom Bradley, the former mayor of Los Angeles. He had joined an LA law firm after twenty years as mayor. I had taken a suit to change into for the interview but absent-mindedly left my dress shoes at the Santa Monica apartment. So I put on the tennis shoes and headed downtown through many detours. Bradley arrived wearing an elegant suit. He said he had encountered little traffic on the way to the office, a comment I found strange under the circumstances. I don't know if he noticed my shoes.

Drought was a recurrent issue in the West before and after the Northridge quake. Water supplies were so low in 1991 that one hard-pressed district in Central California took steps to purchase water from Canada to be transported by ocean liners. Such schemes were dropped when the drought was washed away by unexpected March 1992 rains, but my stories, some written with Jay, continued to explore the long-term water shortage.

We also examined environmental stress. A January story from my hometown of Reno fretted that Nevada, then the fastest growing state in the nation, was importing people and pollution from California. In Hawaii, in March 1991, I reported on the effort to preserve threatened species. Under a Kauai dateline, my story began: "Often called the extinction capital of the nation, Hawaii is becoming a preservation capital as well for endangered species."

The most publicized endangered wild creature in the Pacific Northwest was the northern spotted owl. Until I reported on the clash between loggers and the owl's defenders on Washington State's Olympic Peninsula, I had never seen one of these beautiful nocturnal birds, but didn't have to go deep into the forest to find an owl, as I did my first night in the area. They have white-speckled brown plumage, big brown eyes, and a wingspan of up to four feet. They were controversial only because they live in old-growth forests that are prime sources of timber.

In the visually stunning Olympic Peninsula, out-of-work loggers lived on personal islands of despair. A story I filed from Forks, Washington, in July began with the account of a thirty-one-year-old logger's suicide and told of rising rates of domestic violence, alcoholism, juvenile crime, and mental health breakdowns. One bird-loving reader complained I'd made the loggers more sympathetic than the owls. Perhaps, but for owls and loggers alike, the story has not taken a happy turn. The northern spotted owl was declared an endangered species in 1990, and significant acreage set aside for its protection.

Years later, the first Trump administration decreased this acreage. The Biden administration restored it, but Mother Nature is indifferent to politics. A 2021 study found that the number of northern spotted owls has declined despite the federal effort to save the species.

The California gnatcatcher, by contrast, is a tiny gray bird with a unique catlike call. It flits through coastal sage scrub and desert scrub from Southern California to southern Baja California. In 1991, this songbird became the focus of a battle to save thousands of acres of coastal sage scrubland, much of it marked for housing development. My first story about this conflict quoted an environmental attorney who called the gnatcatcher "the canary in the coal mine" because the fate of fifty other species or plants was entwined with preservation of coastal sage scrub.

The battle over the California gnatcatcher is emblematic of scores of struggles throughout the West between conservation groups and developers. It is not a contest between good and evil. People need homes, and they're not being built nearly fast enough in California and other western states. Homebuilders cite environmental restrictions and lumber costs to explain why demand for housing outpaces supply. But population pressure is the underlying cause. Some eighty million people now live in the West, about half of them in California, according to the Census Bureau. These numbers are growing every day.

The Washington Post prides itself on its political coverage, and I focused on local elections with broader significance. Prime among these was a 1991 Los Angeles County supervisor's race. The Voting Rights Act of 1965 is mostly known for its profound impact on southern states that discriminated against Blacks. But a federal court found in 1990 in a lawsuit brought by the Mexican American Legal Defense Fund and supported by the Justice Department, that Los Angeles County supervisors had deliberately drawn boundaries to dilute Hispanic voting strength. As a result, there were no Hispanics (and no women) on the powerful governing board of the nation's most populous county. The board had an annual budget of $10 billion, greater than most states. The court drew a new district favoring Hispanics.

Gloria Molina, then forty-two, was the first Hispanic woman in the state legislature and the first Hispanic member of the Los Angeles City Council. On February 19, 1991, she became the first Hispanic Los Angeles County supervisor. Molina waged a spirited door-to-door campaign and had the support of the *Los Angeles Times*. She served twenty-three years on the board, earning a reputation as a fiscal watchdog and an advocate for the county's public health-care system, and was succeeded by a Hispanic woman (Hilda Solis), whom she endorsed.

Deedee Corradini, a dynamic businesswoman, was also a trailblazer. She was seeking to become the first female mayor of Salt Lake City. Being a Democrat was no obstacle, as Salt Lake City is a Democratic pond in the Republican lake of Utah. Nor did it matter that she was not Mormon; the outgoing mayor was Catholic. What mattered was that Utah, including Salt Lake, was one of the most male-dominated societies in the nation. Corradini often began her speeches by telling of an incident when she was walking precincts and a woman greeted her at the door enthusiastically, saying it was time for a woman but that she'd have to check with her husband. The woman returned moments later, shook her head and said, "I'm sorry, but we're not voting for Corradini this year."

Mary Kay Lazarus, another Salt Lake businesswoman, introduced me to Corradini and discussed the cultural impact of economic change in Utah. Although Mormon teaching emphasized a woman's role as homemaker, an increasing number of Mormon women had entered the workforce. In these two-earner households, life revolved less around the church. Lazarus, who is Jewish, admired the Mormons. Driven out of American society by violence in the nineteenth century, they had made Salt Lake "a privileged place in which to live," she said.

Corradini, whose father had been a theologian and college president in Lebanon and Syria, had lived abroad until she was fifteen and spoke fluent French and Arabic. I was impressed by her self-confidence and direct way of speaking. Most politicians are on guard in the presence of an unknown reporter, but she seemed entirely at ease with me and discoursed on the record about a variety of subjects. "She'd made it easy to vote for a woman," Lazarus said.

As mayor, Corradini brought light rail to Salt Lake City and helped the city secure the 2002 Winter Olympic Games. In a vintage Corradini moment captured on television, she received the Olympic flag as mayor of the next host city during the closing ceremony of the 1998 Winter Games in Nagano, Japan. Decked out in a red snowsuit on a frigid February night, she beamed with pride as she waved the Olympic flag back and forth. Corradini served as mayor until 2000 and changed the political culture of Salt Lake City. Two of her four successors have been women. Appreciated and mourned, Corradini died of lung cancer in 2015. She was seventy years old and had never smoked.

In San Francisco, the third city I focused on in 1991, Mayor Art Agnos was favored to win reelection. Agnos was heir to a liberal tradition that had peaked in 1975 when state senator George Moscone became mayor in a narrow runoff against a conservative candidate. On November 27, 1978, Moscone and Harvey Milk, the nation's first openly gay county supervisor, were gunned down in their offices by Dan White, a disgruntled former supervisor. To general dismay in the city, White was convicted of manslaughter instead of murder. He served five years in prison and after his release committed suicide. I knew and liked Moscone from his legislative days and had closely followed this shocking story. We'd talked a few days before his murder, and it was still hard for me to accept that he was gone.

The killings of Milk and Moscone cast a malevolent shadow over the 1991 campaign. Gays were a political force in San Francisco, but homophobia still roiled the city's politics. Agnos rallies were disrupted by angry white men shouting "straight, straight," and mouthing crude slurs. The mayor's opponent in a runoff election was Frank Jordan, a former San Francisco police chief who'd spent thirty-three years as a cop without firing his service revolver in anger. He was no bigot and spoke out against what he called "the politics of hate and fear." As chief, Jordan had recruited gays and lesbians as officers, kept officers stricken with AIDS on the force as long as they could work, and instituted sensitivity training.

"I want this city to work for gays and lesbians, for everyone," Jordan told me. He blamed Agnos for littered streets and increasing homelessness, potent issues in a city that valued its image.

Like the elections I'd covered in Los Angeles County and Salt Lake City, the San Francisco mayoralty is nonpartisan. Both candidates were Democrats, but the centrist Jordan was the preference of conservative whites regardless of party. Agnos counted on like-minded liberals and the gay community, then estimated to be one-fifth of the electorate. The mayor led ten-to-one among gays in a *San Francisco Chronicle* poll that otherwise put him narrowly ahead overall. Jordan's campaign manager, Jack Davis, who is gay, told me that Jordan would do better among gays than the poll showed. "It's not socially acceptable among most gays to say you're voting for a cop," Davis said.

Every politician I knew in San Francisco expected Agnos to win, but Jordan told me he would surprise the pundits. I took a day to walk around the city, focusing on downtown, North Beach, and the Mission District. Homeless people were ubiquitous, and streets were strewn with litter. I wrote cautiously that the race was too close to call. The voters were bolder. On December 10, they chose Jordan as mayor by a 4 percent margin. Davis had been right. Agnos carried the gay community but did not approach the ten-to-one margin foreseen in the *Chronicle* poll.

I wrote numerous stories about Governor Wilson in 1991, his first year in office. He made an auspicious start, promising in his inaugural address to introduce an era of "preventive government" that would provide prenatal care for every mother in California and improve programs to address drug use, learning disorders, school dropouts, and gang violence. These lofty aims were undone by California's worst fiscal crisis since the Great Depression. Instead of expanding social programs, Wilson was hard-pressed to accomplish the legally required task of balancing the budget, which he tried to do through a mix of budget reductions, which bothered Democrats, and tax increases, which infuriated Republicans. Democratic Assembly speaker Willie Brown, agreed to the budget cuts, some in programs Wilson had promised to expand. Brown was known for flamboyant behavior and fancy cars, but he was a savvy and responsible legislative leader. He persuaded Democrats to reduce welfare grants and eliminate cost-of-living increases for five years, undoing gains approved by Governor Ronald Reagan a quarter-century earlier. Funds for state university systems were slashed and fees increased as much as 40 percent at some schools. Brown's price for going along with these drastic actions was requiring Wilson to make up the rest of the state's projected deficit by raising state income taxes, particularly on the wealthy.

Conservative Republicans didn't like this compromise. When Wilson asked Republicans in the Assembly to support tax increases, the head of the GOP caucus, an evangelical Christian, told the governor he'd pray about them. Wilson replied that prayers weren't enough; he needed conservative votes. California then required a two-thirds vote to pass the budget, which was stalemated for months while the Republican minority in both chambers of the legislature balked at tax increases and demanded more budget cuts. Eventually, Brown agreed to a minor change in the state's unemployment compensation program, enabling Wilson to round up the necessary votes from a dwindling number of Republican centrists.

Wilson was elected as a moderate Republican who was fiscally conservative but prochoice and protective of the environment. This proved a winning formula for most of his political career. Wilson won an Assembly seat in 1966 and in 1971 was elected mayor of San Diego. He ran for the U.S. Senate in 1982, winning the Republican primary by running to the right of Pete McCloskey and to the left of Barry Goldwater Jr. and Robert Dornan. Wilson faced Governor Jerry Brown in the general election, a race *The Post* detached me from the White House beat to cover. Wilson had an early lead but fell behind in September when it was revealed he'd paid no federal income tax in 1980. Wilson said it was the first he'd heard of it and blamed the tax filing on an accountant.

Down but not out, Wilson persevered. "After a long summer of discontent and a campaign more flawed than a pot-holed road, Wilson has pulled even with and taken the lead while Brown's heavy negatives have reasserted themselves," I wrote. In the end, Wilson won handily. He was reelected in 1988 and defeated Democrat Dianne Feinstein in the 1990 gubernatorial election. Wilson had an executive temperament and found the governorship a better fit than the Senate.

"I really like this job," Governor Wilson told me, saying he enjoyed "the managerial challenge of making something work."

Had he left office in 1994, Wilson would have been remembered as one of California's most constructive politicians. Instead, he tarnished his reputation that year by supporting Proposition 187, an initiative premised on the belief that California's social services were a magnet that had drawn two million unauthorized immigrants across the border from Mexico. Most economists disagreed, saying the immigrants sought jobs, not social services, and were fleeing a country that could not provide them.

The United States has long had a see-saw relationship with immigrants from south of the border, welcoming them during labor shortages, such as in World War II, and turning on them when there was a surplus of labor and immigrants were perceived a threat to American workers. Proposition 187 was the remnant of a failed Republican legislative attempt to deny legal services to unauthorized immigrants. With California mired in economic recession, it was easy for its supporters to gather enough signatures to put the measure on the ballot. Prop 187 would have established a state-run screening system that prohibited immigrants who could not show proof of citizenship from using nonemergency health care, public education, and other services. The initiative was opposed by Kathleen Brown, the Democratic nominee for governor and many newspapers, but voters approved it by 59 to 41 percent.

Prior to Proposition 187, Wilson had sought unsuccessfully for two years to get the Clinton administration to help pay the costs of the immigration influx. Overall, the U.S. government profited from illegal immigration because many migrants pay Social Security taxes without ever receiving benefits. Yet the costs of immigration in health care, law enforcement, and education are disproportionally borne by places such as San Diego where Wilson had been mayor.

So Wilson endorsed Proposition 187 out of frustration after already making immigration a campaign issue. Two months before Proposition 187 qualified for the ballot, his campaign unveiled a commercial that began with a grainy black-and-white video. "They keep coming," an announcer intoned as a dozen Latino immigrants dodged cars and scrambled across the U.S.-Mexican border at San Ysidro. "Two-million illegal immigrants in California. The federal government won't stop them at the border, yet requires us to pay billions to take care of them." The ad went on to make a pitch for Wilson's reelection. It was a scary—and effective—political commercial. Focus groups showed that prospective voters remembered this ad more than any other commercial of the campaign.

Fortunately for California, Proposition 187 was struck down in 1997 by a federal court. I say "fortunately" because health-care professionals made a convincing case that denying health care and vaccinations to large numbers of immigrants would expose all Californians to contagious disease. Nor would it have been in the public interest to have immigrant schoolchildren yanked from classrooms, as sponsors of Proposition 187 said would happen.

Prop 187 haunted Wilson in retirement. He was particularly stung by accusations of racism. Wilson is no racist, and I say that from the perspective of a journalist who is sensitive to racism and has known Wilson throughout his long political career. It's also often said that Wilson's stark anti-immigrant campaign was unnecessary because he defeated Kathleen Brown handedly. Wilson won by 15 percentage points, beating Brown by more than 1.2 million votes. Brown, the daughter of one governor (Pat) and the brother of another (Jerry) carried only seven of California's fifty-eight counties. But when the controversial ad was conceived, Wilson was not ahead. He trailed in early polling, probably because of California's faltering economy. No one foresaw that Brown would conduct such an unfocused campaign or run out of money.

Yet clearing Wilson of a racist motivation does not validate the poor judgment he showed in tying his reelection campaign to Proposition 187. Wilson is a lawyer who knew that immigration is a federal responsibility. That was the heart of the case Wilson had made in trying to get Washington to step up to the plate and help California financially. As Wilson should have anticipated, the courts made short work of the controversial ballot measure. "Proposition 187, as drafted, is not constitutional on its face," Judge Mariana R. Pfaelzer declared in her thirty-two-page opinion striking down the law. Proposition 187 was meant to make a statement, and it did, but there was no way it could have provided the economic relief Wilson had sought from the federal government because it flunked a basic constitutional test. Any lawyer, let alone the governor of California, should have known as much.

Since the passage of Proposition 187, the state that twice elected Reagan governor has become a Democratic bastion in state and federal elections. The only Republican to win the governorship since Wilson was Arnold Schwarzenegger, a celebrity. No Republican now holds statewide office. While this trend is often laid at Wilson's feet, it actually reflects the inexorable impact of demographics. California's electorate has become younger, more Hispanic, and more Asian with each election. Democrats hold an edge in these groupings—and would if Proposition 187 had never existed. At most, Wilson hastened a trend that was already underway.

In the western bureau, I was a general assignment reporter, defined in my book *Reporting: An Inside View* as someone who knows something about everything and nothing about anything. Here are examples of three general assignment stories I covered in 1991.

Jesse Jonathan Turner, known to his friends as Jon, was a mathematics teacher at Beirut University College who had been kidnapped on January 24, 1987, by Shiite militants and held hostage for four-and-a-half years. On Friday afternoon October 25, 1991, I was driving home to Summerland from Los Angeles after an exhausting week in which I'd covered the Oakland firestorm. I was a few miles from home when the car phone rang. On the line was Jim Rowe, an able editor at *The Washington Post* who had the added virtue of knowing the date major league pitchers and catchers report for spring training. Rowe said Turner had been released in Syria and was being flown to his hometown of Boise, Idaho. Karen DeYoung wanted me to fly to Boise and interview him. Knowing I'd had a difficult week, Rowe had tried to talk her out of it, but Karen had persisted. Find out if Lou can get to Boise, she'd said. I understood where Karen was coming from. She'd been a foreign correspondent, accustomed to flying from one country to another on short notice. Santa Barbara is nine hundred miles from Boise, about the distance from London to Rome. These days regional air travel in the West is much diminished, but at the time one could fly from Santa Barbara to many cities in the West. I stopped at home, threw some clothes in an overnight bag, and drove to the airport.

Turner had been flown to a military hospital in Wiesbaden, Germany, where doctors pronounced him fit but out of shape for lack of exercise. I arrived at the Boise airport minutes before Turner's plane touched down, giving me time to secure my rental car and follow his motorcade to the Idaho statehouse, where a sizeable welcoming crowd had gathered in wind and rain. The only parking space I saw was labeled "police," and I parked in it, taking my overnight bag with me in case the car was towed. I found a spot on a corner of the statehouse out of the rain and waited for Turner while the crowd sang patriotic songs. A small stage had been set up for Turner and various dignitaries. He arrived in a limousine and was greeted by Governor Cecil Andrus and Mayor Dirk Kempthorne.

"It's a beautiful day for Idaho when we have you safely here at home," Andrus said, adding that he would proclaim October 27 to be honored annually as "Jesse Turner Day." Turner responded briefly.

"It's cold," he told the crowd. "So, all I want to say is thank you. Thanks for everything."

I retreated to my car, accompanied by a reporter from another newspaper who was staying at the same hotel as me. I told him I'd give him a ride if the car was still there, but he did me a bigger favor. The reporter had a cell phone, which I did not, and said he had no chance of getting a story in his paper at that hour. He loaned me his phone, and I called the national desk. Jo Rector, my favorite night editor, answered. I asked if she wanted a story for the late edition. Nobody was there to take it except Rector.

"You dictate, I'll be rewrite," she said gamely. The story ran the next morning under the headline: "Ex-Hostage Turner Returns to Hometown Welcome."

The next day I awoke early, called the desk, and reached Karen, working on a Saturday. She complimented me for getting a story in the paper late at night and asked if I could follow up by interviewing Turner. I told her I would. Boise was by now overrun with reporters who wanted to see Turner, and he had agreed to make a statement early in the afternoon. So I made some calls and obtained the address of Turner's mother and stepfather, Estelle and Eugene Ronneburg. Turner's own home was only a hundred yards away, but I guessed I'd find him at the Ronneburgs'. My hunch proved right. Turner was there along with his Lebanese-born wife Badr and their four-year-old daughter Joanna.

The Ronneburgs allowed me inside their home and were exceptionally polite. His mother introduced me to Turner, who was friendly but pale. He said he'd be happy to talk about himself and his family but didn't want to discuss what I later learned was a harsh captivity because he didn't want to make it harder for others still held hostage. Three other faculty members had been kidnapped from the university at the same time as Turner by militants posing as police and were still being held.

Turner told me about meeting Badr at a biology laboratory at Beirut University. They were married two years later, and she had been pregnant with their daughter when he was kidnapped. Joanna was born five months into Turner's captivity, and he had not seen her until he was released. Turner otherwise had little to say. He said he was still processing what had happened to him. I thanked him and turned to leave, but Turner asked me to walk out of the house with him and his mother. Reporters were waiting in the street, and one of them asked if I was grandstanding by coming out with him. I shrugged. I slipped away, wrote and filed my story, and made the flight to Santa Barbara. Here is the lede, filed under a Boise dateline: "Walking hand in hand with his mother down the street where he lived as a child, former hostage Jesse Turner today tasted the joys of freedom in his quiet hometown."

Turner, who had degrees in formal language theory and philosophy, continued to teach. In May 2019, thirty-two years after he was kidnapped, the Turners returned to the Beirut campus of what was now Lebanon American University. They visited the lab where they had met and the classroom where he had taught. "I miss the place," Turner said, according to an account in the university newspaper that described him as "visibly emotional."

The second story was a surprise. On a warm November day in Los Angeles I was in *The Post* office in Century City when Elsen called and told me Magic Johnson had tested positive for HIV and would be retiring from the Los Angeles Lakers. Elsen said the national editor had talked to the sports editor, and they'd decided I should cover Johnson's upcoming news conference at the Great Western Forum and write the story. I was stunned. Magic was my favorite basketball player on my favorite team, and I couldn't believe what I was hearing. Here is my lede, filed under an Inglewood dateline: "Earvin 'Magic' Johnson, who transformed the game of professional basketball and won the hearts of millions of Americans with his dazzling passing skills and his smile, announced today that he is retiring from the Los Angeles Lakers because he has contracted the human immunodeficiency syndrome virus (HIV), which causes AIDS."

Johnson was as much in control of the press conference that day as he ever was of a basketball game, dramatically turning a sad event into an upbeat performance in which he cast himself as the good guy. He told reporters he would become a national spokesman about HIV because he wanted young people to understand that "safe sex is the way to go. I think we sometimes think only gay people can get it: it's not going to happen to me. And here I am saying that it could happen to anybody, even me, Magic Johnson."

He didn't say how his wife was taking the news. We learned the next day from Bob Steiner, a Lakers official, that Cookie Johnson was seven months pregnant and did not have HIV. Steiner confirmed that Magic had contracted the disease while having sex but as our story gingerly put it, "could not pinpoint either a specific event or specific partner responsible for transmission of the virus."

That second-day story was headlined "Johnson's HIV Caused by Sex." It had a double byline of "Lou Cannon and Anthony Cotton" and listed Leef Smith as a contributor at the end of the story. If we were following present *Post* practices of multiple bylines, she would have been included at the top.

The story seems to have been written on the premise that readers knew virtually nothing about HIV and included this sentence: "While the AIDS virus can be transmitted heterosexually—and thousands of AIDS cases in the United States have resulted from heterosexual contact—the risk of it happening is far lower than in homosexual contact, largely because the fraction of heterosexuals now infected is very much smaller than that of homosexuals." I don't remember writing this jawbreaker of a sentence. What I do remember about the story is that Cotton, who had good league sources, learned that an NBA official had expressed concern to Johnson about holding a press conference, fearing he would be asked intrusive questions. Johnson knew better. He understood that the supposed tigers of the press were quite timid when questioning someone they adored. Their love for Magic was never in doubt. Our story noted that local sports announcers were near tears as they reported the story. Local politicians were equally worshipful. Los Angeles city councilman Joel Wachs praised "Magic's honesty and courage," and the steps at city hall were renamed in Johnson's honor.

Safe sex received a boost from the Magic Johnson story. Condom sales soared, and a leader of the Minority AIDS Project said Johnson had "made a big difference by proving that HIV is not discriminatory."

Wayne Gretzky, the hockey star, told the Associated Press that fans put stars on a pedestal. "But we bleed, sweat, cry and have ups and downs just like everyone else," he said.

Even Vice President Dan Quayle, in Los Angeles for political appearances, got into the act. He said the Federal Drug Administration would soon announce procedures to speed the approval of new drugs, some dealing with AIDS. Quayle, playing to type, called Johnson a "true champion" but said he would stress abstinence rather than safe sex.

The world had not seen the last of Magic Johnson, on or off the basketball court. He played in the 1992 NBA all-star game and was voted most valuable player. He briefly coached the Lakers in 1994 and played for them in 1996. He was outstanding as a member of the U.S. "Dream Team" that won a gold medal at the 1992 Olympics in Barcelona without breaking a sweat. Johnson said that playing in the Olympics taught him he could live with HIV—and he has lived well. Thirty-one years after his fateful disclosure, Johnson is one of the nation's most successful Black businessmen. He is a motivational speaker, a valued interviewee, and holds a 5 percent ownership stake in the Los Angeles Dodgers and 4 percent of the Washington Commanders football team.

Shortly before the news about Magic, I covered the Oakland firestorm, officially called the Tunnel Fire because of its proximity to the Caldecott Tunnel that runs beneath the Berkeley hills. This fearsome blaze killed 25 people and injured 150 others while destroying 3,469 homes and apartments and two thousand automobiles. Oakland, which had not fully recovered from the Loma Prieta earthquake of 1989, was economically devastated.

October is a dangerous month in California, which receives most of its rain in winter and dries out during the summer months. By autumn, the brush is tinder dry, needing only a spark to become an inferno. Danger is compounded by October winds, called Santa Anas in Southern California and Diablo winds in the San Francisco East Bay. Originating in the desert, these winds sweep offshore from north and east, wiping out the marine layer that is coastal California's saving grace. The Oakland firestorm in the scenic Oakland and Berkeley hills was an avoidable catastrophe.

On Saturday, October 19, Oakland firefighters responded to a five-acre brush fire in steep terrain at 7151 Buckingham Boulevard in Oakland near the Berkeley border. They battled the blaze on a scorching afternoon and left at twilight, believing the fire was under control. But heat from the fire had caused pine needles to fall from the trees. The needles, buried under a crust of ash, smoldered during the night, and the hillside burst into flames late Sunday morning. Driven by gusting winds, the fire swirled south and then west, sweeping down into the Berkeley hills and an upscale development called Hiller Highlands. Within minutes, hillside homes in Oakland and Berkeley were engulfed by flames.

I was home that Sunday, planning to watch a football game on CBS between the San Francisco 49ers and the Detroit Lions when I received a phone call from an occasional stringer who told me a fire was raging in the Oakland hills. I asked him if he was available in case we needed him, and he said he was. Fires were burning all over the West that weekend, including one in Los Padres National Forest, not far from Santa Barbara. But I knew that a fire in the Oakland-Berkeley hills, where the brush hadn't burned in years, was especially perilous. My coverage options were limited. There were no flights to Oakland from Santa Barbara, and I was too late for the Sunday afternoon flight to San Francisco. It was a seven-hour drive. I called the national desk and discussed the situation with the duty editor. He said he'd use the stringer for the Monday story, and I could pick up the coverage the next day. I booked a morning flight to Oakland out of Burbank and watched the football game, during which the sportscasters gave periodic updates on the fire, visible in panoramic camera shots across the bay. At one point ash from the fire drifted onto Candlestick Park.

Firefighters battled the blaze throughout Sunday in treacherous winds, helped by reinforcements from other departments and an air tanker flown by the state forestry department. At the height of the fire, fifteen hundred firefighters and 450 engines were involved. The winds ebbed after dark, enabling firefighters to make a stand, and lower temperatures and fog helped Monday. By the time I arrived in Oakland midmorning Monday, firefighters had established a perimeter around two and a half square miles of the charred rubble of hundreds of homes dotted here and there with intact houses the firestorm had mysteriously spared. What emerged in interviews with firefighters, local and state officials, and survivors of the fire was a stark portrait of nature's power.

A firefighter and a survivor described explosions from eucalyptus trees that had hurled fireballs far and wide. Oakland fire chief Phillip Ewell told me that winds whipped flames through the crowns of the highly flammable trees, spreading the fire from one tree to the next. The fire moved so rapidly it created its own wind system, which is the definition of a firestorm.

"It was like a visit to hell at Ground Zero," wrote Robert Maynard, the publisher of the *Oakland Tribune*, whom I quoted in my story.[1] He and his family fled their expensive Oakland home and were among the fortunate few whose homes were saved by firefighters.

But the firefighters took a beating in early news accounts, which said they had retreated during the firestorm. My Monday story observed that one firefighter, Oakland battalion chief James Riley, had died during such a retreat with his death attributed at the time to a heart attack. On Tuesday it was revealed that Riley had stopped to help a woman who was trapped by a downed power line. Both he and the woman were electrocuted. It's a wonder there weren't more such deaths.

As I wrote Tuesday, officials were trying to control access to the burned-out homes, even by residents, because "downed electrical wires [hung] like Spanish moss over the streets." These downed lines had critically affected the response of the firefighters, who had been forced to retreat because of reduced water pressure in their firehoses. I quoted Chris Hampel, a firefighter from nearby Dublin, who said: "We had to let houses burn. There was nothing we could do. If we had the water, we could have saved every house." This overstated a valid observation. A federal report would determine that eight hundred homes had burned to the ground in the first hour after the flames reignited on Sunday morning, often before firefighters arrived on the scene. But many homes lost later on Sunday might have been saved except for insufficient water pressure.

Most of the deaths occurred as people tried to flee the firestorm in dense smoke on narrow streets. Many died in their cars. Others were killed when they abandoned their vehicles and tried to outrun a fire mov-

1. Maynard, a longtime friend, wrote a vivid first-person account of the firestorm. He'd been an ombudsman at *The Washington Post* and was the first Black owner of a major U.S. daily newspaper. I'd had the privilege of teaching at the nonprofit Institute for Journalism Education that he and his wife, Doris Hicks Maynard, cofounded. Over a thirty-year period, it trained more than a thousand journalists and editors from multicultural backgrounds across the United States.

ing faster than they could sprint. Oakland police officer John Grubensky rushed into one of the fire's worse hot spots on Charring Cross Road in Hiller Highlands, attempting to rescue trapped residents. His body was found in a tunnel with another charred body on his back.

After phoning in my story, I returned to my hotel and sought out survivors among the hotel guests. On Monday, briefers at the fire command post had accounted for twenty-four deaths and listed another twenty people as missing. All but one of the missing was found alive, many of them in the hotel where I was interviewing. Having no easy way to reach loved ones in these pre–cell phone days, survivors waited until relatives reached out to them.

One survivor was a bright-eyed, wizened man who sought me out after learning I worked for *The Washington Post.* He was an eighty-nine-year-old retired attorney named Joseph Edelman who extracted from a briefcase copies of his correspondence with Oakland city officials about a three-acre patch of overgrown chaparral near his home in the Montclair community. Edelman's letters had described the patch as the "Bermuda triangle" and repeatedly urged the city to remove it. Oakland never did, and this patch of shrub had provided the fuel to burn down seventy-five homes, including Edelman's. I quoted him in my story. The next day, via a message from the national desk, I heard from Alison Kutchins in Washington, DC, who said Edelman was her great-uncle and that she had been trying to reach him. The message said Edelman had no children but that Kutchins and her family had found a place for him to stay. Kutchins did not know until she read my story that Edelman had survived the fire. Edelman had not realized he had been listed among the missing.

On Wednesday, I wrote about the lessons of the firestorm. For firefighters, the lesson was clear. "The first thing you're taught is that you don't leave until a fire is thoroughly put out," said James Royce, a former firefighter with the National Park Service at Yosemite National Park. But there was also an important lesson for the rest of us who live in fire-prone communities. The Bermuda Triangle that Edelman had described was replicated throughout the Oakland-Berkeley hills—and many other cities throughout California. I discussed this with Richard Wilson, the California director of forestry, whom I knew from the days when he'd led a fight to prevent the Army Corp of Engineers from building a high dam that would have flooded scenic Round Valley, where he lived. Wilson, a rancher who kept his own home clear of brush, was appalled that Oakland had allowed so much dried vegetation to accumulate.

"Prevention is the key," Wilson said. "We have greater technological ability to fight these fires, but in a contest with nature, nature usually wins. Without prevention, disasters are waiting to happen."

I also talked to Karen Terrell, the well-regarded public information officer for the Department of Forestry, whose factual report contained a lyrical kicker. "Sixty-one percent of California is covered with wildlands," Terrell said. "Fire is just part of California's ecologic makeup. California was built to burn."

These were prescient words. In the three decades between the Oakland firestorm and 2021, California fires became larger and more frequent. The Marble Cone fire in Monterey was the second-worst fire in California history when I covered it in 1977. It is now nineteenth on that list. An analysis by reporters from the Bay Area News Group found that, since 2012, a total of 12.7 million acres have burned in California, which is double the 6.4 million acres that burned in the state in the previous decade. Put another way, one of every eight acres in California has burned since 2012—and that was before five fires devastated Los Angeles County in the first days of 2025.

At the time it happened, the Oakland firestorm ranked as the second deadliest in California history, with twenty-five deaths. The Griffith Park fire of 1933 with twenty-nine deaths topped the list. Both these fires have since been eclipsed by the Camp Fire of 2018, which took eighty lives and destroyed the town of Paradise.

Wildland fires in California are recurrent events that happen at any time of year. Santa Barbara County, where I live, experienced fifteen major fires in just over a decade. The largest of them, the Thomas fire, claimed a thousand homes in Ventura and Santa Barbara counties while burning for forty days in December 2017 and January 2018. The fire's official death toll was only two, but it set in motion a far deadlier catastrophe. In the early morning hours of January 9, 2018, the denuded Santa Barbara hills unleashed rivers of boulders, mud, and debris on the sleeping upscale community of Montecito, home to eighty-six hundred people. Twenty-three people lost their lives, most of them in their own homes. The toll would have been greater had not a savvy fisherman named Marco Farrell warned people in his Montecito neighborhood of the danger of the denuded hillsides.

That morning, Farrell saved his parents' lives and his own after hearing the roar of a river of mud with the consistency of pancake batter barreling down their street.

"Flash flood!" Marco yelled, as he woke his parents and opened the back door of the house to relieve pressure from the mud oozing into the living room and kitchen. The Farrells are personal friends. His father, Jeff, was an Olympic swimming champion. His mother Gabrielle is an artist and exceptional cook. Marco, brave and resilient, sheltered in place for ninety minutes with his parents until the three of them were rescued.[2]

We live next to Montecito in Summerland, which has no mountain behind it on which to gather debris. Nevertheless, our little town was menaced by the Thomas fire, which forced our evacuation for two days. We were spared the trauma of Montecito, but a local fireman later told me that the margin of victory was slight. He said the fire had come within a quarter mile of Summerland and that the entire town might have been lost except for a change in the wind.

A visitor from the East took in the panoramic view of the Pacific Ocean from our deck and proclaimed we live in paradise. I did not dispute him, but it's paradise with an edge. We've enjoyed sunny rainless days while the rest of the country was being pounded with storms. Our enjoyment was tempered by the realization that the lack of rain in 2024 was a harbinger of danger ahead. In California, there is always a next fire.

2. The Farrells' daughter Caroline was safe in Santa Barbara, where she lived with her husband and daughter.

27

WAR AND PEACE

Between Magic Johnson's revelation and the San Francisco mayoralty runoff, I traveled to Hawaii to cover the observance of the fiftieth anniversary of the bombing of Pearl Harbor. I looked forward to Hawaii trips because Mary usually was with me, and we always visited our mutual friends, accomplished journalists John Griffin and Susan Yim Griffin. But I also worked in Hawaii, on this trip filing four long stories in less than six days.

President George H. W. Bush, the last U.S. president to have served in World War II, represented our country at the main event of the Pearl Harbor ceremonies, which took place on December 7, 1991, at the National Memorial Cemetery of the Pacific in the Punchbowl Crater. He was an appropriate choice: Bush enlisted in the Navy the day after his eighteenth birthday and compiled a notable war record as the youngest U.S. aviator in the Pacific. Bush flew fifty-eight missions off the aircraft carrier USS *San Jacinto* in the Avenger, a torpedo bomber with a three-man crew.

On September 2, 1944, Bush's plane was struck by antiaircraft fire as he bombed Japanese targets on the island of Chichi Jima. Bush completed the bombing run with the engine on fire, then maneuvered over the ocean and bailed out. Bleeding profusely from a head wound and vomiting, he spent four hours in an inflatable raft before being rescued by a U.S. submarine.[1] Bush was awarded the Distinguished Flying Cross

1. A Japanese boat based on Chichi Jima tried to capture Bush in the water but was driven off by a U.S. plane. This saved Bush from certain death: Eight other pilots who bailed out over Chichi Jima were captured by the Japanese. All were tortured

for his bravery in completing the bombing run. The other members of his crew perished, one while still inside the plane from antiaircraft fire, the other when his parachute failed to open. Years later, Bush said he was "haunted" by the deaths of his crew. "Why had I been spared and what did God have in store for me?" he said to the writer James Bradley.

Other veterans who gathered in Hawaii that week expressed an enduring sense of loss. Retired Navy lieutenant commander Franklin Van Valkenburgh, son and namesake of the commanding officer who went down with the USS *Arizona,* described receiving his father's Naval Academy class ring after a cleanup crew recovered it from the bridge of the doomed ship.

"Today, I wear it with pride," he said. "I lost the finest shipmate any could have had on that day of infamy, and it left a void in the life of a twenty-two-year-old kid."

The day before the Punchbowl ceremony, the Pearl Harbor veterans marched through Waikiki, where Mary and I were staying at a tiny hotel away from the beach, the only lodging available that week. We walked out in the rain to see the march.

USS *Nevada* survivors formed one of the largest contingents in the parade, marching behind a banner that proclaimed: "USS Nevada—The ship that wouldn't die." At a previous ceremony, retired captain Donald K. Ross had described "on the day hell was in session" maneuvering the *Nevada* away from its berth alongside the *Arizona* and grounding it on a coral reef so that it would not be sunk in the channel. Ross performed this feat of seamanship despite wounds from a Japanese bomb. He was awarded the Medal of Honor. The repaired *Nevada* survived to fight another day and saw action halfway across the world on D-Day. Growing up in Nevada, I'd first heard the thrilling story of the ship's narrow escape when it was recounted by a naval officer at a school assembly in Fallon when I was nine or ten.

Several ceremonies during that week of remembrance emphasized the role of women, particularly Navy nurses, during the war. Lenore Rickert was on duty in a hospital that received seven hundred burned and injured survivors of the Pearl Harbor attack. Sick men gave up their

---

and killed, and four were cannibalized. Four Japanese officers were tried for war crimes after the war and hanged.

beds to the wounded, she said. Hookers from Hotel Street, then Honolulu's red-light district, flocked to the hospital to help.

"It was a good time as well as a bad time," Rickert said. "It was a terrible experience. It was a wonderful experience."

I ended my story of the Waikiki march with the words of Captain Jim Miller, then the highest-ranking survivor of the *Arizona,* about the singular contribution of Pearl Harbor to the war effort: "Our country was unified as never before."

The Pearl Harbor ceremonies roused feelings of patriotism along with compassion for those who had perished in the attack. I'd made three previous tours of the USS Arizona Memorial, a white concrete structure perched gracefully above the sunken ship and many of its entombed crew, and never emerged dry-eyed. That week, on my fourth visit to the memorial, it occurred to me that the anniversary provided an opportunity to correct some of the many myths surrounding the Pearl Harbor attack. My editors liked the idea, and I discussed it with my friend John Griffin, the astute editorial page editor of the *Honolulu Advertiser.* He pointed me to James Harpster, a historian and National Park Service official who was coordinating the week's ceremonies and had devised a myth-busting booklet that was distributed at the USS Arizona Memorial visitor's center. Under the headline "Debunking Myths About the Attack," my story ran in *The Washington Post* the same day as the story about the Waikiki march.

These were the first five paragraphs:

> Honolulu, Dec. 6—Many myths about the Japanese attack on Pearl Harbor persist in the public mind a half century after the event, according to war historians and other scholars.
>
> Most enduring of these myths is the belief that the 68 civilians who were killed on Dec. 7, 1941, were the victims of Japanese bombs. In fact, as a then-secret Pearl Harbor board of inquiry determined in 1943, at least 59 of the civilians were killed by jittery U.S. naval gun crews who fired artillery and antiaircraft weapons long after Japanese planes had returned to their aircraft carriers.
>
> In the most catastrophic example of such "friendly fire," Kikuyo Hirisaki Horikawa was severely wounded when an antiaircraft shell exploded inside her mother's noodle shop an hour after the second

> wave of Japanese bombers had completed their bombing runs. The blast killed her husband, her three young children, a nephew and seven young men from a Japanese Christian Church dormitory.
>
> When Horikawa awoke at the hospital after a five-inch piece of shrapnel had been removed from her chest, she was told by her mother what had happened. "Don't cry or we cannot take you from the hospital," her mother said.
>
> Horikawa, now 84, did not cry. But when she told her story 50 years later to the *Honolulu Advertiser*, she said, "To this day when I see news accounts of a mother whose children have died, I think of my family right away."

Among the debunked myths was a report that Japanese sympathizers cut giant arrows in sugarcane fields to guide attacking planes. My account concluded with a true story that gave birth to a myth in the mind of Ronald Reagan. Dorie Miller, a Black mess attendant on the USS *West Virginia*, had grabbed an abandoned machine gun during the Pearl Harbor attack and fired at Japanese dive bombers. He became the first African American awarded the Navy Cross for heroism. A film version of Miller's actions made a strong but misleading impression on Reagan, who was in Culver City, California, narrating training films for what was then the Army Air Corps. Recounting the story at the beginning of his 1980 presidential campaign, Reagan said racial segregation in the U.S. armed forces had ended at Pearl Harbor.

"In fact, U.S. forces were segregated throughout World War II and desegregated by an executive order issued by President Harry S. Truman after the war," my story concluded.

I wrote two other pieces that week. The main story was about President Bush's powerful speech December 7 at Punchbowl, where he was warmly greeted as "one of us" by the president of the Pearl Harbor Survivors Association. Bush's resonant appeal for an end to "recrimination and rancor" between the United States and Japan and his apology to the 120,000 Japanese Americans for the "great injustice" done them when they were interned by the U.S. government during the war made news throughout the world. My story in *The Post* was headlined, "Bush Issues Call for Reconciliation," along with a boldface quotation pulled from the speech: "Look into your hearts and minds: You will see boys who became men . . . and men who became heroes. Look at the water here—clear and quiet, bidding us to sum up and remember."

Two days earlier, my other story from Hawaii ran on page one under the headline "In Hawaii, Social Liberation and Political Ascent." These are the first four paragraphs:

> Honolulu, Dec. 5—Unlike Japanese Americans on the mainland, most of the 160,000 ethnic Japanese living in Hawaii in 1941 were not rounded up and placed in camps after the attack on Pearl Harbor, though their patriotism was nonetheless challenged.
>
> They met the challenge so brilliantly, however, that it completely transformed the islands. Japanese Americans came home from the war as heroes and in the years that followed wrested political power from a white conservative oligarchy, replacing it with a progressive, multi-racial coalition.
>
> "It is a great irony of the war," said Paul Hooper, a historian at the University of Hawaii. "On one level it was so terrible. But it was literally a liberating war for Americans of Japanese ancestry."
>
> "It was the beginning of our march to first-class citizenship," said Mike Tokunaga, 71, a second-generation, or Nisei, Japanese American who was wounded three times while serving in Italy and France with the 100th Battalion—known as the 'Purple Heart battalion' because of its high rate of casualties during 18 months of combat in Italy and France. Armed with the GI Bill of Rights, Tokunaga came back to Hawaii after the war to get a college education. Then he joined the cadre of Japanese Americans—the most prominent being Sen. Daniel K. Inouye (D)—who led the state's political revolution.

My story went on to relate how Tokunaga, the son of a plantation worker, had been motivated to succeed as a soldier both by U.S. patriotism and by the lessons taught him by his Japan-born parents not to bring shame upon the family.

After the war, Tokunaga did not set out to become a public figure like his friend Inouye but worked as a behind-the-scenes activist who collaborated with other Americans of Japanese ancestry (AJA) to challenge a conservative, planter-oriented political system. They were led by an Irish American police officer named John Burns who formed a Democratic coalition of Japanese American veterans of the 100th Battalion and the 442nd Regimental Combat Team and left-leaning labor unions such as the International Longshoremen's and Warehousemen's Union. This coalition swept to power in the 1954 territorial elections, transforming post–World War II Hawaiian politics. Tokunaga's generation kept a low profile during the observance of the fiftieth anniversary of Pearl Harbor, which did not please all the younger AJAs.

"I am very disappointed in the Japanese American community and how it has handled Pearl Harbor," said Bill Kaneko, an aide to Governor John D. Waihee III and president of the local Japanese American Citizens League. "They buried their heads in the sand. . . . They didn't want to do anything to rock the boat."

Tokunaga shared the ambivalence toward the Pearl Harbor ceremonies of other AJAs of his generation, but he was ebullient about the multicultural diversity of Hawaii, which he expressed by listing the incredibly varied ethnic composition of his nieces and nephews.

"Three, four generations down the line, we'll have so many strains in us that you won't be able to say anything bad about any race or people without saying something bad about yourself," Tokunaga said. We haven't quite reached that multicultural future, but Hawaii comes closer than any other state. According to the 2020 Census, 24.2 percent of Hawaiians are of two or more ethnicities compared with 2.8 percent for the United States as a whole.

Writing in *The Washington Post* four years and eight months after the Pearl Harbor observances, Richard Harwood shared some of his grim memories of his wartime service as a U.S. Marine. It is harrowing reading. Harwood hired me and inspired me at *The Post.* We'd become friends after he was no longer my boss and discussed all manner of things. But Harwood had remained tight-lipped about his wartime service in the Pacific Theater.

In the summer of 1995, nearing the fiftieth anniversary of the end of World War II, *The Post* commissioned a series of stories. Harwood, now retired, was asked to write about the Pacific war, in which he had served with the Fifth Marine Amphibious Corps from 1943 until 1946. He participated in battles on Saipan, Tinian, Guam, and Iwo Jima, where he was seriously wounded. Iwo Jima, a volcanic island 660 miles south of Tokyo, is 2 miles wide by 4 miles long. It was the scene of one of the bloodiest battles in the history of the Marine Corps.

Some 70,000 Marines invaded the island on February 18, 1945, touching off ferocious fighting with a Japanese garrison, 18,000 strong, dug deeply into volcanic rock. The Japanese refused to surrender an island both sides considered strategically valuable. All but 216 of the Japanese defenders were killed. Marine casualties were 6,800 dead and 20,000 wounded, Harwood among them. To put this thirty-six-day battle in perspective, the number of U.S. Marines who died on Iwo Jima is roughly equivalent to all American military fatalities in the Iraq and Afghanistan wars combined.

Harwood wrote about Iwo Jima and other Pacific battles in a twenty-thousand-word article called "A Long Road Home." It's the best condensed history of the Pacific war that I've read, full of spare and unforgiving prose about the ugly realities of war. Harwood's personal experiences are tucked into the remembrances of others. Note in the following passages how he moves from the third-person to the first-person.

After a nostalgic quote from General Douglas MacArthur about the "wondrous beauty" of warfare, Harwood wrote: "In a memoir of his days as a nineteen-year-old mortarman with the Marines at Peleliu in the Palau Islands, E. B. Sledge had no remembrance of 'wondrous beauty.' He remembered dead comrades: One man had been decapitated. His head lay on his chest; his hands had been severed from his wrists. . . . [They] had cut off his penis and stuffed it in his mouth. The corpse next to him had been treated the same. The third had been butchered, chopped up like a carcass torn by some predatory animal."

"At Iwo Jima one day, we came across a Japanese soldier, charbroiled by a flame thrower. He wanted water. He got, instead, the lighted end of a cigarette in his mouth, courtesy of a boy from Brooklyn," Harwood wrote. "One of our unit's favorite snapshots from Saipan was of a dozen or so smiling Marines holding aloft Japanese heads on bamboo poles."

Harwood's account was much more than a collection of horror stories. He examined the racial dimensions of the Pacific war and the impact of technology on modern combat, quoting from historian John Dower's book *War Without Mercy:* "The traditional psychological factors which made ending wars difficult—pride on all sides, desperation and mental paralysis on the part of losers, the winner's drive for revenge and unequivocal victory—were now wedded to unprecedented forces of destruction. War hates were nothing new to the mid-20th century, nor were race hates of the killing of noncombatants. . . . [But] the new capability for rapidly killing large numbers of people were accompanied, almost inevitably, by a general acceptance of the belief that in the total war of the modern age, it was necessary and even proper to do so."

The highest ranks of officialdom in the United States were committed to total war. Paul McNutt, chairman of the War Manpower Commission, favored "the extermination of the Japanese in toto." The United States adopted a prewar plan drawn up by General George Marshall for incendiary attacks to burn the wood-and-paper homes of Japan's densely populated cities. "Before it was over," Harwood wrote, "66 cities had been hit with napalm, white phosphorous and high explosive bombs; 2,210,000 homes were demolished or burned, 9,200,000 people were made homeless, nearly 400,000 killed."

After quoting an angry Japanese survivor of the firebombing, Harwood wrote: "These things, no matter how offensive to our visions of a 'just war,' probably ought to be remembered, not as an excuse for wallowing in guilt but as a reminder of 'what it was like' and of how war can dehumanize the best of men."

Harwood wanted readers to realize that the attack on Pearl Harbor was "merely one of the powerful gusts in the hurricane of war unleashed on December 7, 1941, by Japanese forces." Under the leadership of Fleet Admiral Isoroku Yamamoto, the Japanese began "one of the most brilliant and successful military offensives in the history of warfare."

Within six months they routed the British Army, captured Singapore, and seized Hong Kong, the Philippines, Wake Island, Guam, and the Dutch East Indies—Borneo, Java, and adjoining islands, which provided the Japanese with raw materials for continuing the war. "Virtually everything west of Hawaii—Midway Island, Australia and New Zealand excepted—was under Japanese control, an area of more than six million square miles, an area 50 percent greater than Hitler and his German armies were able to bring under submission," Harwood wrote. But Japanese conduct had undermined its promised racial solidarity of "a thousand million Asiatics" against the white colonialists of France, Britain, the Netherlands, and their American ally. "That solidarity vanished as the occupying armies of Japan enslaved for war purposes millions of Malayans, Burmese, Indonesians, Indochinese, Tamils and other nationalities."

The fortunes of the Pacific war changed in a five-minute period on June 4, 1942, when a huge Japanese fleet on the way to Midway Island was ambushed by the only three U.S. carriers left in the Pacific—the *Hornet*, the *Enterprise*, and the *Yorktown*. Before Midway, the Japanese had never had a defeat. After Midway, they never had a victory. But the war without mercy continued for three more years at terrible human cost. The death toll in China may have reached fifteen million. A million people died from starvation in Indochina.

Okinawa, four hundred miles from southern Japan, was the last big battle of World War II. Harwood's unit, the Fifth Marine Amphibious Corps, had taken heavy casualties at Iwo Jima, and was spared Okinawa, although Harwood's injuries would have kept him out of battle in any case. The United States invaded Okinawa on April 1, 1945, and fierce fighting lasted until June 22. U.S. casualties totaled 49,000, including 12,520 killed. The Japanese lost 110,000, most of its force, which again declined to surrender. Civilian deaths were estimated at from 40,000 to 150,000, a broad range that indicates the uncertainty of the estimates.

Okinawa was supposed to be the stepping stone for U.S. invasion of Kyushu, the southernmost Japanese island. In late July 1945, the War Department estimated that the invasion, codenamed Downfall, would cause between 1.7 million to 4 million U.S. casualties, with as many as 800,000 U.S. dead and 5 to 10 million Japanese dead.

The invasion was forestalled by Japan's announcement of surrender on August 15 after the United States had dropped atomic bombs on Hiroshima and Nagasaki. Harwood quotes Paul Fussell, a U.S. infantry officer in Europe who was readying for the invasion and later wrote a long article for the *New Republic* called *Thank God for the Atom Bomb.*

"That was a common reaction," Harwood wrote. "I have wondered myself if, after all, there is any moral distinction between death from the air and death from a bullet in the brain." Harwood was on Maui where he and his unit were preparing for the invasion of Japan when he heard about the surrender. "In thanks for the outcome, the authorities allowed every man to buy a case of beer," Harwood wrote. "We all got drunk and had a wild time."

I was on book leave when Harwood's essay appeared, and he sent me a copy. On my next visit to Washington, I said to him, "I can see why you didn't want to talk about your wartime experiences." Harwood demurred. He had avoided talking about the war, he said, not because his experiences had been awful but because such talk seemed insensitive to the Marines who had died on Iwo Jima and other islands in the South Pacific. Harwood said he'd decided long ago to share his experiences only if they were part of a larger story. The assignment to write about the Pacific war had provided this opportunity.

I saw Harwood intermittently in the last years of his life. On one of several trips to Washington, I consulted separately with Harwood and Ben Bradlee about my future. They had no say in it, but gave good advice. My assignment to the western bureau had run its course. I could have returned to Washington as a general assignment reporter for *The Post,* but Mary and I liked living in California. Eventually, I reached an agreement with Len Downie, who had succeeded Ben as executive editor, to retire as a staff writer and stay on as a freelance reporter in the West. Once again, *The Post* accommodated me.

Harwood continued to be a presence in my life. On one of my trips back to DC in the late 1990s, we had a party at the Arlington home of Mary's mother, Ann Shinkwin, where Mary and her sister were raised. Ann had been a widow since 1988. Harwood came and spent much of his time there talking to her.

Later, Harwood developed cancer. He described what the disease was doing to his body on one of my trips but did not dwell on it. As best I remember, we spent our time talking about our families and the state of journalism. Harwood was clear as a bell on the deficiencies of our craft. He had been *The Washington Post*'s first ombudsman and done another stint as ombudsman in his last years at the paper. His final column included this assessment.

"We proclaim our 'professionalism' to the gullible. But we do not write well enough. We do not study and report well enough. We do not edit well enough. In our isolation from the main streams of American life and thought we often resemble a Tibetan order, talking primarily to ourselves and other apparatchiks of the political class."[2]

2. "A Call to Excellence," by Richard Harwood, *Washington Post,* December 22, 1991.

I visited Harwood at his home in Bethesda days before he died. He sat upright in bed, calm and courageous, and we talked about politicians we had known—Robert Kennedy and Ronald Reagan in particular—and our days together at the paper. Harwood died at home on March 19, 2001. I wrote a letter to his wife, Bea, telling her what her husband had meant to me, and she responded with a gracious note that I have kept.

"Time is precious," it concluded.

28

THE ORDEAL OF RODNEY KING

The most consequential news stories during my second tour in the western bureau were the Rodney King beating in March 1991 and the riots that erupted after the four Los Angeles police officers who took King into custody were acquitted of using excessive force in April 1992. Fifty-four people died, 2,300 were injured and 12,000 were arrested in five days of rioting.[1] Property damage was more than $1 billion. The fallout from these events reverberates to this day. Los Angeles police chief Daryl Gates was forced into retirement, starting a turnover pattern in which the LAPD had eight subsequent police chiefs. The department was under federal oversight for eight years, but the reforms were fleeting. and use of force by police officers remains a contentious issue. In 2021, LAPD officers shot 37 people, killing 18 of them. Seventeen of those who were shot were experiencing a mental health issue.

Rodney King received $3.8 million in damages as the result of a civil suit but was never the same after the beating. He died in his backyard swimming pool in 2012 with drugs in his system. Two of the four officers acquitted in state court of using excessive force were convicted in federal court of violating King's civil rights and went to prison. The King beating launched an era of trial by videotape, many of them involving encounters between police officers and Black men. Some commentators have drawn a straight line between the King incident and the May 25,

1. There are differing estimates of riot fatalities. I use the figure provided by the Los Angeles Coroner's Office.

2020, killing of George Floyd by a Minneapolis police officer, which was captured by a bystander on a cell-phone camera. This videotape led to the murder conviction of the police officer who held his knee on Floyd's neck for nine minutes and forty-six seconds.

But there were vast differences between the King beating and the Floyd murder beyond the obvious fact that King was not killed. I covered both criminal trials of the LAPD officers and the civil trial in which King was awarded damages. I also studied the King beating in researching my book *Official Negligence: How Rodney King and the Riots Changed Los Angeles and the LAPD.* This meant repeatedly watching the videotape and discussing the incident with use-of-force experts and Taky Tzimeas, the savvy detective who analyzed the beating for the LAPD's Department of Internal Affairs. I interviewed jurors, witnesses, police officers, prosecution and defense attorneys, city officials, riot investigators, people on the streets in South Central Los Angeles. I also interviewed Rodney King.

I wrote *Official Negligence* after Peter Osnos of Random House approached me in the summer of 1992 and asked if I was interested in doing a book about the riots. We knew one another from *The Washington Post,* where Peter had been a senior editor. Osnos is a serious person and, through my trusted agent Kristine Dahl, offered me the highest advance I've ever received. On August 13, 1992, we signed a contract for an untitled book on the riots.

"By understanding the causes of the King case and the riots, we may improve our chances of avoiding another descent into the chaos that gripped Los Angeles during five terrifying spring days in 1992," I wrote in a prologue to *Official Negligence.* "That is the purpose of this book."

What the prologue did not say was that I had seriously underestimated how long it would take me to reach this understanding. *Official Negligence* took me so long to research and write that I burned through the advance, borrowed money on a line of credit, and was on the borderline of depression. My anxiety was compounded when Bertelsmann acquired Random House, prompting Osnos and other key editors to leave, and saddling me with an editor who didn't know what I was writing or why.

Here are the summarized facts of Rodney King's arrest, as revealed at the criminal trials of the four LAPD officers.

King had been drinking the night of March 2, 1981, a Saturday, when he watched a basketball game at the Altadena home of a friend, Bryant Allen. King told a police investigator he had consumed two forty-ounce bottles of malt liquor and another twelve-ounce bottle of malt liquor in the five and one-half hours before the incident. A blood-alcohol test taken more than five hours after King was beaten showed a level of 0.079 percent, just below the 0.08 level that in California was then a presumptive level of intoxication. Extrapolating from this result, state prosecutors and defense attorneys stipulated that, at the time of his arrest, King had a blood-alcohol level of 0.19 percent, more than twice the legal limit.

After the game, King and Allen went for a drive. With them was Freddie Helms, a friend of Allen's whom King had met that night.[2] Helms sat in the front-passenger seat and Allen in the back. King headed west on Interstate 210 for reasons of which he was never certain. His best guess, he said when I interviewed him on December 18, 1995, was that he was heading toward Hansen Dam, where he had fished with his father. As a boy, fishing with his dad had been King's favorite recreation and Hansen Dam his favorite place to fish. He told me they sometimes fished there all night long.

The California Highway Patrol husband-and-wife team of Tim and Melanie Singer was patrolling the 210 freeway that night. Melanie Singer was driving. As she exited at the Sunland Boulevard off-ramp, she glanced in her rear-view mirror and saw a car approaching at high speed. She returned to the freeway and began a 7.8-mile pursuit during which Singer clocked the speed of the car she was following, a white 1988 Hyundai Excel, at speeds of 110 to 115 miles per hour on the freeway and up to 85 miles per hour on residential streets after the car exited the freeway at Paxton Avenue.

By then, patrol cars from other departments had joined in the pursuit, and an LAPD helicopter hovered overhead. King's friend Allen urged him to pull over, but King ignored him. King was on parole from a robbery conviction and knew that driving under the influence—DUI, or "deuce" in police jargon—could lead to the revocation of his parole.

2. Helms was killed in an automobile accident on June 29, 1991, when he was again a passenger in a car whose driver was intoxicated.

"I didn't stop that night because I knew I had been drinking," King told me in that 1995 interview. "I was scared to go back. I had been in prison one time, and I didn't want to go back."

He testified similarly in the federal trial of the officers. Hemmed in by police cars and a pickup that had pulled off the road because of the sirens, King stopped near a darkened entrance to Hansen Park Dam just beyond the Corral (now gone), the bar in which Arnold Schwarzenegger in *Terminator 2* beats up a pool-playing customer who refuses to give up his motorcycle. The CHP car was directly behind the Hyundai. Using a handheld microphone, Tim Singer ordered the occupants of the car to surrender. But his commands were lost in feedback from his phone and the noise of the arrest scene. The driver of a Los Angeles Unified School District patrol car that had joined in the pursuit kept his siren blaring. The LAPD helicopter hovering over the scene added to the din.

While her husband turned his attention to the two Hyundai passengers, who surrendered meekly, Melanie Singer exited the CHP car and eyed King, who she thought looked "almost happy." King put his hands on the roof of his car, looked up at the helicopter waved and did a little dance. Then he dropped down on his knees. "He got down on all fours like a dog," said LAPD officer Tim Wind, watching King in the light of the helicopter. "And he turned around, and he continued to mutter and giggle and smile. At one point he patted the ground."

Officers shouted at King to lie on his stomach and put his hands behind his back. Instead, he moved to what LAPD sergeant Stacey C. Koon thought was a runner's crouch. King looked directly at Koon, who realized that King was intoxicated and suspected he was also using drugs, possibly PCP. Koon reached into the front seat of his car for an electric stun gun known as a Taser, which Koon had often used when he was assigned to the Los Angeles County Jail, where officers are not allowed to carry firearms.

While Koon was unholstering his Taser, Melanie Singer shouted at King to show his hands. King ignored her. He put his hands on his buttocks and shook them at Singer, an action later described by Koon in this way: "He grabbed his butt with both hands and began to shake and gyrate his fanny in a sexually suggestive fashion. As King gyrated, a mixture of fear and offense overcame Melanie. The fear, said Koon in a book about the arrest, was of a "Mandingo sexual encounter." Singer, who later told grand jurors she had "never come into contact with something like this," drew her revolver and directed King to "get your hands away from your butt and lie down." King would remember at the federal trial that a "police lady" had advanced on him, gun drawn, while he was on the ground telling him to obey and repeatedly saying, "I mean it, I mean it, I mean it."

King turned his head and made a clicking noise, a prison sign of disrespect. When Melanie came within five or six feet of King, she heard a voice telling her to stand back. It was Koon, telling her that he was taking over the arrest. Singer looked at him, saw the sergeant's stripes, and yielded to rank.

Koon, then forty-one, was an educated and experienced officer who took pride in controlling dangerous situations. He had a reputation for bravery and stiff-necked rectitude. During more than fourteen years on the LAPD, Koon earned ninety commendations and only three reprimands. Despite his "Mandingo" comment, other cops, including a Black officer I interviewed, did not consider Koon a racist. Working in the tough Seventy-Seventh Street Division in the heart of South Central Los Angeles, Koon once shot and wounded a gang member who was about to shoot another officer. The officer credited Koon with saving his life. Subsequently, Koon became a living legend in the Seventy-Seventh for an occurrence he remembered as much more dangerous than the shooting incident. Koon was on duty when a transvestite prostitute with bleeding, open sores about his lips and mouth was brought into the Seventy-Seventh Street station. Fearing he had AIDS, other cops gave the transvestite, who was Black, a wide berth. While waiting to be booked, he collapsed, apparently of a heart attack. No one moved toward him except Koon, who administered mouth-to-mouth resuscitation.

"His face was pale, he was scared, but he did it anyway," said Greg Baltad, the arresting officer. The prostitute died, but Baltad told me that Koon's futile attempt to save him was the greatest heroism he had ever seen.

On the night he took the arrest from Singer, Koon was more angry than scared. His anger was directed at Singer, whom Koon thought was injecting a gun into a situation that didn't require a lethal weapon. LAPD officers are taught not to approach a suspect with drawn gun, and Singer's "lousy tactic" offended Koon.

"Had she proceeded, either she was going to shoot Rodney King, or he was going take her gun away and shoot her," Koon said in *Presumed Guilty,* a book he wrote defending his actions. Koon reiterated this when I interviewed him on March 17, 1993, during the federal trial, telling me he feared that either King or Singer would be shot. Theodore Briseno, another LAPD officer at the scene, had similar fears. He told me that he thought the likely outcome of what Singer was doing was a "dead cop."

Koon testified at three trials that he formed a "tactical plan" for taking King into custody as he watched him disregard Singer. The first steps of this plan would have arrested King without harming him. After telling others at the noisy scene to "shut up" so King could hear him, Koon repeatedly told King to put his face down. When King ignored these commands, Koon directed four LAPD officers to surround King and "swarm" him. Koon picked the officers nearest him because he was bathed in a cone of light from the helicopter and unable to see that more than a score of other officers had arrived at the scene. But the four officers Koon chose were an unlikely band of brothers for subduing King, a burly man who was six-foot-three-inches tall and 250 pounds. Koon observed that King was "buffed out" and accurately surmised he was an ex-convict who had lifted weights in prison.

Laurence Michael Powell, twenty-eight, whom Koon chose as his lead officer in the swarm of King, had served three and a half years on the LAPD and led the Foothill Division in arrests but was cocky and of uncertain competence. As part of ongoing training, LAPD officers are sometimes called upon at roll call to demonstrate a police technique. Two hours before the King incident, in an improbable coincidence, Powell had been told at Foothill roll call to demonstrate proper use of the "power stroke" with his police baton. The power stroke is a forceful blow, using the entire weight of an officer's body. Powell flunked the test and was told to practice. The correct use of the stroke was then demonstrated by Powell's partner, Tim Wind, a quiet thirty-year-old rookie with more law enforcement experience than Powell, who was his training officer. Wind, a former Green Beret, had served seven years on a small Kansas police force before moving to Southern California and applying to the LAPD. He was nervous about partnering with Powell and told him on their first day together that he didn't want to get "any

81s," the police-manual number for personnel complaints. Powell lied that he had not been the subject of any complaints.

The other two officers in a separate police car who were chosen to swarm King were Briseno, thirty-eight, a wiry nine-year LAPD veteran who was only five feet, seven inches and 135 pounds. He was the training officer for Rolando Solano, twenty-seven, a rookie barely five months out of the police academy.

At Koon's command, the four police officers jumped on King. Powell and Briseno grabbed his arms; Wind and Solano took his legs. Powell kept a knee on King's back, trying to force his left arm back so he could handcuff it. King was drenched in sweat. "His arm was rigid, and it wasn't moving at all," Powell told investigators. "I couldn't move it." Then with a sudden motion, King tossed the officers off his back. Solano retreated and was not seen again until the end of the arrest.

For all the officers, King's exhibition of strength confirmed their suspicions that King was "on something," most probably PCP. The belief that King was on PCP is crucial to understanding Koon's behavior. Los Angeles police stations abounded in horror stories about the exploits of PCP users, who were feared because of their supposed imperviousness to pain. When King threw the officers off his back, Koon's suspicions were confirmed. King had exhibited the "superhuman strength" of the typical PCP user.

"I know if he gets hold of me and he grabs me in [the] neck . . . it's going to be like a death grip, and you can have all the 8,300 members of the police department pull this guy off and it's not going to work," Koon later told Internal Affairs investigators.

But Koon did not want to shoot King, and his only other weapon for controlling him at a distance was his Taser. The sergeant fired the Taser at King, hitting him in the back with the electronic darts. King groaned and fell to his knees, then rose and turned toward Koon. The sergeant, who had shut off the Taser, reactivated it and fired again, this time hitting King's chest from a distance of about nine feet.

Koon had now spent about ten minutes trying to take King into custody without shooting or hitting him, but nothing that happened during this period had been videotaped. Most of the millions of people who have seen the videotape of the King beating do not know that Koon made a considerable effort to arrest King before a single blow was struck.

After King was hit by Koon's second Taser shot, he groaned again and collapsed but braced himself on his right elbow and began to come to his feet. Then he did a 180-degree turn and stared at Powell and Wind from a distance of six feet.

"Does anyone else have a Taser?" Koon asked. No one did.

This was the moment, as King struggled to regain his balance, when George Holliday, awakened by the helicopter and the sirens, began videotaping the scene from the balcony of his second-floor apartment across the street. It was also the moment, or close to it, when a frustrated Koon ordered Powell and Wind to deliver power strokes with their batons, telling them not to hit King in the head. And it was the moment before the moment when King charged in Powell's direction, looking "like he was trying to imitate a mean dog," as Wind put it.

Terrified, Powell swung his baton wildly and not with the power strokes Koon had ordered. Powell's first swing did the most damage of the entire beating, striking King on the right side of the face and fracturing his cheekbone. Solano, the rookie, didn't like the sound Powell's baton made when it hit King's face and turned away. Wind, standing next to Powell, saw two blows by Powell directed at King's arm, but "King's head came up and his body came up. And he moved enough that Powell hit him in the face."

The three-second section of King's charge is moderately clear on the videotape, but Powell's first wild blow was blurred because Holliday moved his camcorder to steady it. The blurred section lasts seven seconds. As the tape becomes clear, King is on his stomach with his torso raised and no blows are being struck. Briseno's arm is coming up to restrain Powell, who stands over King with upraised baton. Wind said this was the moment when Briseno was warning him and Powell that the Taser wires were still attached to King and to avoid touching him because of a possible electric charge. Briseno told me—and twice testified—that he was trying to stop the beating.

Whatever Briseno was trying to do, the beating continued for eighty-one seconds until King stopped moving and yelled, "Please stop!" Koon then ordered officers in the vicinity to jump on King, which they did in what Koon called the "sloppiest swarm I have ever seen."

Powell then handcuffed King, who was hog-tied and dragged to the side of the road, awaiting an ambulance. From evaluations by use-of-force experts, I concluded that King had been struck thirty-one times plus being kicked by Wind and Briseno. These blows injured King, who in addition to the fractured cheekbone suffered multiple fractures on the right side of his face, lacerations on his forehead, a fracture of the distal fibula in the right leg, and various bruises, contusions, and abrasions.

"I felt horrible," King told the grand jury. "I felt beat up and like a crushed can. That's what I felt like, like a crushed can, and my spirits were real low. . . . I was in so much pain."

Koon knew the use of force had been extreme. He reported King's arrest at 12:56 a.m. on Sunday, March 3, 1991, on the portable computer in his police car. "U just had a big time use of force. Tased and beat the suspect of CHP pursuit. Big Time." When he was cross-examined about the King beating at the state trial of the officers on March 20, 1992, Koon said: "I have seen uses of considerable violence, but I have not seen anything as violent as this in my fourteen-and-a-half years [as a Los Angeles police officer]."

Chief Daryl Gates was shocked by the videotape of the King beating. The following morning, Gates played the videotape twenty-five times in his office, staring at the screen in disbelief.

"To see my officers engaged in what appeared to be excessive use of force, possibly criminally excessive, to see them beat a man with their batons *fifty-six times,* to see a sergeant on scene who did nothing to seize control, was something I never dreamed I would witness," Gate wrote in his memoirs. "It was a very, *very* extreme use of force—extreme for any police department in America. But for the LAPD, considered by many to be perhaps the finest, most professional police department in the world, it was more than extreme. It was impossible."

Researching *Official Negligence,* I followed the trail of the videotape. George Holliday, the man who made it, was a thirty-one-year-old Hollywood manager of a national plumbing company. He was a quiet man, with no discernible political agenda, when from a distance of about ninety feet on his second-floor balcony he videotaped the King beating with a Sony camcorder he had received as a birthday present.

Holliday and his wife, Maria, had planned to rise early on Sunday, March 3, to videotape an employee of the plumbing company who was running in the Los Angeles Marathon. They stuck to their schedule, and Holliday also videotaped a wedding later in the day. But he couldn't get the King beating out of his head. Holliday told me he called the LAPD's Foothill station, where the dispatcher "pretty much" hung up on him. It was now Sunday evening. Holliday called CNN, but no one answered. Frustrated, Holliday was now determined to have the videotape aired. On Monday morning he found a taker at KTLA, which made a copy of it.

"We were all shocked by it, and realized from the first that it was important," said Warren Cereghino, the station's news director, whom I knew slightly. Cereghino saw to it that a copy of the tape was sent to LAPD headquarters at Parker Center, where senior officers watched the beating of King in amazement. With Chief Gates out of town, Assistant Chief Robert Vernon moved swiftly, telling Internal Affairs investigators who were off duty, or on their way home, to return to their posts.

The first story of the King beating aired at 10:15 p.m., March 4, 1991, leading the second section of KTLA's late-night broadcast. The story was seen simultaneously at 1:15 a.m. at the Atlanta headquarters of CNN, which had an affiliation agreement with KTLA. The tape made the same strong impression on CNN producers as it had on Cereghino and the senior LAPD officers who viewed it. CNN obtained a microwave feed of the KTLA tape and began using it Tuesday morning. Cereghino soon made the tape available to all Los Angeles stations and their networks. By Tuesday evening, the King beating led national and local newscasts. In the ensuing months, Holliday's videotape would be shown hundreds of times on local television, sometimes as background wallpaper while a voice-over told of developments in the story. The ABC, CBS, and NBC networks would do stories on the evening news using the videotape eighty-seven times during the next thirteen months.

But there was a small yet crucial difference between Holliday's tape and the one most Americans saw on their television screens. In the version KTLA used and sent to other stations, the editors opted for visual clarity at the expense of comprehension and deleted the first ten seconds, which begin with King's charge in the direction of Officer Powell. David Farmer, CNN's Los Angeles bureau chief, subsequently had qualms about this editing. He told me it reflected a "built-in aversion to showing out-of-focus and inexplicable editing."

But the three-second segment of King's charge before the blurry section is only slightly out of focus and hardly inexplicable. The deleted opening section and the events that occurred before the videotape began are crucial to understanding what happened. Including King's charge at the officers doesn't make the beating palatable; I found the videotape hard to watch after seeing it scores of times. But the first three seconds showing King's charge provide a motive for Powell's first (and most destructive) baton swing. Without these first seconds, it looks as if the LAPD officers are beating King for fun.

CNN later received an unedited version of the videotape from Cereghino. When the omission of the first section of the tape became an issue in the trial of the officers nearly a year later, CNN executive vice president Ed Turner directed that the full eighty-one-second Holliday videotape be used whenever it was shown. But at this point the tape was being used sparingly at CNN because of an earlier edict by Turner to stop using the tape as wallpaper in stories about alleged police brutality. Other stations, most importantly local stations in Los Angeles, continued to use the abbreviated version of the videotape.

Meanwhile, events moved swiftly. On March 5, the day after the tape was shown on television, the FBI opened an investigation, and Mayor Tom Bradley promised "appropriate action" against the officers. On March 6, King was released from jail after District Attorney Ira Reiner found insufficient evidence to prosecute him. On March 7, Chief Gates said the officers involved in the beating would be prosecuted, and he suspended fifteen officers who were at the scene. On March 8, Reiner announced he would seek indictments from a grand jury. On March 10, the *Los Angeles Times* published a poll that revealed the negative impression the videotape had made on Southern California viewers. Eighty-six percent of those surveyed had seen the videotape, and 92 percent of those who saw it believed the police officers had used excessive force. On March 12, the American Civil Liberties Union, launching a campaign to fire Gates, ran a full-page ad in the *Los Angeles Times* that asked, "Who do you call when the gang wears blue uniforms?"

Lacking authority to fire Gates, Mayor Bradley became the leader of the campaign to force him into retirement. Bradley had served twenty-one years in the LAPD when it was segregated, rising to the then-unprecedented rank of lieutenant, and leaving the force when legendary Chief William Parker lost confidence in Bradley because he wanted to integrate patrol cars. Jesse Brewer, the highest-ranking Black officer in the history of the LAPD and a friend of the mayor, told me that Bradley remembered other slights during his days as a cop. In the wake of the King affair, Bradley was offended by Gates's remark that the beating was an "aberration." Gates was offended, too. City Council president John

Ferraro, a conciliatory politician, brought Bradley and Gates together in an effort to broker a truce in their war of words.

The police chief used the occasion to tell the mayor, "If it wasn't for you being so absolutely stupid and your office so crass, you'd have known that this incident broke my heart." Gates told me he had been mulling retirement at the time of the Rodney King beating but didn't want to be forced out by Bradley, who had long been a thorn in his side.

Enter Warren Christopher, one of the city's most notable attorneys, who agreed to chair a nonpartisan commission that would investigate the LAPD and the role of Chief Gates. Christopher was chairman of O'Melveny and Myers, a powerful law firm that represented mostly corporate clients. His record of public service included a year and a half as deputy U.S. attorney general in the Johnson administration and four years as deputy secretary of state in the Carter administration. In 1981, Christopher had won national acclaim and the Medal of Freedom for negotiating the release of Americans held hostage in Iran.

I met Christopher during my first tour as western correspondent for *The Washington Post* in the 1970s. He'd read my first book, *Ronnie and Jesse,* and said he'd learned from it even though he thought I was too hard on his old boss Pat Brown. I was pleased when Mayor Bradley on April 1, 1991, announced the creation of the Independent Commission on the Los Angeles Police Department and named Christopher as chairman. I knew Christopher was a straight shooter who would be accessible to reporters. Even better, he gave me an advance warning that President Clinton intended to nominate him as secretary of state. Christopher said I needed to sit down with him and wrap up my questions about the commission before he left for Washington, where he wouldn't have time for book interviews.

What I learned in my last lunch with Christopher—known to everyone as "Chris"—was that he had become unhappy with Bradley, a longtime ally. Christopher said that when Bradley asked him to head the commission he'd extracted a promise from the mayor that he'd soft-pedal comments about Gates while the commission conducted its investigation. Instead, Bradley called publicly the next day for the firing of the police chief.

"He *promised* me," Christopher said, emphasizing the word, as if breaking a promise, hardly uncommon for a politician, was the equivalent of lying under oath. In the process of denouncing Gates, Bradley had also expressed his view that the officers who had beaten Rodney King were guilty. This bothered Christopher, who revered the presumption of innocence.

Christopher told me he'd been on the brink of calling Bradley and resigning when it occurred to him that he owed the investigation of the LAPD to the people of Los Angeles. After deciding to stay, Christopher asked a friend, former prosecutor John Spiegel, to help him staff the commission. Spiegel had misgivings. Christopher told him a story about Marilyn Monroe, "on location in some God-forsaken place and having a miserable time," asking a friend, "Who do I have to fuck to get fired from this picture?"

Warren Christopher was one of the reasons I liked Los Angeles, the second most populous city in the nation but with aspects of a meritocratic frontier town where people rise to important positions because of their abilities. Christopher would not have become a member of the elite in most eastern cities, and Bradley certainly would not have become mayor of another city as white as Los Angeles was when he was first elected. Gates, too, had risen through the ranks on merit. When I first served as western correspondent for *The Washington Post* in the 1970s, Harwood told me I could move the bureau anywhere in California, even San Francisco, where he knew I had lived. That was tempting, but I told him the bureau was in the right place. Los Angeles, for all its faults, is the heart of the West.

One of those faults is widespread alcohol and drug abuse. Everyone I talked to who knew Rodney King had the same opinion of him: He was a gentle giant when sober and a menace to those around him when drinking. "His problem was alcoholism," said King's parole officer, Tim Fowler, a tall and muscular African American who developed an empathetic relationship with King. "He had been drinking from an early age."

Born in Sacramento on April 4, 1965, to an Air Force sergeant who was frequently AWOL and a mother who abandoned him and his sister Angela when they were little, King grew to manhood known by his middle name of "Glen" and a reputation of being friendly when sober and temperamental when he was drinking. Glen was popular at racially mixed John Muir High School in Pasadena, which Jackie Robinson had once attended, and good at sports, particularly baseball. But scholastics were a struggle, and he had been undermined by his father's tendency of taking him out of school to work on construction jobs when the boy was still in grade school. His father, Ronald, died at the age of forty-seven after a life of heavy drinking.

Six months before Rodney would have graduated from John Muir, he dropped out to take a job in construction that he couldn't keep. Tim Fowler is right in thinking of Rodney King as a "basically decent guy of borderline intelligence" whom drink had led to crime. But nothing King had done entitled police officers to beat him like a crushed can.

I think the real reason Christopher didn't quit the oversight panel that would become known to history as the Christopher commission was that he had a historical score to settle with himself. He had been vice chairman of the McCone commission, which investigated the Watts riot of 1965, and principal draftsman of a report that sided with the "disadvantaged Negro" and posed a memorable question: "Of what shall it avail our nation if we can place a man on the moon but cannot cure the sickness in our cities?"

But from this high point, the McCone report descended to generalities about education, health care, transportation, and housing that acted as barriers to full equality. An advisory committee to the U.S. Civil Rights Commission called the report "elemental, superficial, unoriginal and unimaginative." Christopher thought this evaluation unfair and told me the principal shortcoming of McCone was that there had been no follow up on its findings.

Christopher agreed with the most serious criticism of McCone, however, which is that it had fallen short in its examination of Chief William Parker and the LAPD. This reflected the politics of the time. Christopher had been boxed in between the conservative McCone and the liberal but politically nervous Pat Brown, who was struggling to deal with campus unrest and urban riots a year before Ronald Reagan exploited these issues while denying Brown a third term. "It was an impossible position [for Christopher]," wrote Bill Boyarsky in the *Los Angeles Times*. "No wonder the report was a compromise at best, a whitewash at worst."

There would be no whitewash in 1991. Christopher was determined that this commission would follow the facts wherever they led and urged his fellow commissioners to begin by reading the McCone report. Christopher released his 228-page report on July 9, 1991. It called for Los Angeles police chiefs to be chosen by the mayor instead of the Police Commission and limited to two five-year terms. The prevailing attitude on the commission, as I understood it, was that the primary problem with Gates was that he stayed far too long. That said, the recommendation about Gates was pure Christopher.

As he would later demonstrate as secretary of state in negotiating the Dayton Accords, Christopher preferred to give contending parties a face-saving way to change position. But Gates wasn't ready to quit and felt emboldened because the commission recommendation set no time frame for his departure. As Gates saw it, the report was a "travesty" written by lawyers who lacked understanding of police work. Hours after Christopher delivered his report, Gates told reporters at Parker Center that he'd step down only if voters approved a term limit for police chiefs.

The most damning part of the Christopher commission's report found that a "significant number of officers in the LAPD . . . repetitively use excessive force against the public and persistently ignore the written guidelines of the department regarding force. The failure to control these officers is a management issue that is at the heart of the problem."

This finding was bolstered by computerized examination of use-of-force reports involving nearly six thousand officers from January 1987 to March 1991. Sixty-three officers were involved in twenty or more incidents, and 5 percent accounted for more than 20 percent of all use-of-force reports. The data reinforced Christopher's belief that the LAPD's use-of-force problem was primarily a matter of supervision. Relatively few LAPD officers used excessive force on a regular basis but those who did were rarely disciplined effectively.

The commission called the forty-four officers with six or more complaints "problem officers." The Christopher commission also examined the Mobile Digital Terminal (MDT) computer messages sent from patrol cars. The LAPD had stored these messages in a database but not audited them. All told, 6,000,000 computer messages were scrutinized. The commission staff produced a compendium of 693 messages Christopher called "abhorrent" in which officers joked about beating suspects or derogated racial minorities, women, or homosexuals, as gays were called then. Blacks were most frequently disparaged in the offending MDT messages, but derogatory comments were also aimed at Mexicans, Salvadorans, Cubans, Asians, and Jews.

Gates later pointed out, correctly, that only a tiny percentage of the MDT messages were objectionable by any reasonable definition of that term. Even if 600 messages are deemed objectionable, this represented one-tenth of 1 percent of all computer transmissions during the period car messages were audited. How many law enforcement agencies or factory workforces (or even newsrooms) would have fared as well if audited for racial attitudes in 1981? LAPD officers treated the in-car computers as electronic bulletin boards on which they could send ordinary messages like birthday greetings. They didn't expect messages to be audited, as demonstrated by a number of transmissions knocking LAPD management. Given the LAPD's fearsome reputation, remarkably few officers boasted about beating suspects or denigrating Blacks or other minorities.

Nevertheless, prejudice can lurk in dark corners of the mind, ready to evince itself in unguarded moments. In March 1991 an LAPD officer investigated a domestic dispute involving a Black couple and used the MDT system to message a female officer he was trying to impress.

"It was right out of Gorillas in the Mist," the message said, referencing an iconic 1988 film as he compared Black people to animals. The officer was Laurence Powell, on the shift before he encountered Rodney King.

29

JUDICIAL NEGLIGENCE

Dick Harwood would tell reporters to get their stories "down where the goats can get it." By that, he meant to write plainly, avoiding highfalutin words and complicated phrasing. Following that advice, I will say bluntly that I believe the four LAPD officers charged with using excessive force against Rodney King—or at least two of them—were acquitted mainly because the trial was held in Simi Valley in Ventura County. Simi Valley is a conservative suburban city and home to the Ronald Reagan Presidential Library and numerous police officers. Few Black people live there, and none served on the jury that acquitted the officers of abusing King.

The trial wound up in Simi Valley through a convoluted legal process that culminated in a curious decision by Superior Court judge Stanley M. Weisberg. The process began in May 1991 when a Los Angeles County grand jury indicted Sergeant Stacey Koon and officers Laurence Powell, Timothy Wind, and Theodore Briseno on charges of assault with a deadly weapon and excessive use of force by a police officer. Powell and Koon were also charged with filing false police reports. The grand jurors declined to indict any of the nineteen bystander officers who'd been at the scene.

The case was assigned to Superior Court judge Bernard J. Kamins, who wanted a speedy trial in Los Angeles County. Kamins had been on the bench for five years after sixteen years as a public defender. By record and reputation, he was skeptical of police and normally avoided by prosecutors. But since the defendants in *The People of the State of California v. Laurence Powell et al.* were police officers, it was the defense attorneys who wanted nothing to do with Kamins. They filed a motion to remove him while also seeking a change of venue, arguing that the political situation in Los Angeles was too volatile for the defendants to receive a fair trial. Precedents favored the prosecution. A change of venue in Los Angeles had been granted only twice in a quarter-century. Not even the capable attorneys for the notorious Charles Manson had succeeded in getting a court to move his trial out of Los Angeles. These precedents were noted by deputy district attorney Alan Yochelson in arguing against a change of venue.

Yochelson said the King beating was a global sensation and could not be insulated from publicity by moving the trial. Los Angeles, the most diverse big city in California, was the appropriate site for the trial, he said. Judge Kamins agreed. He denied the motion and set the trial date for a month later—June 17, 1991. One never knows with certainty what would have happened on the road not taken, but it's likely that a Los Angeles trial would have resulted in convictions and spared Southern California a deadly riot.

Despite the precedents against them, attorneys for Koon and Powell appealed Kamins'a denial of a change of venue. While not optimistic about winning, one of the attorneys told me the appeal would allow them more time for trial preparation. That need became acute when Koon developed pneumonia.

The appeal landed on the desk of Joan Dempsey Klein, presiding justice of the Second District of the California Court of Appeal. Klein, who died in her sleep on Christmas Eve 2021 at the age of ninety-eight, was a distinguished jurist whose battle for women's rights had won national acclaim. She was considered a fair-minded judge who kept her liberal politics out of the courtroom. Nothing in Klein's record caused district attorney Ira Reiner, who thought well of her, to suspect she would move the trial. But Klein had a keen interest in public affairs and was anguished about what was happening to the city she loved.

"Los Angeles was a cauldron, with Gates and the mayor and the Christopher Commission," Klein told me in 1994. "The tape of the beating was playing on nightly TV every single night, over and over again."

Klein's concerns made her receptive to defense arguments that the situation in Los Angeles was too explosive for the defendants to receive a fair trial. On July 23, 1991, exactly two weeks after the Christopher commission delivered its report, Justice Klein granted the change of venue on behalf of a unanimous four-member court. She never expected that her action would lead to a trial in Simi Valley. It's difficult to understand from a plain reading of her opinion how any reasonable person could have concluded that Ventura County was an "appropriate place" to try the accused officers. Klein's opinion encouraged the trial court to move the trial out of the Los Angeles media market. Simi Valley residents receive the same channels as their Los Angeles counterparts. They read the *Los Angeles Times* and the *Daily News* of the San Fernando Valley, which covered the King beating and its aftermath intensely.

I didn't know about Klein's dismay over the Simi Valley location when I was covering the trial. She wouldn't discuss it publicly. When I talked to her on July 1, 1994, for *Official Negligence,* long after the trial, she said I was the first reporter to whom she'd granted an interview about the change of venue. Rodney King wasn't giving interviews either. I didn't interview him until 1995. King's lawyer, Steven Lerman, believed the officers would be convicted no matter where the trial was held, and he didn't want to risk exposing King to the media.

The next step on the road to Simi Valley was the removal of Kamins as the trial judge. Defense attorneys feared he was hostile to the police, and Kamins validated their fears by sending a cuddly message to prosecutors while the change of venue was being appealed. "Don't panic. You can trust me," the message said. When the sending of this *ex parte* (one-sided) message came to light, Justice Klein said what Kamins had done was "constitutionally unacceptable" and removed him as the trial judge.

Enter Judge Stanley Weisberg, whose quizzical expressions, balding forehead, and dry humor would become familiar to Court TV viewers through a series of nationally televised trials. His appointment did not initially set off alarm bells until Weisberg chose to move the trial to Ventura County. The judge said it was close and "convenient" for all parties. Even better, Ventura had a new and barely used courthouse. One reason it was little used was that it was far away from the county's population center in Ventura and nearby Oxnard. A trial in the downtown courthouse in Ventura might have produced a more diverse jury and a different outcome. We will never know because on November 26, 1991, Weisberg moved the trial to the East Ventura County Courthouse in Simi Valley.

"I have never been so horrified in my life," Roger Gunson, chief deputy of the office's Special Investigations Division, told me after the trial.

Gunson had been in the district attorney's office for twenty-three years and knew how hard it was to convict police officers even in Los Angeles. Gunson could not imagine that a responsible judge would allow Powell to be tried in a suburb of choice for people fleeing the city. And if Ventura was favorable to the defense, Simi Valley was the ideal locale within the county.

I wondered why Sacramento, with an ethnic diversity similar to Los Angeles, had not been on Weisberg's list. Weisberg's answer to the criticism that he had chosen an unrepresentative venue was that he was not allowed to consider demographics.

"As you are aware, the trial court is required to consider the relative costs of transfer and the hardship of the transfer on parties and witnesses," Weisberg wrote me in a May 9, 1994, letter. "There was no legal authority which permitted the court to consider the relative demographic characteristics of the counties."

This was a disingenuous response. "Weisberg screwed up," said one judge I spoke to for my book. "If the court tells you that you have to get out of the media market, how can you put it in Simi Valley? It's the same television, the same news."

So why did the judge choose Simi Valley? The explanation bandied about in the Simi Valley courtroom was that Weisberg selected Ventura County because he saw no risk in holding the trial there because of the presumed strength of the videotaped evidence and he wanted to spend evenings at home. The courtroom was an easy commute for Weisberg against prevailing traffic. If this was the reason, Weisberg wasn't the first, said Darryl Mounger, a decorated LAPD-officer-turned-lawyer who represented Stacey Koon. When a new trial venue is under consideration, Mounger told me, "The only question to ask is where the judge lives."

Weisberg denied that he ordered the change of venue for personal convenience but never gave me an opportunity to question him in person. I wrote to him and quoted his response, but he was one of only two people who would not agree to an interview for *Official Negligence.* The other was Laurence Powell. That mattered less because Powell testified at his trial, and I had access to his responses to police investigators about his actions in the King arrest. Other jurists involved in the cases arising from the King beating—notably Justice Klein and U.S. District Court judge John G. Davies in the federal civil rights trial of the LAPD officers—granted interviews and gave detailed answers to my questions about why they acted as they did. The upshot of Weinberg's shoddy legal reasoning was plain to the prosecution.

"If this case remains in Ventura County, it's a not-guilty verdict," Gunson told a friend. He thought Reiner should appeal Weisberg's decision, while using the district attorney's bully pulpit to "tell the community" that sending the case to Simi Valley meant acquittals for the officers who had abused Rodney King. Reiner respected Gunson but refused to do what he asked. "I thought the videotape would overcome even a bad jury situation," Reiner explained when I interviewed him on September 17, 1993. "I would have been much more reluctant to try a case [in Ventura County] if we were relying solely on testimony."

I had two epiphanies during the early days of the trial, the first of them during jury selection. There were only 6 African Americans on the jury pool of 260 people, 5 of whom were excused for cause on the basis of their responses or because they expressed antipathy toward the defendants during *voir dire*. The one prospective Black juror who cleared these hurdles was removed by a peremptory challenge from defense lawyer Michael Stone. After checking the bus schedules, I realized that discrimination in the jury pool involved class as well as race. There was almost no bus service between the county's population centers and the Simi Valley courthouse. Prospective jurors with travel hardships were excused, keeping nondrivers and people of limited means who couldn't afford daily drives to and from the courthouse off the jury. Oxnard, the largest and most diverse city in Ventura County, was a thirty-mile drive.

The jury of seven men and five women was impaneled on March 2, 1992, one day before the first anniversary of the Rodney King incident. It became a jury of six men and six women in midtrial after a male garbage collector, the only juror from relatively diverse Oxnard, was replaced for personal reasons. This probably benefited the defense. The departed juror had said on his questionnaire that officers who use excessive force "should be treated like everyone else." The woman who replaced him as Juror No. 10 had said on her questionnaire that "police have a very tough . . . a hard job. They need to be respected."

The six male jurors were white. The six women included four whites, a Mexican American housekeeper who'd worked as a security guard, and a Filipino American nurse.

Terry White, an able lawyer who would pay an undeserved price in reputation for the mistakes of judges and his superiors, is African American. He realized that a Black prosecutor ran the risk of not connecting with a white, pro-police jury and briefly considered resigning after Weisberg moved the trial to Simi Valley. But that would have left his replacement with little more than two months to prepare for trial. White concluded that the risk of inadequate preparation was greater than the risk the jury might not warm to a Black prosecutor.

"I said to myself no one knows this case . . . as well as I know it, and no one can be prepared in two months the way I will be prepared," White told me when I interviewed him on October 5, 1993. But he had no illusions that victory would be easy.

Whatever hope the prosecution had of winning rested with the video evidence. Without a videotape, Rodney King would have been just another Black man injured by the police while resisting arrest. No one except family and friends would know his name. But the video that made the trial possible also undermined the criminal case it created.

Of the first thirty-one potential jurors questioned by Weisberg, nine were excused because they had formed an opinion from seeing the videotape that the police had used unreasonable force. The prosecution objected, but Weisberg had little choice. It would have been reversible error for a judge to seat a juror who had announced beforehand that the defendants were guilty as charged. What remained, however, was a panel that did not share the general revulsion at the videotaped beating or doubted if the video told the full story.

"The video gave us a jury panel who had seen the prosecution's best evidence and was not convinced," said John Barnett, the most experienced of the defense attorneys. "The video is our best piece of evidence, as bizarre as that sounds," said Stacey Koon a week before the trial.

Since the videotape was never played during jury selection, prospective jurors based their opinions on the version they'd seen on television. This was the KTLA-edited version, which removed the first three seconds showing King charging toward Officer Powell and ten subsequent seconds, which are blurred because Holliday moved the camera.

Terry White realized that the edited video posed a problem for the prosecution because it eliminated King's charge at the arresting officers. Following a basic strategy of disclosing potentially damaging information before the other side did, White played the entire videotape in his opening statement on March 5, 1992. It would be shown three times more during the first day. White acknowledged that King had been intoxicated and uncooperative. He drew attention to King's charge, which he said "could be viewed as either an attack on Officer Powell or running away from Officer Powell."

White made no attempt to defend King's behavior. But he said Powell responded in an "unreasonable" way, striking King in the face with his baton "much as a baseball batter would swing on a pitch."

This opening statement led to my second epiphany. I had positioned myself in the courtroom so I could see the jurors as they watched the video during White's opening statement. One of them gasped when she saw the opening three seconds in which King charges toward Powell. The faces of others were strained in disbelief. I included some of the jury's reactions in my first-day story of the trial, writing: "Two of the five female jurors appeared to wince when the tape first was shown. A man juror put his hand to his mouth and shook his head."

What I didn't realize at the time was that some of the jury's reaction to the showing of the tape was because its opening segment contradicted the televised version they had watched at home. One of the women who winced was Dorothy Bailey, then known to reporters only by her juror number. Bailey, who became forewoman of the jury, would play a significant role in the deliberations. I interviewed her for *Official Negligence* on January 4, 1995. She told me she'd been amazed by the videotape. Bailey so abhorred violence that she closed her eyes or lowered her head during violent scenes at movies. But as the tape began to roll during White's opening statement, Bailey's fascination overcame her squeamishness. She had not known about King's charge or realized that Powell had taken out his handcuffs early in the incident.

"I was very surprised to see all the things that did happen," she said.

The defense would subsequently dissect the tape in slow motion in a process that Ira Reiner believes gradually desensitized the jurors. But Bailey never became emotionally comfortable with the video at any speed. The value of the unedited tape for Bailey was that it provided motivation for the actions of the officers. "It was the most powerful evidence that we had, but most of America saw only part of the tape," she told me.

I didn't know all this at the time of the trial, but watching the jurors as the tape was played made me skeptical that the prosecution had a slam-dunk case, as was widely believed. When an editor asked me what I thought, I said the prosecution faced an uphill battle. But the prosecution looked strong in my first-day story, which led with the opening statement of John Barnett, representing Officer Briseno. Barnett said the evidence would show that Officer Powell was "out of control" when he struck King with his baton. The story ran on page three of *The Washington Post* under a headline that said: "At L.A. Beating Trial, Officer Accuses Colleague."

Looking back on that trial from a distance, I think Barnett's opening statement and Briseno's subsequent testimony led the media covering the trial into believing the prosecution had a stronger case than it did. Even reporters such as me who understood that the unedited video presented problems for the prosecution could not see how Koon and Powell could escape conviction when the evidence against them included testimony from a participant in the arrest. The attorneys for Koon and Powell addressed this problem by putting the absent Rodney King on trial. King was responsible for everything that happened to him, said Mounger in his opening statement. When he stopped resisting arrest, the beating stopped.

Michael Stone, representing Powell, faced the stiffest challenge of the defense team. His client had delivered most of the baton blows, including the one to the head that accounted for King's most severe injuries. He had also sent computer messages that even Chief Gates had described as racist. But despite never having tried a felony case, Stone was a resourceful lawyer who threw himself into the defense with vigor and determination. He was convinced that Powell had been victimized by the political system, the media, and a spineless LAPD leadership that had bowed to political pressure.

King did not testify, making it easier for jurors to ignore his humanity. These were jurors who respected the police, stopped for red lights, and would have willingly pulled to the side of the road at any police command.

I had a singular problem among reporters covering the trial: I was also expected to cover other stories in the West. Back-to-back storms had eased a severe drought in the region. I filed three pieces on it and collaborated with DC-based colleagues on two other stories about legislation that would have upended water allocations in the West. I also wrote two articles on California governor Jerry Brown's challenge to

Bill Clinton for the Democratic presidential nomination plus a column headlined "The Spoiler." All of these required reporting, which I did while covering the trial, about which I filed more than a dozen stories.

I drove to the Simi Valley courthouse from my home in Summerland via a back road that led through strawberry fields and the small city of Moorpark. One day the largest coyote I have ever seen ran across the road in front of my car from one field to the other, transporting my imagination to the Wild West.

As the trial wore on, I couldn't shake my feeling that two or three of the officers would be acquitted. But the case against Powell seemed strong, even for a pro-police jury. Briseno's testimony ratified the prosecution's contention that Powell was out of control as he rained baton blows on King. Powell also came across as callous. A hospital nurse testified that he had taunted King as he awaited treatment after the beating. After learning that King had worked as an usher at Dodger Stadium, Powell said, "We had a pretty good hardball game tonight. We hit quite a few home runs."

Koon was on the stand for two days and was the strongest of the defense witnesses. He acknowledged without embarrassment the brutality of the King beating and methodically took the jury through all the efforts that preceded the beating to take King into custody peaceably. Koon used a pointer to describe the escalating use of force as if conducting a class. He said he could have subdued King in fifteen seconds with a carotid choke hold. He hadn't done so, he testified, "because in Los Angeles, the choke hold is associated with deaths of Blacks." Here are the opening paragraphs of my first story about Koon's testimony:

> SIMI VALLEY, Calif., March 19—The Los Angeles police sergeant who supervised the beating of black motorist Rodney G. King today said the action of his officers was "violent and brutal" but fully justified by King's actions.
>
> "It was done to control a violent and combative suspect," said Sgt. Stacey Koon, a 20-year-veteran of the police department. "Sometimes police work is brutal. It's just a fact of life."

Koon had a need to tell his story. He had talked candidly with Jaxon Van Derbeken of the *Daily News,* describing the King arrest as a "managed and controlled use of force," and wanted this account to have a wider audience.

In *Official Negligence* I described Koon as a stubborn man and a straight arrow who'd overcome a speech impediment, put himself through college, earned two master's degrees, and succeeded in the profession he had chosen as his life's work. As a police officer, he'd sought demanding assignments and received many commendations. He was a family man, the father of five, and a Roman Catholic. Koon was proud of who he was, perhaps too proud, but also realistic enough to know he would never work again as a police officer no matter how the trial turned out. Testifying gave him the opportunity to tell his story to the world.

Koon was followed on the witness stand by Sergeant Charles Duke of the LAPD, the defense use-of-force expert. He said the LAPD's ban on chokeholds had left officers with few viable options short of deadly force. Duke said it was sometimes necessary "to break a bone" and that every one of the fifty-six baton swings shown on the videotape was justified.

The back-to-back testimony of Koon and Duke, unshaken by cross-examination, filled the defense with confidence and was discouraging to White, who now felt that his only hope for conviction was Laurence Powell. In closing argument on April 22, White zeroed in on Powell, who had testified that King had acted like "an animal" the night of his arrest. Under cross-examination White had prodded Powell to acknowledge that King was human. Mocking Powell, White said to him, "You're not a thug, you're just acting like one."

When the case went to the jury on April 23, there had been a paucity of evidence against Tim Wind, the only one of the four officers who did not testify. I felt certain Wind and Briseno would be acquitted. I was unsure about Koon. If this jury convicts anyone, it probably will be Powell, I told an editor. But I worried that the jury would acquit all of them, causing Los Angeles to blow sky-high.

Was there any way to head off such a calamity or at least inform people it was in the offing? I wasn't sure. I was a faraway journalist not widely read in Los Angeles and realized I could be wrong in my assessment of the case.

But I wanted to do something. While the jury deliberated, I wrote two stories that hinted at impending disaster. The first of these originated with Chief Gates, who sent a video message to every LAPD officer, warning that unnamed community leaders might attempt to create "serious uprisings" if the officers on trial were not convicted. The story ran on April 25 under the headline: "Gates Warns L.A. Police of Possible 'Uprisings.'"

Later, I turned to respected civilian authorities. "Much is at stake for our city, and the longer the jury stays out, the more we tremble," said the Reverend Cecil L. Murray of the First African Methodist Episcopal Church, the oldest Black church in Los Angeles. "The possibility of the verdict being a flash point is very high."

My story said that Murray, working with Mayor Tom Bradley and church and community leaders, had organized a solidarity rally at Murray's church in the heart of South Central Los Angeles for the night of the verdict. This story ran on April 28 under the headline "Bradley, Black Leaders Try to Head Off Violence."

But both Gates and Bradley expected the officers to be convicted. So did Los Angeles city councilman Mark Ridley-Thomas, whose district included the most blighted stretches of South Central. Ridley-Thomas was incensed that Gates had allocated money for police overtime, which proved a sensible precaution, and he denounced the videotaped message the chiefs had sent to officers, saying it had "caused people to be concerned as to whether the department was arming itself" in preparation for a riot. "We should not repeat the errors of the past," Ridley-Thomas said at a news conference. "A massive show of force would be a mistake."

Ridley-Thomas and other Black leaders, except for Murray, were trapped in a historical misperception of their own making. They believed the 1965 Watts riot had been fueled by an excessive police response, which is an oversimplification, and in any case had no bearing on the situation in 1992 when the LAPD had been weakened by internal battles and the attempt to oust Chief Gates. Black leaders, starting with Mayor Bradley, worried about police overreaction, not whether the police would arrive in time and in sufficient numbers to quell a rampage.

On the morning of April 29, the seventh day of deliberations by the sequestered jury, I decided to interview ordinary people in South Central. Cooped up in the courthouse during the trial, I'd had no chance to measure public opinion, as David Broder had taught *Post* reporters to do. So I went door-to-door in Nickerson Gardens, then the largest public housing project west of the Mississippi. It was a troublesome, gang-ridden area on the borderline of Watts that was home to thirty-seven hundred people, 60 percent of whom were Black and most of the others Latino.

I knocked on ten doors, five of which were opened to me, all by Black women. One of the women asked me if I was from the police, and when I said no shut the door. The other four were friendly and answered my questions. All of them knew about Rodney King and the trial of the LAPD officers. They wanted the officers convicted, and one of them said there would be "trouble" if they weren't.

As I was conducting these interviews, I spotted an elderly Black man watching me from across the street. I walked over and introduced myself. He asked when the verdicts would be reached. "Soon, I hope," I said.

The man said it was dangerous for a white man to do interviews in the projects and advised me to leave before the verdicts. I took him seriously and left immediately. After a fast-food lunch, I touched base with my assistant, Leef Smith. She told me someone had called and said verdicts would be announced in the courthouse at 3 p.m. It was Wednesday, April 29. At 1 p.m., Bailey, the jury forewoman, had sent word to Judge Weisberg that the jury had reached ten verdicts and was deadlocked on the remaining charge. Weisberg had agreed beforehand to withhold announcement of verdicts for two hours to give lawyers and their clients time to reach the courtroom. It also gave a two-hour warning to the LAPD that was wasted.

I arrived at the courthouse, which was filling up with reporters, including many who had not covered the trial. There were so many journalists that only eight members of the public were allowed to squeeze into the courtroom, much to the disgust of scores of people who were turned away. The jurors showed no emotion as they filed into the courtroom, but Weisberg's face registered surprise when he saw the verdicts. I saw his look and wondered if he still thought the Simi Valley courthouse was a convenient place to try police officers.

Rodney King's attorney, Steven Lerman, also saw Weisberg's look and was perplexed. "What's he staring at that paper for?" wondered Lerman, who'd assumed the defendants would be convicted.

Some of the defense attorneys had also expected convictions. When John Barnett learned the jury was deadlocked on one charge, he hoped this meant a mistrial for Briseno because he was convinced the other defendants would be found guilty. He could not believe it when the clerk read "not guilty" over and over again. The few members of the public who had been allowed into the courthouse could not believe it either. One of them, John Aguirre, told me he had come to see justice done. He wept as the verdicts were read. Most people in the courtroom were as shocked as Weisberg and Aguirre.

"This is heavy shit," thought Lerman, who would remember deputy district attorney Yochelson approaching him with tears in his eyes. The officers listened stoically until all verdicts were read, then joyously hugged their attorneys. Family members cried tears of happiness and relief. Laurence Powell's sister Leanne, a paralegal who lived with her brother, said it was the first time she had seen him smile since March 3, 1991. The jury acquitted Powell of using excessive force and filing a false police report but deadlocked on another charge of using force under color of authority. This was the cause of the mistrial. Every other officer was acquitted of every charge.

Disbelief was the prominent reaction in the crowded press room. I was surprised so many reporters were surprised. "I was dumbfounded and shocked by the verdicts," said Barbara Murphy of the *Daily News*. "The Black leaders from Los Angeles had warned us, and we hadn't paid any attention to them."

Murphy and a colleague had provided what I believe was the best coverage of the trial. I read them every day. Murphy may have been astonished, but I doubt that readers of her well-written and balanced stories would have been surprised by the acquittals of Wind and Briseno and maybe not of Koon. Powell was another matter. The videotape showed that Powell had hit King on the face with his baton, and undisputed testimony showed that he injured him. It wasn't clear if Powell had acted with malice or was just swinging wildly, but he was a police officer and should have been held responsible for his actions.

As we filed our stories and talked to our editors, legendary Associated Press trial reporter Linda Deutsch entered the press room and announced that disturbances were already beginning in Los Angeles. After filing my story, I told my editors we faced a large-scale riot and needed reporters to cover it. It was an unnecessary request. Karen DeYoung, in charge of the national staff, and executive editor Len Downie had read my stories and memos and arranged for reinforcements even before the verdicts were read.

"Help is on the way," Karen told me.

Before leaving Simi Valley, I interviewed some of the angry people in the parking lot. Don Jones, a retired Black man, had slept in his truck outside the courtroom during the eight-week trial. "I'm dumbstruck," he said. "The video told everything. I could see the video. Ray Charles could see the video."

The crowd was becoming unruly, so I drove back to our office in Century City. Leef greeted me with the news that Pete Wilson had called out the National Guard. I filed a new lede, which led the paper on April 30 under the headline, "National Guard Called to Stem Violence After L.A. Officers' Acquittal in Beating" with a subhead, "Justice Department to Review Case."

I called Mary, who was home in Summerland and had planned to drive to our apartment in Santa Monica if all was well. It wasn't. A curfew was already in place. I didn't tell her about my foray into Nickerson Gardens, but she warned me to be safe and not take chances. I made some phone calls trying to assess the extent of the riot and filed an insert. I was no longer alone. Four other reporters, two in Los Angeles and two in Washington, contributed to the story, as did Leef. I left the office in a darkened building and retrieved my car in the basement parking lot. It was nearly 11 p.m. As I drove west to the apartment along Wilshire Boulevard, I was stopped by a police officer who told me I was out after curfew. I showed him my press pass and explained what I was doing out so late. He thanked me and waved me on. I couldn't help wondering if he would been so courteous if I were Black.

Soon after reaching the apartment, I received a call from Governor Wilson. I had called his office earlier, wanting to know more about why he'd called out the National Guard.[1] Bob White, Wilson's reliable chief of staff, had promised he'd get Wilson back to me. I was so tired I'd forgotten about the request, but White always came through. I'd known Pete since he was a freshman state assemblyman in 1967, and we were on a first-name basis that night. He had flown to Los Angeles after calling out the Guard and sounded exhausted.

The governor apologized for calling hours after my deadline, saying, "It's been a difficult day." "Amen to that," I replied. "It's been a long and difficult day."

1. Wilson was mayor of San Diego when the Watts riot occurred while Governor Pat Brown was out of the country. Lieutenant Governor Glenn Anderson was criticized for being slow to call out the Guard, which Wilson told me he remembered.

30

THE ORDEAL OF LOS ANGELES

On the second day of the riots, I awoke early at the Santa Monica apartment and phoned an acquaintance in Koreatown. In those mostly pre-cell phone days, he returned my call a half-hour later and said he'd been in a firefight with "Black guys" when I phoned him.

"Could I come and see for myself what's happening?" I asked.

"Stay in Santa Monica," he said. "It's not safe in Koreatown."

So instead of going to Koreatown, I went into *The Washington Post* office in Century City, where I was greeted by the amazing sight of a half-dozen reporters whom the editors had flown to Los Angeles. It was the only time we had more reporters than chairs in the bureau, but the chairs weren't really needed because the reporters were soon out in the city covering the ongoing riot.

In addition to these reinforcements from afar, we also had the contributions of my office assistant, Leef Smith, now a special correspondent and finally getting deserved credit from the editors. We shared three bylines that week on major stories of the riots.

One of the newcomers was Paul Taylor, a cheerful and socially conscious reporter who in the week to come would share with me the duties of writing the lead story of the riot. According to an adage of the news business, if you scratch a reporter, you'll find a reformer, and that description fits Paul perfectly. After working fourteen years for *The Post* and serving as the paper's bureau chief in South Africa during that country's transition from apartheid to democracy, Paul would leave the news business to pursue good causes such as election reform.

All of us, newcomers and the home team alike, had our work cut out for us during the six days following the acquittals of the LAPD officers who had beaten Rodney King. It was a week of death and destruction as rioters, mostly Black, responded ferociously to the verdicts. It was a week of burning, as stores and public places and homes were torched, and the Los Angeles Fire Department stopped responding to alarms because firefighters were becoming targets of the rioters. It was a week of looting, as people of all races and ethnicities emptied stores no longer protected by the police. Most of all, it was a week in which the vaunted LAPD gave up on the city it was pledged to serve and protect.

While Los Angeles was at war with itself, communications between civilian authorities and the police broke down, largely because Mayor Tom Bradley and Police Chief Daryl Gates were not on speaking terms. Bradley poured gas on the flames with a fiery televised denunciation of the "senseless" verdicts.[1] Gates shockingly abandoned his post to speak at a fundraiser opposed to a ballot measure that would allow future city mayors to appoint future police chiefs.

Our day-by-day reporting of events ratified Phil Graham's insight about journalism being the first rough draft of history. We capably wrote what we witnessed or were told, but often didn't know the story behind the story. We could see, for instance, that no police were present at the intersection of Florence and Normandie avenues, where a white truck driver was dragged from his vehicle and savagely beaten, but we didn't know why the LAPD was missing in action. One of my main motivations for writing *Official Negligence* was to explain the reasons for the LAPD breakdown. My analysis would be based on multiple interviews and the 222-page report of a commission headed by former federal judge and former FBI director William H. Webster that investigated the "civil disorder in Los Angeles."

The worst violence occurred in the first hours after the verdicts before our larger reporting team was on hand. Seven Los Angeles television stations sent news-gathering helicopters over South Central to see what was happening in the wake of the Simi Valley verdicts. In the

1. "The jury's verdict will never blind the world to what we saw on the videotape," Bradley said. The mayor concluded with a plea for calm, which often pops up first in an internet search of his remarks. But at the time, it was Bradley's fervent denunciation of the verdicts that caught public attention and in the view of his critics stirred passions on the street.

late afternoon of Wednesday, April 29, Leef and I joined thousands of television viewers in watching the horrific events at Florence and Normandie as they unfolded. I felt helpless, as I'm sure did many viewers. Innocent people were being savaged before our eyes, and we could do nothing about it.

The area was under jurisdiction of the LAPD's gritty Seventy-Seventh Street Division, which patrolled twelve square miles awash in poverty, drugs, and violence. It had the city's highest murder rate. "Working 77th" was a badge of honor within the department and often a path to advancement, so the division attracted committed officers. One of these was Lieutenant Michael Moulin, the watch commander on the afternoon of the verdicts, which he viewed from the squad room as they were announced on television. Moulin was an emotional white man of progressive views who was convinced the police officers tried in Simi Valley had used excessive force. When other officers in the Seventy-Seventh cheered as the verdicts were read, Moulin was disgusted.

"White officers were prancing around like someone just had a baby," Moulin said when I interviewed him in 1994. "Frankly, I was disappointed. I thought the criminal justice system had failed the people of Los Angeles."

While Moulin and the officers under his command disagreed on the merit of the verdicts, all of them realized they spelled trouble for the city. That morning the Seventy-Seventh station had received a series of anonymous telephone calls threatening violence. One call seemed particularly ominous to Sergeant Charlie Strong, the assistant watch commander.

"I'm a member of the Eight Tray Gangster Crips, and come this weekend you'll know who we are," the caller said.

The first rocks were thrown when five young Black males made a beer run to the Pay-less Liquor and Deli at Florence and Dalton avenues, a Korean-owned store three blocks west of Normandie known in the neighborhood as "Mr. Lee's." Their beverage of choice was Olde English 800, the malt liquor consumed in quantity by Rodney King before his fateful drive nearly fourteen months earlier. At the store each youth scooped up four or five bottles of the malt liquor and walked toward the entrance, where their path was blocked by David Lee, son of the owner. One of the youths struck Lee on the head with a bottle, and two others hurled bottles at the glass door of the store, shattering it.

"This is for Rodney King!" one of them yelled. From behind a bulletproof counter, Lee's father, Samuel, pushed a silent alarm button that alerted the Seventy-Seventh Street Station of the robbery. It was 4:17 p.m., and one of the deadliest urban riots in the nation's history had begun.

The neighborhood where the riot began was in the relatively safe western side of South Central. I'd done occasional interviews in the area and driven through it en route to Los Angeles Lakers basketball games at the Forum in Inglewood. The crime rate in the Florence-Normandie census tract of 10,000 people was only slightly above the city average and far below the crime rate for South Central as a whole. Nine percent of the residents of Florence-Normandie and neighboring Hyde Park were on public assistance compared to nearly 25 percent of the 672,000 residents of South Central.

But the disorders that erupted in Los Angeles on April 29 had more to do with racial attitudes than with the economy or the crime rate in the neighborhood where they began. Viewed in their totality, the riots had multiple causes. Poverty and social instability would contribute to violence and looting as the disorders spread through South Central and beyond. The extent and ferocity of the riots would prompt some sociologists to describe them as an "uprising" or a "rebellion" against harsh economic conditions and social oppression. Police analysts emphasized the role of organized gangs, noting that the five youths involved in the original attack on Mr. Lee's were gang associates. In their origins, however, the riots were neither a gang conspiracy nor a revolt against bleak economic conditions. They were a cry of Black rage. The riots were "for Rodney King," as the youth said when he hurled the bottle of malt liquor at the door of Mr. Lee's. And they were for Latasha Harlins, whose name was invoked by demonstrators on Florence Avenue and during the systematic destruction of Korean-owned stores throughout the riots.

Latasha was a fifteen-year-old Black girl who walked into a Korean-owned convenience store to buy a $1.79 bottle of orange juice. Approaching the counter with money in hand, she was accosted rudely by Soon Ja Du, forty-nine-year-old female clerk whose family owned the business. Du accused the girl of trying to steal the juice and grabbed her backpack. Latasha responded by punching Du, who pulled out a pistol and shot the teenager in the back of the head as she headed out of the store. Convicted of the killing, Du was inexplicably given probation by Superior Court Judge Joyce Karlin, who was trying her first criminal case. At the sentencing four months before the Simi Valley verdicts, Judge Karlin expressed little solicitude for the victim, but great concern for what would happen to Du in prison.

In the hour after Samuel Lee pushed the button signaling a robbery, the Seventy-Seventh Street Station was flooded with calls for help. A hundred yards away from Mr. Lee's at the corner of Florence and Halldale, police respondents found a young Black man with a goatee and shaved head swinging a silver-and-black aluminum bat at the windshield of a Cadillac with two white men inside. Black youths were cheering the bat wielder, who ran up an alley pursued by officer John Ayala and his partner. The chase ended at an apartment complex known as a hangout of the Eight Tray Gangster Crips, where Ayala arrested the bat wielder in front of a growing crowd.

Four LAPD sergeants from the Seventy-Seventh were present. Sergeant Tom Tavares would remember the crowd as fairly quiet until a television news crew arrived, and the crowd began chanting, "Rodney King, Rodney King, Rodney King." Sergeant Don Schwartzer noticed a mood change in the crowd.

"It was the first call after the verdicts," he said. "We were the friendly neighborhood cops one minute, the next minute we were lunchmeat. It didn't take a genius to figure out we needed to do something. . . . We needed to get out of there."

The sense of urgency felt by officers of the Seventy-Seventh Division was absent at police headquarters at Parker Center. Chief Gates activated the Emergency Operations Center in the subbasement of City Hall East across the street from Parker Center at 3:55 p.m., but this was an empty formality. "In fact, all that appears to have happened was the doors were opened, the lights turned on and the coffee pot plugged in," according to the Webster report. Members of the EOC staff went off shift at their regular 4 p.m. time and were not called back until several hours later. "In the meantime, the EOC was an almost empty room," the report said.

Chief Gates was a mental captive of the Watts riot of 1965, when he was a police captain. In that disorder, begun by a traffic arrest gone awry, rioters were active at night and quiescent during the day. Gates's belief that any future riot would follow the same pattern permeated the LAPD leadership. When Lieutenant Michael Hillmann asked permission a week before the 1992 riots to deploy the LAPD's elite Metro Unit during daytime hours, he was told by Deputy Chief Ronald Frankle, "Riots don't happen during the daytime."

The sun did not set until 7:36 p.m. on that first day of the 1992 Los Angeles riot, and Gates and his deputies were sanguine. At 5:38 p.m., about the time officer Ayala and his partner were depositing the bat-wielding youth they had arrested for vandalism at the Seventy-Seventh Street Station, Gates made an optimistic statement to reporters in Parker Center Auditorium. "If we have disturbances, we are prepared," he said.

Meanwhile, two police cars with four officers inside arrived late at Florence and Normandie in response to Ayala's call for help. Their patrol cars were showered by rocks and bottles thrown by roving bands of youths. Officer Phyllis D'Elia, driving the lead car, tried desperately to make the traffic light at the Florence-Normandie intersection but was blocked by a truck. Officer Timothy McGrath, driving the second car, put out a radio call for help at 5:34 p.m. McGrath, a Black man who had grown up in South Central, was considered an expert on the Eight Tray Gangster Crips. With his patrol car stopped behind D'Elia's car, McGrath spotted a youth approaching with brick-sized stones in both hands. He jumped out of the car and drew his gun. McGrath recognized the youth as Seandel Daniels, a sixteen-year-old gang associate.

Daniels cocked an arm, and McGrath commanded, "Don't do it. Drop the rocks." Daniels looked at McGrath's gun, dropped the rocks and fled. Within five minutes, more than eighteen patrol cars and more than thirty police officers had reached the scene in response to McGrath's call for assistance.

One of the first to arrive was Sergeant Sam Arase, a beefy LAPD veteran. When Daniels reappeared with more rocks, Arase, who is Asian, recognized him as one of the youths who had been throwing rocks at the patrol cars. "We're not going to tolerate that," Arase said. "He's mine." Arase and other officers chased Daniels up an alley between Seventy-First Street and Normandie, northwest of its intersection with Florence. They grabbed him as he climbed a chain-link fence and handcuffed him in a yard.

As Arase turned toward the crowd with the handcuffed Daniels alongside, it seemed to him that there were "millions of people, not only on the sidewalk but in the middle of the street."

As the crowd swelled, it grew in confidence. Police felt under pressure. Officer Perry Alvarez would remember the scene as one of "chaos, constant chaos, with bottles flying everywhere and people yelling 'Fuck the police!'"

Some three dozen officers were outnumbered by a crowd of about two hundred people. Officers formed a loose skirmish line around their cars facing west against the eastbound crowd as people poured in near the Florence-Normandie intersection. Sergeant Tom Tavares, supervising deployment of the skirmish line, was cognizant of a growing crowd to his rear. Bart Bartholomew, a *New York Times* photographer coolly photographing the scene, heard someone say, "Cops going to die tonight."

Lieutenant Moulin, the ranking officer, drove to the scene from the station. He would never forget what he saw. "I found utter chaos, an intersection that was uncontrollable," Moulin told me. "The officers were being subjected to bricks, to huge pieces of concrete, to boards, to flying objects."

Moulin knew the officers were ill-equipped for the situation they faced. "Most of the policemen had no helmets. They had no bulletproof vests, no tear gas, no face shields. . . . I think we're going to have to use deadly force; we could have a massacre here. So I ordered a pullout." Moulin sounded the order to retreat at 5:43 p.m. over a squad-car public address system and repeated it two minutes later. "I want everybody out of the area of Florence and Normandie," Moulin said.

Not every officer at the scene agreed with Moulin, but all of them obeyed his order. The police departed so quickly that Officer D'Elia, first on the scene when she was unable to make the traffic light at Florence and Normandie, was almost left behind. Transfixed by the crowd, she stood momentarily alone as other officers left and her partner, already in their car, beckoned her to join him. D'Elia finally fled, and Bartholomew shot a picture of her running to the patrol car.

"The crowd was very empowered by this," Bartholomew said. "It was clearly a victory for them."

This account is drawn from *Official Negligence* based on my interviews and the Webster commission report. When we filed our story the first night of the riots, Leef and I did not know about the LAPD pullout from the Florence-Normandie area. All we knew was that the police weren't there. Thanks to the TV news helicopters that hovered about

Florence and Normandie after the police retreat, the world saw what happened next.

At 6:43 p.m., an hour after Lieutenant Moulin ordered the police pullback, a white man driving for a Black-owned company entered the intersection in a white delivery truck filled with medical equipment destined for Chile. Larry Tarvin, the fifty-two-year-old driver, was unaware of the Simi Valley verdicts because his truck had no radio. He did not realize that anything was wrong until he saw a man jumping on two cars at the southwest corner of Florence and Normandie. Too late, Tarvin tried to turn back. Before he could do so, Henry Keith (Kiki) Watson pulled Tarvin from his truck and hurled him to the ground as if he were a rag doll. The muscular Watson was six feet one and weighed 215 pounds while Tarvin stood five seven and weighed 130 pounds. Other youths joined in beating Tarvin. One of the first blows knocked off Tarvin's eyeglasses, and he was hit every time he reached for them. An onlooker said, "Now you know how Rodney King felt, white boy."

Reginald Oliver Denny had loaded his red eighteen-wheel truck with twenty-seven tons of sand at an Azusa quarry at 5:39 p.m., as Gates was assuring reporters at Parker Center that the LAPD was prepared to cope with any disturbance. Denny was thirty-six years old, slight of build and mild-mannered. He deplored violence and rarely listened to the news. He was listening to country music when he left the Santa Monica freeway and took a familiar shortcut across Florence Avenue to a plant in Inglewood.

Denny entered the Normandie intersection at 6:46 p.m., a minute after a bystander had helped the battered Tarvin drive away in his looted truck. Denny had not seen what happened to Tarvin, but he noticed from his cab's high vantage point that people were taking items from a truck in front of him. Briefly, he considered making a U-turn but abandoned that idea because his truck lacked power steering. Since he knew his cargo was of no value to looters, Denny reasoned he could "tiptoe across this intersection and get on down the road." But then he heard people shouting at him to stop. Rocks flew though his truck window. Denny would not remember the events that followed the volley of rocks, but they formed a tableau of brutality that much of America would find hard to forget.

As Denny's truck slowly entered the intersection, Antoine Miller yanked open the door of the cab, allowing others to pull Denny onto the street. Henry Watson held Denny's head down with his foot. Another man kicked Denny in the belly. A man in a Malcolm X shirt hurled a five-pound piece of medical equipment taken from Tarvin's truck at Denny's head and hit him three times with a claw hammer. The most damaging blow was administered by Damian Williams, known as "Football," who at point-blank range hurled a slab of concrete at Denny's head. It struck Denny on the right temple and knocked him unconscious. Williams did a victory dance over the hapless man, imitating a football receiver who had caught a touchdown pass. He then flashed the sign of the Eight Tray Gangster Crips and gleefully pointed out Denny's crumpled figure to the helicopter pilots. Gang member Anthony Brown spit on Denny and walked away with Williams, leaving the trucker bleeding and unconscious in the street.

Various men then approached the fallen Denny, hurling liquor bottles at him. Gary Williams strolled over from a nearby gas station and rifled Denny's pockets, holding a liquor bottle in his free hand. As Denny lay unconscious, Lance Parker passed by on a motorcycle and stopped. Parker, a process server for a law firm, took a shotgun from his gym bag and fired a shot at the gas tank of the truck. He missed, which probably spared Denny from being incinerated.

The Denny beating was the most appalling television image of the Los Angeles riots. It would be shown repeatedly during and after the disorders, frequently in tandem with clips of the Rodney King beating. This suggested a false equivalency between the two events, often voiced explicitly by commentators. But the King incident should not be equated with the conduct of Denny's assailants. King had ignored police commands after a high-speed chase and had charged in the direction of Officer Laurence Powell. While the police arguably misjudged the threat King posed, Sergeant Koon had tried to take him into custody without hurting him before the first baton blow was struck. Damian Williams and his fellow gangsters had the unresisting Denny totally in their power and inflicted far graver injuries than the officers did to King. Denny had done nothing to provoke the attack. His only transgressions were to be on the wrong street at the wrong time and to be white.

Denny was rescued from death by four Black people, one of them a woman, who had been watching on television as he was dragged from his truck and beaten. As Titus Murphy, an unemployed aerospace engineer, remembered it, the four friends said to one another: "Somebody's got to get that guy out of there." They decided to do it themselves. They piled into a car and in less than fifteen minutes reached the Florence-Normandie intersection. One of the group was Bobby Green, a trucker with the special license required to drive Denny's truck. With his friends driving ahead of him, Green steered the truck to Daniel Freeman Memorial Hospital three miles away. Denny then had a seizure, and Green thought he was going to die. But paramedics and five doctors, two of them Black, brought Denny back from the brink. The doctors credited the quick action of Green and his friends with saving Denny's life.

Denny's skull was fractured in ninety-one places and pieces of it pushed into his brain. His left eye was so badly dislocated that it would have collapsed into his sinus cavity had not surgeons been able to replace a crushed bone with a piece of plastic. A permanent crater remained in Denny's face after three operations. Tarvin's injuries were less serious but significant. He suffered a cracked pelvis, fractured ribs, a broken nose, and permanent facial scars. In *Official Negligence* I gave brief accounts of seven others who were assaulted at or near Florence-Normandie while Williams and his fellow members of the Eight Tray Gangster Crips were in control. All of those victims were Asian or Latino, and all of the attackers—as well as all the rescuers—were Black. One of the good Samaritans was John Mitchell, a *Los Angeles Times* reporter who helped a victim named Tam Tram after the thirty-four-year-old Vietnamese woman was robbed and hit in the head with a piece of concrete.

The most heroic rescue of the day was performed by Bennie Newton, an ex-convict who ran an inner-city ministry. Newton saw Damian Williams and his cohorts assaulting Fidel Lopez, who was beaten senseless. Williams pulled down the pants of the bleeding man and sprayed black paint on his genitals and body. A voice on an amateur videotape of the assault can be heard saying, "He's black now." As the crowd closed in on Lopez, Newton, with Bible in hand, threw himself over Lopez's body. "Kill him, and you have to kill me, too," he said. The mob backed off. Newton drove Lopez to the hospital and later started a fundraising drive in his church for the badly injured man.

Florence and Normandie was the flashpoint of the riots. The retreat of the police from the area and the subsequent televised violence doomed any chance the LAPD had of maintaining order. One of the few issues on which Chief Gates and the Webster commission agree is that Lieutenant Moulin should have regrouped and returned to Florence-Normandie.

"The lieutenant rightfully pulled the people out, but he should have formed up in squads and gone back in," Gates told me in a post-riot interview. The Webster report said that Moulin's failure to do so was a "critical error."

No one perceived the police failure more keenly than the pilots of the seven news helicopters hovering over Florence and Normandie. They asked an observer in the police helicopter why the LAPD was ignoring calls for help and received the unsatisfactory answer that there were insufficient officers on hand to maintain crowd control. Gang members emboldened by the absence of the police were as puzzled as the pilots at what was happening. Afterwards, several gang members told Lieutenant Bruce Haggerty, head of detectives at the Seventy-Seventh, that there would have been a fight if the police had returned but that the gangs would have backed down. The Webster commission concluded that the police "failure to respond aggressively and in force appears to have been a significant tactical mistake."

It was more than that. The televised images of violence at Florence and Normandie fanned the spread of the riots by advertising to criminals that the LAPD would not stand in their way. Describing the Denny beating, Ted Koppel said: "It is television at its most riveting and horrifying. But live TV also becomes the carrier of a virus. At one and the same time, television conveys the fever of street violence and the impotence of the police."

I don't blame the television stations or the helicopter pilots for that. If the LAPD had been deployed at Florence and Normandie, the aerial reports would have shown the police in control of the intersection and sent the opposite message to would-be criminals.

Bob Tur, a legendary pioneer of helicopter-based traffic reports in Southern California, was an observer in a five-member helicopter crew providing commentary for television station KCOP and radio station KNX that day. Tur's wife, Marika, was shooting the videotape that would provide the most comprehensive record of the violence at Florence and Normandie and that would later surface in the trials of Damian Williams and other gang members. Bob Tur's vivid commentary warned drivers to shun the area.

"This is attempted murder," Tur said as he watched the Denny beating. "Tell LAPD to shut Florence Boulevard down, and Normandie."

Tur was spot on. Parker Center and the Emergency Operations Center across the street knew of Moulin's withdrawal from Florence and Normandie. As the Webster report later observed, the LAPD should have sent police cars to seal freeway exits and kept people away from the deadly intersection.

Webster's report stirred terrible memories among those of us who'd watched the horrifying video of the Denny beating. I remember thinking, "Where are the police?"

In truth I knew the answer to my unspoken question. As the sun set on bloody Los Angeles the night of April 29, 1992, the LAPD was a rudderless police force no longer protecting civilians. Beset by command problems and faulty communications, the LAPD was trying to get its act together in the absence of its chief.

31

"WHERE WERE YOU WHEN WE NEEDED YOU?"

The riots barreled beyond the hundred and five square miles of South Central into Westlake, Pico-Union, Echo Park, Hancock Park, Fairfax, and the mid-Wilshire area. By the second day, looting and fires reached Hollywood Boulevard and the independent cities of Carson, Compton, Gardena, Hawthorne, Huntington Beach, Inglewood, Long Beach, Lynwood, South Gate, and Walnut Park.

This is the top of our story in *The Washington Post* on May 1, 1992, under a dual byline of Lou Cannon and Leef Smith. Casualty figures, which would become much larger, are omitted:

> The nation's second largest city became a war zone tonight, with thousands of National Guard troops and police deployed in riot gear to stop the spread of looting and destruction.
>
> A pall of acrid smoke from hundreds of fires hung over the Los Angeles basin, closing all but one runway at Los Angeles International Airport. Freeways came to a standstill as thousands of frightened residents fled their vast and burning city.
>
> More than 1,700 firefighters battled the stubborn blazes. As night fell, at least 35 fires sent towering smoke into the air in a scene reminiscent of Kuwait's burning oil fields after the Iraqi invasion.
>
> Mayor Tom Bradley declared a dusk-to-dawn curfew for the entire city and said lawbreakers would be arrested and punished. Groceries, drug stores and other businesses were looted and burned. Factories, civic buildings, schools and libraries were closed. Sports

events were canceled or postponed. Sale of ammunition was banned, and gasoline sales were restricted. Postal service was canceled from 10 post offices in 14 zip codes.

"We cannot and will not tolerate any violence as a means to express anger," Bradley said.

Deep in the story we reported that National Guard deployment was slow because many of the troops lacked ammunition for their rifles.

Our story also reported that, in Washington, Attorney General William Barr said the Justice Department would pursue a civil rights investigation of the four LAPD officers whose acquittals had triggered the riots. Barr said it was "important for people to understand that the verdicts on state charges are not the end of the process." The promise to pursue civil rights violations was reiterated by President George H. W. Bush when he toured shattered areas of Los Angeles a week later. Taken together, these statements guaranteed further prosecutions.

Rodney King was dismayed by the acquittal of the officers who had abused him. He watched the verdicts on television in Studio City with bodyguard Tom Owens, who'd become his friend. "King's reaction was one of pure disbelief," Owens told me. "It took him a while to comprehend what had occurred. He sat absolutely motionless throughout the entire reading . . . of the verdicts."

Then King picked up a roller device he used on his right cheek, where he had suffered nerve damage from the beating. He began to move it, slowly at first, then faster, "literally gouging his face with the roller in very short, very forceful strokes."

Distressed as he was by the verdicts, King was deeply troubled that innocent people were being hurt in his name. When King watched the horrific scene at Florence and Normandie, he told his lawyer, Steve Lerman, that he wanted to speak out against violence. Lerman was concerned about putting King before cameras, but King was insistent and his attorney arranged a supervised appearance the next day. Before introducing him, Lerman told reporters that King would not take questions because anything he said might impact his pending civil suit against the acquitted officers and the LAPD.

Paul Taylor and I described King's appearance in our story, saying "he faced the nation on live television, looking uncomfortable amidst the jostling reporters, cameras and enough microphones for a head of state."

"I just want to say, you know, can we all get along?" King said haltingly. "Can we get along? Can we stop making it, making it horrible for the older people and the kids? . . . It's just not right. It's not right. It's not, it's not going to change anything. We'll, we'll get our justice. . . . Please, we can get along here. We all can get along. I mean, we're all stuck here for a while. Let's try to work it out. Let's try to beat it. Let's try to beat it. Let's try to work it out."

And then he was done, whisked away by his lawyer and his bodyguard. King's rhetorical question—"Can we all get along?"—that rioters were answering in the negative would make the history books. But I was also fascinated by "We're all stuck here for a while." It was the way Rodney King looked at the world.

On the day King spoke, President Bush dispatched four thousand Army troops and Marines to Los Angeles along with one thousand riot-trained federal law officers. When added to the six thousand members of the National Guard sent by Governor Wilson and the hundreds of police officers from the LAPD, the Los Angeles County sheriff's office and various cities within the county, they comprised a formidable force that crushed the riot.

On May 4, with calm prevailing, the dusk-to-dawn curfew Mayor Bradley had imposed on the city was lifted, and businesses and schools reopened. Sporadic violence continued, but the mayhem was basically over, leaving behind a city that was physically and emotionally shattered.

The data are staggering. More than 50 people had been killed, 2,383 injured, some grievously, and 12,000 arrested. More than eleven hundred buildings had been destroyed or badly damaged; property loss was estimated at $1 billion.

Mobs had burned and ransacked at will during the riots but were especially destructive in attacking Korean-owned stores, which were destroyed with a systematic ferocity reminiscent of attacks on Jewish-owned stores in Nazi Germany. Black ownership, when the rioters were aware of it, did not necessarily protect a store from looting but often saved it from arson. Korean-owned stores were burned to the ground. While this was in part a legacy of the Latasha Harlins affair, it is likely that Korean-owned stores, many of them isolated from other businesses or concentrated in distinctive pastel-colored strip malls, would have been singled out anyway, given the combustible mix of racial and cultural misunderstanding between African Americans and Korean Americans.

Koreatown, on the fringes of mid-Wilshire, was different. Korean shopkeepers there were less isolated, more numerous, and well-armed. They also had a leader in the form of Richard Rhee, who had come to Los Angeles in 1957 with memories of boyhood hardships in the Korean War and turned a discarded Mayfair market at the corner of Fifth Street and Western Avenue into the California Market, then a premium source of Asian delicacies. Rhee owned fourteen commercial and residential properties throughout Southern California, but the California Market was his jewel, and he was prepared to defend it with his life, if necessary.

After watching the Denny beating on CNN, Rhee summoned his security chief and told him to round up reinforcements. By nightfall, Rhee had posted guards with loaded guns on the market roof, where they could see smoke rising from the fires in South Central. By the time the mob reached Koreatown the next day, Rhee had assembled twenty armed men in the parking lot of the California Market, where they barricaded behind an assortment of trucks and luxury cars. Most had rifles, one a machine gun. The mob, shouting obscenities and threats, moved in after nightfall. The Koreans fired shots in the air, then shots at the feet of the first rank of looters. Breaking ranks, the looters fled. Rhee told me afterward that he thought the machine gun had made an impression. Perhaps, but there is no doubt in my mind that the Koreans were prepared to shoot to kill if the looters had continued their advance.

About the same time the Koreans were making their stand at California Market, Jay Rhee (no relation) and two employees used similar tactics with much less firepower to repel a large crowd at a mini-mall at Santa Monica and Vermont. The looters retreated when a police car drove by, then advanced when it was gone. Rhee and his employees fired five hundred rounds into the air and saved the mini-mall and became disillusioned with law enforcement.

"We have lost our faith in the police," he told the *Los Angeles Times*. "Where were you when we needed you?"

Where were you when we needed you? That was the fundamental question about the LAPD's performance in the riots. Beginning with Chief Parker, the department had created a *Dragnet*-enhanced image of a police force that responded immediately and efficiently to serious crime. It wasn't the kindest and gentlest police force in the nation. But those who ran the LAPD believed it to be the best police force in America, as Gates had said when he watched the video of the Rodney King beating in dismay. What remained of that image went up in the smoke of a thousand burning buildings in Los Angeles.

The LAPD's sorry performance in the riots resulted from a leadership breakdown. Many individual LAPD officers behaved heroically even after their leaders ordered retreat. As an example, officers Lisa Phillips and Daniel Nee were in their patrol car shortly after Lieutenant Michael Moulin ordered the retreat from Florence and Normandie when they heard a dispatcher broadcast an "ADW" (assault with a deadly weapon) in progress. The dispatcher said that "fifty male Blacks [were] throwing rocks at a gray vehicle with a female locked inside."

Moulin came on the air, ordering all Seventy-Seventh Division officers to a command post, saying he didn't want anyone "chasing rocks." But Moulin was not as oblivious to the plight of trapped civilians as his detractors would claim. Three minutes later he was back on the air declaring that the situation was a Code 3 (emergency) call to which any available officer should respond.

Nee and Phillips were young and idealistic officers who answered the Code 3 courageously. Two miles away when they heard the radio call about the trapped woman, they twice called for a police helicopter to fly over and assess the situation. When none was available, they drove back through the intersection of Florence and Normandie while being bombarded with rocks and bottles that broke windows on their patrol car. Ahead of them, one car crashed and another rolled down the street on fire before striking a telephone pole.

"Hordes of people yelling, screaming and throwing huge forty-ounce liquor bottles and beer bottles," Phillips said afterward. "Just crazy. It looked like pictures on the news of Beirut."

As a crowd surrounded their car, Phillips radioed their position and asked for help that did not come. "We were scared to death, very, very scared," she told me later.

The two officers quickly devised a plan. Nee would get the stranded woman out of the car while Phillips covered him. Phillips jumped out of the passenger side of their police car with gun drawn, yelling at the crowd to get back. As Nee turned toward the police car, he was struck in the back of the head with rocks and bottles. He fell, still holding the woman.

"I can remember when Dan hit the ground, the crowd started laughing," Phillips said. "And I'll never forget that.... I thought 'animals.'... I just couldn't think humankind had sunk to such depths. This woman was destroyed, she was a total bloody mess, limp, we thought she was dead already."

Nee regained his feet with the help of Phillips. He put the unconscious woman in the back seat of the police car, which was covered with glass from the broken windows. Phillips, her weapon drawn again, covered him. As they pulled away, a brick smashed through the back window, spraying more glass inside. To Phillips the rescue seemed to take forever, but the entire incident lasted forty seconds.

The officers had rescued Soon Oh, a Korean American who lived in the Wilshire District. Nee and Phillips took her to Daniel Freeman Hospital, the same hospital to which Reginald Denny would be taken, and stayed with her until she was revived. Phillips then called Oh's daughter and told her that her mother had been involved in a car accident and was safe. They also told her not to come to the hospital.

Phillips was interviewed for *Official Negligence* by Jaxon van Derbeken, a top-notch police reporter then with the *Daily News* who helped me gather information for my book. I was also impressed with Lisa Phillips, whom I met several years later when we were both on a television program reprising the lessons of the riots.

The rank-and-file officers whom Jaxon and I interviewed were unanimous in believing the LAPD could and should have done much more than their leaders allowed them to do. "There's no doubt in my mind that we could have saved the city," said Greg Baltad, a member of the LAPD's elite Metro Unit. Baltad, who had once served in the Seventy-Seventh Street Division.

Whether or not the entire city could have been saved is an open question, but great parts of it could have been protected—and lives spared—if the LAPD had followed its proactive doctrine. In retrospect, Daryl Gates also concluded that a more militant police response would have saved lives and property. As chief, Gates was blamed for the tentative police response. He is not blameless, but it took a village of hesitant police officials and fearful civilian authorities to immobilize the LAPD.

In terms of police preparedness, the riots occurred at the worst possible time. Gates was retiring in June, and his subordinates were consumed by a succession struggle. Seven top LAPD officers sought to succeed Gates, and none of them wanted to ruffle political feathers with riot preparation. The Webster report found that nearly a year of succession maneuvering had "seriously impaired" working relationships within the department.

It didn't help that Bradley and Gates were not on speaking terms. For all their faults, they were proud and honorable public men who believed in Los Angeles. Because they weren't talking, Bradley didn't know that Gates had tired of their mutual hostility and was ready to bury the hatchet. At least that's what Gates told me when I interviewed him on February 4, 1994. That's a self-serving recollection to be sure, but the evidence for it is that the two men quickly put aside their long-standing feud once the riot was joined. On the morning of the second day of the riots, Gates went to City Hall to brief Bradley, and the mayor and the chief treated each other with respect. When Gates learned later in the day that his adult son Scott was hospitalized because of a drug overdose, he confided in Bradley and left for the hospital. The mayor told no one that the chief again was away from his post, this time for good reason. Scott recovered after two days on the critical list, and Gates thanked Bradley for his understanding.

By this second day, too late, Gates had resumed leadership of the LAPD. On this day, Assistant Chief Robert Vernon left town on vacation time he'd accumulated in advance of his retirement. David Dotson, the other assistant chief, had been kept out of the loop since testifying against Gates before the Christopher commission. Dotson went home at the end of his shift on the first day of the riots as if it were an ordinary workday. Think of that: As Reginald Denny and others were being savaged at Florence and Normandie, the chief is being driven to a political fundraiser, one assistant chief is preparing for his vacation, and the other is home for the night.

So why did Gates and Bradley, intelligent men with mostly capable subordinates, so badly misjudge the situation? The persuasive answer is that the chief and the mayor and their aides assumed that the graphic videotape of the Rodney King beating assured conviction of at least some of the police officers who had abused him. This misconception was contradicted by the track record of Ventura County juries in cases involving police officers, but it was more powerful than any fact. This misconception undermined the police.

"If we were not prepared for any one thing, we were not prepared for four not-guilty verdicts, LAPD Commander Bayan Lewis told Jaxon Van Derbeken. "We did not prepare for a worst-case scenario."

This complacency filtered downward through the ranks. "Preparedness also involves mental readiness," observed a post-riot LAPD internal review. Because police and civilian authorities had not anticipated acquittals, they were physically and mentally unprepared for the cataclysm that befell Los Angeles.

We didn't know much of this background during riot week in our expanded Los Angeles bureau of *The Washington Post.* The story behind the story would gradually emerge in interviews, reports, investigations, and my book *Official Negligence.* But we did know that the police, civilian leaders, and much of the media had misjudged the explosive situation in South Central Los Angeles. We also knew that the poorer sections of Los Angeles were hurting in the wake of the riots. We wrote what we knew.

One compelling story was written by Ruben Castaneda and Paul Taylor and headlined "L.A. Residents Face Grim Reality of Devastation." Residents in South Central and elsewhere, many lacking a car, had lost the supermarkets at which they shopped to arson and looting.

"Hundreds of other businesses that people relied on in their daily lives—clothing stores, drug stores, discount variety outlets, dry cleaning establishments—were also leveled," the story said. Much of this story was told from the perspective of Marias Posadas, a Guatemalan immigrant, and Linda Nguyen, a Vietnamese immigrant who'd worked in the beauty shop of a mini-mall that had been destroyed. "I feel sad," Nguyen said. "No work. No job. No money. No more market. No more everything."

My May 3 lead story summarized the situation: "A jittery calm, enforced by police and National Guard patrols, returned to this riot-devastated city today as thousands of citizens armed with brooms and shovels began cleaning up the charred ruins of a vast area of south-central Los Angeles."

The following day, under a headline of "Quiet Los Angeles Ends Curfew Today," Paul Taylor and I wrote:

> LOS ANGELES—After three days of terror and a weekend of eerie quiet, the City of Angels anticipated a dose of normalcy Monday when schools are to reopen, a dusk-to-dawn curfew is to be lifted and bus service, most electricity and freeway access are expected to be restored in areas most savaged by the deadliest civil disorder in the nation's modern history.
>
> A massive riot-control force of 22,000 people—police, highway patrol, National Guard, Army, Marines and riot-trained FBI, Border Patrol and Alcohol, Tobacco and Firearms agents—is expected to remain in place at least through midweek, Mayor Tom Bradley announced today.

On May 10, I wrote a story headlined "When Thin Blue Line Retreated, L.A. Riot Went Out of Control." I quoted Chief Gates as saying that a tactical alert putting the LAPD on emergency footing should have been declared sooner than it was. The story also quoted an unnamed officer from the Seventy-Seventh Street Division who'd participated in the retreat from the Florence-Normandie area ordered by Lieutenant Moulin. "We thought we were beating a tactical retreat and would return in force," the officer said. "We didn't know we were abandoning the community."

My editors encouraged me to write a story exploring the fragilities of Los Angeles that might explain why the city was ripe for a riot. My story ran on Sunday, May 10, under the headline "Another Culprit: Weak Government in Los Angeles." Here is the lede:

"Amid the ruins in this land of make-believe, southern Californians are being soothed with scapegoats instead of given reasons for the riots that have forever changed their lives."

After relating how police and civilian authorities blamed one other for the riots while ideologues fell back on bromidic explanations—"permissiveness" for conservatives, "neglect" for liberals—I wrote:

> But the orgy of fault-finding has largely spared the general public or a diffused political system that perfectly mirrors a lifestyle in which personal mobility and individual freedom are the most enduring values. The freeways that crisscross this 500-square-mile city are masterpieces of engineering and vital symbols of this lifestyle. They enable

millions of southern Californians to commute an average of more than 50 miles a day without ever surrendering their individuality. . . .

Southern Californians are not encouraged to form a spirit of community even though their region is one of the nation's most ethnically diverse. The efficient freeways enable motorists to bypass neighborhoods they do not want to enter and to render the residents invisible. Few Angelenos knew where Watts was until it burned down in 1965. Few outsiders drive through south-central Los Angeles after dark, unless, as in the movie "Grand Canyon," they do so by mistake in trying to find a shortcut after a Los Angeles Lakers game.

The political system that serves these freeway riders was designed to share power rather than focus it. It was created early in the century by progressives who distrusted political parties, the spoils system and what they perceived as eastern-style municipal corruption. City and county government were kept nonpartisan, and government employees given civil service protection.

In Los Angeles, the city charter gave everyone a voice and not much else. Only the mayor was elected citywide, and his powers were severely restricted. When a scandal involving pressure on the police chief erupted in the 1930s, municipal reformers persuaded the voters to make the police chief a virtually independent entity with civil service protection that is unique among the major cities of America.

At the time of these so-called reforms, the population of Southern California was largely white, much of it from the Middle West, and homogenous, except for Mexican Americans, who held low-paying manual jobs and rarely voted. The people wanted a government that provided basic services and let them live the good life without interference. Politicians were held in suspicion and disdain here when other regions still considered them public servants. It is no accident, years later, that Ronald Reagan began his rise to power by convincing Southern Californians he was a "citizen-politician."

The result of this system when crisis struck last week was a lack of centralized authority. The result after the crisis is that no one accepts accountability for what went wrong. Chief Gates is five weeks away from a retirement his foes consider long overdue. Mayor Tom Bradley, at 74 and after five terms in office, is admittedly tired. While every community—Hispanic, white, Black and Asian—has talented

> representatives, none commands the broad public support necessary for effective leadership.
>
> The founders of this city sought to diminish politics and strengthen individual freedoms by keeping government weak. They succeeded so well in their intentions they created a system in which no one can lead."

Other reporters on our augmented staff zeroed in on particular communities. One of the best stories was written by Lynne Duke, a talented reporter on *The Post*'s Metro staff who had covered Nelson Mandela's release from prison in 1990 and would return to South Africa to cover his presidency.[1] Duke went to Florence and Normandie and wrote a story that explored the varied reactions of the people who called the area home. It was headlined: "At Normandie and Florence, an Intersection with History."

Samuel Shorts, fifty-seven, had lived around the corner from the intersection for twenty-six years and was mowing his lawn when the riot erupted. "Most of the people in the neighborhood here think it's ridiculous," he told Duke, "and these people didn't have anything to do with it."

But Gemora Knox, an eighteen-year-old high school student, said the opening night of the riot was "kinda fun." He had no feelings about Reginald Denny. "I been beat, and I felt maybe it was his turn," Knox said. Here is an abridged version of the next part of Duke's story:

> Today streets were quiet but for the sirens of police cars escorting National Guard convoys or fire trucks. Gawking motorists and picture-takers jammed two main thoroughfares. A young woman walked around with a bottle of tequila to sell. Menacing-looking youths on bicycles kept a watch on a couple of strangers on foot. People rose and dressed for church, or talked with each other on front porches.
>
> Across Florence Avenue at Art's Famous Chili Dogs, a bright blue and white wooden kiosk with three stools inside for diners, Lee Pate, a quiet man who drives a bus on weekdays, said what happened here represents a new reality.

1. After assignments in Johannesburg and New York, Duke became an editor in the Style section of the *Washington Post*. She died of lung cancer in 2013 at her home in Silver Spring, Maryland. She was fifty-six years old.

> Black men his age were accustomed to waiting for change and accepting what came. But these young Black men won't do that. "No, I don't feel ashamed because you can expect that," Pate said. "Young people today aren't going to take what we've taken. . . ."
>
> Art's, named for its deceased owner who liked to be called by his first name, has been here for 50 years. Twenty years ago the Los Angeles Times called it THE Los Angeles hot-dog stand. Inside are pictures of the Rev. Martin Luther King Jr., Malcolm X, Nelson Mandela and Art, the owner, who was white.

I had eaten at Art's Famous Chili Dogs, which started in 1939 as a pushcart venture by Art Elkind, a chemical engineer from New York reduced to hot dog vendor by the Great Depression. Elkind's claim to inventing the chili dog is disputed; what is undisputed is that he devised an effective steamer for cooking hot dogs. Elkind died in 1990 of a heart attack. He would been pleased that Art's went unscathed during the riots and that, in 1994, Art's would be purchased by a Black family, the Nelmses.

A few weeks earlier on a day when the trial in Simi Valley was not in session I was in Los Angeles for another reason when a Black friend suggested we have lunch at Art's. As it turned out, she needed to cancel, but I went anyway and sampled Art's caseless hot dog without the chili. I was the only white person there, and the Black man who served me called me "Whitey," not in an unfriendly way.

I asked him what he thought about the trial of the cops who had beaten Rodney King, and he assured me they would all be convicted. "They better be," he added.

A few weeks after Duke's story, I went to Art's again. Same guy at the window, and once more I was "Whitey." I stood out not just because of my race but because I was the only customer eating a plain caseless hot dog with mustard. I sat inside on one of the three stools and asked the server if there were any changes in the neighborhood. "Lot more Hispanics," he said, motioning to two of his customers. Art's sold tamales as well as hot dogs, and people were eating them. I visited Art's again on an anniversary of the riot. By then I'd graduated from "Whitey" to "You again" with the server, who suggested I try the full chili dog. I did. It was covered with gooey melted cheese that gave me heartburn and made me vow that next time I'd revert to my plain hot dog. But there was no next time. I moved away to finish my book and never ate again at Art's Famous Chili Dogs.

The iconic hot dog stand had survived the riot and would limp through the Great Recession of 2007–9, which hit Los Angeles hard. But Art's couldn't overcome the massive loss of customers in the COVID-19 pandemic. On March 8, 2020, it closed for good. A long line snaked around the block on Florence Avenue as customers lined up for one last chili dog and the memories that came with it.

The wheels of justice ground unevenly in Los Angeles in the months and years after the riots. Accompanied by FBI agents and his SWAT team and wearing a flak jacket, Chief Daryl Gates woke up Damian Williams at his home at 2 a.m. on May 25 and arrested him for assaulting Reginald Denny. "I wanted very much to personally arrest him," Gates said. "I did it all by myself with the aid of about 200 police officers and the FBI."

"Chief Gates, you're going," Williams said to him.

"Yes, Football, but you're going first, " Gates said.

Williams was tried and convicted by a jury of felony assault. He was sentenced to ten years in prison but released for good behavior in 1997. Williams was arrested again and sentenced to forty-six years to life in prison for the 2000 murder of drug dealer Grover Tinner. As of this writing, he is incarcerated at Centinela State Prison.

Kiki Watson, who assaulted Larry Tarvin and put his foot on Denny's neck, was convicted of misdemeanor assault after a jury deadlocked on a felony charge. He'd spent seventeen months in jail and was freed for time served but subsequently spent three years in prison on a narcotics charge. Watson operates a limousine service in Los Angeles. Antoine Eugene Miller, another of the attackers, served seventeen months for stealing Denny's possessions. He was shot on February 1, 2004, in an altercation outside a Hollywood nightclub and died a week later. Miller was thirty-one years old. After a long recovery from his intensive injuries, Denny left for Lake Havasu, three hundred miles from Los Angeles, where he worked for many years as a boat mechanic. His present whereabouts are unknown—at least by me.

Fifteen thousand people were arrested for riot-related offenses, including curfew violations. Of these, about twelve hundred were felony cases filed by the district attorney for murder, arson, burglary, and other major crimes. Misdemeanors were filed by the city attorney and processed in municipal courts, which were swamped. Prosecutors and defense attorneys alike complained of assembly-line justice in which judges gave cursory examination of the charges if they examined them at all. As best as I can determine from limited data, the majority of misdemeanor defendants pled guilty, and most of them received ten-day jail sentences.

Cheered by his staff, Daryl Gates stepped down as chief on June 26, 1992. Here is the first paragraph of my story in *The Washington Post:* "LOS ANGELES, JUNE 26—Embattled Los Angeles Police Chief Daryl F. Gates walked out of his office for the last time today, leaving behind a demoralized police force, a city rebuilding from the nation's worst urban riot in this century and a legacy of controversy and bitterness in minority communities."

June 1992 marked high water for police reform in Los Angeles. Voters approved Charter F by a nearly two-to-one margin, ending the independence of the city's police chiefs. Mayor Bradley said the results showed "the overwhelming desire of our people for an accountable police department that fights crime instead of being held hostage to the whims of an arrogant, divisive chief of police."

But bringing Daryl Gates to heel and giving the mayor power to appoint his successors did not bring nirvana to Los Angeles or the LAPD. The new police chief appointed by Bradley was William Luther Williams, the hulking son of a meat cutter who'd spent twenty-nine years in the Philadelphia Police Department, rising through the ranks of a force that was investigated by the Justice Department for brutality in the 1970s and rocked by narcotics scandals in the 1980s. In 1988, he became Philadelphia's first Black police chief. He was also the first Black police chief in Los Angeles and the first outsider to hold that position in four decades.

Williams took over a department where the celebrated thin blue line was stretched too thin. In 1978, the year Gates became chief and the tax-limiting Proposition 13 was passed by California voters, Los Angeles spent 20 percent of its city budget on police. By the time Williams became chief, it was 14 percent. Los Angeles had fewer than eight thousand police officers—only fourteen hundred more than Philadelphia—to serve a city three times the geographic size with twice the population. The technological edge that once distinguished the LAPD had vanished. In a city that had invented radio patrols, communications equipment was faulty and out of date, as the riots had shown. Police cars were in sorry condition, sometimes driven until their axles fell off. Because of the shortage of officers and the condition of their cars, the LAPD sent patrol cars only to the most serious emergencies, as Williams was shocked to learn. In Philadelphia the police responded to every emergency call.

More unpleasant surprises were in the offing for the new chief, who was inaugurated in a televised ceremony at the police academy. Williams spoke passionately, promising to heal the city's wounds and refuse to tolerate racism, sexism, or excessive force by police officers. He said he would add officers and expand community policing, enabling citizens to "reclaim their streets and [their] neighborhoods." But Bradley followed Williams to the podium and bluntly warned him that there was no money in the municipal coffers for expanding anything.

"Don't come soon to ask for money," the mayor said. "It simply isn't there."

Williams's tenure was also undermined by problems of his own making: He was so portly he couldn't fit into his police uniform and failed the physical test required of law enforcement officers in California. Ignoring LAPD precedent, Williams also didn't return from a social weekend in Las Vegas when a popular narcotics officer named Charles Heim was shot and killed.

A more serious lapse occurred two months later when it was revealed that Williams had solicited perks and accepted free rooms and meals from Las Vegas casinos. Williams, a slot machine player, made his situation worse by lying to an oversight commission about what he had done, prompting a reprimand. The LAPD, for all its faults, does not tolerate corruption. Officers had been suspended and even fired for lesser offenses. Williams was damaged beyond repair. Mayor Riordan declined to give him a second five-year term, appointing as his replacement Assistant Chief Bernard C. Parks, a hard-boiled officer who had risen through the LAPD ranks. Parks, also an African American, had been a candidate for chief when Williams was selected.

Parks was honest and well-meaning, but a scandal erupted on his watch in 1999 in the Community Resources Against Street Hoodlums (CRASH) anti-gang unit that dwarfed previous allegations of corruption within the LAPD. Because CRASH was part of Rampart Division, it became known as the Rampart scandal. After an intensive internal investigation, CRASH officer Rafael Perez admitted his corruption and implicated seventy other officers in various forms of misconduct, including unprovoked shootings, beatings, planting of false evidence, stealing and dealing narcotics, bank robbery, perjury, and covering up evidence of these activities. Enough evidence was found against fifty-eight of these officers to bring them before an internal administrative board, but only twenty-four were found to have committed wrongdoing. Five officers were fired, seven forced into resignation or retirement, and the other twelve given suspensions of various lengths.

For the U.S. Department of Justice it was the last straw in a pattern of misconduct that had begun with the beating of Rodney King. DOJ sued the city of Los Angeles in May 2000, forcing it into a consent decree that led to nearly twelve years of U.S. oversight and the promise from the city to undertake various reforms of the LAPD under supervision of a federal judge.

That concludes my reporting on the tangled saga of the LAPD. I ceased being a staff writer for *The Washington Post* in 1998. After two additional years of covering the West for *The Post* as a freelancer, I retired from the paper in 2000. As a freelancer, I wrote an article about the Rampart scandal for the *New York Times Magazine* and an article in *National Review* about the officers who had arrested and beaten King. In my post-riot years at *The Post,* the editors encouraged me to write about the recovery in Los Angeles, which I also addressed in *Official Negligence.* Here are the opening paragraphs of an evaluation of the recovery timed to the fifth anniversary of the riots. It appeared in *The Post* with a Los Angeles dateline on April 28, 1997:

> Five years after a violent riot tore apart the social fabric of this multicultural city, Los Angeles is struggling to heal its deep physical and emotional wounds.
>
> A majority of the strip malls that were reduced to smoldering rubble have been rebuilt, many operated by Latino and Asian immigrants. Latinos, long described as the "sleeping giant" of Los Angeles,

> have emerged as a major political force. Tourism has rebounded, and trade is thriving with nations of the Pacific Rim.
>
> But the long, slow struggle for economic recovery has been plagued by racial and ethnic conflicts among blacks, Latinos and Korean Americans. Many middle-class blacks have moved out of Los Angeles.
>
> "We have a lot going for us in terms of economic development, but we need to come to terms with the cultural class and different cultural identities," said Rep. Julian C. Dixon (D), an African American who has long represented a diverse Los Angeles district.

Tensions remained high between Blacks and Koreans. One assessment found that, out of 3,100 businesses destroyed or looted in the riot, 1,867 were Korean owned.

"There is a tremendous amount of bitterness, but it's held in silence," Korean activist Angela Oh told me. "Koreans tend to be that way." Oh added that few Koreans had been compensated for their losses and that some had committed suicide.

A Black-led group, Community Coalition, opposed rebuilding liquor stores in the riot area, many of them Asian-owned. At the time of my writing, the city had issued permits for only thirty-five of more than two hundred stores that had been destroyed. Many of them would never be rebuilt.

After the riots, Mayor Bradley brought in entrepreneur Peter Ueberroth to head a ballyhooed recovery effort called Rebuild Los Angeles. Ueberroth sought $500 million in corporate investment as the down payment on a $6 billion program to make South Central an inner-city showcase and create seventy-five thousand jobs. Ueberroth was supremely confident about the plan, overconfident in retrospect. He told me corporations were eager to play a major role in rebuilding Los Angeles. Some of them heeded Ueberroth's call, but the overall performance never came close to matching the extravagant promises. Ueberroth left in 1994, and Rebuild Los Angeles, renamed RLA, became a research group that early in 1997 closed its doors.

Government action also fell short. The state did nothing. Congress created federal "empowerment zones" providing tax breaks in return for business investment. But the Clinton administration rejected Los Angeles's application for such a zone.

California nonetheless has become the face of America's future led by Los Angeles, the nation's second largest city. Los Angeles has a population of 4 million in a county of 9.8 million people and a metropolitan area of 13 million. Roughly half of the city's population is Latino, 11 percent is Asian, and 10 percent is Black. A popular website ranks Los Angeles first in terms of educational diversity, and the city bounced back quickly from the COVID-19 pandemic.

Ronald Reagan, whom I covered for all those years, believed in the universality of the American experience. He had a shopworn trope he used so often that aides and reporters could recite it by heart.

"America represents something universal in the human spirit," Reagan said in 1988. "I received a letter not long ago from a man who said, 'You can go to Japan to live, but you cannot become Japanese. You can go to France to live and not become a Frenchman. You can go to live in Germany or Turkey, and you won't become a German or a Turk.' Then he added, 'Anybody from any corner of the world can come to America to live and become an American.'"[2]

Notwithstanding the difficulty many foreigners find in assimilating in Europe, Reagan's claim about migrants in France or Germany is half-true at best, But his point about America—especially California—is hard to argue. Nearly 800,000 migrants from Central America now live in Los Angeles County. Some are the sons and daughters of the newcomers who in the 1992 riot looted unguarded markets for food and diapers. They have learned to live in Los Angeles, and they have a higher-labor force participation than foreign-born or U.S.-born populations. They are all Americans, as Reagan would say, and also Californians and Angelenos. They are not going back, and we who were born here are the better for it.

2. There was no such letter. This was a device Reagan often used in speeches. I once asked him why he made up mythical letter writers. Without embarrassment, Reagan answered, "It makes what I'm saying more personal."

32

THE THIRTEENTH JUROR

Robert Almond had a commanding view of South Central Los Angeles from his tenth-floor room in the downtown Los Angeles Hilton Hotel. Every night he peered at this vast area that began a few blocks from the hotel and stretched out to the horizon. The next day he would tell his associates he had seen no fires burning in the city.

Almond was foreman of the sequestered federal jury that was deliberating the fate of the four Los Angeles police officers accused of violating Rodney King's civil rights. The "associates" were his fellow jurors. Almond regarded his reports that South Central wasn't burning as gallows humor. He had learned on combat missions in Vietnam with an automatic-weapons crew that humor helps to ease tensions.

But this was no joke. It was the key to understanding what would unfold in the federal trial of the four officers acquitted in Simi Valley in the beating of Rodney King, Almond saw signs of stress among his fellow jurors that reminded him of the behavior of scared and battle-weary soldiers. He considered himself more stress-resistant than other jurors but realized he was not immune. Almond worried about the safety of his wife and family. He wondered whether people would find out where he lived and throw rocks at his home after the trial was over.

Bob Almond was the foreman, but fear was the thirteenth juror at *U.S. v. Koon*, the federal trial that began on February 25, 1993, at the Edward R. Roybal Federal Building and Courthouse in the Los Angeles Civic Center. Tight security measures were in force. The jurors were driven to and from court in unmarked vans from which they glimpsed barricades and other anti-terrorist precautions around and under the Roybal Building. The heavily armed U.S. marshals who escorted them wore bulletproof vests and were on edge. On what was intended as a relaxed weekend outing at Griffith Park, grim-faced marshals drew their guns when a rattlesnake was spotted slithering across a path.

The snake incident was amusing to some of the jurors and scary to others, but less natural dangers were scary to everyone. When jurors returned to their hotel each afternoon, marshals would block off the sidewalk on Wilshire Boulevard with a tent so they could enter without interference. Once a pedestrian who failed to heed a marshal's instruction to stop was pounced on and pinned to the ground. Another afternoon, marshals learned of a bomb scare at the hotel while transporting the jurors back from the courthouse. The vans returned to the Roybal Building while an excitable male juror screamed, "We're going to die! We're going to die!"

This chilling outburst in the van was a dramatic example of the strains imposed by a trial that jurors thought could ignite another riot. This fear was particularly palpable for a Black man from Watts whom the defense had tried unsuccessfully to keep off the jury. The Watts man told another member of the jury before deliberations began that he feared for the city if the defendants were acquitted. Such fears weighed heavily on the federal jurors, predisposing them to return guilty verdicts because of the terrible prospect of another riot if they did not.

Neither trial was conducted on a level playing field. At the state trial in Simi Valley the jury was composed of like-minded mostly white people who pulled off the road at the sound of sirens and believed in the probity of the police. No juror was Black. Most jurors held such favorable opinions of the police that not even the videotape shook their presumption that the police had acted properly. But at the federal trial the burden of proof that is supposed to be borne by the prosecution fell on the defense. This jury had two Black members united in a common fear with five jurors sympathetic to the defendants that acquittals could spark another momentous riot. This common fear posed an enormous obstacle to a fair trial.

Reporters at the second trial, including me, did not fully realize the extent of these fears. Unlike the jurors, we escaped the hothouse atmosphere of downtown Los Angeles after work and on weekends. More consequently, juror fear went unnoticed by the defense attorneys, two of whom had participated in the successful effort to move the state trial out of Los Angeles. Before the federal trial, defense attorneys talked themselves out of seeking a change of venue, rationalizing that the jury would be chosen from a seven-county area. But it was where the jurors assembled, not their home counties, that mattered. The Roybal Courthouse and the Hilton Hotel where jurors were sequestered were on the edge of the area in which the nation's deadliest modern riot had occurred. Not a day went by without reminders of what had happened when another jury freed the officers who had beaten Rodney King.

Prosecuting attorneys were as unaware as their defense counterparts of the fears of jurors even though it was a boon to them. Steven D. Clymer, the brainy U.S. attorney who coled the prosecution team, told me he'd never heard of the bomb scare until I asked him about it three years after the trial. The only participant in the trial who seems to have recognized the importance of the jurors' emotional state was Almond, who told a fellow juror that a psychologist should visit jurors to help them deal with their problems. No one addressed the terrors that had accumulated in the minds and hearts of a jury whose least fearful member peered through the window of his hotel room each night to see if South Central was burning.

I covered the trial thoroughly for *The Post* and wrote three chapters about it in *Official Negligence*. During the trial, jurors were known only by number, and some chose to remain anonymous afterward. But several key jurors identified themselves and submitted to interviews under various conditions. (For instance, Fred, Juror No. 9, would give only his first name.) I interviewed five jurors and had brief conversations with two others and interviewed all eight attorneys, three of the four defendants, and U.S. district judge John G. Davies, the presiding judge. Davies lived in Santa Barbara and helped when I was writing *Official Negligence*. His perspective from the bench gave my book an added dimension.

Tall and austere, Davies was a naturalized citizen who at the 1952 Olympics won the gold medal for his native Australia in the two-hundred-meter breaststroke. After earning a law degree from UCLA, he practiced business law in Los Angeles for twenty-seven years before being named to the federal bench in 1986 by President Reagan. Although his background was more in civil litigation than criminal law, Davies had substantial trial experience as a lawyer and judge, a droll sense of humor, and a penchant for controlling the courtroom. Jurors liked him. The federal prosecutors thought Davies too conservative, while defense lawyer Harland Braun thought Davies too deferential to federal authority. These perceived deficiencies were transcended by the judge's resolute fair-mindedness, which was evident throughout the trial. He made rulings that alternately disappointed both sides.

The prosecution had more going for it than the fears of jurors that acquittals might spark another riot. U.S. attorney Teree Bowers would call the four lawyers who prosecuted the case "one of the most formidable trial teams ever assembled." Clymer was a rising star in the U.S attorney's office in Los Angeles. He had graduated magna cum laude from Cornell Law School and become an assistant district attorney in Philadelphia, where he'd obtained indictments of police officers involved in a bribery and gambling ring.

Barry Kowalski, diminutive and feisty, had served with distinction as a Marine rifle-platoon leader and had become the nation's best-known civil rights prosecutor. During eleven years at the U.S. Department of Justice, Kowalski had won convictions against an assortment of Ku Klux Klan members, skinheads, and brutal police officers. Alan Tieger, son of a Holocaust survivor and a colleague of Kowalski's in the Civil Rights Division of the Department of Justice, and Lawrence Middleton of the U.S. attorney's office in Los Angeles were capable backups for Clymer and Kowalski.

With the exception of experienced defense lawyer Harlan Braun, who'd taken over as attorney for officer Theodore Briseno, the defense lawyers were no match for the prosecution in trial experience. Michael Stone and Paul DePasquale returned as attorneys for officers Laurence Powell and Timothy Wind, respectively. Stone had been brilliant in Simi Valley, considering it was his first felony trial. But he had never tried a case in federal court. Nor had Ira Salzman, a gentlemanly civil litigator in a one-man office, who replaced Daryl Mounger as the attorney representing Stacey Koon. This was a downgrade. Mounger, a former LAPD officer, had realized his client could come across as brusque and unfeeling and had encouraged Koon to let his emotions show. Koon had done so with reluctance, but his testimony moved the jury.

At the time I wrote a weekly syndicated column that had begun as "Reagan & Company" when I covered the White House. The number of newspaper clients had dwindled since I'd gone west, but *The Post* and a dozen other papers ran the column regularly. Normally, I had many potential subjects, but I was covering the trial full-time and wrote a column examining various aspects of the case. My column, which ran in *The Post* on March 21, 1993, began by saying that prosecutors, defense attorneys, and much of the media shared "a dirty little secret" about the trial of which the public was unaware. "The secret is that this is no open-and-shut case but a difficult prosecution with many comparable outcomes," I wrote.

Most people had formed their opinions of the King beating from a widely televised segment of the videotape. "This segment is sickening, but there is more to the videotape than the segment and more to the case than the videotape," I added. The column went on to discuss various aspects of the case, focusing on whether the officers had used unlawful force.

Rodney King, who had not testified in state court, took the stand March 9 in the trial's main media event. He had not been seen in public since his emotional plea at the height of the riots ("People, I just want to say . . . can we all get along?"), and the televised clip of that speech had added to his celebrity status in a city that dotes on celebrities. A line formed outside the Roybal Building at 6 a.m., more than seven hours before King testified, for the dozen public courtroom seats. The throng included a score of television stations from eight countries. Jurors were curious, too. Their eyes were riveted on King as he strode commandingly into the courtroom at 1:30 p.m., flanked by FBI agents.

King had been carefully prepared. He was neatly dressed in a tailored dark-gray suit, light-colored shirt, and multicolored tie and had lost so much weight that one account described him as "gaunt-looking." Kowalski led King through his opening testimony, pausing to allow his prize witness a glass of water. Rather than let the defense do it, Kowalski brought out King's prison record as well as his heavy drinking on the night of the incident. He then guided King to the jail ward of Los Angeles County–USC Medical Center, where King said he had awakened "horrible and confused and in an enormous amount of pain" on the morning of March 3, 1991.

Under focused but gentle questioning from Kowalski, King then proceeded to give a garbled version of the facts of the case, a narrative that included injecting race into it—remember, this was officially a civil rights-related criminal charge—by saying that officers that night had taunted King with the n-word. King chanted the words in a high-pitched almost falsetto voice in the hushed courtroom.

"Mr. King, do you remember whether the word that was being used was killer or nigger?" Kowalski asked.

"I'm not sure," King said. "I'm not absolutely sure which word it was, if it was killer or nigger."

Sure or not, King had made the trial a racial case even though much of his testimony was inaccurate. His claim that he had complied with Melanie Singer's commands and then was struck or kicked while face down conflicted with every other eyewitness account. The unsubstantiated accusation that officers had used a racial slur and told him to run was contradicted by eyewitnesses, King's grand jury testimony, and government analysis of the videotape.

The defense attorneys were furious at this cynical strategy and in cross-examination the next day tried to expose King as a habitual liar without subjecting him to a verbal beating that might arouse the jurors' sympathy. But when pressed, King took refuge in his clouded memory. By the end of the day, King had repudiated most of his racially charged testimony, but the residue of what he'd said lingered in the courtroom—and in *The Washington Post*.

My story on the first day of King's testimony ran on page one with a fearsome headline: "During Beating, Police Officer Shouted, 'We're Going to Kill You,' King Testifies."

My next-day story, which ran on page three, had a touch of ambivalence that was reflected in the headline: "King Backs Off on Accusation of Racial Slurs" with a deck headline, "L.A. Beating Victim Sticks to Main Story."

One of my editors asked me if I thought the officers had used racist language while beating King. I told her there was no evidence the officers had said anything at all. But I also said that King had made a positive overall impression. How positive I didn't fully realize until I interviewed jurors after the trial. All of them accepted King's claim he had originally lied about his drinking that night because he didn't want to go back to prison. What mattered to the jurors was not King's testimony but his humanity.

"The man was a human being, and no human being deserves to be beat like a wild animal and that's the only thing King did for me," juror Maria Escobel, who is Black, told me in a December 13, 1993, interview. "As for everything else King said about the incident, I was squirming in my seat."

What made Escobel squirm most was King's reaction to documents shown him by Powell's lawyers Michael Stone and Paul DePasquale in a standard courtroom practice of "refreshing the recollection" of witnesses about prior statements that conflicted with their testimony. King pretended to read the documents, but asked the lawyers to repeat their questions.

After DePasquale handed him a document, King blurted out the truth: "I can't read it."

It was a poignant admission greeted by momentary silence in the courtroom. Judge Davies, who had not realized King could not read, ordered the defense attorneys not to show him any more documents. Escobel told me it was "the most embarrassing thing" that happened in the entire trial.

King also came off well with other jurors, including Almond, who initially supported the defendants. Almond told me he wept during King's testimony. Ever since childhood, King had impressed others as decent, friendly, vulnerable, and intellectually limited. He was a different person when in an alcohol-triggered rage, but this side was not on display in the courtroom. On balance, King was an effective witness. Despite difficulty in keeping the facts straight, his emotional memories seemed genuine, as did his unwavering insistence that he kept moving to avoid a brutal beating.

"I was just trying to stay alive, sir, just trying to stay alive," King said to Kowalski. "They never gave me a chance to stay still."

While King changed his story many times, he was consistent on this point. Through a haze of alcohol or drugs, King had feared that the officers who were beating him would kill him—or so it seemed to a sympathetic jury. His declaration that he was trying to stay alive seemed a cry from the heart.

Other aspects of the trial helped determine the fate of the particular defendants. Tim Wind was helped by Clymer, who said in his opening statement that Powell had taken King back to Foothill Station after the beating to exhibit him as a trophy. (In reality, Powell had shown the battered King to a single officer, Daniel Gonzalez, who testified he'd asked to see him.) King was in Powell's patrol car, guarded by Wind. Gonzalez testified he'd looked at King by flashlight. When the light flashed in King's eyes, Wind "made it obvious that I was making Mr. King upset and should just get the heck out of there." Escobel thought this showed compassion.

Timothy Briseno was never really in danger of being convicted. His presence in the docket was little more than a ploy to help the prosecution.

Koon and Powell were damaged by the testimony of Sergeant Mark Conta, the prosecution's use-of-force expert. Conta, who testified that Powell violated LAPD policy by hitting King with his baton the way he did and that Koon, the supervising officer, lost control of the situation.

Many jurors found Conta persuasive, and his analysis of Powell's blow to King's chest fifty-five seconds into the videotape would prove crucial during jury deliberations. As analytical *Los Angeles Times* reporter, Jim Newton, described the significance of Conta's testimony to me in 1994: "Here was a police officer with strong credentials who looked good on the stand and testified knowledgably that LAPD officers had violated policy. It wasn't an outsider saying that what the LAPD had done was wrong but the LAPD itself."

Conta's testimony incensed Koon, who was otherwise fatalistic about a trial he considered an unjust political response to the riots. Koon bore no animus toward the prosecutors or Rodney King, and he could understand why people who had seen the videotape on television thought the treatment of King was unnecessarily brutal. But Koon's image of himself as the good sergeant made him unable to accept suggestions that he had failed to supervise. He found it especially hard to take such criticism from Conta, whom Koon believed had misrepresented LAPD policy in analyzing the video.

After his release from prison, Koon told me that the only time he "lost it" during the trial was when Conta "lied" on the witness stand. But you wouldn't have known that in court, where Koon remained stonily impassive throughout Conta's testimony. Outside the Roybal Building, however, Koon denounced Conta as a "whore" who was trying to ingratiate himself with LAPD management.

LAPD Sergeant Charles Duke, the use-of-force expert who had wowed jurors in the state trial, testified on the third day of the defense presentation. Duke was a decorated star of the LAPD's swat team and a top cop respected even by Clymer, who had no use for other LAPD officers who testified for the defense. If Duke had been the supervising officer at the King arrest, Clymer told me, the incident would have been over quickly without anyone being hurt. I also admired Duke. When I was interviewing LAPD officers in the wake of the King beating, Duke was the only one of them to come to *The Washington Post* office in Century City. He pulled up a chair, looked me straight in the eyes, and answered every question I put to him without once going off the record. My wife, Mary, said Duke would have made an ideal neighbor who would have been there if you needed him.

But despite a mighty effort in the civil rights trial, Duke could not rescue a defense that was on life support by the time he took the stand. Testifying in plain clothes because the LAPD high command wouldn't let him wear his uniform, Duke reviewed the videotape frame by frame and said that every blow and kick by Powell and Wind was warranted by LAPD policy and may have saved Rodney King's life. Duke said that the incident could have escalated into a "deadly force situation" in which someone, probably King, would have been shot. "The safest place for him, and it may be very hard to understand, is on the ground," Duke said.

Even jurors unsympathetic to the defendants respected Duke and recognized he was a good witness. But Duke was not testifying in the vacuum of Simi Valley, where prosecutors had lacked an effective use-of-force witness. Jurors told me after the trial they found both Duke and Conta knowledgeable and did not know which of these experienced sergeants to believe. The defense needed better than a tie. As foreman Bob Almond explained it to me, the conflicting testimony encouraged jurors to rely on their own interpretations of the videotape, which was not favorable to Powell or Koon.

The defense was now dependent on Stacey Koon, who'd waited through a month of testimony to tell his story. Koon believed he had averted a shooting and probably saved King's life. But now he was undergoing a second trial, he believed, solely because Blacks who could not accept the Simi Valley verdicts had reacted violently, and the LAPD responded slowly to a riot for which it was unprepared.

Koon struggled to convey these perceptions to the jury. On the witness stand, Koon was so imperturbable about what had happened the night of the King arrest that he seemed distant and aloof, as if he were reciting a memorized version of events. His sole accomplishment as a witness was to take responsibility for everything that had happened the night of the arrest and absolve the officers who had abused King of blame. This would help two of the officers although it was of no benefit to Koon. Even juror Maria Escobel, who otherwise lacked empathy for Koon, was impressed. "He stood by everything he did," she told me. Answering Salzman's questions for four and a half hours on consecutive days, Koon described his failed attempts to arrest King with shouted commands, the swarm, and the Taser. He said King could have stopped the beating at any time, as he eventually did, by complying with police commands.

"Rodney King has control of the situation," Koon testified. "I have control of the officers." Koon meant to hurt King. "My intent was to cripple Rodney King," Koon said. "That is a better option than having to use deadly force, having to choke or having to shoot Rodney King."

Koon's self-justifying testimony and the prosecution's view that Koon had directed an excessive beating for no good reason left jurors with a choice they would resolve in favor of the prosecution.

Prosecutors had expected Powell to testify, as he'd done in Simi Valley. But after watching Clymer cross-examine Koon, Powell and his attorney had second thoughts. Jessica Crosby and I explained their decision in a double-bylined story April 1 headlined "Defense Rests in King Beating Case to Avoid Grilling of Officer Powell."

Here are the first three paragraphs:

> LOS ANGELES, March 31—Defense Attorney Michael P. Stone abruptly rested his case today in the Rodney G. King civil rights trial without calling his client, Officer Laurence M. Powell, to testify.
>
> The surprise move reflected concern that Powell may have buckled under what Stone said surely would have been "very aggressive" cross-examination by Assistant U.S. Attorney Steven D. Clymer.

> Early today, Powell acknowledged that he was "nervous" about being cross-examined. After Stone had rested, a relaxed Powell told reporters, "They had a big folder and boxes with my name on it. It was going to be one helluva cross-examination."

Then it was Briseno's turn. His attorney, Harland Braun, feared Duke would repeat his testimony in the civil rights trial. Braun talked to Duke, and the two men reached a tacit understanding. Duke would not repeat what he'd said about Briseno in Simi Valley unless asked a direct question under cross-examination. Braun, in turn, would not call Briseno to testify. Braun informed the other defense attorneys about his arrangement with Duke. Testifying was Briseno's decision to make, but he was happy with Braun's attempt to construct a unified defense. Briseno had lived in exile since testifying against Powell and Koon in Simi Valley. He was weary of being seen as the turncoat who had sacrificed other officers to save himself. But Clymer and Kowalski had a surprise of their own: they asked the court to allow them to show jurors a videotape of Briseno's Simi Valley testimony.

Judge Davies, for the only time in the trial, wavered. Listening to the arguments, he appeared first to side with the prosecution, then with the defense. Finally, he decided the taped testimony could be admitted. The defense attorneys filed an emergency appeal with the Ninth Circuit Court of Appeals, asking that the decision be overturned. Appellate courts rarely interfere in the middle of a trial, and Davies was upheld.

Briseno was the beneficiary of this video. Juror Maria Escobel told me that Briseno came off as a highly professional officer. Jury foreman Robert Almond was also impressed.

"I couldn't have planned anything that would have helped Briseno more and hurt the other defendants as much as this ruling [to admit the videotape] by the court," Braun told me after the trial.

What the jurors did not know was that Briseno had changed his mind about the incident based on his viewing of the FBI-enhanced videotape, which did not exist at the time of the Simi Valley trial. He'd become less critical of Koon and also realized that his act in putting a foot on King had resulted in additional blows by Powell. When he no longer faced prosecution, Briseno gave his revised account of the incident to a civil jury and an LAPD Board of Rights hearing. But the federal criminal jury never heard how the enhanced tape had altered Briseno's perceptions of what happened that night.

Perhaps none of this would have mattered. In their closing arguments, Clymer and Kowalski had sprinkled their arguments with reminders to jurors of the riot that had engulfed Los Angeles less than a year earlier. Jurors needed no reminders. They feared another riot if South Central Los Angeles disagreed with their verdicts.

The city was on edge as Judge Davies submitted the case to the jury at 3:07 p.m. on Saturday, April 10. The media took notice of the widespread jitters and may have contributed to them. "Civil War," said a headline on a report by KCOP-TV. "Will It Happen Again?" asked KCAL-TV. Volunteers from Mayor Tom Bradley's "Neighbor to Neighbor" program went door-to-door advocating a nonviolent response to the verdicts. The LAPD went on advanced readiness, adding hundreds of extra officers to patrol duties. "The prospect of new rioting has haunted the federal trial from its opening moments," Jim Newton wrote in the *Los Angeles Times.*

Judge Davies realized that fear of a civil disturbance could influence the verdicts. Without being asked by either side to do so, he raised the issue while instructing the jury. "You should not be influenced by the anticipation and external consequences of your verdicts," he said. Davies was a high-minded judge who wanted verdicts based on the evidence. But his instruction only added to the anxieties of the jurors.

Those anxieties were considerable. During the trial I knew nothing about the attitudes of the jurors, all of whom were anonymous and sequestered. I talked to seven of them for *Official Negligence,* with five of them long enough to qualify as interviews. My most extensive interviews were with Bob Almond and Maria Escobel, Juror No 7.

Almond believed the public expected the jury to reach verdicts. He told me he had been willing to explore the idea that every defendant was innocent but also said, "I think there might have been riots if we had not come up with a decision, if we had a hung jury."

This made him an ideal foreman from Davies's point of view; the judge was obsessed with avoiding a deadlock. During jury selection, Davies had rebuked Braun for attempting to ask prospective jurors if they would hold out if they were in the minority. Braun saw a mistrial as a useful middle ground. He believed it was less likely than acquittals to provoke a riot and thought it improbable the government would try the defendants a third time. A mistrial was the best outcome Powell and Koon could have hoped for since at least three jurors were committed to finding them guilty.

Escobel, the most open-minded of these pro-conviction jurors, had no doubt the officers had used excessive force, perhaps because King was Black but probably because they were "pissed off" at his behavior. Escobel, twenty-nine, was the daughter of Webster Moore, a former Black Panther with ties to radicals Huey Newton and Angela Davis. Raised in a middle-class family in Los Angeles, Escobel told me she had "gone the other way from her father" and avoided politics of any sort. She had attended California State University in Fullerton but dropped out because she could not afford the tuition. She joined the Postal Service and married a Latino coworker. Their son was three months old when Escobel's husband was killed in an automobile accident. At the time of the trial, Escobel was dividing her attention among her son, who was four, a night job operating a sewing machine at the post office, and a beauty shop she owned in Santa Ana with another woman.

Escobel impressed others as strong and intelligent. She had a gift for mimicry and the spunk to stand up to Almond, who was considered "rude" by the female jurors. Like Almond, Escobel had realized she was being asked to serve on a replay of the "Rodney King beating trial." She welcomed the opportunity. Escobel told me she was "tired" of postal work and thought jury service would provide a respite. Almond realized the court had forced the defense to accept the two Black members and decided that Escobel had an agenda because she expressed a firm opinion early in the deliberations that the defendants had used excessive force. I think Escobel's willingness to leave her four-year-old child in the care of others during a long trial suggests she indeed had an agenda. But she was not alone. Others expressed the same view as Escobel and did so just as strongly. Since the jurors were volunteers, it could be said that all of them had agendas, if only to play a part in history.

The deliberations, I later learned, were heated—and troubling. Two male jurors discussed personal experience with drug use. One had attended a rehabilitation program for marijuana users. The other acknowledged ingesting a panoply of drugs, including PCP. If these jurors had truthfully answered questions about drug use on their jury questionnaires, they would not have been accepted on the jury—and they should not have been because their experience with drugs led them to dismiss the issue of whether King's conduct was drug induced. The PCP user was a particular boon to the prosecution, for he minimized the negative effects of this drug in comments to other jurors.

On Wednesday, April 14, the emotions of the jury crested in ways that suggested Almond called Juror No. 8 an "asshole" when she imperiously announced she was going to write a letter to the judge complaining that the jury was quitting too early each day. Later, Almond told another juror he was willing to make peace with Juror No. 8 but was afraid he might hit her in the face if she talked any more about writing a letter of complaint. It is a comment on the state of mind of the jurors that two of them told me that Almond was the calmest person in the room. One juror questioned the masculinity of another. Another ripped off his shirt to show hives he said had been caused by the strain of the deliberations. Another told a terrible family secret that caused jurors to weep. Escobel suggested that some jurors would rather return to the hotel and "get fat" on rich food rather than remain in the jury room and make hard decisions.

Some of the most ferocious arguments were between Escobel and the Watts man, the two Blacks on the jury. Several male jurors felt she unfairly baited him. She felt put upon, too, and at one point broke down and ran crying from the jury room.

By Thursday, however, the jury had coalesced unanimously in favor of finding Powell guilty. They then turned to Tim Wind. Almond took a preliminary vote, which was eight-to-four for acquittal. Wind had been unfortunate to have Powell as a training officer, but he benefited from being compared to him by the jurors. He may also have benefited from the intensity of the Wednesday deliberations, for none of the jurors wanted to go through such an emotional session again. They voted unanimously to acquit Wind. On Friday, April 16, the jury also acquitted Briseno. The vote to acquit was unanimous and swift.

That left only Koon, a hero to the state jury, but on shaky ground with the federal jurors. If the thirteenth juror played a role in the trial's outcome, it was in considering the charges against the sergeant at the heart of the King incident. Jurors were tired and fearful as the trial neared its end and aware of the tension in the courthouse and beyond.

Having acquitted two of the defendants, some jurors were concerned that a third acquittal might spark another riot.

The jury's decisions on Powell, Wind, and Briseno seemed sensible at the time, as they do decades later. Some civil libertarians would dispute the ethics of trying anyone twice for the same actions in differently worded indictments, but the cramped definition of double jeopardy that allows the federal government to do so was not the jury's fault. Powell, given his central role in the beating and his decision not to testify, might well have been convicted in a neutral venue. Wind and Briseno, acquitted by two vastly different juries, were genuinely innocent.

Koon was burdened by the dynamics of the federal trial, a strong prosecution, and the absolutism of his own defense. He seemed at times more concerned with being considered an unprofessional police officer than being convicted of a crime. Powell was the first defendant named in the state indictment. Koon was named first in the federal indictment, suggesting the government's argument that he was, as supervisor on the scene, most responsible for violating Rodney King's civil rights. The defense fought the case on the government's terms. Koon was the only defendant to testify, and defense lawyers rationalized that Powell would be acquitted if the jury accepted Koon's explanation. In the actual deliberations, however, Powell had already been convicted by the time the jurors considered Koon's fate. Since Koon took responsibility for every one of Powell's blows, it stood to reason that, if Powell was guilty, Koon must be guilty, too.

As he considered what happened, Martin De La Rosa, a grocer, realized that Koon had simply let events get away from him. "He wasn't trying to punish King," De La Rosa told me. "It just got out of hand." This statement by a grocery clerk is a more accurate explanation of the incident than the prosecution exaggeration that King was beaten into submission or Koon's fantasy that it was a by-the-book arrest.

Even in the hothouse atmosphere of the Los Angeles courthouse, it's conceivable that Almond and other jurors might have held out for Koon's innocence if he had described the incident as an arrest gone wrong. The jury instructions from Judge Davies told jurors they must find the actions of the defendants intentional to conclude they had violated King's civil rights. Beyond that instruction, Almond expected an act of contrition from Koon or at least an expression that he was sorry King had been so severely beaten. That had not been forthcoming from Koon, who stuck to his narrative that King could have stopped the beating at any time by complying with the officers' commands.

Koon will take to the grave his belief that he followed LAPD policy in the King arrest. We talked in a corridor outside the courtroom after the defense rested its case. Koon said acquittals would be a small victory for the defendants but a "giant verdict for policing."

I asked why. "Use of force is what a policeman's life is all about," Koon replied. "I don't mean that acquittals will be a license for police to go out and rain blows on suspects, but it does mean they will be able to do what they're taught."

Judge Davies was among the many Angelenos who feared civil disorder if the jury acquitted Powell or Koon. By prearrangement, Davies kept the jurors sequestered another night so that verdicts could be announced at the unusual time of 7 a.m. Saturday, April 17. "Fear set the schedule," observed Jim Newton.

The LAPD declared a tactical alert and when Saturday dawned had put thirty-two hundred officers on the street, ten times the normal number. The Los Angeles Sheriff's Department deployed fourteen hundred officers, and six hundred National Guardsmen assembled at local armories. Parking lots near the Roybal Building were cleared and the area ringed with police.

Koon sent a message to Judge Davies the morning of the verdicts, thanking him for conducting a fair trial. He was impassive when court clerk Jim Holmes read the guilty verdict, but Ira Salzman removed his glasses and rubbed his eyes.

Michael Stone held Powell's arm and squeezed the hand of Powell's girlfriend. When the Koon verdict was read, Stone whispered to Powell, "We're going down, bud." Wind bowed his head as he was found not guilty, squeezing the pen with which he had taken notes during the trial. After the verdicts were read, Clymer wished him good luck. Briseno clutched a tiny silver-and-black crucifix during the proceedings. He wept at the convictions of Koon and Powell, as if he had been found guilty as well.

The verdicts were carried over an open line to the press room and broadcast immediately to the world. At First AME Church, the oldest Black church in Los Angeles, a crowd of 150 people roared in delight. As the news spread, motorists drove through Florence and Normandie, ground zero in the riots, honking car horns and playing rap music.

Political leaders praised the verdicts. Mayor Bradley said that Easter Sunday would be "the first day of a new life for Los Angeles." Governor Wilson, in Los Angeles for the weekend, said, "Justice has been done whether or not people agree with the verdicts." President Clinton in Pittsburgh perceived a larger purpose: "Surely the lasting legacy of the Rodney King trial ought to be . . . a determination to reaffirm our common humanity and to make a strength of our diversity."

Prosecutors and defense attorneys offered predictable assessments. "Justice has been done," Kowalski said at a news conference of the prosecutors. "Stacey Koon is not a sacrificial animal to be cast aside for peace in Los Angeles," countered Salzman.

I talked with Harland Braun on Saturday after filing my story. He reflected on the competing verities of peace and justice. "Is it better that two innocent people get convicted, or that fifty people die tomorrow?" he mused. "I don't know."

The clash of those verities and the pressure on the jury to avoid another riot by convicting Powell and Koon might have been avoided had Braun, Salzman, and Stone obtained a change of venue and moved the trial out of Los Angeles. They hadn't even tried. Years later, I asked Davies whether he would have granted a change of venue, and he said that would have depended upon the briefs filed by the competing attorneys.

We'll never know what would have happened if the trial had been conducted, as it should have been, in a neutral venue with no thirteenth juror in the box. But the videotape was a powerful witness.

33

JUDICIAL DISCRETION

When reporters gathered in the Roybal Building courtroom on Wednesday, August 4, 1993, for the sentencing of Laurence Powell and Stacey Koon, Judge John Davies seated the reporters who had covered the trial regularly in the now-vacant jury box. He said it would provide us with another perspective.

Davies was right. Everything looked different from the jury box, where we were closer to the two convicted defendants. I had the seat occupied by Juror No. 6, the Black man from Watts who had been more skeptical of the prosecution's case than many of the white jurors. Seating the journalists in the jury box was the only light-hearted aspect of a day in which Davies put himself at the center of what jurors called "the Rodney King beating case." Davies was primed to challenge federal sentencing guidelines that many judges considered rigid and unfair.

The judge's opening words hinted at what was to come. "The task is not an easy one," he said. "I have tried to treat all of the participants not as symbols, but as individuals." Davies described the defendants in personal terms, observing that Koon was an Air Force veteran, a father of five, and a "successful police officer with an extraordinary record." Powell, Davies said in a massive understatement, did not have quite as distinguished a record but comes from "a family where he has enjoyed the strong support of his parents and four brothers and sisters." The judge had extensively analyzed the King beating and read key portions of his findings from the bench. Then he sentenced Powell and Koon to thirty months in federal prison. The maximum sentence was ten years and a

$250,000 fine, and as I noted in *The Washington Post* the sentence was perceived as lenient by the prosecutors, much of the Black community, and at least one juror I interviewed later. His name was Erik Rasmussen, a Danish-born welder living in Fullerton, who was openly hostile to the police both inside the jury room and in his conversations with me.

On the basis of no evidence whatsoever, Rasmussen asserted that Koon had used his Taser to torture Rodney King and had told other jurors this was common practice in the LAPD.

Davies told me years later that the sentencing of these officers was one of the most difficult decisions he faced in his thirteen years on the bench. His options were limited by complex federal sentencing guidelines that had largely replaced judicial discretion with mathematical formulas for computing sentences. The guidelines, which became law in 1984, were established by the U.S. Sentencing Commission as an antidote to sentencing practices that had varied widely from judge to judge.

According to many legal scholars and trial judges, the guidelines had transferred discretion from judges, who had a duty to be impartial, to prosecutors, who did not. Prosecutors were able to influence sentences by adding various charges, known as "enhancements." As an example, the government in *U.S. v. Koon* sought longer sentences for Koon and Powell because of the seriousness of King's facial injuries even though the prosecution's key witness had testified that the officers were abiding by policy when the injuries were inflicted.

Questionable enhancements such as this one had prompted some jurists to skirt the guidelines in unusual cases. Davies was in this camp. He tried to follow the guidelines but believed they provided insufficient guidance when there were mitigating circumstances.

The guidelines did permit leniency for criminals who accepted responsibility for their actions. In Steven Clymer's view, Koon and Powell were disqualified from any sentence reduction on this ground because they continued to assert their innocence after being convicted. In Koon's case, Clymer did not stop at what was said outside of court. He claimed Koon committed "perjury" when he testified by providing "false justification" for the beating of King. This went too far.

In *Official Negligence* I described both Clymer and Koon as true believers who assumed their motives were pure and their perceptions accurate. Both discounted the opinions of others. Neither gave an inch of ground even when it would have been in their interest to do. Had Koon acknowledged mistakes in the arrest of King, he might have avoided a prison sentence. Had Clymer been willing to acknowledge Koon's sincerity, he would have spared himself and others from a protracted sentencing appeal that reduced the authority of prosecutors.

When I interviewed Clymer after Judge Davies had sentenced Koon and Powell to thirty months in prison, the prosecutor seemed particularly bothered that Koon had shown no "remorse" for his actions. Clymer compared the sergeant to a convicted marijuana dealer who denies wrongdoing because he does not believe that smoking marijuana should be illegal. This was a defective analogy. Koon never claimed that officers should be allowed to use excessive force. In fact, he had turned in a fellow LAPD sergeant who struck two Black transients with a baton. Clymer was familiar with this incident because it was part of the dossier the prosecution had compiled on Koon. But Clymer pushed mitigating information out of his consciousness. To prosecute Koon effectively, Clymer needed to believe he was a bad cop who committed an evil act, not a good cop who had made tactical misjudgments.

In the weeks between the conviction of Koon and Powell and their sentencing, the community pressure that had weighed on jurors shifted to Davies, who was bombarded with letters and telephone calls. Black leaders urged the maximum sentence, while police officers advocated probation.

Davies was, however, receptive to information about the character of the defendants, and received a written testimonial from LAPD detective Roger Richards, who had worked with Koon in uniform patrol early in their careers and remembered him as a "no-nonsense cop" who played by the rules and treated suspects with dignity and respect. "Stacey did not tolerate any deviation from these principles, regardless of his partner's rank or seniority," Richards wrote. "His strength of character earned Stacey a quiet unspoken respect among his contemporaries (as well as fear among those officers who were less than professional or had an inappropriate agenda)."

The judge realized that Richards reflected the prevalent and largely accurate view in the law enforcement community that Koon and Powell had been tried again only because President George H. W. Bush had made a political promise in the wake of the riots. Davies sympathized with the convicted officers, but he also respected the federal jurors and the verdicts they had reached in his court. Beyond that, as Davies told me, even the government acknowledged that the King arrest had begun lawfully and degenerated into an excessive use of force.

The jury had agreed with this contention, as it applied to Koon and Powell, but the verdicts did not say when the behavior of the arresting officers spilled over into illegality. Davies reviewed the testimony and made an extended examination of the videotape in real time and slow motion. The result was a fifty-four-page memorandum about the arrest and beating of Rodney King that stands as a definitive explanation of the incident marred only by the fact that the verdict required Davies to conclude his analysis by finding illegal conduct on the part of two defendants. This was softened by the judge's view that King's "wrongful conduct contributed significantly" to what Powell and Koon had done.

After reading the memorandum, attorneys on both sides suspected that Powell and Koon might have been found not guilty by Davies in a nonjury "bench" trial if the judge had followed his analysis of King's responsibility to its logical conclusion. After completing his fact-finding, Davies launched into a sentencing discussion that was more controversial than his analysis of the incident. Variations from sentences, known as "departures," are permitted by the guidelines. Davies then ticked off four factors he said made the case atypical:

> First, Mr. King's wrongful conduct contributed significantly to provoking the offense behavior. . . .
>
> Second, defendants Koon and Powell have already sustained, and will continue to incur, punishment in addition to the sentence imposed by this court. The extraordinary notoriety and national media coverage of this case, coupled with the defendants' status as police officers, make Koon and Powell unusually susceptible to prison abuse. Moreover, Koon and Powell will be subjected to multiple adversarial proceedings and stripped of their positions and tenure by the LAPD.
>
> Third . . . there is no evidence, and the government does not argue, that Koon and Powell are dangerous or likely to commit crimes in the future.
>
> Fourth, defendants Koon and Powell were indicted for their respective roles in beating Mr. King only after a state court acquitted them of charges based on the same underlying conduct. Under these circumstances, the successive state and federal prosecutions, though legal, raise a specter of unfairness.

Davies said the "combined extraordinary circumstances of this case" warranted departures from the guidelines. Citing a declaration of intent when Congress created the guidelines, Davies said they were never intended to "be imposed in a mechanistic fashion." But he acknowledged he could find "no helpful analogy" on which to base leniency because King's conduct had contributed to the offense. "In fact, very few guideline sections provide for downward adjustments at all," the judge said.

Lacking historical guidance, Davies made an eight-level departure on the basis of the four factors he cited, reducing the score of the offense from twenty-seven to nineteen. Davies sentenced Koon and Powell to thirty months in prison and fined them nothing except a $50 mandatory assessment. Citing a presentence probation report, Davies said that Koon's assets were exhausted. "He has five dependent children who will be unduly burdened if a fine is imposed," Davies said. "Powell is likewise unable to pay a fine, and unlikely to be able to pay." The sentences demonstrated judicial courage. Davies knew the government would probably appeal, as it did on August 27, and that he would be widely criticized.

"In a city struggling to heal itself, the sentencing of two Los Angeles police officers Wednesday was the painful reopening of a wound," began a *Los Angeles Times* story on reaction to the sentences. Joseph Duff, president of the Los Angeles chapter of the NAACP, called the sentences a "travesty of justice." Davies was also assailed by police and their allies. If King was to blame for what happened, why should the officers go to prison? Detective Bill Helm quipped grimly that LAPD cars were being repainted with the motto: "To Protect and Serve Time."

The belief of police officers that the political deck was stacked against them would be enhanced in the months ahead. Jury selection began the day after the sentencing of Koon and Powell in the trial of Damien Williams and Kiki Watson, who had brutalized Reginald Denny and seven other whites, Latinos, or Asians at Florence and Normandie in the wake of the Simi Valley verdicts.

The Los Angeles jury in the Williams trial was the polar opposite of the pro-police jury in Simi Valley, which had no Black members. Williams and Watson were tried before a racially diverse jury whose members overwhelmingly believed that police discriminated against Blacks.

Denny, who had suffered ninety-seven broken bones and permanent facial damage, was a star witness for the prosecution, but he could remember little about the attack and was so forgiving of his assailants that he encouraged similar attitudes on a jury riven by conflict and dropouts. Five alternates were seated during a trial that jury forewoman Walters described to me as "forty days of hell."

On October 18, 1993, the jury acquitted Williams of attempted murder, aggravated mayhem, and causing "great bodily harm" to Denny. He was convicted of simple mayhem for his role in the Denny beating, the lightest felony possible, and of misdemeanor assault against four others. Watson was convicted only of misdemeanor assault for his role in the Denny beating, an offense that carried a maximum jail sentence of six months and required Superior Judge John Ouderkirk to release him for time served.

Particularly revealing of the jury's sympathies was the nine-to-three deadlock in favor of acquittal for the assault charge against the muscular Watson, who had dragged the frail Tarvin from his medical-supply truck and beaten him savagely while an onlooker said, "No pity for the white man."

District Attorney Gil Garcetti was as outraged by this verdict and the acquittal of Williams on the most serious charges against him as his predecessor Ira Reiner had been at the acquittals in Simi Valley and the granting of probation to Soon Ja Du after she shot and killed Latasha Harlins. But *People v. Williams* was another sign, if any was needed, that the composition of the jury or the outlook of the judge carries more weight in a criminal trial than a graphic videotape.

Fear of another riot played a role in *People v. Williams* as it had in *U.S. v. Koon*. An Asian juror said she held out for two days in favor of convicting Williams of attempted murder but changed her vote to not guilty because she feared for her life.

Judge Ouderkirk salvaged what he could by aggregating the misdemeanor charges against Williams with the one felony verdict and sentencing him to ten years in prison. But as Garcetti observed, with credit for time served and additional time off for good behavior, Williams would be eligible for release after four years.

I had been accumulating police sources in preparation for writing *Official Negligence*, and the cops I knew were not surprised by the verdicts in *People v. Williams*. The LAPD had been in a defensive crouch since the riots, not trusting outsiders or even themselves. Many of them were cynical about the judicial system. But there was more to low morale than controversial verdicts. In July, before the sentencing of Koon and Powell and the trial of Williams and Watson, I explored the state of the LAPD in a story written with Jessica Crosby. We quoted a contemplative veteran police sergeant named Joe Cupo that the department "is in a complete state of paralysis."

This story also brought me into contact with Lieutenant John M. Dunkin, newly installed as spokesman for the LAPD. Dunkin had the skills of the wise detective that he was. He could observe a scene and see the missing parts. More than any other police officer, Dunkin helped me in researching *Official Negligence.* I also liked him because he reminded me of my father's friend, Detective Roy Geach of the Reno Police Department, killed in action when I was a boy.

Dunkin cited various statistics to bolster his contention that the LAPD was not performing well. One that caught my eye was an increasing use of deadly force. Koon had speculated that after the King case officers might become reluctant to use their batons and reach for their revolvers instead. I don't know if this was true, but LAPD officers shot seventy-seven suspects in 1992 compared with sixty-one in 1991.

The most telling of Dunkin's statistics was a decline in arrests for major crimes such as robbery, rape, and aggravated assault by more than twenty thousand during the first six months of 1993, while the rate of these crimes remained almost constant. Officers had become so concerned about potential lawsuits that they were reluctant to make the kind of preemptive arrests that often prevent crime, Dunkin said. Many officers were just reporting to work and trying to stay out of trouble.

Koon and Powell asked Judge Davies to allow them to remain at liberty while their convictions were appealed. Davies denied their request, and the two men reported to Camp Parks, one day apart, on October 12 and 13 to begin serving their prison sentences in a federal correctional camp. Camp Parks is in Dublin, twenty-eight miles southeast of Oakland. It was on the fringe of the *Contra Costa Times* circulation area when I was the young editor of the paper in 1960.

Many years later in Santa Barbara when I was no longer a newspaper reporter and Davies no longer a judge, he told me that thirty months in prison is a long time for all but hardened criminals. He had a dim view of long sentences, which he said had scant redemptive value and were necessary only when criminals posed a danger to society. I don't know how he came to this view. It may have been because Davies was a native of Australia, where sentences on the average are half of what they are in the United States. Or it may just have reflected Davies's decency and wisdom. He had a stern visage but a kind heart. After Davies left the bench in 1998, he told me he would not miss the sentencing part of being a judge.

"Welcome to the annual spring Rodney King trial," a guard quipped to me outside the courtroom where King sought $9.5 million in damages from the officers who had beaten him. I omitted his name but led with the guard's comment in a story that ran April 9. 1994, in *The Post* under the headline: "Rodney King: The Jury Is Still Out."

King's lawyers had filed civil suits against everyone in sight, including the city of Los Angeles, and a separate lawsuit against fifteen individuals, including Daryl Gates. Judge Davies pared this lofty litigation by eliminating Gates and eight others as defendants. This left a scaled-down lawsuit against the four police defendants in the criminal trial and two bystander officers.

Judge Davies's finding in the criminal case that King bore some responsibility for what had happened to him had stiffened the spine of the Los Angeles City Council, which rebuffed a claim for $15 million in damages from King's lawyer and left the decision to the courts. On April 19, 1994, a jury awarded King $3.8 million in damages. The city's attorneys were elated, knowing the amount could have been much higher.

I was at this point preoccupied with interviewing jurors in the criminal trial and gave secondary importance to pursuing the civil jurors. *Official Negligence* had become emotionally challenging, and my doctor said I was clinically depressed. My wife, Mary, and my second son, David, who lived in Seattle, realized what was happening. Their affection and understanding enabled me to finish the book.

U.S. v. Koon marched onward, politics entwined with legal issues. Two days after Judge Davies sentenced Koon and Powell, Los Angeles congresswoman Maxine Waters launched a campaign for longer sentences for the former LAPD officers. She secured the signatures of the twenty-five members of the Black Caucus on a letter to Attorney General Janet Reno urging the Department of Justice to appeal the sentence. Reno delivered a high-level review, and prosecutor Steven Clymer lent his voice to the effort. They were all knocking on an open door. Justice Department officials wanted to preserve the sentencing guidelines because of the enormous leverage they gave prosecutors.

The government's appeal of the sentences and the defense appeal of the convictions were heard in 1995 by a randomly chosen three-judge panel of the U.S. Ninth Circuit Court of Appeals headed by Judge Betty Binns Fletcher of Seattle. Fletcher, appointed by President Carter, was a liberal stalwart of the largest appellate court in the United States with a jurisdiction covering nine states and two Pacific territories. It was and remains the nation's most liberal appellate court. Fletcher conducted what is known as a de novo review of the case, meaning that she looked at the trial anew without being bound by conclusions reached by the trial court. In most cases this would have been a boon to the defendants, to whom Fletcher was often sympathetic. But Fletcher's normal standards did not apply in this case.

Judges, no less than jurors, have opinions, and Fletcher, whom I interviewed on May 24, 1996, shared the public revulsion at the beating of Rodney King. She also believed a miscarriage of justice had occurred in the state trial. Her decision in *U.S. v. Koon,* while technically a legal document, can best be read as an expression of Fletcher's strong feelings about the King beating. In her account of the background of the case as well as in my interview she seemed as unaware as a casual viewer of the television-edited clip of the Holliday videotape that King had charged in the direction of Powell before he was hit.

"As the videotape begins," Fletcher wrote, "it shows that King got to his feet in an attempt to escape. Powell and Wind began to strike King with their batons," she wrote as if the officers had set upon King as he was trying to stroll away. Fletcher also emphasized the supposed taunting of King by Powell at Pacific Hospital after the beating. The alleged taunting, a major issue at the state trial, was a minor one in the federal trial because the government had determined that a crucial witness was unreliable and had not called him to testify.

Fletcher's ruling was most one-sided in its finding that the videotape of Briseno's state-trial testimony had not deprived defense attorneys of the chance to cross-examine him in the federal trial. They "*had* the opportunity" to do so at the state trial, she wrote. This is absurd. To conduct the cross-examination Fletcher claimed the defense had an opportunity to make at Simi Valley, the defendants would have needed to know (a) that their clients would be tried again in federal court; (b) that the FBI would have developed a much-enhanced videotape; and (c) that Briseno would see this evidence and change his testimony because of it.

Fletcher accepted as facts assertions by the government that were at best a guess. Neither Fletcher nor the prosecutors knew why the jury had reached its decisions, and the U.S. attorney in Los Angeles made it a policy of not finding out. Nothing in Fletcher's decision reflects awareness of the fearful context in which the jurors deliberated. Fletcher had no way of knowing that the jury foreman scanned South Central every night from his hotel room looking for fires, but she might have considered the probable impact on jurors of the deadly riots. Fletcher apparently knew little about Los Angeles when she wrote her decision hundreds of miles away.

Most telling, Fletcher showed no regard for Davies when she reviewed the sentencing of Powell and Koon. Usually, an appellate judge is reluctant to second-guess the decisions of a trial judge unless he has made an improper legal decision that constitutes reversible error. Furthermore, Fletcher had previously been openly critical of the federal sentencing guidelines.

Given her high opinion of Davies and her low opinion of the sentencing guidelines, it is hard to account for Fletcher's actions except to see them as an expression of her personal feelings about the King beating. Instead of deferring to a trial judge who met Fletcher's standard of knowing more about the case than she did, Fletcher sided with the prosecution on every point. The case was sent back to Davies, who was tasked with imposing longer sentences.

Fletcher's decision was taken stoically by Koon and hard by Powell. "He's shaky and upset," Michael Stone told me after talking to his client. Black leaders hailed the ruling. Harland Braun called the decision "neither intellectually courageous nor politically astute." Daryl Gates called the rejection of Davies's sentences "disgusting." He said the officers had been "put through absolute hell" without taking note of his own contribution to the process.

Judge Stephen Reinhardt, the liberal conscience of the Ninth Circuit, also criticized Fletcher's decision, a rare occasion when he and Gates were on the same page. Reinhardt, a Democratic Party activist who'd been elevated to the bench by President Carter, had served on the Los Angeles Police Commission that selected Gates as chief. Reinhardt had investigated allegations of LAPD misconduct and played a leading role in modifying the department's shooting policy. Gates regarded him as the LAPD's bête noire.

I'd known Reinhardt since 1972, when he was a leader of George McGovern's decisive primary campaign in California. Reinhardt was a critic of the sentencing guidelines, and I sought his comments about Fletcher's ruling. He believed that federal penalties for many crimes were too harsh and made harsher still by the rigid sentencing guidelines.

Reinhardt's experience on the Police Commission had made him aware of cases in which suspects were shot or beaten with much less provocation than Rodney King had provided. While Reinhardt believed Powell had acted brutally, he knew the King incident was not the "aberration" Gates claimed it to be. The officers involved in the King incident, said Reinhardt, "had the bad luck to be caught on videotape but they weren't rogue cops." Reinhart also disagreed that the sentences were "lenient," the word I has used to describe them in *The Post*. "I thought the punishment meted out by Davies was quite severe," Reinhardt said. "Putting a cop in prison for three years is different than just putting anyone in prison for three years."

The validity of Reinhardt's insight would be demonstrated at a halfway house in Rubidoux, California, where Stacey Koon was housed after serving most of his sentence in a medium-security prison in Sheridan, Oregon. Officially known as the Rubidoux Residential Reentry Center, the thirty-bed facility is one of several such centers used by the Bureau of Prisons as halfway houses for inmates with a few months left on their sentences. Koon was sent there on October 14, 1995, and was due to be released exactly two months later.

Until dispatching Koon to Rubidoux, in a low-income area of Riverside County with a substantial Black population, the federal Bureau of Prisons had gone to considerable lengths to keep Koon and Powell safe from harm. They had served the first part of their sentences at a federal prison camp in Dublin, California, a place without walls and gun towers, reserved for nonviolent offenders. When the camp was converted to a women's prison in 1995, the bureau took the unusual step of asking Koon and Powell if they were willing to be transferred to the Boron Correctional Work Camp near Edwards Air Force Base, north of Los Angeles, where the prison population was not exclusively nonviolent. Powell accepted Boron because the transfer brought him within a hundred miles of his family and girlfriend, to whom he'd become engaged while in prison. Koon balked at becoming part of the general prison population where inmates might know him and was transferred instead to relatively safe and isolated Sheridan.

I tried without success to find out who in the Bureau of Prisons approved the transfer of Koon from Sheridan to Rubidoux, sixty miles east of Los Angeles. No one in the bureau wanted to accept responsibility for the final deadly act of official negligence relating to the Rodney King case. The Rubidoux center was unguarded and run by a private company in a high-crime neighborhood. Adding to the blunder, the bureau publicized the transfer, and Koon received a death threat the day he arrived at Rubidoux. Koon told me he was happy to be back in Southern California but that his surroundings reminded him of the dangerous area of Los Angeles he'd patrolled with Seventy-Seventh Street Division.

Koon celebrated his forty-fifth birthday on Thanksgiving Day, November 23, 1995. He received a furlough for the holiday, left Rubidoux early in the morning, and was home at Castaic, north of Los Angeles, when an unhinged thirty-five-year-old Black man named Randall Tolbert burst into the halfway house shortly after noon and demanded to see Koon. Tolbert, a gang member with a long prison and arrest record for violent offenses, including attempted murder, carried a plastic garbage bag that contained liquor, guns, and a sawed-off shotgun. Family members said afterward he had been using PCP for three days. Tolbert became enraged when told that Koon wasn't there and brandished the shotgun at a staff member, insisting he give him Koon's telephone number. Tolbert dialed the number, identified himself as a member of the Westside Project Crips, and shouted into the phone, "Get back down here, motherfucker, you fucking cop faggot, get your ass back here, I'm going to blow you away."[1]

This was the first of three phone conversations Koon had that afternoon with Tolbert, who also called family members and several television stations. In an era before cell phones were commonplace, Koon reported his conversations on a landline to a nearby sheriff's office. He functioned as a hostage negotiator, trying to calm Tolbert and obtain information about his whereabouts in the center. Between calls, Tolbert shot a resident in the chest from a distance, injuring him slightly, and pistol-whipped a woman visitor in the dining hall. Both escaped. Tolbert then moved to another part of the house, taking three hostages—a staff member, a woman who serviced vending machines, and a friend of hers named Karl Milam, who was visiting from his home in Phoenix.

By now, the center was surrounded by a SWAT team from the Riverside County sheriff's office. The standoff continued until 3:30 p.m. when Tolbert killed Milam with a shotgun blast to the head. The SWAT team rushed into the house at the sound of the shot. Koon had told them that Tolbert and the remaining hostages were in a room at the back of the house. As four sheriff's deputies entered the room, Tolbert fired at them, and the deputies shot back, killing him. In a story about the incident the next day the *Los Angeles Times* quoted Tolbert's brother as saying that Koon's presence in Rubidoux had been "eating at all of them."

Koon never returned to Rubidoux. He spent the last few weeks of his sentence in house arrest, from which he was released December 14. Powell, who had been sent to a reentry center in a quiet neighborhood of Garden Grove, had been discharged a day earlier. Although free, the two men spent an uneasy first six months of 1996, awaiting the outcome of an appeal of Judge Fletcher's decision to the U.S. Supreme Court. If the appeal was lost, Koon and Powell faced additional years in prison.

More was at stake than the freedom of two former police officers. The federal sentencing guidelines were under fire from many quarters, and advocates of judicial discretion hoped the high court would use *U.S. v. Koon* to restore the weakened authority of district court judges. A principal objection to the guidelines was the mandatory lengthy sen-

1. Quoted by Robert Deitz in his book *Willful Injustice: A Post-O.J. Look at Rodney King, American Justice and Trial by Race,* 1996.

tences they imposed on drug offenders, a provision that particularly affected crack cocaine users, a disproportionate percentage of whom were Black.[2] A 1994 report to the Connecticut General Assembly from its chief attorney, George Coppolo, summarized objections to the guidelines as "too complex, inflexible, and severe." These complaints were well known to the justices, especially after Stephen Breyer, a former head of the Sentencing Commission, was appointed to the U.S. Supreme Court in 1994.

On June 13, 1996, the high court cautiously seized its opportunity. While failing to issue as sweeping a decision as advocates of judicial discretion would have liked, the court unanimously overturned the Ninth Circuit and found that Judge Davies had used mostly valid factors in rejecting the lengthy sentences sought by the government. Although there were dissents to some aspects of the ruling, the fact that an ideologically divided court could achieve unanimity on its main conclusions was a testament to the legal prowess and collegial skills of Justice Anthony Kennedy.

"It has been uniform and constant in the federal judicial tradition for the sentencing judge to consider every convicted person as an individual and every case as a unique study in the human failings that sometimes mitigate, sometimes magnify, the crime and punishment to ensue," Kennedy wrote in his decision. "We do not understand it to have been the congressional purpose to withdraw all sentencing discretion from the United States District Judge." With that, the court unanimously ordered the case be sent back to Davies for resentencing.

U.S v. Koon proved a stepping stone in a series of Supreme Court decisions that eventually invalidated the federal sentencing guidelines. On January 12, 2005, in *U.S. v. Booker* with Justice Breyer in the majority, the Supreme Court ruled in a five-to-four decision that federal sentencing guidelines should be advisory, not mandatory.

Booker was nine years in the future when Davies resentenced Koon and Powell on September 26, 1996, in the judge's eighth-floor courtroom in the Roybal Federal Building in downtown Los Angeles. I attended the proceedings and interviewed Koon afterward. The standing-room-only

2. A 1986 federal law imposed a minimum five-year sentence for distribution of five grams of crack cocaine, a drug favored by Black users. For powder cocaine, more apt to be used by whites, the minimum five-year sentence was five hundred grams, a hundred-to-one disparity.

days of the King case were long gone. Only forty people attended, mostly attorneys, family members, and others with a connection to the case. Most of the media were preoccupied with jury selection in the second O.J. Simpson trial across town in Santa Monica.

Those in the courtroom seemed pleased to see one another. Powell was unusually relaxed and chatty. Barry Kowalski, who had flown in from Washington to represent the Justice Department, was also in good spirits. He reminisced with a marshal about their Marine Corps days in Vietnam and told me he felt as if he were attending a college reunion. It was an apt metaphor. Jim Newton wrote in the *Los Angeles Times* that "the once-bitter disputes that gripped Davies' courtroom in the winter and spring of 1993 gave way to a reunion air." But it was an odd reunion, like a ceremony in which soldiers from opposing sides who had once tried to kill each other met to talk nostalgically about the war.

Lawrence Middleton, the assistant U.S. attorney who was the only Black member of the prosecution's trial team, dispelled the festive mood with a passionate plea to Davies to punish Koon financially. Recalling that Davies had reduced the sentences of the former officers in part because their notoriety had exposed them to prison abuse, Middleton said, "The defendant (Koon) has used the same notoriety to profit. He's profited to the tune of $10 million."

Middleton slightly exaggerated the money raised by the Koon Defense Fund, of which a little more than one-fourth had gone to Koon and his family. (Outside the courtroom, Koon's lawyer, Ira Salzman, said bitingly that Koon hadn't asked to lose his career and become a convicted felon.) Davies was courteous to Middleton but unimpressed by his argument. The judge made short work of the contention that he should give Koon and Powell longer prison terms because the Supreme Court had struck down two of the mitigating factors he had used.

Powell and Koon, on the advice of counsel, declined to address the court. Davies reimposed the thirty-month sentences. Koon shook hands with his lawyers and Powell hugged his sister. Protected by armed guards, the two men slipped out a side door.

Mike Stone, who had fought a good fight for Powell and won and lost (and won again in the civil trial) believed the Rodney King case was finally over. "It's done," he said, as he left the courtroom. "It's finally over."

Jim Newton, whose informed coverage had impressed both sides and

Judge Davies, agreed. He wrote the next day in the *Los Angeles Times* that the sentencing hearing had "effectively closed out the episode that had reshaped the city's legal and political landscape."

Stacey Koon wasn't so sure. When I interviewed him after the resentencing, his normal fatalism had given way to pessimism about the government's intentions.

"It was a privilege to be a defendant in a case that helped restore sentencing discretion," he told me. When I said to him that Blacks would likely benefit the most from this ruling, he responded, "That's fine with me."

Nonetheless, I sensed that Koon was troubled. He'd tried to make good use of his time in prison, reading serious nonfiction and losing weight and becoming stronger with regular workouts. Koon had gone over the events of March 3, 1991, repeatedly in his mind and was convinced he had done the best he could with the weapons at his disposal and the officers at hand. He seemed almost to regret this analysis. "If I thought I'd done wrong, I would have pled guilty," Koon told me. "I wouldn't have put the city or my family through this."

Koon was bothered by the realization he'd become a symbol of police brutality and especially of racism, which he abhors. The Rubidoux incident weighed on him, particularly the killing of the innocent hostage. Stacey Koon is not a racist. Powell had responded to a domestic dispute involving African Americans just before the King incident and in a message to a colleague compared the scene to *Gorillas in the Mist.* Both the LAPD and the FBI had comprehensively searched Koon's computer messages to find a comparable comment. They never did. Even Clymer, who disliked Koon, acknowledged that the FBI could not find any evidence of racism by Koon. To the contrary, Koon had turned in a white police officer who had abused Black homeless people. Koon had dropped to his knees and given mouth-to-mouth resuscitation to a Black suspect with AIDS and open sores. None of the other officers in the Seventy-Seventh Street Division station house, white or Black, would go near the suspect.

On the matter of resentencing, Stone and Newton were right and Koon was wrong. The government realized that an appeal was fruitless and did not ask a higher court to impose fines. Koon learned about the decision from a lawyer's message on his answering machine when he returned one afternoon after taking his children to Magic Mountain, a popular amusement park in nearby Valencia. He called me with the news, saying the case was indeed over. For the first time since he'd taken over the arrest of Rodney King, Stacey Koon sounded happy.

But Koon had been right in a larger sense when he told me after the resentencing that the King case would never end. The incident changed the way Los Angeles looked at its police force, and in time it changed the LAPD as well. More broadly, the videotape of the King incident launched an era in which civilians used videotape recorders and their ubiquitous successors, mobile cell phones, to record encounters between police officers and criminal suspects, all too often Black men. As cops and courts became more accustomed to such recordings, they were counted on to supply decisive evidence, as happened in the highly publicized killing of George Floyd. Some police departments fought back by issuing officers body cameras. This proved a two-way street, as body cameras, like DNA, can lead to exoneration or indictment.

Rodney King has passed away, as has George Holliday, the amateur photographer who videotaped his beating and arrest. Judge John Davies has also passed. I have lost track of Koon and the other officers whose encounter with King led to several trials and a deadly riot.

The tangled narrative of the Rodney King case awakened Americans to the harsh reality of police work and changed police practices in many jurisdictions as well as federal sentencing procedures. It casts a long shadow. In time, the name Rodney King would be replaced by the names of other African Americans in notorious cases with lethal consequences. The killings of Philando Castile, Breonna Taylor, and yes George Floyd—along with many other civilians—would produce a harsh reckoning about the cost of lingering racism and panicked and overzealous policing.

34

REFLECTIONS AND MEMORIES

"All we have is our memories," Nancy Reagan told me sadly while describing the memory-erasing impact of Alzheimer's disease on her husband. Once the Great Communicator of American politics, Ronald Reagan could no longer remember being president of the United States or the personal history of their life together, Mrs. Reagan said.

The loss of personal memories mattered more to her than his inability to remember the White House, for there is a substantial record of the Reagan presidency. Nancy wanted the world to know that Ronnie, as she called him, was a loving and caring husband. To this end, she commissioned a book of his love letters, many written when they were dating or when he was traveling in the early years of their marriage. *I Love You, Ronnie* is a tender remembrance of the Reagans in springtime.

I interviewed Mrs. Reagan on November 5, 1999, midway through the long goodbye after the shuttering of Ronald Reagan's brain. He was in tremendous physical shape because of workouts and good health habits, which were not entirely a blessing. Ronald Reagan would live another five and a half years, cared for by Nancy, whom he loved without remembering.

Reagan was eighty-three years old when he wrote a poignant farewell letter to the American people disclosing that he had Alzheimer's disease. I'm ninety-one as I write these words and don't have Alzheimer's or any form of dementia, but I've had two strokes and worry that I could become a burden to my wife, who is ten years younger than me and struggling with her own medical issues. My family history does not encourage illusions about longevity. My second son, David, a competitive long-distance runner, died at age sixty of pancreatic cancer. My father, Jack, a heavy smoker, also died when he was sixty. Nathan McMorris, my grandson and my daughter's only son, died of a drug overdose when he was twenty. My mother, Irene, died when she was eighty-three, and my younger brother, Bob, my only sibling, died at seventy-seven.

I covered Ronald Reagan as a journalist or wrote about him as a biographer for more than fifty years. He remains of interest to people too young to remember him and has grown in stature in the misty precincts of memory. When he was president, Reagan was scorned by the liberals who dominate the academic landscape, but his reputation has risen even in academe. Harvard political scientist Joseph S. Nye Jr., one my favorite scholars, calls Reagan a saboteur of the status quo. Reagan has held his own in various polls, but that wouldn't have mattered much to him. Reagan cared more about results than rankings. Although he took little stock in polls, he valued the judgments of history.

The extended mental twilight of Ronald Reagan is a cautionary reminder that good health has downsides. Still, I'd rather be healthy than not. On Saturday, December 29, 2018, I was driving home after taking a walk and planning to watch Notre Dame play Clemson in the Cotton Bowl. I was nearly home when I lost feeling on the right side of my body, including my right leg. I made it into our steep driveway, steering with my left hand. As I drove down the driveway, I reached across my body and shoved the shift lever into park to avoid plowing into our garage. But I was not in pain, and didn't realize I'd had a stroke. I told my wife I'd watch the game and call our doctor on Monday. Mary ignored me. She called our next-door neighbor Cherie, a retired medical professional known in Summerland as the neighborhood nurse.

Cherie did a brief test and told us to go immediately to Cottage Hospital and tell whoever was on duty that I'd had a stroke. Mary drove us to the emergency room seven miles away. I had barely sat down in the waiting room when I was escorted inside the hospital by my neurologist Dr. Philip R. Delio, who happened to be on duty. He gently directed nurses who seemed to move at warp speed. They injected a vein in my right arm with a drug called tPA (tissue plasminogen activator), which can reverse a stroke if given within three hours. Thanks to Mary and Cherie and the quick action of Dr. Delio and the nurses, little more than an hour elapsed between the onset of the stroke and the amazing treatment I received.

Cottage Hospital, Santa Barbara County's main medical facility, is a stroke center headed by Dr. Delio, a respected physician who makes it a point of always returning patients' telephone calls. What a wonderful medical system we would have if we could clone him. I regained feeling in my right leg that night in the ICU, where I asked my nurse, Paris, if she knew the score of the Cotton Bowl game.

"If you're for Notre Dame, you don't want to know," she said. Notre Dame had lost thirty-one to three. I said I was disappointed. Not as disappointed as her father, Paris said. He is a Notre Dame alum.

My next stroke occurred on December 16, 2022, when my wife was at the grocery story, and it was a long while before I reached the hospital. I'm still paying for that as I write these words two years later.

The great discovery of my old age has been Tai Chi, an Asian discipline of slow and rapid movements descended from martial arts. It is meditative and magical. Richard Dogvin, a Tai Chi master, leads a score or more of us in practice twice a week in a quiet clearing in Alice Keck Memorial Reserve in Santa Barbara. The reserve is a 4.6-acre gem with trees from many corners of the world. A towering sweetgum tree with leaves that turn bright red in November overhangs the clearing where we practice. The leaves are lovely, but I've stumbled more than once on the seed-containing burrs shed by the tree. Nonetheless, Alice Keck is my favorite place in Santa Barbara. We end each practice with a Qigong exercise known as Longevity. At home I do it every day.

My twenty-nine years with *The Washington Post*, the last two as a freelancer, ended in 2000. I'd had an option two years earlier of returning to Washington as a general assignment reporter on the national staff, but I'd been there and done that and wanted to stay in the West. My two turns as western bureau chief of *The Washington Post* had been productive and rewarding, but as a freelancer I'd lost the opportunity to shape the coverage and felt it was time to move on.

At sixty-seven I wasn't ready to retire but was unsure if I could make a decent living on my own. Soon after I stepped away from *The Post*, my fears were dispelled by a phone call from David Shipley, who was then editor of the *New York Times Magazine* (and later the opinion page of

The Washington Post). David was a committed editor who knew what he wanted. What he wanted then was an explanation of an LAPD scandal that threatened to upend Los Angeles. It was a perfect assignment for me. I'd developed sources within the LAPD while researching *Official Negligence* and have been intrigued by police practices since boyhood.

My story appeared in the October 1, 2000, edition of the *Times* magazine under the headline "One Bad Cop." Although I later wrote occasional op-ed pieces for the *New York Times,* this is the only story I ever wrote for the Sunday magazine. The story fulfilled my need to follow up on the shortfalls of a police department that fascinated me while announcing to the world that I was a writer for hire. In the years ahead I would write for *Time, National Review, George, Smithsonian, RealClearPolitics,* and other publications and websites.

"One Bad Cop" was the story of Rafael Perez, a Puerto Rican–born, Philadelphia-reared former U.S. Marine who joined the LAPD in 1989. He became the golden boy of an elite anti-gang unit called CRASH—Community Resources Against Street Hoodlums—that operated in an area I described this way: "Rampart, west of downtown, is a compact warren of dense, dangerous neighborhoods that leads Los Angeles in homicides, narcotics sales and violent crimes. Out-of-town visitors to other poor sections of the city, even South Central, are often surprised to find homes surrounded by tidy lawns and neighborhoods sprinkled with parks and greenery. Such amenities are rare in Rampart, where open space is scarce, crowded high-rises abound and trees do not grow easily."

Perez started in the LAPD as a patrol officer, won an assignment to a narcotics unit, and advanced in 1995 to Rampart CRASH, which had its own station out of which Perez operated in plainclothes. He was valued by fellow officers because of his fluency in Spanish and knowledge of gang ways. Ethan Cohan, another officer in Rampart CRASH, told me that officers in the unit sometimes bet on which team would find a gun on a gang member that night.

"Perez always won," said Cohen. "I just thought this guy was really good."

It turned out that Perez and the cops who conspired with him were stealing narcotics and framing gang members by planting firearms and drugs on them. Perez had no compunction about falsifying evidence. As Perez saw it, he was evening the score.

"When I planted a case on someone, did I feel bad?" I quoted him as saying. "Not once. I felt good. I felt, you know, I'm taking this guy off the streets."

What began as overaggressive law enforcement evolved into a life of crime. In 1997, Perez told investigators, he and another officer arrested a suspect and found a bag containing a pound of powder cocaine. They kept the drugs—along with the suspect's pager. When the pager went off, Perez pretended to be a dealer and took an order for a quarter pound of cocaine. Instead of arresting the buyer, the officers decided to make the sale. Soon they were dealing drugs with product they had confiscated from gang members.

Perez was tripped up in 1998 after two Rampart CRASH officers detained a young gang suspect and choked and beat him until he vomited blood. When the gang member was released, he checked into a hospital and reported the incident, which came to the attention of Chief Bernard Parks, who was appalled. Parks ordered that administrative charges be brought against the officers, who were then fired. During the investigation, officers in the property division discovered that six pounds of cocaine had been checked out for a court appearance and never returned. The officer who signed for the cocaine was Rafael Perez. Following up further, officers from Internal Affairs discovered that Perez had checked out cocaine in other cases, including some in which he had not been involved as a police officer.

Perez was tried in December 1998 for possession of cocaine for sale, grand theft, and forgery. The jury, split eight-to-four in favor of conviction, could not reach a verdict. While Perez awaited retrial, investigators examined his financial records and found unexplained deposits. He had remodeled his home extensively, far beyond the means of his salary. Prosecutors played hardball. They threatened to file charges against Perez's wife, a civilian employee of the LAPD who they believed knew of his illegal activities. With a young daughter at home, Perez didn't want to risk his wife going to jail. He decided to cut a deal.

The concessions Perez's lawyer, William K. McKesson, extracted from District Attorney Gil Garcetti on September 8, 1999, was sweet for Perez and useful for the LAPD, which was swamped with lawsuits and administrative cases. In exchange for a five-year prison sentence, immunity from further prosecution, and total immunity for his wife, Perez implicated seventy officers from the Rampart CRASH unit in unprovoked shootings, beatings, planting of false evidence, stealing and dealing narcotics, bank robbery, perjury, and covering up these activities. Garcetti knew Perez was getting off light but felt he had no choice since McKesson told him that an innocent man shot in the neck by Perez was serving twenty-three years in prison for a crime he did not commit.

The fallout from Perez's revelations would have more impact on the LAPD and Los Angeles than the Rodney King incident, although not all of it was apparent when I wrote "One Bad Cop." As a result of falsified evidence and perjury by officers in the Rampart division, 106 criminal convictions were overturned and 140 civil lawsuits were filed against the city of Los Angeles, which settled them at a cost of $125 million. On November 2, 2000, the city and the U.S. Department of Justice entered into a consent agreement that would bring the LAPD under federal oversight for nearly twelve years.

The political impact of the Rampart scandal was also far-reaching. On November 7, Los Angeles voters rejected Garcetti's bid for a third term by a nearly two-to-one margin. The new district attorney was Stephen Cooley, who had made the scandal a campaign issue. The ripple effect of Rampart swept away Chief Parks, whom Mayor James Hahn declined to reappoint for a second five-year term. Parks was replaced as chief in 2002 by the renowned William Bratton, who embraced the consent agreement. Discarding Parks did not save Hahn, who was damaged by the residual effects of the Rampart scandal. Seeking a second term in 2002, he was soundly defeated by Anthony Villaraigosa.

Rafael Perez was imprisoned in a secure wing of the Los Angeles County jail and kept away from inmates with gang ties. He was a model prisoner who served only three years of his five-year sentence. When Perez was paroled in 2002, the court took the unusual step of allowing him to move to another state. He was a wanted man in gangland and within the Rampart division of the LAPD. The police department's proximity to Hollywood had another ancillary effect: In the hit 2001 movie *Training Day,* Denzell Washington played a corrupt LAPD detective based on Rafael Perez. Washington won an Academy Award for his performance.

I gained something, too. The *Times* magazine story was a reminder that there were still stories to be pursued—and that I could write them for a variety of audiences.

Nevertheless, I stepped away from freelance work to write again about the actor-turned-politician I'd been chronicling since 1966. My first book, *Ronnie and Jesse: A Political Odyssey,* examined Ronald Reagan's life through the first two years of his governorship. My second Reagan book, called *Reagan* without a subtitle, dealt with the remainder of the governorship, Reagan's 1976 and 1980 presidential campaigns, and the early part of his presidency. My third and best book, *President Reagan: The Role of a Lifetime,* reviewed the entire presidency. First published in 1992 by Simon and Schuster, *President Reagan* was updated and published by Public Affairs Books in 2000. Public Affairs, founded by Peter Osnos, a former colleague at *The Washington Post,* has kept it in print.

The timetables of my Reagan books had shortchanged the second and more productive term of his governorship. After a discussion with my agent, Kris Dahl, who was always there for me, I proposed a book examining all aspects of Reagan's rise, including his formative years as president of the Screen Actors Guild. This idea was embraced by Public Affairs, where Robert Kimzey was my valued editor. In 2005, Public Affairs published *Ronald Reagan: His Rise to Power,* which incorporated parts of *Reagan* and expanded my examination of his second term as governor. It received good reviews and was subsequently issued by Public Affairs in a set with *President Reagan: The Role of a Lifetime.*

Three years later, Public Affairs also published *Reagan's Disciple: George W. Bush's Quest for a Presidential Legacy,* a book coauthored with my eldest son, Carl M. Cannon. Carl's insights about Bush were special, and our book received strong and complimentary reviews.

I couldn't shake Ronald Reagan. Despite being absorbed in other projects, I was for a time bombarded with requests to write about Reagan or give a speech about him. One of the most interesting requests brought me in 2014 to a conference on presidential leadership sponsored by the Departments of History, International Studies, and Political Science at the Virginia Military Institute. The participants in this conference included two of the best-informed officials of the Reagan years: Suzanne Ridgway of the State Department and Jack Matlock of the National Security Council. The same year, I accepted an offer from *Time* to write the lead article for a special issue the magazine was doing on Reagan. *Time* later expanded this issue into a book, *The Reagan Paradox: The Conservative Icon and Today's GOP.*

I never had any illusion that I'd written the last word about Ronald Reagan. Biographers from Craig Shirley to Max Boot have produced recent books, and others will as well. There was always more to learn about him—and there always will be. Historians and biographers stand on the shoulders of those who have gone before them. Others will stand on our shoulders as well.

California Journal was a pioneer magazine of state government and politics that was the brainchild of my friend Judson Clark and two other former staff members in the state legislature who had founded State Net, a Sacramento-based firm that tracked legislation for a variety of clients. The *Journal* began in 1970, when I was a Washington correspondent for Ridder Publications. At Jud's request I wrote a "Letter from Washington" for the first few issues.

During the thirty-five years of its existence, when it was largely published by Tom Hoeber and edited by A. G. Block, *California Journal* made a significant contribution to civic reporting in the Golden State. This was a time when California was setting the national agenda on air pollution and other issues. I learned how useful the magazine could be when researching *Governor Reagan: His Rise to Power.*

When I left Ridder Publications for *The Washington Post* in 1972, I showed the magazine to national staff editor Richard Harwood, who'd hired me. Harwood valued state capital reporting, which he'd done himself. He said he liked *California Journal* and had no objections to me writing for it but accurately predicted that I wouldn't have time for magazine writing once I became immersed in political coverage for *The Post.*

Fast-forward twenty-nine years later when I'd retired from *The Post.* I now had time to write for *California Journal*—and did. So did a number of distinguished journalists and authors whose work had graced the magazine's pages over the years. Among them were Bill Boyarsky, Ed Cray, Gladwin Hill, Sherry Bebitch Jeffe, Joel Kotkin, Richard Reeves, Peter Schrag, Steve Scott, Michele Willens, and my eldest son, Carl. I respected all of them, but a change in State Net policy in 2003 stripped *California Journal* from the comfort zone of company sponsorship and forced the magazine to become a nonprofit in every meaning of the term.

Jud Clark asked me in 2004 to become president of *California Journal* and assist in fundraising, which is not my strong suit, but we raised enough money to keep the magazine alive for another year. What we needed was an ongoing institutional sponsor. The resolute Bill Hauck was the point man in our fundraising effort. We raised more than a million dollars, but even Bill could not save the magazine. We came close. Hauck and I sat down with a billionaire politician who said he was tempted to fund *California Journal* in perpetuity. After much discussion, he decided not to do so. *California Journal* shut its doors in January 2005.

Closing the magazine was a blow to Jud and Tom and also A.G., even though he no longer worked there. They and many others, including David Lesher, the editor who succeeded A.G., had worked creatively to make *California Journal* a success. I took it hard, too. *California Journal* had produced high-quality political journalism in the nation's most populous state. The death of the magazine was California's loss.

An offshoot of *California Journal* that arrived on the heels of the magazine's closing was *State Net Capitol Journal,* hereinafter *Cap J.* It has been published online since 2005, first by State Net and then by LexisNexis, which acquired State Net in 2010. I wrote a monthly column for *Cap J* through December 2021, when I stepped away to complete this memoir. The publication had a small but influential audience. Most of *Cap J* was written by Rich Ehisen, an accomplished journalist who became a close friend, and by me and Korey Clark, one of Jud's four sons. Rich had our backs, which mattered after LexisNexis took control of *Cap J* and occasionally pressured us to write something that was more promotional than newsworthy. I wouldn't do it, and Rich saw to it that I wasn't asked.

In my columns I tried to illuminate aspects of state government neglected in most daily news coverage, using as my inspiration a phrase popularized by Supreme Court justice Louis Brandeis who said in a famous 1932 dissent that states could operate as "laboratories" of democracy by testing policies—even unorthodox or unwise ones—without running afoul of the U.S. Constitution.

In this long memoir I've largely avoided writing about the hearth-and-home experiences of my adult life. I've learned, however, that some of these experiences define me as much as any news story I have written. That is especially true of fishing with my four children. I'd fished sparingly as a child because my father didn't know how, and resolved early that if I became a dad I'd fish with my kids.

I kept that promise even though I'm not a particularly adept fisherman. My first fish after my family moved back to Reno in 1949 was a trout caught on a worm in the Truckee River in Reno when I was a sophomore in high school. I had recently read "Big Two-Hearted River," a favorite Ernest Hemingway story, and released the trout the way Nick Adams did in the story by dipping my hand in the water before touching the fish. I later became inspired by catch-and-release fishing. Fishing with others on the Kenai River in Alaska, we caught three dozen rainbows over sixteen inches in length on barbless hooks, releasing them all except for a trout that hit its head on a rock as I reeled it in.

The trout in the Truckee were small by comparison, and I didn't keep any I caught as a sophomore. I returned to the river as a junior on the first day of fishing season—then an excused absence from school in Nevada—and caught two small trout. I took them home and my father, no fisherman but an accomplished short-order cook, showed me how to clean them and fry them in bacon grease. The technique is simple, really, and I passed it on to Carl when he was only five or six. We had fished a tributary of the Merced River in Mariposa County and caught several trout.

In Sacramento, after the legislators had scattered to their home districts by midday Thursday, I'd pick up Carl and we'd head for bass ponds in the rolling hills east of Sacramento. The ponds were on private land, but the landowner didn't mind us fishing there as long as we didn't litter. We parked on the side of a dirt road, navigated a field of cows and an occasional bull, and walked a mile or so to the isolated and peaceful ponds.

I remember the day Carl caught his first big bass. I was instructing him how to pull back on his rod and set the hook when he said, "Dad, I've already got him." He was eleven years old. That first big fish was a breakthrough, and Carl caught his share after that. By next summer, he was fishing on his own in a neighboring pond.

Judy, my daughter, was seven and begged to come. I didn't want to bring her on a long walk amidst the cows and settled instead on taking her without the boys to a small pond near the road brimming with bluegill, which were easy to catch. Our expeditions ended abruptly in 1968 when Judy and I fished the bluegill pond and returned to my Volkswagen to find a bullet hole in the door on the driver's side. Judy says I told her that there was a note from someone who had been hunting rabbits and hit the car by mistake. I don't remember any note, and in any case abruptly decided these fishing visits weren't safe. To Carl's disappointment, I stopped all future visits to the ponds. I assured him we'd find other places to fish, and we did.

I had other adventures with the children, the most harrowing of which occurred in 1969 in the Pacific Ocean off Año Nuevo Point, a small island midway between San Mateo and Santa Cruz Counties. Carl was away at church camp. Dave, then nine years old, was with me and a friend named Paul Azevedo in search of abalone, a mollusk that when prepared properly is a great delicacy. We would search under rocks for abalone we couldn't see, then pry them off with a tire iron. Paul worked in the Advertising Department of the *Contra Costa Times,* where I was editor. He was passionate about the Roman Catholic Church and abalone fishing, in that order, and he had a folder in his car listing the times of every Mass at every church in Central California. His wife, Lydia, said Paul never missed Mass. Another folder listed the time of every minus tide, ideal for taking abalone, and Paul didn't miss many low tides either.

Paul had gathered our limit—five abalone each of legal size—and started wading back to the mainland at Año Nuevo when I noticed we were bucking a crosscurrent that I later learned was frequent in the channel. Paul realized immediately this could be dangerous for David, who was drifting away from the small inner-tube raft we used to carry the abalone. With a single scooping motion, Paul grabbed Dave in one hand and discarded the gunny sack containing our abalone catch with the other. He then planted Dave where our catch had been between two of us. Although furious with myself for putting Dave in danger, I remained calm.

"This is not working," I told Paul. "We have to go back to the island."

Without a word, Paul turned around, with Dave between us in our makeshift raft. We made our way, with some difficulty, through the rising surf back to the island. Upon reaching shore, we headed to an abandoned building adjacent to the island lighthouse. Having interviewed local scientists who monitored wildlife there, I knew there were supplies in this building. We broke a lock and entered. David was shivering, and we dried him off, changed him into warm clothes, and contemplated our situation. This was long before cell phones, and we planned to spend the night in the building and catch the next minus tide at dawn.

Instead, several hours later, we heard an unexpected and welcome sound: A U.S. Coast Guard helicopter landed on Año Nuevo Island. We were surprised to see them; they were equally surprised to see us. When we explained what we doing there, a young Coast Guard officer said, "This is your lucky day."

Dave, by then warm and safe, thought it was exciting to fly in a helicopter and considered the whole day a wonderful adventure. But Paul and I knew that we'd narrowly escaped a catastrophe.

These abalone-gathering expeditions happened before my youngest son, Jack, born November 1, 1965, was of fishing age. When Jack was four, we moved to Washington, DC, where I was a correspondent for Ridder Publications until joining *The Washington Post* in 1972. There was scant time for fishing in Washington, but Jack and I made up for lost time after I was transferred to the newspaper's western bureau. On vacation in 1978, we fished for kokanee salmon in Lake Tahoe. I sautéed the keepers that night at the small cabin where we stayed. Kokanee turn pink when cooked, the color of sockeye salmon, to which they are related. It was my favorite day of fishing with Jack.

These outings were rare because I was busy covering the White House. Later in the Reagan years, when I had more balance in my life, Jack and I fished at a pond owned by Arthur W. "Nick" Arundel, a wealthy newspaper publisher and like my old friend Pete McCloskey a U.S. Marine Corps combat officer in the Korean War.

I haven't fished in years, but these remembrances open a window to the past. As Nancy Reagan said, all we have is our memories, and the times I spent fishing with my children are precious memories to me.

35

JOURNALISM'S CRUCIBLE

I've had the great good fortune to be a journalist, most often a reporter, for much of my life. I've won my share of awards. Despite occasional setbacks, it's been a privilege. It's also been fun. Some publishers were eager for exposés, while others valued solid day-to-day reporting—and I liked doing both. I enjoyed coming to work each day, particularly at *The Washington Post.* As Marty Nolan of the *Boston Globe* put it, journalism was inside work with no heavy lifting.

For newspaper publishers in the twentieth century, owning a newspaper was a path to riches. They profited from display advertising by department stores and auto agencies and the hundreds of classified ads for which newspapers charged more than the pittance it cost them to print. These advantages vanished in the twenty-first century as the growth of the internet, the shrinkage of display advertising, and the exodus of classified advertisers to Craigslist made newspapers unprofitable. A study by Northwestern University's Medill School found newspapers shut down at the rate of two per week in the early decades of this century. The circulation areas of these lost papers become "news deserts," the study asserted, because few were served by online or digital replacements.

In California, the metaphor brought to mind by the 2023 passing of the *Salinas Californian* was a lake more than a desert. In the winter of 2022–23, a six-year drought ended in California, producing floods across the state. In Central California the rain-swollen Salinas River inundated thousands of acres of farmland and left thousands of farmworkers homeless. It was a big news story with few reporters to report it. The last reporter at the *Californian* left at the end of December. I learned about the Salinas River flood from a brief televised report I watched in a Santa Barbara hospital while recovering from a stroke.

James Rainey of the *Los Angeles Times* reported on the economics of the *Californian* in an April 1, 2023, story that no one mistook for an April Fool's Day joke. "Owned by Gannett, the largest newspaper publisher in the nation, the venerable *Californian* now carries stories from the chain's *USA Today* and its other California papers," Rainey wrote. "The only original content from Salinas comes in the form of paid obituaries, making death virtually the only sign of life at an institution once considered a must-read by many Salinans."

John Steinbeck was born in Salinas. I read his short stories as I boy and, of course, *The Grapes of Wrath*, and as an adult visited the Salinas museum that honors him. I liked the *Californian*. It was not a great newspaper, but its best issues reflected the tone and texture of the Salinas Valley, one of the most agriculturally productive places in America.

In 2023 I found myself indulging in magical thinking: The *Californian* would be resurrected and I would work there, perhaps writing a column about state politics. In reality, there was no chance that the *Californian* would enjoy a second life. Newspapers were closing all over the land and still are. In the twenty years since 2005, the United States had lost nearly three thousand newspapers employing some forty-three thousand journalists, according to a Northwestern University tabulation.

The plight of the news business was underscored in March 2024 when two major chains, Gannett and McClatchy, announced in a cost-saving move that they would no longer take the services of the Associated Press, the world's largest wire service.

With their own staffs having been decimated, the obvious question is: Where will these papers—and their readers—get their news?

From the time he burst out of his bubble as a real estate operator, tabloid personality, and reality television star, Donald J. Trump tested journalistic norms. In his 2015 announcement speech, he infamously labeled Mexican immigrants "rapists" and drug mules, branded orthodox newspapers "fake news," and disparaged elected officials in both major political parties in the manner of a New York insult comic. Traditional journalists were at a loss on how to cover this man. In an influential August 2016 column, *New York Times* media critic Jim Rutenberg laid out the problem: "If you're a working journalist and you believe that Donald J. Trump is a demagogue playing to the nation's worst racist and nationalistic tendencies, that he cozies up to anti-American dictators and that he would be dangerous with control of the United States nuclear codes, how the heck are you supposed to cover him?"

Rutenberg suggested that reporters who find a Trump presidency a potential danger to the country naturally "move closer than you've ever been to being oppositional." He conceded that a news organization deciding, even in its supposedly straight reporting, to openly take sides was perilous, uncharted territory. Although his essay was nuanced, much of mainstream journalism saw it as a blessing by no less an august authority than the *New York Times* to discard long-understood rules of objectivity when covering Trump.

Even before Trump reclaimed the presidency in 2024, many influential journalists were saying that the news business shouldn't even strive to be impartial. One of them was my old colleague Len Downie, retired from *The Washington Post* and teaching journalism at Arizona State University. Len authored a much-read op-ed in our old newspaper asserting that even the pursuit of journalistic objectivity "can lead to false balance or misleading 'bothsidesism' in covering stories about race, the treatment of women, LGBTQ+ rights, income inequality, climate change and many other subjects."

But "false balance" is a problematic concept for journalism. So is "misleading bothsidesism." Is a news organization supposed to decide by fiat which side doesn't get a hearing on public policy issues such as race and the treatment of women?

The political parties have conflicting views on these issues and most other topics. Democracy can't function very well, it seems to me, if half the electorate receives a steady stream of news that conforms to Democratic Party policies while the other half gets whatever excites Republicans or so-called MAGA voters in the minds of Fox News executives or other right-leaning outlets. The ultimate result of this approach isn't journalism; it's competing versions of political propaganda. "Objectivity" to me and many other journalists always meant being fair, not a sterile exercise of giving each side an equal number of paragraphs.

If we don't trust our readers and viewers to decide for themselves after being fully informed, how are Americans ever supposed to find consensus on topics ranging from Donald Trump's fitness to hold office (or Joe Biden's) to whether the United States should protect Ukraine from destruction?

Certainly reporters, editors, photographers, columnists, and cartoonists at *The Washington Post* when Len and I worked there, and the *New York Times* (at least until Trump came along) believed they could make the world a better place under journalism's existing rules of the road. Objective reporting doesn't mean timid reporting. Often it takes great courage, which both those papers exhibited for instance when publishing the Pentagon Papers.

In 1896, Adolph S. Ochs put these principles in writing when he assumed control of the *Times*. The newspaper, Ochs told his readers, would endeavor "to give the news impartially, without fear or favor, regardless of party, sect, or interests involved." Ochs added that his aim was to make the *Times* "a forum for the consideration of all questions of public importance, and to that end to invite intelligent discussion from all shades of opinion."

This model served me and other reporters well for a long time. I believe it also served the country well. As I was finishing this memoir, I received validation that the traditional ethics still had adherents. It didn't come in a widely discussed op-ed in a prestigious news outlet, but in a personal email, after I had my second stroke, from David Hoffman, who covered the Reagan White House with me when he was in his late twenties and early thirties: "I remember so much of our work together. It was hugely formative in my career and my life. I learned from you lessons that I use now every day and try to pass along to the younger journalists—not always successfully. One of those lessons was to talk to everyone. . . . You told me that was one of the secrets of covering Reagan and the White House: make sure you talk to all sides, don't let them pigeonhole you into one or the other."

A year earlier, David had written a book about a courageous Cuban dissident who had battled Fidel Castro. In writing it, he had to walk a minefield between sources on the left who want increased U.S. engagement with Cuba and those on the right who want another Bay of Pigs—and those in the middle.

"Just last week, I was talking to all of them," David told me. "And it works."

I freely acknowledge that Ronald Reagan, the fortieth U.S. president, whom Hoffman and I covered together, wasn't nearly as challenging to deal with as Donald Trump, the forty-fifth (and forty-seventh) president. But despite Trump's many provocations—not least of which is consciously seeking to undermine the legitimacy of the media itself—I believe that abandoning a journalistic model that served this country during crucibles ranging from the civil rights movement to Vietnam and Watergate out of antipathy to the occupant of the Oval Office sells our craft short. It's also a disservice to the American people.

Ultimately, we must trust our readers, listeners, and viewers to get it right. Our job should still be to report the news without fear or favor. Explore all sides of a question. Don't be afraid of what we might learn—or what the voters might do with the information.

The line Ronald Reagan loved so much comes to my mind—one he used repeatedly until he even won over Mikhail Gorbachev. "Trust, but verify," he'd say. I believe that ultimately journalists must verify the facts ourselves with honest reporting—and then trust the people to do their best with it.

INDEX